CYNNWYS
CONTENTS

D1635579

FOREWORD
RHAGAIR

The *Teach Yourself Welsh Dictionary* is a modern dictionary specifically designed for use by Welsh learners. The Welsh–English section is based on a basic vocabulary formulated to meet their particular needs. It differs significantly from the traditional type of dictionary, in as much as it also contains mutated forms of nouns, verbs, adjectives and prepositions integrated into the main alphabetical structure. Learners thereby are able to trace the standard form of a mutated word without difficulty. Irregularly formed plural nouns are systematically included, and each Welsh verb is complete with its first person singular form in the present tense. In addition, many of the prepositions governed by various verbs are included.

An attempt has been made to supply sufficient grammatical detail with each entry in the English–Welsh section to facilitate cross-reference and easy access to the fuller definition in the Welsh–English section.

Throughout, the dictionary is well illustrated with examples of language in action, with an emphasis on Welsh idiomatic usage.

The supplement contains a short introduction to some of the salient features of Welsh grammar including the conjugation of verbs and prepositions, the comparison of adjectives, forms of personal pronouns, and a summary of the main rules of consonantal mutation.

I am indebted to Mr Cennard Davies, M.A., for his sustained interest and encouragement during the preparation of the work, for reading the manuscript, and for his many valuable suggestions.

I gratefully acknowledge that a section of the dictionary was awarded First Prize at the 1989 Llanrwst National Eisteddfod. Its completion was commissioned by the Eisteddfod Council, and it is now published by kind permission of the National Eisteddfod Court.

Edwin C. Lewis.

Llangyfelach,
SWANSEA.

GEIRIADUR
Cymraeg–Saesneg

BYRFODDAU
ABBREVIATIONS

a.	ansoddair	*adjective*
a.b.	ansoddair benywaidd	*feminine adjective*
ad.	adferf	*adverb*
a.g.	ansoddair gwrywaidd	*masculine adjective*
ardd.	arddodiad	*preposition*
At.	Atodiad	*Supplement, Appendix*
b.	benywaidd	*feminine*
be.	berfenw	*verb-noun* (followed in brackets by the first person present tense)
bf.	berf	*verb*
c.	cysylltair	*conjunction*
D.C.	De Cymru	*South Wales (S.W.)*
e.b.	enw benywaidd	*feminine noun*
* e.b.g.	enw benywaidd/gwrywaidd	*feminine/masculine noun*
ebych	ebychiad	*interjection*
e.e.	er enghraifft	*for example*
e.g.	enw gwrywaidd	*masculine noun*
* e.g.b.	enw gwrywaidd/benywaidd	*masculine/feminine noun*
e.ll.	enw lluosog	*plural noun*
e.torf.	enw torfol	*collective noun*
g.	gwrywaidd	*masculine*
G.C.	Gogledd Cymru	*North Wales (N.W.)*
geir.	geiryn	*particle*
geir. gof.	geiryn gofynnol	*interrogative particle*
geir. perth.	geiryn perthynol	*relative particle*
gw.	gweler	*see*
lit.	yn llythrennol	*literally*
ll.	lluosog	*plural*
N.W.	Gogledd Cymru	*North Wales (dialect)*
[pron.]	dywedir	*[pronounced]*
rhag.	rhagenw	*pronoun*
rhagdd.	rhagddodiad	*prefix*
rhag. gof.	rhagenw gofynnol	*interrogative pronoun*
rhag. perth.	rhagenw perthynol	*relative pronoun*
S.W.	De Cymru	*South Wales (dialect)*
S.W.W.	De Orllewin Cymru	*South West Wales (dialect)*
y fan.	y fannod	*definite article*
ymad. ad.	ymadrodd adferfol	*adverbial phrase*

*The gender of some nouns varies in different dialects, for example:
munud (*minute*); llygad (*eye*).

a *geir. gof. o flaen berf (interrogative particle before a verb).* **A oes heddwch?** Is there peace?

a *rhag. perth. (followed by soft mutation)* who, whom, which (**a** *is often omitted in everyday speech, but the mutated form of the verb remains).* **Y ferch a welais** The girl whom I saw; **y llyfr a ddarllenais** the book which I read.

a:ac [**ac** *pron.* **ag**] *c.* (**a** *before a consonant,* **ac** *before a vowel;* **a** *followed by spirant mutation)* and. **du a gwyn** black and white; **pensil a phapur** pencil and paper; **afal ac oren** apple and orange.

â *bf.* he/she/it goes. *gw.* **mynd.**

â: ag **1** *ardd,* (**â** *before a consonant,* **ag** *before a vowel;* **â** *followed by spirant mutation)* with (*an instrument*), by means of. **torri cig â chyllell** cutting meat with a knife; **crynu ag ofn** shivering with fear. **2** *c.* (**â** before a consonant, **ag** before a vowel; **â** followed by spirant mutation) as. **cyn goched â thân** as red as fire; **mor ysgafn â phluen** as light as a feather; **mor wyn ag eira** as white as snow.

aber *e.g.b.* *ll.* **-oedd** estuary, mouth of river; confluence; stream.

aberth *e.g.b.* *ll.* **-au** sacrifice.

aberthu *be.* **(aberthaf)** to sacrifice.

absennol *a.* absent.

ac *gw.* **a.**

acen *e.b.* *ll.* **-nau, -ion** accent; intonation.

act *e.b.* *ll.* **-au** act; statute.

actio *be.* **(actiaf)** to act.

acw: cw *ad.* (**cw** *in everyday speech)* there, yonder.

achlysur *e.g.* *ll.* **-on** occasion; cause, opportunity

achos **1** *e.g.* *ll.* **-ion** reason, cause; action; case, factor. **2** *ardd.* because, for.

achosi *be.* **(achosaf)** to cause.

achub *be.* **(achubaf)** to save. **achub bywyd** to save life; **achub cyfle** to seize an opportunity.

adael *gw.* **gadael.**

adain: aden *e.b.* *ll.* **adenydd** wing.

adar *gw.* **aderyn.**

adeg *e.b.* *ll.* **-au** opportunity; period of time. **adeg y Nadolig** Christmas time; **ar adegau** at (certain) times.

adeilad *e.g.* *ll.* **-au** building.

adeiladu *be.* **(adeiladaf)** to build, to construct.

adeiladwr *e.g.* *ll.* **adeiladwyr** builder.

adenydd *gw.* **aden.**

aderyn *e.g.* *ll.* **adar** bird.

adfer *be.* **(adferaf)** to return; to revive; to restore *(to health, former condition, etc.).*

adferf *e.f.* *ll.* **-au** adverb.

adlais *e.g.* *ll.* **adleisiau** echo.

adleisiau *gw.* **adlais.**

adloniannau *gw.* **adloniant.**

adloniant *e.g.* *ll.* **adloniannau** entertainment; recreation.

adnabod *be.* **(adnabyddaf)** to recognise; to be familiar with; to identify; to know *(person or place);* to diagnose.

adnod *e.b.* *ll.* **-au** verse *(in Bible);* clause; section.

adran *e.b.* *ll.* **-nau** division, section; department. **Adran Addysg** Education Department.

adref *ad.* homewards.

adrodd *be.* **(adroddaf)** to relate; to recite; to report.

adroddiad   **ail**

adroddiad *e.g. ll.* **-au** account, report; recitation; narration.
addas *a.* fitting, suitable, proper.
addewid *e.g.b. ll.* **-ion** promise.
addo (i), *be* **(addawaf)** to promise. **Addewais iddo y byddwn yn mynd.** I promised him that I would go.
addoldai *gw.* **addoldy.**
addoldy *e.g. ll.* **addoldai** place of worship.
addoli *be.* **(addolaf)** to worship.
addoliad *e.g. ll.* **-au** worship; religious service.
addysg *e.b. ll.* **-au** learning, knowledge; education, instruction. **addysg grefyddol** religious education; **addysg gynradd** primary education; **addysg uwchradd** secondary education.
aeaf *gw.* **gaeaf.**
aeddfed *a.* ripe, mature.
ael *e.b. ll.* **-iau** brow.
aelod *e.g. ll.* **-au** limb; member. **Aelod Seneddol** Member of Parliament.
aelodaeth *e.b.* membership.
aelwyd *e.b. ll.* **-ydd** hearth; home.
aer **1** *e.g.* air, atmosphere. **2** *e.g. ll.* **-(i)on** heir.
aeres *e.b. ll.* **-au** heiress.
aerion *gw.* **aer.**
aeron *gw.* **aer, aeronen.**
aeronen *e.b. ll.* **aeron** berry, fruit.
aeth *gw.* **mynd.**
afael *gw.* **gafael.**
afaelgar *gw.* **gafaelgar.**
afal *e.g. ll.* **-au** apple.
afan(s)en *e.b. ll.* **afan(s)** raspberry *(S.W.)*.
afiach *a.* unhealthy, sick; dirty, unwholesome.
afiechyd *e.g. ll.* **-on** disease, illness.
afon *e.b. ll.* **-ydd** river; straits. **Afon Tawe** River Tawe; **Afon Menai** Menai Straits.
afonydd *gw.* **afon.**
afr *gw.* **gafr.**
agor *be.* **(agoraf)** to open.
agored *a.* open; unobstructed; liable.

agoriad *e.g. ll.* **-au** key *(N.W.);* opening, aperture. **agoriad llygad** eye-opener.
agos *a.* (**at** *person,* **i** *place*) near. *gw. At. Ansoddeiriau.*
agosach *gw.* **agos.**
agosaf *gw.* **agos.**
agosáu (at, i) *be.* **(agosâf)** to draw near to, to approach. **agosáu at** *(person)*; **agosáu i** *(place)*.
agosed *gw.* **agos.**
agwedd *e.g. ll.* **-au** attitude.
angau *e.g. ll.* **angheuoedd** death.
angel *e.g. ll.* **angylion, engyl** angel.
angenrheidiau *gw.* **anghenraid.**
angenrheidiol *a.* necessary.
anghenraid *e.g. ll.* **angenrheidiau** necessity.
angheuoedd *gw.* **angau.**
anghofio *be.* **(anghofiaf)** to forget.
anghyfarwydd *a.* unfamiliar, unaccustomed. **anghyfarwydd â** unfamiliar with, unaccustomed to.
anghywir *a.* inaccurate, wrong; false.
angladd *e.g.b. ll.* **-au** funeral.
angylion *gw.* **angel.**
ai 1 *geir. gof. heb dreiglad ar ei ôl, a geir o flaen enw, rhagenw, berfenw ac ansoddair (interrogative particle not followed by mutation, and used before a noun, pronoun, verb-noun, or adjective)* (**ai** *is often omitted in spoken Welsh).* **Ai te sy'n y cwpan?** Is it tea in the cup? **Ai Twm sy yno?** Is it Twm that's there? **2** *c.* either . . . or; **naill ai Marc neu Ioan** Either Marc or Ioan.
âi *bf.* he/she/it was going/would go/ used to go; *gw.* **mynd.**
ail *a. (followed by soft mutation)* second; like, similar. **yr ail fachgen** the second boy; **yr ail dŷ** the second house; **yr ail gadair** the second chair; **heb (ei) ail** unequalled; **bob (yn) ail** alternate, alternately.
ail *rhagdd.* re-, second; secondary. **ail achos** secondary cause; **ailadroddiad** repetition; **ailfeddwl** second thought, afterthought; **ailgyfrif** a recount; **ail-law** second-hand; **ailystyried** to reconsider.

ailgylchu   **amyneddgar**

ailgylchu *be.* (**ailgylchaf**) to recycle.
air *gw.* **gair.**
alar *gw.* **galar.**
alarch *e.g. ll.* **-od, elyrch** swan.
alaru *gw.* **galaru.**
alaw *e.b. ll.* **-on** music; air, melody,
tune; lily. **alaw werin** folk tune.
Alban, Yr *eb.* Scotland.
Almaen, Yr *eb.* Germany.
alw *gw.* **galw.**
alwad *gw.* **galwad.**
alwedigaeth *gw.* **galwedigaeth.**
alwyn *gw.* **galwyn.**
allan *ad.* out, outside.
allanfa *e.b. ll.* **allanfeydd** exit.
allanfeydd *gw.* **allanfa.**
allanol *a.* external, outward, exterior.
allt *e.b. ll.* **elltydd** hill *(N.W.)*; cliff
(N.W.); wood *(S.W.)*.
alltud *e.g. ll.* **-ion** exile; alien.
alltudion *gw.* **alltud.**
allu *gw.* **gallu.**
alluog *gw.* **galluog.**
allwedd *e.b. ll.* **-au, -i** key *(S.W.)*;
clef.
allweddell *e.b. ll.* **-au** keyboard.
am 1 *ardd. (followed by soft mutation)*
(personal forms: **amdana, amdanat,**
amdano/amdani, amdanon,
amdanoch, amdanyn*) about, at,
around, for, on. **am ddeg o'r gloch**
at ten o'clock; **Galwodd am Emyr**
He called for Emyr; **am y tro** for the
time being; *gw. At. Arddodiaid.* **2** *c.*
because, for, since; provided that.
amaethwr *e.g. ll.* **amaethwyr**
farmer; *gw.* **ffarmwr: ffermwr.**
amaethyddiaeth *e.b.* agriculture.
amau 1 *be.* (**amheuaf**) to doubt; to
suspect; to dispute. **2** *e.g. ll.*
amheuon doubt.
ambell *a. (followed by soft mutation)*
occasional. **ambell waith**
occasionally, sometimes; **ambell un**
an occasional one.
ambiwlans *e.g. ll.* **-ys** ambulance.
amcan *e.g. ll.* **-ion** purpose, notion,
guess.
amcanion *gw.* **amcan.**
amddiffyn 1 *be.* (**amddiffynnaf**) to
defend; to protect. **2** *e.g. ll.* **-ion**

defence.
Americanwr *e.g. ll.* **Americanwyr**
an American.
amgaeëdig *a.* enclosed.
amgáu *be.* (**amgaeaf**) to enclose; to
envelop.
amgueddfa *e.b. ll.* **amgueddfeydd**
museum; **Amgueddfa**
Genedlaethol National Museum;
Amgueddfa Werin Folk Museum.
amgueddfeydd *gw.* **amgueddfa.**
amgylch *e.g. ll.* **-oedd** circuit,
environs; **o amgylch** round about,
about.
amgylchedd *e.g. ll.* **-au, -ion**
environment.
amharod *a.* unprepared, unready,
unwilling.
amherffaith *a.* imperfect.
amheuaeth *e.b. ll.* **-au** doubt,
suspicion.
amheuon *gw.* **amau.**
amhosibl *a.* impossible.
aml *a. (followed by soft mutation)*
frequent, abundant; **aml (i) gyfle**
frequent opportunity; **gan amlaf**
most often, mostly.
amlen *e.b. ll.* **-ni** envelope.
amlenni *gw.* **amlen.**
amlosgfa *e.b. ll.* **amlosgfeydd**
crematorium.
amlosgfeydd *gw.* **amlosgfa.**
amlosgi *be.* (**amlosgaf**) to cremate.
amlwg *a.* evident, clear, plain;
famous; prominent.
amod *e.g.b. ll.* **-au** condition; term;
proviso.
amrwd *a.* raw, crude.
amryw *a. (followed by soft mutation)*
several; various. **amryw fath** various
kinds.
amrywiaeth *e.g. ll.* **-au** variety;
variation.
amser *e.g. ll.* **-au, -oedd** time,
period; season; tense; rhythm,
measure *(in music and poetry)*.
amserau *gw.* **amser.**
amserlen *e.b. ll.* **-ni** timetable.
amseroedd *gw.* **amser.**
amynedd *e.g.* patience.
amyneddgar *a.* patient.

anabl *a.* disabled.
anabledd *e.g.* disability.
anadl *[pron.* **anal** *in S.W.] e.g.b. ll.*
-au, -on breath.
anadlu *be.* **(anadlaf)** to breathe.
anaddas *a.* unfit, unsuitable.
anafu *be.* **(anafaf)** to receive hurt or injury; to injure, to wound, to mutilate.
anaml *a.* infrequent; scarce, rare.
anarferol *a.* unusual.
anawsterau *gw.* **anhawster.**
aned *gw.* **ganed.**
aneffeithiol *a.* ineffectual.
aneglur *a.* obscure.
anerchion *gw.* **annerch.**
anferth *a.* huge, gigantic, monstrous, prodigious.
anfodlon *a.* unwilling, discontented.
anfoesgar *a.* rude, ill-mannered.
anfon *be.* **(i** *place,* **at** *person)* **(anfonaf)** to send; to transmit.
anffodus *a.* unfortunate.
anhapus *a.* unhappy; unlucky.
anhawster *e.g. ll.* **anawsterau** difficulty.
anhwyldeb *e.g. ll.* **-au** sickness.
anhwylder *e.g. ll.* **-au** sickness.
anhwylus *a.* unwell; inconvenient.
anialwch *e.g.* desert, wilderness.
anifail *e.g. ll.* **anifeiliaid** animal, beast. **anifail anwes** pet.
anifeiliaid *gw.* **anifail.**
anlwcus *a.* unlucky.
annerch 1 *be.* **(anerchaf)** to greet; to address. **2** *e.g. ll.* **anerchion** greetings.
anerchiadau addresses, speeches.
annhebyg *a.* unlike, dissimilar, different.
annheg *a.* unfair, unjust.
annheilwng *a.* unworthy.
anniben *a.* untidy.
annibyniaeth *e.b.* independence.
Annibynnwr *e.g. ll.* **Annibynwyr** Independent, Congregationalist.
annoeth *a.* unwise.
annwyd *e.g. ll.* **-au, -on** cold, chill. **Mae annwyd arno fe(fo)** He has a cold.
annwyl *a. (when the adjective*

precedes the noun soft mutation occurs) dear, beloved; precious.
Annwyl Blant Dear Children;
Annwyl Gyfaill Dear Friend *(used to begin a speech or a letter).* **anwylyd** darling.
anochel *a.* unavoidable, inevitable.
anodd *a.* difficult, hard.
anos *a.* more difficult, harder.
anrheg *e.b. ll.* **-ion** gift, present.
anrhydedd *e.g. ll.* **-au** honour.
ansicr *a.* uncertain, doubtful.
ansicrwydd *e.g.* uncertainty, doubt.
ansoddair *e.g. ll.* **ansoddeiriau** adjective.
ansoddeiriau *gw.* **ansoddair.**
antur *e.g.b. ll.* **-iau, -iaethau** adventure; danger, risk.
anturus *a.* adventurous.
anweledig *a.* invisible, unseen.
anwes *e.g. ll.* **-au** fondness, pampering, fondling; indulgence. **anifail anwes** pet.
anwesu *be.* **(anwesaf)** to fondle, to cherish.
anwiredd *e.g. ll.* **-au** untruth, iniquity.
anwyd *gw.* **ganwyd.**
anwylaf 1 *a.* dearest. **2** *e.g.* beloved one.
anwyliaid *e.ll.* beloved ones.
ar *ardd. (followed by soft mutation) (personal forms:* **arna, arnat, arno/arni, arnon, arnoch, arnyn)** on, upon; by, in, at. **ar fynydd Epynt** on Epynt mountain; **ar lawr y gegin** on the kitchen floor; **ar hap a damwain** by chance; *gw. At. Arddodiaid.*
araf *a.* slow, leisurely. **yn araf deg** slowly, gently; by degrees.
arafu *be.* **(arafaf)** to slow, to retard, to decelerate.
araith *e.b. ll.* **areithiau** speech, address.
arall *a. ll.* **eraill** another, other, else. **bachgen arall** another boy; **bechgyn eraill** other boys.
arbed *be.* **(arbedaf)** to spare, to save. **arbed amser** to save time.
arbennig *a.* specialist, distinct.

arch

awduraeth

arch 1 *e.b.* *ll.* **eirchion** request, petition. **2** *e.b.* *ll.* **eirch** coffin, ark.
arch- *rhagdd.* chief, principal, high, arch-; worst. **archesgob** archbishop; **archdderwydd** archdruid; **archoffeiriad** chief priest; **archelyn** worst enemy.
archeb *e.b.* *ll.* **-ion** order *(especially for goods).*
archebu *be.* **(archebaf)** to order.
archfarchnad *e.b.* *ll.* **-oedd** hypermarket.
ardal *e.b.* *ll.* **-oedd** region, district, area.
ardd *gw.* **gardd.**
arddangosfa *e.b.* *ll.* **arddangosfeydd** show, exhibition.
ardderchog *a.* excellent, splendid.
arddio *gw.* **garddio.**
arddodiad *e.g.* *ll.* **arddodiaid** preposition.
arddodiaid *gw.* **arddodiad.**
arddwr *gw.* **garddwr.**
arddwrn *e.g.* *ll.* **arddyrnau** wrist.
areithiau *gw.* **araith.**
arf *e.g.b.* *ll.* **-au** weapon; tool; **arfau** arms.
arfer 1 *be.* **(arferaf)** to use; to practise; to accustom; to partake of. **2** *e.g.b.* *ll.* **-ion** usage, custom, practice; rule; habit.
arferion *gw.* **arfer.**
arferol *a.* usual, customary.
arfog *a.* armed.
arfordir *e.g.* *ll.* **-oedd** sea-coast, maritime district.
arglwydd *e.g.* *ll.* **-i** lord. **Tŷ'r Arglwyddi** House of Lords.
arglwyddes *e.b.* *ll.* **-au** lady.
arglwyddi *gw.* **arglwydd.**
argraff *e.b.* *ll.* **-iadau, -au** impression, imprint.
argraffiad *e.g.* *ll.* **-au** edition.
argraffu *be.* **(argraffaf)** to print, to impress.
argymell *be.* **(argymhellaf)** to urge.
arholiad *e.g.* *ll.* **-au** examination. **arholiad llafar** oral examination; **arholiad ysgrifenedig** written examination; **sefyll arholiad** to take *(sit)* an examination.

arian *e.g.* silver; money, coin, cash. **arian byw** quicksilver, mercury; **arian gleision** small change, **arian parod** cash; **arian pen** exact money; **arian poced** pocket money.
arlleg *gw.* **garlleg.**
arllwys *be.* **(arllwysaf)** to pour, to empty. **arllwys y glaw** to pour with rain *(S.W.).*
arogl *e.g.* *ll.* **-au** scent, perfume *(N.W.).*
arogli: aroglu *be.* **(aroglaf)** to scent, to smell *(N.W.).*
aros (am) *be.* **(arhosaf)** to wait (for), to stay; to stop, to remain.
arth *e.g.* *ll.* **eirth** bear.
arw *gw.* **garw.**
arwain *be.* **(arweiniaf)** to lead, to guide, to conduct.
arweinydd *e.g.* *ll.* **-ion** leader, guide, conductor.
asesu *be.* **(asesaf)** to assess.
asgellwr *e.g.* *ll.* **asgellwyr** wing: **blaenasgellwr** flanker *(rugby).*
asgwrn *e.g.* *ll.* **esgyrn** bone.
asiant *e.g.* *ll.* **-au** agent.
asiantaeth *e.b.* *ll.* **-au** agency.
asyn *e.g.* *ll.* **-nod** ass, donkey.
asynnod *gw.* **asyn.**
at *ardd.* *(followed by soft mutation) (personal forms:* **ata, atat, ato/ati, aton, atoch, atyn)** to, towards, for, at, by. *gw.* **At. Arddodiaid.**
atal *rhag.* *be.* **(ataliaf)** to stop; to prevent; to withhold. **atal dweud** to stammer.
ateb 1 *be.* **(atebaf)** to answer, to reply. **2** *e.g.* *ll.* **-ion** answer, reply.
atebion *gw.* **ateb.**
atgoffa *be.* **(atgoffaf)** to recall, to remind.
atodiad *e.g.* *ll.* **-au.** appendix.
atyniadol *a.* attractive.
athrawes *e.b.* *ll.* **-au** female teacher.
athrawon *gw.* **athro.**
athro *e.g.* *ll.* **athrawon** teacher. professor: **yr Athro Thomas Parry** Professor Thomas Parry.
aur *e.g.* gold.
awdur *e.g.* *ll.* **-on** author.
awduraeth *e.b.* *ll.* **-au** authorship.

awdurdod   **awyren**

awdurdod *e.g.b. ll.* **-au** authority.
  awdurdod iechyd health authority.
awduron *gw.* **awdur.**
awel *e.b. ll.* **-on** breeze.
awelon *gw.* **awel.**
awgrymu *be.* **(agrymaf)** to suggest.
awn *bf.* we go. *gw.* **mynd.**

awr *e.b. ll.* **oriau** hour; time.
Awst *e.g.* August.
awyddus *a.* desirous, eager, zealous.
  yn awyddus i fynd eager to go.
awyr *e.b.* air; sky. **awyr agored** open
  air; **awyr iach** fresh air.
awyren *e.b. ll.* **-nau** aeroplane.

ba *gw.* **pa.**
bab *gw.* **pab.**
baban *e.g. ll.* **-od** baby.
babanaidd *a.* babyish, childish,
puerile.
babell *gw.* **pabell.**
babi *e.g.* baby; *gw.* **pabi.**
babydd *gw.* **pabydd.**
bac *gw.* **pac.**
baced *gw.* **paced.**
bacio *be.* **(baciaf)** to back; to move
backward; to bet (on). **bacio car** to
reverse a car; **bacio ceffyl** to bet on
success of a horse; *gw.* **pacio.**
bach 1 *e.g. ll.* **-au** hook, hinge. **2** *a.*
small, little; dear. **araf bach** slowly,
very slowly; **bore bach** very early
morning, crack of dawn.
bachau *gw.* **bach; bachyn.**
bachgen *e.g. ll.* **bechgyn** boy.
bachgennaidd *a.* boyish, childish,
puerile.
bachu *be.* **(bachaf)** to hook, to
grapple.
bachyn *e.g. ll.* **bachau** hook.
bad *e.g. ll.* **-au** boat. **bad achub**
lifeboat.
badell *gw.* **padell.**
bader *gw.* **pader.**
bae *e.g. ll.* **-au** bay. **Bae Abertawe**
Swansea Bay.
baent *gw.* **paent.**
bafiliwn *gw.* **pafiliwn.**
bafin *gw.* **pafin.**

bag *e.g. ll.* **-iau** bag.
bagan *gw.* **pagan.**
bagiau *gw.* **bag.**
bai *e.g. ll.* **beiau** fault, blame; defect.
baich *e.g. ll.* **beichiau** load, burden.
bais *gw.* **pais.**
bâl *gw.* **pâl.**
balas *gw.* **palas.**
balch *a.* proud, fine, stately; glad.
Roedd e'n falch ein gweld ni he
was glad to see us.
balchder *e.g.* pride, glory.
baled *e.b. ll.* **-i** ballad.
baledwr *e.g. ll.* **baledwyr** composer
of ballads, ballad-monger.
balot *e.g. ll.* **-au** ballot.
balu *gw.* **palu.**
balŵn *e.b. ll.* **balwnau** balloon.
ballu *gw.* **pallu.**
bamffled *gw.* **pamffled.**
ban *e.g.b. ll.* **-nau** peak, mountain,
beacon, height; top, summit; corner,
quarter; arm, branch; verse, section
of line. **Bannau Brycheiniog**
Brecon Beacons; **o bedwar ban y
byd** from the four corners of the
world.
banana *e.g. ll.* **-s, bananâu** banana.
banasen *gw.* **panasen.**
banc 1 *e.g. ll.* **-au** bank. **gŵyl banc**
bank holiday. **2** *e.g. ll.* **bencydd**
mound, bank, hillock.
bancio *be.* **(banciaf)** to bank.
band *e.g. ll.* **-au, -iau** band, binding.
band pres brass band.
banel *gw.* **panel.**
baner *e.b. ll.* **-i** banner, flag.
bannas *gw.* **panasen.**
bannau *gw.* **ban.**
bannod *e.b. ll.* **banodau 1** line,
clause, part. **2** definite article *gw.* **y,
yr, 'r.**
banodau *gw.* **bannod.**
bant *gw.* **pant.**
bapur *gw.* **papur**
bapuro *gw.* **papuro.**
bar *e.g. ll.* **-rau** bar.
bâr *gw.* **pâr.**
bara *e.g.* bread. **bara brith** currant
bread; **bara lawr** laver bread; **bara
menyn** bread and butter. *gw.* **para.**

baragraff   **beisiau**

baragraff *gw.* **paragraff.**
baratoi *gw.* **paratoi.**
barbeciw *e.g. ll.* **barbeciwiau**
barbecue.
barc *gw.* **parc.**
barch *gw.* **parch.**
barchedig *gw.* **parchedig.**
barchu *gw.* **parchu.**
barchus *gw.* **parchus.**
bardwn *gw.* **pardwn.**
bardd *e.g. ll.* **beirdd** bard, poet.
barddoniaeth *e.b.* poetry.
barf *e.b. ll.* **-au** beard.
barhad *gw.* **parhad.**
barhau *gw.* **parhau.**
barn *e.b. ll.* **-au** opinion, judgement.
  Dydd y Farn the Day of Judgement.
barnwr *e.g. ll.* **barnwyr** judge.
barod *gw.* **parod.**
barrau *gw.* **bar.**
barsel *gw.* **parsel.**
barti *gw.* **parti.**
bas 1 *e.g.* bass *(voice)*; base. **2** *a.*
  shallow.
Basg, Gwlad y *e.b.* the Basque
  Country. *gw.* **Pasg.**
basged *e.b. ll.* **-i** basket. **basgedaid**
  basketful.
basiant *gw.* **pasiant.**
basn *e.g. ll.* **-au, -ys** basin. **basn**
  siwgr sugar basin.
basnau *gw.* **basn.**
basnys *gw.* **basn.**
baswn i. *bf.* I would (be). *gw.* **bod.**
baswr *e.g. ll.* **baswyr** bass *(singer)*.
bat *e.g. ll.* **-iau** bat.
batrwm *gw.* **patrwm.**
batrymau: batrynau *gw.* **patrwm.**
bath 1 *e.g. ll.* **-au** kind; bath; such a.
  Dim byd o'r fath nothing of the
  kind; **Welais i erioed y fath le.** I
  never saw such a place. **2** *a.* minted.
bathdai *gw.* **bathdy.**
bathdy *e.g. ll.* **bathdai** mint.
bathodyn *e.g. ll.* **-nau** badge.
bathu *be.* **(bathaf)** to form, to shape,
  to coin, to mint. **bathu gair** to coin a
  word.
baw *e.g.* dirt *(S.W.)*, dung, filth,
  mucus.
bawb *gw.* **pawb.**

bawd *e.g. ll.* **bodiau** thumb; big toe.
  bys bawd thumb, big toe.
bawen *gw.* **pawen.**
becso *be.* **(becsaf)** to worry, to vex
  (S.W.).
becyn *gw.* **pecyn.**
bechadur *gw.* **pechadur.**
bechan *a.b.* little, small. *gw.* **bychan.**
bechgyn *gw.* **bachgen.**
bechod *gw.* **pechod.**
bechu *gw.* **pechu.**
bedair *gw.* **pedair.**
bedol *gw.* **pedol.**
bedw *gw.* **bedwen.**
bedwar *gw.* **pedwar.**
bedwaredd *gw.* **pedwaredd.**
bedwen *e.b. ll.* **bedw** birch. **gwialen**
  fedw birch-rod.
bedwerydd *gw.* **pedwerydd.**
bedyddio *be.* **(bedyddiaf)** to baptise.
Bedyddiwr *e.g. ll.* **Bedyddwyr**
  Baptist. **Ioan Fedyddiwr** John the
  Baptist.
bedd *e.g. ll.* **-au** grave, tomb.
beg *gw.* **peg.**
begwn *gw.* **pegwn.**
beiau *gw.* **bai.**
Beibl *e.g. ll.* **-au** Bible. **Y Beibl**
  Cymraeg Newydd The New Welsh
  Bible.
beic *e.g. ll.* **-iau** bicycle.
beicio *be.* **(beiciaf)** to cycle.
beichiau *gw.* **baich.**
beichiog *a.* pregnant; burdened.
beidio *gw.* **peidio (â).**
beiddio *be.* **(beiddiaf)** to dare, to
  venture.
beilot *gw.* **peilot.**
beint *gw.* **peint.**
beintio *gw.* **peintio.**
beintiwr *gw.* **peintiwr.**
beio *be.* **(beiaf)** to blame, to accuse,
  to censure.
beirdd *gw.* **bardd.**
beiriant *gw.* **peiriant.**
beirniad *e.g. ll.* **beirniaid**
  adjudicator, critic.
beirniadu *be.* **(beirniadaf)** to
  adjudicate, to criticise.
beirniaid *gw.* **beirniad.**
beisiau *gw.* **pais.**

bêl   **bicil**

bêl *gw.* **pêl.**
belydr *gw.* **pelydr.**
bell *gw.* **pell.**
bellach *ad.* now, at length, further.
  gw. **pell.**
bellaf *gw.* **pell.**
belled *gw.* **pell.**
bellter *gw.* **pellter.**
ben *gw.* **pen.**
benaethiaid *gw.* **pennaeth.**
benawdau *gw.* **pennawd.**
ben-blwydd *gw.* **pen-blwydd.**
bencadlys *gw.* **pencadlys.**
bencampwr *gw.* **pencampwr.**
bencydd *gw.* **banc.**
bendant *gw.* **pendant.**
benderfyniad *gw.* **penderfyniad.**
benderfynol *gw.* **penderfynol.**
benderfynu *gw.* **penderfynu.**
bendigedig *a.* blessed, glorious,
  wonderful.
bendith *e.b.* *ll.* **-ion** blessing.
bendithio *b.e.* **(bendithiaf)** to bless.
benelin *gw.* **penelin.**
benfoel *gw.* **penfoel.**
ben-glin *gw.* **pen-glin.**
benigamp *gw.* **penigamp.**
benillion *gw.* **pennill.**
ben-lin *gw.* **pen-glin.**
benlinio *gw.* **penlinio.**
bennaeth *gw.* **pennaeth.**
bennaf *gw.* **pennaf.**
bennau *gw.* **pen.**
bennawd *gw.* **pennawd.**
bennill *gw.* **pennill.**
bennod *gw.* **pennod.**
benodau *gw.* **pennod.**
benodi *gw.* **penodi.**
benodiad *gw.* **penodiad.**
benrhyn *gw.* **penrhyn.**
bensaer *gw.* **pensaer.**
bensil *gw.* **pensil.**
bensiwn *gw.* **pensiwn.**
bensiynau *gw.* **pensiwn.**
bensiynwr *gw.* **pensiynwr.**
benteulu *gw.* **penteulu.**
bentref *gw.* **pentref.**
bentwr *gw.* **pentwr.**
bentyrrau *gw.* **pentwr.**
benthyca *be.* **(benthycaf)** to borrow,
  to lend.

benwythnos *gw.* **penwythnos.**
benyw *e.b.* *ll.* **-od** woman, female.
benywaidd *a.* female, feminine.
ber *a.b.* short, brief. *gw.* **byr.**
bêr *gw.* **pêr.**
berchen: berchennog *gw.*
  perchen.
beren *gw.* **peren.**
bererin *gw.* **pererin.**
berf *e.b.* *ll.* **-au** verb.
berfa *e.b.* *ll.* **berfâu** wheelbarrow
  (*N.W.*); *gw.* **whilber.**
berfedd *gw.* **perfedd.**
berfenw *e.b.* *ll.* **-au** verb-noun.
berffaith *gw.* **perffaith.**
berffeithio *gw.* **perffeithio.**
beri *gw.* **peri.**
berl *gw.* **perl.**
berlysiau *gw.* **perlysiau.**
berllan *gw.* **perllan.**
bersli *gw.* **persli.**
berson *gw.* **person.**
bersonol *gw.* **personol.**
bersonoliaeth *gw.* **personoliaeth.**
bert *gw.* **pert.**
berth *gw.* **perth.**
berthnasau *gw.* **perthynas.**
berthnasol *gw.* **perthnasol.**
berthyn *gw.* **perthyn.**
berthynas *gw.* **perthynas.**
berw **1** *e.g.* boiling, tumult, turmoil. **2**
  a. boiling, seething; **dŵr berw**
  boiling water. **3** *e.g.* cress: **berw'r**
  dŵr water cress.
berwi *be.* **(berwaf)** to boil.
bergyl *gw.* **perygl.**
beryglus *gw.* **peryglus.**
beswch *gw.* **peswch.**
besychiad *gw.* **pesychiad.**
betrol *gw.* **petrol.**
beth *rhag.* what? **beth am ginio?**
  what about dinner? **beth mae e'n**
  wneud? what's he doing? **beth**
  sydd yma? what's here? **beth ydy**
  ei enw? what's his name? **beth**
  bynnag anyway. *gw.* **peth.**
biano *gw.* **piano.**
bianydd *gw.* **pianydd.**
bib *gw.* **pib.**
biben *gw.* **piben.**
bicil: bicl *gw.* **picil.**

bictiwr

bictiwr *gw.* **pictiwr.**
bicwnen *gw.* **picwnen.**
bigfain *gw.* **pigfain.**
bigiad *gw.* **pigiad.**
bigo *gw.* **pigo.**
bigog *gw.* **pigog.**
bil *e.g. ll.* **-iau** bill. *gw.* **pil.**
biler *gw.* **piler.**
bilio *gw.* **pilio.**
bilion *gw.* **pil.**
bili-pala *gw.* **pili-pala.**
bilsen *gw.* **pilsen.**
bilyn *gw.* **pilyn.**
bin *e.g. ll.* **iau** bin. *gw.* **pin.**
bîn *gw.* **pîn.**
bînafal *gw.* **pînafal.**
binc *gw.* **pinc.**
binnau *gw.* **pin.**
binsio *gw.* **pinsio.**
binwydden *gw.* **pinwydden.**
bioden *gw.* **pioden.**
bioleg *e.b.* biology.
bisged *e.b. ll.* **bisgedi** biscuit.
bisgïen *e.b. ll.* **bisgis** biscuit.
bisyn *gw.* **pisyn.**
biti *gw.* **piti.**
bitw *a.* tiny. **bws bitw** minibus.
blaen 1 *e.g. ll.* **-au, -ion** point, end, top, tip; front, van; edge; source, limit, lead. **2** *a.* foremost, front, first.
blaendal *e.g. ll.* **-iadau** deposit.
blaenor *e.g. ll.* **-iaid** leader; deacon; predecessor.
blaenwr *e.g. ll.* **blaenwyr** forward (*rugby and soccer*); leader (*of orchestra*).
blaguro *be.* **(blaguraf)** to bud.
blaguryn *e.g. ll.* **blagur** bud.
blaid *gw.* **plaid.**
blaidd *e.g. ll.* **bleiddiaid, bleiddiau** wolf.
blan *gw.* **plan.**
blanced *e.b. ll.* **-i** blanket. **blanced wlân** woollen blanket; **blanced drydan** electric blanket.
blanhigyn *gw.* **planhigyn.**
blannu *gw.* **plannu.**
blant *gw.* **plant.**
blas *e.g.* taste, flavour; fervour, zest. **colli blas ar** to lose one's taste for. *gw.* **plas.**

blasty *gw.* **plasty.**
blasu *be.* **(blasaf)** to taste, to relish.
blasus *a.* tasty, delicious, savoury.
blât *gw.* **plât.**
blawd *e.g. ll.* **blodiau, blodion** flour, meal; **blawd codi** self-raising flour; **blawd llif** sawdust.
ble *rhag.* where?
bleidiau *gw.* **plaid.**
bleidlais *gw.* **pleidlais.**
bleidleisio *gw.* **pleidleisio.**
bleidleisiwr *gw.* **pleidleisiwr.**
bleiddiaid: bleiddiau *gw.* **blaidd.**
blentyn *gw.* **plentyn.**
blentynnaidd *gw.* **plentynnaidd.**
bleser *gw.* **pleser.**
bleserus *gw.* **pleserus.**
blesio *gw.* **plesio.**
blew *gw.* **blewyn.**
blewyn *e.g. ll.* **blew** hair (*on body, not on head*), fur; small fish bone. **hollti blew** to split hairs.
blin *a.* tired, tiresome, cross; sorry.
blinder *e.g. ll.* **-au** weariness, trouble, adversity.
blinedig *a.* wearisome, tired.
blino *be.* **(blinaf)** to tire, to vex, to weary. **Rydw i wedi blino** I am tired; **Mae e wedi blino** he is tired; **blino ar** to grow tired of.
blisgyn *gw.* **plisgyn.**
blisman: blismon *gw.* **plisman.**
blith *gw.* **plith.**
blodau *gw.* **blodyn.**
blodeugerdd *e.b. ll.* **-i** anthology.
blodfresychen *e.b. ll.* **blodfresych** cauliflower.
blodiau: blodion *gw.* **blawd.**
blodyn *e.g. ll.* **blodau** flower, blossom, bloom.
bloedd *e.g. ll.* **-iau, -iadau** shout.
bloeddio *be.* **(bloeddiaf)** to shout (*N.W.*).
blows *e.b. ll.* **-ys** blouse.
blu *gw.* **pluen.**
bluen *gw.* **pluen.**
bluf *gw.* **plufyn.**
blufyn *gw.* **plufyn.**
blwc *gw.* **plwc.**
blwch *e.g. ll.* **blychau** box, chest.
blwg *gw.* **plwg.**

14

blwm   **bos**

blwm *gw.* **plwm.**
blwydd 1 *e.b. ll.* -i year-old, year of
age. **tair blwydd oed** three years of
age. 2 *a.* year old. *gw. At Treiglad
Trwynol.*
blwyddyn *e.b. ll.* **blynyddoedd**
year. **dwy flynedd** two years; **tair
blynedd** three years; **pedair
blynedd** four years; **pum mlynedd**
five years. *gw. At. Treiglad Trwynol.*
blwyf *gw.* **plwyf.**
blychau *gw.* **blwch.**
blygu *gw.* **plygu.**
blynedd *gw.* **blwyddyn.**
blynedd *e.b.ll.* years (*used usually
after cardinal numbers*).
blynyddoedd *gw.* **blwyddyn.**
bob *gw.* **pob. bob bore** every
morning; **bob nos** every night; **bob
dydd** every day.
bobi *gw.* **pobi.**
bobl *gw.* **pobl.**
boblogaeth *gw.* **poblogaeth.**
boblogaidd *gw.* **poblogaidd.**
bobman *gw.* **pobman.**
bobydd *gw.* **pobydd.**
boced *gw.* **poced.**
bocs *e.g. ll.* -ys box.
boch *e.b. ll.* -au cheek.
bod 1 *e.g. ll.* -au existence; being.
Y Bod Mawr God. 2 *be.* (**rydw i**) to
be; **rydw i** I am, **rwyt ti** you are,
mae e/o he/it is, **mae hi** she/it is,
etc. gw. At. Berfau.
bodau *gw.* **bod.**
bodiau *gw.* **bawd.**
bodio *be.* (**bodiaf**) to thumb, to
finger.
bodlon: boddlon *a.* willing, pleased,
content. **bodlon ar** satisfied with.
bodloni *be.* (**bodlonaf**) to please, to
satisfy, to be contented.
bodd *e.g.* will, pleasure; consent.
rhyngu bodd to please; **trwy fodd**
with consent or permission; **wrth ei
fodd** happy, contented.
boddhad *e.g.* satisfaction, pleasure.
boddi *be.* (**boddaf**) to drown, to be
drowned, to flood.
boddlon *gw.* **bodlon.**
boen *gw.* **poen.**

boeni *gw.* **poeni.**
boenus *gw.* **poenus.**
boenydio *gw.* **poenydio.**
boer: boeri *gw.* **poer, poeri.**
boeth *gw.* **poeth.**
boeth *gw.* **poethi.**
bol *e.g. ll.* -iau belly, stomach,
abdomen.
bola *e.g. ll.* **bolâu, boliau** belly,
stomach, abdomen.
bolâu *gw.* **bola.**
boliau *gw.* **bol.**
bolion *gw.* **polyn.**
boliticaidd *gw.* **politicaidd.**
bolyn *gw.* **polyn.**
bollt *e.g.b. ll.* -au, **byllt** bolt, dart;
thunderbolt.
bolltau *gw.* **bollt.**
bolltio *be.* (**bolltiaf**) to bolt.
bom *e.g. ll.* -iau bomb.
bôn *e.g. ll.* **bonau, bonion** base,
trunk, stump, counterfoil. **yn y bôn**
basically, in reality.
boneddiges *e.b. ll.* -au lady.
boneddigion *gw.* **bonheddwr.**
bonheddig *a.* noble, gentle.
bonheddwr *e.g. ll.* **bonheddwyr,
boneddigion** gentleman, nobleman.
Foneddigion a Boneddigesau
Ladies and Gentlemen (*in addressing
an audience*).
bonion *gw.* **bôn.**
bont *gw.* **pont.**
bontydd *gw.* **pont.**
bopeth *g.w.* **popeth.**
bopty *gw.* **popty.**
bord *e.b. ll.* -ydd, -au table (*S.W.*),
board (*S.W.*).
bordau: bordydd *gw.* **bord.**
bore *e.g. ll.* -au morning. **yn fore**
early; **bore trannoeth** next
morning.
borfa *gw.* **porfa.**
borfeydd *gw.* **porfa.**
borffor *gw.* **porffor.**
bori *gw.* **pori.**
bortread *gw.* **portread.**
borth *gw.* **porth.**
borthladd *gw.* **porthladd.**
bos *e.g. ll.* -ys boss, chief. **Pwy ydy'r
bos yma?** Who's the boss here?

bos   **brigyn**

bos *gw.* **pos.**
bosibilrwydd *gw.* **posibilrwydd.**
bosibl *gw.* **posibl.**
bost *gw.* **post.**
bostio *gw.* **postio.**
bostman: bostmon *gw.* **postman.**
bostmyn *gw.* **postman.**
bostyn *gw.* **postyn.**
bosys *gw.* **bos.**
botel *gw.* **potel.**
botwm *e.g. ll.* **botymau** button.
botymu *be.* **(botymaf)** to button.
bowdr: bowdwr *gw.* **powdr.**
bowdrau *gw.* **powdr.**
bowlen: powlen *e.b. ll.* **-ni,**
  bowliau: powliau bowl.
braf *a.* fine, nice, pleasant. **bore braf**
  a fine morning; **Mae hi'n braf** (*no*
  mutation), it is fine (*weather-wise*).
bragdy *e.g. ll.* **bragdai** brewery.
braich *e.b.g. ll.* **breichiau** arm.
braidd *ad.* near, almost, just, rather,
  scarcely. **o'r braidd** hardly. *gw.*
  praidd.
brain *gw.* **brân.**
braint *e.b. ll.* **breintiau, breiniau**
  privilege, right, honour, status.
bram *gw.* **pram.**
brân *e.b. ll.* **brain** crow.
bras *a.* thick, fat; greasy; coarse; rich;
  rough, approximate.
braslun *e.g. ll.* **-iau** outline, sketch.
braster *e.g. ll.* **-au** grossness, fat.
braw *e.g. ll.* **-iau** terror, fright.
brawd *e.g. ll.* **brodyr** brother.
brawddeg *e.b. ll.* **-au** sentence.
brawf *gw.* **prawf.**
brawiau *gw.* **braw.**
brecwast *e.g. ll.* **-au** breakfast.
i frecwast for breakfast.
brech *e.b. ll.* **-au** eruption,
  vaccination, pox. **brech goch**
  measles; **brech yr ieir** chickenpox.
brechdan *e.b. ll.* **-au** slice of
  buttered bread, sandwich.
brechiad *e.g. ll.* **-au** inoculation,
  vaccination.
bregeth *gw.* **pregeth.**
bregethu *gw.* **pregethu.**
bregethwr *gw.* **pregethwr.**
breichiau *gw.* **braich.**

breichled *e.b. ll.* **-au** bracelet,
  bangle.
breiddiau *gw.* **praidd.**
breifat *gw.* **preifat.**
breiniau: breintiau *gw.* **braint.**
bren *gw.* **pren.**
brenhines *e.b. ll.* **breninesau**
  queen.
brenhinoedd *gw.* **brenin.**
brenhinol *a.* royal.
brenin *e.g. ll.* **brenhinoedd** king.
brennau *gw.* **pren.**
brentis *gw.* **prentis.**
brentisiaeth *gw.* **prentisiaeth.**
bres *e.g. ll.* **-i,-ys** brace. *gw.* **pres.**
breseb *gw.* **preseb.**
bresennol *gw.* **presennol.**
bresenoldeb *gw.* **presenoldeb.**
bresgripsiwn *gw.* **presgripsiwn.**
brest *e.b. ll.* **-iau** breast; chest.
breswyl: breswylfod *gw.* **preswyl.**
breswylfeydd *gw.* **preswyl.**
bresychen *e.b. ll.* **bresych** cabbage.
brethyn *e.g. ll.* **-nau** cloth. **brethyn**
  cartref home-spun cloth.
breuddwyd *e.b.g. ll.* **-ion** dream.
breuddwydio *be.* **(breuddwydiaf)** to
  dream.
breuddwydion *gw.* **breuddwyd.**
bridwerth *gw.* **pridwerth.**
bridd *gw.* **pridd.**
brif *gw.* **prif.**
brifardd *gw.* **prifardd.**
brifathrawes *gw.* **prifathrawes.**
brifathro *gw.* **prifathro.**
brifddinas *gw.* **prifddinas.**
brifeirdd *gw.* **prifardd.**
brifio *gw.* **prifio.**
brifo *be.* **(brifaf)** to hurt, to wound; to
  crumble (*N.W.*).
brifysgol *gw.* **prifysgol.**
briffordd *gw.* **priffordd.**
briffyrdd *gw.* **priffordd.**
brig *e.g. ll.* **-au** top, summit; outcrop;
  twig(s). **brig y don** crest of the
  wave; **brig y goeden** the tree top;
  brig y nos dusk; **brig y to** the roof-
  top; **o'r brig i'r bôn** from top to
  bottom; **glo brig** open-cast coal.
brigau *gw.* **brig, brigyn.**
brigyn *e.g. ll.* **brigau** twig.

brin   **bunnau**

brin *gw.* prin.
brinder *gw.* prinder.
brintio *gw.* printio.
briod *gw.* priod.
briodas *gw.* priodas.
briodi *gw.* priodi.
briodol *gw.* priodol.
bris *gw.* pris.
britho: brithio *be.* (brithaf: brithiaf) to turn grey (of hair, beard).
briwsionyn *e.g. ll.* briwsion crumb, fragment.
bro *e.b. ll.* bröydd region, country, vale, lowland. bro a bryn vale and hill; Bro Morgannwg Vale of Glamorgan.
broblem *gw.* problem.
brodor *e.g. ll.* -ion native.
brodorol *a.* native.
brodyr *gw.* brawd.
brofi *gw.* profi.
brofiad *gw.* profiad.
brofiadol *gw.* profiadol.
brofion *gw.* profion.
broffid *gw.* proffid.
broffidiol *gw.* proffidiol.
broffwyd *gw.* proffwyd.
broffwydo *gw.* proffwydo.
broga *e.g. ll.* -od frog. *gw.* ffroga.
bron 1 *e.b. ll.* -nau breast. 2 *e.b. ll.* -nydd breast of hill. 3 *ad.* almost nearly, just about to.
bronfraith *e.b. ll.* bronfreithod thrush.
bronnau: bronnydd *gw.* bron.
Brotestant *gw.* Protestant.
brown *a.* brown.
bröydd *gw.* bro.
brudd *gw.* prudd.
brwdfrydig *a.* enthusiastic.
brwnt *a.* dirty (*S.W.*), foul, cruel (*N.W.*).
brws: brwsh *e.g. ll.* brwsys: brwshys brush, broom.
brwsio: brwshio *be.* (brwsiaf: brwshiaf) to sweep, to brush.
brwsys: brwshys *gw.* brws.
brwydr *e.b. ll.* -au battle, conflict.
brwydrau *gw.* brwydr.
bryd *e.g. ll.* -iau mind, thought, intent. *gw.* pryd.

Brydain *gw.* Prydain.
brydau *gw.* pryd.
Brydeinig *gw.* Prydeinig.
bryder *gw.* pryder.
bryderu *gw.* pryderu.
bryderus *gw.* pryderus.
brydferth *gw.* prydferth.
brydferthwch *gw.* prydferthwch.
brydiau *gw.* bryd, pryd.
brydlon *gw.* prydlon.
bryf: bryfedyn: bryfyn *gw.* pryf.
bryfed *gw.* pryf.
bryfocio *gw.* profocio.
bryfyn *gw.* pryf.
bryn *e.g. ll.* -iau hill.
brynhawn *gw.* prynhawn.
bryniau *gw.* bryn.
brynu *gw.* prynu.
brynwr *gw.* prynwr.
brys *e.g.* haste, hurry. ar frys in haste, hurriedly; ar frys gwyllt in a mad rush.
brysio *be.* (brysiaf) to hasten, to hurry.
brysurdeb *gw.* prysurdeb.
brysuro *gw.* prysuro.
brysur *gw.* prysur.
buan *a.* swift, quick, fast; soon. *gw.* At. Ansoddeiriau.
buarth *e.g. ll.* -au farmyard, yard.
buchod *gw.* buwch.
budr *a.* dirty (*N.W.*), nasty (*N.W.*), foul (*N.W.*), vile (*N.W.*). bachgen budr a bit of a lad (*S.W.*).
buddsoddi *b e.* (buddsoddaf) to invest.
buddugol *a.* victorious, winning.
buddugoliaeth *e.b. ll.* -au victory.
bues i *bf.* I was, I have been. *gw.* bod.
bugail *e.g. ll.* bugeiliaid shepherd; pastor.
bugeiliaid *gw.* bugail.
bugeilio *be.* (bugeiliaf) to shepherd, to watch.
bulpud *gw.* pulpud.
bum: bump *gw.* pump.
bûm: bues *bf.* I was, I have been. *gw.* bod.
b'un *gw.* p'un.
bunnau: bunnoedd *gw.* punt.

bunt   **byrth**

bunt *gw.* **punt.**
bupur *gw.* **pupur.**
bur *gw.* **pur.**
burfa *gw.* **purfa.**
buro *gw.* **puro.**
busnes *e.g.b.* *ll.* **-ion, -au** business, affairs.
buwch *e.b.* *ll.* **buchod, da** (*S.W.*) cow.
bwced *e.g.b.* *ll.* **-i** bucket.
bwdin *gw.* **pwdin.**
bwdr *gw.* **pwdr.**
bwdryn *gw.* **pwdryn.**
bwdu *gw.* **pwdu.**
bwlch *e.g.* *ll.* **bylchau** gap, pass.
bŵer *gw.* **pŵer.**
bwll *gw.* **pwll.**
bwmp *gw.* **pwmp.**
bwnc *gw.* **pwnc.**
bwrdd *e.g.* *ll.* **byrddau** table (*N.W.*); board, plank; deck. **bwrdd brecwast** breakfast table; **bwrdd du** blackboard.
bwriad *e.g.* *ll.* **-au** purpose, intention, resolution.
bwriadu *be.* (**bwriadaf**) to intend.
bwrpas *gw.* **pwrpas.**
bwrs *gw.* **pwrs.**
bwrw *be.* (**bwriaf**) to cast; to shed; to strike. **bwrw glaw** to rain; **bwrw cesair** to hail; **bwrw eira** to snow.
bws *e.g.* *ll.* **bysiau, bysys** bus.
bwthyn *e.g.* *ll.* **bythynnod** cottage, cabin.
bwy *gw.* **pwy.**
bwyd *e.g.* *ll.* **-ydd** food.
bwyda *gw.* **bwydo.**
bwydlen *e.b.* *ll.* **-ni** menu.
bwydo: bwyda *be.* (**bwydaf**) to feed, to nourish. **bwydo'r adar** to feed the birds.
bwydydd *gw.* **bwyd.**
bwyll *gw.* **pwyll.**
bwyllgor *gw.* **pwyllgor.**
bwyllo *gw.* **pwyllo.**
bwynt *gw.* **pwynt.**
bwys *gw.* **pwys.**
bwysedd *gw.* **pwysedd.**
bwysig *gw.* **pwysig.**
bwysigrwydd *gw.* **pwysigrwydd.**
bwyslais *gw.* **pwyslais.**

bwyso *gw.* **pwyso.**
bwyta: byta (*S.W.*) *be.* (**bwytâf**) to eat; to consume, to ravage; to corrode (*S.W.*). **Bwytâf ginio bob dydd** I eat dinner every day. *gw. At. Berfau.*
bwyty *e.g.* *ll.* **bwytai** restaurant.
bwyth *gw.* **pwyth.**
bychan *a.g.* little, small, petty. *gw.* **bechan.**
byd *e.g.* *ll.* **-oedd** world; life; state. **byd caled** a hard struggle; **byd da** good living, a sumptuous life; **byd o wahaniaeth** a world of difference; **gwyn ei fyd!** blessed is he, how fortunate! **beth yn y byd. . .?** what in the world. . .? what on earth. . .?
bydoedd *gw.* **byd.**
bydru *gw.* **pydru.**
bydd (e/hi) *bf.* he/she/it will be. **Bydd Mair yno** Mair will be there; **bydd plant yno hefyd** Children will be there also. *gw.* **bod.**
byddar 1 *e.g.* *ll.* **-iaid** deaf person **2** *a.* deaf.
byddin *e.b.* *ll.* **-oedd** army, host.
byddinoedd *gw.* **byddin.**
byg *e.g.* *ll.* **bygiau** bug.
bylchai *gw.* **bwlch.**
byllau *gw.* **pwll, pyllyn.**
byllt *gw.* **bollt.**
byllyn *gw.* **pyllyn.**
bymtheg: bymtheng *gw.* **pymtheg.**
bymthegfed *gw.* **pymthegfed.**
bynciau *gw.* **pwnc.**
bynnag *rhag.* **-ever, -soever. beth bynnag** whatsoever; **ble bynnag** wherever; **pryd bynnag** whenever; **pwy bynnag** whoever.
byped *gw.* **pyped.**
byr *a.g.* *ll.* **-ion** short, brief. **dyn byr** a short man; **stori fer** a short story; **straeon byrion** short stories. *gw.* **ber.**
byrbryd *e.g.* *ll.* **-iau** snack.
byrddaid *e.g.* *ll.* **byrddeidiau** tableful.
byrddau *gw.* **bwrdd.**
byrfodd *e.g.* *ll.* **-au** abbreviation.
byrsau *gw.* **pwrs.**
byrth *gw.* **porth.**

bys   **bywydeg**

bys *e.g. ll.* **-edd** finger. **bys bawd**
thumb, big toe; **bysedd y blaidd**
lupins; **bysedd y cŵn** foxgloves.
gw. **pysen.**
bysedd *gw.* **bys.**
bysen *gw.* **pysen.**
bysgod *gw.* **pysgodyn.**
bysgodyn *gw.* **pysgodyn.**
bysgota *gw.* **pysgota.**
bysgotwr *gw.* **pysgotwr.**
bysiau *gw.* **bws.**
byst *gw.* **post,** *gw.* **postyn.**
bysys *gw.* **bws.**
byta *(S.W.) gw.* **bwyta.**
byth 1 *ad.* ever, still, always. **am
byth** for ever; **byth a hefyd**
continually. **2** (**byth** *is frequently
used in negative sentences in the
present, future, imperfect and*

*conditional tense to convey the
meaning* never). **Ddaw e byth** He
will never come; **Doedd hi byth yn
hwyr** She was never late. **3** *e.g. ll.* **-
oedd** eternity. **byth bythoedd** for
ever and ever, world without end.
bythefnos *gw.* **pythefnos.**
bythynnod *gw.* **bwthyn.**
byw 1 *be.* **(bywiaf)** to live, to exist, to
dwell, to inhabit; to animate, to
revive, to restore to life. **byw a bod**
to be habitually present; **Mae e'n
byw yma** He lives here.
2 *a.* alive, living. **Ydy e'n fyw?** Is
he alive? **3** *e.g.* life. **yn fy myw** for
the life of me.
bywiog *a.* lively, vivacious.
bywyd *e.g. ll.* **-au** life, existence.
bywydeg *e.b.* biology.

caban *e.g. ll.* **-au** booth, cabin, hut.
cacen *e.b. ll.* **-nau, -ni** cake *(N.W.).*
cacwn *gw.* **cacynen.**
cacynen *e.b. ll.* **cacwn** wasp
(N.W.). **yn gacwn gwyllt** furious.
cadach *e.g. ll.* **-au** cloth, rag;
handkerchief, bandage *(N.W.).*
cadach llawr cloth for wiping
floor; **cadach llestri** dish cloth.
cadair *e.b. ll.* **cadeiriau** chair.
cadair esmwyth easy chair; **cadair
freichiau** arm chair.
cadeirio *be.* **(cadeiriaf)** to chair.
cadeiriol *a.* chaired. **eglwys
gadeiriol** cathedral.
cadeirydd *e.g. ll.* **-ion** chairman.
cadno *e.g. ll.* **cadnoaid, cadnawon**
fox. **cadnawes: cadnöes** vixen
(S.W.).
cadw (rhag.) *be.* **(cadwaf)** to keep,
to preserve (from). **cadw ar gof** to
keep on record; **cadw draw** to stay
away; **cadw sŵn** to make a noise,
to complain; **cadw'n heini** to keep
fit; **cadw ystafell** to reserve a
room; **cadw-mi-gei** money box;
cyfrif cadw deposit account.
cadwrol *a.* conservative.
cadwyn *e.b. ll.* **-au, -i** chain; series.
cadwyno *be.* **(cadwynaf)** to chain,
to enslave.
cae *e.g. ll.* **-au** field.
caeau *gw.* **cae.**

cael *be.* **(caf)** to have, to find. **ar
gael** in existence, available; **cael
annwyd** to catch a cold; **cael blas
ar** to enjoy; **cael a chael** a close
call. *gw. At. Berfau.*
caer *a.b. ll.* **-au, ceyrydd** fort,
castle.
Caer *e.b.* Chester.
Caerdydd *e.b.* Cardiff.
Caeredin *e.b.* Edinburgh.
Caerfyrddin *e.b.* Carmarthen.
Caergybi *e.b.* Holyhead.
Caerloyw *e.b.* Gloucester.
Caersalem: Jerwsalem *e.b.*
Jerusalem.
caets *e.g. ll.* **-ys** cage.
caf *bf.* I have, I shall have. *gw.* **cael.**
cafodd *bf.* he/she/it had. *gw.* **cael.**
caffe *e.g. ll.* **-s** café.
cangen *e.b. ll.* **canghennau**
branch.
canghennau *gw.* **cangen.**
caiff *bf.* he/she/it will have. *gw.* **cael.**
cais *e.g. ll.* **ceisiadau, ceisiau**
attempt; try *(rugby)*; request;
application. **gwneud cais** to make
an application, to apply.
calan *e.g. ll.* **-nau** first day *(of
month or season).* **Dydd Calan**
New Year's Day; **Calan Gaeaf** All
Saints' Day; **Calan Mai** May Day.
caled *a.* hard, hardy, difficult. *gw.
At. Ansoddeiriau.*
caledi *e.g.* hardship, severity.
caledu *be.* **(caledaf)** to harden; to
dry. **caledu dillad** to air clothes;
caledu gwely to air a bed.
caledwch *e.g.* hardness; difficulty.
calendr *e.g. ll.* **-au** calendar.
calenigion *gw.* **calennig.**
calennig *e.g. ll.* **calenigion** New
Year's Gift.
caletach *gw.* **caled.**
caletaf *gw.* **caled.**
caleted *gw.* **caled.**
calon *e.b. ll.* **-nau** heart. **diolch o
galon** heartfelt thanks; **calon lân**
pure heart; **calon y gwir** the
absolute truth.
call *a.* wise, sensible, **hanner call a
chrac** foolish, stupid. *gw. At.*

callach   **cantor**

Ansoddeiriau.
callach *gw.* **call.**
callaf *gw.* **call.**
called *gw.* **call.**
cam 1 *e.g. ll.* **-au** stride, step; injury.
o gam i gam step by step.
2 *a.* crooked, false. **coesgam**
bandy-legged.
camarwain *be.* **(camarweiniaf)** to
mislead.
camddeall *be.* **(camddeallaf)** to
misunderstand.
camera *e.g. ll.* **camerâu** camera.
camp *e.b. ll.* **-au** feat, game;
excellence. **campau** sports.
campfa *e.b. ll.* **campfeydd**
gymnasium.
campfeydd *gw.* **campfa.**
campus *a.* excellent, splendid.
campwaith *e.g. ll.* **campweithiau**
masterpiece.
campweithiau *gw.* **campwaith.**
camsyniad *e.g. ll.* **-au** mistake
(S.W.).
camu *be.* **(camaf)** to step, to stride;
to bend, to stoop.
cân *e.b. ll.* **caniadau, caneuon**
song, poem. **cân actol** action song;
cân bop pop song; **cân serch** love
song; **cân werin** folksong; **cân
ysgafn** ballad.
can 1 *a.* white; hundred. **canpunt** a
hundred pounds (sterling);
canmlwydd a hundred years old;
canmil a hundred thousand; **canrif**
a century. *gw.* **cant.**
2 *e.g.* white flour, flour; **bara cân**
white bread. **3** *e.g. ll.* **-iau** *(tin)* can.
caneuon *gw.* **cân.**
canfed *a.* hundredth.
canhwyllau *gw.* **cannwyll.**
canhwyllbren *e.g. ll.* **-nau, -ni**
candlestick.
caniad *e.g. ll.* **-au** song, singing;
ring *(telephone).* **Rhowch ganiad i
fi** Telephone me.
caniadaeth *e.b.* music, singing.
Caniadaeth y Cysegr Songs of
Praise.
caniadau *gw.* **cân, caniad.**
caniatâd *e.g.* permission, consent.

caniatáu *be.* **(caniatâf)** to allow.
caniedydd *e.g. ll.* **-ion** song-book,
hymn-book.
canmlwydd *e.ll. & e.b. ll.* **-i** a
hundred years old, hundred years;
century.
canmlwyddiannau *gw.*
canmlwyddiant.
canmlwyddiant *e.g. ll.*
canmlwyddiannau centenary.
canmol 1 *be.* **(canmolaf)** to praise.
2 *e.g.* praise.
canmoliaeth *e.b. ll.* **-au** praise.
cannoedd *gw.* **cant.**
cannu *be.* to bleach, to whiten.
cannwyll *e.b. ll.* **canhwyllau**
candle. **cannwyll y llygad** pupil of
the eye; apple of the eye.
canol 1 *e.g. ll.* **-au** centre, middle.
canol dydd midday; **canol nos**
midnight. **2** *a.* middle.
canolbarth *e.g. ll.* **-au** midland;
Canolbarth Cymru Mid Wales;
Canolbarth Lloegr The Midlands;
Canolbarth Ffrainc Central
France.
canolbwyntio (ar) *be.*
(canolbwyntiaf) to concentrate, to
focus (on).
canoldir *e.g. ll.* **-oedd** inland
region. **Y Môr Canoldir**
Mediterranean Sea.
canolfan *e.b. ll.* **-nau** centre.
canolfan ddinesig civic centre;
canolfan hamdden leisure centre.
canolog *a.* central.
canolwr *e.g. ll.* **canolwyr** referee,
umpire.
canradd *a.* centigrade.
canran *e.b. ll.* **canrannau**
percentage.
canrif *e.b. ll.* **canrifau, canrifoedd**
century.
canrifau: canrifoedd *gw.* **canrif.**
cant: can *e.g. ll.* **cannoedd**
hundred. **cant a mil** a hundred and
one, a large number; **cant y cant**
hundred per cent; **deg y cant** ten
per cent; **can diolch** many thanks;
canwaith a hundred times.
cantor *e.g. ll.* **-ion** precentor. *gw.*

cantores; canwr.
cantores *e.b. ll.* **-au** female singer, female vocalist. *gw.* **cantor; canwr.**
canu *be.* **(canaf)** to sing, to play. **canu cloch** to ring a bell; **canu'n iach** to bid goodbye; **canu'r piano** to play the piano; **wedi canu ar** too late, all up. *gw. At. Berfau.*
canŵ *e.g. ll.* **-od** canoe.
canŵio *be.* **(canŵiaf)** to canoe.
canwr *e.g. ll.* **canwyr** male singer, vocalist. *gw.* **cantor; cantores.**
canwriad *e.g. ll.* **canwriaid** centurion.
cap *e.g. ll.* **-iau** cap.
capel *e.g. ll.* **-i, -au** chapel.
capteiniaid *gw.* **capten.**
capten *e.g. ll.* **-iaid, capteiniaid** captain.
capteniaid *gw.* **capten.**
car *e.g. ll.* **ceir** car. **car heddlu** police car; **car rasio** racing car; **car llusg** sled.
carafán *e.b. ll.* **-au** caravan.
carafana *be.* **(carafanaf)** to go caravanning.
carco *be.* **(carcaf)** to take care of *(S.W.).*
carcus *a.* careful *(S.W.).*
carchar *e.g. ll.* **-au** prison.
carcharor *e.g. ll.* **-ion** prisoner.
carcharu *be.* **(carcharaf)** to imprison.
cardiau *gw.* **cerdyn.**
caredig *a.* kind.
caredigrwydd *e.g.* kindness.
cariad *e.g.b. ll.* **-on** love, lover. **Dere 'ma, cariad!** Come here, love!
cariadon *gw.* **cariad.**
cariadus *a.* beloved; loving.
cario *be.* **(cariaf)** to carry.
carlamu *be.* **(carlamaf)** to gallop.
carol *e.b. ll.* **-ai** carol. **carol Nadolig** Christmas carol.
carped *e.g. ll.* **-i** carpet.
carreg *e.b. ll.* **cerrig** stone. **carreg aelwyd** hearthstone; **carreg fedd** tombstone; **carreg filltir** milestone; **carreg y drws** doorstep; **cerrig mân** pebbles, chippings.

cartref *e.g. ll.* **-i** home. **gartref** at home; **adref** homewards.
cartrefi *gw.* **cartref.**
cartrefu *be.* **(cartrefaf)** to dwell.
caru *b e.* **(caraf)** to love, to like, to court.
carwriaeth *e.b. ll.* **carwriaethau** affair, romance.
cas *e.g.* enmity, hated person or thing; case. **2** *a.* nasty.
casáu *be.* **(casâf)** to detest.
casgen *e.b. ll.* **casgenni** barrel.
casgenni *gw.* **casgen.**
casgliad *e.g. ll.* **-au** collection; gathering; conclusion. **Fe ddaeth i'r casgliad** He came to the conclusion.
casglu *be.* **(casglaf)** to collect, to infer. **casglu dros** to collect on behalf of.
Cas-gwent *e.b.* Chepstow.
Casllwchwr *e.b.* Loughor.
Casnewydd *e.b.* Newport *(Mon.).*
castell *e.g. ll.* **cestyll** castle.
Castell-nedd *e.b.* Neath.
cath *e.b. ll.* **-od** cat. **cath fach** kitten; **cwrcath, cwrcyn** tomcat.
cau **1** *be.* **(caeaf)** to close. **2** *a.* enclosed; hollow.
cawl **1** *e.g.* soup, broth. **cawl cennin** leek broth; **cawl pys** pea soup. **2** *e.g.* mess. **Fe wnaeth e gawl o'r trefniadau** He made a mess of the arrangements.
cawod *e.b. ll.* **cawodydd** shower. **cawodydd Ebrill** April showers.
cawr *e.g. ll.* **cewri** giant. **cawr o wleidydd** a great politician.
caws *e.g.* cheese. **caws Caer** Cheshire cheese; **caws Caerffili** Caerffili cheese; **cael caws o fola ci** to get blood out of a stone. *gw.* **cosyn.**
cefn *e.g. ll.* **-au** back; ridge; support. **cefn gwlad** heart of the countryside. **Roedd e'n gefn i'r teulu** He was a great help to the family.
cefnder *e.g. ll.* **-wyr, cefndyr** cousin *(male); gw.* **cyfnither.**
cefnderwyr *gw.* **cefnder.**

cefndir *e.g. ll.* -**oedd** background.
cefndiroedd *gw.* **cefndir.**
cefndyr *gw.* **cefnder.**
cefnogi *be.* (**cefnogaf**) to support.
cefnu (ar) *be.* (**cefnaf**) to turn one's back upon, to forsake.
cefnwr *e.g. ll.* **cefnwyr** back, full-back.
ceffyl *e.g. ll.* -**au** horse. **ceffyl blaen** leading horse, pushy person; **ceffyl brith** piebald horse; **ceffyl gwinau** bay (horse); **ceffyl siglo** rocking horse; **ar gefn ei geffyl** on his high horse, exultant.
ceg *e.b. ll.* -**au** mouth. (**cael, rhoi**) **llond ceg** *(to receive, to give)* a telling off.
cegin *e.b. ll.* -**au** kitchen. **cegin fach** kitchenette; **cegin gefn** back kitchen.
cei *e.g. ll.* **ceiau** quay. *gw.* **cael.**
ceidwad *e.g. ll.* **ceidwaid** keeper.
ceiliog *e.g. ll.* -**od** cockerel. **ceiliog y gwynt** weathercock; **ceiliog y rhedyn** grasshopper.
Ceinewydd *e.b.* Newquay.
ceiniog *e.b. ll.* -**au** penny. **heb geiniog goch** without a brass farthing or penny.
ceir *gw.* **car.**
ceiriosen *e.b. ll.* **ceirios** cherry.
ceisiadau: ceisiau *gw.* **cais.**
ceisio *be.* (**ceisiaf**) to seek, to ask. **ceisio am** to try for, to apply for.
celf *e.b. ll.* -**au** art, craft; **Adran Celf** Art Department.
celfi *gw.* **celficyn.**
celficyn *e.g. ll.* **celfi** a piece of furniture; a tool.
Celtaidd *a.* Celtic.
celwydd *e.g. ll.* -**au** lie, untruth. **celwydd golau** white lie; **celwydd noeth** barefaced lie; **celwyddgi** a liar.
celwyddog *a.* untruthful.
celyn *gw.* **celynnen.**
celynnen *e.b. ll.* **celyn** holly. **llwyn celyn** holly bush.
cell *e.b. ll.* -**oedd,** -**au** cell.
cellau: celloedd *gw.* **cell.**
cemeg *e.b.* chemistry.

cenadaethau *gw.* **cenhadaeth.**
cenedl *e.b. ll.* **cenhedloedd** nation; species, kind; gender *(grammar)*. **Cenedl y Cymry** the Welsh nation; **Y Cenhedloedd** the Gentiles; **y Cenhedloedd Unedig** the United Nations; **cenedl enwau** gender of nouns.
cenedlaethau *gw.* **cenhedlaeth.**
cenedlaethol *a.* national. **Llyfrgell Genedlaethol Cymru** National Library of Wales.
cenedlaetholdeb *e.b.* nationalism.
cenedlaetholwr *e.g. ll.* **cenedlaetholwyr** a nationalist.
cenedlaetholwyr *gw.* **cenedlaetholwr.**
cenedligrwydd *e.g.* nationality.
cenfigennus *a.* jealous.
cenhadaeth *e.b. ll.* **cenadaethau** mission; embassy.
cenhadol *a.* missionary.
cenhadon *gw.* **cenhadwr.**
cenhadu *be.* (**cenhadaf**) to conduct a mission; to allow.
cenhadwr *e.g. ll.* **cenhadon** a missionary; **cenhades** a female missionary.
cenhedlaeth *e.b. ll.* **cenedlaethau** generation; nation.
cenhedloedd *gw.* **cenedl.**
cenhinen *e.b. ll.* **cennin** leek. **cenhinen Bedr** daffodil.
cenllysg *e.torf.* hailstones.
cennin *gw.* **cenhinen.**
cer *bf.* go! *(singular). gw.* **mynd.**
cerdyn *e.g. ll.* **cardiau** card. **cerdyn Nadolig** Christmas card; **cerdyn pen-blwydd** birthday card.
cerdd *e.b. ll.* -**au,** -**i** song, poem; music. **cerdd dafod** poetic art, poetry; music; **cerdd dant** instrumental music; penillion singing.
cerdded *be.* (**cerddaf**) to walk.
cerddi *gw.* **cerdd.**
cerddor *e.g. ll.* -**ion** musician.
cerddorfa *e.b. ll.* **cerddorfeydd** orchestra. **Cerddorfa Ieuenctid** Youth Orchestra.
cerddorfeydd *gw.* **cerddorfa.**

cerddoriaeth   **Clwyd**

cerddoriaeth *e.b.* music.
cerddorol *a.* musical.
cerddwr *e.g. ll.* **cerddwyr** walker.
  Cymdeithas Cerddwyr Llanelli
  Llanelli Ramblers' Association.
cerddwyr *gw.* **cerddwr.**
cerfio *be.* **(cerfiaf)** to carve.
cerflun *e.g. ll.* **-iau** statue.
cerrig *gw.* **carreg.**
cerwch *bf.* go! *(plural). gw.* **mynd.**
ces *bf.* I had. *gw.* **cael.**
cesair *e. torf.* hailstones *(S.W.).*
cestyll *gw.* **castell.**
ceubren *e.g. ll.* **-nau** hollow tree.
cewri *gw.* **cawr.**
cewyn *e.g. ll.* **-nau, -ion** napkin
  (S.W.).
ceyrydd *gw.* **caer.**
ci *e.g. ll.* **cŵn** dog. **ci bach** pup, **ci**
  defaid sheepdog; **ci hela** hound;
  corgi corgi; **milgi** greyhound.
cig *e.g. ll.* **-oedd** meat; gum. **cig**
  eidion beef; **cig oen** lamb; **cig**
  moch bacon.
cigydd *e.g. ll.* **-ion** butcher.
cigyddion *gw.* **cigydd.**
cilio (i, rhag.) *be.* **(ciliaf)** to flee; to
  retreat (to, from). **cilio i** to flee
  towards; **cilio rhag** to flee from, to
  retreat from.
ciniawau *gw.* **cinio.**
cinio *e.g.b. ll.* **ciniawau** dinner.
cipolwg *e.g. ll.* **cipolygon** glance.
cist *e.b. ll.* **-iau** chest, coffer.
claf 1 *e.g. ll.* **cleifion** sick person.
  2 *a.* ill.
clai *e.g. ll.* **cleiau, cleion** clay.
  traed o glai mortal.
clasur *e.g. ll.* **-on** a classic.
clasurol *a.* classical.
clawdd *e.g. ll.* **cloddiau** wall made
  of earth, ditch. **Clawdd Offa** Offa's
  Dyke.
clawr *e.g. ll.* **cloriau** cover, lid. **ar**
  glawr on record.
clebran *be.* **(clebraf)** to chatter.
cledr *e.b. ll.* **-au** pole, rafter; rail;
  palm *(of hand).* **cledrau** rails *(of*
  railway).
clefyd *e.g. ll.* **-au, -on** sickness.
  clefyd melyn jaundice; **clefyd**

melys/siwgr diabetes.
cleifion *gw.* **claf.**
clêr *gw.* **cleren.**
clerc *e.g. ll.* **-od** clerk.
cleren *e.b. ll.* **clêr** fly *(S.W.).* **cleren**
  lwyd horse-fly.
clir *a.* clear.
clirio *be.* **(cliriaf)** to clear.
clo *e.g. ll.* **-eau, -eon** lock. **ar glo**
  locked; **dan glo** locked, locked up,
  under lock and key; **yng nghlo**
  locked; **twll y clo** keyhole.
cloc *e.g. ll.* **-iau** clock. **cloc larwm**
  alarm-clock.
clocwedd *a.* clockwise.
cloch *be. ll.* **clychau** bell. **cloch y**
  llan chuch-bell; **clychau'r gog**
  bluebells; **dau o'r gloch** two
  o'clock.
clod *e.g.b. ll.* **-ydd** praise.
clodfori *be.* **(clodforaf)** to praise.
cloddiau *gw.* **clawdd.**
cloeau *gw.* **clo.**
cloeon *gw.* **clo.**
cloff *a.* lame.
cloffi 1 *be.* **(cloffaf)** to become lame.
  cloffi rhwng dau feddwl to
  hesitate.
  2 *e.g.* lameness.
clogwyn *e.g. ll.* **-au, -i** cliff, crag.
clogwyni: clogwynau *gw.* **clogwyn.**
clogyn *e.g. ll.* **-au** cloak.
cloi *be.* **(cloaf, clof)** to lock; to
  conclude. **cloi allan** to lock out, to
  exclude; **cload allan** lock-out;
  Nawr i gloi Now to conclude.
clorian *e.b. ll.* **-nau** scales.
cloriau *gw.* **clawr.**
clown *e.g. ll.* **-iaid** clown.
clun *e.b. ll.* **-iau** hip; thigh; leg.
clust *e.b. ll.* **-iau** ear. **bonclust** box
  on the ear.
clustog *e.b. ll.* **-au** pillow, cushion.
clwm *e.g. ll.* **clymau** knot; tie. *gw.*
  cwlwm.
clwtyn *e.g. ll.* **clytiau** rag *(S.W.).*
  clwtyn llawr floor cloth; **clwtyn**
  llestri dish cloth; **clwtyn ymolch**
  face cloth. **ar y clwt** stranded,
  abandoned; without work.
Clwyd *e.b.* Former County in N.E.

24

clwyd   **cornel**

Wales.

clwyd *e.b.* *ll.* **-i, -au** gate.

clwydi: clwydau *gw.* **clwyd.**

clwyf *e.g.* *ll.* **-au** wound, injury.
  clwyf y traed a'r genau foot and
  mouth disease.

clychau *gw.* **cloch.**

clymau *gw.* **clwm, cwlwm.**

clymu *be.* **(clymaf)** to tie.

clytiau *gw.* **clwtyn.**

clyw 1 *e.g.* hearing, earshot. **trwm ei
  glyw** hard of hearing; **yn fy nghlyw**
  within my hearing. **2** *bf.* hear!
  (singular), listen! *(singular), gw.*
  clywed.

clywed (am, oddi wrth) *be.* **(clywaf)**
  to hear (of, from); to feel; to taste; to
  smell. **Clywch, clywch!** Hear, hear!

cnau *gw.* **cneuen.**

cneuen *e.b.* *ll.* **cnau** nut.

cnoc *e.g.b.* *ll.* **-au** a knock; a fool
  (S.W.). **tipyn o gnoc:** quite a fool;
  cnocell y coed woodpecker.

cnocio; cnoco *be.* **(cnociaf:
  cnocaf)** to knock, to strike.

cnoi *be.* **(cnoaf)** to bite, to chew.
  cnoi cil to chew the cud; to mull
  over.

coban *e.b.* *ll.* **cobannau** night-shirt.

cobannau *gw.* **coban.**

coch *a.* *ll.* **-ion** red. **yn goch**
  obscene; of poor quality; **coch y
  berllan** bullfinch. *gw. At.
  Ansoddeiriau.*

cochach *gw.* **coch.**

cochaf *gw.* **coch.**

coched *gw.* **coch.**

cochen *e.b.* red-haired female.

cochyn *e.b.* red-haired male.

codi *be.* **(codaf)** to rise, to erect, to
  pick up; to withdraw *(money)*, to
  charge (fee).

coed *gw.* **coeden.**

Coed-duon Blackwood.

coeden *e.b.* *ll.* **coed** tree.

coedwig *e.b.* *ll.* **-oedd** forest, wood.

coes *e.b.* *ll.* **-au** leg. **tynnu coes** to
  leg pull.

cof *e.g.* *ll.* **-ion** memory;
  remembrance. **er cof am** in
  memory of; **o fewn cof** within

living memory; **o'i gof** angry; mad;
  ar gof a chadw recorded and
  preserved, on record; **cofion
  cynnes** warmest regards.

cofio (am) *be.* **(cofiaf)** to remember.

cofion *gw.* **cof.**

cofleidio *be.* **(cofleidiaf)** to
  embrace.

cofrestr *e.b.* *ll.* **-au, -i** register.

cofrestru *be.* **(cofrestraf)** to
  register.

coffi *e.g.* coffee; **noson goffi** coffee
  evening.

cog 1 *e.b.* *ll.* **-au** cuckoo. *gw.*
  cwcw.
  2 *e.g.* *ll.* **-au** cook.

coginio *be.* **(coginiaf)** to cook.

cogydd *e.g.* *ll.* **-ion** cook.

coleg *e.g.* *ll.* **-au** college.

coler *e.g.b.* *ll.* **-au, -i** collar.

colofn *e.b.* *ll.* **-au** column, pillar.

coluro *be.* **(coluraf)** to colour, to
  make up.

colled *e.g.b.* *ll.* **-ion** loss. **Roedd
  colled arni** She was angry.

collen *e.b.* *ll.* **cyll** hazel. **cnau cyll**
  hazelnuts.

colli *be.* **(collaf)** to lose, to spill, to
  fail, to miss. **ar goll** lost, missing,
  mislaid.

copi *e.g.* *ll.* **copïau** a copy.

copïo *be.* **(copïaf)** to copy.

copyn *e.g.* *ll.* **-nau, -nod** spider.
  pryf copyn spider.

côr *e.g.* *ll.* **corau** choir, pew (in
  church or chapel); stall, crib. **côr
  cymysg** mixed choir; **côr merched**
  ladies' choir.

corau *gw.* **côr.**

cordyn *e.g.* *ll.* **-ion** cord, string.

corff *e.g.* *ll.* **cyrff** body; corpse;
  capital. **Yr Hen Gorff** Calvinistic
  Methodists.

corfforol *a.* bodily, physical.
  Addysg Gorfforol physical
  education.

corgi *e.g.* *ll.* **corgwn** corgi.

corn *e.g.* *ll.* **cyrn** horn; corn; cairn;
  chimney. **corn simdde** chimney
  stack; **Siôn Corn** Father Christmas.

cornel *e.b.g.* *ll.* **-au, -i** corner.

coron   **cron**

coron *e.b. ll.* **-au** crown.
coroni *be.* **(coronaf)** to crown. **i goroni'r cwbl** to cap it all.
corryn *e.g. ll.* **corynnod** spider *(S.W.)*.
corynnod *gw.* **corryn.**
cosb *e.b. ll.* **-au** punishment, penalty. **y gosb eithaf** capital punishment; **cic gosb** penalty kick.
cosbi *be.* **(cosbaf)** to punish.
cosi 1 *be.* **(cosaf)** to itch. **2** *e.g.* itch.
costus *a.* expensive.
cosyn *e.g. ll.* **-nau** a small cheese. *gw.* **caws.**
cot: côt *e.b. ll.* **cotau: cotiau** coat. **cot fawr** overcoat; **cot law** raincoat.
cotau: cotiau *gw.* **cot.**
cotwm *e.g. ll.* **cotymau** cotton.
crac 1 *e.g. ll.* **-au, -iau** crack. **2** *a.* angry *(S.W.)*.
crachach *e.ll.* snobs *(S.W.)*.
crafu 1 *be.* **(crafaf)** to scratch; to scrape. **2** *e.g.* itch.
crafiad *e.g. ll.* **-au** scratch.
cragen *e.b. ll.* **cregyn** shell.
craig *e.b. ll.* **creigiau** rock, cliff. **Mae e'n graig o arian.** He's very wealthy.
cras *a. ll.* **creision** baked; scorched; harsh. **llai cras** not so highly baked; **tafod cras** a harsh tongue; **llais cras** a raucous voice. *gw.* **creisionyn.**
crasu *be.* **(crasaf)** to bake; to scorch.
credu (yn) *be.* **(credaf)** to believe, to trust (in).
crefydd *e.b. ll.* **-au** religion.
crefft *e.b. ll.* **-au** skill, craft.
crefftwr *e.g. ll.* **crefftwyr** craftsman.
crefftwyr *gw.* **crefftwr.**
cregyn *gw.* **cragen.**
creigiau *gw.* **craig.**
creigiog *a.* rocky.
creision *gw.* **cras, creisionyn.**
creisionyn *e.g. ll.* **creision** crisp, flake. **creision ŷd** corn flakes.
crempog *e.b. ll.* **-au** pancake *(N.W.). gw.* **ffroesen.**

creulon *a.* cruel.
creulondeb *e.g. ll.* **-au** cruelty.
cri *e.g.b. ll.* **-au** cry, lament.
crib *e.b. ll.* **-au** comb; bird's comb; crest, summit, ridge. **crib y ceiliog** the cock's comb; **crib y mynydd** the mountain's ridge; **mynd â chrib fân** to examine minutely.
cribo *be.* **(cribaf)** to comb; to card.
criced *e.g.* cricket (game).
cricedwr *e.g. ll.* **cricedwyr** cricketer.
cricsyn *e.g. ll.* **criciaid, crics** a cricket *(insect)*.
crio (am, ar) *be.* **(criaf)** to shout, to weep *(N.W.)*.
Cristion *e.g. ll.* **Cristnogion** Christian.
criw *e.g. ll.* **-iau** crew, crowd. **criw o bobl ifainc** a gang of young people.
croen *e.g. ll.* **crwyn** skin, hide; peel. **croendenau** thin-skinned; sensitive; **croendew** thick-skinned; insensitive; **croenddu** black-skinned; negroid; **croen ei din ar ei dalcen** in a bad mood.
croes *e.b. ll.* **-au** cross. **croes Crist** Christ's cross.
croesair *e.g. ll.* **croeseiriau** crossword; **pos croeseiriau** crossword puzzle.
croesau *gw.* **croes.**
croesawu *be.* **(croesawaf)** to welcome.
croesawus *a.* hospitable.
croeseiriau *gw.* **croesair.**
croesfan *e.g. ll.* **-nau** crossing.
croesffordd *e.b. ll.* **croesffyrdd** crossroad.
croeshoelio *be.* **(croeshoeliaf)** to crucify.
croesholi *be.* **(croesholaf)** to cross-examine. **croesholiad** a cross-examination.
croesi *be.* **(croesaf)** to cross, to oppose.
croeso *e.g.* welcome. **y Bwrdd Croeso** the Welsh Tourist Board.
Croesoswallt *e.b.* Oswestry.
cron *a.b.* round. *gw.* **crwn.**

cronfa *e.b. ll.* **cronfeydd** reservoir; fund.
cronfeydd *gw.* **cronfa.**
crud *e.g. ll.* **-au, -iau** cradle.
crwn *a.g.* round. *gw.* **cron.**
crwst *e.g. ll.* **crystiau** crust. *gw.* **crystyn.**
crwyn *gw.* **croen.**
cryd *e.g. ll.* **-iau** shivering, fever. **Mae'r cryd arna i** I've got the shivers; **cryd y cymalau** rheumatism.
cryf *a. ll.* **-ion** strong, powerful. *gw. At. Ansoddeiriau.*
cryfach *gw.* **cryf.**
cryfaf *gw.* **cryf.**
cryfed *gw.* **cryf.**
crynhoi *be.* **(crynhoaf)** to collect, to gather, to summarise. **i grynhoi** to sum up.
cryno *a.* tidy; suitable; compact. **ffurfiau cryno'r ferf** compact forms of the verb; **cryno ddisg** compact disc.
crynodeb *e.g.b. ll.* **-au** precis, summary; tidiness.
crynu *be.* **(crynaf)** to shiver, to quake. **daeargryn** earthquake.
crys *e.g. ll.* **-au** shirt. **crys T** T-shirt; **Y Crysau Cochion** The Welsh Rugby Team.
crystiau *gw.* **crwst, crystyn.**
crystyn *e.g. ll.* **crystiau, crust.** *gw.* **crwst.**
cu *a.* dear, fond, beloved. **mam-gu** grandmother *(S.W.).* **tad-cu** grandfather *(S.W.).*
cuddio (rhag) *be.* **(cuddiaf)** to hide (from), to cover, to bury.
cul *a. ll.* **-ion** narrow, narrow-minded. **culfor** *e.g.* strait, channel.
curo *be.* **(curaf)** to strike, to knock, to defeat. **curo dwylo** to clap hands.
cusan *e.g.b. ll.* **-au** kiss.
cusanu *be.* **(cusanaf)** to kiss.
cw *gw.* **acw.**
cwb *e.g. ll.* **cybiau** kennel, coop.
cwbl 1 *a.* all, complete, entire. **cwbl iach** completely healthy; **cwbl gyfan** quite complete; **cwbl sicr** completely certain.
2 *e.g. ll. (used with the definite article)* all, everything. **y cwbl** everything, all: **y cwbl oll** everything, the whole lot; **dim o gwbl** nothing at all; **dyna'r cwbl** that's all; **Prynodd e'r cwbl** He bought everything.
cwblhau *be.* **(cwblhaf)** to finish, to complete.
cwcw *e.b. ll.* **cwcŵod** cuckoo *(S.W.). gw.* **cog.**
cwch *e.g. ll.* **cychod** boat; hive. **cwch hwylio** sailing boat; **cwch modur** motor boat; **cwch pysgota** fishing boat; **cwch rhwyfo** rowing boat; **cwch gwenyn** beehive.
cwd *e.g. ll.* **cydau** bag; purse; sack.
cwdyn *e.g. ll.* **cydau** bag; purse; sack.
cweryl *e.g. ll.* **-au, -on** quarrel.
cweryla (â) *be.* **(cwerylaf)** to quarrel (with).
cwerylau: cwerylon *gw.* **cweryl.**
cwestiwn *e.g. ll.* **cwestiynau** question.
cwestiyna *be.* **(cwestiynaf)** to question.
cwestiynau *gw.* **cwestiwn.**
cwlwm *e.g. ll.* **clymau** knot; bunch. *gw.* **clwm.**
cwm *e.g. ll.* **cymoedd** valley. **Cwm Tawe** Swansea Valley.
cwmni *e.g. ll.* **cwmnïau, cwmnïoedd** company. **cwmni yswiriant** insurance company.
cwmnïau *gw.* **cwmni.**
cwmnïoedd *gw.* **cwmni.**
cwmwl *e.g. ll.* **cymylau** cloud.
cŵn *gw.* **ci.**
cwningen *e.b. ll.* **cwningod** rabbit.
cwningod *gw.* **cwningen.**
cwpan *e.g.b. ll.* **-au** cup.
cwpla *be.* **(cwplâf)** to finish *(S.W.).*
cwpwrdd *e.g. ll.* **cypyrddau** cupboard. **cwpwrdd cornel** corner cupboard.
cwr *e.g. ll.* **cyrrau, cyrion** corner, end; edge, border; outskirts. **ar gwr y dref** on the outskirts of the town.
cwrdd 1 *e.g. ll.* **cyrddau** meeting

cwrs   **cyfleu**

(S.W.), religious service, congregation. **cwrdd gweddi** prayer-meeting; **cyrddau mawr** special preaching meetings; **tŷ cwrdd** chapel *(nonconformist)*. 2 *be.* **(cwrddaf)** to meet, to come together; to touch. **cwrdd â** to meet, meeting.

cwrs *e.g. ll.* **cyrsau, cyrsiau** course.

cwrtais *a.* courteous.

cwrw *e.g. ll.* **-au** beer.

cwsg 1 *e.g.* sleep; numbness. **2** *a.* asleep; numb. **ynghwsg** asleep; lifeless, numb.

cwsmer *e.g. ll.* **-iaid** customer.

cwstwm *e.g. ll.* **cystymau** custom, patronage.

cwt *e.b.g. ll.* **cytiau** hut, sty, wound; tail; queue. **cwt ieir** chicken coop.

cwta *a.* short, abrupt.

cwymp *e.g. ll.* **-au, -iau** fall, slope; collapse.

cwympo *be.* **(cwympaf)** to fall; to fell.

cwyn *e.b.g. ll.* **-au, -ion** complaint.

cwyno (am, i) *be.* **(cwynaf)** to complain (about, to).

cwyr *e.g. ll.* **-au** beeswax; wax.

cychod *gw.* **cwch.**

cychwyn 1 *e.g.* beginning, start. **2** *be.* **(cychwynnaf)** to begin, to start. **ar y cychwyn** at first, at the start.

cydadrodd *be.* **(cydadroddaf)** to recite together. **parti cydadrodd** choral speaking party.

cydau *gw.* **cwd, cwdyn.**

cydio (yn) *be.* **(cydiaf)** to join, to connect, to couple, to take hold (of).

cydnabod 1 *be.* **(cydnabyddaf)** to acknowledge; to honour, to remunerate. **2** *e.g.* acquaintance.

cydwybodol *a.* conscientious.

cydymdeimlad *e.g. ll.* **cydymdeimladau** sympathy.

cyfagos *a.* neighbouring.

cyfaill *e.g. ll.* **cyfeillion** friend, companion. **Annwyl Gyfeillion** Dear Friends *(form of address)*. *gw.* **cyfeilles.**

cyfan *e.g. ll.* **-ion** all, total, entirety. **y cyfan** all, the lot, everything: **ar y cyfan** on the whole; **wedi'r cyfan** after all.

cyfangwbl *a.* altogether, complete, whole. **yn gyfangwbl** completely, wholly; **Roedd e'n gyfangwbl ddu** He was completely black.

cyfansoddi *be.* **(cyfansoddaf)** to compose; to establish.

cyfansoddwr *e.g. ll.* **cyfansoddwyr** composer.

cyfanswm *e.g. ll.* **cyfansymiau** total, amount.

cyfarch *be.* **(cyfarchaf)** to greet.

cyfarchion *e.ll.* greetings.

cyfarfod 1 *e.g. ll.* **-ydd** meeting. **2** *be.* **(cyfarfyddaf)** to meet, to encounter. **cyfarfod â** to meet.

cyfarfodydd *gw.* **cyfarfod.**

cyfarth *be.* **(cyfarthaf)** to bark.

cyfarwyddiadur *e.g. ll.* **-on** directory.

cyfarwyddo (â) *be.* **(cyfarwyddaf)** to familiarise, to instruct.

cyfarwyddwr *e.g. ll.* **cyfarwyddwyr** director.

cyfeilles *e.b. ll.* **-au** female friend. *gw.* **cyfaill.**

cyfeillgar *a.* friendly, sociable. *gw. At. Ansoddeiriau.*

cyfeillgarwch *e.g.* friendship.

cyfeillion *gw.* **cyfaill.**

cyfeiriad *e.g. ll.* **-au** direction, reference, address.

cyfeirio (at, i) *be.* **(cyfeiriaf)** to direct, to refer.

cyfenw *e.g. ll.* **-au** surname.

cyferbyn (â) *a.* opposite, contrary. **cyferbyn â** opposite.

cyfiawn *a.* righteous, just.

cyfiawnder *e.g. ll.* **-au** righteousness, justice.

cyfieithiad *e.g. ll.* **-au** translation.

cyfieithu *be.* **(cyfieithaf)** to translate.

cyfieithydd *e.g. ll.* **-ion** translator, interpreter.

cyfle *e.g. ll.* **-oedd** opportunity, chance.

cyfleu *be.* **(cyfleaf)** to convey, to imply.

cyfleus   **cyngor**

cyfleus *a.* convenient, expedient.
cyflog *e.b. ll.* **-au** salary, wages, hire.
cyflogi *be.* **(cyflogaf)** to employ, to
hire.
cyflogwr *e.g. ll.* **cyflogwyr**
employer.
cyflwr *e.g. ll.* **cyflyrau** state,
condition, case.
cyflwyno (i) *be.* **(cyflwynaf)** present
(to), to dedicate (to).
cyflym *a.* quick, swift, speedy. *gw.*
At. Ansoddeiriau.
cyflymach *gw.* **cyflym.**
cyflymaf *gw.* **cyflym.**
cyflymder *e.g. ll.* **-au** speed,
velocity, swiftness.
cyflymed *gw.* **cyflym.**
cyflymu *be.* **(cyflymaf)** to accelerate,
to hasten.
cyflymydd *e.g. ll.* **-ion** accelerator.
cyflyrau *gw.* **cyflwr.**
cyfnither *e.b. ll.* **-oedd** female
cousin. *gw.* **cefnder.**
cyfnod *e.g. ll.* **cyfnodau** period.
cyfoeth *e.g.* wealth, riches.
cyfoethog *a.* rich, wealthy.
cyfradd *e.b. ll.* **-au** rate. **cyfraddau**
llog interest rates.
cyfraith *e.b. ll.* **cyfreithiau** law.
cyfrannu (i, at) *be.* **(cyfrannaf)** to
contribute; to impart.
cyfreithiwr *e.g. ll.* **cyfreithwyr**
solicitor, lawyer.
cyfreithwyr *gw.* **cyfreithiwr.**
cyfres *e.b. ll.* **-au, -i** series, suite
(musical). **drama gyfres** a serial.
cyfresau: cyfresi *gw.* **cyfres.**
cyfrif 1 *be.* **(cyfrifaf)** to count, to
reckon. **2** *e.g.* account, reckoning.
cyfrif trafod current account; **cyfrif**
cadw deposit account.
cyfrifiadur *e.g. ll.* **-on** computer.
cyfrifiannell *e.g. ll.* **-au** calculator.
cyfrifol *a.* responsible; calculable.
cyfrifol am responsible for.
cyfrifoldeb *e.g. ll.* **-au** responsibility.
cyfrifydd *e.g. ll.* **-ion** accountant.
cyfrinach *e.b. ll.* **-au** secret, mystery.
cyfrinachol *a.* secret, confidential,
private.
cyfrol *e.b. ll.* **-au** volume, book.

cyfrwng *e.g. ll.* **cyfryngau** agent;
agency; medium; means. **trwy**
gyfrwng through the medium of; **y**
cyfryngau the media.
cyfrwys *a.* cunning, crafty.
cyfryngau *gw.* **cyfrwng.**
cyfun *a.* agreeing, comprehensive,
united. **Ysgol Gyfun Treforys**
Morriston Comprehensive School.
cyfuwch *gw.* **uchel.**
cyfweld (â) *be.* **(cyfwelaf)** to
interview.
cyfweliad *e.g. ll.* **-au** interview.
cyfyng *a.* narrow, confined,
restricted. **Mae hi'n gyfyng arni**
She is in dire straits.
cyfyngu (ar) *be.* **(cyfyngaf)** to
narrow, to confine, to restrict.
cyfystyr 1 *e.g. ll.* **-on** synonym.
2 *a* synonymous. **cyfystyr â**
synonymous with.
cyfforddus: cyffyrddus *a.*
comfortable *(S.W.).*
cyffredin *a.* common, ordinary,
vulgar. **enw cyffredin** common
noun; **pobl gyffredin** ordinary
people.
cyffrous *a.* exciting, moving.
cyffur *e.g. ll.* **-iau** drug, medicine.
cyffwrdd (â) *be.* **(cyffyrddaf)** to
touch, to contact, to meet.
cyngerdd *e.g.b. ll.* **cyngherddau**
concert.
cyngherddau *gw.* **cyngerdd.**
cynghori (i) *be.* **(cynghoraf)** to
advise, to counsel, to exhort.
cynghorion *gw.* **cyngor.**
cynghorwr *e.g. ll.* **cynghorwyr**
adviser, councillor.
cynghrair *e.g. ll.* **cynghreiriau**
alliance, league.
cynghreiriad *e.g. ll.* **cynghreiriaid**
ally.
cynghreiriau *gw.* **cynghrair.**
cyngor 1 *e.g. ll.* **cynghorion** advice,
counsel. **2** *e.g. ll.* **cynghorau**
council. **cyngor cymuned**
community council; **cyngor**
dosbarth district council; **cyngor**
sir county council; **Cyngor y**
Celfyddydau the Arts Council.

cyhoedd   **cyn**

cyhoedd 1 *a.* public. **2** *e.g.* public. **ar gyhoedd, ar goedd** publicly; **y cyhoedd** the public.

cyhoeddi *be.* **(cyhoeddaf)** to announce, to proclaim; to publish.

cyhoeddiad *e.g. ll.* **-au** publication; announcement; engagement.

cyhoeddus *a.* public. **neuadd gyhoeddus** public hall; **cyfarfod cyhoeddus** public meeting.

cyhoeddusrwydd *e.g.* publicity.

cyhoeddwr *e.g. ll.* **cyhoeddwyr** publisher; announcer.

cyhuddiad *e.g. ll.* **-au** accusation.

cyhuddo *be.* **(cyhuddaf)** to accuse.

cyhyd *gw.* **hir.**

cyhyrog *a.* muscular, strong.

cylch *e.g. ll.* **-au, -oedd** circle, hoop; class; region. **o gylch** around.

cylchfan *e.g. ll.* **-nau** roundabout.

cylchgrawn *e.g. ll.* **cylchgronau** magazine, periodical.

cylchgronau *gw.* **cylchgrawn.**

cylchlythyr *e.g. ll.* **-au, -on** a circular.

cyll *bf.* he/she/it loses. *gw.* **collen, colli.**

cyllell *e.b. ll.* **cyllyll** knife. **cyllell boced** penknife; **cyllell fara** bread knife.

cyllyll *gw.* **cyllell.**

cymaint *gw.* **mawr.**

cymal *e.g. ll.* **-au** joint; clause, phrase.

cymanfa *e.b. ll.* **-oedd** assembly, singing festival.

cymanfaoedd *gw.* **cymanfa.**

cymar *e.g. ll.* **cymheiriaid** partner.

cymdeithas *e.b. ll.* **-au** society, association.

cymdogion *gw.* **cymydog.**

cymeriad *e.g. ll.* **-au** character.

cymryd *be.* **(cymeraf)** to accept, to take. **cymryd ar** to pretend *(N.W.).*

cymharu (â) *be.* **(cymharaf)** to compare.

cymhleth *a.* complex, involved.

cymhlethdod *e.g. ll.* **-au** complication, complexity.

cymhlethu *be.* **(cymhlethaf)** to complicate.

cymhorthion *gw.* **cymorth.**

cymoedd *gw.* **cwm.**

cymorth *e.g. ll.* **cymhorthion** aid, assistance. **cymorth cyntaf** first aid.

Cymraeg 1 *e.b.g.* Welsh *(language).* **2** *a.* Welsh *(in language).* **Y Gymraeg** The Welsh language; **yn Gymraeg** in Welsh; **Cymraeg da** good *(spoken or written)* Welsh.

Cymraes; Cymreiges *e.b. ll.* **-au** Welshwoman.

Cymreictod *e.g.* Welsh quality, Welshness.

Cymreig *a.* Welsh, pertaining to Wales or to the Welsh. **arferion Cymreig** Welsh traditions; **brethyn Cymreig** Welsh woollen cloth; **Swyddfa Gymreig** The Welsh Office.

Cymreiges *gw.* **Cymraes.**

Cymro *e.g. ll.* **Cymry** Welshman. **Cymro i'r carn** thorough Welshman; **Cymro uniaith** monoglot Welshman; **Cymry alltud** exiled Welsh; **Cymry Llundain** London Welsh.

Cymru *e.b.* Wales.

Cymry *gw.* **Cymro.**

cymryd *gw.* **cymeryd.**

cymundeb *e.g. ll.* **-au** communion, fellowship.

cymuned *e.b. ll.* **-au** community.

cymwynas *e.b. ll.* **-au** favour, kindness. **talu'r gymwynas olaf** to pay the last respects *(attendance at funeral).*

cymydog *e.g. ll.* **cymdogion** neighbour.

cymylau *gw.* **cwmwl.**

cymylog *a.* cloudy.

cymysg *a.* mixed.

cymysgu (â) *be.* **(cymysgaf)** to mix, to confuse.

cymysgwch 1 *e.g.* jumble, medley. **2** *bf.* mix! *(plural). gw.* **cymysgu.**

cyn 1 *ardd.* before, previous to. **Dewch cyn cinio** Come before dinner. **2** *rhagdd.* (followed by soft mutation) first, former, ex-; **cyn-brifathro** former headteacher; **cyn-lôwr** former miner;

cynaeafau   **cysur**

cyn-weinidog former minister. **3** *c.*
& ad. (followed by soft mutation) as.
cyn dewed â mochyn as fat as a
pig; **cyn ddued â'r frân** as black as
the crow; **cyn goched â thân** as
red as fire; *gw. At. Treigladau.*
cynaeafau *gw.* **cynhaeaf.**
cynddrwg *gw.* **drwg.**
cynffon *e.b. ll.* **-nau** tail *(N.W.).*
cynffonnau ŵyn bach hazel
catkins. *gw.* **cwt.**
cynhadledd *e.b. ll.* **cynadleddau**
conference.
cynhaeaf *e.g. ll.* **cynaeafau** harvest.
cynhesu *be.* **(cynhesaf)** to warm, to
get warm.
cynhwysion *gw.* **cynnwys.**
cynhyrfus *a.* exciting, agitated.
cynigion *gw.* **cynnig.**
cynilion *e.ll.* savings.
cynilo *be.* **(cynilaf)** to save, to
economise.
cynllun *e.g. ll.* **-iau** plan, design,
scheme, project.
cynllunio *be.* **(cynlluniaf)** to plan, to
design.
cynlluniwr: cynllunydd *e.g. ll.*
cynllunwyr planner, designer,
architect.
cynnal *be.* **(cynhaliaf)** to support, to
hold, to maintain. **gwaith cynnal a
chadw** maintenance work.
cynnar *a.* early, soon. *gw. At.
Ansoddeiriau.*
cynnes *a.* warm.
cynnig 1 *be.* **(cynigiaf)** to attempt, to
try, to propose. **rhoi cynnig ar** to
attempt to.
2 *e.g. ll.* **cynigion** attempt; offer,
proposal; motion, bid.
cynnwys 1 *e.g. ll.* **cynhwysion.**
content, contents. **2** *be.* **(cynhwysaf)**
to contain, to include. **gan gynnwys**
including.
cynnyrch *e.g. ll.* **cynhyrchion**
produce.
cynorthwy-ydd *e.g. ll.*
cynorthwywyr helper, assistant.
cynorthwywr *e.g. ll.* **cynorthwywyr**
helper, assistant.
cynradd *a.* primary. **ysgol gynradd**
primary school.
cynrychioli *be.* to represent.
cynt: gynt *ad.* formerly, previously
née. **Siân Owen, gynt Lewis** Siân
Owen, *née* Lewis; **y flwyddyn gynt**
the previous year. *gw.* **buan,**
cynnar.
cyntaf *a.* first, chief, earliest. *gw.*
cynnar.
cynted *gw.* **cynnar.**
cyntedd *e.g. ll.* **cynteddau,**
cynteddoedd porch, court, lobby,
hall.
cynteddau: cynteddoedd *gw.*
cyntedd.
cynulleidfa *e.b. ll.* **-oedd**
congregation.
cynwysedig *a.* included.
cypyrddau *gw.* **cwpwrdd.**
cyrddau *gw.* **cwrdd.**
cyrff *gw.* **corff.**
cyrion *gw.* **cwr.**
cyrliog *a.* curly.
cyrn *gw.* **corn.**
cyrraedd *be.* **(cyrhaeddaf)** to reach,
to arrive, to attain. **Cyrhaeddodd y
tŷ** He arrived at the house.
cyrrau *gw.* **cwr.**
cyrsau *gw.* **cwrs.**
cyrsiau *gw.* **cwrs.**
cysglyd *a.* sleepy.
cysgod *e.g. ll.* **-ion, -au** shadow;
shelter.
cysgodau *gw.* **cysgod.**
cysgodi (rhag) *be.* **(cysgodaf)** to
shade; to shelter.
cysgodion *gw.* **cysgod.**
cysgu *be.* **(cysgaf)** to sleep.
cystadlaethau *gw.* **cystadleuaeth.**
cystadleuaeth *e.b. ll.*
cystadlaethau competition.
cystadleuwr: cystadleuydd *e.g. ll.*
cystadleuwyr competitor.
cystadleuwyr *gw.* **cystadleuwr.**
cystadlu (â) *be.* **(cystadlaf)** to
compete.
cystal *a.* as well. **yn ogystal** in
additon. *gw.* **da.**
cystymau *gw.* **cwstwm.**
cysur *e.g. ll.* **-on** comfort,
consolation.

cysuro   **cywiro**

cysuro *be.* **(cysuraf)** to comfort, to console.

cysurus *a.* comfortable.

cyswllt *e.g.* *ll.* **cysylltau** joint, junction, connection.

cytgan *e.b.* *ll.* **-au** chorus.

cytsain 1 *e.b.* *ll.* **cytseiniaid** consonant.

2 *e.b.* *ll.* **cytseiniau** harmony.

cytseiniaid *gw.* **cytsain.**

cytseiniau *gw.* **cytsain.**

cytundeb *e.g.* *ll.* **-au** agreement, pact, contract.

cytuno **(â)** *be.* **(cytunaf)** to agree (with), consent (to).

cyw *e.g.* *ll.* **-ion** chick. **cyw iâr** chicken *(N.W.)*; *gw.* **ffowlyn.**

cywaith *e.g.* *ll.* **cyweithiau** project; collective work.

cyweithiau *gw.* **cywaith.**

cywilydd *e.g.* shame.

cywion *gw.* **cyw.**

cywir *a.* correct, sincere, true, honest.

cywiriad *e.g.* *ll.* **-au** correction.

cywiro *be.* **(cywiraf)** to correct, to amend, to verify.

'**ch** *rhag.* you, your. *gw. At.*
Rhagenwau Personol.
chaban *gw.* **caban.**
chacen *gw.* **cacen.**
chacwn *gw.* **cacwn.**
chacynen *gw.* **cacynen.**
chadach *gw.* **cadach.**
chadair *gw.* **cadair.**
chadeirio *gw.* **cadeirio.**
chadeiriol *gw.* **cadeiriol.**
chadeirydd *gw.* **cadeirydd.**
chadnawes *gw.* **cadno.**
chadno *gw.* **cadno.**
chadnoaid *gw.* **cadno.**
chadw *gw.* **cadw.**
chadwyn *gw.* **cadwyn.**
chadwyno *gw.* **cadwyno.**
chae *gw.* **cae.**
chael *gw.* **cael.**
chaer *gw.* **caer.**
Chaerdydd *gw.* **Caerdydd.**
Chaerfyrddin *gw.* **Caerfyrddin.**
Chaergybi *gw.* **Caergybi.**
chaets *gw.* **caets.**
chaf *gw.* **caf.**
chafodd *gw.* **cafodd.**
chaffe *gw.* **caffe.**
changen *gw.* **cangen.**
changhennau *gw.* **cangen.**
chaiff *gw.* **caiff.**
chais *gw.* **cais.**
chalan *gw.* **calan.**
chaled *gw.* **caled.**

chaledi *gw.* **caledi.**
chaledu *gw.* **caledu.**
chaledwch *gw.* **caledwch.**
chalendr *gw.* **calendr.**
chalenigion *gw.* **calennig.**
chalennig *gw.* **calennig.**
chaletach *gw.* **caled.**
chaletaf *gw.* **caled.**
chaleted *gw.* **caled.**
chalon *gw.* **calon.**
chall *gw.* **call.**
challach *gw.* **call.**
challaf *gw.* **call.**
challed *gw.* **call.**
cham *gw.* **cam.**
chamarwain *gw.* **camarwain.**
chamddeall *gw.* **camddeall.**
chamera *gw.* **camera.**
champ *gw.* **camp.**
champfa *gw.* **campfa.**
champfeydd *gw.* **campfa.**
champus *gw.* **campus.**
champwaith *gw.* **campwaith.**
chamsyniad *gw.* **camsyniad.**
chamu *gw.* **camu.**
chân *gw.* **cân.**
chan *gw.* **can, gan.**
chaneuon *gw.* **cân.**
chanfed *gw.* **canfed.**
chanhwyllau *gw.* **cannwyll.**
chanhwyllbren *gw.* **canhwyllbren.**
chaniad *gw.* **caniad.**
chaniadaeth *gw.* **caniadaeth.**
chaniadau *gw.* **cân, caniad.**
chaniatâd *gw.* **caniatâd.**
chaniatáu *gw.* **caniatáu.**
chaniedydd *gw.* **caniedydd.**
chanmlwydd *gw.* **canmlwydd.**
chanmlwyddiannau *gw.*
  canmlwydd.
chanmol *gw.* **canmol.**
chanmoliaeth *gw.* **canmoliaeth.**
channoedd *gw.* **cant.**
channwyll *gw.* **cannwyll.**
chanol *gw.* **canol.**
chanolbarth *gw.* **canolbarth.**
chanolbwyntio *gw.* **canolbwyntio.**
chanoldir *gw.* **canoldir.**
chanolfan *gw.* **canolfan.**
chanolog *gw.* **canolog.**
chanolwr *gw.* **canolwr.**

chanradd   **chenhadu**

chanradd *gws.* canradd.
chanran *gw.* canran.
chanrif *gw.* canrif.
chanrifau: chanrifoedd *gw.* canrif.
chant *gw.* cant.
chantor *gw.* cantor.
chantores *gw.* cantores.
chanu *gw.* canu.
chanŵ *gw.* canŵ.
chanŵio *gw.* canŵio.
chanwr *gw.* canwr.
chap *gw.* cap.
chapel *gw.* capel.
chapteiniaid *gw.* capten.
chapten *gw.* capten.
chapteniaid *gw.* capten.
char *gw.* car.
charafán *gw.* carafán.
charafana *gw.* carafana.
charco *gw.* carco.
charcus *gw.* carcus.
charchar *gw.* carchar.
charcharor *gw.* carcharor.
charcharu *gw.* carcharu.
chardiau *gw.* cerdyn.
charedig *gw.* caredig.
charedigrwydd *gw.* caredigrwydd.
chariad *gw.* cariad.
chariadon *gw.* cariad.
chariadus *gw.* cariadus.
chario *gw.* cario.
charlamu *gw.* carlamu.
charol *gw.* carol.
charped *gw.* carped.
charreg *gw.* carreg.
chartref *gw.* cartref.
chartrefi *gw.* cartref.
chartrefu *gw.* cartrefu.
charu *gw.* caru.
charwriaeth *gw.* carwriaeth.
chas *gw.* cas.
chasáu *gw.* casáu.
chasgen *gw.* casgen.
chasgenni *gw.* casgen.
chasgliad *gw.* casgliad.
chasglu *gw.* casglu.
Chas-gwent *gw.* Cas-gwent.
Chasllwchwr *gw.* Casllwchwr.
Chasnewydd *gw.* Casnewydd.
chastell *gw.* castell.
Chastell-nedd *gw.* Castell-nedd.

chath *gw.* cath.
chau *gw.* cau.
chawl *gw.* cawl.
chawod *gw.* cawod.
chawr *gw.* cawr.
chaws *gw.* caws.
chefn *gw.* cefn.
chefnder *gw.* cefnder.
chefndir *gw.* cefndir.
chefndiroedd *gw.* cefndir.
chefndyr *gw.* cefnder.
chefnogi *gw.* cefnogi.
chefnu *gw.* cefnu.
chefnwr *gw.* cefnwr.
chefnwyr *gw.* cefnwr.
cheffyl *gw.* ceffyl.
cheg *gw.* ceg.
chegin *gw.* cegin.
chei *gw.* cael, cei.
cheidwad *gw.* ceidwad.
cheiliog *gw.* ceiliog.
Cheinewydd *gw.* Ceinewydd.
cheiniog *gw.* ceiniog.
cheiriosen *gw.* ceiriosen.
cheisio *gw.* ceisio.
chelf *gw.* celf.
chelfi *gw.* celficyn.
chelficyn *gw.* celficyn.
Cheltaidd *gw.* Celtaidd.
chelwydd *gw.* celwydd.
chelwyddog *gw.* celwyddog.
chelyn *gw.* celynnen.
chelynnen *gw.* celynnen.
chell *gw.* cell.
chellau: chelloedd *gw.* cell.
chemeg *gw.* cemeg.
chenadaethau *gw.* cenhadaeth.
chenedl *gw.* cenedl.
chenedlaethau *gw.* cenhedlaeth.
chenedlaethol *gw.* cenedlaethol.
chenedlaetholdeb *gw.*
  cenedlaetholdeb.
chenedlaetholwr *gw.*
  cenedlaetholwr.
chenedlaetholwyr *gw.*
  cenedlaetholwr.
chenfigennus *gw.* cenfigennus.
chenhadaeth *gw.* cenhadaeth.
chenhadol *gw.* cenhadol.
chenhadon *gw.* cenhadwr.
chenhadu *gw.* cenhadu.

chenhadwr   chog

chenhadwr *gw.* cenhadwr.
chenhedlaeth *gw.* cenhedlaeth.
chenhedloedd *gw.* cenedl.
chenhinen *gw.* cenhinen.
chennin *gw.* cenhinen.
cher *gw.* mynd.
cherdyn *gw.* cerdyn.
cherdd *gw.* cerdd.
cherdded *gw.* cerdded.
cherddor *gw.* cerddor.
cherddorfa *gw.* cerddorfa.
cherddorfeydd *gw.* cerddorfa.
cherddoriaeth *gw.* cerddoriaeth.
cherddorol *gw.* cerddorol.
cherddwr *gw.* cerddwr.
cherddwyr *gw.* cerddwr.
cherflun *gw.* cerflun.
cherrig *gw.* carreg.
cherwch *gw.* mynd.
ches *gw.* ces.
chesair *gw.* cesair.
chestyll *gw.* castell.
chewri *gw.* cawr.
chewyn *gw.* cewyn.
cheyrydd *gw.* caer.
chi: chwi *rhag.* you. *gw.* ci.
chig *gw.* cig.
chigydd *gw.* cigydd.
chigyddion *gw.* cigydd.
chilio *gw.* cilio.
chiniawau *gw.* cinio.
chinio *gw.* cinio.
chipolwg *gw.* cipolwg.
chist *gw.* cist.
chithau: chwithau *rhag.* you also.
chlaf *gw.* claf.
chlai *gw.* clai.
chlasur *gw.* clasur.
chlasurol *gw.* clasurol.
chlawdd *gw.* clawdd.
chlawr *gw.* clawr.
chlebran *gw.* clebran.
chledr *gw.* cledr.
chlefyd *gw.* clefyd.
chleifion *gw.* claf.
chlêr *gw.* cleren.
chlerc *gw.* clerc.
chleren *gw.* cleren.
chlir *gw.* clir.
chlirio *gw.* clirio.
chlo *gw.* clo, cloi.

chloc *gw.* cloc.
chloch *gw.* cloch.
chlod *gw.* clod.
chlodfori *gw.* clodfori.
chloff *gw.* cloff.
chloffi *gw.* cloffi.
chlogwyn *gw.* clogwyn.
chlogyn *gw.* clogyn.
chloi *gw.* cloi.
chlorian *gw.* clorian.
chloriau *gw.* clawr.
chlown *gw.* clown.
chlun *gw.* clun.
chlust *gw.* clust.
chlustog *gw.* clustog.
chlwm *gw.* clwm.
chlwtyn *gw.* clwtyn.
Chlwyd *gw.* Clwyd.
chlwyd *gw.* clwyd.
chlwydau: chlwydi *gw.* clwyd.
chlwyf *gw.* clwyf.
chlychau *gw.* cloch.
chlymau *gw.* clwm.
chlymu *gw.* clymu.
chlytiau *gw.* clwtyn.
chlyw *gw.* clyw.
chlywed *gw.* clywed.
chnau *gw.* cneuen.
chneuen *gw.* cneuen.
chnoc *gw.* cnoc.
chnocio *gw.* cnocio.
chnoi *gw.* cnoi.
choban *gw.* coban.
chobannau *gw.* coban.
choch *gw.* coch.
chochach *gw.* coch.
chochaf *gw.* coch.
choched *gw.* coch.
chodi *gw.* codi.
Choed-duon *gw.* Coed-duon.
choeden *gw.* coeden.
choedwig *gw.* coedwig.
choes *gw.* coes.
chof *gw.* cof.
chofio *gw.* cofio.
chofion *gw.* cof.
chofleidio *gw.* cofleidio.
chofrestr *gw.* cofrestr.
chofrestru *gw.* cofrestru.
choffi *gw.* coffi.
chog *gw.* cog.

choginio   **chwaneg**

choginio *gw.* coginio.
chogydd *gw.* cogydd.
choleg *gw.* coleg.
choler *gw.* coler.
cholofn *gw.* colofn.
choluro *gw.* coluro.
cholled *gw.* colled.
chollen *gw.* collen.
cholli *gw.* colli.
chopïo *gw.* copïo.
chopyn *gw.* copyn.
chôr *gw.* côr.
chorau *gw.* côr.
chordyn *gw.* cordyn.
chorff *gw.* corff.
chorfforol *gw.* corfforol.
chorgi *gw.* corgi.
chorn *gw.* corn.
chornel *gw.* cornel.
choron *gw.* coron.
choroni *gw.* coroni.
chorryn *gw.* corryn.
chorynnod *gw.* corryn.
chosb *gw.* cosb.
chosbi *gw.* cosbi.
chostus *gw.* costus.
chot *gw.* cot.
chotau: chotiau *gw.* cot.
chotwm *gw.* cotwm.
chrac *gw.* crac.
chrachach *gw.* crachach.
chrafu *gw.* crafu.
chragen *gw.* cragen.
chraig *gw.* craig.
chras *gw.* cras.
chrasu *gw.* crasu.
chredu *gw.* credu.
chrefydd *gw.* crefydd.
chrefft *gw.* crefft.
chrefftwr *gw.* crefftwr.
chrefftwyr *gw.* crefftwr.
chregyn *gw.* cragen.
chreigiau *gw.* craig.
chreigiog *gw.* creigiog.
chreision *gw.* creisionyn.
chrempog *gw.* crempog.
chreulon *gw.* creulon.
chreulondeb *gw.* creulondeb.
chri *gw.* cri.
chrib *gw.* crib.
chribo *gw.* cribo.

chriced *gw.* criced.
chricedwr *gw.* cricedwr.
chrio *gw.* crio.
Christion *gw.* Cristion.
Christnogion *gw.* Cristion.
chriw *gw.* criw.
chroen *gw.* croen.
chroes *gw.* croes.
chroesair *gw.* croesair.
chroesau *gw.* croes.
chroesawu *gw.* croesawu.
chroesawus *gw.* croesawus.
chroeseiriau *gw.* croesair.
chroesfan *gw.* croesfan.
chroesffordd *gw.* croesffordd.
chroesholi *gw.* croesholi.
chroesi *gw.* croesi.
chroeso *gw.* croeso.
chron *gw.* cron.
chronfa *gw.* cronfa.
chronfeydd *gw.* cronfa.
chrud *gw.* crud.
chrwn *gw.* crwn.
chrwst *gw.* crwst.
chryd *gw.* cryd.
chryf *gw.* cryf.
chryfach *gw.* cryf.
chryfaf *gw.* cryf.
chryfed *gw.* cryf.
chrynhoi *gw.* crynhoi.
chryno *gw.* cryno.
chrynodeb *gw.* crynodeb.
chrynu *gw.* crynu.
chrys *gw.* crys.
chrystiau *gw.* crwst, crystyn.
chrystyn *gw.* crystyn.
chu *gw.* cu.
chuddio *gw.* cuddio.
chul *gw.* cul.
churo *gw.* curo.
chusan *gw.* cusan.
chusanu *gw.* cusanu.
chwaer *e.b.* *ll.* chwiorydd sister,
   maiden.
chwain *gw.* chwannen.
chwaith: ychwaith *ad.* neither, nor
   . . . either, not . . . either.
chwalu *be.* (chwalaf) to crumble; to
   scatter, to disperse. chwalu cartref
   to break up a home.
chwaneg: ychwaneg *a. & e.g.*

more, additional.
chwanegu *gw.* **ychwanegu.**
chwannen *e.b. ll.* **chwain** flea.
chwant *e.g. ll.* **-au** desire, appetite; lust. **Mae chwant bwyd arnaf i** I desire food; **Does dim chwant mynd arni** She doesn't feel like going.
chwap *a. & ad.* at once, instantly.
chwarae: 1 *be.* **(chwaraeaf)** to play, to perform. **2** *e.g. ll.* **-on** game, sport; play. **amser chwarae** playtime; **chwarae teg** fair play; **meysydd chwarae** playing fields.
chwaraewr *e.g. ll.* **chwaraewyr** player, actor.
chwaraewyr *gw.* **chwaraewr.**
chwarddaf *g.w.* **chwerthin.**
chwarel 1 *e.b.g. ll* **-i, -au** quarry. **2** *e.g.b. ll.* **-au, -i** pane of glass.
chwarelau: chwareli *gw.* **chwarel.**
chwareus *a.* playful.
chwarter *e.g. ll.* **-au, -i** quarter.
chwb *gw.* **cwb.**
chwbl *gw.* **cwbl.**
chwcw *gw.* **cwcw.**
chwch *gw.* **cwch.**
chwd *gw.* **cwd.**
chwdyn *gw.* **cwdyn.**
chwe: chwech *a.* six. **chwe** *before singular nouns (followed by spirant mutation)*; **chwe bachgen, chwe llyfr; chwech** *on its own or with* **o** + *plural noun* **chwech o dai, chwech o blant; chwe deg** sixty.
chweched *a.* sixth.
chwedl *e.b. ll.* **-au, -euon** story, legend, fable; report, rumour; saying.
chwedlau: chwedleuon *gw.* **chwedl.**
Chwefror *e.g.* February.
chwerthin 1 *be.* **(chwarddaf)** to laugh, to smile. **chwerthin am ei ben** to laugh at him. **2** *e.g.* laughter.
chwerthinllyd *a.* laughable.
chwerw *a.* bitter; severe, sharp, spiteful.
chweryl *gw.* **cweryl.**
chweryla *gw.* **cweryla.**
chwerylau: chwerylon *gw.* **cweryl.**
chwestiwn *gw.* **cwestiwn.**

chwestiyna *gw.* **cwestiyna.**
chwestiynau *gw.* **cwestiwn.**
chwi *gw.* **chi.**
chwiban *e.g. ll.* **-au** a whistling, whistle.
chwiban: chwibanu (ar) *be,* **(chwibanaf)** to whistle.
chwifio (at) *be.* **(chwifiaf)** to wave.
chwilen *e.b. ll.* **chwilod** beetle. **Mae chwilen yn ei ben** He has a bee in his bonnet.
chwilio (am) *be.* **(chwiliaf)** to search (for), to examine.
chwiliwr *e.g. ll.* **chwilwyr** investigator, searcher.
chwilod *gw.* **chwilen.**
chwilota *be.* **(chwilotaf)** to rummage, to pry.
chwilwyr *gw.* **chwiliwr.**
chwilotwr *e.g. ll.* **chwilotwyr** rummager, one engaged in research.
chwiorydd *gw.* **chwaer.**
chwip 1 *e.b.g. ll.* **-au, -iau** whip. **2** *a.* swift, quick. **3** *ad.* instantly.
chwipio *be.* **(chwipiaf)** to whip.
chwistrelliad *e.g. ll.* **-au** injection.
chwith *a.* left; strange; sad. **o chwith** the wrong way about, awkwardly; **tu chwith** inside out.
chwithau *gw.* **chithau.**
chwithig *a.* strange; awkward.
chwlwm *gw.* **cwlwm.**
chwm *gw.* **cwm.**
chwmni *gw.* **cwmni.**
chwmnïau *gw.* **cwmni.**
chwmnïoedd *gw.* **cwmni.**
chwmwl *gw.* **cwmwl.**
chŵn *gw.* **ci.**
chwningen *gw.* **cwningen.**
chwningod *gw.* **cwningen.**
chwpan *gw.* **cwpan.**
chwpla *gw.* **cwpla.**
chwpwrdd *gw.* **cwpwrdd.**
chwr *gw.* **cwr.**
chwrdd *gw.* **cwrdd.**
chwrs *gw.* **cwrs.**
chwrtais *gw.* **cwrtais.**
chwrw *gw.* **cwrw.**
chwsg *gw.* **cwsg.**
chwsmer *gw.* **cwsmer.**
chwstwm *gw.* **cwstwm.**

chwt   chyfrol

chwt *gw.* **cwt.**
chwta *gw.* **cwta.**
chwydu *be.* **(chwydaf)** to vomit.
chwyddiant *e.g. ll.* **chwyddiannau**
  inflation; inflammation.
chwyddo *be.* **(chwyddaf)** to swell,
  to increase.
chwyddwydr *e.g. ll.* **-au** magnifying
  glass.
chwyldro: chwyldroad *e.g. ll.*
  chwyldroadau revolution.
  y Chwyldro Diwydiannol the
  Industrial Revolution; **y Chwyldro
  Ffrengig** the French Revolution.
chwymp *gw.* **cwymp.**
chwympo *gw.* **cwympo.**
chwyn *e. torf.* weeds. *gw.* **cwyn;** *gw.*
  chwynnyn.
chwynladdwr *e.g.* weed-killer.
chwynnyn *e.g. ll. & e.torf.* **chwyn**
  weed.
chwynnu *be.* **(chwynnaf)** to weed.
chwyno *gw.* **cwyno.**
chwyro *gw.* **cwyro.**
chwyrnu *be.* **(chwyrnaf)** to snore, to
  snarl; to whirl.
chwys *e.g.* perspiration, sweat. **yn
  chwys domen** dripping with
  perspiration.
chwysu *be.* **(chwysaf)** to perspire, to
  sweat.
chwythu *be.* **(chwythaf)** to blow.
chychod *gw.* **cwch.**
chychwyn *gw.* **cychwyn.**
chydadrodd *gw.* **cydadrodd.**
chydau *gw.* **cwd; cwdyn.**
chydio *gw.* **cydio.**
chydnabod *gw.* **cydnabod.**
chydwybodol *gw.* **cydwybodol.**
chydymdeimlad *gw.*
  cydymdeimlad.
chyfagos *gw.* **cyfagos.**
chyfaill *gw.* **cyfaill.**
chyfan *gw.* **cyfan.**
chyfangwbl *gw.* **cyfangwbl.**
chyfansoddi *gw.* **cyfansoddi.**
chyfansoddwr *gw.* **cyfansoddwr.**
chyfanswm *gw.* **cyfanswm.**
chyfarch *gw.* **cyfarch.**
chyfarfod *gw.* **cyfarfod.**
chyfarfodydd *gw.* **cyfarfod.**

chyfarwyddiadur *gw.*
  cyfarwyddiadur.
chyfarwyddo *gw.* **cyfarwyddo.**
chyfarwyddwr *gw.* **cyfarwyddwr.**
chyfeilles *gw.* **cyfeilles.**
chyfeillgar *gw.* **cyfeillgar.**
chyfeillgarwch *gw.* **cyfeillgarwch.**
chyfeiriad *gw.* **cyfeiriad.**
chyfeirio *gw.* **cyfeirio.**
chyfenw *gw.* **cyfenw.**
chyferbyn *gw.* **cyferbyn.**
chyfiawn *gw.* **cyfiawn.**
chyfiawnder *gw.* **cyfiawnder.**
chyfieithiad *gw.* **cyfieithiad.**
chyfieithu *gw.* **cyfieithu.**
chyfieithydd *gw.* **cyfieithydd.**
chyfle *gw.* **cyfle.**
chyfleu *gw.* **cyfleu.**
chyfleus *gw.* **cyfleus.**
chyflog *gw.* **cyflog.**
chyflogi *gw.* **cyflogi.**
chyflogwr *gw.* **cyflogwr.**
chyflwr *gw.* **cyflwr.**
chyflwyno *gw.* **cyflwyno.**
chyflym *gw.* **cyflym.**
chyflymach *gw.* **cyflymach.**
chyflymaf *gw.* **cyflymaf.**
chyflymder *gw.* **cyflymder.**
chyflymed *gw.* **cyflymed.**
chyflymu *gw.* **cyflymu.**
chyflymydd *gw.* **cyflymydd.**
chyflyrau *gw.* **cyflwr.**
chyfnither *gw.* **cyfnither.**
chyfnod *gw.* **cyfnod.**
chyfoeth *gw.* **cyfoeth.**
chyfoethog *gw.* **cyfoethog.**
chyfraith *gw.* **cyfraith.**
chyfrannu *gw.* **cyfrannu.**
chyfreithiwr *gw.* **cyfreithiwr.**
chyfreithwyr *gw.* **cyfreithiwr.**
chyfres *gw.* **cyfres.**
chyfresau: chyfresi *gw.* **cyfres.**
chyfrif *gw.* **cyfrif.**
chyfrifiadur *gw.* **cyfrifiadur.**
chyfrifiannell *gw.* **cyfrifiannell.**
chyfrifol *gw.* **cyfrifol.**
chyfrifoldeb *gw.* **cyfrifoldeb.**
chyfrifydd *gw.* **cyfrifydd.**
chyfrinach *gw.* **cyfrinach.**
chyfrinachol *gw.* **cyfrinachol.**
chyfrol *gw.* **cyfrol.**

chyfrwng   **chynradd**

chyfrwng *gw.* cyfrwng.
chyfrwys *gw.* cyfrwys.
chyfryngau *gw.* cyfrwng.
chyfun *gw.* cyfun.
chyfuwch *gw.* uchel.
chyfweld *gw.* cyfweld.
chyfweliad *gw.* cyfweliad.
chyfyng *gw.* cyfyng.
chyfyngu *gw.* cyfyngu.
chyfystyr *gw.* cyfystyr.
chyfforddus *gw.* cyfforddus.
chyffredin *gw.* cyffredin.
chyffrous *gw.* cyffrous.
chyffur *gw.* cyffur.
chyffwrdd *gw.* cyffwrdd.
chyffyrddus *gw.* cyffyrddus.
chyngerdd *gw.* cyngerdd.
chyngherddau *gw.* cyngerdd.
chynghori *gw.* cynghori.
chynghorion *gw.* cyngor.
chynghorwr *gw.* cynghorwr.
chynghrair *gw.* cynghrair.
chynghreiriad *gw.* cynghreiriad.
chyngor *gw.* cyngor.
chyhoedd *gw.* cyhoedd.
chyhoeddi *gw.* cyhoeddi.
chyhoeddiad *gw.* cyhoeddiad.
chyhoeddus *gw.* cyhoeddus.
chyhoeddusrwydd *gw.*
  cyhoeddusrwydd.
chyhoeddwr *gw.* cyhoeddwr.
chyhuddiad *gw.* cyhuddiad.
chyhuddo *gw.* cyhuddo.
chyhyd *gw.* cyhyd.
chyhyrog *gw.* cyhyrog.
chylch *gw.* cylch.
chylchfan *gw.* cylchfan.
chylchgrawn *gw.* cylchgrawn.
chylchgronau *gw.* cylchgrawn.
chylchlythyr *gw.* cylchlythyr.
chyll *gw.* collen; colli.
chyllell *gw.* cyllell.
chyllyll *gw.* cyllell.
chymaint *gw.* cymaint.
chymal *gw.* cymal.
chymanfa *gw.* cymanfa.
chymanfaoedd *gw.* cymanfa.
chymar *gw.* cymar.
chymdeithas *gw.* cymdeithas.
chymdogion *gw.* cymydog.
chymeriad *gw.* cymeriad.

chymeryd *gw.* cymryd.
chymharu *gw.* cymharu.
chymhleth *gw.* cymhleth.
chymhlethdod *gw.* cymhlethdod.
chymhlethu *gw.* cymhlethu.
chymhorthion *gw.* cymorth.
chymoedd *gw.* cwm.
chymorth *gw.* cymorth.
Chymraeg *gw.* Cymraeg.
Chymraes *gw.* Cymraes.
Chymreictod *gw.* Cymreictod.
Chymreig *gw.* Cymreig.
Chymreiges *gw.* Cymreiges.
Chymro *gw.* Cymro.
Chymru *gw.* Cymru.
Chymry *gw.* Cymro.
chymryd *gw.* cymryd.
chymundeb *gw.* cymundeb.
chymuned *gw.* cymuned.
chymwynas *gw.* cymwynas.
chymydog *gw.* cymydog.
chymylau *gw.* cwmwl.
chymylog *gw.* cymylog.
chymysg *gw.* cymysg.
chymysgu *gw.* cymysgu.
chymysgwch *gw.* cymysgwch.
chyn *gw.* cyn.
chynaeafau *gw.* cynhaeaf.
chynddrwg *gw.* cynddrwg.
chynffon *gw.* cynffon.
chynhadledd *gw.* cynhadledd.
chynhaeaf *gw.* cynhaeaf.
chynhesu *gw.* cynhesu.
chynhyrfus *gw.* cynhyrfus.
chynigion *gw.* cynnig.
chynilion *gw.* cynilion.
chynilo *gw.* cynilo.
chynllun *gw.* cynllun.
chynllunio *gw.* cynllunio.
chynlluniwr *gw.* cynlluniwr.
chynllunydd *gw.* cynlluniwr.
chynnal *gw.* cynnal.
chynnar *gw.* cynnar.
chynnes *gw.* cynnes.
chynnig *gw.* cynnig.
chynnwys *gw.* cynnwys.
chynnyrch *gw.* cynnyrch.
chynorthwywr *gw.* cynorthwywr.
chynorthwy-ydd *gw.* cynorthwy-
  ydd.
chynradd *gw.* cynradd.

chynt   **chywiro**

chynt *gw.* **cynnar.**
chyntaf *gw.* **cyntaf, cynnar.**
chynted *gw.* **cynnar.**
chyntedd *gw.* **cyntedd.**
chynteddau *gw.* **cyntedd.**
chynteddoedd *gw.* **cyntedd.**
chynulleidfa *gw.* **cynulleidfa.**
chynwysiedig *gw.* **cynwysiedig.**
chypyrddau *gw.* **cwpwrdd.**
chyrddau *gw.* **cwrdd.**
chyrff *gw.* **corff.**
chyrion *gw.* **cwr.**
chyrliog *gw.* **cyrliog.**
chyrn *gw.* **corn.**
chyrraedd *gw.* **cyrraedd.**
chyrrau *gw.* **cwr.**
chyrsau *gw.* **cwrs.**
chyrsiau *gw.* **cwrs.**
chysglyd *gw.* **cysglyd.**
chysgod *gw.* **cysgod.**
chysgodau *gw.* **cysgod.**
chysgodi *gw.* **cysgodi.**
chysgodion *gw.* **cysgod.**
chysgu *gw.* **cysgu.**
chystadlaethau *gw.* **cystadleuaeth.**

chystadleuaeth *gw.* **cystadleuaeth.**
chystadleuwr *gw.* **cystadleuwr.**
chystadleuwyr *gw.* **cystadleuwr.**
chystadleuydd *gw.* **cystadleuwr.**
chystadlu *gw.* **cystadlu.**
chystal *gw.* **cystal.**
chystymau *gw.* **cwstwm.**
chysur *gw.* **cysur.**
chysuro *gw.* **cysuro.**
chysurus *gw.* **cysurus.**
chyswllt *gw.* **cyswllt.**
chytgan *gw.* **cytgan.**
chytsain *gw.* **cytsain.**
chytseiniaid *gw.* **cytsain.**
chytseiniau *gw.* **cytsain.**
chytundeb *gw.* **cytundeb.**
chytuno *gw.* **cytuno.**
chyw *gw.* **cyw.**
chywaith *gw.* **cywaith.**
chyweithiau *gw.* **cywaith.**
chywilydd *gw.* **cywilydd.**
chywion *gw.* **cyw.**
chywir *gw.* **cywir.**
chywiriad *gw.* **cywiriad.**
chywiro *gw.* **cywiro.**

da 1 *a.* good, well. **bore da** good morning; **da iawn** very good, very well (*in health*); **Mae'n dda gen i weld** I'm glad to see. *gw. At. Ansoddeiriau.* **2** *e.g.* good, goodness. **3** *e. torf.* goods, stock; cattle *(S.W.).*
dabl *gw.* **tabl.**
dablet *gw.* **tablet.**
dacl *gw.* **tacl.**
daclo *gw.* **taclo.**
daclu *gw.* **taclu.**
daclus *gw.* **taclus.**
dacluso *gw.* **tacluso.**
daclwr *gw.* **taclwr.**
dacsi *gw.* **tacsi.**
dacw *ad.* There is/are, behold (*far away*) (*followed by soft mutation*).
Dachwedd *gw.* **Tachwedd.**
dad *gw.* **tad.**
dadansoddi *be.* **(dadansoddaf)** to analyse.
dad-cu *gw.* **tad-cu.**
dadl *e.b. ll.* **-euon** debate, argument, dispute.
dadlau *be.* **(dadleuaf)** to argue, to debate, to dispute.
dadrewi *be.* **(dadrewaf)** to defrost.
daear *e.b. ll.* **-oedd** earth, ground, soil, land. **Beth ar y ddaear ydy e?** What on earth is it? **Ble ar y ddaear mae e?** Where on earth is he/it?
daeareg *e.b.* geology.

daeargryn *e.g.b. ll.* **-fâu, -feydd** earthquake.
daearyddiaeth *e.b.* geography.
daeth *bf.* he/she/it came. *gw.* **dod.**
dafad *e.b. ll.* **defaid** sheep, ewe; wart.
dafarn *gw.* **tafarn.**
dafarnwr *gw.* **tafarnwr.**
dafell *gw.* **tafell.**
daflegryn *gw.* **taflegryn.**
daflen *gw.* **taflen.**
daflu *gw.* **taflu.**
dafod *gw.* **tafod.**
dafodiaith *gw.* **tafodiaith.**
dafol *gw.* **tafol.**
dagfa *gw.* **tagfa.**
dagrau *gw.* **deigryn.**
dagu *gw.* **tagu.**
dangnefedd *gw.* **tangnefedd.**
daid *gw.* **taid.**
dail *gw.* **dalen, deilen.**
daioni *e.g.* goodness. **er daioni** for the good of. *gw.* **da.**
dair *gw.* **tair.**
daith *gw.* **taith.**
dal *gw.* **tal.**
dal: dala *(S.W.) be.* **(daliaf, dalaf)** to hold, to capture, to seize, to catch; to maintain; to keep, to wager, to bet; to continue; to rely, to trust. **dal annwyd** to catch a cold; **dal ati** to persevere, to stick at it; **dal dŵr** to hold water; **dal dig** to bear or retain a grudge; **dal ei dir** to hold his ground; **dal i fyny** to bear up, to uphold; **dal i lawr** to subjugate; **dal perthynas â** to be related to; **dal sylw** to take notice; **dal wrth/at** to adhere to, to persevere in; **dal y slac yn dynn** to pretend to work; **does dim dal arno.** He cannot be relied upon; **Ydy e'n dal i ganu?** Does he still sing?
dâl *gw.* **tâl.**
dalai *gw.* **talai.**
dalaith *gw.* **talaith.**
dalcen *gw.* **talcen.**
daleb *gw.* **taleb.**
daleion *gw.* **talai.**
dalen *e.g. ll.* **dail, -nau** leaf (*of a book*); sheet (*of paper*); leaf (*of tree,*

dalent   **datod**

plant, etc.). **troi dalen newydd** to turn over a new leaf; **ymyl y ddalen** margin of a page. *gw.* **deilen, tudalen.**
dalent *gw.* **talent.**
dalentog *gw.* **talentog.**
dalgylch *e.g. ll.* **-oedd** catchment area.
dalu *gw.* **talu.**
dalwr *gw.* **talwr.**
dalwrn *gw.* **talwrn.**
dall 1 *a.* blind. 2 *e.g. ll.* **deillion, deilliaid** blind person(s).
dallu *be.* **(dallaf)** to blind, to dazzle.
damaid *gw.* **tamaid.**
dameg *e.b. ll.* **damhegion** parable.
dameidiau *gw.* **tamaid.**
damhegion *gw.* **dameg.**
damwain *e.b. ll.* **damweiniau** accident; chance. **ar ddamwain, trwy ddamwain, wrth ddamwain** by chance.
dan: tan *ardd.* **(dana, danat, dano/dani, danon, danoch, danyn)** under, until, as far; *(followed by soft mutation). gw. At. Arddodiaid.* **dan + verb-noun: aeth adref dan ganu** he went home singing; **cododd hi dan chwerthin** she got up laughing; **aethon nhw i'r capel dan wylo** they went to the chapel weeping.
dân *gw.* **tân.**
danau *gw.* **tân.**
dancer *gw.* **tancer.**
danddaear *gw.* **tanddaear.**
danfon *be.* **(danfonaf)** to send, to dispatch; to conduct, to accompany. *gw.* **anfon.**
danfor *gw.* **tanfor.**
dangos (i) *be.* **(dangosaf)** to show, to reveal.
danio *gw.* **tanio.**
danlinellu *gw.* **tanlinellu.**
danlwybr *gw.* **tanlwybr.**
danllyd *gw.* **tanllyd.**
dannau *gw.* **tant.**
dannedd *gw.* **dant.**
dannoedd *e.b.* toothache.
danseilio *gw.* **tanseilio.**
dant *e.g. ll.* **dannedd** tooth; cog;

tine. **dant blaen** front tooth; incisor; **dannedd gosod/dodi** false teeth; **at ei ddant** to his taste; **dant y llew** dandelion. *gw.* **tant.**
danwydd *gw.* **tanwydd.**
dap *gw.* **tap.**
dâp *gw.* **tâp.**
daran *gw.* **taran.**
daranu *gw.* **taranu.**
darddiad *gw.* **tarddiad.**
darddu *gw.* **tarddu.**
darfod (i) *be.* **(darfodaf)** to end; to finish, to die; to waste away; to happen (*N.W.*).
darganfod *be.* **(darganfyddaf)** to discover.
darged *gw.* **targed.**
darian *gw.* **tarian.**
darlith *e.b. ll.* **-iau** lecture.
darlithio *be.* **(darlithiaf)** to lecture.
darlithiwr: darlithydd *e.g. ll.* **darlithwyr** lecturer.
darlun *e.g. ll.* **-iau** picture.
darlunio *be.* **(darluniaf)** to describe, to draw, to illustrate.
darlledu *be.* **(darlledaf)** to broadcast.
darllen *be.* **(darllenaf)** to read.
darllenwr: darllenydd *e.g. ll.* **darllenwyr** reader.
darn *e.g. ll.* **-au** part, piece.
daro *gw.* **taro.**
darw *gw.* **tarw.**
dasg *gw.* **tasg.**
dasgu *gw.* **tasgu.**
datblygiad *e.g. ll* **-au** development, evolution.
datblygu *be.* **(datblygaf)** to develop, to evolve.
daten *gw.* **taten.**
datgan *be.* **(datganaf)** to declare, to recite.
datganiad *e.g. ll.* **-au** declaration, rendering.
datganoli *be.* **(datganolaf)** to devolve, to decentralise.
datgelu *be.* **(datgelaf)** to reveal.
datguddio *be.* **(datguddiaf)** to reveal, to disclose.
dato: datws *gw.* **taten.**
datod *be.* **(datodaf)** to undo, to

datrys   **delwi**

solve, to loose; to dissolve (*N.W.*).
datrys *be.* **(datrysaf)** to solve, to
  unravel.
datws *gw.* **taten.**
dathliad *e.g. ll.* **dathliadau**
  celebration.
dathlu *be.* **(dathlaf)** to celebrate.
dau 1 *a.g.* (*followed by soft mutation*)
  two. **2** *e.g. ll.* **deuoedd** two. **y**
  ddau both. *gw.* **dwy.**
dawel *gw.* **tawel.**
dawelu *gw.* **tawelu.**
dawelwch *gw.* **tawelwch.**
dawelydd *gw.* **tawelydd.**
dawelyn *gw.* **tawelyn.**
dawns *e.b. ll.* **-iau** dance. **dawns**
  werin folk dance.
dawnsio *be.* **(dawnsiaf)** to dance.
  dawnsio gwerin folk dancing.
de 1 *a.* southern; right. **y llaw dde**
  the right hand. **2** *e.g.* south. **pegwn**
  y de south pole. **3** *e.b.* right side.
  ar y dde on the right (hand) side.
  gw. **te.**
deall 1 *be.* **(deallaf)** to understand.
  2 *e.g.* understanding, intelligence,
  intellect.
deallus *a.* intelligent.
debot *gw.* **tebot.**
debyg *gw.* **tebyg.**
debygrwydd *gw.* **tebygrwydd.**
decell *gw.* **tegell.**
dechneg *gw.* **techneg.**
dechnegol *gw.* **technegol.**
dechnegwr *gw.* **technegwr.**
dechnoleg *gw.* **technoleg.**
dechrau 1 *be.* **(dechreuaf)** to begin,
  originate. **Mae e'n dechrau tyfu**
  He/it is beginning to grow.
  2 *e.g.* beginning, origin.
dechreuad *e.g.* beginning.
  'Yn y dechreuad . . .' 'In the
  beginning . . .'
dedwydd *a.* happy, blessed.
deddf *e.b. ll.* **-au** law, statute, act.
  Deddf Gwlad law of the land;
  Deddf Uno 1536 Act of Union
  1536; **Deddf yr Iaith** (Welsh)
  Language Act.
deddfu *be.* **(deddfaf)** to legislate.
defnydd *e.g. ll.* **-au** material, cloth,

fabric; use, purpose.
defnyddio *be.* **(defnyddiaf)** to use.
defnyddiol *a.* useful.
deffro *be.* **(deffroaf)** to awake, to
  awaken.
deg: deng 1 *a.* ten. **deng mlynedd**
  ten years, decade; **deng mlwydd**
  ten years (*of age*); **deng niwrnod**
  ten days; **a'm deg ewin** (*doing*) my
  level best. *gw. At. Tr. Trwynol.* **2** *e.g.*
  ll. **degau** ten. *gw.* **teg.**
degan *gw.* **tegan.**
degawd *e.g. ll.* **-au** decade.
degell *gw.* **tegell.**
degwch *gw.* **tegwch.**
deng *a.* ten; (*used before* **blwydd,**
  blynedd *and* **diwrnod**) (followed
  by nasal mutation). *gw.* **deg.**
deheuol *a.* southern.
dei *gw.* **tei.**
deialog *e.g.b. ll.* **-au** dialogue.
deiar *gw.* **teiar.**
deidiau *gw.* **taid.**
deigr *gw.* **teigr.**
deigryn *e.g. ll.* **dagrau** tear.
deilen *e.b. ll.* **dail** leaf (*of tree*); *gw.*
  dalen.
deiliwr *gw.* **teiliwr.**
deilsen *gw.* **teilsen.**
deilwng *gw.* **teilwng.**
deilwres *gw.* **teilwres.**
deilyngdod *gw.* **teilyngdod.**
deilliaid: deillion *gw.* **dall.**
deimlad *gw.* **teimlad.**
deimlo *gw.* **teimlo.**
deintydd *e.g. ll.* **-ion** dentist.
deipiadur *gw.* **teipiadur.**
deirgwaith *gw.* **teirgwaith.**
deiseb *e.b. ll.* **-au** petition.
deisen *gw.* **teisen.**
deitl *gw.* **teitl.**
deithio *gw.* **teithio.**
deithiwr *gw.* **teithiwr.**
del *a.* pretty, neat (*N.W.*).
deledu *gw.* **teledu.**
deleffon *gw.* **teleffon.**
delw *e.b. ll.* **-au** image, idol, form,
  manner. **ar ddelw** in the image of.
delwi *be.* **(delwaf)** to become
  motionless, to be paralysed with
  fright.

delyn   **diffuant**

delyn *gw.* **telyn.**
delyneg *gw.* **telyneg.**
delynor *gw.* **telynor.**
delynores *gw.* **telynores.**
deml *gw.* **teml.**
denau *gw.* **tenau.**
deniadol *a.* attractive, enticing.
denu *be.* **(denaf)** to attract, to entice.
derbyn *be.* **(derbyniaf, derbynnaf)** to receive.
derbynebau: derbynebion *gw.* **derbynneb.**
derbyniol *a.* acceptable, approved, receptive.
derbynneb *e.g. ll.* **derbynebau, derbynebion** receipt, voucher.
derbynnydd *e.g. ll.* **derbynyddion** receiver; receptionist. **derbynnydd swyddogol** official receiver.
derfyn *gw.* **terfyn.**
deri *e. ll.* oak-trees, oak. *gw.* **derwen.**
derm *gw.* **term.**
derw *a.* of oak, oaken. *gw.* **derwen.**
derwen *e.b. ll.* **derw** oak-tree, oak. *gw.* **deri, derw.**
des *gw.* **tes.**
desg *e.b. ll.* **-iau** desk.
desog *gw.* **tesog.**
destun *gw.* **testun.**
detholiad *e.g. ll.* **-au** selection, anthology.
deuawd *e.g.b. ll.* **-au** duet.
deuddeg 1 *a.* twelve. **2** *e.g.* twelve.
deuddegfed *a.* twelfth.
deugain 1 *a.* forty. **deugain mlynedd** forty years. **2** *e.g.* forty.
deulu *gw.* **teulu.**
deunaw 1 *a.* eighteen. **deunaw mlynedd** eighteen years. **2** *e.g.* eighteen.
deuoedd *gw.* **dau.**
dew *gw.* **tew.**
dewch *bf.* come! (*plural*). *gw.* **dod.**
dewin *e.g. ll.* **-iaid** magician, wizard, diviner.
dewis 1 *be.* **(dewisaf)** to choose, to select. **2** *e.g. ll.* **-au** choice, desire.
dewr 1 *a. ll* **-ion** brave, valiant. **2** *e.g. ll.* **-ion** brave man, hero.
deyrnas *gw.* **teyrnas.**

di *gw.* **ti.** *gw. At. Rhagenwau.*
diacon *e.g. ll.* **-iaid** deacon.
diafol *e.g. ll.* **diawliaid** devil.
dial (ar) 1 *be.* **(dialaf)** to avenge; to revenge. **2** *e.g. ll.* **-au, -on** vengeance.
dianc (rhag) *be.* **(dihangaf)** to escape, to avoid.
diarfogi *be.* **(diarfogaf)** to disarm.
diarhebion *gw.* **dihareb.**
diawl *e.g. ll.* **-iaid** devil. **Cer i'r diawl!** To hell with you! **diawl o beth** a devil of a thing.
diawledig *a.* devilish.
diawliaid *gw.* **diafol, diawl.**
di-baid *a.* unceasing, constant.
diben *e.g. ll.* **-ion** end, object, aim. **di-ben-draw** endless, interminable.
dibennu *be.* **(dibennaf)** to end, to finish, to terminate.
di-blwm *a.* unleaded.
dibynnu (ar) *be.* **(dibynnaf)** to depend (on), to rely (on).
diced *gw.* **ticed.**
diderfyn *a.* unlimited.
diddordeb *e.g. ll.* **-au** interest, hobby.
diddorol *a.* interesting, of interest.
dieithr *a.* strange, unfamiliar.
dieithryn *e.g. ll.* **dieithriaid** stranger.
diferyn *e.g. ll.* **-nau, diferion** drop.
difetha *be.* **(difethaf)** to destroy, to spoil.
diflannu *be.* **(diflannaf)** to vanish, to disappear.
diflas *a.* distasteful, dull.
difrifol *a.* serious, earnest, solemn.
difyr: difyrrus *a.* pleasant, amusing, entertaining.
difyrru *be.* **(difyrraf)** to amuse, to entertain.
diffiniad *e.g. ll.* **-au** definition.
diffinio *be.* **(diffiniaf)** to define.
diffodd *be.* **(diffoddaf)** to extinguish, to quench. **diffodda'r golau/stôf/tân/teledu** switch off the light/stove/fire/television.
diffuant *a.* genuine, sincere. **Yr eiddoch yn ddiffuant** Yours sincerely.

diffyg   **disgybl**

diffyg *e.g. ll.* **-ion** defect, want, lack, failure, flaw.
digon 1 *e.g.* enough, sufficiency; plenty.
2 *a.* enough; plentiful, ample. 3 *ad.* enough, sufficiently, adequately.
Dyna ddigon! That's enough! **yn ddigon da** good enough (*no mutation*).
digonedd *e.g.* abundance, plenty.
digrif *a.* merry, amusing.
digwydd *be.* **(digwyddaf)** to happen, to occur. **Digwyddodd hi weld y dyn.** She happened to see the man.
digwyddiad *e.g. ll.* **-au** happening, event.
dihareb *e.b. ll.* **diarhebion** proverb.
diheintydd *e.g. ll.* **-ion** disinfectant.
dihuno *be.* **(dihunaf)** to waken, to awaken (*S.W.*).
dileu *be.* **(dileaf)** to delete, to abolish, to exterminate, to erase.
dilyn *be.* **(dilynaf)** to follow, to pursue.
dillad *gw.* **dilledyn.**
dilledyn *e.g. ll.* **dillad** garment, dress, item of clothing. **dillad bob dydd** everyday clothes; **dillad diwedydd** clothes changed into after work; **dillad gwaith** working clothes; **dillad gwely** bedclothes; **dillad isa(f)** underclothing; **dillad nos** pyjamas; **dillad parch** Sunday best, best clothes.
dim 1 *e.g.* any, no. **am ddim** for nothing, gratis; **dim byd** nothing at all; **dim ond** nothing but, only, merely; **dim un** not a single one; **i'r dim** exactly.
dîm *gw.* **tîm.**
dinas *e.b. ll.* **-oedd** city.
dinasyddion *gw.* **dinesydd.**
dinesig *a.* civic, urban.
dinesydd *e.g. ll.* **dinasyddion** citizen.
dinistrio *be.* **(dinistriaf)** to destroy.
diniwed *a.* innocent, harmless, simple.
diod *e.b. ll.* **-ydd** drink, beverage. **diod gadarn** strong drink; **diod o**

ddŵr a drink of water.
dioddef **(o)** 1 *be.* **(dioddefaf)** to suffer, to endure, to allow. 2 *e.g. ll.* **-au, -iadau** suffering, passion.
diofal *a.* careless.
diog: dioglyd *a.* lazy, sluggish, indolent.
diogel *a.* safe, secure, certain.
diogi 1 *be.* **(diogaf)** to be lazy or idle, to laze. 2 *e.g.* laziness.
dioglyd *gw.* **diog.**
diogyn *e.g. ll.* **-nod** idler, sluggard.
diolch **(i, am)** 1 *be.* **(diolchaf)** to thank, to give thanks. 2 *e.g. ll.* **-iadau** thanks; thanksgiving. **diolch byth!** thank heaven! **diolch yn fawr** many thanks (*to you*). **diolch i'r nef (drefn)** thank goodness.
diolchgar *a.* thankful, grateful.
diolchgarwch *e.g.* thankfulness, thanksgiving. **Cwrdd Diolchgarwch** Harvest Thanksgiving Service.
diolchiadau *gw.* **diolch.**
diota *be.* **(diotaf)** to drink (*alcohol*).
dip *gw.* **tip.**
dipyn *gw.* **tipyn.**
dir *gw.* **tir.**
dirgelwch *e.g. ll.* **dirgelion** mystery, secret, secrecy.
dirion *gw.* **tirion.**
dirlun *gw.* **tirlun.**
diroedd *gw.* **tiroedd.**
dirprwy *e.g. ll.* **-on** deputy, delegate, proxy, substitute. **dirprwy brifathro** deputy headmaster.
dirprwyaeth *e.b. ll.* **-au** deputation, delegation.
dirwy *e.b. ll.* **-on** fine, penalty.
disg *e.g.b. ll.* **-iau** disc, record.
disglair *a.* bright, brilliant.
disgleirio *be.* **(disgleiriaf)** to shine, to glitter.
disgrifiad *e.g. ll.* **-au** description.
disgrifio *be.* **(disgrifiaf)** to describe.
disgwyl (am) *be.* **(disgwyliaf)** to expect, to look, to wait for. **Mae hi'n disgwyl baban** She is expecting a baby. **Mae e'n disgwyl bws.** He is waiting for a bus.
disgybl *g. ll.* **-ion** disciple, pupil, novice, follower, adherent.

disgyblaeth *e.b.* *ll.* **-au** discipline.
disgyn *be.* **(disgynnaf)** to descend, to fall.
disian *gw.* **tisian.**
distaw *a.* silent, calm, quiet.
distawrwydd *e.g.* silence, quiet.
distewi *be.* **(distewaf)** to silence, to be silent, to calm.
diswyddo *be.* **(diswyddaf)** to dismiss, to depose, to sack, to make redundant.
dithau *gw.* **tithau.**
di-waith *a.* unemployed, idle.
diwallu *be.* **(diwallaf)** to satisfy, to supply.
diwedd **1** *e.g.* **ll** **-ion, -au** end, close, conclusion; death; purpose. **2** *a.* last, final. **o'r dechrau i'r diwedd** from start to finish.
diweddar *a.* recent; modern, late (*S.W.*); late (*of person*); lately, deceased. **y diweddar Tom Jones** the late Tom Jones. **Ydych chi wedi nofio'n ddiweddar?** Have you been swimming lately? **Cymraeg Diweddar** Modern Welsh.
diweddglo *e.g.* *ll.* **diweddgloeon** conclusion, close, epilogue.
diweddarach *a.* later. *gw.* **diweddar.**
diwerth *a.* worthless.
diwethaf *a.* last; previous; latest. **Rydw i'n dal y trên nesa achos collais yr un diwethaf** I'm catching the next train because I missed the previous one.
diwrnod *e.g.* *ll.* **-au** day. **diwrnod braf/teg** fine day; **diwrnod gwaith** working day; **diwrnod gŵyl** holyday, holiday; **diwrnod mawr** red letter day, 'big day'; **diwrnod i'r brenin** a thoroughly enjoyable day; **y diwrnod o'r blaen** the day before, the other day; **ers diwrnodau** for many days (*past*).
diwtor *gw.* **tiwtor.**
diwydiant *e.g.* *ll.* **diwydiannau** industry. **diwydiant dur** steel industry; **diwydiant glo** coal industry; **diwydiant ymwelwyr** tourist industry; **diwydiant ysgafn**

light industry.
diwygiad *e.g.* *ll.* **-au** reform, reformation; revival. **Diwygiad Protestannaidd** Protestant Reformation.
diwygio *be.* **(diwygiaf)** to amend, to reform, to revise.
diwylliant *e.g.* *ll.* **diwylliannau** culture.
dlawd *gw.* **tlawd.**
dlodi *gw.* **tlodi.**
dlodion *gw.* **tlawd.**
dlos *gw.* **tlos.**
dlws *gw.* **tlws.**
dlysau *gw.* **tlws.**
do *ad.* yes (*affirmative answer to questions using verbs in the past tense*). **Fuest ti'n siopa heddiw? Do** Were you shopping today? Yes. **Welaist ti'r dyn? Do** Did you see the man? Yes. *gw.* **to.**
doc *e.g.* *ll.* **-iau** dock. **docfa** berth.
doctor *e.g.* *ll.* **-iaid** doctor (always used in title); **Y Dr Tom Huws** Dr Tom Huws.
docyn *gw.* **tocyn.**
docynnwr *gw.* **tocynnwr.**
dod: dyfod (at, dros, yn, i) *be.* **(deuaf)** to come, to arrive; to occur; to become. *gw. At. Berfau.*
dodi *be.* **(dodaf)** to put, to place (*S.W.*); to give. **dodi ar ddeall** to explain to; **dodi bai ar** to blame; **dodi (un) ar waith** to set (one) to work.
dodrefnyn *e.g.* *ll.* **dodrefn** piece of furniture (*N.W.*). *gw.* **celficyn.**
dodwy *be.* **(dodwaf)** to lay eggs.
doddi *gw.* **toddi.**
doe *ad. & e.g.b.* yesterday. **bore ddoe** yesterday morning; **echdoe** the day before yesterday.
does *gw.* **toes.**
doeth *a.* wise. **Y Tri Gŵr Doeth** The Three Wise Men.
doethineb *e.b.* *ll.* **-au** wisdom, discretion.
dof *a.* *ll.* **-ion** tame, domesticated.
dogfen *e.b.* *ll.* **-ni, nau** document.
doiled *gw.* **toiled.**
dol *e.b.* *ll.* **-iau** doll.

dôl   **dreisgar**

dôl *e.b. ll.* **dolydd, dolau** meadow.
dôl *e.g.* dole. **ar y dôl** on the dole.
dolc *gw.* **tolc.**
dolcio *gw.* **tolcio.**
dolen *e.b. ll.* **-nau, -ni** handle, link,
ring. **dolen gydiol** connecting link.
dolur *e.g. ll.* **-iau** hurt, ailment, pain,
ache. **dolur rhydd** diarrhoea; **dolur
y galon** heart disease.
dolydd *gw.* **dôl.**
doll *gw.* **toll.**
dom *gw.* **tom.**
don *gw.* **ton.**
dôn *gw.* **tôn.**
donau *gw.* **tôn.**
donfedd *gw.* **tonfedd.**
doniol *a.* witty, humorous.
donnau *gw.* **ton.**
dorch *gw.* **torch.**
doreithiog *gw.* **toreithiog.**
doreth *gw.* **toreth.**
dorf *gw.* **torf.**
dorfeydd *gw.* **torf.**
dorheulo *gw.* **torheulo.**
Dori *gw.* **Tori.**
doriad *gw.* **toriad.**
Dorïaid *gw.* **Torïaid.**
Dorïaidd *gw.* **Torïaidd.**
dorri *gw.* **torri.**
dors *gw.* **tors.**
dorth *gw.* **torth.**
dosau *gw.* **tosyn.**
dosbarth *e.g. ll.* **-au, -iadau** class,
standard; district. **dosbarth canol**
middle class; **dosbarth gweithiol**
working class; **dosbarth isaf** lower
class; **dosbarth uchaf** upper class;
dosbarthiadau meithrin nursery
classes; **cyngor dosbarth** district
council; **dosbarth nos** evening
class.
dost *gw.* **tost.**
dostrwydd *gw.* **tostrwydd.**
dosyn *gw.* **tosyn.**
drachfen: trachefn *ad.* again.
draddodiad *gw.* **traddodiad.**
draddodiadol *gw.* **traddodiadol.**
draed *gw.* **traed.**
draen *e.b. ll.* **-iau** drain. **draeniau
dŵr** water drains.
draen: draenen *e.b. ll.* **drain** thorn.

draenen ddu blackthorn; **draenen
wen** hawthorn; **ar bigau'r drain**
on tenterhooks.
draenog *e.g. ll.* **-od, -iaid, -ion**
hedgehog.
draeth *gw.* **traeth.**
draethau *gw.* **traeth.**
draethawd *gw.* **traethawd.**
draethodau *gw.* **traethawd.**
drafnidiaeth *gw.* **trafnidiaeth.**
drafod *gw.* **trafod.**
drafferth *gw.* **trafferth.**
drafferthu *gw.* **trafferthu.**
draffordd *gw.* **traffordd.**
draffyrdd *gw.* **traffordd.**
dragwyddol *gw.* **tragwyddol.**
drai *gw.* **trai.**
draig *e.b. ll.* **dreigiau** dragon.
Y Ddraig Goch the Red Dragon.
drain *e. ll.* thorns; *gw.* **draen:
draenen.**
drais *gw.* **trais.**
drallod *gw.* **trallod.**
drallwysiad *gw.* **trallwysiad.**
drama *e.b. ll.* **dramâu** drama.
drama radio radio play; **drama
deledu** television play; **drama
gyfres** serial; **drama un act** one-
act play.
dramodwr: dramodydd *e.g. ll.*
dramodwyr dramatist.
dramor *gw.* **tramor.**
drannoeth *gw.* **trannoeth.**
drap *gw.* **trap.**
draul *gw.* **traul.**
draw *ad.* yonder, there, beyond.
Mae'r tŷ draw fanna The house is
over there.
drawsblannu *gw.* **trawsblannu.**
drawst *gw.* **trawst.**
drechu *gw.* **trechu.**
dref: dre *gw.* **tref.**
drefi *gw.* **tref.**
drefn *gw.* **trefn.**
drefnu *gw.* **trefnu.**
drefnus *gw.* **trefnus.**
dreigiau *gw.* **draig.**
dreiglad *gw.* **treiglad.**
dreiglo *gw.* **treiglo.**
dreisio *gw.* **treisio.**
dreisgar *gw.* **treisgar.**

drem

drem *gw.* **trem.**
drên *gw.* **trên.**
drenau *gw.* **trên.**
drennydd *gw.* **trennydd.**
dreser: dresel *e.g. ll.* **-i, -ydd**
dresser.
dreth *gw.* **treth.**
drethdalwr *gw.* **trethdalwr.**
drethu *gw.* **trethu.**
dreuliau *gw.* **traul.**
dreulio *gw.* **treulio.**
drewdod *e.g.* stink, stench.
drewi (o) 1 *be.* **(drewaf)** to stink.
2 *e.g.* stench.
dri *gw.* **tri.**
driawd *gw.* **triawd.**
dric *gw.* **tric.**
dridiau *gw.* **tridiau.**
drigain *gw.* **trigain.**
drigfan *w.* **trigfan.**
drigo *gw.* **trigo.**
drigolion *gw.* **trigolion.**
dringo *be.* **(dringaf)** to climb.
dringwr *e.g. ll.* **dringwyr** climber.
drin *gw.* **trin.**
drindod *gw.* **trindod.**
drioedd *gw.* **trioedd.**
driongl *gw.* **triongl.**
drist *gw.* **trist.**
dristwch *gw.* **tristwch.**
dro *gw.* **tro.**
drochi *gw.* **trochi.**
droeau *gw.* **tro.**
droed *gw.* **troed.**
droedfedd *gw.* **troedfedd.**
droedffordd *gw.* **troedffordd.**
dröedig *gw.* **tröedig.**
dröedigaeth *gw.* **tröedigaeth.**
droedio *gw.* **troedio.**
droednoeth *gw.* **troednoeth.**
droeon *gw.* **tro.**
drogylch *gw.* **trogylch.**
droi *gw.* **troi.**
dros: tros *ardd. (followed by soft mutation)* **(drosto, drostot, drosto/drosti, droston, drostoch, drostyn).** over, for, instead of, on behalf of. **drosodd** finished; **drosodd a throsodd** over and over again; **dros ben** exceedingly; **mynd dros ben llestri** to go over

drychineb

the top; **dros dro** temporary; **dros nos** overnight; **dros y Sul** over the weekend. *gw. At. Arddodiaid.*
drosedd *gw.* **trosedd.**
droseddu *gw.* **troseddu.**
droseddwr *gw.* **troseddwr.**
drosgais *gw.* **trosgais.**
drosglwyddo *gw.* **trosglwyddo.**
drosi *gw.* **trosi.**
drosiad *gw.* **trosiad.**
droswr *gw.* **troswr.**
drothwy *gw.* **trothwy.**
drowsus *gw.* **trowsus.**
druan *gw.* **truan.**
drud *a.* expensive, dear, precious, valuable.
drudwy *e.g. ll.* **-od** starling.
drueni *gw.* **trueni.**
druenus *gw.* **truenus.**
drugaredd *gw.* **trugaredd.**
drugarhau *gw.* **trugarhau.**
drwbl *gw.* **trwbl.**
drwchus *gw.* **trwchus.**
drwg 1 *e.g.* evil, iniquity, wickedness. **o ddrwg i waeth** from bad to worse; **y drwg yn y caws** the source of the evil.
2 *a.* evil; bad; wicked; rotten. **afal drwg** rotten apple; **wy drwg** rotten egg. *gw. At. Ansoddeiriau.*
drwm *e.g. ll.* **drymiau** drum. *gw.* **trwm.**
drws *e.g. ll.* **drysau** door, entrance, gap. **drws cefn** a back door; **drws nesaf** next door; **wrth y drws** at hand, close, near; **carreg y drws** doorstep.
drwser *gw.* **trwser.**
drwsio *gw.* **trwsio.**
drwsiwr *gw.* **trwsiwr.**
drwy: trwy *ardd. (followed by soft mutation)* **(drwyddo, drwyddot, drwyddo/drwyddi, drwyddon, drwyddoch, drwyddyn)** through, by, by means of. *gw. At. Arddodiaid.*
drwydded *gw.* **trwydded.**
drwyn *gw.* **trwyn.**
drwynol *gw.* **trwynol.**
drych *e.g. ll.* **-au** mirror; image, form; spectacle; vision.
drychineb *gw.* **trychineb .**

drychiolaeth   **dybied**

drychiolaeth *e.b. ll.* **-au** apparition, illusion.
drydan *gw.* **trydan.**
drydanol *gw.* **trydanol.**
drydanwr *gw.* **trydanwr.**
drydedd *gw.* **trydedd.**
drydydd *gw.* **trydydd.**
drydyddol *gw.* **trydyddol.**
drygioni *e.g.* evil, wickedness. *gw.* **drwg.**
drygionus *a.* bad, wicked. *gw.* **drwg.**
dryloyw *gw.* **tryloyw.**
dryll *e.g.b. ll.* **-iau** gun (*S.W.*), rifle (*S.W.*), cannon.
drysau *gw.* **drws.**
drysor *gw.* **trysor.**
drysorfa *gw.* **trysorfa.**
drysori *gw.* **trysori.**
drysorydd *gw.* **trysorydd.**
drysu *be.* **(drysaf)** to confuse, to entangle, to disarrange.
dryw *e.g.b. ll.* **-od** wren.
drywydd *gw.* **trywydd.**
du *a. ll* **-on** black; dark.
dudalen *gw.* **tudalen.**
dueddiad *gw.* **tueddiad.**
dull *e.g. ll* **-iau** form, mode, manner.
dun *gw.* **tun.**
dunnell *gw.* **tunnell.**
duo *be.* **(duaf)** to blacken, to darken.
duon *a.ll.* black. *gw.* **du.**
dur 1 *e.g. ll.* **-oedd** steel. **2** *a.* steel.
duw *e.g. ll.* **-iau** god. **Duw Dad** God the Father; **Duw Hollalluog** Almighty God; **Duw Tragwyddol** Eternal God; **bendith Duw** the blessing of God; **Duw Duw!** Good God!
duwies *e.b. ll.* **-au** goddess.
duwiol *a.* devout, godly.
dwbl *a.* double, twice.
dweud (am, wrth) *be.* **(dwedaf, dywedaf)** to say, to speak; to mention. **dweud a dweud** to keep on saying; **dweud anwiredd** to tell a lie; **dweud ei feddwl** to say what one thinks; **dweud yn dda (am)** to speak well (of); **dweud yn ddrwg (am)** to speak ill (of); **dywedais wrtho am gau ei geg** I told him to shut up.

dwfn *a.* deep; profound.
dwfr *gw.* **dŵr.**
dwl *a.* dull, foolish.
dwlc *gw.* **twlc.**
dwll *gw.* **twll.**
dwmpath *gw.* **twmpath.**
dwndis *gw.* **twndis.**
dwnel *gw.* **twnel.**
dwp *gw.* **twp.**
dwpsyn *gw.* **twpsyn.**
dŵr: dwfr *e.g. ll.* **dyfroedd** water. **dŵr berw(edig)** boiling water, **dŵr glaw** rainwater; **dŵr golchi llestri** dishwater; **dŵr (y) môr** sea water; **gwneud dŵr** to urinate. *gw.* **tŵr.**
dwr *gw.* **twr.**
dwrci *gw.* **twrci.**
dwristiaeth *gw.* **twristiaeth.**
dwrn *e.g. ll.* **dyrnau** fist.
dwrw *gw.* **twrw.**
dwsin *e.g. ll.* **-au** dozen.
dwt *gw.* **twt.**
dwy *a.b.* two. **y ddwy** the two, both (feminine). *gw.* **dau.**
dwyieithog *a.* bilingual.
dwyieithrwydd *e.g.* bilingualism.
dwylo *e.ll.* hands. *gw.* **llaw.**
dwyll *gw.* **twyll.**
dwyllo *gw.* **twyllo.**
dwym *gw.* **twym.**
dwymo *gw.* **twymo.**
dwymyn *gw.* **twymyn.**
dwyn *be.* **(dygaf)** to take away, to bear, to convey; to bring; to steal. **dwyn ar gof** to bring to mind; **dwyn i ben** to accomplish, to complete; **dwyn ffrwyth** to bear fruit; **dwgyd** to steal (*S.W.*).
dwyrain *e.g.* east. **y Dwyrain Canol** the Middle East; **y Dwyrain Pell** the Far East.
dwys *a.* grave; intense; profound; thick, dense, concentrated. **cwrs dwys** crash course.
dwywaith *ad.* twice.
dy *rhag.* (*followed by soft mutation*) your (*singular*). **dy chwaer** your sister; **dy lyfr** your book; **dy hunan** yourself.
dŷ *gw.* **tŷ.**
dybied: dybio *gw.* **tybied.**

dychmygion   **dysgl**

dychmygion *gw.* **dychymyg.**
dychmygu *be.* **(dychmygaf)** to
imagine, to think, to contrive.
dychrynllyd *a.* frightful, dreadful,
horrendous.
dychwelyd *be.* **(dychwelaf)** to
return.
dychymyg *e.g. ll.* **dychmygion**
imagination, fancy; idea; riddle.
dydy e/hi ddim *bf.* he/she/it does
not. *gw.* **bod.**
dydd *e.g. ll.* **-iau** day. **Dydd da!**
Good Day; **o ddydd i ddydd** from
day to day; **dyddiau'r wythnos**
days of the week; **ers dyddiau**
many days ago; **Dydd Nadolig**
Christmas Day; **Dydd Gŵyl Dewi**
St David's Day; **Dydd Gwener y
Groglith** Good Friday; **Dydd Llun
(y) Pasg** Easter Monday.
dyddiad *e.g. ll.* **-au** date, dating.
dyddiau *gw.* **dydd.**
dyddio *be.* **(dyddiaf) to date**
(*something*).
dyddyn *gw.* **tyddyn.**
dyddynnwr *gw.* **tyddynnwr.**
dyfalu *be.* **(dyfalaf)** to conjecture, to
guess; to devise.
dyfarniad *e.g. ll.* **-au** verdict,
decision.
dyfarnu *be.* **(dyfarnaf)** to adjudicate;
to adjudge; to decide.
dyfarnwr *e.g. ll.* **dyfarnwyr** judge,
umpire.
dyfiant *gw.* **tyfiant.**
dyfnder *e.g. ll.* **-au, -oedd** deep,
depth.
dyfod *gw.* **dod.**
dyfodol 1 *a.* future, coming. **2** *e.g.*
future. **amser dyfodol** future tense;
yn y dyfodol in the future; **dyfodol
disglair** a brilliant future.
dyfroedd *gw.* **dŵr.**
dyfu *gw.* **tyfu.**
dyfyniad *e.g. ll.* **-au** quotation.
dyffryn *e.g. ll.* **-noedd** valley.
dynged *gw.* **tynged.**
dyngedfennol *gw.* **tyngedfennol.**
dyngu *gw.* **tyngu.**
dylanwad *e.g. ll.* **-au** influence.
dyle *gw.* **tyle.**

dyled *e.b. ll.* **-ion** debt, due, claim,
obligation.
dyledus *a.* due, indebted, obligatory.
dyletswydd *e.b. ll.* **-au** duty,
obligation.
dylino *gw.* **tylino.**
dylwyth *gw.* **tylwyth.**
dyllau *gw.* **twll.**
dyllu *gw.* **tyllu.**
dylluan *gw.* **tylluan.**
dyma *ad.* here is/are; this is; these
are.
dymer *gw.* **tymer.**
dymestl *gw.* **tymestl.**
dymherau *gw.* **tymheredd.**
dymheredd *gw.* **tymheredd.**
dymhestlog *gw.* **tymhestlog.**
dymhorau *gw.* **tymor.**
dymor *gw.* **tymor.**
dymuniad *e.g. ll.* **-au** wish, desire;
request. **gyda phob dymuniad da**
with all best wishes; **dymuniadau
gorau** best wishes.
dymuno *be.* **(dymunaf)** to wish, to
desire.
dymunol *a.* desirable, pleasant;
desired.
dyn *e.g. ll.* **-ion** man, person. **dyn
cyffredin** common man; **dyn
dieithr** stranger; **dyn eira**
snowman. *gw.* **tyn(n).**
dyna *ad.* there is/are. **dyna chi** there
you are; **dyna dro** what bad luck!
dyna drueni what a pity! **dyna fe**
there it is.
dyner *gw.* **tyner.**
dynerwch *gw.* **tynerwch.**
dynes *e.b. ll.* **-au** woman (*N.W.*).
dynion *gw.* **dyn.**
dyn(n) *gw.* **tyn(n).**
dynnu *gw.* **tynnu.**
dyrau *gw.* **tŵr.**
dyrfa *gw.* **tyrfa.**
dyrfau *gw.* **twrw.**
dyrnaid *e.g. ll.* **dyrneidiau** handful,
little, few.
dyrnau *gw.* **dwrn.**
dyrneidiau *gw.* **dyrnaid.**
dyrrau *gw.* **twr.**
dysgedig *a.* learned.
dysgl *e.b. ll.* **-au** dish, plate; cup;

dysgu   **dywysoges**

disk. **dysgl de** tea cup; **dysgl gawl** soup-plate, soup-bowl.

dysgu (i) *be.* **(dysgaf)** to learn, to teach, to educate; **dysgu ar gof** to learn by heart.

dysgwr *e.g. ll.* **dysgwyr** learner.

dysgwyr *gw.* **dysgwr.**

dyst *gw.* **tyst.**

dystio *gw.* **tystio.**

dystiolaeth *gw.* **tystiolaeth.**

dystion *gw.* **tyst.**

dystysgrif *gw.* **tystysgrif.**

dywediad *e.g. ll.* **-au** saying.

dyweddïad *e.g. ll.* **-au** engagement, betrothal.

dyweddïo *be.* **(dyweddïaf)** to get engaged.

dywel *gw.* **tywel.**

dywod *gw.* **tywod.**

dywydd *gw.* **tywydd.**

dywyll *gw.* **tywyll.**

dywyllu *gw.* **tywyllu.**

dywyllwch *gw.* **tywyllwch.**

dywys *gw.* **tywys.**

dywysog *gw.* **tywysog.**

dywysoges *gw.* **tywysoges.**

dderbynneb

dda *gw.* da.
ddadansoddi *gw.* dadansoddi.
ddadl *gw.* dadl.
ddadlau *gw.* dadlau.
ddadrewi *gw.* dadrewi.
ddaear *gw.* daear.
ddaeareg *gw.* daeareg.
ddaeargryn *gw.* daeargryn.
ddaearyddiaeth *gw.*
  daearyddiaeth.
ddaeth *gw.* daeth.
ddafad *gw.* dafad.
ddagrau *gw.* deigryn.
ddail *gw.* deilen.
ddaioni *gw.* daioni.
ddal: ddala *gw.* dal.
ddalen *gw.* dalen.
ddalgylch *gw.* dalgylch.
ddall *gw.* dall.
ddallu *gw.* dallu.
ddameg *gw.* dameg.
ddamhegion *gw.* dameg.
ddamwain *gw.* damwain.
ddanfon *ge.* danfon.
ddangos *gw.* dangos.
ddannedd *gw.* dant.
ddannoedd *gw.* dannoedd.
ddant *gw.* dant.
ddarfod *gw.* darfod.
ddarganfod *gw.* darganfod.
ddarlith *gw.* darlith.
ddarlithio *gw.* darlithio.
ddarlithiwr: darlithydd *gw.*

darlithiwr.
ddarlun *gw.* darlun.
ddarlunio *gw.* darlunio.
ddarlledu *gw.* darlledu.
ddarllen *gw.* darllen.
ddarllenwr: ddarllenydd *gw.*
  darllenwr.
ddarn *gw.* darn.
ddatblygiad *gw.* datblygiad.
ddatblygu *gw.* datblygu.
ddatgan *gw.* datgan.
ddatganiad *gw.* datganiad.
ddatganoli *gw.* datganoli.
ddatgelu *gw.* datgelu.
ddatguddio *gw.* datguddio.
ddatod *gw.* datod.
ddatrys *gw.* datrys.
ddathliad *gw.* dathliad.
ddathlu *gw.* dathlu.
ddau *gw.* dau.
ddawns *gw.* dawns.
ddawnsio *gw.* dawnsio.
dde *gw.* de.
ddeall *gw.* deall.
ddeallus *gw.* deallus.
ddechrau *gw.* dechrau.
ddechreuad *gw.* dechreuad.
ddedwydd *gw.* dedwydd.
ddeddf *gw.* deddf.
ddeddfu *gw.* deddfu.
ddefnydd *gw.* defnydd.
ddefnyddio *gw.* defnyddio.
ddefnyddiol *gw.* defnyddiol.
ddeffro *gw.* deffro.
ddeg: ddeng *gw.* deg.
ddegawd *gw.* degawd.
ddeheuol *gw.* deheuol.
ddeialog *gw.* deialog.
ddeigryn *gw.* deigryn.
ddeilen *gw.* deilen.
ddeilliaid: ddeillion *gw.* dall.
ddeintydd *gw.* deintydd.
ddeiseb *gw.* deiseb.
ddel *gw.* del.
ddelw *gw.* delw.
ddelwi *gw.* delwi.
ddeniadol *gw.* deniadol.
ddenu *gw.* denu.
dderbyn *gw.* derbyn.
dderbyniol *gw.* derbyniol.
dderbynneb *gw.* derbynneb.

dderbynnydd   **ddiwrnod**

dderbynnydd *gw.* derbynnydd.
dderi *gw.* deri.
dderw *gw.* derw.
dderwen *gw.* derwen.
ddesg *gw.* desg.
ddetholiad *gw.* detholiad.
ddeuawd *gw.* deuawd.
ddeuddeg *gw.* deuddeg.
ddeuddegfed *gw.* deuddegfed.
ddeugain *gw.* deugain.
ddeunaw *gw.* deunaw.
ddeuoedd *gw.* deuoedd.
ddewin *gw.* dewin.
ddewis *gw.* dewis.
ddewr *gw.* dewr.
ddiacon *gw.* diacon.
ddiafol *gw.* diafol.
ddial *gw.* dial.
ddianc *gw.* dianc.
ddiarfogi *gw.* diarfogi.
ddiawl *gw.* diawl.
ddiawledig *gw.* diawledig.
ddiawliaid *gw.* diafol, diawl.
ddi-baid *gw.* di-baid.
ddiben *gw.* diben.
ddibennu *gw.* dibennu.
ddi-blwm *gw.* di-blwm.
ddibynnu *gw.* dibynnu.
ddiderfyn *gw.* diderfyn.
ddiddordeb *gw.* diddordeb.
ddiddorol *gw.* diddorol.
ddieithr *gw.* dieithr.
ddieithryn *gw.* dieithryn.
ddiferyn *gw.* diferyn.
ddifetha *gw.* difetha.
ddiflannu *gw.* diflannu.
ddiflas *gw.* diflas.
ddifrifol *gw.* difrifol.
ddifyr: ddifyrrus *gw.* difyr.
ddifyrru *gw.* difyrru.
ddiffiniad *gw.* diffiniad.
ddiffinio *gw.* diffinio.
ddiffodd *gw.* diffodd.
ddiffuant *gw.* diffuant.
ddiffyg *gw.* diffyg.
ddigon *gw.* digon.
ddigonedd *gw.* digonedd.
ddigrif *gw.* digrif.
ddigwydd *gw.* digwydd.
ddigwyddiad *gw.* digwyddiad.
ddihareb *gw.* dihareb.

ddiheintydd *gw.* diheintydd.
ddihuno *gw.* dihuno.
ddileu *gw.* dileu.
ddilyn *gw.* dilyn.
ddillad *gw.* dilledyn.
ddilledyn *gw.* dilledyn.
ddim *gw.* dim.
ddinas *gw.* dinas.
ddinasyddion *gw.* dinesydd.
ddinesig *gw.* dinesig.
ddinesydd *gw.* dinesydd.
ddinistrio *gw.* dinistrio.
ddiniwed *gw.* diniwed.
ddiod *gw.* diod.
ddioddef *gw.* dioddef.
ddiofal *gw.* diofal.
ddiog: ddioglyd *gw.* diog.
ddiogel *gw.* diogel.
ddiogi *gw.* diogi.
ddioglyd *gw.* diog.
ddiogyn *gw.* diogyn.
ddiolch *gw.* diolch.
ddiolchgar *gw.* diolchgar.
ddiolchgarwch *gw.* diolchgarwch.
ddiota *gw.* diota.
ddirgelwch *gw.* dirgelwch.
ddirprwy *gw.* dirprwy.
ddirprwyaeth *gw.* dirprwyaeth.
ddirwy *gw.* dirwy.
ddisg *gw.* disg.
ddisglair *gw.* disglair.
ddisgleirio *gw.* disgleirio.
ddisgrifiad *gw.* disgrifiad.
ddisgrifio *gw.* disgrifio.
ddisgwyl *gw.* disgwyl.
ddisgybl *gw.* disgybl.
ddisgyblaeth *gw.* disgyblaeth.
ddisgyn *gw.* disgyn.
ddistaw *gw.* distaw.
ddistawrwydd *gw.* distawrwydd.
ddistewi *gw.* distewi.
ddiswyddo *gw.* diswyddo.
ddi-waith *gw.* di-waith.
ddiwallu *gw.* diwallu.
ddiwedd *gw.* diwedd.
ddiweddar *gw.* diweddar.
ddiweddarach *gw.* diweddar.
ddiweddglo *gw.* diweddglo.
ddiwerth *gw.* diwerth.
ddiwethaf *gw.* diwethaf.
ddiwrnod *gw.* diwrnod.

ddiwydiant   **ddysgl**

ddiwydiant *gw.* diwydiant.
ddiwygiad *gw.* diwygiad.
ddiwygio *gw.* diwygio.
ddiwylliant *gw.* diwylliant.
ddoc *gw.* doc.
ddoctor *gw.* doctor.
ddod: ddyfod *gw.* dod.
ddodi *gw.* dodi.
ddodrefnyn *gw.* dodrefnyn.
ddodwy *gw.* dodwy.
ddoe *gw.* doe.
ddoeth *gw.* doeth.
ddoethineb *gw.* doethineb.
ddof *gw.* dof.
ddogfen *gw.* dogfen.
ddol *gw.* dol.
ddôl *gw.* dôl.
ddolen *gw.* dolen.
ddolur *gw.* dolur.
ddoniol *gw.* doniol.
ddosbarth *gw.* dosbarth.
ddraen: ddraenen *gw.* draen.
ddraenog *gw.* draenog.
ddraig *gw.* draig.
ddrain *gw.* draen.
ddrama *gw.* drama.
ddramodwr *gw.* dramodwr.
ddramodydd *gw.* dramodwr.
ddreser: ddresel *gw.* dreser.
ddrewdod *gw.* drewdod.
ddrewi *gw.* drewi.
ddringo *gw.* dringo.
ddringwr *gw.* dringwr.
ddrud *gw.* drud.
ddrudwy *gw.* drudwy.
ddrwg *gw.* drwg.
ddrwm *gw.* drwm.
ddrws *gw.* drws.
ddrych *gw.* drych.
ddrychiolaeth *gw.* drychiolaeth.
ddrygioni *gw.* drygioni.
ddrygionus *gw.* drygionus.
ddryll *gw.* dryll.
ddrylliau *gw.* dryll.
ddrysau *gw.* drws.
ddrysu *gw.* drysu.
ddryw *gw.* dryw.
ddu *gw.* du.
ddull *gw.* dull.
dduo *gw.* duo.
ddur *gw.* dur.

dduw *gw.* duw.
dduwies *gw.* duwies.
ddwbl *gw.* dwbl.
ddweud *gw.* dweud.
ddwfn *gw.* dwfn.
ddwfr *gw.* dŵr.
ddwl *gw.* dwl.
ddŵr *gw.* dŵr.
ddwrn *gw.* dwrn.
ddwsin *gw.* dwsin.
ddwy *gw.* dwy.
ddwyieithog *gw.* dwyieithog.
ddwyieithrwydd *gw.*
  dwyieithrwydd.
ddwylo *gw.* dwylo.
ddwyn *gw.* dwyn.
ddwyrain *gw.* dwyrain.
ddwys *gw.* dwys.
ddwywaith *gw.* dwywaith.
ddychmygion *gw.* dychymyg.
ddychmygu *gw.* dychmygu.
ddychrynllyd *gw.* dychrynllyd.
ddychwelyd *gw.* dychwelyd.
ddychymyg *gw.* dychymyg.
ddydd *gw.* dydd.
ddyddiad *gw.* dyddiad.
ddyddiau *gw.* dydd.
ddyfalu *gw.* dyfalu.
ddyfarniad *gw.* dyfarniad.
ddyfarnu *gw.* dyfarnu.
ddyfarnwr *gw.* dyfarnwr.
ddyfnder *gw.* dyfnder.
ddyfod *gw.* dod.
ddyfodol *gw.* dyfodol.
ddyfroedd *gw.* dŵr.
ddyfyniad *gw.* dyfyniad.
ddyffryn *gw.* dyffryn.
ddylanwad *gw.* dylanwad.
ddyled *gw.* dyled.
ddyledus *gw.* dyledus.
ddyletswydd *gw.* dyletswydd.
ddymuniad *gw.* dymuniad.
ddymuno *gw.* dymuno.
ddymunol *gw.* dymunol.
ddyn *gw.* dyn.
ddynes *gw.* dynes.
ddyrnaid *gw.* dyrnaid.
ddyrnau *gw.* dwrn.
ddyrneidiau *gw.* dyrnaid.
ddysgedig *gw.* dysgedig.
ddysgl *gw.* dysgl.

ddysgu *gw.* **dysgu.**
ddysgwr *gw.* **dysgwr.**
ddysgwyr *gw.* **dysgwyr.**

ddywediad *gw.* **dywediad.**
ddyweddïad *gw.* **dyweddïad.**
ddyweddïo *gw.* **dyweddïo.**

e: o *gw.* **ef.**
eang *a.* broad, wide, extensive.
eb: ebe: ebr *bf.* says, said (I, he/she, they, etc.).
ebol *e.g. ll.* **-ion** colt; buck.
e-bost *e.g.ll.* **e-bostiau** e-mail.
Ebrill *e.g.* April.
economeg *e.b.* economics.
echdoe *e.g. ll. & ad.* the day before yesterday.
echnos *e.b. ll. & ad.* the night before last.
edau *e.b. ll.* **edafedd** thread.
edifar: edifeiriol *a.* sorry, penitent, contrite. **Mae'n edifar gen i** I regret.
edmygu *be.* **(edmygaf)** to admire.
edrych *be.* **(edrychaf)** to look, to observe, to search, to examine; to expect. **edrych am** to look for, to expect; **edrych ar** to look on, to look upon; **edrych ar ôl** to look after, to mind; **edrych at** to look towards; **edrych dros** to overlook, to survey; **edrych allan** to look out, to seek; **edrych ymlaen** to look forward.
ef: efe: efô *rhag.* he, him, it (*N.W.*).
efallai *ad.* perhaps.
efengyl *e.b. ll.* **-au** gospel. **Efengyl Iesu Grist** the Gospel of Jesus Christ.
efeilliaid *gw.* **gefell.**

efo *ardd.* with, by means of (*N.W.*).
efô *gw.* **ef.**
Efrog *e.b.* York.
Efrog Newydd *e.b.* New York.
effaith *e.b. ll.* **effeithiau** effect.
effeithiau *gw.* **effaith.**
effeithiol *a.* effective.
effro *a.* awake (*N.W.*).
egin *gw.* **eginyn.**
eginyn *e.g. ll.* **egin** shoot, sprout, (young) blade.
eglur *a.* clear, evident, plain.
egluro *be.* **(egluraf)** to reveal; to explain; to manifest.
eglwys *e.b. ll.* **-i** church, the church.
egni *e.g. ll.* **egnïon, egnïoedd** energy, might; effort, endeavour.
egnïoedd *gw.* **egni.**
egnïol *a.* vigorous, energetic.
egnïon *gw.* **egni.**
egwyddor *e.b. ll.* **-ion** principle; rudiment; alphabet.
egwyddorol *a.* having principles. *gw.* **gwyddor.**
egwyl *e.b. ll.* **-iau, -ion** break, interval; spell.
enghraifft *e.b. ll.* **enghreifftiau** example, instance. **er enghraifft** for example.
enghreifftiau *gw.* **enghraifft.**
englyn *e.g. ll.* **-ion** an epigrammatic four-line stanza in Welsh poetry.
engyl *gw.* **angel.**
ehedydd *e.g. ll.* **-ion** lark.
ei *rhag.* his, her, its. **ei hunan** himself/herself. *gw. At. Treigladau.*
eich *rhag.* your. **eich hunan** yourself; **eich hunain** yourselves.
Eidal, Yr *e.b.* Italy.
Eidaleg *e.b.* Italian language.
Eidales *e.b. ll.* **-au** Italian woman.
Eidalwr *e.g. ll.* **Eidalwyr** Italian man.
eiddo 1 *e.g.* possession(s), property, estate. **ei eiddo** his possession. **2** *ad.* his, hers, etc.
eifr *gw.* **gafr.**
Eingl-Gymro *e.g. ll.* **Eingl-Gymry** Anglo-Welshman.
eiliad *e.g.b. ll.* **-au** second, moment.
eilwaith *ad.* again, a second time.

ein *rhag.* our. **ein hunain** ourselves.
eira *e.g. ll.* **-oedd** snow.
eirch *gw.* **arch.**
eirchion *gw.* **arch.**
eirfa *gw.* **geirfa.**
eiriadur *gw.* **geiriadur.**
eiriau *gw.* **gair.**
eirin *gw.* **eirinen.**
eirinen *e.b. ll.* **eirin** plum, damson;
berry. **eirin gwlanog** peaches.
eirio *gw.* **geirio.**
eirlys *e.g. ll.* **-iau** snowdrop. *gw.*
tlws yr eira.
eirth *gw.* **arth.**
eisiau *e.g.* need, want, lack, poverty.
Rydw i eisiau – I need –, I want –.
Mae eisiau – arnaf i I need –, I
want –.
eisoes *ad.* already.
eistedd *be.* **(eisteddaf)** to sit, to seat.
eisteddfod *e.b. ll.* **-au** eisteddfod.
eisteddfodwr *e.g. ll.* **eisteddfodwyr**
a frequenter of *eisteddfodau.*
eitem *e.b. ll.* **-au** item.
eithaf 1 *e.g. ll.* **-ion, -oedd, -edd**
end, extremity, uttermost part.
2 *a.* farthest, surperlative. **y gosb
eithaf** capital punishment.
3 *ad.* very, quite.
eithafol *a.* extreme.
eithr 1 *rhag.* except, besides. **2** *c.* but.
eithrio *be.* **(eithriaf)** to except, to
exclude. **ac eithrio** except,
excepting.
eleni *ad.* this year.
elfen *e.b. ll.* **-nau** element, particle,
factor, tendency. **yn fy elfen** in my
element.
elfennau *gw.* **elfen.**
elfennol *a.* elementary, constituent,
simple.
eliffant *e.g. ll.* **-od** elephant.
elw *e.g. ll.* **-on** profit, gain.
elwa *be.* **(elwaf)** to profit, to gain.
elyn *gw.* **gelyn.**
elltydd *gw.* **allt.**
em *gw.* **gem.**
emyn *e.g. ll.* **-au** hymn. **emyn-dôn**
hymn-tune.
emynydd *e.g. ll.* **emynwyr** hymn-
writer.

ên *gw.* **gên.**
enaid *e.g. ll.* **eneidiau** soul, spirit;
life.
enau *gw.* **genau.**
enedigaeth *gw.* **genedigaeth.**
eneidiau *gw.* **enaid.**
eneth *gw.* **geneth.**
eneuau *gw.* **genau.**
enfawr *a.* enormous, vast, immense,
huge.
enfys *e.b. ll.* **-au** rainbow.
eni *gw.* **geni.**
enillwr: enillydd *e.g. ll.* **enillwyr**
earner; victor, winner.
ennill 1 *be.* **(enillaf)** to gain, to
profit, to get; to win. **2** *e.g. ll.*
enillion winnings; salary; profit.
ennyd *e.g.b.* a while, moment.
enw *e.g. ll.* **-au** name; noun; **enw
anwes** pet name; **enw benywaidd**
feminine noun; **enw gwrywaidd**
masculine noun; **enw torfol**
collective noun; **ffugenw** *nom de
plume,* pseudonym.
enwad *e.g. ll.* **-au** religious
denomination.
enwedig *a.* especial.
enwi *be.* **(enwaf)** to name.
enwog 1 *a.* famous renowned,
eminent. **2** *e.ll.* **-ion** persons of
renown or fame; celebrities.
enwogrwydd *e.g.* fame.
enyn *gw.* **genyn.**
eos *e.b. ll.* **-iaid** nightingale.
epa *e.g. ll.* **-od** ape.
er *ardd.* because of, for, in order to;
since (*a fixed point in time*); despite.
er anrhydedd in honour; **er bod**
although; **er cof** in memory, *in
memoriam*; **er gwaethaf** in spite of,
despite; **er hynny** yet, since then; **er
lles/budd** for the benefit of; **er
mwyn** for the sake of, in order to;
er dydd Llun since Monday.
eraill *gw.* **arall.**
erbyn *ardd.* against, facing, opposite;
by, for, in preparation for. **erbyn
hyn** by this time, by now; **mynd yn
erbyn** to oppose, to go against;
erbyn meddwl coming to think of
it.

erchyll   **ewythr**

erchyll *a.* atrocious, terrible.
erddi *gw.* **gardd.**
erfin *gw.* **erfinen.**
erfinen *e.b. ll.* **erfin** turnip, swede.
erfyn 1 *be.* **(erfyniaf)** to beg, to
entreat, to pray, to implore. **2** *e.g. ll.*
arfau weapon, tool. *gw.* **arf.**
ergyd *e.g.b. ll.* **-ion** blow, knock,
shot, hit, bang, detonation.
erioed *ad.* ever.
erlid *be.* **(erlidiaf)** to pursue, to
persecute.
erlyn *be.* **(erlynaf)** to prosecute.
erlyniad *e.g. ll.* **-au** prosecution.
erlynydd *e.g. ll.* **-ion** prosecutor.
ernes *e.b. ll.* **-au** security, pledge;
deposit.
ers *ardd.* for, since (*a continuing
period*). **ers pythefnos** for the last
fortnight. **ers tro** for some time.
erthygl *e.b. ll.* **-au** article, literary
composition; clause.
erthyliad *e.g. ll.* **-au** abortion,
miscarriage.
erthylu *be.* **(erthylaf)** to abort, to
miscarry.
erw *e.b. ll.* **-au** acre.
eryr *e.g. ll.* **-od** eagle.
Eryri *e.b.* Snowdonia.
es i *bf.* I went. *gw.* **mynd.**
esboniad *e.g. ll.* **-au** commentary;
explanation, exposition .
esbonio (i) *be.* **(esboniaf)** to explain
(to).
esgeulus *a.* negligent.
esgeuluso *be.* **(esgeulusaf)** to
neglect.
esgeulustod: esgeulustra *e.g.*
negligence.
esgid *e.b. ll.* **-iau** boot; shoe:
esgidiau mawr/uchel high boots;
esgidiau ysgafn light boots or
shoes; **yr esgid yn gwasgu** a
difficult financial situation.
esgob *e.g. ll.* **-ion** bishop. **Esgob
Tyddewi** Bishop of St David's;
esgobaeth diocese; **Esgob!** Oh
Lord!

esgus *e.g. ll.* **-ion, -odion** excuse;
pretence (*S.W.*). **mae e'n esgus
cysgu** he's pretending to sleep.
esgusion *gw.* **esgus.**
esgusodi *be.* **(esgusodaf)** to make
an excuse, to excuse; **Esgusodwch
fi** Excuse me.
esgusodion *gw.* **esgus.**
esgyrn *gw.* **asgwrn. Esgyrn
Dafydd!** Good heavens!
esiampl *e.b. ll.* **-au** example.
esmwyth *a.* soft, easy, comfortable.
estron *e.g. ll.* **-iaid** foreigner, alien,
stranger.
estyn *be.* **(estynnaf)** to extend, to
reach; to stretch, to lengthen; to give.
estyniad *e.g. ll.* **-au** extension.
etifeddu *be.* **(etifeddaf)** to inherit.
eto *c. & ad.* again a second time, yet,
still, nevertheless.
ethol *be.* **(etholaf)** to elect, to
choose, to select.
etholaeth *e.b. ll.* **-au** constituency;
electorate.
etholiad *e.g. ll.* **-au** election;
etholiad cyffredinol general
election; **is-etholiad** by-election.
eu *rhag.* (*words beginning with a
vowel are aspirated when preceded
by* **eu**) their. **eu hafalau** their
apples; **eu hemynau** their hymns;
eu hysgolion their schools. **eu
hunain** themselves. *gw. At.
Rhagenwau.*
euog *a.* guilty; **euog neu ddieuog**
guilty or not guilty.
euogrwydd *e.g.* guilt.
euraid: euraidd *a.* gold, golden.
ewch *bf.* go! (*plural*). *gw.* **mynd.**
ewin *e.g.b. ll.* **-edd** nail, claw, talon;
hoof. **â'i ddeg ewin** with all his
might.
Ewrop *e.b.* Europe.
ewyllys *e.b. ll.* **-iau, -ion** will;
desire; testament. **yn erbyn ei
ewyllys** against his will.
ewyn *e.g.* foam, froth. *gw.* **gewyn.**
ewythr *e.g. ll.* **-edd, -od** uncle.

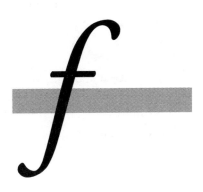

fab *gw.* **mab.**
faban *gw.* **baban.**
fabanaidd *gw.* **babanaidd.**
fabi *gw.* **babi.**
fabolgamp *gw.* **mabolgamp.**
facio *gw.* **bacio.**
fach *gw.* **bach.**
fachau *gw.* **bach, bachyn.**
fachgen *gw.* **bachgen.**
fachgennaidd *gw.* **bachgennaidd.**
fachlud *gw.* **machlud.**
fachu *gw.* **bachu.**
fachyn *gw.* **bach.**
fad *gw.* **bad.**
fadarch *gw.* **madarch.**
fae *gw.* **bae.**
faer *gw.* **maer.**
faeres *gw.* **maeres.**
faes *gw.* **maes.**
faestref *gw.* **maestref.**
fafon *gw.* **mafonen.**
fag *gw.* **bag.**
fagddu, y *e.b.* utter darkness.
fagiau *gw.* **bag.**
fagu *gw.* **magu.**
Fai *gw.* **Mai.**
fai *gw.* **bai.**
faich *gw.* **baich.**
fain *gw.* **main.**
faint *rhag. gof.* how much? how
  many? *gw.* **maint.**
falch *gw.* **balch.**
falchder *gw.* **balchder.**

faldod *gw.* **maldod.**
faldodi *gw.* **maldodi.**
faled *gw.* **baled.**
faledwr *gw.* **baledwr.**
falot *gw.* **balot.**
falu *gw.* **malu.**
falŵn *gw.* **balŵn.**
falwoden *gw.* **malwoden.**
fam *gw.* **mam.**
fam-gu *gw.* **mam-gu.**
famiaith *gw.* **mamiaith.**
fân *gw.* **mân.**
fan *e.b. ll.* **-iau** van. *gw.* **ban, man.**
fanana *gw.* **banana.**
fanc *gw.* **banc.**
fancio *gw.* **bancio.**
fand *gw.* **band.**
fandal *e.g. ll.* **-iaid** vandal.
fandaleiddio *be.* **(fandaleiddiaf)** to
  vandalise.
fandaliaeth *e.b.* vandalism.
faneg *gw.* **maneg.**
faner *gw.* **baner.**
fannau *gw.* **ban, man.**
fannod *gw.* **bannod.**
fans *gw.* **mans.**
fantais *gw.* **mantais.**
fanteisio *gw.* **manteisio.**
fanteision *gw.* **mantais.**
fantell *gw.* **mantell.**
fanwl *gw.* **manwl.**
fanylion *gw.* **manylyn.**
fanylu *gw.* **manylu.**
fanylyn *gw.* **manylyn.**
fap *gw.* **map.**
far *gw.* **bar.**
fara *gw.* **bara.**
farbeciw *gw.* **barbeciw.**
farc *gw.* **marc.**
farcio *gw.* **marcio.**
farchnad *gw.* **marchnad.**
farchog *gw.* **marchog.**
fardd *gw.* **bardd.**
farddoniaeth *gw.* **barddoniaeth.**
farf *gw.* **barf.**
farn *gw.* **barn.**
farnwr *gw.* **barnwr.**
farrau *gw.* **bar.**
fart *gw.* **mart.**
farw *gw.* **marw.**
farwaidd *gw.* **marwaidd.**

farwol   **fenywaidd**

farwol *gw.* marwol.
farwolaeth *gw.* marwolaeth.
fas *gw.* bas.
fasged *gw.* basged.
fasn *gw.* basn.
fasnach *gw.* masnach.
fasnachwr *gw.* masnachwr.
fasnau: fasnys *gw.* basn.
faswr *gw.* baswr, maswr.
fat *gw.* bat, mat.
fater *gw.* mater.
fatsen: fatsien *gw.* matsen.
fath *gw.* bath, math.
fathdy *gw.* bathdy.
fathemateg *gw.* mathemateg.
fathemategol *gw.* mathemategol.
fathemategwr *gw.* mathemategwr.
fathodyn *gw.* bathodyn.
fathu *gw.* bathu.
faw *gw.* baw.
fawd *gw.* bawd.
fawl *gw.* mawl.
fawn *gw.* mawn.
fawr *gw.* mawr.
fawredd *gw.* mawredd.
Fawrth *be.* Mawrth.
fe 1 *rhag.* he, him, it. 2 *geir.* particle
(*may be used before verbs (S.W.)*). fe
welais; fe glywais; fe gwympodd.
gw. At. Berfau – Fe/Mi.
feallai *ad.* perhaps.
fecso *gw.* becso.
fechan *gw.* bechan.
fechgyn *gw.* bachgen.
fechnïaeth *gw.* mechnïaeth.
Fedi *gw.* Medi.
fedi *gw.* medi.
fedru *gw.* medru.
fedrus *gw.* medrus.
fedwen *gw.* bedwen.
fedyddio *w.* bedyddio.
Fedyddiwr *gw.* Bedyddiwr.
fedd *gw.* bedd, meddu.
feddal *gw.* meddal.
feddalu *gw.* meddalu.
feddalwedd *gw.* meddalwedd.
feddu *gw.* meddu.
feddw *gw.* meddw.
feddwi *gw.* meddwi.
feddwl *gw.* meddwl.
feddyg *gw.* meddyg.

feddygfa *gw.* meddygfa.
feddyginiaeth *gw.* meddyginiaeth.
feddylgar *gw.* meddylgar.
feddyliau *gw.* meddwl.
fefus *gw.* mefusen.
Fehefin *gw.* Mehefin.
feiau *gw.* bai.
feibion *gw.* mab.
Feibl *gw.* Beibl.
feic *gw.* beic.
feicrodon *gw.* meicrodon.
feichiau *gw.* baich.
feichiog *gw.* beichiog.
feiddio *gw.* meiddio.
feim *gw.* meim.
feinir *gw.* meinir.
feio *gw.* beio.
feirdd *gw.* bardd.
feirioli *gw.* meirioli.
feirniad *gw.* beirniad.
feirniadu *gw.* beirniadu.
feirniaid *gw.* beirniad.
feistr *gw.* meistr.
feistres *gw.* meistres.
feistri: feistriaid *gw.* meistr.
feistroli *gw.* meistroli.
feithrin *gw.* meithrin.
fel *c.* as, so, like. fel arfer as usual,
usually; fel pe bai/petai/petasai as
if.
fêl *gw.* mêl.
felen *gw.* melen.
felin *gw.* melin.
felyn *gw.* melyn.
felys *gw.* melys.
felysfwyd *gw.* melysfwyd.
fellten *gw.* mellten.
felltith *gw.* melltith.
felly *ad.* so, thus.
fendigedig *gw.* bendigedig.
fendith *gw.* bendith.
fenig *gw.* maneg.
fenter *gw.* menter.
fentrau *gw.* menter.
fentro *gw.* mentro.
fentrus *gw.* mentrus.
fenthyca *gw.* benthyca.
fenyn *gw.* menyn.
fenyw *gw.* benyw, menyw.
fenywaidd *gw.* benywaidd,
menywaidd.

fer   **fodiau**

fer *gw.* **ber.**
fêr *gw.* **mêr.**
ferch *gw.* **merch.**
Fercher *gw.* **Mercher.**
ferchetaidd *gw.* **merchetaidd.**
ferf *gw.* **berf.**
ferfa *gw.* **berfa.**
ferfenw *gw.* **berfenw.**
ferlod *gw.* **merlyn.**
ferlota *gw.* **merlota.**
ferlotwr *gw.* **merlotwr.**
ferlyn *gw.* **merlyn.**
fersiwn *e.g. ll.* **fersiynau** version.
ferthyr *gw.* **merthyr.**
ferw *gw.* **berw.**
ferwi *gw.* **berwi.**
fes *gw.* **mesen.**
fesen *gw.* **mesen.**
festri *e.b. ll.* **festrïoedd** vestry.
fesul *gw.* **mesul.**
fesur *gw.* **mesur.**
fesurydd *gw.* **mesurydd.**
fetel *gw.* **metel.**
fetr *gw.* **metr.**
fetrig *gw.* **metrig.**
fethiant *gw.* **methiant.**
fewn *gw.* **mewn.**
fewnwr *gw.* **mewnwr.**
feysydd *gw.* **maes.**
fi: mi *rhag.* I, me. *gw.* **mi.**
ficer *e.g. ll.* **-iaid** vicar.
ficerdai *gw.* **ficerdy.**
ficerdy *e.g. ll.* **ficerdai** vicarage.
ficrodon *gw.* **microdon.**
figwrn *gw.* **migwrn.**
fil *gw.* **mil.**
filfeddyg *gw.* **milfeddyg.**
filgi *gw.* **milgi.**
filiwn *gw.* **miliwn.**
filoedd *gw.* **mil.**
filwr *gw.* **milwr.**
filltir *gw.* **milltir.**
fin *gw.* **bin.**
fin *gw.* **min.**
finegr *e.g. ll.* **-au** vinegar.
finiog *gw.* **miniog.**
finlliw *gw.* **minlliw.**
finnau *gw.* **minnau.**
fiola *e.b. ll.* **-s** viola.
fioled *e.b. ll.* **-au** violet.
fioleg *gw.* **bioleg.**

firi *gw.* **miri.**
firws *e.g. ll.* **-au** virus.
fis *gw.* **mis.**
fisged *gw.* **bisged.**
fisgïen *gw.* **bisgïen.**
fisglwyf *gw.* **misglwyf.**
fisoedd *gw.* **mis.**
fisol *gw.* **misol.**
fisolyn *gw.* **misolyn.**
fitw *gw.* **bitw.**
fiwsig *gw.* **miwsig.**
flaen *gw.* **blaen.**
flaendal *gw.* **blaendal.**
flaenor *gw.* **blaenor.**
flaenwr *gw.* **blaenwr.**
flaguro *gw.* **blaguro.**
flaguryn *gw.* **blaguryn.**
flaidd *gw.* **blaidd.**
flanced *gw.* **blanced.**
flas *gw.* **blas.**
flasu *gw.* **blasu.**
flasus *gw.* **blasus.**
flawd *gw.* **blawd.**
fleiddiaid *gw.* **blaidd.**
flew *gw.* **blewyn.**
flewyn *gw.* **blewyn.**
flin *gw.* **blin.**
flinder *gw.* **blinder.**
flinedig *gw.* **blinedig.**
flino *gw.* **blino.**
flodau *gw.* **blodyn.**
flodeugerdd *gw.* **blodeugerdd.**
flodfresychen *gw.* **blodfresychen.**
flodyn *gw.* **blodyn.**
floedd *gw.* **bloedd.**
floeddio *gw.* **bloeddio.**
flows *gw.* **blows.**
flwch *gw.* **blwch.**
flwydd *gw.* **blwydd.**
flwyddyn *gw.* **blwyddyn.**
flychau *gw.* **blwch.**
flynedd *gw.* **blwyddyn.**
flynyddoedd *gw.* **blwyddyn.**
fo *rhag.* he, it (*N.W.*).
focs *gw.* **bocs.**
foch *gw.* **boch, mochyn.**
fochyn *gw.* **mochyn.**
fod *gw.* **bod.**
fodau *gw.* **bod.**
fodfedd *gw.* **modfedd.**
fodiau *gw.* **bodiau.**

fodio

fodio *gw.* bodio.
fodlon: foddlon *gw.* bodlon.
fodloni *w.* bodloni.
fodrwy *gw.* modrwy.
fodryb *gw.* modryb.
fodur *gw.* modur.
fodurwr *gw.* modurwr.
fodd *gw.* bodd, modd.
foddhad *gw.* boddhad.
foddi *gw.* boddi.
foddion *gw.* moddion.
foel *gw.* moel.
foelni *gw.* moelni.
foes *gw.* moes.
foesol *gw.* moesol.
foethus *gw.* moethus.
fogi *gw.* mogi.
fol *gw.* bol.
fola *gw.* bola.
foli *gw.* moli.
foliau *gw.* bol.
follt *gw.* bollt.
folltau *gw.* bollt.
fom *gw.* bom.
Fôn *gw.* Môn.
fôn *gw.* bôn.
foneddiges *gw.* boneddiges.
foneddigion *gw.* bonheddwr.
fonheddig *gw.* bonheddig.
fonheddwr *gw.* bonheddwr.
fonion *gw.* bôn.
fôr *gw.* môr.
ford *gw.* bord.
fordaith *gw.* mordaith.
fordau: fordydd *gw.* bord.
forddwyd *gw.* morddwyd.
fore *gw.* bore.
forfa *gw.* morfa.
forfil *gw.* morfil.
forgais *gw.* morgais.
Forgannwg *gw.* Morgannwg.
forgeisiau *gw.* morgais.
forgrugyn *gw.* morgrugyn.
forio *gw.* morio.
fôr-leidr *gw.* môr-leidr.
forio *gw.* morio.
foroedd *gw.* môr.
foron *gw.* moronen.
foronen *gw.* moronen.
forthwyl *gw.* morthwyl.
forwr *gw.* morwr.

forwyn *gw.* morwyn.
fory: yfory *ad.* tomorrow.
fos *gw.* bos.
fotwm *gw.* botwm.
fotymu *gw.* botymu.
fowlen *gw.* bowlen.
fragdy *gw.* bragdy.
fraich *gw.* braich.
fraint *bw.* braint.
frân *gw.* brân.
fras *gw.* bras.
fraslun *gw.* braslun.
fraster *gw.* braster.
fraw *gw.* braw.
frawd *gw.* brawd.
frawddeg *gw.* brawddeg.
frecwast *gw.* brecwast.
frech *gw.* brech.
frechdan *gw.* brechdan.
frechiad *gw.* brechiad.
freichiau *gw.* braich.
freichled *gw.* breichled.
freiniau: freintiau *gw.* braint.
frenhines *gw.* brenhines.
frenhinoedd *gw.* brenin.
frenhinol *gw.* brenhinol.
frenin *gw.* brenin.
fres *gw.* bres.
frest *gw.* brest.
fresychen *gw.* bresychen.
frethyn *gw.* brethyn.
freuddwyd *gw.* breuddwyd.
freuddwydio *gw.* breuddwydio.
freuddwydion *gw.* breuddwyd.
frifo *gw.* brifo.
frig *gw.* brig.
frigau *gw.* brig, brigyn.
frigyn *gw.* brigyn.
fritho: frithio *gw.* britho.
friwsion *gw.* briwsionyn.
friwsionyn *gw.* briwsionyn.
fro *gw.* bro.
frodor *gw.* brodor.
frodyr *gw.* brawd.
froga *gw.* broga.
fron *gw.* bron.
fronfraith *gw.* bronfraith.
fronnau: fronnydd *gw.* bron.
frown *gw.* brown.
fröydd *gw.* bro.
frwdfrydig *gw.* brwdfrydig.

frwnt *gw.* **brwnt.**
frws: frwsh *gw.* **brws.**
frwsio: frwshio *gw.* **brwsio.**
frwsys: frwshys *gw.* **brws.**
frwydr *gw.* **brwydr.**
frwydrau *gw.* **brwydr.**
fryd *gw.* **bryd.**
fryn *gw.* **bryn.**
fryniau *gw.* **bryn.**
frys *gw.* **brys.**
frysio *gw.* **brysio.**
fuan *gw.* **buan.**
fuarth *gw.* **buarth.**
fuchod *gw.* **buwch.**
fud *gw.* **mud.**
fudiad *gw.* **mudiad.**
fudr *gw.* **budr.**
fuddsoddi *gw.* **buddsoddi.**
fuddugol *gw.* **buddugol.**
fuddugoliaeth *gw.* **buddugoliaeth.**
fues i *bf.* I was, I have been. *gw.* **bod.**
fugail *gw.* **bugail.**
fugeiliaid *gw.* **bugail.**
fugeilio *gw.* **bugeilio.**
ful *gw.* **mul.**
fûm: fues *bf.* I was, I have been. *gw.*
  bod.
funud *gw.* **munud.**
fur *gw.* **mur.**
fusnes *gw.* **busnes.**
fuwch *gw.* **buwch.**
fwced *gw.* **bwced.**
fwg *gw.* **mwg.**
fwgwd *gw.* **mwgwd.**
fwlch *gw.* **bwlch.**
fwnci *gw.* **mwnci.**
fwrdeistref *gw.* **bwrdeistref.**
fwrdd *gw.* **bwrdd.**
fwriad *gw.* **bwriad.**
fwriadu *gw.* **bwriadu.**
fwrw *gw.* **bwrw.**
fws *gw.* **bws.**
fwstash *gw.* **mwstash.**
fwstwr *gw.* **mwstwr.**
fwthyn *gw.* **bwthyn.**
fwy *gw.* **mawr.**
fwyaf *gw.* **mawr.**
fwyar *gw.* **mwyaren.**
fwyaren *gw.* **mwyaren.**
fwyd *gw.* **bwyd.**
fwydo: fwyda *gw.* **bwydo.**

fwydlen *gw.* **bwydlen.**
fwydydd *gw.* **bwyd.**
fwydyn *gw.* **mwydyn.**
fwyn *gw.* **mwyn.**
fwynhad *gw.* **mwynhad.**
fwynhau *gw.* **mwynhau.**
fwyta: fyta *gw.* **bwyta.**
fwyty *gw.* **bwyty.**
fy *rhag.* (*followed by nasal mutation*)
  my, of me. *gw. At. Rhagenwau.*
fychan *gw.* **bychan.**
fyd *gw.* **byd.**
fydoedd *gw.* **byd.**
fydd e/o/hi *bf.* he/she/it will be. *gw.*
  bod.
fyddar *gw.* **byddar.**
fyddin *gw.* **byddin.**
fyddinoedd *gw.* **byddin.**
fyfyrdod *gw.* **myfyrdod.**
fyfyrio *gw.* **myfyrio.**
fyfyriwr *gw.* **myfyriwr.**
fyglyd *gw.* **myglyd.**
fygu *gw.* **mygu.**
fygydau *gw.* **mwgwd.**
fylchau *gw.* **bwlch.**
fynach *gw.* **mynach.**
fynachlog *gw.* **mynachlog.**
fynachod *gw.* **mynach.**
fynaich *gw.* **mynach.**
fynd: fyned *gw.* **mynd.**
fynedfa *gw.* **mynedfa.**
fynedfeydd *gw.* **mynedfa.**
fynediad *gw.* **mynediad.**
fynegai *gw.* **mynegai.**
fynegeion *gw.* **mynegai.**
fynegi *gw.* **mynegi.**
fynnu *gw.* **mynnu.**
fynwent *gw.* **mynwent.**
fyny, i *ad.* up, upwards. **oddi fyny**
  from above; **ar i fyny** upwards; in
  good spirits, in a cheerful mood.
fynychu *gw.* **mynychu.**
fynydd *gw.* **mynydd.**
fynyddig: fynyddog *gw.* **mynyddig.**
fyr *gw.* **byr.**
fyrbryd *gw.* **byrbryd.**
fyrddau *gw.* **bwrdd.**
fyrfodd *gw.* **byrfodd.**
fyrr *gw.* **myrr.**
fys *gw.* **bys.**
fysedd *gw.* **bys.**

fystyrau   **fywydeg**

fystyrau *gw.* **mwstwr.**
fysys *gw.* **bws.**
fyth, *gw.* **byth,** *gw.* **myth.**
fythynnod *gw.* **bwthyn.**

fyw *gw.* **byw.**
fywiog *gw.* **bywiog.**
fywyd *gw.* **bywyd.**
fywydeg *gw.* **bywydeg.**

ffa *gw.* **ffäen.**
ffäen: ffeuen *e.b. ll.* **ffa** bean. **ffa pob** baked beans.
ffactor *e.g.b. ll.* **-au** factor.
ffaelu (â) *be.* **(ffaelaf)** to fail, to miss, to mistake (*S.W.*).
ffafr *e.b. ll.* **-au** favour, respect.
ffair *e.b. ll.* **ffeiriau** fair. **ffair haf** summer fair; **ffair lyfrau** book fair; **ffair sborion** jumble sale; **fel ffair** an utter mess, very busy.
ffaith *e.b. ll.* **ffeithiau** fact.
ffarm: fferm *e.b. ll.* **ffermydd** farm. **tŷ fferm** farmhouse.
ffarmio: ffermio *be.* **(ffarmiaf: ffermiaf)** to farm.
ffarmwr: ffermwr *e.g. ll.* **ffermwyr** farmer, agriculturist.
ffárwel: ffarwél *e.b.* farewell. **Ffárwel haf** Michaelmas daisy.
ffarwelio (â) *be.* **(ffarweliaf)** to bid farewell; to say goodbye.
ffatri *e.b. ll.* **ffatrïoedd** factory.
ffau *e.b. ll.* **ffeuau** den, lair, burrow, set.
ffawydden *e.b. ll.* **ffawydd** beech tree.
ffefryn *e.g. ll.* **-nau** favourite.
ffeiriau *gw.* **ffair.**
ffeithiau *gw.* **ffaith.**
ffel *a.* dear; knowing – especially of a dog.
ffenestr *e.b. ll.* **-i** window.

fferm *gw.* **ffarm.**
ffermdai *gw.* **ffermdy.**
ffermdy *e.g. ll.* **ffermdai** farmhouse.
ffermio *gw.* **ffarmio.**
ffermwr *gw.* **ffarmwr.**
ffermwyr *gw.* **ffarmwr.**
fferyllydd *e.g. ll.* **-ion** pharmacist, chemist.
ffeuau *gw.* **ffau.**
ffeuen *gw.* **ffäen.**
ffiaidd *a.* foul, loathsome, odious.
ffigur *e.g. ll.* **-au** figure, type, form; diagram.
ffin *e.b. ll.* **-iau** boundary, border, frontier, limit.
ffiniau *gw.* **ffin.**
ffiniol *a.* bordering.
ffiseg *e.b.* physics.
fflachio *be.* **(fflachiaf)** to flash.
fflam *e.b. ll.* **-au, -iau** flame, blaze.
fflamau: fflamiau *gw.* **fflam.**
ffoadur *e.g. ll.* **-iaid** fugitive, refugee; deserter.
ffoaduriaid *gw.* **ffoadur.**
ffodus *a.* fortunate, lucky, prosperous.
ffoi (rhag) *be.* **(ffoaf)** to flee, to escape; to desert.
ffôl *a.* foolish, unwise, silly, foolhardy.
ffolineb *e.g. ll.* **-au** foolishness, folly.
ffon *e.b. ll.* **ffyn** stick, walking-stick, staff; rod; club.
ffôn *e.g. ll.* **ffonau** telephone, phone. *gw.* **teleffon.**
ffonio *be.* **(ffoniaf)** to phone.
fforc *e.b. ll.* **ffyrc** fork.
fforchio *be.* **(fforchiaf)** to fork; to straddle.
ffordd *e.b. ll.* **ffyrdd** road, way, street, route. **ffordd allan** exit; **ffordd fawr** highway; **ffordd osgoi** bypass; **priffordd** highway; **traffordd** motorway; **ffordd ddeuol** dual carriageway; **pontffordd** viaduct; **trosffordd** fly-over.
ffortiwn *e.b. ll.* **ffortiynau** fortune.
ffortiynau *gw.* **ffortiwn.**
ffos *e.b. ll.* **-ydd** ditch, trench.

ffosydd *gw.* **ffos.**
ffowls *gw.* **ffowlyn.**
ffowlyn *e.g. ll.* **ffowls** chicken, fowl *(S.W.).*
ffraeo (â) *be.* **(ffraeaf)** to quarrel, to bicker.
Ffrangeg *e.b.* French (language).
Ffrainc *e.b.* France.
Ffrances *e.b. ll.* **-au** Frenchwoman.
Ffrancod *gw.* **Ffrancwr.**
Ffrancwr *e.g. ll.* **Ffrancwyr, Ffrancod** Frenchman.
Ffrancwyr *gw.* **Ffrancwr.**
Ffrengig *a.* French.
ffres *a.* fresh.
ffrind *e.g. ll.* **-au** friend.
ffrindiau *gw.* **ffrind.**
ffrio *be.* **(ffriaf)** to fry.
ffroen *e.b. ll.* **-au** nostril.
ffroesen *e.b. ll.* **ffroes** pancake *(S.W.). gw.* **crempog.**
ffrog: ffroc *e.b. ll.* **-iau** frock. **ffrog felen** a yellow frock; **ffrog wen** a white frock.
ffroga *e.g. ll.* **ffrogaod** frog. *gw.* **broga.**
ffrwd *e.b. ll.* **ffrydiau** swift stream; torrent, flood; current.
ffrwydro *be.* **(ffrwydraf)** to explode.
ffrwyth *e.g. ll.* **ffrwythau** fruit; produce; result, effect.
ffrwythlon *a.* fruitful, fertile.
ffrwythloni *be.* **(ffrwythlonaf)** to become or be fruitful; to fertilise.
ffrydiau *gw.* **ffrwd.**
ffrynt *e.g.b. ll.* **-iau** fron. **ffrynt gynnes** warm front; **ffrynt oer** cold front; **drws (y) ffrynt** front door; **o'r ffrynt** from the front.
ffug *a.* deceptive, sham, counterfeit, false. **dogfen ffug** forged document.
ffug-bas *e.b. ll.* **-ys** dummy-pass *(rugby).*

ffugenw *e.g. ll.* **-au** pseudonym, *nom de plume.*
ffugio *be.* **(ffugiaf)** to pretend, to disguise, to forge, to feign.
ffuglen *e.b.* fiction. **ffuglen wyddonol** *e.b.* science fiction.
ffurf *e.b. ll.* **-iau** form, shape; appearance, likeness; substance.
ffurfafen *e.b. ll.* **-nau** sky; heavens.
ffurfiau *gw.* **ffurf.**
ffurfio *be.* **(ffurfiaf)** to form, to fashion, to create.
ffurflen *e.b. ll.* **-ni** form, chart. **ffurflen gais** application form.
ffurflenni *gw.* **ffurflen.**
ffŵl *e.g. ll.* **ffyliaid** fool.
ffwr *e.g. ll.* **ffyrrau** fur.
ffwrdd, i *ad.* away. **ffwrdd-â-hi** *a. & ad.* slap-dash, precipitate.
ffwrn *e.b. ll.* **ffyrnau** oven, furnace. **ffwrn microdon** microwave oven.
ffws *e.g.* fuss.
ffydd *e.b. ll.* **-iau** faith, belief, confidence.
ffyddlon *a.* faithful, loyal.
ffyliaid *gw.* **ffŵl.**
ffyn *gw.* **ffon.**
ffynhonnau *gw.* **ffynnon.**
ffynhonnell *e.b. ll.* **ffynonellau** source, spring, fount; origin.
ffynidwydden *e.b. ll.* **ffynidwydd** fir-tree, pine-tree.
ffynnon *e.b. ll.* **ffynhonnau** spring, fountain, well; source, origin.
ffynonellau *gw.* **ffynhonnell.**
ffyrc *gw.* **fforc.**
ffyrdd *gw.* **ffordd.**
ffyrnau *gw.* **ffwrn.**
ffyrnig *a.* fierce, savage, furious, wild.
ffyrnigrwydd *e.g.* ferocity.
ffyrrau *gw.* **ffwr.**

g

ga i *bf.* may I . . .? *gw.* **cael.**
gaban *gw.* **caban.**
gacen *gw.* **cacen.**
gacwn *gw.* **cacynen.**
gacynen *gw.* **cacynen.**
gadach *gw.* **cadach.**
gadael *be.* **(gadawaf)** to leave, to desert; to allow. **gadewais** I left; **gadewaist** you left.
gadair *gw.* **cadair.**
gadeiriau *gw.* **cadair.**
gadeirio *gw.* **cadeirio.**
gadeiriol *gw.* **cadeiriol.**
gadeirydd *gw.* **cadeirydd.**
gadno *gw.* **cadno.**
gadw *gw.* **cadw.**
gadwyn *gw.* **cadwyn.**
gadwyno *gw.* **cadwyno.**
gae *gw.* **cae.**
gaeaf *e.g. ll.* **-au** winter.
gaeau *gw.* **cae.**
gael *gw.* **cael.**
gaer *gw.* **caer.**
Gaer *gw.* **Caer.**
Gaerdydd *gw.* **Caerdydd.**
Gaeredin *gw.* **Caeredin.**
Gaerfyrddin *gw.* **Caerfyrddin.**
Gaergybi *gw.* **Caergybi.**
gaets *gw.* **caets.**
gaf *gw.* **cael.**
gafael (yn) *be.* **(gafaelaf)** to hold tight, to clutch; to grip. **Gafael yn fy llaw** Take my hand.

gafaelgar *a.* gripping.
gafodd *gw.* **cael.**
gafr *e.b. ll.* **geifr** goat.
gaffe *gw.* **caffe.**
gangen *gw.* **cangen.**
ganghennau *gw.* **cangen.**
gaiff *gw.* **caiff.**
gair *e.g. ll.* **geiriau** word. **gair bach** short address, brief note; **geirda** good report, commendation, reference; **gair drwg** bad reputation; **ar y gair** instantly: **cadw at ei air** to keep his word; **dweud gair** to speak or address (a meeting, etc.); **Gair Duw** God's word; **gair yn ei bryd** timely advice.
gais *gw.* **cais.**
galan *gw.* **calan.**
galar *e.g.* mourning, grief.
galaru *be.* **(galaraf)** to mourn.
galed *gw.* **caled.**
galedi *gw.* **caledi.**
galedwch *gw.* **caledwch.**
galendr *gw.* **calendr.**
galennig *gw.* **calennig.**
galetach *gw.* **caled.**
galetaf *gw.* **caled.**
galeted *gw.* **caled.**
galon *gw.* **calon.**
galw (ar, am) *be.* **(galwaf)** to call, to summon; to visit; to name.
galwad *e.b.g. ll.* **-au** a call; vocation, calling, profession. **Cafodd y gweinidog alwad i Lanelli** The minister received a call to Llanelli.
galwedigaeth *e.b. ll.* **-au** occupation, vocation.
galwyn *e.g. ll.* **-i, -au** gallon.
gall *gw.* **call.**
gallach *gw.* **call.**
gallaf *gw.* **call.** *gw.* **gallu.**
galled *gw.* **call.**
gallu 1 *be.* **(gallaf)** to be able. **2** *e.g. ll.* **-oedd** ability, power, wealth.
galluog *a.* able, powerful.
gam *gw.* **cam.**
gamarwain *gw.* **camarwain.**
gamddeall *gw.* **camddeall.**

gamera   **gasáu**

gamera *gw.* **camera.**
gamp *gw.* **camp.**
gampfa *gw.* **campfa.**
gampfeydd *gw.* **campfa.**
gampus *gw.* **campus.**
gampwaith *gw.* **campwaith.**
gampweithiau *gw.* **campwaith.**
gamsyniad *gw.* **camsyniad.**
gamu *gw.* **camu.**
gan *ardd.* (*followed by soft mutation*)
(*personal forms*: **gen i, gen ti,**
ganddo/ganddi, gennyn,
gennych, ganddyn). with, by,
from, since. **gan amlaf** usually,
mostly: **gan hynny** therefore; **gan**
mwyaf mostly, almost. *gw. At.*
Arddodiaid; gw. **can; cant.**
gân *gw.* **cân.**
ganddi: ganddo *gw.* **gan.**
ganddyn *gw.* **gan.**
ganed *bf.* he/she was born.
ganeuon *gw.* **cân.**
ganfed *gw.* **canfed.**
ganhwyllbren *gw.* **canhwyllbren.**
ganiad *gw.* **caniad.**
ganiadaeth *gw.* **caniadaeth.**
ganiadau *gw.* **cân, caniad.**
ganiatâd *gw.* **caniatâd.**
ganiatáu *gw.* **caniatáu.**
ganiedydd *gw.* **caniedydd.**
ganmlwydd *gw.* **canmlwydd.**
ganmlwyddiannau *gw.*
  canmlwyddiant.
ganmlwyddiant *gw.*
  canmlwyddiant.
ganmol *gw.* **canmol.**
ganmoliaeth *gw.* **canmoliaeth.**
gannoedd *gw.* **cant.**
gannwyll *gw.* **cannwyll.**
ganhwyllau *gw.* **cannwyll.**
ganol *gw.* **canol.**
ganolbarth *gw.* **canolbarth.**
ganolbwyntio *gw.* **canolbwyntio.**
ganoldir *gw.* **canoldir.**
ganolfan *gw.* **canolfan.**
ganolog *gw.* **canolog.**
ganolwr *gw.* **canolwr.**
ganradd *gw.* **canradd.**
ganran *gw.* **canran.**
ganrif *gw.* **canrif.**
ganrifau: ganrifoedd *gw.* **canrif.**

gant *gw.* **cant.**
gânt *gw.* **cael.**
gantor *gw.* **cantor.**
gantores *gw.* **cantores.**
ganu *gw.* **canu.**
ganŵ *gw.* **canŵ.**
ganŵio *gw.* **canŵio.**
ganwr *gw.* **canwr.**
ganwriad *gw.* **canwriad.**
ganwyd *bf.* he/she was born.
  Ganwyd ef yng Nghymru He was
  born in Wales. *gw.* **geni.**
gap *gw.* **cap.**
gapel *gw.* **capel.**
gapten *gw.* **capten.**
gar *gw.* **car.**
garafán *gw.* **carafán.**
garafana *gw.* **carafana.**
garco *gw.* **carco.**
garcus *gw.* **carcus.**
garchar *gw.* **carchar.**
garcharor *gw.* **carcharor.**
garcharu *gw.* **carcharu.**
gardiau *gw.* **cerdyn.**
gardd *e.b. ll.* **gerddi** garden.
garddio *be.* (**garddiaf**) to garden, to
  cultivate a garden.
garddwr *e.g. ll.* **garddwyr** gardener.
garedig *gw.* **caredig.**
garedigrwydd *gw.* **caredigrwydd.**
garej *e.g. ll.* **-ys** garage.
gariad *gw.* **cariad.**
gariadon *gw.* **cariad.**
gariadus *gw.* **cariadus.**
gario *gw.* **cario.**
garlleg *e.g.* garlic. **ewin(edd)**
  garlleg clove of garlic.
garol *gw.* **carol.**
garped *gw.* **carped.**
garreg *gw.* **carreg.**
gartref *ad.* at home. **Mae e'n byw**
  gartref He's living at home. *gw.*
  cartref.
gartrefi *gw.* **cartref.**
gartrefu *gw.* **cartrefu.**
garu *gw.* **caru.**
garw *a. ll.* **geirwon** coarse, rough,
  harsh.
garwriaeth *gw.* **carwriaeth.**
gas *gw.* **cas.**
gasáu *gw.* **casáu.**

gasgen *gw.* casgen.
gasgenni *gw.* casgen.
gasgliad *gw.* casgliad.
gasglu *gw.* casglu.
Gas-gwent *gw.* Cas-gwent.
Gasllwchwr *gw.* Casllwchwr.
Gasnewydd *gw.* Casnewydd.
gastell *gw.* castell.
Gastell-nedd *gw.* Castell-nedd.
gât *e.b. ll.* gatiau, gâts, gatsys
  (*never undergoes soft mutation*) gate.
  yr hen gât the old gate; dwy gât
  two gates; y gât wen the white
  gate. *gw.* clwyd. *gw.* iet.
gath *gw.* cath.
gau *a.* (*precedes noun*) false. gau
  broffwyd a false prophet. *gw.* cau.
gawl *gw.* cawl.
gawod *gw.* cawod.
gawr *gw.* cawr.
gaws *gw.* caws.
gefell *e.g.b. ll.* gefeilliaid twin.
  gefell twin brother; gefeilles twin
  sister; yr efeilliaid the twins.
gefn *gw.* cefn.
gefnder *gw.* cefnder.
gefndir *gw.* cefndir.
gefndiroedd *gw.* cefndir.
gefndyr *gw.* cefnder.
gefnogi *gw.* cefnogi.
gefnu *gw.* cefnu.
gefnwr *gw.* cefnwr.
geffyl *gw.* ceffyl.
geg *gw.* ceg.
gegin *gw.* cegin.
gei *gw.* cei.
geidwad *gw.* ceidwad.
geifr *gw.* gafr.
geiliog *gw.* ceiliog.
Geinewydd *gw.* Ceinewydd.
geiniog *gw.* ceiniog.
geir *gw.* car.
geirfa *e.b. ll.* -oedd vocabulary.
geiriadur *e.g. ll.* -on dictionary.
geiriau *gw.* gair.
geirio *be.* (geiriaf) to word, to
  phrase.
geiriosen *gw.* ceiriosen.
geirwon *gw.* garw.
geisiadau: geisiau *gw.* cais.
geisio *gw.* ceisio.

gelf *gw.* celf.
gelfi *gw.* celficyn.
gelficyn *gw.* celficyn.
Geltaidd *gw.* Celtaidd.
gelwydd *gw.* celwydd.
gelwyddog *gw.* celwyddog.
gelyn *e.g. ll.* -ion enemy. gelyn
  pennaf chief enemy. *gw.*
  celynnen.
gelynnen *gw.* celynnen.
gell *gw.* cell.
gellau: gelloedd *gw.* cell.
gem *e.b.g. ll.* -au gem.
gêm *e.b. ll.* gêmau (*doesn't mutate*)
  game. Dyma gêm dda Here's a
  good game; dwy gêm rygbi two
  rugby games; dewch i gêmau'r
  ysgol Come to the school's games.
gemeg *gw.* cemeg.
gen *gw.* gan.
gên *e.b. ll.* genau chin, jaw.
genau *e.g. ll.* geneuau mouth; *gw.*
  gên.
genedigaeth *e.b. ll.* -au birth.
genedl *gw.* cenedl.
genedlaethol *gw.* cenedlaethol.
genedlaetholdeb *gw.*
  cenedlaetholdeb.
genedlaetholwr *gw.*
  cenedlaetholwr.
genetig: genetaidd: genynnol *a.*
  genetic.
geneth *e.b. ll.* -od girl (*N.W.*).
geneuau *gw.* genau.
genfigennus *gw.* cenfigennus.
genhadaeth *gw.* cenhadaeth.
genhadol *gw.* cenhadol.
genhadu *gw.* cenhadu.
genhadwr *gw.* cenhadwr.
genhedlaeth *gw.* cenhedlaeth.
genhedloedd *gw.* cenedl.
genhinen *gw.* cenhinen.
geni *be.* to be born, to give birth to.
  dyddiad geni date of birth.
gennin *gw.* cenhinen.
gennych *gw.* gan.
gennym *gw.* gan.
genyn *e.g. ll.* -au gene.
ger *ardd.* at, by, near, before, in front
  of. gerllaw close to.
gêr *e.ll.* gear, tackle; rubbish.

gerbron *gw.* **ger.**
gerdyn *gw.* **cerdyn.**
gerdd *gw.* **cerdd.**
gerdded *gw.* **cerdded.**
gerddi *gw.* **cerdd, gardd.**
gerddor *gw.* **cerddor.**
gerddorfa *gw.* **cerddorfa.**
gerddoriaeth *gw.* **cerddoriaeth.**
gerddorol *gw.* **cerddorol.**
gerddwr *gw.* **cerddwr.**
gerddwyr *gw.* **cerddwr.**
gerfio *gw.* **cerfio.**
gerflun *gw.* **cerflun.**
gerllaw *gw.* **ger.**
gerrig *gw.* **carreg.**
ges *gw.* **cael.**
gesair *gw.* **cesair.**
gestyll *gw.* **castell.**
gewri *gw.* **cawr.**
gewyn *gw. ll.* **-nau, -ion** sinew, tendon, ligament; nerve. *gw.* **cewyn.**
geyrydd *gw.* **caer.**
gi *gw.* **ci.**
gig *gw.* **cig.**
gigydd *gw.* **cigydd.**
gilio *gw.* **cilio.**
gilydd *rhag.* other, another, another of the same class or kind. **ei gilydd** each other; **gyda'i gilydd** together (they); **gyda'ch gilydd** together (you); **gyda'n gilydd** together (we).
ginio *gw.* **cinio.**
gipolwg *gw.* **cipolwg.**
gist *gw.* **cist.**
glaf *gw.* **claf.**
glai *gw.* **clai.**
glan *e.b. ll.* **-nau, glennydd** bank, shore. **glan y môr** sea-shore; **glan yr afon** river's bank; **glan y bedd** the grave-side; **gwyliwr y glannau** coast-guard.
glân *a.* clean, pure, holy; beautiful, fair.
glanhau *be.* **(glanhaf)** to clean, to purify; to heal.
glanio *be.* **(glaniaf)** to land, to come or go ashore, disembark; bring to land.
glannau *gw.* **glan.**
glas 1 *a. ll.* **gleision** blue, green, grey, silver; wan, pallid; raw. **arian**

gleision silver (money), silver coins; **glas y dorlan** kingfisher. **2** *e.g.* blue.
glaswelltyn *e.g. ll.* **glaswellt** green grass.
glasur *gw.* **clasur.**
glasurol *gw.* **clasurol.**
glaw *e.g. ll.* **-ogydd** rain. **bwrw glaw** to rain; **eirlaw** sleet; **glaw mân** drizzle.
glawdd *gw.* **clawdd.**
glawr *gw.* **clawr.**
glebran *gw.* **clebran.**
glefyd *gw.* **clefyd.**
gleision *gw.* **glas.**
glendid *e.g.* cleanness, cleanliness, purity; beauty; piety, holiness.
glennydd *gw.* **glan.**
glêr *gw.* **cleren.**
glerc *gw.* **clerc.**
gleren *gw.* **cleren.**
glin *e.g.b. ll.* **-iau** knee.
glir *gw.* **clir.**
glirio *gw.* **clirio.**
glo *e.g.* coal. **glo brig** open-cast coal; **glo carreg** anthracite coal; **glo mân** small coal; **glo rhwym** bituminous coal. *gw.* **clo.**
gloc *gw.* **cloc.**
glocwedd *gw.* **clocwedd.**
gloch *gw.* **cloch.**
glod *gw.* **clod.**
glodfori *gw.* **clodfori.**
gloddiau *gw.* **clawdd.**
glofa *e.b. ll.* **glofeydd** colliery.
glofeydd *gw.* **glofa.**
gloff *gw.* **cloff.**
gloffi *gw.* **cloffi.**
glogwyn *gw.* **clogwyn.**
glogyn *gw.* **clogyn.**
gloi *gw.* **cloi.**
glorian *gw.* **clorian.**
glown *gw.* **clown.**
glöwr *e.g. ll.* **glowyr** collier, coal-miner.
glöyn byw *e.g. ll.* **glöynnod byw** butterfly (*N.W.*).
gloyw *a. ll.* **-on** clear, bright, shiny. **Cymro glân gloyw** a thoroughbred Welshman.
glud *e.g. ll.* **-ion** glue.

gludio   **goler**

gludio: gludo *be.* **(gludiaf: gludaf)**
to glue; to adhere.
glun *gw.* **clun.**
glust *gw.* **clust.**
glustog *gw.* **clustog.**
glwm *gw.* **clwm.**
glwtyn *gw.* **clwtyn.**
Glwyd *gw.* **Clwyd.**
glwyd *gw.* **clwyd.**
glwyf *gw.* **clwyf.**
glychau *gw.* **cloch.**
glymau *gw.* **clwm, cwlwm.**
glymu *gw.* **clymu.**
glyn *e.g.* *ll.* **-noedd** valley, glen.
Glynebwy *e.b.* Ebbw Vale.
glynu (wrth) *be.* **(glynaf)** to adhere,
to cling.
glyw *ge.* **clyw.**
glywed *gw.* **clywed.**
gnau *gw.* **cneuen.**
gneuen *gw.* **cneuen.**
gnoc *gw.* **cnoc.**
gnocio *gw.* **cnocio.**
gnoi *gw.* **cnoi.**
go *ad.* (*precedes noun and causes soft
mutation*) rather, somewhat; small,
little, exceeding (*N.W.*). **go ddrud**
somewhat expensive.
gobaith *e.g.* *ll.* **gobeithion** hope.
goban *gw.* **coban.**
gobeithio *gw.* **(gobeithiaf)** to hope.
gobeithion *gw.* **gobaith.**
gobennydd *e.g.* *ll.* **gobenyddion**
pillow, bolster.
goch *gw.* **coch.**
gochach *gw.* **coch.**
gochaf *gw.* **coch.**
goched *gw.* **coch.**
godi *gw.* **codi.**
godidog *gw.* excellent, splendid.
godre *e.g.* *ll.* **-on** edge, hem, fringe;
foot or bottom (*of mountain, hill,
etc.*); foot (*of page*).
godro *be.* **(godraf)** to milk.
goddef *be.* **(goddefaf)** to suffer, to
bear, to endure, to tolerate.
goddefgar *a.* tolerant.
goddrych *e.g.* *ll.* **-au** subject.
Goed-duon *gw.* **Coed-duon.**
goeden *gw.* **coeden.**
goedwig *gw.* **coedwig.**

goes *gw.* **coes.**
gof *e.g.* *ll.* **-aint** smith, blacksmith.
gw. **cof.**
gofal *e.g.* *ll.* **-on** care; charge.
gofalu (am) *be.* **(gofalaf)** to take
care; to worry, to vex.
gofalus *a.* careful, anxious, worried.
gofalwr *e.g.* *ll.* **gofalwyr** caretaker,
custodian.
gofid *e.g.* *ll.* **-iau** trouble, sorrow,
grief, affliction.
gofidio (am) *be.* **(gofidiaf)** to grieve,
to vex.
gofio *gw.* **cofio.**
gofleidio *gw.* **cofleidio.**
gofod *e.g.* *ll.* **-au** space, gap. *gw.*
gwagle.
gofodwr *e.g.* *ll.* **gofodwyr**
astronaut.
gofrestr *gw.* **cofrestr.**
gofrestru *gw.* **cofrestru.**
gofyn (am) 1 *be.* **(gofynnaf)** to ask
(for).
2 *e.g.* *ll.* **-ion** request, requirement,
demand. **yn ôl y gofyn** according to
demand.
goffi *gw.* **coffi.**
gog *gw.* **cog.**
goginio *gw.* **coginio.**
gogledd 1 *e.g.* north. 2 *a.* north,
northern. **Pegwn y Gogledd** North
Pole.
gogleddol *a.* northern.
gogleddwr *e.g.* *ll.* **gogleddwyr**
northerner.
gogleisio *be.* **(gogleisiaf)** to tickle.
gogoniant *e.g.* *ll.* **gogoniannau**
glory.
gogydd *gw.* **cogydd.**
gogystal *a.* comparable.
gohirio *be.* **(gohiriaf)** to postpone.
gôl *e.b.* *ll.* **goliau** goal (*soccer*).
golau 1 *e.g.* light. 2 *a.* light, fair
(*colour*). *gw.* **goleuni. golau
diogelwch** safety light; **golau
dydd** daylight; **golau (l)leuad**
moonlight.
golchi *be.* **(golchaf)** to wash; to
flow over or past.
goleg *gw.* **coleg.**
goler *gw.* **coler.**

goleudy

goleudy *e.g. ll.* **goldeudai** lighthouse.
goleuni *e.g.* light; *gw.* **golau.**
goleuo *be.* **(goleuaf)** to light, to enlighten; to set fire to.
goliau *gw.* **gôl.**
golofn *gw.* **colofn.**
golud *e.g. ll.* **-oedd** wealth, riches.
goluro *gw.* **coluro.**
golwg *e.g.b. ll.* **golygon** sight; appearance, view. **golygon** eyes; **i bob golwg** to all appearances; **o'r golwg** out of sight; **y fath olwg!** what a sight; **rhagolygon y tywydd** weather prospects; **roedd golwg wael arni** she looked ill.
golygfa *e.b. ll.* **golygfeydd** view, scenery, scene.
golygon *gw.* **golwg.**
golygu *be.* **(golygaf)** to view; to mean, to imply, to intend; to edit. **Beth rwyt ti'n ei olygu?** What do you mean?
golygus *a.* handsome.
golygydd *e.g. ll.* **-ion** editor.
golled *gw.* **colled.**
gollen *gw.* **collen.**
golli *gw.* **colli.**
gollwng *be.* **(gollyngaf)** to release; to leak.
gonest *a.* honest, sincere.
gopïo *gw.* **copïo.**
gopyn *gw.* **copyn.**
gôr *gw.* **côr.**
gorau *a.* best. **o'r gorau** okay. *gw.* **da.** *gw.* **côr.**
gorchfygu *be.* **(gorchfygaf)** to defeat, to conquer, to subdue, to beat.
gorchymyn (i) 1 *be.* **(gorchmynnaf)** to command, to order, to decree, to charge. 2 *e.g. ll.* **gorch(y)mynion** commandment, command, decree, order. **Y Deg Gorchymyn** The Ten Commandments.
gordyn *gw.* **cordyn.**
gorfod 1 *e.g.b. ll.* **-au** compulsion, obligation; victory, success. 2 *a.* enforced, compulsory, obligatory; conquering, victorious. 3 *be.* **(gorfodaf)** to be obliged, forced or

gorymdaith

compelled to, to have (to). **Rwyt ti'n gorfod mynd** You have to go.
gorfodaeth *e.b.g. ll.* **-au** compulsion, obligation. **gorfodaeth filwrol** military conscription.
gorfodi (i) *be.* **(gorfodaf)** to compel, to oblige; to conquer, to overcome.
gorfodol *a.* compulsory, obligatory.
gorfoleddus *a.* joyful.
gorff *gw.* **corff.**
gorffen *be.* **(gorffennaf)** to finish, to conclude.
Gorffennaf *e.g.* July.
gorffennol 1 *e.g.* the past. 2 *a.* past.
gorfforol *gw.* **corfforol.**
gorffwys *e.g.* rest.
gorffwyso *be.* **(gorffwysaf)** to rest.
gorgi *gw.* **corgi.**
gorlawn *a.* overflowing, overcrowded.
gorllewin *e.g.* west. **Gorllewin Morgannwg** West Glamorgan.
gormod 1 *e.g.* excess; too many. 2 *a. & ad.* too much, excessive. **gormod o gwynion** too many complaints; **gormod o straeon** too many stories; **gormod o stŵr** too much noise; **gormod o drafferth** too much trouble; **bwyta gormod** to eat too much.
gorn *gw.* **corn.**
gornel *gw.* **cornel.**
gornest *e.b. ll.* **-au** contest, battle; match.
goron *gw.* **coron.**
goroni *gw.* **coroni.**
gorryn *gw.* **corryn.**
gorsaf *e.b. ll.* **-oedd** station. **gorsaf betrol** petrol station; **gorsaf bŵer** power station; **gorsaf dân** fire station.
gorsedd *e.b. ll.* **-au** throne. **Gorsedd y Beirdd** the Gorsedd of Bards (*bardic institution*).
goruchaf *a.* most high, supreme.
goruwchnaturiol *a.* supernatural.
gorwedd *be.* **(gorweddaf)** to lie, to lie down.
gorwel *e.g. ll.* **-ion** horizon.
gorymdaith *e.b. ll.* **gorymdeithiau** procession.

gosb *gw.* **cosb.**
gosbi *gw.* **cosbi.**
gosi *gw.* **cosi.**
gosod 1 *be.* **(gosodaf)** to put; to plant; to let; to bestow; to fix. **gosod gerbron** to set before; **gosod mewn trefn** to set in order; **gosod pris** to fix a price; **gosod yr ardd** to plant the garden. **2** *a.* false, artificial, applied. **dannedd gosod** false teeth, denture. **gwallt gosod** false hair, wig.
gostus *gw.* **costus.**
gostwng *be.* **(gostyngaf)** to lower, to reduce; to diminish; to ease.
gostyngedig *a.* humble.
gostyngiad *e.g. ll.* **-au** reduction.
gosyn *gw.* **cosyn.**
got: gôt *gw.* **cot.**
gotwm *gw.* **cotwm.**
grac *gw.* **crac.**
grachach *gw.* **crachach.**
gradd *e.b. ll.* **-au** step, grade, degree, university degree. **gradd anrhydedd** an honours degree; **i'r fath raddau** to such an extent; **mewn graddau** by degrees, gradually; **o radd i radd** step by step, by degrees.
graddfa *e.b. ll.* **graddfeydd** scale. **ar raddfa eang** on a large scale; **graddfa Celsius** Celsius Scale.
graddio *be.* **(graddiaf)** to graduate, to grade, to scale.
graddol *a.* gradual. **yn raddol** by degrees.
graenus *a.* of good quality, glossy, sleek.
grafu *gw.* **crafu.**
gragen *gw.* **cragen.**
graig *gw.* **craig.**
gramadeg *e.g. ll.* **-au** grammar. **llyfr gramadeg** grammar book.
gramadegol *a.* grammatical.
grant *e.g. ll.* **-iau** grant.
gras *e.g. ll.* **-au, -usau** grace. *gw.* **cras.**
grasu *bw.* **crasu.**
grawnffrwyth *e.g. ll.* **-au** grapefruit.
gredu *gw.* **credu.**
grefydd *gw.* **crefydd.**

grefft *gw.* **crefft.**
grefftwr *gw.* **crefftwr.**
gregyn *gw.* **cragen.**
greigiau *gw.* **craig.**
greigiog *gw.* **creigiog.**
greision *gw.* **cras, creisionyn.**
grempog *gw.* **crempog.**
gresyn *e.g. ll.* **-au** pity (*N.W.*). **Gresyn iddo farw** Pity that he died; **Gresyn o beth** It's a shame.
gresynu *be.* **(gresynaf)** to deplore, to be sorry, to pity.
greulon *gw.* **creulon.**
greulondeb *gw.* **creulondeb.**
gri *gw.* **cri.**
grib *gw.* **crib.**
gribo *gw.* **cribo.**
griced *gw.* **criced.**
gricedwr *gw.* **cricedwr.**
grio *gw.* **crio.**
gris *e.g. ll.* **-iau** step, stair.
Gristion *gw.* **Cristion.**
griw *gw.* **criw.**
Groeg 1 *e.b.* Greece. **2** *e.b. & a.* the Greek language, Greek; pertaining to the Greek language, to Greece or to the Greeks.
Groegaidd *a.* Grecian, Greek.
Groeges *e.b. ll.* **-au** Greek female.
Groegwr *e.g. ll.* **Groegwyr** Greek, Grecian.
groen *gw.* **croen.**
groes *gw.* **croes.**
groesair *gw.* **croesair.**
groesawu *gw.* **croesawu.**
groesawus *gw.* **croesawus.**
groesfan *gw.* **croesfan.**
groesffordd *gw.* **croesffordd.**
groesholi *gw.* **croesholi.**
groesi *gw.* **croesi.**
groeso *gw.* **croeso.**
gron *gw.* **cron.**
gronfa *gw.* **cronfa.**
grud *gw.* **crud.**
grudd *e.b.g. ll.* **-iau** cheek.
grug *e.g.* heather.
grwn *gw.* **crwn.**
grŵp *e.g. ll.* **grwpiau** group. **grŵp pop** pop group.
grwst *gw.* **crwst.**
gryd *gw.* **cryd.**

gryf   **gwarchod**

gryf *gw.* **cryf.**
gryfach *gw.* **cryf.**
gryfaf *gw.* **cryf.**
gryfed *gw.* **cryf.**
grym *e.g. ll.* **-oedd** force; energy; power.
grymus *a.* powerful, strong, mighty.
grynhoi *gw.* **crynhoi.**
gryno *gw.* **cryno.**
grynodeb *gw.* **crynodeb.**
grynu *gw.* **crynu.**
grys *gw.* **crys.**
grystyn *gw.* **crystyn.**
gu *gw.* **cu.**
guddio *gw.* **cuddio.**
gul *gw.* **cul.**
guro *gw.* **curo.**
gusan *gw.* **cusan.**
gusanu *gw.* **cusanu.**
gwadu *be.* **(gwadaf)** to deny, to disown.
gwaed *e.g.* blood. **yn y gwaed** in the blood as a family trait; **Cymro o waed coch cyfan** a thoroughbred Welshman.
gwaedu *be.* **(gwaedaf)** to bleed. **gwaedu fel mochyn** to bleed like a (slaughtered) pig.
gwaedd *e.b. ll.* **-au** shout.
gwael *a.* poor; miserable; sick; vile. **tro gwael â** an unworthy act (with).
gwaelod *e.g. ll.* **-ion** bottom, base, foundation. **ar waelod** at the bottom; **yng ngwaelod** in the bottom; **gwaelodion** sediment, dregs.
gwaeth *gw.* **drwg.**
gwaethaf *gw.* **drwg. er gwaethaf** in spite of; **gwaetha'r modd** the more the pity; worse luck.
gwaethed *gw.* **drwg.**
gwaethygu *be.* **(gwaethygaf)** to worsen.
gwag *a. ll.* **gweigion** empty; desolate; vacant.
gwagedd *e.g. ll.* **-au** vanity; void.
gwagio: gwagu *be.* **(gwagiaf: gwagaf)** to empty.
gwagle *e.g. ll.* **-oedd** space, void. *gw.* **gofod.**
gwagu *gw.* **gwagio.**

gwahân *e.g.* separation; difference. **ar wahân** apart; separately; independently; **byw ar wahân** to live apart.
gwahaniaeth *e.g.* difference, separation.
gwahaniaethu *be.* **(gwahaniaethaf)** to differ.
gwahanol *a.* different, various.
gwahanu *be.* **(gwahanaf)** to separate.
gwahardd *be.* **(gwaharddaf)** to prohibit.
gwahodd 1 *be.* **(gwahoddaf)** to invite, to ask. **2** *e.g. ll.* **-ion** invitation, bidding.
gwahoddedig *e.g. ll.* **-ion** invited, bidden, called. **gwahoddedigion** guests.
gwahoddiad *e.g. ll.* **-au** invitation.
gwahoddion *gw.* **gwahodd.**
gwair *e.g. ll.* **gweiriau** grass (*grown for harvesting*); hay (*S.W.*).
gwaith 1 *e.g. ll.* **gweithiau** work; composition; works. **gwaith annwyd** cold sores; **gwaith cartref** homework; **gwaith glo** coal-mine, colliery; **gwaith tŷ** house work. **2** *e.b. ll.* **gweithiau** time, occasion, turn. **unwaith** once; **dwywaith** twice; **teirgwaith** three times; **canwaith** a hundred times; **y waith honno** that occasion. **3** *c.* for, because.
gwal *e.b. ll.* **gwaliau, gwelydd** wall.
gwâl *e.b. ll.* **gwalau** lair; bed.
gwall *e.g. ll.* **-au** mistake, defect, want.
gwallgof *a.* insane, mad.
gwallt *e.g. ll.* **-au, -iau** hair. **blewyn** (*one*) hair.
gwallus *a.* faulty, inaccurate, erroneous.
gwan *a. ll.* **gweiniaid, gweinion** weak, feeble. **esgus wan** a feeble excuse.
gwanwyn *e.g. ll.* **-au** spring.
gwar *e.b.g. ll.* **-rau** nape of the neck.
gwâr *a.* cultured.
gwarchod *be.* **(gwarchodaf)** to

74

watch, to guard, to baby-sit.
gwaredu (rhag) *be.* **(gwaredaf)** to
save, to redeem, to deliver, to rid.
gwaredwr *e.g.* *ll.* **gwaredwyr**
saviour, deliverer.
gwario *be.* **(gwariaf)** to spend
(*money*).
gwarrau *gw.* **gwar.**
gwartheg *e.ll.* cattle. *gw.* **buwch,
da.**
gwarthus *a.* shameful.
gwas *e.g.* *ll.* **gweision** male
servant; boy, lad. *gw.* **morwyn.**
gwasanaeth *e.g.* *ll.* **-au** service;
use.
gwasanaethu *be.* **(gwasanaethaf)**
serve, to minister.
gwasg 1 *e.b.* *ll.* **-au, -oedd, gweisg**
press, pressure; waist. **gwasg
argraffu** printing-press; **gwasg
gaws** cheese-press; **gwŷr y wasg**
the press (*reporters*). 2 *e.g.* *ll.* **-au,
-oedd** stress; waist.
gwasgedd *e.g.* *ll.* **-au** pressure.
gwasgedd isel low pressure;
gwasgedd uchel high pressure.
gwasgfa *e.b.* *ll.* **gwasgfeydd**
squeeze.
gwasgod *e.b.* *ll.* **-au** waistcoat.
gwasgu *be.* **(gwasgaf)** to press, to
squeeze, to wring, to crush.
gwastad 1 *e.g.ll.* **-au** plain. 2 *a.* flat,
level, even; constant. **yn wastad**
always (*S.W.*).
gwastraff *e.g.* *ll.* **-au, -oedd** waste.
gwastraff niwclear nuclear waste.
gwastraffu *be.* **(gwastraffaf)** to
waste.
gwau *be.* **(gweaf, gweuaf)** to
weave; to knit. **dillad gwau** knitted
garments. *gw.* **gweu.**
gwaun *e.b.* *ll.* **gweunydd** meadow;
moor.
gwawd *e.g.* *ll.* **-iau, -ion** scorn,
satire.
gwawdio *be.* **(gwawdiaf)** to scorn,
to mock, to jeer.
gwawr *e.b.g.* *ll.* **-iau, -oedd** dawn;
hue; shade. **ar doriad gwawr** at
daybreak; **roedd gwawr las yn y
brethyn** there was a shade of blue

in the material.
gwawrio *be.* **(gwawriaf)** to dawn.
gwawroedd *gw.* **gwawr.**
gwb *gw.* **cwb.**
gwbl *gw.* **cwbl.**
gwcw *gw.* **cwcw.**
gwch *gw.* **cwch.**
gwd *gw.* **cwd.**
gwdihŵ *e.b.* *ll.* **-aid, -s** owl (*S.W.*).
gw. **tylluan.**
gwdyn *gw.* **cwdyn.**
gwddf *e.g.* *ll.* **gyddfau** neck, throat;
neckline. **gwddf crwn** round neck;
gwddf ffrog neckline; **gwddf
sgwâr** square neck; **gwddf V**
V-neck.
gwddwg *e.g.* *ll.* **gwddygau** neck,
throat; neckline (*S.W.*).
gwe *e.b.* *ll.* **-oedd** web, cobweb.
gwe corryn: gwe pry' cop
cobweb; **safle ar y we: gwefan**
website.
gweddi *e.b.* *ll.* **gweddïau** prayer.
Gweddi'r Arglwydd The Lord's
Prayer; **cwrdd gweddi** prayer
meeting.
gweddill *e.g.* *ll.* **-ion** remnant.
gweddïo *be.* **(gweddïaf)** to pray.
gweddol 1 *a.* fair. **pris gweddol** a
fairly good price; **cyflog gweddol**
a fairly good wage. 2 *ad.* (*precedes
the adjective and is followed by soft
mutation*). **yn weddol dawel** fairly
quiet; **yn weddol gyflym** fairly
quick.
gweddw 1 *e.b.* *ll.* **-on** widow.
2 *a.* widowed. **gŵr gweddw**
widower.
gwefus *e.b.* *ll.* **-au** lip.
gweiddi *be.* **(gwaeddaf)** to shout.
gweigion *gw.* **gwag.**
gweiniaid *gw.* **gwan.**
gweinidog *e.g.* *ll.* **-ion** minister,
servant. **Gweinidog yr Efengyl**
Minister of the Gospel; **Prif
Weinidog** Prime Minister;
Gweinidog Gwladol Minister of
State.
gweinion *gw.* **gwan.**
gweinydd *e.g.* *ll.* **-ion** waiter.
gweinyddes *e.b.* *ll.* **-au** waitress,

gweiriau   **gwesty**

female attendant; nurse.
gweinyddes feithrin nursery nurse.
gweiriau *gw.* **gwair.**
gweisg *gw.* **gwasg.**
gweision *gw.* **gwas.**
gweithdy *e.g. ll.* **gweithdai**
workshop.
gweithgar *a.* hardworking,
industrious.
gweithiau *gw.* **gwaith.**
gweithio *be.* **(gweithiaf)** to work; to
ferment; to operate.
gweithiwr *e.g. ll.* **gweithwyr**
worker.
gweithred *e.b. ll.* **-oedd** act, deed.
gweithredu *be.* **(gweithredaf)** to
act, to operate, to execute.
gweithwyr *gw.* **gweithiwr.**
gwelâu *gw.* **gwely.**
gweld: gweled *be.* **(gwelaf)** to see,
to perceive. **gweler** see (*when
referring to something*).
gwelw *a.* pale.
gwely *e.g. ll.* **-au, gwelâu** bed.
gwelydd *gw.* **gwal.**
gwell *a.* better (*note: nouns following
gwell do not mutate*).
gwella *be.* **(gwellaf)** to improve, to
better; to cure; to mend.
gwellt *e. torf.* grass, sward; straw.
gw. **gwelltyn.**
gwelltyn *e.g. ll.* **gwellt** blade of
grass; a straw. *gw.* **gwellt.**
gwen *a.b.* white. **ffrog wen** a white
frock; **torth wen** a white loaf. *gw.*
gwyn.
gwên *e.b. ll.* **gwenau** smile.
gwenau *gw.* **gwên.**
gwendid *e.g. ll.* **-au** weakness; wane
(*of the moon*). **y lleuad yn ei
gwendid** the wane of the moon.
Gwener *e.b.* Venus. **dydd Gwener**
Friday.
gwenith *e.ll.* wheat. **gwenithen** a
grain of wheat.
gwennol *e.b. ll.* **gwenoliaid**
swallow.
Gwent *e.b.* a former county in S.E.
Wales.
gwenu (ar) *be.* **(gwenaf)** to smile.
gwenwyn *e.g. ll.* **-au** poison;

venom; malice; spite.
gwenwynig: gwenwynol *a.*
poisonous.
gwenynen *e.b. ll.* **gwenyn** bee.
gwêr *e.g. ll.* **gwerau** tallow.
gwerdd *a.b.* green. **ffrog werdd** a
green frock; **deilen werdd** a green
leaf; **y Blaid Werdd** The Green
Party. *gw.* **gwyrdd.**
gwerin *e.b. & e.torf. ll.* **-oedd, -edd**
ordinary people, peasantry, folk;
proletariat. **amgueddfa werin** folk
museum; **cân werin** folk dance.
gweriniaeth *e.b. ll.* **-au** democracy,
republic.
Gweriniaeth Iwerddon *e.b.* Eire.
gwers *e.b. ll.* **-i** lesson; stanza of
poetry. **gwers Gymraeg** Welsh
lesson; **gwers hanes** history lesson.
gwerslyfr *e.g. ll.* **-au** text-book.
gwersyll *e.g. ll.* **-oedd** camp.
gwerth *e.g. ll.* **-oedd** worth, value.
mae'n werth y drafferth it's worth
the trouble; **ar werth** for sale;
mae'n werth punt It's worth a
pound; **Ga i werth pum punt o
betrol?** May I have five pounds'
worth of petrol?
gwerthfawr *a.* valuable, precious.
gwerthfawrogi *be.*
(gwerthfawrogaf) to appreciate.
gwerthfawrogiad *e.g. ll.* **-au**
appreciation.
gwerthiant *e.g. ll.* **gwerthiannau**
sale.
gwerthoedd *gw.* **gwerth.**
gwerthu *be.* **(gwerthaf)** to sell.
gwerthwr *e.g. ll.* **gwerthwyr** seller,
salesman.
gweryl *gw.* **cweryl.**
gweryla *gw,* **cweryla.**
gwestai *e.g. ll.* **gwesteion** guest.
gw. **gwesty.**
gwesteion *gw.* **gwestai.**
gwesteiwr *e.g. ll.* **gwesteiwyr** host.
gwesteiwraig hostess.
gwestiwn *gw.* **cwestiwn.**
gwestiyna *gw.* **cwestiyna.**
gwestiynau *gw.* **cwestiwn.**
gwesty *e.g. ll.* **gwestai, gwestyau**
hotel, inn.

gweu *be.* **(gweuaf)** to weave; to knit. *gw.* **gwau.**

gweunydd *gw.* **gwaun.**

gwg *e.g. ll.* **-on, gygau** frown, scowl.

gwgu (ar) *be.* **(gwgaf)** to frown, to scowl, to glower.

gwiail *gw.* **gwialen.**

gwialen *e.b. ll.* **gwiail, gwialennod** rod, cane, stick. **gwialen fedw** birch-rod.

gwialennod *gw.* **gwialen.**

gwin *e.g. ll.* **-oedd** wine. **gwin coch** red wine; **gwin gwyn** white wine.

gwir 1 *e.g.* truth. **yn wir** in truth, indeed. **2** *a.* true; real; net. **stori wir** a true story; (*the adjective may also precede a noun and convey additional emphasis; it then causes a soft mutation*). **gwir bwysau** net weight; **gwir Gymro** a real Welshman; **y gwir ystyr** the real meaning.

gwirionedd *e.g. ll.* **-au** truth, reality.

gwisg *e.b. ll.* **-oedd** dress. **gwisg briodas** wedding-dress; **gwisg nos** night-dress.

gwisgo *be.* **(gwisgaf)** to dress; to wear.

gwiwer *e.b. ll.* **-od** squirrel. **y wiwer goch** the red squirrel; **y wiwer lwyd** the grey squirrel.

gwlad *e.b. ll.* **gwledydd** country, land. **gwlad fy nhadau** land of my fathers.

Gwlad Belg *e.b.* Belgium.

gwladfa *e.b. ll.* **gwladfaoedd, gwladfeydd** colony; settlement. **Y Wladfa** Patagonia.

gwladgarwr *e.g. ll.* **gwladgarwyr** patriot.

gwladol *a.* civil; country; state; national. **Ysgrifennydd Gwladol** Secretary of State.

Gwlad Pwyl *e.b.* Poland.

Gwlad y Basg *e.b.* Basque Country.

Gwlad yr Haf *e.b.* Somerset.

Gwlad yr Iâ *e.b.* Iceland.

gwlân *e.g. ll.* **gwlanoedd** wool.

gwlanen *e.b. ll.* **-ni** home-spun, home-made cloth or flannel.

gwlanen goch red flannel;

gwlanen wen white flannel;

gwlanen ymolchi face-cloth; **crys gwlanen** flannel shirt.

gwledig *a.* rural; rustic; boorish. **Cymru Wledig** Rural Wales.

gwledydd *gw.* **gwlad.**

gwledd *e.b. ll.* **-oedd** feast; **gwledd briodas** marriage-feast.

gwledda *be.* **(gwleddaf)** to feast.

gwleidydd *e.g. ll.* **-ion** politician, statesman.

gwleidyddiaeth *e.b.* politics.

gwleidyddol *a.* political.

gwlff *e.g. ll.* **gylffau** gulf.

gwlith *e.g. ll.* **-oedd** dew.

gwlwm *gw.* **cwlwm.**

gwlyb *a. ll.* **-ion** wet.

gwlybaniaeth *e.g.* moisture, wet, humidity.

gwlychu *be.* **(gwlychaf)** to wet, to moisten; to get wet.

gwm *e.g. ll.* **gymiau** gum. *gw.* **cwm.**

gwmni *gw.* **cwmni.**

gwmnïau *gw.* **cwmni.**

gwmnïoedd *gw.* **cwmni.**

gwmwl *gw.* **cwmwl.**

gwn *e.g. ll.* **gynnau** gun. *gw.* **gwybod.**

gŵn *e.g. ll.* **gynau** gown. **gŵn gwisgo** dressing gown; **gŵn nos** night-gown; *gw.* **ci.**

gwneud: gwneuthur *be.* **(gwnaf)** to make; to do. *gw. At. Berfau.*

gwningen *gw.* **cwningen.**

gwniadyddes: gwniyddes *e.b. ll.* **-au** dressmaker, seamstress.

gwnïo *be.* **(gwnïaf)** to sew, to stitch. **peiriant gwnïo** sewing machine.

gwnïyddes *gw.* **gwniadyddes.**

gwobr *e.b. ll.* **-au** prize, reward. **y wobr gyntaf** the first prize; **gwobr gysur** consolation prize.

gwobrwyo *be.* **(gwobrwyaf)** to reward, to award prize to.

gwpan *gw.* **cwpan.**

gwpla *gw.* **cwpla.**

gwpwrdd *gw.* **cwpwrdd.**

gwr *gw.* **cwr.**

gŵr   **gwydryn**

gŵr *e.g. ll.* **gwŷr** man; husband. **gŵr
dieithr** stranger; **gŵr gwadd** guest,
guest speaker; **gwŷr y wasg**
pressmen, the press.
gwrach *e.b. ll.* **-od, -ïod** hag, witch.
gwragedd *gw.* **gwraig.**
gwraidd *gw.* **gwreiddyn.**
gwraig *e.b. ll.* **gwragedd** wife;
woman.
gwrandawiad *e.g. ll.* **-au** listening,
hearing.
gwrandawr *e.g. ll.* **gwrandawyr**
listener, hearer.
gwrando (ar) *be.* **(gwrandawaf)** to
listen. **Gwrandewais ar** I listened
to; **Gwrandewaist ar** You listened
to.
gwrdd *gw.* **cwrdd.**
gwreichionen *e.b. ll.* **gwreichion**
spark.
gwreiddiau *gw.* **gwreiddyn.**
gwreiddio *be.* **(gwreiddiaf)** to root,
to ground.
gwreiddiol *a.* original.
gwreiddyn *e.g. ll.* **gwraidd,
gwreiddiau** root; stock.
gwres *e.g. ll.* **-au** heat, warmth; zeal.
gwres canolog central heating.
gwresog *a.* hot, warm; fervent.
gwresogi *be.* **(gwresogaf)** to heat.
gwresogydd *e.g. ll.* **-ion** heater.
gwrido *be.* **(gwridaf)** to blush.
gwridog *a.* rosy-cheeked, ruddy.
gwrol *a.* brave, courageous.
gwrs *gw.* **cwrs.**
gwrtais *gw.* **cwrtais.**
gwrtaith *e.g. ll.* **gwrteithiau**
manure, fertiliser.
gwrth *rhagdd.* (*Prefix with the sense
'against, contra-, counter-, anti-' in
nouns, adjectives and verbs, and
followed by soft mutation*). **gwrth-
ddweud** to contradict.
gwrthblaid *e.b. ll.* **gwrthbleidiau**
opposition (*party*).
gwrthchwyswr *e.b. ll.*
gwrthchwyswyr antiperspirant.
gwrthdaro *be.* **(gwrthdrawaf)** to
clash, to collide.
gwrthdystio *be.* **(gwrthdystiaf)** to
protest.

gwrthglocwedd *a.* anticlockwise.
gwrthod *be.* **(gwrthodaf)** to refuse;
to reject. **Fe wrthododd e fynd
adref** He refused to go home.
gwrthrych *e.g. ll.* **-au** object.
gwrthrychol *a.* objective.
gwrthryfel *e.g. ll.* **-oedd** rebellion,
mutiny, insurrection.
gwrthryfela *be.* **(gwrthryfelaf)** to
rebel.
gwrthwyneb **1** *e.g. ll.* **-au** in
opposition to. **2** *a.* contrary,
opposite. **i'r gwrthwyneb** to the
contrary, in the opposite direction.
gwrthwynebu *be.* **(gwrthwynebaf)**
to oppose; to object.
gwrthwynebwr; gwrthwynebydd
e.g. ll. **gwrthwynebwyr** opponent;
objector; antagonist.
gwrthwynebydd cydwybodol
conscientious objector.
gwrw *gw.* **cwrw.**
gwrych *e.g. ll.* **-oedd** hedge; *e.ll.*
bristles
gwryw **1** *e.g. ll.* **-od** male. **gwryw a
benyw** male and female. **2** *a.* male.
gwrywaidd: gwrywol *a.* male.
gwrywgydiaeth *e.b.* homosexuality.
gwrywgydiwr homosexual.
gwsg *gw.* **cwsg.**
gwsmer *gw.* **cwsmer.**
gwstwm *gw.* **cwstwm.**
gwt *gw.* **cwt.**
gwta *gw.* **cwta.**
gwthiad *e.g. ll.* **-au** heave, thrust.
gwthio *be.* **(gwthiaf)** to push, to
thrust.
gwthiwr *e.g. ll.* **gwthwyr** pusher.
gwybedyn *e.g. ll.* **gwybed** gnat.
gwybod (am) **1** *be.* **(gwn)** to know.
gw. At. Berfau. **2** *e.g. ll.* **-au**
knowledge. **heb yn wybod (i)**
without knowing, unwittingly.
gwybodaeth *e.b.ll.* **-au** knowledge.
gwych *a.* fine, splendid; brilliant.
gwydr *e.g. ll.* **-au** glass. **gwydr gwin**
wineglass; **gwydr lliw** coloured
glass, stained glass; **gwydr nadd**
cut-glass; **tŷ gwydr** glasshouse.
gwydrau *gw.* **gwydr, gwydryn.**
gwydryn *e.g. ll.* **gwydrau** drinking-

glass. **gwydraid** glassful.
gŵydd 1 *e.b. ll.* **gwyddau** goose.
  croen gŵydd goose-flesh. **2** *e.g.*
  presence. **yng ngŵydd fy**
  ngelynion in the presence of my
  enemies.
gwyddbwyll *e.b.* chess.
Gwyddel *e.g. ll.* **-od, Gwyddyl**
  Irishman.
Gwyddeleg *e.g.* Irish language.
Gwyddeles *e.b. ll.* **-au** Irishwoman.
Gwyddelig *a.* Irish.
gwyddoniaeth *e.b.* science.
gwyddonol *a.* scientific.
gwyddonydd *e.g. ll.* **gwyddonwyr**
  scientist.
gwyddor *e.b. ll.* **-ion** rudiment,
  science: **yr wyddor** the alphabet.
gwyfyn *e.g. ll.* **-od** moth.
gŵyl *e.b. ll.* **gwyliau** feast, festival;
  holiday. **Gŵyl Dewi** Saint David's
  Day. **gŵyl y banc** bank holiday.
gwylan *e.b. ll.* **-od** seagull.
gwyliadwrus *a.* watchful, cautious.
gwyliau *gw.* **gŵyl.**
gwylio (dros) *be.* **(gwyliaf)** to mind;
  watch (over); to guard.
gwyliwr *e.g. ll.* **gwylwyr** sentry,
  guard, watchman.
gwylnos *e.b. ll.* **-au** vigil,
  watchnight.
gwylwyr *gw.* **gwyliwr.**
gwyll *e.g.* darkness.
gwyllt *a.* wild, mad. **yn wyllt gacwn**
  furiously cross, in a mad rage.
gwylltio: gwylltu *be.* **(gwylltiaf:**
  gwylltaf) to lose one's temper, to
  excite violently.
gwymon *e.g.* seaweed.
gwymp *gw.* **cwymp.**
gwympo *gw.* **cwympo.**
gwyn *a. ll.* **-ion** white; holy. **Gwlad**
  y menig gwynion Land of the
  white gloves (*alluding to the*
  frequent presentation of white gloves
  to assize judges in Wales, when there
  were no cases for trial). *gw.* **cwyn.**
  gw. **gwen.**
Gwynedd *e.b.* County in N.W.
  Wales.
gwynegon *e.g.* rheumatism (*S.W.*).

gwynegu *be.* **(gwynegaf)** to ache
  (*S.W.*).
gwynfa *e.b.* paradise.
gwynfyd *e.g. ll.* **-au** blessedness,
  bliss. **Y Gwynfydau** The
  Beatitudes.
gwyngalch *e.g.* white-lime,
  whitewash.
gwynion *gw.* **cwyn.** *gw.* **gwyn.**
gwynnu *be.* **(gwynnaf)** to whiten, to
  bleach.
gwynt *e.g. ll.* **-oedd** wind; smell. **a'i**
  wynt yn ei ddwrn breathless,
  panting, having one's heart in one's
  mouth; **prin ei wynt** short of breath.
gwyntog *a.* windy; bombastic;
  hirwyntog longwinded.
gwyr *gw.* **cwyr.**
Gŵyr *e.b.* Gower.
gŵyr 1 *a.* crooked, inclined, aslant.
  2 *bf.* he/she/it knows. *gw.* **gwybod.**
gwŷr *gw.* **gŵr.**
gwyrdd 1 *a. ll.* **-ion** green. **2** *e.g.*
  green. *gw.* **gwerdd.**
gwyriad *e.g. ll.* **-au** deviation.
gwyro: gwyrio *be.* **(gwyraf:**
  gwyriaf) to bend, to deviate, to
  incline, to swerve.
gwyrth *e.b. ll.* **-iau** miracle.
gwyrthiol *a.* miraculous. **Roedd**
  hi'n wyrthiol ei weld It was
  miraculous to see him.
gwyryf *e.b. ll.* **-on** virgin.
gwysion *gw.* **gwŷs.**
gwŷs *e.b. ll.* **gwysion** summons.
gwystl *e.g. ll.* **-on** hostage; pledge.
gwywo *be.* **(gwywaf)** to wither, to
  fade.
gychod *gw.* **cwch.**
gychwyn *gw.* **cychwyn.**
gyd, i *ad.* (*always immediately*
  follows the noun to which it refers)
  all. **Roedd y plant i gyd yn dost**
  All the children were ill.
gyda: gydag *ardd.* together with; in
  company of.
gydadrodd *gw.* **cydadrodd.**
gydio *gw.* **cydio.**
gydnabod *gw.* **cydnabod.**
gyddfau *gw.* **gwddf.**
gyfaill *gw.* **cyfaill.**

gyfan   **gymhlethu**

gyfan *gw.* **cyfan.**
gyfangwbl *gw.* **cyfangwbl.**
gyfansoddi *gw.* **cyfansoddi.**
gyfansoddwr *gw.* **cyfansoddwr.**
gyfanswm *gw.* **cyfanswm.**
gyfarch *gw.* **cyfarch.**
gyfarfod *gw.* **cyfarfod.**
gyfarwyddiadur *gw.*
　cyfarwyddiadur.
gyfarwyddo *gw.* **cyfarwyddo.**
gyfarwyddwr *gw.* **cyfarwyddwr.**
gyfeilles *gw.* **cyfeilles.**
gyfeillgar *gw.* **cyfeillgar.**
gyfeillgarwch *gw.* **cyfeillgarwch.**
gyfeillion *gw.* **cyfaill.**
gyfeiriad *gw.* **cyfeiriad.**
gyfeirio *gw.* **cyfeirio.**
gyfenw *gw.* **cyfenw.**
gyferbyn (â) *ardd.* opposite. **yn y tŷ**
　gyferbyn in the opposite house;
　gyferbyn â'n tŷ ni opposite our
　house.
gyfiawn *gw.* **cyfiawn.**
gyfiawnder *gw.* **cyfiawnder.**
gyfieithiad *gw.* **cyfieithiad.**
gyfieithu *gw.* **cyfieithu.**
gyfieithydd *gw.* **cyfieithydd.**
gyfle *gw.* **cyfle.**
gyfleu *gw.* **cyfleu.**
gyfleus *gw.* **cyfleus.**
gyflog *gw.* **cyflog.**
gyflogi *gw.* **cyflogi.**
gyflogwr *gw.* **cyflogwr.**
gyflwr *gw.* **cyflwr.**
gyflwyno *gw.* **cyflwyno.**
gyflym *gw.* **cyflym.**
gyflymach *gw.* **cyflym.**
gyflymaf *gw.* **cyflym.**
gyflymder *gw.* **cyflymder.**
gyflymed *gw.* **cyflym.**
gyflymu *gw.* **cyflymu.**
gyflymydd *gw.* **cyflymydd.**
gyfnither *gw.* **cyfnither.**
gyfnod *gw.* **cyfnod.**
gyfoeth *gw.* **cyfoeth.**
gyfoethog *gw.* **cyfoethog.**
gyfraith *gw.* **cyfraith.**
gyfrannu *gw.* **cyfrannu.**
gyfreithiwr *gw.* **cyfreithiwr.**
gyfres *gw.* **cyfres.**
gyfrif *gw.* **cyfrif.**

gyfrifiadur *gw.* **cyfrifiadur.**
gyfrifol *gw.* **cyfrifol.**
gyfrifoldeb *gw.* **cyfrifoldeb.**
gyfrifydd *gw.* **cyfrifydd.**
gyfrinach *gw.* **cyfrinach.**
gyfrinachol *gw.* **cyfrinachol.**
gyfrol *gw.* **cyfrol.**
gyfrwng *gw.* **cyfrwng.**
gyfrwys *gw.* **cyfrwys.**
gyfun *gw.* **cyfun.**
gyfuwch *gw.* **uchel.**
gyfweld *gw.* **cyfweld.**
gyfweliad *gw.* **cyfweliad.**
gyfyng *gw.* **cyfyng.**
gyfyngu *gw.* **cyfyngu.**
gyfystyr *gw.* **cyfystyr.**
gyfforddus *gw.* **cyfforddus.**
gyffredin *gw.* **cyffredin.**
gyffrous *gw.* **cyffrous.**
gyffur *gw.* **cyffur.**
gyffwrdd *gw.* **cyffwrdd.**
gygau *gw.* **gwg.**
gyngerdd *gw.* **cyngerdd.**
gynghori *gw.* **cynghori.**
gynghorwr *gw.* **cynghorwr.**
gyngor *gw.* **cyngor.**
gyhoedd *gw.* **cyhoedd.**
gyhoeddi *gw.* **cyhoeddi.**
gyhoeddiad *gw.* **cyhoeddiad.**
gyhoeddus *gw.* **cyhoeddus.**
gyhoeddusrwydd *gw.*
　cyhoeddusrwydd.
gyhoeddwr *gw.* **cyhoeddwr.**
gyhyd *gw.* **cyhyd.**
gyhyrog *gw.* **cyhyrog.**
gylch *gw.* **cylch.**
gylchgrawn *gw.* **cylchgrawn.**
gylchlythyr *gw.* **cylchlythyr.**
gyll *gw.* **cyll.**
gyllell *gw.* **cyllell.**
gyllyll *gw.* **cyllell.**
gymaint *gw.* **mawr.**
gymal *gw.* **cymal.**
gymanfa *gw.* **cymanfa.**
gymdeithas *gw.* **cymdeithas.**
gymdogion *gw.* **cymydog.**
gymeriad *gw.* **cymeriad.**
gymharu *gw.* **cymharu.**
gymhleth *gw.* **cymhleth.**
gymhlethdod *gw.* **cymhlethdod.**
gymhlethu *gw.* **cymhlethu.**

gymoedd *gw.* **cwm.**
gymorth *gw.* **cymorth.**
Gymraeg *gw.* **Cymraeg.**
Gymraes *gw.* **Cymraes.**
Gymreictod *gw.* **Cymreictod.**
Gymreig *gw.* **Cymreig.**
Gymreiges *gw.* **Cymraes.**
Gymro *gw.* **Cymro.**
Gymru *gw.* **Cymru.**
Gymry *gw.* **Cymro.**
gymryd *gw.* **cymryd.**
gymundeb *gw.* **cymundeb.**
gymuned *gw.* **cymuned.**
gymwynas *gw.* **cymwynas.**
gymydog *gw.* **cymydog.**
gymylau *gw.* **cwmwl.**
gymylog *gw.* **cymylog.**
gymysg *gw.* **cymysg.**
gymysgu *gw.* **cymysgu.**
gymysgwch *gw.* **cymysgwch.**
gyn *gw.* **cyn.**
gynaeafau *gw.* **cynhaeaf.**
gynau *gw.* **gŵn.**
gynddrwg *gw.* **cynddrwg.**
gynffon *gw.* **cynffon.**
gynhadledd *gw.* **cynhadledd.**
gynhaeaf *gw.* **cynhaeaf.**
gynhesu *gw.* **cynhesu.**
gynhyrfus *gw.* **cynhyrfus.**
gynigion *gw.* **cynnig.**
gynilion *gw.* **cynilion.**
gynilo *gw.* **cynilo.**
gynllun *gw.* **cynllun.**
gynllunio *gw.* **cynllunio.**
gynlluniwr *gw.* **cynlluniwr.**
gynllunydd *gw.* **cynlluniwr.**
gynnal *gw.* **cynnal.**
gynnar *gw.* **cynnar.**
gynnau *ad.* a short while ago, just now. *gw.* **gwn.**
gynnes *gw.* **cynnes.**
gynnig *gw.* **cynnig.**
gynradd *gw.* **cynradd.**
gynt *ad.* formerly; *née*; long since; ages ago. **Rhian Smith (gynt Jones)** Rhian Smith (*née* Jones); **yr**

hen ddyddiau gynt the old days, ages ago. *gw.* **cynnar.**
gyntaf *gw.* **cynnar.**
gynted *gw.* **cynnar.**
gyntedd *gw.* **cyntedd.**
gynulleidfa *gw.* **cynulleidfa.**
gynulliad *gw.* **cynulliad.**
gyrddau *gw.* **cwrdd.**
gyrfa *e.b.* *ll.* **-oedd, gyrfeydd** race; career; course.
gyrfeydd *gw.* **gyrfa.**
gyrff *gw.* **corff.**
gyrion *gw.* **cwr.**
gyrliog *gw.* **cyrliog.**
gyrn *gw.* **corn.**
gyrraedd *gw.* **cyrraedd.**
gyrrau *gw.* **cwr.**
gyrru *be.* **(gyrraf)** to drive; to send; to push.
gyrrwr *e.g.* *ll.* **gyrwyr** driver; sender.
gyrwyr *gw.* **gyrrwr.**
gysglyd *gw.* **cysglyd.**
gysgod *gw.* **cysgod.**
gysgodi *gw.* **cysgodi.**
gysgu *gw.* **cysgu.**
gystadleuaeth *gw.* **cystadleuaeth.**
gystadleuwr *gw.* **cystadleuwr.**
gystadleuydd *gw.* **cystadleuwr.**
gystadlu *gw.* **cystadlu.**
gystal *gw.* **da.**
gystymau *gw.* **cwstwm.**
gysur *gw.* **cysur.**
gysuro *gw.* **cysuro.**
gysurus *gw.* **cysurus.**
gyswllt *gw.* **cyswllt.**
gytgan *gw.* **cytgan.**
gytsain *gw.* **cytsain.**
gytundeb *gw.* **cytundeb.**
gytuno *gw.* **cytuno.**
gyw *gw.* **cyw.**
gywaith *gw.* **cywaith.**
gywir *gw.* **cywir.**
gywiriad *gw.* **cywiriad.**
gywiro *gw.* **cywiro.**

nghaniatâd

ngadael *gw.* gadael.
ngaeaf *gw.* gaeaf.
ngafael *gw.* gafael.
ngafr *gw.* gafr.
ngair *gw.* gair.
ngalar *gw.* galar.
ngalw *gw.* galw.
ngalwad *gw.* galwad.
ngalwedigaeth *gw.* galwedigaeth.
ngalwyn *gw.* galwyn.
ngallu *gw.* gallu.
ngardd *gw.* gardd.
ngarddio *gw.* garddio.
ngarddwr *gw.* garddwr.
ngarej *gw.* garej.
ngarlleg *gw.* garlleg.
ngat *gw.* gât.
ngefeilliaid *gw.* gefell.
ngeirfa *gw.* geirfa.
ngeiriadur *gw.* geiriadur.
ngeiriau *gw.* gair.
ngelyn *gw.* gelyn.
ngên *gw.* gên.
ngenau *gw.* gên, genau.
ngenetaidd *gw.* genetig.
ngenetig *gw.* genetig.
ngeneth *gw.* geneth.
ngeneuau *gw.* genau.
ngeni *gw.* geni.
ngenyn *gw.* genyn.
ngenynnol *gw.* genetig.
ngêr *gw.* gêr.
ngewyn *gw.* gewyn.

nghaban *gw.* caban.
nghacen *gw.* cacen.
nghacwn *gw.* cacynen.
nghacynen *gw.* cacynen.
nghadach *gw.* cadach.
nghadair *gw.* cadair.
nghadeirio *gw.* cadeirio.
nghadeirydd *gw.* cadeirydd.
nghadnawes *gw.* cadno.
nghadno *gw.* cadno.
nghadw *gw.* cadw.
nghadwyn *gw.* cadwyn.
nghadwyno *gw.* cadwyno.
nghae *gw.* cae.
nghael *gw.* cael.
Nghaer *gw.* Caer.
nghaer *gw.* caer.
Nghaerdydd *gw.* Caerdydd.
Nghaerfyrddin *gw.* Caerfyrddin.
Nghaergybi *gw.* Caergybi.
Nghaerloyw *gw.* Caerloyw.
Nghaersalem *gw.* Caersalem.
nghaets *gw.* caets.
nghaffe *gw.* caffe.
nghangen *gw.* cangen.
nghais *gw.* cais.
nghalan *gw.* calan.
nghaledi *gw.* caledi.
nghaledu *gw.* caledu.
nghaledwch *gw.* caledwch.
nghalendr *gw.* calendr.
nghalennig *gw.* calennig.
nghalon *gw.* calon.
ngham *gw.* cam.
nghamarwain *gw.* camarwain.
nghamddeall *gw.* camddeall.
nghamera *gw.* camera.
nghamp *gw.* camp.
nghampfa *gw.* campfa.
nghampwaith *gw.* campwaith.
nghamsyniad *gw.* camsyniad.
nghan *gw.* can.
nghân *gw.* cân.
nghaneuon *gw.* cân.
nghanfed *gw.* canfed.
nghanhwyllau *gw.* cannwyll.
nghanhwyllbren *gw.* canhwyllbren.
nghaniad *gw.* caniad.
nghaniadaeth *gw.* caniadaeth.
nghaniadau *gw.* cân. *gw.* caniad.
nghaniatâd *gw.* caniatâd.

nghaniatáu   nghenhadwr

nghaniatáu *gw.* caniatáu.
nghaniedydd *gw.* caniedydd.
nghanmlwydd *gw.* canmlwydd.
nghanmol *gw.* canmol.
nghanmoliaeth *gw.* canmoliaeth.
nghannoedd *gw.* cant.
nghannwyll *gw.* cannwyll.
nghanol *gw.* canol.
nghanolbarth *gw.* canolbarth.
nghanoldir *gw.* canoldir.
nghanolfan *gw.* canolfan.
nghanolwr *gw.* canolwr.
nghanradd *gw.* canradd.
nghanran *gw.* canran.
nghanrif *gw.* canrif.
nghanrifau: nghanrifoedd *gw.*
  canrif.
nghant *gw.* cant.
nghantor *gw.* cantor.
nghantores *gw.* cantores.
nghanu *gw.* canu.
nghanŵ *gw.* canŵ.
nghanŵio *gw.* canŵio.
nghanwr *gw.* canwr.
nghap *gw.* cap.
nghapel *gw.* capel.
nghapten *gw.* capten.
nghar *gw.* car.
ngh�arafán *gw.* carafán.
nghar�afana *gw.* carafana.
ngharco *gw.* carco.
ngharchar *gw.* carchar.
ngharcharor *gw.* carcharor.
ngharcharu *gw.* carcharu.
nghardiau *gw.* cerdyn.
ngharedigrwydd *gw.*
  caredigrwydd.
nghariad *gw.* cariad.
nghariadon *gw.* cariad.
nghariadus *gw.* cariadus.
nghario *gw.* cario.
ngharol *gw.* carol.
ngharped *gw.* carped.
ngharreg *gw.* carreg.
nghartref *gw.* cartref.
nghartrefi *gw.* cartref.
nghartrefu *gw.* cartrefu.
ngharu *gw.* caru.
ngharwriaeth *gw.* carwriaeth.
nghas *gw.* cas.
nghasáu *gw.* casáu.

nghasgen *gw.* casgen.
nghasgliad *gw.* casgliad.
nghasglu *gw.* casglu.
Nghas-gwent *gw.* Cas-gwent.
Nghasllwchwr *gw.* Casllwchwr.
Nghasnewydd *gw.* Casnewydd.
nghastell *gw.* castell.
Nghastell-nedd *gw.* Castell-nedd.
nghath *gw.* cath.
nghau *gw.* cau.
nghawl *gw.* cawl.
nghawod *gw.* cawod.
nghawr *gw.* cawr.
nghaws *gw.* caws.
nghefn *gw.* cefn.
nghefnder *gw.* cefnder.
nghefndir *gw.* cefndir.
nghefndiroedd *gw.* cefndir.
nghefndyr *gw.* cefnder.
nghefnogi *gw.* cefnogi.
nghefnu *gw.* cefnu.
nghefnwr *gw.* cefnwr.
nghefnwyr *gw.* cefnwr.
ngheffyl *gw.* ceffyl.
ngheg *gw.* ceg.
nghegin *gw.* cegin.
nghei *gw.* cei.
ngheidwad *gw.* ceidwad.
ngheiliog *gw.* ceiliog.
Ngheinewydd *gw.* Ceinewydd.
ngheiniog *gw.* ceiniog.
ngheiriosen *gw.* ceiriosen.
ngheisio *gw.* ceisio.
nghelf *gw.* celf.
nghelfi *gw.* celficyn.
nghelficyn *gw.* celficyn.
nghelwydd *gw.* celwydd.
nghelyn *gw.* celynnen.
nghelynnen *gw.* celynnen.
nghell *gw.* cell.
nghellau: nghelloedd *gw.* cell.
nghemeg *gw.* cemeg.
nghenedl *gw.* cenedl.
nghenedlaetholdeb *gw.*
  cenedlaetholdeb.
nghenedlaetholwr *gw.*
  cenedlaetholwr.
nghenhadaeth *gw.* cenhadaeth.
nghenhadon *gw.* cenhadwr.
nghenhadu *gw.* cenhadu.
nghenhadwr *gw.* cenhadwr.

nghenhedlaeth   **nghornel**

nghenhedlaeth *gw.* cenhedlaeth.
nghenhinen *gw.* cenhinen.
nghennin *gw.* cennin.
ngherdyn *gw.* cerdyn.
ngherdd *gw.* cerdd.
ngherddor *gw.* cerddor.
ngherddorfa *gw.* cerddorfa.
ngherddoriaeth *gw.* cerddoriaeth.
ngherddwr *gw.* cerddwr.
ngherfio *gw.* cerfio.
ngherflun *gw.* cerflun.
ngherrig *gw.* carreg.
nghesair *gw.* cesair.
nghestyll *gw.* castell.
nghewri *gw.* cawr.
nghewyn *gw.* cewyn.
ngheyrydd *gw.* caer.
nghi *gw.* ci.
nghig *gw.* cig.
nghigydd *gw.* cigydd.
nghinio *gw.* cinio.
nghipolwg *gw.* cipolwg.
nghist *gw.* cist.
nghlaf *gw.* claf.
nghlai *gw.* clai.
nghlasur *gw.* clasur.
nghlawdd *gw.* clawdd.
nghlawr *gw.* clawr.
nghlebran *gw.* clebran.
nghledr *gw.* cledr.
nghlefyd *gw.* clefyd.
nghleifion *gw.* claf.
nghlêr *gw.* cleren.
nghlerc *gw.* clerc.
nghleren *gw.* cleren.
nghlirio *gw.* clirio.
nghlo *gw.* clo.
nghloc *gw.* cloc.
nghloch *gw.* cloch.
nghlod *gw.* clod.
nghlodfori *gw.* clodfori.
nghloddiau *gw.* clawdd.
nghloffi *gw.* cloffi.
nghlogwyn *gw.* clogwyn.
nghlogyn *gw.* clogyn.
nghloi *gw.* cloi.
nghlorian *gw.* clorian.
nghloriau *gw.* clawr.
nghlown *gw.* clown.
nghlun *gw.* clun.
nghlust *gw.* clust.

nghlustog *gw.* clustog.
nghlwm *gw.* clwm.
nghlwtyn *gw.* clwtyn.
Nghlwyd *gw.* Clwyd.
nghlwyd *gw.* clwyd.
nghlwydau: nghlwydi *gw.* clwyd.
nghlwyf *gw.* clwyf.
nghlychau *gw.* cloch.
nghlymau *gw.* clwm.
nghlymu *gw.* clymu.
nghlytiau *gw.* clwtyn.
nghlyw *gw.* clyw.
nghlywed *gw.* clywed.
nghnau *gw.* cneuen.
nghneuen *gw.* cneuen.
nghnoc *gw.* cnoc.
nghnocio *gw.* cnocio.
nghnoi *gw.* cnoi.
nghoban *gw.* coban.
nghoch *gw.* coch.
nghodi *gw.* codi.
nghoed *gw.* coeden.
Nghoed-duon *gw.* Coed-duon.
nghoeden *gw.* coeden.
nghoedwig *gw.* coedwig.
nghoes *gw.* coes.
nghof *gw.* cof.
nghofion *gw.* cof.
nghofleidio *gw.* cofleidio.
nghofrestr *gw.* cofrestr.
nghofrestru *gw.* cofrestru.
nghoffi *gw.* coffi.
nghog *gw.* cog.
nghoginio *gw.* coginio.
nghogydd *gw.* cogydd.
ngholeg *gw.* coleg.
ngholer *gw.* coler.
ngholofn *gw.* colofn.
ngholuro *gw.* coluro.
ngholled *gw.* colled.
nghollen *gw.* collen.
ngholli *gw.* colli.
nghopïo *gw.* copïo.
nghopyn *gw.* copyn.
nghôr *gw.* côr.
nghorau *gw.* côr.
nghordyn *gw.* cordyn.
nghorff *gw.* corff.
nghorgi *gw.* corgi.
nghorn *gw.* corn.
nghornel *gw.* cornel.

84

nghoron   **nghyfanswm**

nghoron *gw.* **coron.**
nghoroni *gw.* **coroni.**
nghorryn *gw.* **corryn.**
nghosb *gw.* **cosb.**
nghosbi *gw.* **cosbi.**
nghot *gw.* **cot.**
nghôt *gw.* **cot.**
nghotwm *gw.* **cotwm.**
nghrac *gw.* **crac.**
nghrachach *gw.* **crachach.**
nghrafu *gw.* **crafu.**
nghragen *gw.* **cragen.**
nghraig *gw.* **craig.**
nghrasu *gw.* **crasu.**
nghredu *gw.* **credu.**
nghrefydd *gw.* **crefydd.**
nghrefft *gw.* **crefft.**
nghrefftwr *gw.* **crefftwr.**
nghregyn *gw.* **cragen.**
nghreigiau *gw.* **craig.**
nghreision *gw.* **creision.**
nghrempog *gw.* **crempog.**
nghreulondeb *gw.* **creulondeb.**
nghri *gw.* **cri.**
nghrib *gw.* **crib.**
nghribo *gw.* **cribo.**
nghriced *gw.* **criced.**
nghricedwr *gw.* **cricedwr.**
nghricsyn *gw.* **cricsyn.**
nghrio *gw.* **crio.**
Nghristion *gw.* **Cristion.**
Nghristnogion *gw.* **Cristion.**
nghriw *gw.* **criw.**
nghroen *gw.* **croen.**
nghroes *gw.* **croes.**
nghroesair *gw.* **croesair.**
nghroesau *gw.* **croes.**
nghroesawu *gw.* **croesawu.**
nghroesfan *gw.* **croesfan.**
nghroesffordd *gw.* **croesffordd.**
nghroesholi *gw.* **croesholi.**
nghroesi *gw.* **croesi.**
nghroeso *gw.* **croeso.**
nghronfa *gw.* **cronfa.**
nghronfeydd *gw.* **cronfa.**
nghrud *gw.* **crud.**
nghrwst *gw.* **crwst.**
nghrwyn *gw.* **croen.**
nghryd *gw.* **cryd.**
nghrynodeb *gw.* **crynodeb.**
nghrynu *gw.* **crynu.**

nghrys *gw.* **crys.**
nghrystiau *gw.* **crwst, crystyn.**
nghrystyn *gw.* **crystyn.**
nghuddio *gw.* **cuddio.**
nghuro *gw.* **curo.**
nghusan *gw.* **cusan.**
nghusanu *gw.* **cusanu.**
nghwb *gw.* **cwb.**
nghwbl *gw.* **cwbl.**
nghwcw *gw.* **cwcw.**
nghwch *gw.* **cwch.**
nghwd *gw.* **cwd.**
nghwdyn *gw.* **cwdyn.**
nghweryl *gw.* **cweryl.**
nghwestiwn *gw.* **cwestiwn.**
nghwestiyna *gw.* **cwestiyna.**
nghwestiynau *gw.* **cwestiwn.**
nghwlwm *gw.* **cwlwm.**
nghwm *gw.* **cwm.**
nghwmni *gw.* **cwmni.**
nghwmnïau: nghwmnïoedd *gw.* **cwmni.**
nghwmwl *gw.* **cwmwl.**
nghŵn *gw.* **ci.**
nghwningen *gw.* **cwningen.**
nghwningod *gw.* **cwningen.**
nghwpan *gw.* **cwpan.**
nghwpla *gw.* **cwpla.**
nghwpwrdd *gw.* **cwpwrdd.**
nghwr *gw.* **cwr.**
nghwrdd *gw.* **cwrdd.**
nghwrs *gw.* **cwrs.**
nghwrw *gw.* **cwrw.**
nghwsg *gw.* **cwsg.**
nghwsmer *gw.* **cwsmer.**
nghwstwm *gw.* **cwstwm.**
nghwt *gw.* **cwt.**
nghwymp *gw.* **cwymp.**
nghwyn *gw.* **cwyn.**
nghwyno *gw.* **cwyno.**
nghwyr *gw.* **cwyr.**
nghychod *gw.* **cwch.**
nghychwyn *gw.* **cychwyn.**
nghydadrodd *gw.* **cydadrodd.**
nghydau *gw.* **cwd, cwdyn.**
nghydnabod *gw.* **cydnabod.**
nghyfaill *gw.* **cyfaill.**
nghyfan *gw.* **cyfan.**
nghyfansoddi *gw.* **cyfansoddi.**
nghyfansoddwr *gw.* **cyfansoddwr.**
nghyfanswm *gw.* **cyfanswm.**

nghyfarch

nghyntedd

nghyfarch *gw.* cyfarch.
nghyfarfod *gw.* cyfarfod.
nghyfarfodydd *gw.* cyfarfod.
nghyfarwyddiadur *gw.*
 cyfarwyddiadur.
nghyfarwyddo *gw.* cyfarwyddo.
nghyfarwyddwr *gw.* cyfarwyddwr.
nghyfeilles *gw.* cyfeilles.
nghyfeillgarwch *gw.* cyfeillgarwch.
nghyfeillion *gw.* cyfaill.
nghyfeiriad *gw.* cyfeiriad.
nghyfeirio *gw.* cyfeirio.
nghyfenw *gw.* cyfenw.
nghyfiawnder *gw.* cyfiawnder.
nghyfieithiad *gw.* cyfieithiad.
nghyfieithu *gw.* cyfieithu.
nghyfieithydd *gw.* cyfieithydd.
nghyfle *gw.* cyfle.
nghyflog *gw.* cyflog.
nghyflogi *gw.* cyflogi.
nghyflogwr *gw.* cyflogwr.
nghyflwr *gw.* cyflwr.
nghyflwyno *gw.* cyflwyno.
nghyflymder *gw.* cyflymder.
nghyflymu *gw.* cyflymu.
nghyflymydd *gw.* cyflymydd.
nghyfnither *gw.* cyfnither.
nghyfoeth *gw.* cyfoeth.
nghyfraith *gw.* cyfraith.
nghyfreithiwr *gw.* cyfreithiwr.
nghyfres *gw.* cyfres.
nghyfrif *gw.* cyfrif.
nghyfrifiadur *gw.* cyfrifiadur.
nghyfrifiannell *gw.* cyfrifiannell.
nghyfrifoldeb *gw.* cyfrifoldeb.
nghyfrifydd *gw.* cyfrifydd.
nghyfrinach *gw.* cyfrinach.
nghyfrol *gw.* cyfrol.
nghyfrwng *gw.* cyfrwng.
nghyfweliad *gw.* cyfweliad.
nghyfyngu *gw.* cyfyngu.
nghyffur *gw.* cyffur.
nghyffwrdd *gw.* cyffwrdd.
nghyngerdd *gw.* cyngerdd.
nghynghori *gw.* cynghori.
nghynghorwr *gw.* cynghorwr.
nghynghrair *gw.* cynghrair.
nghyngor *gw.* cyngor.
nghyhoeddi *gw.* cyhoeddi.
nghyhoeddiad *gw.* cyhoeddiad.
nghyhoeddusrwydd *gw.*

 cyhoeddusrwydd.
nghyhoeddwr *gw.* cyhoeddwr.
nghylch *gw.* cylch.
nghylchfan *gw.* cylchfan.
nghylchgrawn *gw.* cylchgrawn.
nghylchgronau *gw.* cylchgrawn.
nghylchlythyr *gw.* cylchlythyr.
nghyll *gw.* collen.
nghyllell *gw.* cyllell.
nghyllyll *gw.* cyllell.
nghymal *gw.* cymal.
nghymanfa *gw.* cymanfa.
nghymdeithas *gw.* cymdeithas.
nghymdogion *gw.* cymydog.
nghymeriad *gw.* cymeriad.
nghymharu *gw.* cymharu.
nghymhlethdod *gw.* cymhlethdod.
nghymoedd *gw.* cwm.
nghymorth *gw.* cymorth.
Nghymraeg *gw.* Cymraeg.
Nghymraes *gw.* Cymraes.
Nghymreictod *gw.* Cymreictod.
Nghymreiges *gw.* Cymreiges.
Nghymro *gw.* Cymro.
Nghymru *gw.* Cymru.
Nghymry *gw.* Cymro.
nghymryd *gw.* cymryd.
nghymundeb *gw.* cymundeb.
nghymwynas *gw.* cymwynas.
nghymydog *gw.* cymydog.
nghymylau *gw.* cwmwl.
nghymysgu *gw.* cymysgu.
nghymysgwch *gw.* cymysgwch.
nghyn- *gw.* cyn-.
nghynaeafau *gw.* cynhaeaf.
nghynffon *gw.* cynffon.
nghynhadledd *gw.* cynhadledd.
nghynhaeaf *gw.* cynhaeaf.
nghynhesu *gw.* cynhesu.
nghynilion *gw.* cynilion.
nghynllun *gw.* cynllun.
nghynllunio *gw.* cynllunio.
nghynlluniwr *gw.* cynlluniwr.
nghynnal *gw.* cynnal.
nghynnig *gw.* cynnig.
nghynnwys *gw.* cynnwys.
nghynorthwywr *gw.* cynorthwywr.
nghynorthwy-ydd *gw.* cynorthwy-
 ydd.
nghyntaf *gw.* cyntaf.
nghyntedd *gw.* cyntedd.

nghynulleidfa

nghynulleidfa *gw.* **cynulleidfa.**
nghypyrddau *gw.* **cwpwrdd.**
nghyrddau *gw.* **cwrdd.**
nghyrff *gw.* **corff.**
nghyrn *gw.* **corn.**
nghyrraedd *gw.* **cyrraedd.**
nghyrsau: nghyrsiau *gw.* **cwrs.**
nghysgod *gw.* **cysgod.**
nghysgodi *gw.* **cysgodi.**
nghysgodion *gw.* **cysgod.**
nghysgu *gw.* **cysgu.**
nghystadlaethau *gw.*
  cystadleuaeth.
nghystadleuaeth *gw.*
  cystadleuaeth.
nghystadleuwr *gw.* **cystadleuwr.**
nghystadlu *gw.* **cystadlu.**
nghystymau *gw.* **cwstwm.**
nghysur *gw.* **cysur.**
nghysuro *gw.* **cysuro.**
nghyswllt *gw.* **cyswllt.**
nghytgan *gw.* **cytgan.**
nghytsain *gw.* **cytsain.**
nghytundeb *gw.* **cytundeb.**
nghytuno *gw.* **cytuno.**
nghyw *gw.* **cyw.**
nghywaith *gw.* **cywaith.**
nghywiriad *gw.* **cywiriad.**
nghywiro *gw.* **cywiro.**
nglan *gw.* **glan.**
nglân *gw.* **glân.**
nglanhau *gw.* **glanhau.**
nglanio *gw.* **glanio.**
nglannau *gw.* **glan.**
nglas *gw.* **glas.**
nglaswelltyn *gw.* **glaswelltyn.**
nglaw *gw.* **glaw.**
nglendid *gw.* **glendid.**
nglin *gw.* **glin.**
nglo *gw.* **glo.**
nglofa *gw.* **glofa.**
nglöwr *gw.* **glöwr.**
nglöyn byw *gw.* **glöyn byw.**
nglud *gw.* **glud.**
ngludio *gw.* **gludio.**
ngludo *gw.* **gludio.**
nglyn *gw.* **glyn.**
nglynu *gw.* **glynu.**
ngobaith *gw.* **gobaith.**
ngobeithion *gw.* **gobaith.**
ngobennydd *gw.* **gobennydd.**

ngodre *gw.* **godre.**
ngodro *gw.* **godro.**
ngoddef *gw.* **goddef.**
ngoddrych *gw.* **goddrych.**
ngof *gw.* **gof.**
ngofaint *gw.* **gof.**
ngofal *gw.* **gofal.**
ngofalwr *gw.* **gofalwr.**
ngofid *gw.* **gofid.**
ngofidio *gw.* **gofidio.**
ngofod *gw.* **gofod.**
ngofodwr *gw.* **gofodwr.**
ngofynion *gw.* **gofyn.**
ngogledd *gw.* **gogledd.**
ngogleisio *gw.* **gogleisio.**
ngogogiant *gw.* **gogoniant.**
ngôl *gw.* **gôl.**
ngolau *gw.* **golau.**
ngolchi *gw.* **golchi.**
ngoleudy *gw.* **goleudy.**
ngoleuni *gw.* **goleuni.**
ngoleuo *gw.* **goleuo.**
ngolud *gw.* **golud.**
ngolwg *gw.* **golwg.**
ngolygfa *gw.* **golygfa.**
ngolygfeydd *gw.* **golygfa.**
ngolygon *gw.* **golwg.**
ngolygydd *gw.* **golygydd.**
ngollwng *gw.* **gollwng.**
ngorau *gw.* **gorau.**
ngorchfygu *gw.* **gorchfygu.**
ngorchymyn *gw.* **gorchymyn.**
ngorfodaeth *gw.* **gorfodaeth.**
ngorfodi *gw.* **gorfodi.**
Ngorffennaf *gw.* **Gorffennaf.**
ngorffennol *gw.* **gorffennol.**
ngorffwys *gw.* **gorffwys.**
ngorffwyso *gw.* **gorffwyso.**
ngorllewin *gw.* **gorllewin.**
ngornest *gw.* **gornest.**
ngorsaf *gw.* **gorsaf.**
ngorsedd *gw.* **gorsedd.**
ngorwel *gw.* **gorwel.**
ngosod *gw.* **gosod.**
ngostwng *gw.* **gostwng.**
ngostyngiad *gw.* **gostyngiad.**
ngradd *gw.* **gradd.**
ngraddfa *gw.* **graddfa.**
ngramadeg *gw.* **gramadeg.**
ngrant *gw.* **grant.**
ngras *gw.* **gras.**

ngrawnffrwyth   **ngwerthfawrogiad**

ngrawnffrwyth *gw.* **grawnffrwyth.**
ngris *gw.* **gris.**
Ngroeg *gw.* **Groeg.**
ngrudd *gw.* **grudd.**
ngrug *gw.* **grug.**
ngrŵp *gw.* **grŵp.**
ngrym *gw.* **grym.**
ngwadu *gw.* **gwadu.**
ngwaed *gw.* **gwaed.**
ngwaedu *gw.* **gwaedu.**
ngwaedd *gw.* **gwaedd.**
ngwaelod *gw.* **gwaelod.**
ngwaelodion *gw.* **gwaelod.**
ngwaethaf *gw.* **gwaethaf.**
ngwagedd *gw.* **gwagedd.**
ngwagle *gw.* **gwagle.**
ngwahanol *gw.* **gwahanol.**
ngwahodd *gw.* **gwahodd.**
ngwahoddedigion *gw.*
  gwahoddedig.
ngwahoddiad *gw.* **gwahoddiad.**
ngwair *gw.* **gwair.**
ngwaith *gw.* **gwaith.**
ngwal *gw.* **gwal.**
ngwâl *gw.* **gwâl.**
ngwalau *gw.* **gwâl.**
ngwaliau *gw.* **gwal.**
ngwall *gw.* **gwall.**
ngwallt *gw.* **gwallt.**
ngwanwyn *gw.* **gwanwyn.**
ngwar *gw.* **gwar.**
ngwarchod *gw.* **gwarchod.**
ngwaredu *gw.* **gwaredu.**
ngwaredwr *gw.* **gwaredwr.**
ngwario *gw.* **gwario.**
ngwartheg *gw.* **gwartheg.**
ngwas *gw.* **gwas.**
ngwasanaeth *gw.* **gwasanaeth.**
ngwasanaethu *gw.* **gwasanaethu.**
ngwasg *gw.* **gwasg.**
ngwasgedd *gw.* **gwasgedd.**
ngwasgfa *gw.* **gwasgfa.**
ngwasgod *gw.* **gwasgod.**
ngwasgu *gw.* **gwasgu.**
ngwastraff *gw.* **gwastraff.**
ngwastraffu *gw.* **gwastraffu.**
ngwau *gw.* **gwau.**
ngwaun *gw.* **gwaun.**
ngwawdio *gw.* **gwawdio.**
ngwawr *gw.* **gwawr.**
ngwdihŵ *gw.* **gwdihŵ.**

ngwddf *gw.* **gwddf.**
ngwddwg *gw.* **gwddwg.**
ngweddi *gw.* **gweddi.**
ngweddill *gw.* **gweddill.**
ngweddïo *gw.* **gweddïo.**
ngwefus *gw.* **gwefus.**
ngweiddi *gw.* **gweiddi.**
ngweigion *gw.* **gwag.**
ngweiniaid *gw.* **gwan.**
ngweinidog *gw.* **gweinidog.**
ngweinion *gw.* **gwan.**
ngweinydd *gw.* **gweinydd.**
ngweinyddes *gw.* **gweinyddes.**
ngweiriau *gw.* **gwair.**
ngweisg *gw.* **gwasg.**
ngweision *gw.* **gwas.**
ngweithdy *gw.* **gweithdy.**
ngweithiau *gw.* **gwaith.**
ngweithio *gw.* **gweithio.**
ngweithiwr *gw.* **gweithiwr.**
ngweithred *gw.* **gweithred.**
ngweithwyr *gw.* **gweithiwr.**
ngwelâu *gw.* **gwely.**
ngweld *gw.* **gweld.**
ngwely *gw.* **gwely.**
ngwelyau *gw.* **gwely.**
ngwell *gw.* **da.**
ngwella *gw.* **gwella.**
ngwellt *gw.* **gwellt, gwelltyn.**
ngwelltyn *gw.* **gwelltyn.**
ngwên *gw.* **gwên.**
ngwenau *gw.* **gwên.**
ngwendid *gw.* **gwendid.**
Ngwener *gw.* **Gwener.**
ngwenith *gw.* **gwenith.**
ngwennol *gw.* **gwennol.**
Ngwent *gw.* **Gwent.**
ngwenu *gw.* **gwenu.**
ngwenwyn *gw.* **gwenwyn.**
ngwenynen *gw.* **gwenynen.**
ngwêr *gw.* **gwêr.**
ngwerin *gw.* **gwerin.**
ngweriniaeth *gw.* **gweriniaeth.**
ngwers *gw.* **gwers.**
ngwerslyfr *gw.* **gwerslyfr.**
ngwersyll *gw.* **gwersyll.**
ngwerth *gw.* **gwerth.**
ngwerthfawrogi *gw.*
  gwerthfawrogi.
ngwerthfawrogiad *gw.*
  gwerthfawrogiad.

ngwerthiant　　　　　　　　　　　　　　**ngwynegon**

ngwerthiant *gw.* gwerthiant.
ngwerthu *gw.* gwerthu.
ngwerthwr *gw.* gwerthwr.
ngwestai *gw.* gwestai, gwesty.
ngwesteion *gw.* gwestai.
ngwesteiwr *gw.* gwesteiwr.
ngwesteiwraig *gw.* gwesteiwr.
ngwesty *gw.* gwesty.
ngweu *gw.* gweu.
ngweunydd *gw.* gwaun.
ngwg *gw.* gwg.
ngwgu *gw.* gwgu.
ngwiail *gw.* gwialen.
ngwialen *gw.* gwialen.
ngwialennod *gw.* gwialen.
ngwin *gw.* gwin.
ngwir *gw.* gwir.
ngwirionedd *gw.* gwirionedd.
ngwisg *gw.* gwisg.
ngwisgo *gw.* gwisgo.
ngwiwer *gw.* gwiwer.
ngwlad *gw.* gwlad.
ngwladfa *gw.* gwladfa.
ngwladgarwyr *gw.* gwladgarwr.
ngwlân *gw.* gwlân.
ngwlanen *gw.* gwlanen.
ngwledydd *gw.* gwlad.
ngwledd *gw.* gwledd.
ngwledda *gw.* gwledda.
ngwleidydd *gw.* gwleidydd.
ngwleidyddiaeth *gw.*
  gwleidyddiaeth.
ngwlff *gw.* gwlff.
ngwlith *gw.* gwlith.
ngwlybaniaeth *gw.* gwlybaniaeth.
ngwlychu *gw.* gwlychu.
ngwn *gw.* gwn.
ngŵn *gw.* gŵn.
ngwneud *gw.* gwneud.
ngwyniadyddes *gw.* gwniadyddes.
ngwnïo *gw.* gwnïo.
ngwniadyddes *gw.* gwniadyddes.
ngwobr *gw.* gwobr.
ngwobrwyo *gw.* gwobrwyo.
ngŵr *gw.* gŵr.
ngwrach *gw.* gwrach.
ngwragedd *gw.* gwraig.
ngwraidd *gw.* gwreiddyn.
ngwraig *gw.* gwraig.
ngwrandawiad *gw.* gwrandawiad.
ngwrandawr *gw.* gwrandawr.

ngwrando *gw.* gwrando.
ngwreichion *gw.* gwreichionen.
ngwreiddiau *gw.* gwreiddyn.
ngwreiddio *gw.* gwreiddio.
ngwreiddyn *gw.* gwreiddyn.
ngwres *gw.* gwres.
ngwresogi *gw.* gwresogi.
ngwresogydd *gw.* gwresogydd.
ngwrtaith *gw.* gwrtaith.
ngwrthblaid *gw.* gwrthblaid.
ngwrthdystio *gw.* gwrthdystio.
ngwrthod *gw.* gwrthod.
ngwrthrych *gw.* gwrthrych.
ngwrthryfel *gw.* gwrthryfel.
ngwrthwyneb *gw.* gwrthwyneb.
ngwrthwynebu *gw.* gwrthwynebu.
ngwrthwynebwr *gw.*
  gwrthwynebwr.
ngwrthwynebydd *gw.*
  gwrthwynebwr.
ngwrywgydiaeth *gw.*
  gwrywgydiaeth.
ngwthiad *gw.* gwthiad.
ngwthio *gw.* gwthio.
ngwthiwr *gw.* gwthiwr.
ngwybod *gw.* gwybod.
ngwybodaeth *gw.* gwybodaeth.
ngwydr *gw.* gwydr.
ngwydrau *gw.* gwydr, gwydryn.
ngwydryn *gw.* gwydryn.
ngwŷdd *gw.* gwŷdd.
ngwyddbwyll *gw.* gwyddbwyll.
Ngwyddel *gw.* Gwyddel.
Ngwyddeleg *gw.* Gwyddeleg.
ngwyddoniaeth *gw.* gwyddoniaeth.
ngwyddonydd *gw.* gwyddonydd.
ngwyddor *gw.* gwyddor.
ngwyfyn *gw.* gwyfyn.
ngwŷl *gw.* gwŷl.
ngwylan *gw.* gwylan.
ngwyliau *gw.* gwŷl.
ngwylio *gw.* gwylio.
ngwyliwr *gw.* gwyliwr.
ngwylnos *gw.* gwylnos.
ngwylwyr *gw.* gwyliwr.
ngwyll *gw.* gwyll.
ngwylltio *gw.* gwylltio.
ngwymon *gw.* gwymon.
ngwyn *gw.* gwyn.
Ngwynedd *gw.* Gwynedd.
ngwynegon *gw.* gwynegon.

ngwynfa

ngwynfa *gw.* **gwynfa.**
ngwynfyd *gw.* **gwynfyd.**
ngwyngalch *gw.* **gwyngalch.**
ngwynt *gw.* **gwynt.**
ngwŷr *gw.* **gŵr.**
ngwyrdd *gw.* **gwyrdd.**
ngwyriad *gw.* **gwyriad.**
ngwyro *gw.* **gwyro.**
ngwyrth *gw.* **gwyrth.**

ngwŷs *gw.* **gwŷs.**
ngwystion *gw.* **gwystl.**
ngynau *gw.* **gŵn.**
ngynnau *gw.* **gwn.**
ngyrfa *gw.* **gyrfa.**
ngyrfeydd *gw.* **gyrfa.**
ngyrru *gw.* **gyrru.**
ngyrrwr *gw.* **gyrrwr.**
ngyrwyr *gw.* **gyrrwr.**

In certain circumsances **h** is prefixed to words beginning with a vowel. If the word you require does not appear in this section ignore the initial **h** and look it up in the appropriate section, for example, **hawr**, see **awr**. See Appendix Pronouns.

had *e. torf.* seed. *gw.* **hadyn, hedyn.**
hadu *be.* **(hadaf)** to sow, to propagate; to run to seed.
hadyn; hedyn *e.g. ll.* **had** a seed. *gw.* **had.**
haearn 1 *e.g. ll.* **heyrn** iron. **2** *a.* of iron, iron.
haeddu *be.* **(haeddaf)** to deserve, to merit. **haeddu ennill** to deserve to win; **haeddu clod** to deserve praise.
hael *a.* generous, liberal.
haelioni *e.g.* generosity, liberality.
haelionus *a.* generous, liberal.
haenen *e.b. ll.* **haenau** layer, stratum, seam (*of rock*).
haerllug *a.* impudent.
haerllugrwydd *e.g.* cheek, impudence.
haeru *be.* **(haeraf)** to assert, to affirm.
haf *e.g. ll.* **-au** summer, summertime.
hafaidd *a.* summer-like, summery.
hafal *a.* like, similar, equal.

hafaliad *e.g. ll.* **-au** equation.
hafaliad cydamserol simultaneous equation; **hafaliad dwyradd** quadratic equation; **hafaliad syml** simple equation; **hafaliad unradd** linear equation.
hafan *e.b. ll.* **-au** haven, port, harbour.
hafdy *e.g. ll.* **hafdai** summerhouse. **tŷ haf** holiday cottage.
hafddydd *e.g. ll.* **-iau** summer's day.
hafod *e.g. ll.* **-ydd** (*often seen in place names*) summer residence formerly occupied by the family and its stock during the summer months only. *gw.* **hendref.**
hafoty *e.g. ll.* **hafotai** chalet, holiday cottage.
Hafren *e.b.* Severn. **Afon Hafren** River Severn, the Severn; **Pont Hafren** Severn Bridge.
hagr *a.* ugly, unsightly (*N.W.*).
hagrwch *e.g.* ugliness.
haid *e.b. ll.* **heidiau** swarm, flock, drove. **haid o wenyn** swarm of bees.
haidd *e. torf.* barley. *gw.* **heidden.**
haig *e.b. ll.* **heigiau** shoal. **haig o bysgod** shoal of fish.
haint *e.b. ll.* **heintiau** disease, infection, plague; faint, fit. **Fe ges i haint pan welais i'r ysbryd** I had a fit when I saw the ghost.
hala *be.* **(halaf)** to spend; to send; to drive; to spread (*S.W.*).
halen *e.g. ll.* **-au** salt, brine. **halen y ddaear** salt of the earth.
hallt *a.* salty, briny; harsh, severe. **talu'n hallt** to pay dearly.
halltu *be.* **(halltaf)** to salt, to cure.
hamdden *e.g.b.* leisure, respite. **canolfan hamdden** leisure centre; **oriau hamdden** leisure hours, spare time.
hamddena *be.* **(hamddenaf)** to concern oneself with leisure pursuits.
hamddenol *a.* leisurely.
hances *e.b. ll.* **-i** handkerchief.
hanerau *gw.* **hanner.**
haneri *gw.* **hanner.**

hanerwr   **heintus**

hanerwr *e.g. ll.* **hanerwyr** half-back
(games).
hanes *e.g. ll.* **-ion** history; story of
the past, tale, record, report.
Glywaist ti'r hanes am Wil? Did
you hear the tale about Wil?
haneswyr *gw.* **hanesydd.**
hanesydd: haneswr *e.g. ll.*
hanesyddion: haneswyr historian.
hanesyn *e.g. ll.* **-nau** story,
anecdote, tale.
hanfodol *a.* essential; integral.
haniaethol *a.* abstract.
hanner *e.g. ll.* **hanerau, haneri**
half. **hanner awr** half an hour;
hanner call foolish, half-witted;
hanner cylch semicircle; **hanner
dydd** midday, noon; **hanner
munud!** half-a-minute! half-a-
moment! **hanner nos** midnight;
hanner-pan half-soaked; half-wit;
hanner pris half-price.
hap *e.b. ll.* **-au, -iau** chance, luck,
fortune. **chwarae hap** to gamble. **ar
hap a damwain** by chance, by luck.
hapus *a.* happy, cheerful.
hapusrwydd *e.g.* happiness, bliss,
blessedness.
harbwr *e.g. ll.* **-s** harbour, port.
hardd *a. ll.* **heirdd** beautiful,
comely, handsome, fine, splendid (*of
person or object*).
harddwch *e.g.* beauty, fairness,
comeliness.
hau: heu *be.* **(heuaf)** to sow, to
scatter; to disseminate.
haul *e.g. ll.* **heuliau** sun.
hawdd *a.* easy. **Mae'n hawdd
gweld** It is easy to see; **Mae'n
hawdd nofio** It is easy to swim;
Mae'n hawdd siopa It is easy to
shop. *gw. At. Ansoddeiriau.*
hawl *e.b.g. ll.* **-iau** legal claim, right,
demand; question. **hawliau
dyn/dynol** the rights of man, human
rights; **hawliau sifil** civil rights.
hawlfraint *e.b. ll.* **hawlfreintiau**
privilege; copyright.
hawlio *be.* **(hawliaf)** to claim, to
demand.
haws *gw.* **hawdd.**

hawsaf *gw.* **hawdd.**
hawsed *gw.* **hawdd.**
heb *ardd.* (*followed by soft mutation*)
**(hebddo, hebddot,
hebddo/hebddi, hebddon,
hebddoch, hebddyn)** without,
minus, free from, besides. *gw. At.
Arddodiaid.*
heblaw *ardd.* besides, without.
hebog *e.g. ll.* **-au, -iaid** hawk,
falcon. **gwylio fel hebog** to watch
like a hawk, to watch intensely.
Hebraeg *e.g.* Hebrew language.
Hebreig *a.* Hebrew.
Hebrëwr *e.g. ll.* **Hebrëwyr** Hebrew;
Hebrëes female Hebrew.
hebrwng *be.* **(hebryngaf)** to lead, to
accompany, to escort. **cynhebrwng**
funeral, funeral procession; **tŷ
hebrwng** funeral home, chapel of
rest.
hecsagon *e.g. ll.* **-au** hexagon.
hedeg *be.* **(hedaf)** to fly.
hedfan *be.* **(hedfanaf)** to fly.
hedydd *e.g. ll.* **-ion** lark. *gw.*
ehedydd.
hedyn *gw.* **hadyn.**
hedd *e.g.b. ll.* **-au** peace,
tranquillity, serenity, calm.
heddiw *ad.* today.
heddlu *e.g. ll.* **-oedd** police force.
heddwas *e.g. ll.* **heddweision**
policeman.
heddwch *e.g.* peace, tranquillity,
stillness.
heddweision *gw.* **heddwas.**
hefo *gw.* **efo** (*N.W.*).
hefyd *c. & ad.* also, too, in addition;
likewise.
heibio *ad.* past; aside, beside, by.
heibio i'r tŷ past the house.
heidiau *gw.* **haid.**
heidden *e.b. ll.* **haidd** grain of
barley.
heigiau *gw.* **haig.**
heini *a.* active, lively, agile, nimble.
dosbarth cadw'n heini keep fit
class.
heintiau *gw.* **haint.**
heintus *a.* diseased, infectious,
contagious.

heirdd *gw.* **hardd.**
hel: hela *be.* **(heliaf: helaf)** to drive;
to chase, to pursue; to send; to hunt;
to gather, to collect; to fetch. **hel
achau** to genealogise *(N.W.).* **hel
straeon** to gossip *(N.W.).*
helaeth *a.* ample, large, broad;
plentiful.
helfa *e.b.* *ll.* **helfâu, helfeydd** a
hunting, hunt, chase, catch. **helfa
drysor** treasure hunt; **helfa dda** a
good catch.
helgi *e.g.* *ll.* **helgwn** hound.
heliwr *e.g.* *ll.* **helwyr** huntsman,
gatherer.
help *e.g.b.* help, aid; assistance;
support. **help llaw** helping hand.
help (i) *be.* **(helpaf)** to help, to assist.
helygen *e.b.* *ll.* **helyg** willow.
helynt *e.g.* *ll.* **-ion** course or way *(of
life, etc.)*; fuss, bother; business.
Beth yw ei hynt a'i helynt? What
has become of him?
hem *e.b.* *ll.* **-iau** hem, border, seam.
hen *a.* old, aged; ancient *(precedes
the noun and causes soft mutation)*
hen bryd high time; **hen ddigon**
quite enough; **henffasiwn** old-
fashioned; **hen gariad** former
sweetheart, 'old flame'; **hen gownt**
outstanding account, debit; grudge;
hen lanc (old) bachelor; **wedi hen
farw** long since dead; **yr Hen Wlad**
the Old Country, term of endearment
for Wales. *gw. At. Ansoddeiriau.*
henach *gw.* **hen.**
henaf *gw.* **hen.**
henaidd *a.* oldish, old-fashioned.
henaint *e.g.* old age; senility.
hendaid *e.g.* *ll.* **hendeidiau** great-
grandfather; forefather, ancestor.
hendeidiau *gw.* **hendaid.**
hendref *e.b.* *ll.* **hendrefi,
hendrefydd** winter dwelling
located in the valley, to which the
family and its stock returned after
the summer months in the **hafod** on
the mountain. *gw.* **hafod.**
hendrefi *gw.* **hendref.**
hendrefydd *gw.* **hendref.**
henebion *e.ll.* ancient monuments.

hened *gw.* **hen.**
heneiddio *be.* **(heneiddiaf)** to grow
old, to become old.
heneiniau *gw.* **hennain.**
henffasiwn *gw.* **hen.**
hennain *e.b.* *ll.* **heneiniau** great-
grandmother *(N.W.).*
heno *ad.* tonight, (on) this night.
henoed *e.g. & e.torf. & a.* old age,
great age; old person; old people,
old, elderly. **cartref henoed** old
people's home.
henwr *e.g.* *ll.* **henwyr** old man.
heol: hewl *e.b.* *ll.* **-ydd** street, road,
way. **heol ddeuol** dual
carriageway; **heol fawr** highway;
heol gefn back-road, byway.
heolydd *gw.* **heol.**
her *e.b.* *ll.* **-iau** challenge, defiance,
provocation.
hercyd *be.* **(hercaf)** to fetch, to
reach *(S.W.).*
herio *be.* **(heriaf)** to challenge, to
defy, to dare.
herwfilwr *e.g.* *ll.* **herwfilwyr**
guerilla.
herwgipiad *e.g.* *ll.* **-au** hijack.
herwgipio *be.* **(herwgipiaf)** to
hijack.
herwgipiwr *e.g.* *ll.* **herwgipwyr**
hijacker.
herwgydiad *e.g.* *ll.* **-au** kidnap.
herwgydio *be.* **(herwgydiaf)** to
kidnap.
herwgydiwr *e.g.* *ll.* **herwgydwyr**
kidnapper.
herwydd *ardd.* according to, by. **o'r
herwydd** on account of that.
het *e.b.* *ll.* **-au, -iau** hat.
heu *gw.* **hau.**
heuad *e.g.* a sowing.
heulog *a.* sunny.
heuliau *gw.* **haul.**
heulwen *e.b.* sunshine; a girl's name.
Heulwen ydy enw'r ferch The
girl's name is Heulwen.
heuwr *e.g.* *ll.* **heuwyr** sower.
hewl *gw.* **heol.**
hewlydd *gw.* **heol.**
heyrn *gw.* **haearn.**
hi *rhag.* she, her, it.

hidio   **hun**

hidio (am) *be.* **(hidiaf)** to heed, to care, to mind (*S.W.*).
hil *e.b. ll.* **-ion, -iau** race, lineage; offspring, descendants.
hiliol *a.* racial.
hin *e.b. ll.* **-oedd** weather.
hindda *e.b.* fine weather. **hindda a drycin** fair weather and foul.
hinsawdd *e.b. ll.* **hinsoddau** climate.
hir *a. ll.* **-ion** long, lengthy. *gw. At. Ansoddeiriau.*
hirach *gw.* **hir.**
hiraeth *e.g. ll.* **-au** longing, nostalgia, homesickness, grief.
hiraethu (am) *be.* **(hiraethaf)** to long (for), to yearn (for), to sorrow, to grieve.
hiraf *gw.* **hir.**
hirbell *a.* distant, remote. **o hirbell** from afar; **dysgu o hirbell** distance learning.
hired *gw.* **hir.**
hirgylch *e.g. ll.* **-au, -oedd** ellipse.
hirion *gw.* **hir.**
hirlwm *e.g.* lean period at the end of winter.
hirnod *e.g. ll.* **-au** circumflex accent (^).
hithau *rhag.* she, she too.
hiwmor *e.g.* humour.
hoe *e.g. ll.* **-au** pause, break, respite. **Sioni hoe** a layabout (*S.W.*).
hoel: hoelen *e.g.b. ll.* **hoelion, hoelon** nail. **taro'r hoelen ar ei phen** to comment appropriately with a fitting remark; to hit the nail on the head.
hoelio *be.* **(hoeliaf)** to nail.
hofrennydd *e.g. ll.* **hofrenyddion** helicopter.
hoff *a.* (*precedes the noun and causes soft mutation*) dear, beloved, favourite. **fy hoff le bwyta** my favourite eating place.
hoffi *be.* **(hoffaf)** to like, to be pleased (with).
hoffter *e.g. ll.* **-au** liking, fondness.
hogen *e.b. ll.* **-nod** girl, lass (*N.W.*).
hogi *be.* **(hogaf)** to sharpen, to whet. **carreg hogi** whetstone.

hogiau *gw.* **hogyn.**
hogyn *e.g. ll.* **hogiau, hogynnau** boy, lad (*N.W.*).
hongian *be.* **(hongiaf)** to hang, to suspend.
hôl *be.* **(holaf)** to fetch (*S.W.*). *gw.* **holi, nôl.**
holi *be.* **(holaf)** to question, to inquire, to ask (about). **holi am** to ask about, to ask after.
holiadur *e.g. ll.* **-on** questionnaire.
holwr *e.g. ll.* **holwyr** questioner, examiner, interrogator.
holwyddoreg *e.b. ll.* **-au** catechism.
holl *a.* (*precedes the noun and causes soft mutation*) all, whole. **yr holl bobl** all the people; **yr holl fyd** the whole world.
hollalluog *a.* almighty.
hollfyd *e.g.* universe.
holliach *a.* **whole, sound (of health).**
hollol *a. & ad.* (*precedes the adjective and causes soft mutation*) whole, entire, complete. **yn hollol dawel** completely quiet; **yn hollol gywir** wholly correct.
hollt *e.g. ll.* **-au** a split.
hollti *be.* **(holltaf)** to split.
hon *a.b. & rhag.* this (one), she (her), it.
honedig *a.* alleged, reputed.
honiad *e.g. ll.* **-au** assertion, claim.
honni *be.* **(honnaf)** to allege, to assert, to profess, to pretend, to claim.
honno, honna *a.b. & rhag.* that (one), she (her), it. *gw.* **hwnnw.**
hosan *e.b. ll.* **-au** stocking, sock.
hoyw *a.* lively, sprightly; gay, homosexual.
hud *e.g. ll.* **-ion** magic, charm, spell.
hudo *be.* **(hudaf)** to charm, to allure.
hudol *a.* enchanting.
huddygl *e.g.* soot.
hufen *e.g. ll.* **-nau** cream. **hufen lâ** ice-cream.
hugain *gw.* **ugain.**
hun: hunan 1 *rhag. ll.* **hunain** self. **fi fy hun(an)** I myself; **ti dy hun(an)** you yourself; **ef ei**

hun(an) he himself; **nhw eu hunain** they themselves; **ei hunan bach** alone. **2** *a.* self-.
hunanwasanaeth self-service.
hunain *gw.* **hun.**
hunanarlwyol *a.* self-catering.
hunan-barch *e.g.* self-respect.
hunangofiant *e.g.* autobiography.
hunanhyderus *a.* self-confident.
hunanladdiad *e.g. ll.* **-au** suicide.
hunanlanhaol *a.* self-cleaning.
hunanol *a.* selfish.
hunllef *e.b.* nightmare.
huno *be.* **(hunaf)** to sleep, to fall asleep.
Hunodd, 5 Mai 1940 Died 5 May 1940 (*on gravestones*).
hurt *a.* stupid, dull, stunned. **hurtyn** stupid person, blockhead.
hwch *e.b. ll.* **hychod** sow. **Mae hi'n hen hwch** She is slovenly.
hwiangerdd *e.b. ll.* **-i** lullaby; nursery-rhyme.
hwn *a.g. & rhag.* this (one).
hwnnw, hwnna *a.g. & rhag.* that (one). *gw.* **honno.**
hwnt *ad.* beyond, aside, away. **tu hwnt** beyond; **yn gyflym tu hwnt** exceedingly fast.
hwp *e.g.* push, thrust, shove.
hwrdd *e.g. ll.* **hyrddod** ram (*S.W.*).
hwrê *ebych. & e.b.* hooray!
hwy: hwynt: nhw *rhag.* they, them. *gw.* **hir.**
hwyaf *gw.* **hir.**
hwyad: hwyaden *e.b. ll.* **hwyaid** duck.
hwyaid *gw.* **hwyad.**
hwyl *e.b. ll.* **-iau** sail; journey; religious fervour; mood; fun; goodbye. **mewn hwyliau da** in a good mood; **hwyl!** bye! **Pob hwyl ichi** All the best.
hwyliau *gw.* **hwyl.**
hwylio *be.* **(hwyliaf)** to sail, to set out on a journey.
hwylus *a.* ease, comfortable, expedient, convenient.
hwyluso *be.* **(hwylusaf)** to facilitate.
hwylustod *e.g.* easy, convenience, facility, expediency.

hwynt *gw.* **hwy.**
hwyr 1 *a.* late. **2** *e.g.* (late) evening.
hwyrach *ad.* perhaps (*N.W.*). *gw. At. Ansoddeiriau.*
hwythau *rhag.* they, they also.
hyblyg *a.* flexible, pliable, pliant.
hybu *be.* **(hybaf)** to recover; to promote.
hychod *gw.* **hwch.**
hyd 1 *ardd.* (*followed by soft mutation*) to, till, for, as far as. **hyd yn hyn** up till now; **hyd at bum punt** up to £5. *gw. At. Treigladau.* **2** *e.g. ll.* **-au, -oedd, -ion** length; while.
hyder *e.g.* confidence, trust.
hyderu *be.* **(hyderaf)** to be confident; to trust, rely or depend (on).
hyderus *a.* confident.
Hydref *e.g.* October.
hydref *e.g. ll.* **-au** autumn.
hydrefol *a.* autumnal.
hydrogen *e.g.* hydrogen.
hydd *e.g. ll.* **-od** stag.
hyddysg *a.* learned, well-versed.
hyf *a.* bold.
hyfdra *e.g.* boldness.
hyfryd *a.* pleasant, delightful, fine, agreeable.
hyfrydwch *e.g.* delight, pleasure.
hyfforddi *be.* **(hyfforddaf)** to train, to direct, to instruct.
hyfforddiant *e.g. ll.* **hyfforddiannau** training, instruction.
hyfforddwr *e.g. ll.* **hyfforddwyr** instructor, guide, trainer, coach.
hyhi *rhag.* she, her (*emphatic*).
hylif *a. & e.g. ll.* **-au** liquid, flowing; fluid; a liquid, a fluid; a flow.
hyll *a.* ugly, hideous.
hyn *a. & rhag.* this, these.
hŷn *gw.* **hen.**
hynaf *gw.* **hen.**
hynafiad *e.g. ll.* **hynafiaid** ancestor.
hynafol *a.* ancient.
hyned *gw.* **hen.**
hynny *a. & rhag.* that, those.
hynod *a.* remarkable, notable; exceptional. **yn hynod o dda**

hynt   **hytrach**

exceptionally well; **yn hynod o
gyfoethog** exceptionally rich.
hynt *e.b.* *ll.* **-au, -oedd** way, course,
journey; career; (one's) fate or lot,
condition, state. **Beth yw ei hynt
erbyn hyn?** What's his fate by
now?
hyrddod *gw.* **hwrdd.**
hysbyseb *e.b.g.* *ll.* **-ion**
advertisement, announcement.
hysbysebiad *e.g.* *ll.* **-au**
advertisement.

hysbysebu *be.* **(hysbysebaf)** to
advertise.
hysbysebwr *e.g.* *ll.* **hysbysebwyr**
advertiser.
hysbysfwrdd *e.g.* *ll.*
hysbysfyrddau noticeboard.
hysbysiad *e.g.* *ll.* **-au**
announcement, notice,
advertisement.
hysbysu *be.* **(hysbysaf)** to
announce, to inform; to advertise.
hytrach *ad.* rather; more so.

i 1 *ardd.* (*followed by soft mutation*)
(i fi/mi, i ti, iddo/iddi, i ni, i chi,
iddyn nhw) to, into, for. i'r dim
exactly, precisely; i fyny up,
upwards; i ffwrdd away; i gyd all;
i lawr down; i mewn into; i fod i
supposed to; i'w gilydd to each
other. *gw. At. Arddodiaid.* 2 *rhag.* I,
me. *gw. At. Rhagenwau Personol.*
iâ *e.g.* ice. cloch iâ icicle.
iach *a.* healthy, well.
iacháu *be.* (iacháf) to heal, to cure.
iachawdwr *e.g. ll.* iachawdwyr
saviour.
iachawdwriaeth: iechydwriaeth
e.b. salvation, healing.
iachus *a.* healthy, wholesome.
iaith *e.b. ll.* ieithoedd language.
iaith lafar spoken language;
mamiaith first language, mother
tongue; ail iaith second language;
dwyieithog bilingual.
iâr *e.b. ll.* ieir hen. iâr fach yr haf
butterfly.
iard *e.b. ll.* ierdydd yard (of school,
etc.).
iarll *e.g. ll.* ieirll earl.
iarlles *e.b. ll.* -au countess.
ias *e.b. ll.* -au thrill, shiver; temper.
iasol *a.* thrilling; intensely cold.
Iau *e.g.* Thursday.
iau 1 *e.g. ll.* ieuau liver. 2 *e.b. ll.*
ieuau yoke. *gw.* ieuanc.

iawn 1 *ad.* very. yn dda iawn very
good. 2 *e.g.* rightness, truth;
compensation; atonement; talu'r
iawn am to compensate. 3 *a.* right,
true, correct.
iawndal *e.g. ll.* -oedd
compensation, damages, indemnity.
iawnder *e.g. ll.* -au justice, right,
rightness. iawnderau dynol:
iawnderau sifil civil rights, civil
liberties.
idiom *e.b. ll.* -au idiom.
Iddew *e.g. ll.* -on Jew.
Iddewes *e.b. ll.* -au Jewess.
Iddewig *a.* Jewish.
Iddewaeth *e.b.* Judaism.
ie *ad.* yes (*positive response to a
question that does not begin with a
verb*).
iechyd *e.g.* health, soundness, well-
being.
iechyd da! good health! (*in drinking
a toast*).
ieir *gw.* iâr.
ieirll *gw.* iarll.
ieithoedd *gw.* iaith.
ierdydd *gw.* iard.
Iesu *e.g.* Jesus. Iesu Grist Jesus
Christ; Iesu Mab Duw Jesus Son of
God.
iet *e.b. ll.* -au, -iau gate. *gw.* clwyd.
ieuangach *gw.* ieuanc.
ieuangaf *gw.* ieuanc.
ieuanged *gw.* ieuanc.
ieuainc *gw.* ieuanc.
ieuanc: ifanc *a. ll.* ieuainc: ifainc.
young. *gw. At. Ansoddeiriau.*
ieuau *gw.* iau.
ieuenctid *e.g. & e.ll.* youth. côr
ieuenctid youth choir.
ifainc *gw.* ieuanc.
ifanc *gw.* ieuanc.
ifancach *gw.* ieuanc.
ifancaf *gw.* ieuanc.
ig *e.b. l.* -ion hiccup.
igam-ogam *a.* zigzag.
igian *be.* (igiaf) to hiccup.
ing *e.g. ll.* -oedd anguish, agony,
distress.
ildio *be.* (ildiaf) to yield.
ill *rhag.* both, they, them. ill dau

(dwy) both of them.
imwnedd *e.g.* immunity.
imwneiddiad *e.g. ll.* **-au** immunisation.
imwneiddio *be.* **(imwneiddiaf)** to immunise.
incwm *e.g.* income. **Treth Incwm** Income Tax.
India, Yr *e.b.* India.
Indiad *e.g. ll.* **Indiaid** an Indian. **Un o'r India yw e/hi** He/she is Indian.
injan: injin *e.b. ll.* **-s** engine.
Ionawr *e.g.* January.
iorwg *e.g.* ivy (*S.W.*).
iro *be.* **(iraf)** to grease; to anoint; to oil; to lubricate.
is 1 *ardd.* below, under. *gw.* **isel.**
2 *rhagdd.* (*followed by soft mutation*) sub-, under-, vice-.

isaf *gw.* **isel.**
ised *gw.* **isel.**
isel *a.* low; humble; base; depressed. *gw. At. Ansoddeiriau.*
Iseldiroedd, Yr *e.b.* The Netherlands.
is-etholiad *e.g. ll.* **-au** by-election.
is-gadeirydd *e.g. ll.* **-ion** vice-chairman.
islaw *ardd.* below, beneath.
is-lywydd *e.g. ll.* **-ion** vice-president.
israddol *a.* inferior; subordinate.
isymwybod *e.g.* subconscious.
Iwerddon Ireland. **byw yn Iwerddon** to live in Ireland; **dod o Iwerddon** to come from Ireland; **mynd i Iwerddon** to go to Ireland.

jac: Jac *e.g.* *ll.* **-s** jack.
jac-codi-baw *e.g.* 'J.C.B.',
  mechanical excavator.
jac-do: jac-y-do *e.g.* *ll.* **-s** jackdaw.
jac-y-do *gw.* **jac-do.**
jam *e.g.* *ll.* **-iau** jam.
Japán Japan.
Japanëad *e.g.* *ll.* **Japanëaid** a
  Japanese.
Japanëaidd *a.* Japanese.
Japanëeg *e.b.* Japanese (language).
jar: jâr *e.b.* *ll.* **jariau, jarrau** jar.

jas *e.g.* jazz.
jeli *e.g.* *ll.* **-s, jeliau** jelly.
jersi: jyrsi: siersi *e.b.* *ll.* **-s** jersey.
jet *e.g.* *ll.* **-iau** jet (of water, gas,
  etc.); jet (nozzle); jet plane. **awyren
  jet** jet aircraft, jet plane; **peiriant jet**
  jet engine.
ji-binc *e.b.* *ll.* **-od** chaffinch.
jig-so *e.g.* jigsaw: **pos jig-so** jigsaw
  puzzle.
jîns *e.g.* jeans.
jîp *e.g.* jeep.
jiráff *e.g.* *ll.* **jiraffod** giraffe.
jiwbilî: jubilî *e.b.* *ll.* **jiwbilïau**
  jubilee, occasion or season of
  rejoicing.
job *e.g.b.* *ll.* **-iau, -s** job, piece of
  work; occupation.
jobyn *e.g.* *ll.* **jobiau** a small job.
  Jobyn da! Good job!
jôc *e.b.* *ll.* **-s** a joke, witticism;
  object of ridicule.
jocan *bf.* **(jocaf)** to joke (*S.W.*).
joio *bf.* **(joiaf)** to enjoy.
jubilî *gw.* **jiwbilî.**
jwg: siwg *e.b.* *ll.* **jygiau: siygiau**
  jug. **jwg laeth** milk jug.
jygiau *gw.* **jwg.**
jyngl *e.b.* *ll.* **-oedd** jungle.
jyrsi *gw.* **jersi.**

rear-lamp, tail-light of vehicle; **lamp
olew** oil lamp.
lamplen *e.b.* lampshade.
lamu *gw.* **llamu.**
lan *ad.* up; *gw.* **glan, llan.**
lân *gw.* **glân.**
lanastr *gw.* **llanastr.**
lanc *gw.* **llanc.**
lances *gw.* **llances.**
lanciau *gw.* **llanc.**
lanhau *gw.* **glanhau.**
lanio *gw.* **glanio.**
lannau *gw.* **glan, llan.**
lanw *gw.* **llanw.**
lapio (am) *be.* **(lapiaf)** to lap, to
wrap. **papur lapio** wrapping paper.
larwm *e.g.* alarm: **cloc larwm**
alarm-clock.
las *gw.* **glas.**
laswelltyn *gw.* **glaswelltyn.**
lathen *gw.* **llathen.**
lau *gw.* **lleuen.**
law *gw.* **glaw, llaw.**
lawdriniaeth *gw.* **llawdriniaeth.**
lawen *gw.* **llawen.**
lawenhau *gw.* **llawenhau.**
lawenydd *gw.* **llawenydd.**
lawer *gw.* **llawer.**
lawes *gw.* **llawes.**
lawfeddyg *gw.* **llawfeddyg.**
lawfeddygaeth *gw.*
llawfeddygaeth.
lawfeddygol *gw.* **llawfeddygol.**
lawlif *gw.* **llawlif.**
lawlyfr *gw.* **llawlyfr.**
lawn *gw.* **llawn.**
lawnder *gw.* **llawnder.**
lawnt *e.g.b.* *ll.* **-iau, -ydd** lawn.
lawr, i *ad.* down. *gw.* **llawr.**
lawysgrif *gw.* **llawysgrif.**
lawysgrifen *gw.* **llawysgrifen.**
le *gw.* **lle.**
lecyn *gw.* **llecyn.**
lechen *gw.* **llechen.**
lechi *gw.* **llechen.**
led *gw.* **lled.**
ledled *gw.* **lledled.**
ledr *gw.* **lledr.**
ledrith *gw.* **lledrith.**
ledu *gw.* **lledu.**
lef *gw.* **llef.**

labed *gw.* **llabed.**
label *e.g.* *ll.* **-i** label.
labelu *be.* **(labelaf)** to label.
labordy *e.g.* *ll.* **labordai** laboratory.
labrwr *e.g.* *ll.* **labrwyr** labourer.
lac *gw.* **llac.**
lacio *gw.* **llacio.**
lacs *gw.* **llacs.**
lacsog *gw.* **llacsog.**
lachar *gw.* **llachar.**
Ladin *gw.* **Lladin.**
ladrad *gw.* **lladrad.**
ladrata *gw.* **lladrata.**
ladron *gw.* **lleidr.**
ladd *gw.* **lladd.**
ladd-dy *gw.* **lladd-dy.**
laes *gw.* **llaes.**
laesu *gw.* **llaesu.**
laeth *gw.* **llaeth.**
lafant *e.g.* lavender.
lafar *gw.* **llafar.**
lafariad *gw.* **llafariad.**
lafn *gw.* **llafn.**
lafur *gw.* **llafur.**
lafurio *gw.* **llafurio.**
lafurus *gw.* **llafurus.**
lafurwr *gw.* **llafurwr.**
lai *gw.* **llai.**
lain *gw.* **llain.**
lais *gw.* **llais.**
laith *gw.* **llaith.**
lam *gw.* **llam.**
lamp *e.b.* *ll.* **-au** lamp. **lamp ôl**

lefain   **long**

lefain *e.g.b.* leaven. *gw.* **llefain.**
lefaru *gw.* **llefaru.**
lefarwr *gw.* **llefarwr.**
lefarwyr *gw.* **llefarwr.**
lefarydd *gw.* **llefarydd.**
lefau *gw.* **llef.**
lefel *e.b.g.* *ll.* **-au, -ydd, leflau**
level. **lefel y môr** sea-level.
lefelyn *gw.* **llefelyn.**
leflau *gw.* **lefel.**
lefrith *gw.* **llefrith.**
lefydd *gw.* **lle.**
leiaf *gw.* **bach.**
leiafrif *gw.* **lleiafrif.**
leian *gw.* **lleian.**
leidr *gw.* **lleidr.**
leihau *gw.* **lleihau.**
lein *e.b.* *ll.* **-iau, leins** line, cord;
telephone line; line-out. **lein ddillad**
clothes line; **lein fach** narrow-gauge
railway.
leiniau *gw.* **lein, llain.**
leinio *be.* **(leiniaf)** to line up; to form
a line-out; to thrash, to give (one) a
hiding (*N.W.*).
leisiau *gw.* **llais.**
leisio *gw.* **lleisio.**
leithder *gw.* **lleithder.**
len *gw.* **llen.**
lên *gw.* **llên.**
lencyndod *gw.* **llencyndod.**
lendid *gw.* **glendid.**
lenni *gw.* **llen.**
lennydd *gw.* **glan.**
lenor *gw.* **llenor.**
lenwi *gw.* **llenwi.**
lenyddiaeth *gw.* **llenyddiaeth.**
lenyddol *gw.* **llenyddol.**
leoedd *gw.* **lle.**
leol *gw.* **lleol.**
leoli *gw.* **lleoli.**
leoliad *gw.* **lleoliad.**
Lerpwl *e.b.* Liverpool.
les 1 *e.b.* *ll.* **-oedd** lease. 2 *e.b.* *ll.* **-
au** lace. *gw.* **lles.**
lesol *gw.* **llesol.**
lestr *gw.* **llestr.**
letchwith *gw.* **lletchwith.**
lety *gw.* **llety.**
letya *gw.* **lletya.**
letys *gw.* **letysen.**

letysen *e.b.* *ll.* **letys** lettuce.
leuad *gw.* **lleuad.**
leuen *gw.* **lleuen.**
lew *gw.* **llew.**
lewygu *gw.* **llewygu**
lewyrch *gw.* **llewyrch.**
lewyrchu *gw.* **llewyrchu.**
lewyrchus *gw.* **llewyrchus.**
lewys *gw.* **llawes.**
liain *gw.* **lliain.**
lid *gw.* **llid.**
lieiniau *gw.* **lliain.**
lif *gw.* **llif.**
lifio *gw.* **llifio.**
lifo *gw.* **llifo.**
lifogydd *gw.* **llif.**
lifft *e.g.* *ll.* **-iau** lift.
lili *e.b.* *ll.* **-s, liliau** lily; **lili wen**
fach snowdrop.
lin *gw.* **glin.**
lindysyn *e.g.* *ll.* **lindys** caterpillar.
linell *gw.* **llinell.**
linyn *gw.* **llinyn.**
lipa *gw.* **llipa.**
litr *e.g.* *ll.* **-au** litre.
lithren *gw.* **llithren.**
lithriad *gw.* **llithriad.**
lithrig *gw.* **llithrig.**
lithro *gw.* **llithro.**
liw *gw.* **lliw.**
liwgar *gw.* **lliwgar.**
liwiau *gw.* **lliw.**
liwio *gw.* **lliwio.**
liwiog *gw.* **lliwiog.**
liwo *gw.* **lliwo.**
lo *gw.* **glo, llo.**
loches *gw.* **lloches.**
lochesu *gw.* **llochesu.**
Loegr *gw.* **Lloegr.**
loer *gw.* **lloer.**
loeren *gw.* **lloeren.**
lofa *gw.* **glofa.**
lofnod *gw.* **llofnod.**
lofnodi *gw.* **llofnodi.**
lofrudd *gw.* **llofrudd.**
lofruddiaeth *gw.* **llofruddiaeth.**
lofruddio *gw.* **llofruddio.**
lofft *gw.* **llofft.**
log *gw.* **llog.**
logi *gw.* **llogi.**
long *gw.* **llong.**

longddrylliad | **lygaid**

longddrylliad *gw.* **llongddrylliad.**
longwr *gw.* **llongwr.**
loi *gw.* **llo.**
lol *e.b.* frivolity; nonsense. **Paid â siarad lol!** Don't talk nonsense!.
lolfa *e.b.* *ll.* **lolfeydd** lounge, sitting-room.
lolian: lolian *be.* **(lolaf: loliaf)** to lounge; to joke, to talk nonsense (*S.W.*).
lon *gw.* **llon.**
lôn *e.b.* *ll.* **lonydd** lane, road. **y Lôn Goed** the Tree-Lined Way (*place name in N.W. Wales*); **y lôn gefn** the back-lane; **lôn ddianc** escape lane.
loncian *be.* **(lonciaf)** to jog.
lonciwr *e.g.* *ll.* **loncwyr** jogger.
lond *gw.* **llond.**
longyfarch *gw.* **llongyfarch.**
longyfarchiad *gw.* **llongyfarchiad.**
lonydd *gw.* **lôn.** *gw.* **llonydd.**
lonyddwch *gw.* **llonyddwch.**
loriau *gw.* **llawr.**
lorïau *gw.* **lorri.**
lorri *e.b.* *ll.* **lorïau, lorris** lorry. **lorri laeth** milk-lorry; **lorri lo** coal-lorry; **lorri wartheg** cattle-lorry.
losg *gw.* **llosg.**
losgi *gw.* **llosgi.**
losin *gw.* **losinen.**
losinen: losen *e.b.* *ll.* **losin** sweet, lozenge.
löwr *gw.* **glöwr.**
löyn byw *gw.* **glöyn byw.**
loyw *gw.* **gloyw.**
lu *gw.* **llu.**
lud *gw.* **glud.**
ludio: ludo *gw.* **gludio.**
ludw *gw.* **lludw.**
Lun *gw.* **Llun.**
lun *gw.* **llun.**
Lundain *gw.* **Llundain.**
luniaidd *gw.* **lluniaidd.**
lunio *gw.* **llunio.**
luoedd *gw.* **llu.**
luosi *gw.* **lluosi.**
luosog *gw.* **lluosog.**
lusern *gw.* **llusern.**
lusgo *gw.* **llusgo.**
luwch *gw.* **lluwch.**

luwchfa *gw.* **lluwchfa.**
lw *gw.* **llw.**
lŵans: lwfans *e.g.b.* allowance, concession.
lwc *e.b.g.* luck, fate, chance. **Pob lwc i ti!** Good luck to you! **Lwc dda!** Good luck! Prosperity! Success!
lwcus *a.* lucky, fortunate.
lwch *gw.* **llwch.**
lwfans *gw.* **lŵans.**
lwfr *gw.* **llwfr.**
lwgu *gw.* **llwgu.**
lwnc *gw.* **llwnc.**
lwncdestun *gw.* **llwncdestun.**
lwon *gw.* **llw.**
lwy *gw.* **llwy.**
lwyaid *gw.* **llwyaid.**
lwybr *gw.* **llwybr.**
lwyd *gw.* **llwyd.**
lwydo *gw.* **llwydo.**
lwydrew *gw.* **llwydrew.**
lwydrewi *gw.* **llwydrewi.**
lwydd *gw.* **llwydd.**
lwyddiannus *gw.* **llwyddiannus.**
lwyddiant *gw.* **llwydd.**
lwyddo *gw.* **llwyddo.**
lwyfan *gw.* **llwyfan.**
lwyfannu *gw.* **llwyfannu.**
lwyn *gw.* **llwyn.**
lwynog *gw.* **llwynog.**
lwyr *gw.* **llwyr.**
lwyrymwrthodwr *gw.* **llwyrymwrthodwr.**
lwyth *gw.* **llwyth.**
lwytho *gw.* **llwytho.**
lwythog *gw.* **llwythog.**
lydan *gw.* **llydan.**
lydanu *gw.* **llydanu.**
Lydaw *gw.* **Llydaw.**
lyfelyn *gw.* **llyfelyn.**
lyfn *gw.* **llyfn.**
lyfr *gw.* **llyfr.**
lyfrgell *gw.* **llyfrgell.**
lyfrgellydd *gw.* **llyfrgellydd.**
lyfryn *gw.* **llyfryn.**
lyfu *gw.* **llyfu.**
lyffant *gw.* **llyffant.**
lygad *gw.* **llygad.**
lygadu *gw.* **llygadu.**
lygaid *gw.* **llygad.**

lygod   **lywyddu**

lygod *gw.* llygoden.
lygoden *gw.* llygoden.
lygredig *gw.* llygredig.
lygredd *gw.* llygredd.
lygru *gw.* llygru.
lynges *gw.* llynges.
lyn *gw.* glyn, llyn.
lynciau *gw.* llwnc.
lyncu *gw.* llyncu.
lynnau *gw.* llyn.
lynnoedd *gw.* glyn, llyn.
lynu *gw.* glynu.
lys *gw.* llys.
lysenw *gw.* llysenw.
lysenwi *gw.* llysenwi.
lysfam *gw.* llysfam.
lysfwytäwr *gw.* llysfwytäwr.

lysgenhadaeth *gw.*
 llysgenhadaeth.
lysgennad *gw.* llysgennad.
lysiau *gw.* llysieuyn.
lysieuol *gw.* llysieuol.
lysieuyn *gw.* llysieuyn.
lythrennau *gw.* llythyren.
lythrennog *gw.* llythrennog.
lythyr *gw.* llythyr.
lythyren *gw.* llythyren.
lyw *gw.* llyw.
lywio *gw.* llywio.
lywodraeth *gw.* llywodraeth.
lywodraethu *gw.* llywodraethu.
lywodraethwr *gw.* llywodraethwr.
lywydd *gw.* llywydd.
lywyddu *gw.* llywyddu.

llabed *e.b.* *ll.* **-au** lapel, flap.
llac *a.* slack, loose; lax.
llacio *be.* **(llaciaf)** to slacken; to loosen; to relax.
llacs *e.g.* mud, dirt (*S.W.*).
llacsog *a.* muddy, dirty (*S.W.*).
llachar *a.* bright, brilliant, dazzling.
Lladin *e.b. & a.* Latin. **America Ladin** Latin America.
lladrad *e.g.* *ll.* **-au** theft, robbery.
lladrata *be.* **(lladrataf)** to rob, to steal, to thieve.
lladron *gw.* **lleidr.**
lladd *be.* **(lladdaf)** to kill, to stay, to slaughter; to cut, to mow, to fell. **lladd ar** to run down, to criticise adversely; **lladd gwair** to mow (*hay*); **lladd mawn** to cut peat; **fel lladd nadroedd** at full speed, with might and main (*lit. like killing snakes*).
lladd-dy *e.g.* *ll.* **lladd-dai** slaughterhouse.
llaes *a.* loose, long, flowing.
llaesu *be.* **(llaesaf)** to slacken, to loosen, to relax. **llaesu dwylo** to become idle, weak or indifferent, to stay one's hand(s).
llaeth *e.g.* *ll.* **-au** milk (*S.W.*). *gw.* **llefrith.**
llafar 1 *e.g.* (*verbal*) expression, spoken or colloquial language. **iaith lafar** the spoken language.

2 *a.* loud, clear, vociferous; pertaining to the voice; oral **arholiad llafar** oral (*as opposed to written*) examination.
llafariad *e.b.* *ll.* **llafariaid** vowel.
llafn *e.g.* *ll.* **-au** blade.
llafur *e.g.* *ll.* **-iau** labour, toil; tillage; corn. **llafur cariad** labour of love; **Y Blaid Lafur** The Labour Party.
llafurio: llafuro *be.* **(llafuriaf: llafuraf)** to labour, to toil, to work.
llafurus *a.* laborious, painstaking, industrious.
llafurwr *e.g.* *ll.* **llafurwyr** labourer, worker, husbandman.
llai *gw.* **bach.**
llain *e.b.* *ll.* **lleiniau** (*long narrow*) strip of land, cloth &c., piece, patch, pitch, wicket (*cricket*), plot (*of land*). **llain galed** hard shoulder (*of motorway*); **llain lanio** landing-strip, airstrip; **llain o dir** strip of land, isthmus.
llais *e.g.* *ll.* **lleisiau** voice, sound.
llaith *a.* damp, moist, dank.
llall *rhag.* *ll.* **lleill** the other (*one*), another. **y llall** the other (*person, thing*); **y lleill** the others, the other persons/things.
llam *e.g.* *ll.* **-au** leap, jump, bound, stride.
llamu *be.* **(llamaf)** to leap, to jump, to bound, to stride.
llan *e.b.* *ll.* **-nau** (parish) church, churchyard; enclosure, yard.
llanast(r) *e.g.* mess.
llanc *e.g.* *ll.* **-iau** youth, lad.
llances *e.b.* *ll.* **-i, -au** young woman, lass.
llanciau *gw.* **llanc.**
llannau *gw.* **llan.**
llanw 1 *e.g.* *ll.* **-au** flow (of tide). **trai a llanw** ebb and flow. **2** *be.* **(llanwaf)** to fill, to fill up.
llathen *e.b.* *ll.* **-ni** yard, yardstick. **Doedd e ddim yn llawn llathen** He wasn't all there.
llau *gw.* **lleuen.**
llaw *e.b.* *ll.* **dwylo** hand. **i law** to hand: **llawchwith** left-handed; **llawdde** skilful, dextrous; **llawfer**

llawdriniaeth   **llenor**

shorthand; **llaw galed** trouble, rough time, hard time (*especially with sick person*); **llaw yn llaw** hand in hand; **ail-law** second-hand; **hen law ar** one who possesses the 'know how', (*lit. an old hand*); **rhoi help llaw** to give a helping hand.
llawdriniaeth *e.b. ll.* **-au** surgery.
llawen *a.* cheerful, merry, glad.
llawenhau (yn) *be.* **(llawenhaf)** to rejoice, to be joyful.
llawenydd *e.g.* joy, jubilation, rejoicing.
llawer 1 *e.g. ll.* **-oedd** many, much; abundant. **2** *ad.* by far, much (*with comparative adjective*). **o lawer** by far, by a great deal, by much; **llawer gwaith** many times; **yn llawer gwell** much better; **llawer tro** many a time.
llawes *e.b. ll.* **llewys** sleeve.
llawfeddyg *e.g. ll.* **-on** surgeon.
llawfeddygaeth *e.b.* surgery.
llawfeddygol *a.* surgical.
llawlif *e.b. ll.* **-iau** hand-saw.
llawlyfr *e.g. ll.* **-au** handbook, manual.
llawn *a. ll.* **-ion** full; **yn llawn bryd** high time.
llawnder *e.g.* abundance, fullness.
llawnion *gw.* **llawn.**
llawr *e.g. ll.* **lloriau** floor, ground; storey; earth. **ar lawr** down, exhausted, on (to) the ground, on the ground floor, downstairs, up (*from bed*), not yet gone to bed; **ar lawr gwlad** on the lowlands; **y llawr cyntaf** the first floor.
llawysgrif *e.g. ll.* **-au** manuscript.
llawysgrifen *e.b. ll.*
llawysgrifennau handwriting.
lle *e.g. ll.* **-oedd, llefydd** place, room, accommodation.
lle bwyd café, restaurant. **lle chwech** toilet; **lle tân** fireplace; **o'i le** out of (its) place or order, wrong, inappropriate.
llecyn *e.g. ll.* **-nau** spot, place.
llechen *e.b. ll.* **llechi** slate.
llechi *gw.* **llechen.**
lled 1 *e.g. ll.* **-au** breadth, width.

Mae stori ar led yn a pentref There is a story going around the village. **2** *ad.* rather, partly, almost.
lledled *ardd.* throughout. **lledled y byd** throughout the world.
lledr *e.g. ll.* **-au** leather.
lledrith *e.g. ll.* **-oedd** magic, enchantment; spectre; fantasy: **hud a lledrith** magic and fantasy.
lledu *be.* **(lledaf)** to spread, to widen, to open, to expand.
llef *e.g. ll.* **-au** voice, cry.
llefain *be.* **(llefaf)** to cry (*S.W.*).
llefaru *be.* **(llefaraf)** to speak, to utter.
llefarwr *e.g. ll.* **llefarwyr** speaker.
llefarwyr *gw.* **llefarwr.**
llefarydd *e.g. ll.* **-ion** speaker, spokesman. **Y Llefarydd** (the) Speaker of the House of Commons.
llefau *gw.* **llef.**
llefelyn *e.g. ll* **-od** stye (*in eye*). *gw.* **llyfelyn, llefrithen.**
llefrith *e.g.* milk (*N.W.*). *gw.* **llaeth.**
llefrithen *e.b.* stye (in eye) (*N.W.*); *gw.* **llefelyn, llyfelyn.**
llefydd *gw.* **lle.**
lleiaf *a.* smallest, least. **o leiaf** at least; **gorau po leiaf** the fewer the better.
lleiafrif *e.g. ll.* **-au, -oedd** minority.
lleian *e.b. ll.* **-od** nun.
lleidr *e.g. ll.* **lladron** thief, robber, bandit. **lleidr pen ffordd** highwayman.
lleihau *be.* **(lleihaf)** to become smaller, to diminish, to shrink.
lleill *gw.* **llall.**
lleiniau *gw.* **llain.**
lleisiau *gw.* **llais.**
lleisio *be.* **(lleisiaf)** to use the voice (*in speaking, shouting, etc.*), to sound, to cry out.
lleithder *e.g. ll.* **-au** damp, moisture.
llen *e.b. ll.* **-ni** curtain, veil, sheet. **Y Llen Haearn** The Iron Curtain.
llên *e.b.* literature. **llên gwerin** folklore; **ffuglen** fiction.
llencyndod *e.g.* adolescence.
llenni *gw.* **llen.**
llenor *e.g. ll.* **-ion** author, writer,

llenwi **llongwr**

literary person .
llenwi *be.* **(llenwaf)** to fill.
llenyddiaeth *e.b.* *ll.* **-au** literature.
llenyddol *a.* literary.
lleoedd *gw.* **lle.**
lleol *a.* local. **llywodraeth leol** local
government.
lleoli *be.* **(lleolaf)** to locate, to
localise, to place.
lleoliad *e.g.* *ll.* **-au** location, setting.
lles *e.g.* *ll.* **-au** benefit, profit,
advantage, welfare. **er lles** for the
benefit of, to the advantage of: **o les**
of benefit;
Y Wladwriaeth Les The Welfare
State.
llesol *a.* beneficial, profitable,
advantageous.
llestr *e.g.* *ll.* **-i** vessel; cup, dish, pot.
lletchwith *a.* awkward, clumsy.
llety *e.g.* *ll.* **-au** lodging(s).
lletya *be.* **(lletyaf)** to lodge.
lleuad *e.b.* *ll.* **-au** moon. **lleuad
lawn** full moon; **lleuad newydd**
new moon. *gw.* **lloer.**
lleuen *e.b.* *ll.* **llau** louse.
llew *e.g.* *ll.* **-od** lion. **llewes** lioness.
llewygu *be.* **(llewygaf)** to faint, to
swoon.
llewyrch *e.g.* brightness, light,
gleam, lustre.
llewyrchu *be.* **(llewyrchaf)** to shine,
to gleam.
llewyrchus *a.* bright, prosperous.
llewys *gw.* **llawes.**
lliain *e.g.* *ll.* **llieiniau** line, cloth,
towel, napkin.
llid *e.g.* *ll.* **-iau, -ion** wrath;
irritation, inflammation; passion. **llid
yr ymennydd** meningitis.
llieiniau *gw.* **lliain.**
llif 1 *e.g.* *ll.* **-ogydd** stream, flow,
flood, deluge, current. **2** *e.b.* *ll.* **-iau**
saw. **llif gadwyn** chain saw.
llifio *be.* **(llifiaf)** to saw; to rasp, to
file.
llifo *be.* **(llifaf)** to flow, to stream, to
flood.
llifogydd *gw.* **llif.**
llinell *e.b.* *ll.* **-au** line, axis; line-out.
llinell gam crooked line; **llinell**

syth straight line.
llinyn *e.g.* *ll* **-nau** line, string, cord,
tape, twine. **llinyn mesur**
measuring tape.
llipa *a.* limp, flaccid, weak.
llithren *e.b.* *ll.* **-nau** chute, slide.
llithriad *e.g.* *ll.* **-au** a slip, glide,
slur; error, mistake.
llithrig *a.* slippery; fluent.
llithro *be.* **(llithraf)** to slip, to slide;
to slur.
lliw *e.g.* *ll.* **-iau** colour, countenance,
hue. **lliw dydd** by day; **lliw nos** by
night; **lliwiau'r hydref** autumn
colours.
lliwgar *a.* colourful.
lliwiau *gw.* **lliw.**
lliwio: lliwo *be.* **(lliwiaf: lliwaf)** to
colour, to dye.
lliwiog *a.* coloured, tinted.
lliwo *gw.* **lliwio.**
llo *e.g.* *ll.* **lloi, lloeau** calf; **fel llo**
gormless.
lloches *e.g.* *ll.* **-au** refuge, shelter,
lair.
llochesu *be.* **(llochesaf)** to harbour,
to shelter.
lloeau *gw.* **llo.**
Lloegr *e.b.* England.
lloer *e.b.* *ll.* **-au** moon (*literary
usage*); *gw.* **lleuad.**
lloeren *e.b.* *ll.* **-ni, -nau** satellite,
sputnik.
llofnod *e.b.* *ll.* **-au, -ion** signature.
llofnodi *be.* **(llofnodaf)** to sign.
llofrudd *e.g.* *ll.* **-ion** murderer.
llofruddiaeth *e.g.* *ll.* **-au** murder.
llofruddio *be.* **(llofruddiaf)** to
murder.
llofft *e.b.* *ll.* **-ydd** loft, upstairs;
gallery; bedroom: **ar y llofft**
upstairs; **lan llofft** upstairs (*S.W.*).
llog *e.g.* *ll.* **-au** interest, hire; **ar log**
for hire.
llogi *be.* **(llogaf)** to hire.
llong *e.b.* *ll.* **-au** ship. **llong
hwyliau** sailing ship; **llong danfor**
submarine; **llong ryfel** warship.
llongddrylliad *e.g.* *ll.* **-au**
shipwreck.
llongwr *e.g.* *ll.* **llongwyr** sailor.

106

lloi *gw.* **llo.**
llon *a.* merry, cheerful.
llond *e.g.* as much as something will hold; fullness, sufficiency. **llond llwy de o siwgr** a teaspoonful of sugar; **llond tŷ o blant** a houseful of children.
llongyfarch (ar) *be.* **(llongyfarchaf)** to congratulate.
llongyfarchiad *e.g.* *ll.* **-au** congratulation. **Llongyfarchiadau!** Congratulations!
llonydd *a.* quiet, still, calm; **Gad lonydd i fi!** Let me have some peace!
llonyddwch *e.g.* stillness, tranquillity, quietness; peace.
lloriau *gw.* **llawr.**
llosg 1 *e.g.* *ll.* **-iadau** burning, arson.
2 burning, burnt. **llosgfynydd** volcano; **pwnc llosg** burning issue.
llosgi *be.* **(llosgaf)** to burn, to scorch, to smart.
llosgydd *e.g.* *ll.* **-ion** incinerator, burner.
llu *e.g.* *ll.* **-oedd** host, multitude; *(follows plural noun and undergoes soft mutation)* crowd. **Daeth milwyr lu o rywle** A host of soldiers came from somewhere.
lluched *e. torf.* flash of lightning; lighting flashes.
lludw *e.g.* ash, ashes. **Lludw i ludw** Ashes to ashes; **dydd Mercher y Lludw** Ash Wednesday; **lorri ludw** ashcart.
Llun *e.g.* Monday. **Llun y Pasg** Easter Monday.
llun *e.g.* *ll.* **-iau** picture, drawing, image.
Llundain *e.b.* London.
lluniaidd *a.* shapely, graceful.
lluniau *gw.* **llun.**
llunio *be.* **(lluniaf)** to form, to fashion, to shape.
lluoedd *gw.* **llu.**
lluosi *be.* **(lluosaf)** to multiply.
lluosog *a.* numerous, plural.
llusern *e.b.* *ll.* **-au** lamp, lantern.
llusgo *be.* **(llusgaf)** to drag, to trail,

to draw, to crawl: **llusgo traed** to drag (one's) feet.
lluwch *e.g.* *ll.* **-au** snow-drift; dust, specks.
lluwchfa *e.b.* *ll.* **lluwchfeydd** snowdrift.
llw *e.g.* *ll.* **-on** oath; curse. **ar fy llw** on oath, on my word; **cymryd llw** to take an oath.
llwch *e.g.* *ll.* **llychau** dust, powder; ashes; lake, loch.
llwfr *a.* cowardly, timid.
llwgu *be.* **(llwgaf)** to starve, to be ravenously hungry.
llwm *a.* poor, bare.
llwnc *e.g.* *ll.* **llynciau** gullet, throat; draught, gulp.
llwncdestun *e.g.* *ll.* **-au** toast (health).
llwon *gw.* **llw.**
llwy *e.b.* *ll.* **-au** spoon. **llwy bren** wooden spoon; **llwy de** teaspoon; **llwy gawl** soup-spoon; **llwy garu** love-spoon.
llwyaid *e.b.* *ll.* **llwyeidiau** spoonful.
llwybr *e.g.* *ll.* **-au** path, track, route. **llwybr tarw** straight path, short cut; **ar y llwybr iawn** on the right track.
llwyd *a.* grey, pale, hoary. **Brawd Llwyd** Grey Friar, Cistercian Friar.
llwydo *be.* **(llwydaf)** to turn grey; to become mouldy.
llwydrew *e.g.* *ll.* **-ogydd** hoarfrost *(S.W.).*
llwydrewi *be.* **(llwydrewaf)** to cast a hoarfrost, to be frosty *(S.W.).*
llwydd: llwyddiant *e.g.* *ll.* **llwyddiannau** success, prosperity.
llwyddiannus *a.* successful, prosperous.
llwyddo (i) *be.* **(llwyddaf)** to succeed, to prosper.
llwyfan *e.g.b.* *ll.* **-nau** platform, stage. **llwyfan olew** oil rig.
llwyfannu *be.* **(llwyfannaf)** to stage.
llwyn 1 *e.g.* *ll.* **-i** grove, bush. **o lech i lwyn** furtively, stealthily, slyly *(literally from rock to bush).*
2 *e.b.* *ll.* **-au** loin.
llwynog *e.g.* *ll.* **-od** fox *(N.W.).*
llwynoges vixen.

llwyr 1 *a.* complete, entire, utter, total. **2** *ad.* entirely, altogether. **3** *rhag.* total.
llwyrymwrthodwr *e.g. ll.*
llwyrymwrthodwyr teetotaller.
llwyth *e.g. ll.* **-au** tribe, clan; *e.g. ll.* **-i** load, burden, freight.
llwytho *be.* **(llwythaf)** to load, to burden.
llwythog *a.* laden, burdened.
llydan *a.* wide, broad.
llydanu *be.* **(llydanaf)** to widen.
Llydaw *e.b.* Britanny.
Llydawr *e.g.* Breton.
Llydawes *e.b.* Breton woman.
Llydaweg *e.b.* Breton language.
llyfelyn *e.g. ll.* **llyfelod** stye (in eye). *gw.* **llefelyn, llefrithen.**
llyfn *a.* smooth, sleek.
llyfr *e.g. ll.* **-au** book. **llyfr emynau** hymn-book; **llyfr gosod** set book (*in syllabus*); **llyfr lloffion** scrapbook; **llyfr lluniau** picture book; **llyfr sieciau** cheque book; **llawlyfr** handbook, manual.
llyfrgell *e.b. ll.* **-oedd** library.
llyfrgell y sir county library.
llyfrgellydd *e.g. ll.* **-ion, llyfrgellwyr** librarian.
llyfryn *e.g. ll.* **-nau** booklet, pamphlet.
llyfu *be.* **(llyfaf)** to lick.
llyffant *e.g. ll.* **-od, llyffaint** toad. **caws llyffant** toadstool.
llygad *e.g.b. ll.* **llygaid** eye. **llygad tro** squint; **llygad y ffynnon** fountain head, original source of information; **yn llygad ei le** perfectly right, quite correct. **yn llygaid i gyd** all eyes, all attention; **(dim ond) dau lygad a thrwyn** '(only) two eyes and a nose', said of a thin person.
llygadu *be.* **(llygadaf)** to eye, to watch, to have (one's) eye upon.
llygaid *gw.* **llygad.**
llygod *gw.* **llygoden.**
llygoden *e.b. ll.* **llygod** mouse. **llygoden fach** mouse; **llygoden fawr/Ffrengig** rat.
llygredig *a.* corrupt, degraded, defiled.

llygredd *e.g. ll.* **-au** corruption; pollution, contamination.
llygru *be.* **(llygraf)** to corrupt, to pollute, to contaminate.
llynges *e.b. ll.* **-au** fleet, navy. **Y Llynges** The Navy.
llym *a.* sharp, keen, severe.
llyn *e.g.b. ll.* **-noedd, -nau** lake, pool.
llynciau *gw.* **llwnc.**
llyncu *be.* **(llyncaf)** to swallow, to devour, to gulp.
llynedd *ad.* (*the definite article is used with the adverb*) last year. **Gwelais ef y llynedd** I saw him last year.
llynnau *gw.* **llyn.**
llynnoedd *gw.* **llyn.**
llyo *be.* **(llyaf)** to lick (*S.W.*).
llys *e.g. ll.* **-oedd** court, hall, place. **Llys y Goron** The Crown Court; **Llys yr Ynadon** The Magistrates' Court; **Yr Uchel Lys** The High Court.
llysenw *e.g. ll.* **-au** nickname.
llysenwi *be.* **(llysenwaf)** to nickname.
llysfam *e.b. ll.* **-au** stepmother.
llysfwytäwr *e.g. ll.* **llysfwytawyr** vegetarian (male). **llysfwytäwraig** vegetarian (female).
llysgenhadaeth *e.b. ll.* **llysgenadaethau** embassy.
llysgennad *e.g. ll.* **llysgenhadon** ambassador.
llysiau *gw.* **llysieuyn.**
llysieuol *a.* herbal, vegetable, botanical; spiced. **te llysieuol** herbal tea.
llysieuyn *e.g. ll.* **llysiau** vegetable, herb.
llythrennau *gw.* **llythyren.**
llythrennog *a.* literate.
llythyr *e.g. ll.* **-au, -on** letter, epistle. **llythyr caru** love-letter; **llythyr cyfreithiwr** solicitor's letter.
llythyren *e.b. ll.* **llythrennau** letter of the alphabet. **llythrennau'r abiec** letters of the alphabet; **priflythrennau** capital letters; **llythyren y ddeddf** letter of the law.

llyw   **llywyddu**

llyw *e.g. ll.* **-iau** leader, ruler; rudder,
helm. **(bod) wrth y llyw** (to be) at
the helm, (to be) in charge.
llywio *be.* **(llywiaf)** to govern, to
rule; to steer, to pilot.
llywodraeth *e.b. ll.* **-au** government.
llywodraeth ganolog central
government; **llywodraeth leol** local

government.
llywodraethu *be.* **(llywodraethaf)**
to govern, to rule, to control.
llywodraethwr *e.g. ll.*
llywodraethwyr governor.
llywydd *e.g. ll.* **-ion** president (*of*
society). *gw.* **arlywydd.**
llywyddu *be.* **(llywyddaf)** to preside.

m

mab *e.g. ll.* **meibion** boy, son, man, male.
maban *gw.* **baban.**
mabi *gw.* **babi.**
mabolgamp *e.b. ll.* **-au** game, sport, feat. **mabolgampau'r ysgol** school sports.
mach *gw.* **bach.**
machau *gw.* **bach; bachyn.**
machgen *gw.* **bachgen.**
machlud *e.g. ll.* **-oedd** setting (*of the sun*), going down. **machlud haul** sunset.
machu *gw.* **bachu.**
machyn *gw.* **bachyn.**
mad *gw.* **bad.**
madarch *e. torf.* mushrooms; **madarchen** *e.b.* a mushroom.
mae *gw.* **bae, bod.**
maer *e.g. ll.* **meiri** mayor. **maer y dre** the town mayor.
maeres *e.b. ll.* **-au** mayoress.
maes *e.g. ll.* **meysydd** field, square; syllabus. **maes chwarae** playing field; **maes o law** shortly.
maestref *e.b. ll.* **-i, -ydd** suburb.
mafonen *e.b. ll.* **mafon** raspberry.
mag *gw.* **bag.**
magiau *gw.* **bag.**
magu *be.* **(magaf)** to breed, to nurse, to gain. **magu bola** to acquire a pot belly; **magu hyder** to gain confidence.

Mai *e.g.* May.
mai *c.* that (*emphatic*). **rwy'n sicr mai Tom yw e** I'm sure that it is Tom (and nobody else). *gw.* **bai.**
maich *gw.* **baich.**
main *a.* thin, lean, slim, shrill, fine.
maint *e.g.b. ll.* **meintiau** size, dimension; magnitude; amount, quantity; extent.
malchder *gw.* **balchder.**
maldod *e.g.* indulgence, pampering, spoiling; caresses; affectation.
maldodi *be.* **(maldodaf)** to pamper, to fondle, to pet.
maled *gw.* **baled.**
maledwr *gw.* **baledwr.**
malot *gw.* **balot.**
malu *be.* **(malaf)** to grind, to crush, to smash. **malu awyr** to talk nonsense, to talk idly.
malŵn *gw.* **balŵn.**
malwen: (*N.W.*) **malwoden** (*S.W.*) *e.b. ll.* **malwod** snail, slug.
malwoden (*S.W.*) *gw.* **malwen.**
mam *e.b. ll.* **-au** mother. **mam faeth** foster-mother; **mam-yng-nghyfraith** mother-in-law.
mam-gu *e.b.* grandmother (*S.W.*); *gw.* **nain.**
mamiaith *e.b. ll.* **mamieithoedd** mother tongue.
mân *a.* tiny, small, minute; fine; petty. **arian mân** small change, small coin; **glaw mân** fine rain, drizzle; **glo mân** small coal, slack; **yn fân ac yn fuan** quickly and in short gasps (*of breath*); with small quick steps or movements.
man *e.g.b. ll.* **-nau** place, spot; mark; blemish. **man a man (i fi, i ti . . .)** (it is) all the same (to me, to you . . .), (it makes) no difference; **man cychwyn** starting-point; **man cyfarfod** meeting place; **man gwan** weak spot; **yn y fan a'r lle** in the (very) place, on the (very) spot; **yn y man** soon, before (very) long, presently; on the spot, immediately, at once, now. *gw.* **ban.**
manana *gw.* **banana.**
manc *gw.* **banc.**

mancio   **medru**

mancio *gw.* **bancio.**
mand *gw.* **band.**
mandiau *gw.* **band.**
maneg *e.b. ll.* **menig** glove,
gauntlet. **Gwlad y menig gwynion**
Land of the white gloves (alluding to
the frequent presentation of white
gloves to assize judges in Wales,
when there were no cases for trial).
maner *gw.* **baner.**
mannau *gw.* **ban, man.**
mans *e.g.* manse.
mantais *e.b. ll.* **manteision**
advantage. **o fantais** of advantage;
cymryd mantais (ar) to take
advantage (of).
manteisio (ar) *be.* **(manteisiaf)** to
take advantage to profit (from).
manteision *gw.* **mantais.**
mantell *e.b. ll.* **-oedd, mentyll**
mantle, cloak, robe.
manwl *a.* exact, careful, strict; fine;
particular; **yn fanwl** in detail.
manylion *e.ll.* details, particulars.
manylu (ar) *be.* **(manylaf)** to
particularise, to go into detail
(about), to be exact.
manylyn *e.g. ll.* **manylion** detail.
map *e.g. ll.* **-iau** map.
mar *gw.* **bar.**
mara *gw.* **bara.**
marbeciw *gw.* **barbeciw.**
marc *e.g. ll.* **-iau, -au** mark.
gwneud marc to make one's mark.
marcio *be.* **(marciaf)** to mark, to
mark out.
marchnad *e.b. ll.* **-oedd** market.
y Farchnad Gyffredin the
Common market; **y farchnad rydd**
the free market.
marchog *e.g. ll.* **-ion** horseman,
rider; knight.
mardd *gw.* **bardd.**
marddoniaeth *gw.* **barddoniaeth.**
marf *gw.* **barf.**
marn *gw.* **barn.**
marnwr *gw.* **barnwr.**
mart *e.g. ll.* **-iau** mart (*S.W.*).
marw 1 *be.* **(marwaf)** to die; **wedi
marw: yn farw** dead. **2** *a. ll.*
meirw, meirwon dead, deceased. **3**

e.g. ll. **meirw, meirwon** the dead.
marwaidd *a.* lifeless, listless,
sluggish.
marwol *a.* deadly, fatal, mortal.
ergyd farwol mortal blow.
marwolaeth *e.b. ll.* **-au** death.
mas *gw.* **bas.**
masged *gw.* **basged.**
masn *gw.* **basn.**
masnach *e.b. ll.* **-au** trade,
commerce.
masnachwr *e.g. ll.* **masnachwyr**
merchant, tradesman, dealer.
masnau: masnys *gw.* **basn.**
maswr *e.g. ll.* **maswyr** outside-half
(*rugby*).
mat *e.g. ll.* **-iau** mat. *gw.* **bat.**
mater *e.g. ll.* **-ion** matter, subject.
matsen: matsien *e.b. ll.* **matsys**
match. **fel matsien** wild tempered,
fiery (*lit. like a match*).
math *e.g. ll.* **-au** sort, kind, species.
gw. **bath.**
mathemateg *e.g.* mathematics.
mathemategol *a.* mathematical.
mathemategwr *e.g. ll.*
mathemategwyr mathematician.
mathodyn *gw.* **bathodyn.**
maw *gw.* **baw.**
mawd *gw.* **bawd.**
mawl *e.g.* praise.
mawn *e.g.* peat. **lladd mawn** to cut
peat.
mawnog *e.b. ll.* **-ydd** a peat bog.
mawr *a. ll.* **-ion** great, big, large.
gw. At. Ansoddeiriau.
mawredd *e.g.* greatness, majesty
grandeur. **Mawredd mawr!** Good
gracious!
Mawrth *e.g.* March; Tuesday; Mars.
mecso *gw.* **becso.**
mechan *gw.* **bechan.**
mechgyn *gw.* **bachgen.**
mechnïaeth *e.b.* bail, suretyship.
Medi *e.g.* September.
medi *be.* **(medaf)** to reap, to harvest,
to cut.
medru *be.* **(medraf)** to be able to do
or accomplish (*a thing*); to be able to
speak, know (*a language*); to hit, to
strike, to shoot. **medru'r Gymraeg**

medrus   **menthyca**

to know Welsh, to be able to speak
Welsh.
medrus *a.* skilful, able, clever (*with
one's hand*); correct.
medw *gw.* **bedwen.**
medwen *gw.* **bedwen.**
medyddio *gw.* **bedyddio.**
medd *e.g.* mead. *gw.* **bedd, meddaf.**
meddaf *bf.* I say, I said. **meddwn i**
I would say; **medd** he/she/it
says/said. *gw.* **meddu.**
meddai *bf.* he/she/it was saying,
he/she/it was used to saying.
meddal *a.* soft, tender, pliable.
meddalu *be.* **(meddalaf)** to soften,
to become soft; to thaw.
meddalwedd *e.b.* software.
meddu *be.* **(meddaf)** to possess, to
own.
meddw *a.* *ll.* **-on** drunk. **yn feddw
gaib** blind drunk.
meddwi (ar) *be.* **(meddwaf)** to be
drunk, to become drunk.
meddwl (am) 1 *be.* **(meddyliaf,
meddylaf)** to think, to mean, to
intend. **meddwl y byd o** to think
the world of.
2 *e.g.* *ll.* **meddyliau**
thought, mind, meaning, opinion.
meddyg *e.g.* *ll.* **-on** doctor of
medicine.
meddygfa *e.b.* *ll.* **meddygfeydd**
surgery.
meddyginiaeth *e.b.* *ll.* **-au** remedy,
medicine.
meddylgar *a.* thoughtful, pensive.
meddyliau *gw.* **meddwl.**
mefusen *e.b.* *ll.* **mefus** strawberry.
Mehefin *e.g.* June.
meiau *gw.* **bai.**
meibion *gw.* **mab.**
Meibl *gw.* **Beibl.**
meic *e.g.* *ll.* **-iau** microphone. *gw.*
beic.
meicrodon *gw.* **microdon.**
meichiau *gw.* **baich.**
meiddio *be.* **(meiddiaf)** to dare, to
venture. *gw.* **beiddio.**
meim *e.g.b.* *ll.* **-iau** mime.
meinir *e.b.* maiden.
meintiau *gw.* **maint.**

meio *gw.* **beio.**
meirdd *gw.* **bardd.**
meiri *gw.* **maer.**
meirioli *be.* **(meiriolaf)** to thaw, to
melt.
meirniad *gw.* **beirniad.**
meirniadu *gw.* **beirniadu.**
meirniaid *gw.* **beirniad.**
meistr *e.g.* *ll.* **-i, -iaid** master,
owner.
meistres *e.b.* *ll.* **-i** mistress.
meistri: meistriaid *gw.* **meistr.**
meistroli *be.* **(meistrolaf)** to master.
meithrin *be.* **(meithrinaf)** to nurture,
to rear, to foster. **meithrinfa**
nursery; **ysgol feithrin** nursery
school.
mêl *e.g.* honey. **mis mêl**
honeymoon; **yn fêl ar ei fysedd**
music to his ears, to his extreme
gratification.
melen *a.b.* yellow: **ffrog felen**
yellow frock. *gw.* **melyn.**
melin *e.b.* *ll.* **-au** mill: **melin ddŵr**
water mill; **melin wlân** woollen
mill; **melin wynt** windmill;
gwneud melin ac eglwys to make
a great to-do of, to make a fuss about
nothing.
melyn *a.g.* yellow. **crys melyn**
yellow shirt, **cyw melyn olaf**
youngest child of family, last of the
brood; **melynwy** yolk of an egg.
gw. **melen.**
melys *a.* sweet; **melysion** sweets.
melysfwyd *e.g.* *ll.* **-ydd** dessert.
mellt *gw.* **mellten.**
mellten *e.b.* *ll.* **mellt** lightning. **fel
mellten** like a flash (*of lightning*),
fast.
melltith *e.b.* *ll.* **-ion** curse. **Melltith
arno!** Curse him!
menig *gw.* **maneg.**
menter *e.b.* *ll.* **mentrau** venture,
hazard.
mentrau *gw.* **menter.**
mentro (ar) *be.* **(mentraf)** to
venture.
mentrus *a.* venturesome.
mentyll *gw.* **mantell.**
menthyca *gw.* **benthyca.**

112

menyn   **mhatrymau**

menyn: ymenyn *e.g.* butter. **blodau menyn** buttercups.
menyw 1 *e.b. ll.* **-od** woman. **2** *a.* female (*S.W.*).
mêr *e.g. ll.* **merion** marrow (*bone*).
merch *e.b. ll.* **-ed** girl, daughter.
Mercher *e.g.* Wednesday; Mercury. **Dydd Mercher Lludw** Ash Wednesday.
merchetaidd *a.* effeminate.
merf *gw.* **berf.**
merfa *gw.* **berfa.**
merfenw *gw.* **berfenw.**
merlod *gw.* **merlyn.**
merlota *bf.* to go pony-trekking.
merlotwr *e.g. ll.* **merlotwyr** pony-trekker.
merlyn *e.g. ll.* **-nod, merlod** pony.
merthyr *e.g. ll.* **-on** martyr. **Merthyr Tudful** valley town in South Wales.
merw *gw.* **berw.**
merwi *gw.* **berwi.**
mesen *e.b. ll.* **mes** acorn.
mesul *ad.* in the measure of. **Daeth y plant i mewn fesul un** The children came in one by one; **fesul tri** three at a time.
mesur *e.g. ll.* **-au 1** measure, metre. **ffon fesur** rule, ruler. **2** *be.* to measure.
mesurydd *e.g. ll.* **-ion** measurer, meter, gauge. **mesurydd glaw** rain gauge.
metel *e.g. ll.* **-oedd, -au** metal; mettle.
metr *e.g. ll.* **-au** metre. **metr sgwâr** square metre.
metrig *a.* metric.
methiant *e.g. ll.* **methiannau** failure.
methu (â) *be.* (**methaf**) to fail.
meudwy *e.g. ll.* **-aid, -od** hermit, recluse.
mewian *be.* (**mewiaf**) to mew.
mewn *ardd.* in, within. **i mewn: i fewn** in, inward(s): **mewn a maes** in and out; **mewn bod** in being, extant; **mewn cariad** in love; **mewn eiliad** in a moment, at once, instantly; **mewn gwaith** in work, employed; **mewn llaw** in hand,

receiving attention, under consideration; **mewn trefn** in order; **o fewn y mis** within the month; **y tu mewn: y tu fewn** inside.
mewnwr *e.g. ll.* **mewnwyr** scrum-half (*rugby*), inside-forward (*soccer*).
meysydd *gw.* **maes.**
mha *gw.* **pa.**
Mhab *gw.* **Pab.**
mhabell *gw.* **pabell.**
mhabi *gw.* **pabi.**
mhabydd *gw.* **pabydd.**
mhac *gw.* **pac.**
mhaced *gw.* **paced.**
mhacio *gw.* **pacio.**
mhadell *gw.* **padell.**
mhader *gw.* **pader.**
mhaent *gw.* **paent.**
mhafiliwn *gw.* **pafiliwn.**
mhafin *gw.* **pafin.**
mhagan *gw.* **pagan.**
mhais *gw.* **pais.**
mhâl *gw.* **pâl.**
mhalas *gw.* **palas.**
mhalau:mhalod *gw.* **pâl.**
mhalu *gw.* **palu.**
mhamffled *gw.* **pamffled.**
mhamffledyn *gw.* **pamffledyn.**
mhanasen *gw.* **panasen.**
mhanel *gw.* **panel.**
mhannas *gw.* **panasen.**
mhant *gw.* **pant.**
mhapur *gw.* **papur.**
mhapuro *gw.* **papuro.**
mhâr *gw.* **pâr.**
mharadwys *gw.* **paradwys.**
mharagraff *gw.* **paragraff.**
mharatoi *gw.* **paratoi.**
mharc *gw.* **parc.**
mharch *gw.* **parch.**
mharchu *gw.* **parchu.**
mharchus *gw.* **parchus.**
mhardwn *gw.* **pardwn.**
mharhad *gw.* **parhad.**
mharsel *gw.* **parsel.**
mharti *gw.* **parti.**
Mhasg *gw.* **Pasg.**
mhasiant *gw.* **pasiant.**
mhatrwm *gw.* **patrwm.**
mhatrwn *gw.* **patrwn.**
mhatrymau *gw.* **patrwm.**

mhatrynau   **mhlannu**

mhatrynau *gw.* patrwn.
mhawb *gw.* pawb.
mhawen *gw.* pawen.
mhebyll *gw.* pabell.
mhecyn *gw.* pecyn.
mhechadur *gw.* pechadur.
mhechod *gw.* pechod.
mhedair *gw.* pedair.
mhedol *gw.* pedol.
mhedwar *gw.* pedwar.
mhedwaredd *gw.* pedwaredd.
mhedwerydd *gw.* pedwerydd.
mheg *gw.* peg.
mhegwn *gw.* pegwn.
mhegynau *gw.* pegwn.
mheilot *gw.* peilot.
mheint *gw.* peint.
mheintio *gw.* peintio.
mheintiwr *gw.* peintiwr.
mheiriannau *gw.* peiriant.
mheiriannydd *gw.* peiriannydd.
mheiriant *gw.* peiriant.
mheisiau *gw.* pais.
mhêl *gw.* pêl.
mhelydr *gw.* pelydr.
mhellter *gw.* pellter.
mhen *gw.* pen.
mhenaethiaid *gw.* pennaeth.
mhenawdau *gw.* pennawd.
mhen-blwydd *gw.* pen-blwydd.
mhencadlys *gw.* pencadlys.
mhencampwr *gw.* pencampwr.
mhenderfyniad *gw.* penderfyniad.
mhenelin *gw.* penelin.
mhenillion *gw.* pennill.
mhennaeth *gw.* pennaeth.
mhennau *gw.* pen.
mhennawd *gw.* pennawd.
mhennill *gw.* pennill.
mhennod *gw.* pennod.
mhenodau *gw.* pennod.
mhenodi *gw.* penodi.
mhenodiad *gw.* penodiad.
mhenrhyn *gw.* penrhyn.
mhensaer *gw.* pensaer.
mhensil *gw.* pensil.
mhensiwn *gw.* pensiwn.
mhensiynwr *gw.* pensiynwr.
mhenteulu *gw.* penteulu.
mhentref *gw.* pentref.
mhentwr *gw.* pentwr.

mhenwythnos *gw.* penwythnos.
mhêr *gw.* pêr.
mherchen: mherchennog *gw.*
   perchen.
mheren *gw.* peren.
mhererin *gw.* pererin.
mherfedd *gw.* perfedd.
mherffaith *gw.* perffaith.
mherffeithio *gw.* perffeithio.
mheri *gw.* peri.
mherl *gw.* perl.
mherlysiau *gw.* perlysiau.
mherllan *gw.* perllan.
mhersli *gw.* persli.
mherson *gw.* person.
mhersonoliaeth *gw.* personoliaeth.
mherth *gw.* perth.
mherthynas *gw.* perthynas.
mherygl *gw.* perygl.
mheswch *gw.* peswch.
mhesychiad *gw.* pesychiad.
mheth *gw.* peth.
mhiano *gw.* piano.
mhianydd *gw.* pianydd.
mhib *w.* pib.
mhiben *gw.* piben.
mhicil *gw.* picil.
mhictiwr *gw.* pictiwr.
mhicwn *gw.* picwnen.
mhicwnen *gw.* picwnen.
mhigiad *gw.* pigiad.
mhigo *gw.* pigo.
mhil *gw.* pil.
mhiler *gw.* piler.
mhilion *gw.* pil.
mhili-pala *gw.* pili-pala.
mhilsen *gw.* pilsen.
mhilyn *gw.* pilyn.
mhin *gw.* pin.
mhîn *gw.* pîn.
mhînafal *gw.* pînafal.
mhinnau *gw.* pin.
mhinsio *gw.* pinsio.
mhinwydden *gw.* pinwydden.
mhioden *gw.* pioden.
mhisyn *gw.* pisyn.
mhlaid *gw.* plaid.
mhlan *gw.* plan.
mhlanced *gw.* blanced, planced.
mhlanhigyn *gw.* planhigyn.
mhlannu *gw.* plannu.

mhlant   mhryd

mhlant *gw.* plant.
mhlas *gw.* plas.
mhlasty *gw.* plasty.
mhlât *gw.* plât.
mhlatiau *gw.* plât.
mhleidiau *gw.* plaid.
mhleidlais *gw.* pleidlais.
mhleidleisiau *gw.* pleidlais.
mhleidleisio *gw.* pleidleisio.
mhleidleisiwr *gw.* pleidleisiwr.
mhlentyn *gw.* plentyn.
mhleser *gw.* pleser.
mhleserus *gw.* pleserus.
mhlesio *gw.* plesio.
mhlisgyn *gw.* plisgyn.
mhlisman: mhlismon *gw.* plisman.
mhlu *gw.* pluen.
mhluen *gw.* pluen.
mhluf *gw.* plufyn.
mhlufyn *gw.* plufyn.
mhlwc *gw.* plwc.
mhlwg *gw.* plwg.
mhlwm *gw.* plwm.
mhlwyf *gw.* plwyf.
mhlygu *gw.* plygu.
mhob *gw.* pob.
mhobi *gw.* pobi.
mhobl *gw.* pobl.
mhoblogaeth *gw.* poblogaeth.
mhobman *gw.* pobman.
mhobydd *gw.* pobydd.
mhoced *gw.* poced.
mhoen *gw.* poen.
mhoeni *gw.* poeni.
mhoenus *gw.* poenus.
mhoenydio *gw.* poenydio.
mhoer: mhoeri *gw.* poer, poeri.
mhoethi *gw.* poethi.
mholyn *gw.* polyn.
mhont *gw.* pont.
mhopeth *gw.* popeth.
mhopty *gw.* popty.
mhorfa *gw.* porfa.
mhorfeydd *gw.* porfa.
mhorffor *gw.* porffor.
mhortread *gw.* portread.
mhorth *gw.* porth.
mhorthladd *gw.* porthladd.
mhos *gw.* pos.
mhosibilrwydd *gw.* posibilrwydd.
mhost *gw.* post.

mhostman: mhostmon *gw.*
    postman.
mhostyn *gw.* postyn.
mhotel *gw.* potel.
mhowdr: mhowdwr *gw.* powdr.
mhowdrau *gw.* powdr.
mhowlen *gw.* bowlen.
mhraidd *gw.* praidd.
mhram *gw.* pram.
mhrawf *gw.* prawf.
mhregeth *gw.* pregeth.
mhregethu *gw.* pregethu.
mhregethwr *gw.* pregethwr.
mhreiddiau *gw.* praidd.
mhren *gw.* pren.
mhrennau *gw.* pren.
mhrentis *gw.* prentis.
mhrentisiaeth *gw.* prentisiaeth.
mhrentisiaid *gw.* prentis.
mhres *gw.* pres.
mhreseb *gw.* preseb.
mhresennol *gw.* presennol.
mhresenoldeb *gw.* presenoldeb.
mhresgripsiwn *gw.* presgripsiwn.
mhreswyl: mhreswylfod *gw.*
    preswyl.
mhridwerth *gw.* pridwerth.
mhridd *gw.* pridd.
mhrifardd *gw.* prifardd.
mhrifathrawes *gw.* prifathrawes.
mhrifathro *gw.* prifathro.
mhrifddinas *gw.* prifddinas.
mhrifeirdd *gw.* prifardd.
mhrifysgol *gw.* prifysgol.
mhriffordd *gw.* priffordd.
mhrinder *gw.* prinder.
mhrintio *gw.* printio.
mhriod *gw.* priod.
mhriodas *gw.* priodas.
mhriodi *gw.* priodi.
mhriodol *gw.* priodol.
mhris *gw.* pris.
mhroblem *gw.* problem.
mhrofi *gw.* profi.
mhrofiad *gw.* profiad.
mhrofion *gw.* prawf.
mhrofocio : mhryfocio *gw.*
    profocio.
mhroffid *gw.* proffid.
mhroffwyd *gw.* proffwyd.
mhryd *gw.* pryd.

Mhrydain *gw.* **Prydain.**
mhrydau *gw.* **pryd.**
mhryder *gw.* **pryder.**
mhrydferthwch *gw.* **prydferthwch.**
mhrydiau *gw.* **pryd.**
mhryf: mhryfedyn: mhryfyn *gw.* **pryf.**
mhryfocio *gw.* **profocio.**
mhrynhawn *gw.* **prynhawn.**
mhrynu *gw.* **prynu.**
mhrynwr *gw.* **prynwr.**
mhrysurdeb *gw.* **prysurdeb.**
mhulpud *gw.* **pulpud.**
mhum: mhump *gw.* **pum.**
mhunnau *gw.* **punt.**
mhunnoedd *gw.* **punt.**
mhunt *gw.* **punt.**
mhupur *gw.* **pupur.**
mhurfa *gw.* **purfa.**
mhuro *gw.* **puro.**
mhwdin *gw.* **pwdin.**
mhwdryn *gw.* **pwdryn.**
mhŵer *gw.* **pŵer.**
mhwll *gw.* **pwll.**
mhwllyn *gw.* **pwllyn.**
mhwmp *gw.* **pwmp.**
mhwnc *gw.* **pwnc.**
mhwrpas *gw.* **pwrpas.**
mhwrs *gw.* **pwrs.**
mhwyll *gw.* **pwyll.**
mhwyllgor *gw.* **pwyllgor.**
mhwynt *gw.* **pwynt.**
mhwys *gw.* **pwys.**
mhwysedd *gw.* **pwysedd.**
mhwysigrwydd *gw.* **pwysigrwydd.**
mhwyslais *gw.* **pwyslais.**
mhwyso *gw.* **pwyso.**
mhwyth *gw.* **pwyth.**
mhyllau *gw.* **pwll** *gw.* **pyllyn.**
mhyllyn *gw.* **pyllyn.**
mhymtheg *gw.* **pymtheg.**
mhymthegfed *gw.* **pymthegfed.**
mhynciau *gw.* **pwnc.**
mhyped *gw.* **pyped.**
mhyrsau *gw.* **pwrs.**
mhyrth *gw.* **porth.**
mhys *gw.* **pysen.**
mhysen *gw.* **pysen.**
mhysgodyn *gw.* **pysgodyn.**
mhysgota *gw.* **pysgota.**
mhysgotwr *gw.* **pysgotwr.**

mhyst *gw.* **postyn**
mhythefnos *gw.* **pythefnos.**
mi *gw.* **fi;** *geiryn (particle used before a verb) (N.W.). gw.* **fe.**
microdon: meicrodon *e.b.g.* microwave; microwave oven.
migwrn *e.g. ll.* **migyrnau.** ankle, knuckle.
mil *e.b. ll.* **-oedd** thousand.
mil *gw.* **bil.**
milfeddyg *e.g. ll.* **-on** veterinary surgeon.
milgi *e.g. ll.* **milgwn** greyhound. **fel milgi** swift, like a greyhound.
miliwn *e.b. ll.* **miliynau** million. **miliynydd** millionaire.
miloedd *gw.* **mil.**
milwr *e.g. ll.* **milwyr** soldier.
milltir *e.b. ll.* **-oedd** mile. **milltir sgwâr** square mile; immediate locality.
min *e.g. ll.* **-ion** lip; side, bank; (cutting) edge (of blade). **min y gyllell** the edge of the knife; **min y ffordd** the wayside; **min y môr** the sea-shore, seaside; **byw wrth fin y gyllell** to live from hand to mouth. *gw.* **bin.**
miniog *a.* sharp, keen, edged.
minlliw *e.g.* lipstick.
minnau *rhag.* I also, me.
mioleg *gw.* **bioleg.**
miri *e.g.* merriment, fun.
mis *e.g. ll.* **-oedd** month.
Mis Bach February.
misged *gw.* **bisged.**
misgedi *gw.* **bisged.**
misgïen *gw.* **bisgïen.**
misglwyf *e.g.* menstruation, period.
misoedd *gw.* **mis.**
misol *a.* monthly.
misolyn *e.g. ll.* **misolion** monthly (magazine).
miwsig *e.g.* music.
mlaen *gw.* **blaen.**
mlaendal *gw.* **blaendal.**
mlaenor *gw.* **blaenor.**
mlaenwr *gw.* **blaenwr.**
mlagur *gw.* **blaguryn.**
mlaguryn *gw.* **blaguryn.**
mlaidd *gw.* **blaidd.**

mlanced · **morgrugyn**

mlanced *gw.* blanced.
mlas *gw.* blas.
mlasu *gw.* blasu.
mlawd *gw.* blawd.
mleiddiaid *gw.* blaidd.
mlew *gw.* blewyn.
mlewyn *gw.* blewyn.
mlinder *gw.* blinder.
mlino *gw.* blino.
mlodau *gw.* blodyn.
mlodeugerdd *gw.* blodeugerdd.
mlodfresychen *gw.* blodfresychen.
mlodyn *gw.* blodyn.
mloedd *gw.* bloedd.
mloeddio *gw.* bloeddio.
mlows *gw.* blows.
mlwch *gw.* blwch.
mlwydd *gw.* blwydd.
mlwyddyn *gw.* blwyddyn.
mlychau *gw.* blwch.
mlynedd *gw.* blwyddyn.
mlynyddoedd *gw.* blwyddyn.
mocs *gw.* bocs.
moch *gw.* boch, mochyn.
mochyn *e.g. ll.* moch pig. fel
mochyn dirty, filthy, fat, like a pig.
mod *gw.* bod.
modfedd *e.b. ll.* -i inch.
modiau *gw.* bawd.
modloni *gw.* bodloni.
modrwy *e.b. ll.* -on ring. modrwy
aur gold ring; modrwy briodas
wedding-ring; modrwy glust
ear-ring.
modryb *e.g. ll.* -edd aunt.
modur *e.g. ll.* -on motor.
modurwr *e.g. ll.* modurwyr
motorist.
modd *e.g. ll.* -ion manner; means,
wealth. gwaetha'r modd worse
luck; modd bynnag however; pa
fodd? how? *gw.* bodd.
moddhad *gw.* boddhad.
moddi *gw.* boddi.
moddion *e.ll.* means; medicine:
moddion gras means of grace. *gw.*
modd.
moel *a.* bare; bald.
moelni *e.g.* bareness; baldness.
moes *e.b. ll.* -au usual behaviour,
habit, wont; *in plural:* manners;

morals. moesau da good manners;
good morals.
moesol *a.* ethical; moral.
moethus *a.* luxurious, comfortable.
mogi *be.* (mogaf) to suffocate, to
smother; Brawd mogi yw tagu
Suffocating is akin to choking, one is
as bad as the other.
mol *gw.* bol.
mola *gw.* bola.
moli *be.* (molaf) to praise.
moliau *gw.* bol.
mollt *gw.* bollt.
mom *gw.* bom.
Môn, Ynys *e.b.* Anglesey. Môn
Mam Cymru Anglesey Mother of
Wales.
môn *gw.* bôn.
moneddiges *gw.* boneddiges.
moneddigion *gw.* bonheddwr.
monheddwr *gw.* bonheddwr.
môr *e.g. ll.* moroedd sea, ocean. Y
Môr Canoldir Mediterranean Sea;
Môr Iwerydd Atlantic Ocean; Môr
Tawel Pacific Ocean.
mor *ad.* (*followed by soft mutation,
except for adjectives beginning with
ll and rh*) as, so, how. mor dew â
mochyn as fat as a pig; mor ddu
â'r nos as black as the night; mor
goch â thân as red as fire; mor
wyn ag eira as white as snow.
mord *gw.* bord.
mordaith *e.b. ll.* mordeithiau (sea)
voyage.
mordau: mordydd *gw.* bord.
morddwyd *e.b. ll.* -ydd thigh.
more *gw.* bore.
morfa *e.b.g. ll.* morfeydd sea-marsh,
bog, fen.
morfeydd *gw.* morfa.
morfil *e.g. ll.* -od whale.
morgais *e.g. ll.* morgeisiau
mortgage.
Morgannwg *e.b.* Glamorgan. De
Morgannwg South Glamorgan;
Gorllewin Morgannwg West
Glamorgan; Morgannwg Ganol
Mid Glamorgan.
morgeisiau *gw.* morgais.
morgrugyn *e.g. ll.* morgrug ant.

morio

morio *be.* **(moriaf)** to sail.
môr-leidr *e.g. ll.* **môr-ladron** pirate.
morlo *e.g. ll.* **morloi** seal.
moroedd *gw.* **môr.**
moron *gw.* **moronen.**
moronen *e.b. ll.* **moron** carrot.
morthwyl *e.g. ll.* **-ion** hammer.
morwr *e.g. ll.* **morwyr** sailor, seaman.
morwyn *e.b. ll.* **morynion** maid, girl, virgin. **y Forwyn Fair** the Virgin Mary.
morwyr *gw.* **morwr.**
mos *gw.* **bos.**
mosys *gw.* **bos.**
motwm *gw.* **botwm.**
motymau *gw.* **botwm.**
mowlen *gw.* **bowlen.**
mragdy *gw.* **bragdy.**
mraich *gw.* **braich.**
mrain *gw.* **brân.**
mraint *gw.* **braint.**
mrân *gw.* **brân.**
mraslun *gw.* **braslun.**
mraster *gw.* **braster.**
mraw *gw.* **braw.**
mrawd *gw.* **brawd.**
mrawddeg *gw.* **brawddeg.**
mrecwast *gw.* **brecwast.**
mrech *gw.* **brech.**
mrechdan *gw.* **brechdan.**
mrechiad *gw.* **brechiad.**
mreichiau *gw.* **braich.**
mreichled *gw.* **breichled.**
mrenhines *gw.* **brenhines.**
mrenin *gw.* **brenin.**
mres *gw.* **bres.**
mrest *gw.* **brest.**
mresychen *gw.* **bresychen.**
mrethyn *gw.* **brethyn.**
mreuddwyd *gw.* **breuddwyd.**
mreuddwydio *gw.* **breuddwydio.**
mreuddwydion *gw.* **breuddwyd.**
mrifo *gw.* **brifo.**
mrig *gw.* **brig.**
mrigau *gw.* **brig, brigyn.**
mrigyn *gw.* **brigyn.**
mriwsionyn *gw.* **briwsionyn.**
mro *gw.* **bro.**
mrodorion *gw.* **brodor.**
mrodyr *gw.* **brawd.**

mwy

mroga *gw.* **broga.**
mron *gw.* **bron.**
mronfraith *gw.* **bronfraith.**
mronnau: mronnydd *gw.* **bron.**
mrown *gw.* **brown.**
mröydd *gw.* **bro.**
mrws: mrwsh *gw.* **brws.**
mrwsio: mrwsho *gw.* **brwsio.**
mrwsys: mrwshys *gw.* **brws.**
mrwydr *gw.* **brwydr.**
mrwydrau *gw.* **brwydr.**
mryd *gw.* **bryd.**
mryn *gw.* **bryn.**
mryniau *gw.* **bryn.**
mrys *gw.* **brys.**
mrysio *gw.* **brysio.**
muarth *gw.* **buarth.**
muchod *gw.* **buwch.**
mud *a.* dumb, mute.
mudiad *e.g. ll.* **-au** movement. **Mudiad Ysgolion Meithrin** (Welsh) Nursery Schools' Movement.
muddugoliaeth *gw.* **buddugoliaeth.**
mugail *gw.* **bugail.**
mugeiliaid *gw.* **bugail.**
mugeilio *gw.* **bugeilio.**
mul *e.g. ll.* **-od** donkey; mule.
munud *e.g.b. ll.* **-au** minute. **Arhoswch funud!** Wait a minute!
mur *e.g. ll.* **-iau** wall.
musnes *gw.* **busnes.**
muwch *gw.* **buwch.**
mwced *gw.* **bwced.**
mwg *e.g.* smoke.
mwgwd *e.g. ll.* **mygydau** mask.
mwlch *gw.* **bwlch.**
mwnci *e.g. ll.* **mwncïod** monkey.
mwrdeistref *gw.* **bwrdeistref.**
mwrdd *gw.* **bwrdd.**
mwriad *gw.* **bwriad.**
mws *gw.* **bws.**
mwstash *e.g. ll.* **mwstashis** moustache.
mwstwr *e.g. ll.* **mystyrau** noise, commotion, bustle (*S.W.*).
mwthyn *gw.* **bwthyn.**
mwy 1 *a.* bigger, larger, greater, more, louder, longer, further.
2 *ad.* more (*often followed by* **na**).
mwy na more than. **mwy na digon**

mwyach   **mywydeg**

too much, excessive; **mwy na mwy**
a lot, a great deal, very many, too
much, exceedingly; **mwy na thebyg**
more than likely; **mwy neu lai**
more or less. *gw.* **mawr.**
mwyach *ad.* any more, any longer,
again, henceforth.
mwyaf *gw.* **mawr.**
mwyar *gw.* **mwyaren.**
mwyaren *e.b. ll.* **mwyar** blackberry.
mwyd *gw.* **bwyd.**
mwydlen *gw.* **bwydlen.**
mwydo: mwyda *gw.* **bwydo.**
mwydod *gw.* **mwydyn.**
mwydyn *e.g. ll.* **mwydod** worm.
mwyn 1 *e.g. ll.* **-au** mineral; ore.
2 *e.g.* sake. **er mwyn** for the sake
of; **er mwyn Duw** for God's sake. **3**
a. gentle, mild, dear.
mwynhad *e.g.* enjoyment, pleasure.
mwynhau *be.* **(mwynhaf)** to enjoy;
to become mild.
mwyta: myta *gw.* **bwyta.**
mwyty *gw.* **bwyty.**
mychan *gw.* **bychan.**
myd *gw.* **byd.**
myddin *gw.* **byddin.**
myfi *rhag.* I, me, myself.
myfyrdod *e.g. ll.* **-au** meditation.
myfyrio *be.* **(myfyriaf)** to study, to
meditate.
myfyriwr *e.g. ll.* **myfyrwyr** student.
myfyriwr hŷn mature student.
myglyd *a.* smoky, close, stifling.
mygu *be.* **(mygaf)** to smoke; to
smother; to suffocate.
mygydau *gw.* **mwgwd.**
mylchau *gw.* **bwlch.**
mynach *e.g. ll.* **-od, mynaich** monk.
mynachlog *e.b. ll.* **-ydd** monastery.

mynachod *gw.* **mynach.**
mynaich *gw.* **mynach.**
mynd: myned *be.* **(af)** to go, to
proceed. *gw. At. Berfau.*
mynedfa *e.b. ll.* **mynedfeydd**
entrance, passage.
mynedfeydd *gw.* **mynedfa.**
mynediad *e.g. ll.* **-au** admission,
access, entry; going. **mynediad am
ddim** admission free.
mynegai *e.g. ll.* **mynegeion** index,
concordance.
mynegeion *gw.* **mynegai.**
mynegi (i) *be.* **(mynegaf)** to tell, to
indicate.
mynnu *be.* **(mynnaf)** to will, to
insist, to wish, to obtain.
mynwent *e.b. ll.* **-ydd** graveyard,
churchyard, cemetery.
mynychu *be.* **(mynychaf)** to attend.
mynydd *e.g. ll.* **-oedd** mountain;
llosgfynydd volcano.
mynyddig: mynyddog *a.*
mountainous.
myrbryd *gw.* **byrbryd.**
myrddau *gw.* **bwrdd.**
myrfodd *gw.* **byrfodd.**
myrfoddau *gw.* **byrfodd.**
myrr *e.g.* myrrh.
mys *gw.* **bys.**
mysedd *gw.* **bys.**
mysiau *gw.* **bws.**
mystyrau *gw.* **mwstwr.**
mysys *gw.* **bws.**
myta *gw.* **bwyta.**
myth *e.g. ll.* **-au** myth.
mythynnod *gw.* **bwthyn.**
myw *gw.* **byw.**
mywyd *gw.* **bywyd.**
mywydeg *gw.* **bywydeg.**

n

na 1 *c.* (*followed by spirant mutation*)
nor, neither, than. 2 *ad.* no, not. *gw.*
da.
   gw. At. Treigladau.
nabod *gw.* **adnabod.**
nac 1 *c.* neither, nor. 2 *ad.* no, not.
nad *ad.* not.
nadansoddi *gw.* **dadansoddi.**
nadl *gw.* **dadl.**
nadlau *gw.* **dadlau.**
Nadolig *e.g. ll.* **-au** Christmas.
   Nadolig Llawen Merry Christmas.
nadredd: nadroedd *gw.* **neidr.**
naddo *ad.* no (*negative answer to
   questions using verbs in the past
   tense*) **Fuest ti yn y dre ddoe?
   Naddo** Were you in the town
   yesterday? No. **Ganodd e gyda'r
   côr? Naddo** Did he sing with the
   choir? No. **Fuoch chi yn Rhos
   erioed? Naddo** Were you ever in
   Rhos? No.
naddu *be.* (**naddaf**) to chip, to hew,
   to whittle.
naear *gw.* **daear.**
naeareg *gw.* **daeareg.**
naeargryn *gw.* **daeargryn.**
naearyddiaeth *gw.* **daearyddiaeth.**
nafad *gw.* **dafad.**
nag *c.* than.
nage *ad.* not so, no.
nagrau *gw.* **deigryn.**

nai *e.g. ll.* **neiaint** nephew.
naid *e.g. ll.* **neidiau** jump, leap,
   bound.
nail *gw.* **dalen, deilen.**
naill *rhag.* the one, either: **y naill
   neu'r llall** the one or the other; **naill
   ai Ebrill neu Fai** either April or
   May.
nain *e.b. ll.* **neiniau** grandmother
   (*N.W.*). *gw.* **mam-gu.**
naioni *gw.* **daioni.**
nal: nala *gw.* **dal.**
nalen *gw.* **dalen.**
nalgylch *gw.* **dalgylch.**
nallu *gw.* **dallu.**
nam *e.g. ll.* **-au** flaw, blemish, mark.
nameg *gw.* **dameg.**
namhegion *gw.* **dameg.**
namwain *gw.* **damwain.**
nanfon *gw.* **danfon.**
nangos *gw.* **dangos.**
nannedd *gw.* **dannedd.**
nannoedd *gw.* **dannoedd.**
nant *e.b. ll.* **nentydd** brook, stream.
   gw. **dant.**
narganfod *gw.* **darganfod.**
narlith *gw.* **darlith.**
narlithio *gw.* **darlithio.**
narlithiwr: narlithydd *gw.*
   darlithiwr.
narlun *gw.* **darlun.**
narlunio *gw.* **darlunio.**
narlledu *gw.* **darlledu.**
narllen *gw.* **darllen.**
narllenwr: narllenydd *gw.*
   darllenwr.
narn *gw.* **darn.**
natblygiad *gw.* **datblygiad.**
natblygu *gw.* **datblygu.**
natgan *gw.* **datgan.**
natganiad *gw.* **datganiad.**
natganoli *gw.* **datganoli.**
natguddio *gw.* **datguddio.**
natod *gw.* **datod.**
natrys *gw.* **datrys.**
natur *e.b.* nature; temper.
naturiol *a.* natural.
nathliad *gw.* **dathliad.**
nathlu *gw.* **dathlu.**
nau *gw.* **dau.**
naw 1 *a.* nine. 2 *e.g.* nine. **naw deg**

nawdd   **newydd**

ninety; **naw deg un** ninety one;
deunaw eighteen; **naw wfft ichi!**
blow you!
nawdd *e.g.* refuge; patronage,
support.
nawns *gw.* **dawns.**
nawnsio *gw.* **dawnsio.**
nawr *ad.* now. *gw.* **rŵan.**
naws *e.b. ll.* **-au** feeling, nature,
tingle, disposition, nuance. **naws y
gaeaf** feeling of winter; **naws oer**
cold feeling.
ne *gw.* **de.**
neall *gw.* **deall.**
neb *e.g.* anyone, no one. **Does neb
yma** There's no one here.
nechrau *gw.* **dechrau.**
nechreuad *gw.* **dechreuad.**
neddf *gw.* **deddf.**
neddfu *gw.* **deddfu.**
nef: nefoedd *e.b.* heaven. **Nefoedd
Wen!** Good heavens!
nefol: nefolaidd *a.* heavenly.
nefnydd *gw.* **defnydd.**
nefnyddio *gw.* **defnyddio.**
neffro *gw.* **deffro.**
neg: neng *gw.* **deg.**
negawd *gw.* **degawd.**
neges *e.b. ll.* **-au, -euon** message,
errand. **negesydd** messenger.
negyddol *a.* negative.
neiaint *gw.* **nai.**
neialog *gw.* **deialog.**
neidiau *gw.* **naid.**
neidio *be.* **(neidiaf)** to jump, to leap.
neidiwr *e.g. ll.* **neidwyr** jumper,
leaper.
neidr *e.b. ll.* **nadroedd, nadredd**
snake.
neidwyr *gw.* **neidiwr.**
neigryn *gw.* **deigryn.**
neilen *gw.* **deilen.**
neilliaid: neillion *gw.* **dall.**
neilltu *e.g.* one side. **o'r neilltu**
apart, aside.
neilltuo *be.* **(neilltuaf)** to reserve, to
set aside, to earmark.
neilltuol *a.* special, particular,
peculiar. **yn neilltuol o oer**
particularly cold.
neiniau *gw.* **nain.**

neintydd *gw.* **deintydd.**
neis *a.* nice.
neiseb *gw.* **deiseb.**
neithiwr *ad.* last night.
nelw *gw.* **delw.**
nen *e.b. ll.* **-nau, -noedd** ceiling;
heaven, sky.
nenfwd *e.g. ll.* **nenfydau** ceiling.
nentydd *gw.* **nant.**
nenu *gw.* **denu.**
nerbyn *gw.* **derbyn.**
nerbynneb *gw.* **derbynneb.**
nerbynnydd *w.* **derbynnydd.**
nerf *e.b. ll.* **-au** nerve.
nerfus *a.* nervous.
neri *gw.* **deri.**
nerth *e.g. ll.* **-oedd** strength, might,
power.
nerthoedd *gw.* **nerth.**
nerw *gw.* **derw.**
nerwen *gw.* **derwen.**
nes *c. & ardd.* until. *gw.* **agos.**
nesaf *a.* next. *gw.* **agos.**
nesáu (at) *be.* **(nesâf)** to approach,
to draw near.
nesed *gw.* **agos.**
nesg *gw.* **desg.**
netholiad *gw.* **detholiad.**
neu *c. (followed by soft mutation)* or.
bachgen neu ferch boy or girl;
eira neu law rain or snow. *(Note:
conjugated forms of verbs do* not
mutate after neu) **Rhedodd neu
cerddodd** He walked or ran; **Holais
neu gofynnais** I questioned or
asked.
neuadd *e.b. ll.* **-au** hall: **Neuadd
Gyhoeddus** Public Hall; **Neuadd
Les** Welfare Hall.
neuawd *gw.* **deuawd.**
neuddeg *gw.* **deuddeg.**
neuddegfed *gw.* **deuddegfed.**
neugain *gw.* **deugain.**
neunaw *gw.* **deunaw.**
neuoedd *gw.* **dau.**
newid 1 *be.* **(newidiaf)** to change, to
alter. 2 *e.g. ll.* **-iadau** change.
newin *gw.* **dewin.**
newis *gw.* **dewis.**
newydd 1 *a.* new. **newydd sbon**
brand new. 2 *e.g. ll.* **-ion** news.

newydd-ddyfodiad

nhelyneg

papur newydd newspaper. **Mae e
newydd ganu.** He has just sung.
newydd-ddyfodiad *e.g.ll.* **newydd-
ddyfodiaid** newcomer.
newyddiadurwr *e.g. ll.*
newyddiadurwyr journalist.
newyddion *gw.* **newydd.**
newyn *e.g.* famine, hunger.
nhabl *gw.* **tabl.**
nhabled *gw.* **tabled.**
nhacl *gw.* **tacl.**
nhaclo *gw.* **taclo.**
nhaclu *gw.* **taclu.**
nhaclwr *gw.* **taclwr.**
nhacsi *gw.* **tacsi.**
Nhachwedd *gw.* **Tachwedd.**
nhad *gw.* **tad.**
nhad-cu *gw.* **tad-cu.**
nhafarn *gw.* **tafarn.**
nhafarnwr *gw.* **tafarnwr.**
nhafell *gw.* **tafell.**
nhaflegryn *gw.* **taflegryn.**
nhaflen *gw.* **taflen.**
nhaflu *gw.* **taflu.**
nhafod *gw.* **tafod.**
nhafodiaieth *gw.* **tafodiaith.**
nhafol *gw.* **tafol.**
nhagfa *gw.* **tagfa.**
nhagu *w.* **tagu.**
nhangnefedd *gw.* **tangnefedd.**
nhai *gw.* **tŷ.**
nhaid *gw.* **taid.**
nhair *gw.* **tair.**
nhaith *gw.* **taith.**
nhâl *gw.* **tâl.**
nhalai *gw.* **talai.**
nhalaith *gw.* **talaith.**
nhalcen *gw.* **talcen.**
nhaleb *gw.* **taleb.**
nhalent *gw.* **talent.**
nhaloedd *gw.* **tâl.**
nhalu *gw.* **talu.**
nhalwr *gw.* **talwr.**
nhalwrn *gw.* **talwrn.**
nhamaid *gw.* **tamaid.**
nhameidiau *gw.* **tamaid.**
nhân *gw.* **tân.**
nhanau *gw.* **tân.**
nhancer *gw.* **tancer.**
nhanio *gw.* **tanio.**
nhannau *gw.* **tant.**

nhanseilio *gw.* **tanseilio.**
nhant *gw.* **tant.**
nhanwydd *gw.* **tanwydd.**
nhap *gw.* **tap.**
nhâp *gw.* **tâp.**
nhapiau *gw.* **tap, tâp.**
nharan *gw.* **taran.**
nharddiad *gw.* **tarddiad.**
nharged *gw.* **targed.**
nharian *gw.* **tarian.**
nhariannau *gw.* **tarian.**
nharo *gw.* **taro.**
nharw *gw.* **tarw.**
nhasg *gw.* **tasg.**
nhasgu *gw.* **tasgu.**
nhaten *gw.* **taten.**
nhato: nhatws *gw.* **taten.**
nhawelu *gw.* **tawelu.**
nhawelwch *gw.* **tawelwch.**
nhawelydd *gw.* **tawelydd.**
nhawelyn *gw.* **tawelyn.**
nhe *gw.* **te.**
nhebot *gw.* **tebot.**
nhebygrwydd *gw.* **tebygrwydd.**
nhecell *gw.* **tecell.**
nhechneg *gw.* **techneg.**
nhechnegwr *gw.* **technegwr.**
nhechnoleg *gw.* **technoleg.**
nhegan *gw.* **tegan.**
nhegell *gw.* **tecell.**
nhegwch *gw.* **tegwch.**
nhei *gw.* **tei.**
nheiar *gw.* **teiar.**
nheidiau *gw.* **taid.**
nheigr *gw.* **teigr.**
nheiliwr *gw.* **teiliwr.**
nheilsen *gw.* **teilsen.**
nheilwres *gw.* **teilwres.**
nheilyngdod *gw.* **teilyngdod.**
nheimlad *w.* **teimlad.**
nheimlo *gw.* **teimlo.**
nheipiadur *gw.* **teipiadur.**
nheisen *gw.* **teisen.**
nheitl *gw.* **teitl.**
nheithiau *gw.* **taith.**
nheithio *gw.* **teithio.**
nheithiwr *gw.* **teithiwr.**
nhelediad *gw.* **telediad.**
nheledu *gw.* **teledu.**
nheleffon *gw.* **teleffon.**
nhelyn *gw.* **telyn.**

nhelyneg *gw.* telyneg.
nhelynor *gw.* telynor.
nhelynores *gw.* telynores.
nhelynorion *gw.* telynor.
nheml *gw.* teml.
nherfyn *gw.* terfyn.
nherfysg *gw.* terfysg.
nherfysgaeth *gw.* terfysgaeth.
nherfysgwr *gw.* terfysgwr.
nherm *gw.* term.
nhes *gw.* tes.
nhestun *gw.* testun.
nheulu *gw.* teulu.
nheyrnas *gw.* teyrnas.
nhiced *gw.* ticed.
nhîm *gw.* tîm.
nhip *gw.* tip.
nhipyn *gw.* tipyn.
nhir *gw.* tir.
nhirlun *gw.* tirlun.
nhiroedd *gw.* tir.
nhiwtor *gw.* tiwtor.
nhlodi *gw.* tlodi.
nhlws *gw.* tlws.
nhlysau *gw.* tlws.
nho *gw.* to.
nhocyn *gw.* tocyn.
nhocynnwr *gw.* tocynnwr.
nhoddi *gw.* toddi.
nhoes *gw.* toes.
nhoiled *gw.* toiled.
nholc *gw.* tolc.
nholl *gw.* toll.
nhon *gw.* ton.
nhôn *gw.* tôn.
nhonau *gw.* tôn.
nhonfedd *gw.* tonfedd.
nhonnau *gw.* ton.
nhorch *gw.* torch.
nhorf *gw.* torf.
nhorfeydd *gw.* torf.
nhoriad *gw.* toriad.
nhorri *gw.* torri.
nhors *gw.* tors.
nhorth *gw.* torth.
nhosau *gw.* tosyn.
nhost *gw.* tost.
nhostrwydd *gw.* tostrwydd.
nhosyn *gw.* tosyn.
nhrachwant *gw.* trachwant.
nhraddodiad *gw.* traddodiad.

nhraed *gw.* troed.
nhraeth *gw.* traeth.
nhraethau *gw.* traeth.
nhraethawd *gw.* traethawd.
nhrafnidiaeth *gw.* trafnidiaeth.
nhrafod *gw.* trafod.
nhrafferth *gw.* trafferth.
nhrafferthu *gw.* trafferthu.
nhraffordd *gw.* traffordd.
nhraffyrdd *gw.* traffordd.
nhrai *gw.* trai.
nhrais *gw.* trais.
nhrallod *gw.* trallod.
nhrallwysiad *gw.* trallwysiad.
nhrap *gw.* trap.
nhraul *gw.* traul.
nhrawsblannu *gw.* trawsblannu.
nhrawst *gw.* trawst.
nhrechu *gw.* trechu.
nhref: nhre *gw.* tref.
nhrefn *gw.* trefn.
nhrefnu *gw.* trefnu.
nhrefnydd *gw.* trefnydd.
nhrefydd *gw.* tref.
nhreial *gw.* treial.
nhreiglad *gw.* treiglad.
nhreiglo *gw.* treiglo.
nhreisio *gw.* treisio.
nhrên *gw.* trên.
nhrenau *gw.* trên.
nhreth *gw.* treth.
nhrethdalwr *gw.* trethdalwr.
nhrethu *gw.* trethu.
nhreuliau *gw.* traul.
nhreulio *gw.* treulio.
nhri *gw.* tri.
nhriawd *gw.* triawd.
nhric *gw.* tric.
nhrigain *gw.* trigain.
nhrigfan *gw.* trigfan.
nhrigolion *gw.* trigolion.
nhrin *gw.* trin.
nhrindod *gw.* trindod.
nhrioedd *gw.* trioedd.
nhriongl *gw.* triongl.
nhristwch *gw.* tristwch.
nhro *gw.* tro.
nhrochi *gw.* trochi.
nhroeau *gw.* tro.
nhroed *gw.* troed.
nhroedfedd *gw.* troedfedd.

nhröedigaeth   **nifetha**

nhroedffordd *gw.* troedffordd.
nhröedigaeth *gw.* tröedigaeth.
nhroedio *gw.* troedio.
nhroeon *gw.* tro.
nhrogylch *gw.* trogylch.
nhroi *gw.* troi.
nhrosedd *gw.* trosedd.
nhroseddwr *gw.* troseddwr.
nhrosgais *gw.* trosgais.
nhrosglwyddo *gw.* trosglwyddo.
nhrosiad *gw.* trosiad.
nhroswr *gw.* troswr.
nhrothwy *gw.* trothwy.
nhrowsus *gw.* trowsus.
nhruan *gw.* truan.
nhrueni *gw.* trueni.
nhrugaredd *gw.* trugaredd.
nhrwbl *gw.* trwbl.
nhrwser *gw.* trwser.
nhrwsiwr *gw.* trwsiwr.
nhrwydded *gw.* trwydded.
nhrwyn *gw.* trwyn.
nhrychineb *gw.* trychineb.
nhrydan *gw.* trydan.
nhrydanwr *gw.* trydanwr.
nhrydedd *gw.* trydedd.
nhrydydd *gw.* trydydd.
nhrysor *gw.* trysor.
nhrysorfa *gw.* trysorfa.
nhrysori *gw.* trysori.
nhrysorydd *gw.* trysorydd.
nhrywydd *gw.* trywydd.
nhudalen *gw.* tudalen.
nhueddiad *gw.* tueddiad.
nhun *gw.* tun.
nhunnell *gw.* tunnell.
nhw: hwy *rhag.* they, them. **Ble maen nhw?** Where are they? **Gwelodd nhw** He/she saw them.
nhwlc *gw.* twlc.
nhwll *gw.* twll.
nhwmpath *gw.* twmpath.
nhwndis *gw.* twndis.
nhwnel *gw.* twnel.
nhwpsyn *gw.* twpsyn.
nhŵr *gw.* tŵr.
nhwr *gw.* twr.
nhwrci *gw.* twrci.
nhwristiaeth *gw.* twristiaeth.
nhwrw *gw.* twrw.
nhwyll *gw.* twyll.

nhwyllo *gw.* twyllo.
nhwymo *gw.* twymo.
nhwymyn *gw.* twymyn.
nhŷ *gw.* tŷ.
nhybied: nhybio *gw.* tybied.
nhyddyn *gw.* tyddyn.
nhyddynnwr *gw.* tyddynnwr.
nhyfiant *gw.* tyfiant.
nhyfu *gw.* tyfu.
nhynged *gw.* tynged.
nhyle *gw.* tyle.
nhylwyth *gw.* tylwyth.
nhyllau *gw.* twll.
nhyllu *gw.* tyllu.
nhylluan *gw.* tylluan.
nhymer *gw.* tymer.
nhymestl *gw.* tymestl.
nhymheredd *gw.* tymheredd.
nhymhorau *gw.* tymor.
nhymor *gw.* tymor.
nhyner *gw.* tyner.
nhynerwch *gw.* tynerwch.
nhynnu *gw.* tynnu.
nhyrfa *gw.* tyrfa.
nhyst *gw.* tyst.
nhystiolaeth *gw.* tystiolaeth.
nhystysgrif *gw.* tystysgrif.
nhywel *gw.* tywel.
nhywod *gw.* tywod.
nhywydd *gw.* tywydd.
nhywyllu *gw.* tywyllu.
nhywyllwch *gw.* tywyllwch.
nhywys *gw.* tywys.
nhywysog *gw.* tywysog.
nhywysoges *gw.* tywysoges.
ni *rhag.* we, us.
ni: nid *ad.* not.
niacon *gw.* diacon.
niafol *gw.* diafol.
nial *gw.* dial.
nianc *gw.* dianc.
niawl *gw.* diawl.
niawliaid *gw.* diafol, diawl.
niben *gw.* diben.
nid *gw.* ni.
niddordeb *gw.* diddordeb.
nieithryn *gw.* dieithryn.
nifer (o) *e.g.b. ll.* -oedd, -i number, quantity. **nifer o fechgyn** a number of boys.
niferyn *w.* diferyn.

nifetha *gw.* **difetha.**
nifyrru *gw.* **difyrru.**
niffiniad *gw.* **diffiniad.**
niffinio *gw.* **diffinio.**
niffodd *gw.* **diffodd.**
niffyg *gw.* **diffyg.**
nigon *gw.* **digon.**
nigonedd *gw.* **digonedd.**
nigwyddiad *gw.* **digwyddiad.**
nihareb *gw.* **dihareb.**
niheintydd *gw.* **diheintydd.**
nihuno *gw.* **dihuno.**
nileu *gw.* **dileu.**
nilyn *gw.* **dilyn.**
nillad *gw.* **dilledyn.**
nilledyn *gw.* **dilledyn.**
nim *gw.* **dim.**
ninas *gw.* **dinas.**
ninasyddion *gw.* **dinesydd.**
ninesydd *gw.* **dinesydd.**
ninistrio *gw.* **dinistrio.**
ninnau *rhag.* we also.
niod *gw.* **diod.**
nioddef *gw.* **dioddef.**
niogi *gw.* **diogi.**
niogyn *gw.* **diogyn.**
niolch *gw.* **diolch.**
niolchgarwch *gw.* **diolchgarwch.**
nirgelwch *gw.* **dirgelwch.**
nirprwy *gw.* **dirprwy.**
nirprwyaeth *gw.* **dirprwyaeth.**
nirwy *gw.* **dirwy.**
nis *ad.* not . . . him/her/it/them. **nis gwelais** I did not see him/etc.
nisg *gw.* **disg.**
nisgrifiad *gw.* **disgrifiad.**
nisgrifio *gw.* **disgrifio.**
nisgwyl *gw.* **disgwyl.**
nisgybl *gw.* **disgybl.**
nisgyblaeth *gw.* **disgyblaeth.**
nisgyn *gw.* **disgyn.**
nistawrwydd *gw.* **distawrwydd.**
nistewi *gw.* **distewi.**
niswyddo *gw.* **diswyddo.**
nith *e.b. ll.* **-oedd** niece.
niwallu *gw.* **diwallu.**
niwed *e.g. ll.* **niweidiau** harm, damage, injury. **gwneud niwed i** to harm.
niwedd *gw.* **diwedd.**
niweddglo *gw.* **diweddglo.**

niweidiau *gw.* **niwed.**
niwl *e.g. ll.* **-oedd** mist, haze.
niwl trwchus fog.
niwlog *a.* misty, foggy, hazy.
niwrnod *gw.* **diwrnod.**
niwydiant *gw.* **diwydiant.**
niwygiad *gw.* **diwygiad.**
niwygio *gw.* **diwygio.**
niwylliant *gw.* **diwylliant.**
noc *gw.* **doc.**
noctor *gw.* **doctor.**
nod *e.g.b. ll.* **-au, -ion** note; mark, token, aim.
nodau *gw.* **nod, nodyn.**
nodedig *a.* remarkable, noted, appointed, specified.
nodi *be.* (**nodaf**) to note, to mark, to appoint, to state. *gw.* **dodi.**
nodrefn *gw.* **dodrefnyn.**
nodrefnyn *gw.* **dodrefnyn.**
nodwedd *e.b. ll.* **-ion** character, feature, characteristic. **rhaglen nodwedd** feature programme.
nodweddiadol *a.* characteristic, typical.
nodwydd *e.b. ll.* **-au** needle.
nodyn *e.g. ll.* **nodau** note.
noddwr *e.g. ll.* **noddwyr** protector, patron.
noe *gw.* **doe.**
noeth *a.* naked, bare, exposed, raw, sheer.
noethineb *gw.* **doethineb.**
nofel *e.b. ll.* **-au** novel.
nofelwr: nofelydd *e.g. ll.* **nofelwyr** novelist.
nofiad *e.g.* a swim.
nofio *be.* (**nofiaf**) to swim.
nogfen *gw.* **dogfen.**
nol *gw.* **dol.**
nôl: hôl *be.* (**nolaf: holaf**) to fetch; *gw.* **dôl.**
nolen *gw.* **dolen.**
nolur *gw.* **dolur.**
Norman *e.g. ll.* **-iaid** Norman. **castell Normanaidd** Norman castle.
nos *e.b. ll.* **-au** night. **nos da** good night; **nos Sul** Sunday night; **nos yfory** tomorrow night.
nosbarth *gw.* **dosbarth.**

nosweithiau   **nyweddïo**

noson: noswaith *e.b. ll.*
  nosweithiau evening: **noswaith
  dda** good evening; **noson lawen**
  merry evening; **am ddwy noson** for
  two evenings.
nosweithiau *gw.* **noson.**
nraen: nraenen *gw.* **draen.**
nraenog *gw.* **draenog.**
nraig *gw.* **draig.**
nrain *gw.* **draen.**
nrama *gw.* **drama.**
nramodwr *gw.* **dramodwr.**
nramodydd *gw.* **dramodwr.**
nreigiau *gw.* **draig.**
nreser: nresel *gw.* **dreser.**
nrewdod *gw.* **drewdod.**
nringwr *gw.* **dringwr.**
nrudwy *gw.* **drudwy.**
nrwg *gw.* **drwg.**
nrwm *gw.* **drwm.**
nrws *gw.* **drws.**
nrych *gw.* **drych.**
nrychiolaeth *gw.* **drychiolaeth.**
nrygioni *gw.* **drygioni.**
nryll *gw.* **dryll.**
nryllau *gw.* **dryll.**
nrysau *gw.* **drws.**
nrysu *gw.* **drysu.**
nryw *gw.* **dryw.**
null *gw.* **dull.**
nuo *gw.* **duo.**
nur *gw.* **dur.**
nuw *gw.* **duw.**
nuwies *gw.* **duwies.**
nwfr *gw.* **dŵr.**
nŵr *gw.* **dŵr.**
nwrn *gw.* **dwrn.**
nwsin *gw.* **dwsin.**
nwy *e.g. ll.* **-on, -au** gas. **Nwy Môr y
  Gogledd** North Sea gas. *gw.* **dwy.**

nwyau *gw.* **nwy.**
nwydd *e.g. ll.* **-au** material, article.
  nwyddau goods (*note: only the
  plural form is used*).
nwyon *gw.* **nwy.**
nwyieithrwydd *gw.* **dwyieithrwydd.**
nwylo *gw.* **dwylo.**
nwyn *gw.* **dwyn.**
nwyrain *gw.* **dwyrain.**
nychmygion *gw.* **dychymyg.**
nychmygu *gw.* **dychmygu.**
nychymyg *gw.* **dychymyg.**
nydd *gw.* **dydd.**
nyddiad *gw.* **dyddiad.**
nyfarniad *gw.* **dyfarniad.**
nyfarnu *gw.* **dyfarnu.**
nyfarnwr *gw.* **dyfarnwr.**
nyfnder *gw.* **dyfnder.**
nyfodol *gw.* **dyfodol.**
nyfroedd *gw.* **dŵr.**
nyfyniad *gw.* **dyfyniad.**
nyffryn *gw.* **dyffryn.**
nylanwad *gw.* **dylanwad.**
nyled *gw.* **dyled.**
nyletswydd *gw.* **dyletswydd.**
nymuniad *gw.* **dymuniad.**
nyn *gw.* **dyn.**
nynes *gw.* **dynes.**
nyni *rhag.* we, us.
nyrnaid *gw.* **dyrnaid.**
nyrnau *gw.* **dwrn.**
nyrs *e.g.b. ll.* **-ys** nurse.
nyrsio *be.* **(nyrsiaf)** to nurse.
nysgl *gw.* **dysgl.**
nysgu *gw.* **dysgu.**
nysgwr *gw.* **dysgwr.**
nyth *e.b. ll.* **-od** nest. **nyth y dryw**
  the wren's nest.
nywediad *gw.* **dywediad.**
nyweddïad *gw.* **dyweddïad.**

nyweddïo *gw.* **dyweddïo.**
o *ardd.* (*followed by soft mutation*)
(*personal forms:* **ohono, ohonot,
ohono/ohoni, ohonon, ohonoch,
ohonyn**) from, of, out of. **o
amgylch** around; **o chwith**
wrongly, the wrong way about; **o
flaen** before, ahead of; **o gwbl** at
all; **o gwmpas** around, round
about; **o hyd** still; **o'r blaen**
beforehand, earlier, previously; **o'r
diwedd** at last; **o'r gloch** o'clock;
o'r gorau very well. *gw. At.
Arddodiaid. gw.* **ef.**
obaith *gw.* **gobaith.**
obeithio *gw.* **gobeithio.**
obeithion *gw.* **gobaith.**
obennydd *gw.* **gobennydd.**
oblegid *c. & ardd.* because, for.
ochenaid *e.b. ll.* **ocheneidiau** sigh.
ochneidio *be.* (**ochneidiaf**) to sigh,
to groan.
ochr *e.b. ll.* **-au** side. **ochr yn ochr**
side by side; **wrth ochr** beside; **yr
ochr draw i** (on) the other side to.
od *a.* odd, bizarre; remarkable.
odidog *gw.* **godidog.**
odl *e.b. ll.* **-au** rhyme; ode, song.
odli *be.* (**odlaf**) to rhyme.
odre *gw.* **godre.**
odro *gw.* **godro.**
oddef *gw.* **goddef.**
oddefgar *w.* **goddefgar.**

oddeutu *ardd. & ad.* about, around.
oddi *ardd.* out of, from. **oddi allan**
outside; **oddi ar** from off; since;
oddieithr except, unless; **oddi
mewn** within; **oddi wrth** from;
oddi yma from here.
oddrych *gw.* **goddrych.**
oed *e.g. ll.* **-au** age; time. **blwydd
oed** year old; **saith oed** seven
years of age; **gwneud oed â** to
arrange a tryst, to make a date.
oedfa *e.b. ll.* **-on, oedfeuon**
service, meeting.
oedi *be.* (**oedaf**) to delay, to
postpone; to linger.
oedolion *gw.* **oedolyn.**
oedolyn *e.g. ll.* **oedolion** adult.
oedran *e.g. ll.* **-nau** age.
oedrannus *a.* aged, elderly.
oedd *bf.* was, were. *gw.* **bod.**
oen *e.g. ll.* **ŵyn** lamb.
oer *a.* cold, chill, chilly; frigid.
oerfel *e.g.* cold.
oergell *e.b. ll.* **-oedd** refrigerator.
oeri *be.* (**oeraf**) to cool, to become
cold.
oes 1 *e.b. ll.* **-au, -oedd** age,
lifetime. **ers oes** from an age; **o
oes i oes** from age to age; **yn oes
oesoedd** for ever and ever. **2** *bf.* is,
are. *gw.* **bod.** *gw. At. Berfau –
Affirmative & Negative answers.*
of *gw.* **gof.**
ofal *w.* **gofal.**
ofalu *gw.* **gofalu.**
ofalus *gw.* **gofalus.**
ofalwr *gw.* **gofalwr.**
ofer *a.* vain; prodigal; waste. **ymgais
ofer** a vain attempt.
oferedd *e.g.* vanity, dissipation,
frivolity.
ofergoel *e.b. ll.* **-ion** superstition.
ofergoeledd: ofergoeliaeth *e.g.*
superstition.
ofergoelus *a.* superstitious.
ofid *gw.* **gofid.**
ofidio *gw.* **gofidio.**
ofn *e.g. ll.* **-au** fear, terror, dread.
Mae ofn arno fe He is afraid; **Mae
ofn llygod arna i** I am afraid of
mice.

ofnadwy   **organ**

ofnadwy *a.* awful, dreadful,
horrendous.
ofnau *gw.* **ofn.**
ofni *be.* **(ofnaf)** to fear, to dread.
ofnus *a.* timid, nervous.
ofod *gw.* **gofod.**
ofodwr *gw.* **gofodwr.**
ofyn *gw.* **gofyn.**
offeiriad *e.g. ll.* **offeiriaid** priest,
parson.
offer *gw.* **offeryn.**
offeren *e.b.* mass (*Roman Catholic*).
offeryn *e.g. ll.* **-nau, offer**
instrument, tool, apparatus,
equipment. **offeryn cerdd** musical
instrument; **offeryn chwyth** wind
instrument; **offeryn llinynnol**
stringed instrument; **offerynnau
taro** percussion instruments.
offerynnol *a.* instrumental. **darn
offerynnol** instrumental piece (*of
music*).
ogledd *gw.* **gogledd.**
ogleddol *gw.* **gogleddol.**
ogleddwr *gw.* **gogleddwr.**
ogleisio *gw.* **gogleisio.**
ogof *e.b. ll.* **-âu, -eydd** cave,
cavern; den.
ogoniant *gw.* **gogoniant.**
ogylch *ardd.* about.
ogystal *gw.* **gogystal.**
ongl *e.b. ll.* **-au** angle. **ongl sgwâr**
right angle; **triongl** triangle.
onglog *a.* angular.
oherwydd *c. & ardd.* because, for.
ohirio *gw.* **gohirio.**
ôl 1 *e.g. ll.* **olion** mark, print; track;
trace. **ôl bysedd** finger-marks; **ôl
traed** footprints. **2** *a.* back, hind:
ar ôl after; **pen ôl** behind, bottom
(buttocks); **yn ôl** according to; ago;
y tu ôl behind.
olaf *a.* last (*the very last*). *gw.* **hwyr.**
olau *gw.* **golau.**
olchi *gw.* **golchi.**
oleudy *gw.* **goleudy.**
oleuni *gw.* **goleuni.**
oleuo *gw.* **goleuo.**
olew *e.g. ll.* **-au** oil. **maes olew**
oilfield.
olion *gw.* **ôl.**

ôl-nodiad *e.g. ll.* **ôl-nodiadau**
postscript.
ôl-ofal *e.g. ll.* **ôl-ofalon** after-care.
olrhain *be.* **(olrheiniaf)** to trace, to
track.
olud *gw.* **golud.**
olwg *gw.* **golwg.**
olwr *e.g. ll.* **olwyr** back (*rugby,
etc.*).
olwyn *e.b. ll.* **-ion** wheel. **cadair
olwyn/olwynion** wheelchair;
olwyn fesur trundle wheel.
olwyr *gw.* **olwr.**
olygfa *gw.* **golygfa.**
olygon *gw.* **golwg.**
olygu *gw.* **golygu.**
oll *ad.* all, wholly; ever, at all.
ollwng *gw.* **gollwng.**
ond 1 *c.* but, only. **2** *ardd.* except;
save; but.
onest *gw.* **gonest.**
oni: onid 1 *ad.* not? is it not? **2** *c.* if
not, unless. **3** *ardd.* except; save;
but: **onid e?** otherwise; else; is it
not?
onibai (am) *c.* were it not (for).
onid *gw.* **oni.**
onnen *e.b. ll.* **ynn** ash-tree.
opera *e.b. ll.* **operâu** opera. **opera
ddigri** comic opera; **opera
fawreddog** grand opera; **opera
ysgafn** light opera; **opera sebon**
soap opera.
optegwr: optegydd *e.g. ll.*
optegwyr optician.
orau *gw.* **da.**
orchfygu *gw.* **gorchfygu.**
orchymyn *gw.* **gorchymyn.**
oren *e.g. ll.* **-au** orange.
orfod *gw.* **gorfod.**
orfodaeth *gw.* **gorfodaeth.**
orfodi *gw.* **gorfodi.**
orfodol *gw.* **gorfodol.**
orfoleddus *gw.* **gorfoleddus.**
orffen *gw.* **gorffen.**
Orffennaf *gw.* **Gorffennaf.**
orffennol *gw.* **gorffennol.**
orffwys *gw.* **gorffwys.**
orffwyso *gw.* **gorffwyso.**
organ *e.g.b. ll.* **-au** organ. **organ
geg** mouth-organ.

organig   **owns**

organig *a.* organic.
organydd *e.g. ll.* **-ion** organist.
oriau *gw.* **awr.**
oriel *e.b. ll.* **-au** gallery.
orlawn *gw.* **gorlawn.**
orllewin *gw.* **gorllewin.**
ormod *gw.* **gormod.**
ornest *e.b. ll.* **-au** contest, combat,
duel, match. *gw.* **gornest.**
orsaf *gw.* **gorsaf.**
orsedd *gw.* **gorsedd.**
oruchaf *gw.* **goruchaf.**
oruwchnaturiol *gw.*
goruwchnaturiol.
orwedd *gw.* **gorwedd.**

orwel *gw.* **gorwel.**
orymdaith *gw.* **gorymdaith.**
os *c.* if (*definite not conjecture*). **Os
daw Tom, dof i hefyd** If Tom
comes, I will come too.
osgoi *be.* **(osgoaf)** to avoid, to
swerve, to evade; to shirk. **ffordd-
osgoi** bypass.
osod *gw.* **gosod.**
ostwng *gw.* **gostwng.**
ostyngedig *gw.* **gostyngedig.**
ostyngiad *gw.* **gostyngiad.**
owns *e.b. ll.* **-ys** ounce; **dwy owns**
two ounces.

cease, to lack.
pam: paham: pa *ad.* why?
pamffled *e.g. ll.* **-i, -au** pamphlet.
pamffledyn *e.g.* pamphlet.
pan *c.* when.
panasen *e.b. ll.* **pannas** parsnip.
panel *e.g. ll.* **-i** panel.
pannas *gw.* **panasen.**
pant *e.g. ll.* **-au, -iau** valley, hollow; dent. *following Soft Mutation after* **i > i bant, bant** *ad.* away, off. **Mae e bant** He's away; **o bant** from away; **o bant i bentan** everywhere, from pillar to post.
papur *e.g. ll.* **-au** paper. **papur newydd** newspaper; **papur deg punt** ten-pound note; **papur wal** wallpaper.
papuro *be.* **(papuraf)** to paper.
pâr *e.g. ll.* **parau** pair.
para (i): parhau (i) *be.* **(paraf)** to continue (to).
paradwys *e.b. ll.* **-au** paradise.
paragraff *e.g. ll.* **-au** paragraph.
paratoi *be.* **(paratoaf)** to prepare to. **paratoi i fynd** to prepare to go.
parau *gw.* **pâr.**
parc *e.g. ll.* **-au, -iau** park; field *(S.W.W.).*
parch *e.g.* respect. **dillad parch** Sunday best, best clothes *(lit. the clothes of respect).*
parchedig *a. ll.* **-ion** *(often abbreviated to* **y parchg**) reverend, reverent. **Y Parchedig Ifan Rhys** Reverend Ifan Rhys.
parchu *be.* **(parchaf)** to respect.
parchus *be.* respectable, respectful.
pardwn *e.g. ll.* **pardynau** pardon.
parhad *e.g.* continuation.
parhau *gw.* **para.**
parod *a.* ready, willing, prepared. **yn barod** already; **arian parod** ready cash.
parsel *e.g. ll.* **-au, -i** parcel.
parti *e.g. ll.* **-ion** party.
Pasg *e.g.* Easter. **Dydd Llun y Pasg** Easter Monday; **wy Pasg** Easter egg; **y Pasg** Easter.
pasiannau *gw.* **pasiant.**

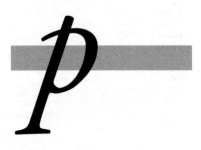

pa *a.* Which? What? **(Pa) beth?** What (thing)? **Pa bryd? Pryd?** When? **Pa fodd?** How? **P'un?** Which one? *gw.* **pam.**
Pab *e.g. ll.* **-au** Pope.
pabell *e.b. ll.* **pebyll** tent, pavilion.
pabi *e.b. ll.* **pabïau** poppy.
pabydd *e.g. ll.* **-ion** papist.
pac *e.g. ll.* **-au, -iau** pack, bundle.
paced *e.g. ll.* **-i** packet, package.
paciau *gw.* **pac.**
pacio *be.* **(paciaf)** to pack.
padell *e.b. ll.* **-i** bowl, pan.
pader *e.g. ll.* **-au** the Lord's prayer, prayers. **dweud pader/dysgu pader i berson** *'to teach your grandmother to suck eggs'.*
paent *e.g. ll.* **-iau** paint.
pafiliwn *e.g.* pavilion.
pafin *e.g. ll.* **-au** pavement *(S.W).*
pagan *e.g.* **-iaid** pagan.
paham *gw.* **pam.**
pais *e.b. ll.* **peisiau** petticoat.
pâl 1 *e.b. ll.* **palau** spade *(S.W.).* **2** *e.g. ll.* **palod** puffin.
palas *e.g. ll.* **-au, -oedd** palace.
palau *gw.* **pâl.**
palmant *e.g. ll.* **-au** pavement *(N.W.).*
palod *gw.* **pâl.**
palu *be.* **(palaf)** to dig over *(not down).*
pallu *be.* **(pallaf)** to refuse, to fail, to

pasiant   **penodi**

pasiant *e.g. ll.* **pasiannau** pageant.
patrwm *e.g. ll.* **patrymau** pattern.
patrwn *e.g. ll.* **patrynau** pattern.
patrymau *gw.* **patrwm.**
patrynau *gw.* **patrwn.**
pawb *e.g.* everybody, all.
pawen *e.b. ll.* **-nau** paw.
pe *c. if.* **Pe bawn i yno** If I were
there.
pebyll *gw.* **pabell.**
pecyn *e.g. ll.* **-nau** package, packet.
pechadur *e.g. ll.* **-iaid** sinner.
pechod *e.g. ll.* **-au** sin: **Dyna
bechod!** What a pity!
pechu *be.* **(pechaf)** to sin; **pechu
yn erbyn** to sin against.
pedair *eb. & a.b. (adjective placed
before feminine noun)* four. **pedair
merch** four girls; **pedair cadair**
four chairs. *gw.* **pedwar.**
pedol *e.b. ll.* **-au** horseshoe.
pedwar *e.g. ll. & a.g.* four. *gw.*
pedair.
pedwaredd *a.b.* fourth. **y
bedwaredd ferch** the fourth girl.
pedwerydd *a.g.* fourth. **y
pedwerydd bachgen** the fourth
boy.
peg *e.g. ll.* **-iau** peg.
pegwn *e.g. ll.* **pegynau** pole.
Pegwn y De South Pole; **Pegwn y
Gogledd** North Pole.
pegynau *gw.* **pegwn.**
peidio (â) *be.* **(peidiaf)** to cease, to
stop. **Paid (â) siarad** Don't talk.
peilot *e.g. ll.* **-iaid** pilot.
peint *e.g. ll.* **-iau** pint. **peint a
hanner** a pint and a half.
peintio *be.* **(peintiaf)** to paint.
peintiwr *e.g. ll.* **peintwyr** painter.
peiriannau *gw.* **peiriant.**
peiriannydd: peiriannwr *e.g. ll.*
peirianwyr engineer.
peiriant *e.g. ll.* **peiriannau** engine,
machine. **peiriant golchi** washing
machine; **peiriant car** car engine;
peiriant gwnïo sewing machine.
peisiau *gw.* **pais.**
pêl *e.b. ll.* **peli, pelau** ball.
pêl-droed football; **pêl rygbi**
rugby ball.

pelydr *e.g. ll.* **-au** ray, beam.
pelydr X X ray.
pell *a.* far. *gw. At. Ansoddeiriau.*
pellach *gw.* **pell.**
pellaf *gw.* **pell.**
pelled *gw.* **pell.**
pellter *e.g. ll.* **-au, -oedd** distance.
yn y pellter in the distance. **o
bellter** from a distance.
pen 1 *e.g. ll.* **-nau** head, top, end,
mouth. **ar ben** on top of, ended; **ar
ei phen ei hun** by herself; **pen y
bryn** top of the hill; **pen ôl** behind,
bottom (buttocks). 2 *a.* chief,
supreme.
penaethiaid *gw.* **pennaeth.**
penawdau *gw.* **pennawd.**
pen-blwydd *e.g. ll.* **-i** birthday.
pencadlys *e.g. ll.* **-oedd**
headquarters.
pencampwr *e.g. ll.* **pencampwyr**
champion.
pendant *a.* positive, definite,
emphatic.
penderfyniad *e.g. ll.* **-au** resolution,
determination.
penderfynol *a.* resolute, determined.
yn benderfynol o determined to.
penderfynu *be.* **(penderfynaf)** to
decide, to resolve: **Fe
benderfynodd fynd** He decided to
go.
penelin *e.g.b. ll.* **-oedd** elbow.
penfoel *a.* bald-headed.
pen-glin: pen-lin *e.b. ll.*
pengliniau: penliniau knee.
penigamp *a.* splendid, excellent.
penillion *gw.* **pennill.**
pen-lin *gw.* **pen-glin.**
penlinio *be.* **(penliniaf)** to kneel.
pennaeth *e.g. ll.* **penaethiaid** chief.
pennaf *a.* principal, chief.
pennau *gw.* **pen.**
pennawd *e.g. ll.* **penawdau**
heading; headline; **penawdau'r
newyddion** the news headlines.
pennill *e.g. ll.* **penillion** stanza,
verse.
pennod *e.b. ll.* **penodau** chapter.
penodau *gw.* **pennod.**
penodi *be.* **(penodaf)** to appoint.

penodiad   **pînafal**

penodiad *e.g. ll.* **-au** appointment.
penrhyn *e.g. ll.* **-au** promontory,
headland.
pensaer *e.g. ll.* **penseiri** architect.
penseiri *gw.* **pensaer.**
pensil *e.g. ll.* **-iau** pencil.
pensiwn *e.g. ll.* **pensiynau**
pension.
pensiynau *gw.* **pensiwn.**
pensiynwr *e.g. ll.* **pensiynwyr**
pensioner.
penteulu *e.g. ll.* **-oedd** head of
family.
pentref *e.g. ll.* **-i** village.
pentwr *e.g. ll.* **pentyrrau** heap,
mass, pile.
pentyrrau *gw.* **pentwr.**
penwythnos *e.g. ll.* **-au** weekend.
pêr *a.* sweet *(of sound). gw.* **peren.**
perlysiau *e.ll.* herbs.
perchen: perchennog *e.g. ll.*
perchenogion owner, proprietor.
Roedd e'n berchen ar dŷ He was
a house owner.
perchenogaeth *e.b.* ownership.
perchenogi *be.* to own.
peren *e.b. ll.* **pêr** pear.
pererin *e.g. ll.* **-ion** pilgrim.
perfedd *e.g. ll.* **-ion** entrails, guts,
middle. **perfedd gwlad** heart of
countryside; **perfedd nos** dead of
night.
perffaith *a.* perfect.
perffeithio *be.* **(perffeithiaf)** to
perfect.
peri (i) *be.* **(peraf)** to cause.
perl *e.g. ll.* **-au** pearl.
perllan *e.b. ll.* **-nau** orchard.
persawr *e.g. ll.* **-au** perfume,
fragrance.
persli *e.g.* parsley.
person 1 *e.g. ll.* **-au** person.
2 *e.g. ll.* **-iaid** parson.
personol *a.* personal.
personoliaeth *e.b. ll.* **-au**
personality.
pert *a.* pretty.
perth *e.b. ll.* **-i** bush; hedge *(S.W.).*
perthnasau *gw.* **perthynas.**
perthnasol *a.* relevant.
perthyn (i) *be.* **(perthynaf)** to

belong, to be related.
perthynas *e.b.g. ll.* **perthnasau**
relation; relationship.
perygl *e.g. ll.* **peryglon** danger.
peryglus *a.* dangerous.
peswch 1 *be.* **(pesychaf)** to cough.
2 *e.g.* a cough.
pesychiad *e.g. ll.* **-au** cough.
petai *bf.* if it were *(conjecture).* **pe
bai** if; **pe basai** if.
petrol *e.g. ll.* **-au** petrol. **petrol di-
blwm** unleaded petrol.
peth *e.g. ll.* **-au** thing, some, part.
pa beth? what (thing)? **oes peth
ar ôl** is there some left?
piano *e.g.b. ll.* **-s** piano.
pianydd *e.g. ll.* **-ion** pianist.
pib *e.b. ll.* **-au: pibell** *e.b. ll.* **-au, -i**
pipe *(smoking, musical variety).*
canu'r pibau to play the pipes;
tanio pib to light a pipe.
piben *e.b. ll.* **-ni** pipe *(drainpipe,
etc.).*
picil *e.g.* pickle, trouble. **mewn picil**
in trouble.
pictiwr *e.g. ll.* **pictiyrau** picture.
picwn *gw.* **picwnen.**
picwnen *e.b. ll.* **picwn** wasp *(S.W.).*
pigfain *a.* tapering.
pigiad *e.g. ll.* **-au** prick, sting;
injection.
pigo *be.* **(pigaf)** to pick, to sting, to
prick, to peck.
pigog *a.* prickly, irritable.
pil *e.g. ll.* **-ion** peel.
piler *e.g. ll.* **-au** pillar, column **o
biler i bost** from pillar to post.
pilio *be.* **(piliaf)** to peel.
pilion *gw.* **pil.**
pili-pala *e.g. ll.* **pili-palod** butterfly
(S.W.).
pilsen *e.b. ll.* **pils** pill.
pilyn *e.g. ll.* **-nau** garment *(S.W.)*
rag. **pilyn gorau** best garment;
pilyn parch Sunday garment, best
garment.
pin *e.g. ll.* **-nau** pin; pen. **pin
ysgrifennu** writing pen; **pinnau
bawd** drawing pins.
pîn *gw.* **pinwydden.**
pînafal *e.g. ll.* **-au** pineapple.

pinc   **popeth**

pinc *a.* pink: **yn y pinc** in very good
health.
pinnau *gw.* **pin.**
pinsio *be.* **(pinsiaf)** to pinch.
pinwydden *e.b. ll.* **pîn, pinwydd**
pine.
piod *gw.* **pioden.**
pioden *e.b. ll.* **piod** magpie.
pisyn *e.g. ll.* **-nau** piece *(S.W.).* **Mae
hi'n bisyn!** She's good looking!
piti *e.g.* pity.
plaid *e.b. ll.* **pleidiau** party, side. **o
blaid** in favour; **Y Blaid
Geidwadol** The Conservative Party;
Y Blaid Lafur The Labour Party; **Y
Blaid (Plaid Cymru)** The Welsh
Nationalist Party; **Y Blaid Werdd**
The Green Party.
plan *e.g. ll.* **-iau** plan.
planced *e.b. ll.* **-i** blanket. *gw.*
blanced
planhigyn *e.g. ll.* **planhigion** plant.
planiau *gw.* **plan.**
plannu *be.* **(plannaf)** to plant.
plant *gw.* **plentyn.**
plas *e.g. ll.* **-au** palace, mansion.
plastai *gw.* **plasty.**
plasty *e.g. ll.* **plastai** palace,
mansion.
plât *e.g. ll.* **platiau** plate.
platiau *gw.* **plât.**
pleidiau *gw.* **plaid.**
pleidlais *e.b. ll.* **pleidlesiau** vote.
pleidleisiau *gw.* **pleidlais.**
pleidleisio *be.* **(pleidleisliaf)** to
vote. **bwrw pleidlais** to cast a vote.
pleidleisiwr *e.g. ll.* **pleidleiswyr**
voter.
plentyn *e.g. ll.* **plant** child.
plentynnaidd *a.* childish.
pleser *e.g. ll.* **-au** pleasure. **rhoi
pleser i** to give pleasure to.
plesurus *a.* pleasant, pleasurable.
plesio *be.* **(plesiaf)** to please.
plisgyn *e.g. ll.* **plisg** shell, pod,
casing.
plisman: plismon *e.g. ll.* **plismyn**
policeman.
plismyn *gw.* **plisman.**
plith *e.g.* midst. **i blith** into the
midst of; **o blith** from among;

ymhlith among; **blith draphlith** in
confusion, intermingled.
plu *gw.* **pluen.**
pluen *e.b. ll.* **plu** feather; fly
(fishing-bait). **clymu plu** to fashion
fishing-flies; **yn ysgafn fel pluen**
light as a feather.
pluf *gw.* **plufyn.**
plufyn *e.g. ll.* **pluf** feather *(S.W.).*
plwc *e.g. ll.* **plyciau** pull, jerk.
plwg *e.g. ll.* **plygiau** plug.
plwm 1 *e.g.* lead; 2 *a.* leaden;
vertical.
plwyf *e.g. ll.* **-i** parish. **ar y plwyf**
on the parish, destitute.
plyciau *gw.* **plwc.**
plygiau *gw.* **plwg.**
plygu *be.* **(plygaf)** to fold, to bend,
to stoop, to bow, to submit.
pob *a.* each, every, all; roast. **pob
cynnig** every attempt, every offer;
pob dydd every day; **pob tro**
every occasion; **pob un** everyone;
tatws pob roast potatoes.
pobi *be.* **(pobaf)** to bake, to roast.
pobl *e.b. ll.* **-oedd** people. **y bobl
hyn** these people.
poblogaeth *e.b. ll.* **-au** population.
poblogaidd *a.* popular.
pobman *ad.* everywhere.
pobydd *e.g. ll.* **-ion** baker.
poced *e.b. ll.* **-i** pocket.
poen *e.g.b. ll.* **-au** pain, ache, agony.
poeni *be.* **(poenaf)** to pain, to worry,
to tease. **Paid poeni!** Don't worry!
poenus *a.* painful.
poenydio *be.* **(poenydiaf)** to torture,
to torment.
poer: poeri *e.g.* spittle, saliva.
poeri (at, i'r) *be.* **(poeraf)** to spit.
gw. **poer.**
poeth *a.* hot.
poethi *be.* **(poethaf)** to heat, to be
heated.
polion *gw.* **polyn.**
politicaidd *a.* political.
polyn *e.g. ll.* **polion** pole, stake.
pont *e.b. ll.* **-ydd** bridge.
pontydd *gw.* **pont.**
Pont-y-pŵl *e.b.* Pontypool.
popeth *e.g.* everything.

poptai   **priod**

poptai *gw.* **popty.**
popty *e.g. ll.* **poptai** bakehouse;
  oven.
porfa *e.b. ll.* **porfeydd** pasture;
  grass *(S.W.).*
porfeydd *gw.* **porfa.**
porffor *e.g. ll. & a.* purple.
pori *be.* **(poraf)** to graze.
portread *e.g. ll.* **-au** portrait,
  portrayal.
porth *e.g. ll.* **pyrth** door; porch.
porthladd *e.g. ll.* **-oedd** harbour.
pos *e.g. ll.* **posau** puzzle, riddle.
  pos croeseiriau crossword puzzle.
posibilrwydd *e.g.* possibility.
posibl *a.* possible.
post 1 *e.g. ll.* **pyst** post, pillar. 2
  e.g. ll.
  -iau post, mail.
postio *be.* **(postiaf)** to post.
postman: postmon *e.g. ll.*
  postmyn postman.
postmyn *gw.* **postman.**
postyn *e.g. ll.* **pyst** post. **fel postyn**
  deaf *(as a post).*
potel *e.b. ll.* **-i** bottle. **potel ddŵr**
  poeth hotwater bottle.
powdr: powdwr *e.g. ll.* **powdrau**
  powder.
powdrau *gw.* **powdr.**
powlen *gw.* **bowlen.**
praidd *e.g. ll.* **preiddiau** flock.
pram *e.g. ll.* **-lau** pram.
prawf *e.g. ll.* **profion** trial, test,
  proof. **prawf darllen** reading test;
  prawf gyrru driving test; **ar brawf**
  on trial, on probation; **blwyddyn**
  brawf probationary year;
  Gwasanaeth Prawf Probation
  Service; **swyddog prawf** probation
  officer.
pregeth *e.b. ll.* **-au** sermon.
pregethu *be.* **(pregethaf)** to preach.
pregethwr *e.g. ll.* **pregethwyr**
  preacher.
preiddiau *gw.* **praidd.**
preifat *a.* private.
pren *e.g. ll.* **-nau** tree, wood, timber.
  pren afalau apple-tree; **pren caled**
  hardwood; **pren meddal** softwood;
  llwy bren a wooden spoon.

prennau *gw.* **pren.**
prentis *e.g. ll.* **-iaid** apprentice.
prentisiaeth *e.b. ll.* **-au**
  apprenticeship.
prentisiaid *gw.* **prentis.**
pres 1 *e.g.* brass, bronze; money. 2
  a. brass. **band pres** brass band;
  jwg bres brass jug.
preseb *e.g. ll.* **-au** crib, stall,
  manger.
presennol *a.* present. **yr amser**
  presennol the present tense.
presenoldeb *e.g. ll.* **-au** presence,
  attendance.
presgripsiwn *e.g. ll.*
  presgripsiynau prescription.
preswyl: preswylfod *e.g. ll.*
  preswylfeydd dwelling place.
  ysgol breswyl boarding school;
  neuadd breswyl hall of residence.
pridwerth *e.g.* ransom.
pridd *e.g. ll.* **-oedd** soil, earth.
prif *a. (precedes the noun it qualifies*
  and is followed by soft mutation)
  prime, chief, major, principal. **prif**
  ddiddordeb chief interest; **prif**
  westeion principal guests; **prif**
  lyfrgell main library.
prifardd *e.g. ll.* **prifeirdd** chief bard
  (one who has won chair or crown at
  National Eisteddfod).
prifathrawes *e.b. ll.* **-au**
  headmistress, principal.
prifathro *e.g. ll.* **prifathrawon**
  headmaster, principal.
prifddinas *e.b. ll.* **-oedd** capital
  city.
prifeirdd *gw.* **prifardd.**
prifio *be.* **(prifiaf)** to grow *(S.W.).*
prifysgol *e.b. ll.* **-ion** university:
  Prifysgol Cymru University of
  Wales.
priffordd *e.b. ll.* **priffyrdd** highway.
priffyrdd *gw.* **priffordd.**
prin *a.* rare, scarce, hardly.
prinder *e.g. ll.* **-au** scarcity.
printio *be.* **(printiaf)** to print.
priod 1 *a.* own, proper; married. 2
  e.g.b. husband or wife. **ei phriod**
  her husband; **fy mhriod** my partner
  (husband/wife). **ei briod le** his

priodas   **pwy**

proper place; **priodfab** bridegroom;
priodferch bride; **gŵr priod**
married man; **gwraig briod** married
woman; **Ydych chi'n briod?** Are
you married?
priodas *e.b. ll.* **-au** marriage,
wedding.
priodi (â) *be.* **(priodaf)** to marry.
priodol *a.* appropriate, proper.
pris *e.g. ll.* **-iau, -oedd** price.
problem *e.g. ll.* **-au** problem.
profi *be.* **(profaf)** to prove, to test, to
taste.
profiad *e.g. ll.* **-au** experience.
profiadol *a.* experienced.
profion *gw.* **prawf.**
profocio: pryfocio *be.* **(profociaf:**
pryfociaf) to provoke.
proffid *e.b. ll.* **-iau** profit.
proffiddiol *a.* profitable.
proffwyd *e.g. ll.* **-i** prophet;
proffwydes prophetess.
proffwydo *be.* **(proffwydaf)** to
prophesy.
Protestant *e.g. ll.* **Protestaniaid**
Protestant.
prudd *a.* sad, grave, serious.
pryd 1 *e.g. ll.* **-au** meal. **byrbryd**
snack; **tamaid i aros pryd**
temporary provision while awaiting
arrival of something more
substantial. 2 *e.g. ll.* **-iau** time,
season: **Pryd? Pa bryd?** What
time? **mewn pryd** in time; **ar y**
pryd at the time; impromptu; **hen**
bryd about time.
Prydain *e.b.* Britain.
prydau *gw.* **pryd.**
Prydeinig *a.* British.
pryder *e.g. ll.* **-on** anxiety, care,
worry.
pryderu *be.* **(pryderaf)** to be
anxious.
pryderus *a.* anxious.
prydferth *a.* beautiful, handsome.
prydferthwch *e.g.* beauty.
prydiau *gw.* **pryd.**
prydlon *a.* punctual.
pryf: pryfedyn: pryfyn *e.g. ll.*
pryfed insect; vermin; animal;
worm. **pryf copyn** spider *(N.W.).*

pryfed *gw.* **pryf.**
pryfocio *gw.* **profocio.**
pryfyn *gw.* **pryf.**
prynhawn *e.g. ll.* **-au** afternoon.
prynhawn da! good afternoon!
prynu *be.* **(prynaf)** to buy.
prynwr *e.g. ll.* **prynwyr** buyer,
redeemer.
prysur *a.* busy, hasty; diligent,
serious.
prysurdeb *e.g.* haste, hurry; busyness.
prysuro (i) *be.* **(prysuraf)** to hasten
(to), to hurry. **Rwy'n prysuro i**
esbonio I hasten to explain.
pulpud *e.g. ll.* **-au** pulpit.
pum: pump *e.g. ll. & a.* five.
pumed fifth.
p'un *gw.* **pa.**
punnau *gw.* **punt.**
punnoedd *gw.* **punt.**
punt *e.b. ll.* **punnau, punnoedd**
pound *(£).*
pupur *e.g. ll.* **-au** pepper. **fel melin**
bupur very talkative.
pur 1 *a.* pure, sincere. **Yr eiddoch**
yn bur Yours sincerely. 2 *ad.* very,
fairly. **yn bur wael** very poorly; **yn**
bur dda fairly good.
purfa *e.b. ll.* **purfeydd** refinery.
purfa olew oil refinery.
puro *be.* **(puraf)** to purify.
pwdin *e.g. ll.* **-au** pudding, sweet
(after dinner). **Bydd pwdin yn**
dilyn There's a sweet to follow.
pwdr *a.* rotten, corrupt, lazy *(S.W.).*
pwdryn *e.g* idler, sluggard (S.W.).
pwdu *be.* **(pwdaf)** to sulk, to pout.
pŵer *e.g. ll.* **-au** power.
pwll *e.g. ll.* **pyllau** pit, pool, pond.
pwll glo coal-pit, coal-mine.
pwmp *e.g. ll.* **pympiau** pump.
pwnc *e.g. ll.* **pynciau** subject, topic.
pynciau craidd core subjects;
pynciau sylfaen foundation
subjects; **Cymanfa Bwnc** assembly
for cathechising and discussing
prepared portions of Scripture.
pwrpas *e.g. ll.* **-au** purpose.
pwrs *e.g. ll.* **pyrsau** purse.
pwy *rhag. gof.* who? **pwy bynnag**
whosoever.

pwyll   **pythefnos**

pwyll *e.g.* sense, discretion. **colli ei
bwyll** to lose his senses, to become
enraged; **cymryd pwyll** to take
time; **mynd gan bwyll** to go
steadily.
pwllgor *e.g. ll.* **-au** committee.
pwllgor addysg education
committee; **pwyllgor brys**
emergency committee; **pwyllgor
gwaith** executive committee.
pwyllo *be.* **(pwyllaf)** to pause, to
consider, to reflect.
pwynt *e.g. ll.* **-iau** point. **dau bwynt
pump** 2.5 (two point five);
rhewbwynt freezing-point.
pwys 1 *e.g. ll.* **-au** weight,
importance. **ar bwys** near; **ennill
pwysau** to put on weight; **o bwys**
important; **codi pwys ar** to make
one feel sick. 2 *e.g. ll.* **-i** pound *(lb).*
pwysedd *e.g.* pressure. **pwysedd
gwaed** blood pressure.
pwysig *a.* important.
pwysigrwydd *e.g.* importance.
pwyslais *e.g. ll.* **pwysleisiau**
emphasis.

pwyso (ar) *be.* **(pwysaf)** to weigh,
to lean (on), to rest.
pwyth *e.g. ll.* **-au** stitch. **talu'r
pwyth** to avenge; retaliate.
pydru *be.* **(pydraf)** to rot, to decay.
pyllau *gw.* **pwll,** *gw.* **pyllyn.**
pyllyn *e.g. ll.* **pyllau** pool, pond.
pympiau *gw.* **pwmp.**
pymtheg 1 *e.g. ll.* **-au** fifteen 2 *a.*
fifteen.
pymthegfed *a.* fifteenth.
pynciau *gw.* **pwnc.**
pyped *e.g. ll.* **-au** puppet.
pyrsau *gw.* **pwrs.**
pyrth *gw.* **porth.**
pys *gw.* **pysen.**
pysen *e.b. ll.* **pys** pea. **pys pêr**
sweet peas.
pysgod *gw.* **pysgodyn.**
pysgodyn *e.g. ll.* **pysgod** a fish.
pysgodyn aur a goldfish.
pysgota *be.* **(pysgotaf)** to fish.
pysgotwr *e.g. ll.* **pysgotwyr**
fisherman.
pyst *gw.* **post, postyn.**
pythefnos *e.g.b. ll.* **-au** fortnight.

pha *gw.* pa.
Phab *gw.* Pab.
phabell *gw.* pabell.
phabi *gw.* pabi.
phabydd *gw.* pabydd.
phac *gw.* pac.
phaced *gw.* paced.
phacio *gw.* pacio.
phadell *gw.* padell.
phader *gw.* pader.
phaent *gw.* paent.
phafiliwn *gw.* pafiliwn.
phafin *gw.* pafin.
phagan *gw.* pagan.
phaham *gw.* paham.
phais *gw.* pais.
phâl *gw.* pâl.
phalas *gw.* palas.
phalau *gw.* pâl.
phalod *gw.* pâl.
phalu *gw.* palu.
phallu *gw.* pallu.
pham *gw.* pam.
phamffled *gw.* pamffled.
phamffledyn *gw.* pamffled.
phan *gw.* pan.
phanasen *gw.* panasen.
phanel *gw.* panel.
phannas *gw.* panasen.
phant *gw.* pant.
phapur *gw.* papur.
phapuro *gw.* papuro.
phâr *gw.* pâr.

phara *gw.* para.
pharadwys *gw.* paradwys.
pharagraff *gw.* paragraff.
pharatoi *gw.* paratoi.
pharc *gw.* parc.
pharch *gw.* parch.
pharchedig *gw.* parchedig.
pharchu *gw.* parchu.
pharchus *gw.* parchus.
pharhad *gw.* parhad.
pharhau *gw.* parhau.
pharod *gw.* parod.
pharsel *gw.* parsel.
pharti *gw.* parti.
Phasg *gw.* Pasg.
phasiannau *gw.* pasiant.
phasiant *gw.* pasiant.
phatrwm *gw.* patrwm.
phatrwn *gw.* patrwn.
phatrymau *gw.* patrwm.
phatrynau *gw.* patrwn.
phawb *gw.* pawb.
phawen *gw.* pawen.
phe *gw.* pe.
phebyll *gw.* pabell.
phecyn *gw.* pecyn.
phechadur *gw.* pechadur.
phechod *gw.* pechod.
phechu *gw.* pechu.
phedair *gw.* pedair.
phedol *gw.* pedol.
phedwar *gw.* pedwar.
phedwaredd *gw.* pedwaredd.
phedwerydd *gw.* pedwerydd.
pheg *gw.* peg.
phegwn *gw.* pegwn.
phegynau *gw.* pegwn.
pheidio *gw.* peidio.
pheilot *gw.* peilot.
pheint *gw.* peint.
pheintio *gw.* peintio.
pheintiwr *gw.* peintiwr.
pheiriannydd: pheiriannwr *gw.*
   peiriannydd.
pheiriannau *gw.* peiriant.
pheiriant *gw.* peiriant.
pheisiau *gw.* pais.
phêl *gw.* pêl.
phelydr *gw.* pelydr.
phell *gw.* pell.
phellach *gw.* pell.

phellaf

phlanhigyn

phellaf *gw.* **pell.**
phelled *gw.* **pell.**
phellter *gw.* **pellter.**
phen *gw.* **pen.**
phenaethiaid *gw.* **pennaeth.**
phenawdau *gw.* **pennawd.**
phen-blwydd *gw.* **pen-blwydd.**
phencadlys *gw.* **pencadlys.**
phencampwr *gw.* **pencampwr.**
phendant *gw.* **pendant.**
phenderfyniad *gw.* **penderfyniad.**
phenderfynol *gw.* **penderfynol.**
phenderfynu *gw.* **penderfynu.**
phenelin *gw.* **penelin.**
phenfoel *gw.* **penfoel.**
phen-glin *gw.* **pen-glin.**
phenigamp *gw.* **penigamp.**
phenillion *gw.* **pennill.**
phen-lin *gw.* **pen-glin.**
phenlinio *gw.* **penlinio.**
phennaeth *gw.* **pennaeth.**
phennaf *gw.* **pennaf.**
phennau *gw.* **pen.**
phennawd *gw.* **pennawd.**
phennill *gw.* **pennill.**
phennod *gw.* **pennod.**
phenodau *gw.* **pennod.**
phenodi *gw.* **penodi.**
phenodiad *gw.* **penodiad.**
phenrhyn *gw.* **penrhyn.**
phensaer *gw.* **pensaer.**
phenseiri *gw.* **pensaer.**
phensil *gw.* **pensil.**
phensiwn *gw.* **pensiwn.**
phensiynau *gw.* **pensiwn.**
phensiynwr *gw.* **pensiynwr.**
phenteulu *gw.* **penteulu.**
phentref *gw.* **pentref.**
phentwr *gw.* **pentwr.**
phenwythnos *gw.* **penwythnos.**
pher *gw.* **pêr.**
pherchen *gw.* **perchen.**
pherchennog *gw.* **perchen.**
pheren *gw.* **peren.**
phererin *gw.* **pererin.**
pherfedd *gw.* **perfedd.**
pherffaith *gw.* **perffaith.**
pherffeithio *gw.* **perffeithio.**
pheri *gw.* **peri.**
pherl *gw.* **perl.**
pherlysiau *gw.* **perlysiau.**

pherllan *gw.* **perllan.**
phersli *gw.* **persli.**
pherson *gw.* **person.**
phersonol *gw.* **personol.**
phersonoliaeth *gw.* **personoliaeth.**
phert *gw.* **pert.**
pherth *gw.* **perth.**
pherthnasau *gw.* **perthynas.**
pherthnasol *gw.* **perthnasol.**
pherthyn *gw.* **perthyn.**
pherthynas *gw.* **perthynas.**
pherygl *gw.* **perygl.**
pheryglus *gw.* **peryglus.**
pheswch *gw.* **peswch.**
phesychiad *gw.* **pesychiad.**
phetai *gw.* **petai.**
phetrol *gw.* **petrol.**
pheth *gw.* **peth.**
phiano *gw.* **piano.**
phianydd *gw.* **pianydd.**
phib *gw.* **pib.**
phiben *gw.* **piben.**
phicil *gw.* **picil.**
phictiwr *gw.* **pictiwr.**
phicwn *gw.* **picwnen.**
phicwnen *gw.* **picwnen.**
phigfain *gw.* **pigfain.**
phigiad *gw.* **pigiad.**
phigo *gw.* **pigo.**
phigog *gw.* **pigog.**
phil *gw.* **pil.**
philer *gw.* **piler.**
philio *gw.* **pilio.**
philion *gw.* **pil.**
phili-pala *gw.* **pili-pala.**
philsen *gw.* **pilsen.**
philyn *gw.* **pilyn.**
phin *gw.* **pin.**
phîn *gw.* **pîn.**
phînafal *gw.* **pînafal.**
phinc *gw.* **pinc.**
phinnau *gw.* **pin.**
phinsio *gw.* **pinsio.**
phinwydden *gw.* **pinwydden.**
phioden *gw.* **pioden.**
phisyn *gw.* **pisyn.**
phiti *gw.* **piti.**
phlaid *gw.* **plaid.**
phlan *gw.* **plan.**
phlanced *gw.* **blanced.**
phlanhigyn *gw.* **planhigyn.**

phlaniau

phlaniau *gw.* **plan.**
phlannu *gw.* **plannu.**
phlant *gw.* **plant.**
phlas *gw.* **plas.**
phlastai *gw.* **plasty.**
phlasty *gw.* **plasty.**
phlât *gw.* **plât.**
phlatiau *gw.* **plât.**
phleidiau *gw.* **plaid.**
phleidlais *gw.* **pleidlais.**
phleidleisiau *gw.* **pleidlais.**
phleidleisio *gw.* **pleidleisio.**
phleidleisiwr *gw.* **pleidleisiwr.**
phlentyn *gw.* **plentyn.**
phlentynnaidd *gw.* **plentynnaidd.**
phleser *gw.* **pleser.**
phleserus *gw.* **pleserus.**
phlesio *gw.* **plesio.**
phlisgyn *gw.* **plisgyn.**
phlisman: phlismon *gw.* **plisman.**
phlismyn *gw.* **plisman.**
phlu *gw.* **pluen.**
phluen *gw.* **pluen.**
phluf *gw.* **plufyn.**
phlufyn *gw.* **plufyn.**
phlwc *gw.* **plwc.**
phlwg *gw.* **plwg.**
phlwm *gw.* **plwm.**
phlwyf *gw.* **plwyf.**
phlyciau *gw.* **plwc.**
phlygiau *gw.* **plwg.**
phlygu *gw.* **plygu.**
phob *gw.* **pob.**
phobi *gw.* **pobi.**
phobl *gw.* **pobl.**
phoblogaeth *gw.* **poblogaeth.**
phoblogaidd *gw.* **poblogaidd.**
phobman *gw.* **pobman.**
phobydd *gw.* **pobydd.**
phoced *gw.* **poced.**
phoen *gw.* **poen.**
phoeni *gw.* **poeni.**
phoenus *gw.* **poenus.**
phoenydio *gw.* **poenydio.**
phoer *gw.* **poer.**
phoeri *gw.* **poer, poeri (at, i'r).**
phoeth *gw.* **poeth.**
phoethi *gw.* **poethi.**
pholion *gw.* **polyn.**
pholiticaidd *gw.* **politicaidd.**
pholyn *gw.* **polyn.**

phrifathrawes

phont *gw.* **pont.**
phontydd *gw.* **pont.**
Phont-y-pŵl *gw.* **Pont-y-pŵl.**
phopeth *gw.* **popeth.**
phoptai *gw.* **popty.**
phopty *gw.* **popty.**
phorfa *gw.* **porfa.**
phorfeydd *gw.* **porfa.**
phorffor *gw.* **porffor.**
phori *gw.* **pori.**
phortread *gw.* **portread.**
phorth *gw.* **porth.**
phorthladd *gw.* **porthladd.**
phos *gw.* **pos.**
phosibilrwydd *gw.* **posibilrwydd.**
phosibl *gw.* **posibl.**
phost *gw.* **post.**
phostio *gw.* **postio.**
phostman: phostmon *gw.* **postman.**
phostmyn *gw.* **postman.**
phostyn *gw.* **postyn.**
photel *gw.* **potel.**
phowdr: phowdwr *gw.* **powdr.**
phowdrau *gw.* **powdr.**
phowlen *gw.* **bowlen.**
phraidd *gw.* **praidd.**
phram *gw.* **pram.**
phrawf *gw.* **prawf.**
phregeth *gw.* **pregeth.**
phregethu *gw.* **pregethu.**
phregethwr *gw.* **pregethwr.**
phreiddiau *gw.* **praidd.**
phreifat *gw.* **preifat.**
phren *gw.* **pren.**
phrennau *gw.* **pren.**
phrentis *gw.* **prentis.**
phrentisiaeth *gw.* **prentisiaeth.**
phrentisiaid *gw.* **prentis.**
phres *gw.* **pres.**
phreseb *gw.* **preseb.**
phresennol *gw.* **presennol.**
phresenoldeb *gw.* **presenoldeb.**
phresgripsiwn *gw.* **presgripsiwn.**
phreswyl: phreswylfod *gw.* **preswyl.**
phridwerth *gw.* **pridwerth.**
phridd *gw.* **pridd.**
phrif *gw.* **prif.**
phrifardd *gw.* **prifardd.**
phrifathrawes *gw.* **prifathrawes.**

phrifathro **phythefnos**

phrifathro *gw.* prifathro.
phrifddinas *gw.* prifddinas.
phrifeirdd *gw.* prifardd.
phrifio *gw.* prifio.
phrifysgol *gw.* prifysgol.
phriffordd *gw.* priffordd.
phriffyrdd *gw.* priffordd.
phrin *gw.* prin.
phrinder *gw.* prinder.
phrintio *gw.* printio.
phriod *gw.* priod.
phriodas *gw.* priodas.
phriodi *gw.* priodas.
phriodol *gw.* priodol.
phris *gw.* pris.
phroblem *gw.* problem.
phrofi *gw.* profi.
phrofiad *gw.* profiad.
phrofiadol *gw.* profiadol.
phrofion *gw.* prawf.
phrofocio *gw.* profocio.
phroffid *gw.* proffid.
phroffidiol *gw.* proffidiol.
phroffwyd *gw.* proffwyd.
phroffwydo *gw.* proffwydo.
Phrotestant *gw.* Protestant.
phrudd *gw.* prudd.
phryd *gw.* pryd.
Phrydain *gw.* Prydain.
phrydau *gw.* pryd.
Phrydeinig *gw.* Prydeinig.
phryder *gw.* pryder.
phryderu *gw.* pryderu.
phryderus *gw.* pryderus.
phrydferth *gw.* prydferth.
phrydferthwch *gw.* prydferthwch.
phrydiau *gw.* pryd.
phrydlon *gw.* prydlon.
phryf: phryfedyn: phryfyn *gw.*
 pryf.
phryfed *gw.* pryf.
phryfocio *gw.* profocio.
phryfyn *gw.* pryf.
phrynhawn *gw.* prynhawn.
phrynu *gw.* prynu.
phrynwr *gw.* prynwr.
phrysur *gw.* prysur.
phrysurdeb *gw.* prysurdeb.
phrysuro *gw.* prysuro.
phulpud *gw.* pulpud.

phum: phump *gw.* pum.
ph'un *gw.* pa.
phunnau *gw.* punt.
phunnoedd *gw.* punt.
phunt *gw.* punt.
phupur *gw.* pupur.
phur *gw.* pur.
phurfa *gw.* purfa.
phuro *gw.* puro.
phwdin *gw.* pwdin.
phwdr *gw.* pwdr.
phwdryn *gw.* pwdryn.
phwdu *gw.* pwdu.
phŵer *gw.* pŵer.
phwll *gw.* pwll.
phwllyn *gw.* pwllyn.
phwmp *gw.* pwmp.
phwnc *gw.* pwnc.
phwrpas *gw.* pwrpas.
phwrs *gw.* pwrs.
phwy *gw.* pwy.
phwyll *gw.* pwyll.
phwyllgor *gw.* pwyllgor.
phwyllo *gw.* pwyllo.
phwynt *gw.* pwynt.
phwys *gw.* pwys.
phwysedd *gw.* pwysedd.
phwysig *gw.* pwysig.
phwysigrwydd *gw.* pwysigrwydd.
phwyslais *gw.* pwyslais.
phwyso *gw.* pwyso.
phwyth *gw.* pwyth.
phwytho *gw.* pwytho.
phydru *gw.* pydru.
phyllau *gw.* pwll, pyllyn.
phyllyn *gw.* pyllyn.
phympiau *gw.* pwmp.
phymtheg *gw.* pymtheg.
phymthegfed *gw.* pymthegfed.
phynciau *gw.* pwnc.
phyped *gw.* pyped.
phyrsau *gw.* pwrs.
phyrth *gw.* porth.
phys *gw.* pysen.
physgod *gw.* pysgodyn.
physgodyn *gw.* pysgodyn.
physgota *gw.* pysgota.
physgotwr *gw.* pysgotwr.
physt *gw.* post, postyn.
phythefnos *gw.* pythefnos.

raca *gw.* rhaca.
raced *e.b.g. ll.* -i racket.
racs *gw.* rhecsyn.
rad *gw.* rhad.
radio *e.g. ll.* -s radio.
radd *gw.* gradd.
raddfa *gw.* graddfa.
raddio *gw.* graddio.
raddol *gw.* graddol.
raeadr *gw.* rhaeadr.
raenus *gw.* graenus.
raff *gw.* rhaff.
ragair *gw.* rhagair.
ragbrawf *gw.* rhagbrawf.
ragbrofion *gw.* rhagbrawf.
ragenw *gw.* rhagenw.
ragfarn *gw.* rhagfarn.
ragfarnllyd *gw.* rhagfarnllyd.
ragflas *gw.* rhagflas.
Ragfyr *gw.* Rhagfyr.
raglen *gw.* rhaglen.
raglenni *gw.* rhaglen.
ragor *gw.* rhagor.
ragori *gw.* rhagori.
ragorol *gw.* rhagorol.
rai *gw.* rhai.
raid *gw.* rhaid.
ramadeg *gw.* gramadeg.
ramadegol *gw.* gramadegol.
ramantaidd *gw.* rhamantus.
ramantus *gw.* rhamantus.
ran *gw.* rhan.
ranbarth *gw.* rhanbarth.

randir *gw.* rhandir.
raniad *gw.* rhaniad.
rannau *gw.* rhan.
rannu *gw.* rhannu.
ras *e.b. ll.* -ys race *(competitive)*.
  ras-gyfnewid relay race. *gw.* gras.
raw *gw.* rhaw.
rawnffrwyth *gw.* grawnffrwyth.
record *e.b. ll.* -iau record.
recsyn *gw.* rhecsyn.
redeg *gw.* rhedeg.
redwr *gw.* rhedwr.
redyn *gw.* rhedynen.
redynen *gw.* rhedynen.
reg *gw.* rheg.
regfeydd *gw.* rheg.
regi *gw.* rhegi.
reidiau *gw.* rhaid.
reilffordd *gw.* rheilffordd.
reilffyrdd *gw.* rheilffordd.
reis *e.g.* rice. pwdin reis rice
  pudding.
reol *gw.* rheol.
reolaidd *gw.* rheolaidd.
reoli *gw.* rheoli.
reolwr *gw.* rheolwr.
reolwyr *gw.* rheolwr.
res *gw.* rhes.
resi *gw.* rhes.
restr *gw.* rhestr.
restrau *gw.* rhestr.
restri *gw.* rhestr.
reswm *gw.* rheswm.
resymau *gw.* rheswm.
resynu *gw.* gresynu.
rew *gw.* rhew.
rewgell *gw.* rhewgell.
rewi *gw.* rhewi.
rewlif *gw.* rhewlif.
rëydr *gw.* rhaeadr.
riant *gw.* rhiant.
rieni *gw.* rhiant.
rif *gw.* rhif.
rifau *gw.* rhif.
rifo *gw.* rhifo.
rifyddeg *gw.* rhifyddeg.
rifyn *gw.* rhifyn.
rifynnau *gw.* rhifyn.
riffl *e.g. ll.* -au rifle.
rigwm *gw.* rhigwm.
rigymau *gw.* rhigwm.

rihyrsal **rywun**

rihyrsal *e.b.* *ll.* **-s** rehearsal.
rinwedd *gw.* **rhinwedd.**
ris *gw.* **gris.**
risiau *gw.* **gris.**
riw *gw.* **rhiw.**
robin goch *e.g.* robin.
roced *e.b.* *ll.* **-i, -au** rocket.
rodd *gw.* **rhodd.**
roddi *gw.* **rhoddi.**
roddion *gw.* **rhodd.**
roedd **-e/-hi** *bf.* he/she/it/was. *gw.*
 bod.
Roeg *gw.* **Groeg.**
Roegaidd *gw.* **Groegaidd.**
Roegwr *gw.* **Groegwr.**
rofiau *gw.* **rhaw.**
roi *gw.* **rhoddi.**
Romania *e.b.* Romania.
rolio *gw.* **rholio.**
ros *gw.* **rhos.**
rosydd *gw.* **rhos.**
rosyn *gw.* **rhosyn.**
rosynnau *gw.* **rhosyn.**
ruban *e.g.* *ll.* **-au** ribbon.
rudd *gw.* **grudd.**
Rufain *gw.* **Rhufain.**
Rufeinig *gw.* **Rhufeinig.**
rug *gw.* **grug.**
ruo *gw.* **rhuo.**
ruthro *gw.* **rhuthro.**
rŵan *ad.* now *(N.W.).* *gw.* **nawr.**
rwbio *gw.* **rhwbio.**
rwber *e.g.* rubber.
Rwsia *e.b.* Russia.
Rwsiad *e.g.* *ll.* **Rwsiaid** a Russian.
Rwsieg *e.g.* Russian (language).

rwyd *gw.* **rhwyd.**
rwydi *gw.* **rhwyd.**
rwydd *gw.* **rhwydd.**
rwyfo *gw.* **rhwyfo.**
rwyfus *gw.* **rhwyfus.**
rwygo *gw.* **rhwygo.**
rwymo *gw.* **rhwymo.**
rwystr *gw.* **rhwystr.**
rybudd *gw.* **rhybudd.**
rybuddio *gw.* **rhybuddio.**
ryd *gw.* **rhyd.**
rydw i *bf.* I am. *gw.* **bod.**
Rydychen *gw.* **Rhydychen.**
rydd *gw.* **rhydd.**
ryddhau *gw.* **rhyddhau.**
ryddid *gw.* **rhyddid.**
ryddion *gw.* **rhydd.**
ryfedd *gw.* **rhyfedd.**
ryfeddod *gw.* **rhyfeddod.**
ryfeddol *gw.* **rhyfeddol.**
ryfeddu *gw.* **rhyfeddu.**
ryfel *gw.* **rhyfel.**
ryngwladol *gw.* **rhyngwladol.**
rym *gw.* **grym.**
rymus *gw.* **grymus.**
rysáit *eb.* *ll.* **-s.** recipe, prescription.
ryw *gw.* **rhyw.**
rywbeth *gw.* **rhywbeth.**
rywbryd *gw.* **rhywbryd.**
rywdro *gw.* **rhywdro.**
rywfaint *gw.* **rhywfaint.**
rywiol *gw.* **rhywiol.**
rywle *gw.* **rhywle.**
rywrai *gw.* **rhywun.**
rywsut *gw.* **rhywsut.**
rywun *gw.* **rhywun.**

rhaca *e.b. ll.* **-nau** rake. **fel rhaca** very thin, like a rake.

rhacs *gw.* **rhecsyn.**

rhad 1 *a.* cheap; free. **yn rhad ac am ddim** absolutely free. **2** *e.g. ll.* **-au** blessing, grace.

rhaeadr *e.b. ll.* **-au, rhëydr** cataract, waterfall.

rhaff *e.b. ll.* **-au** rope.

rhag 1 *ardd.* before; lest; against, from. **2** *rhag.* pre-, for-, ante-.

rhagair *e.g.* preface.

rhagbrawf *e.g. ll.* **rhagbrofion** preliminary test; foretaste.

rhagbrofion *gw.* **rhagbrawf.**

rhagenw *e.g. ll.* **-au** pronoun. **rhagenw gofynnol** interrogative pronoun; **rhagenw perthynol** relative pronoun.

rhagfarn *e.b. ll.* **-au** prejudice.

rhagfarnllyd *a.* prejudiced.

rhagflas *e.g.* foretaste.

Rhagfyr *e.g.* December.

rhaglen *e.b. ll.* **-ni** programme. **rhaglen deledu** television programme; **rhaglen fyw** live programme; **rhaglen nodwedd** feature programme.

rhaglenni *gw.* **rhaglen.**

rhagor *e.g. ll.* **-au, -ion** difference, more, excess. **rhagor o fwyd** more food.

rhagori (ar) *be.* **(rhagoraf)** to excel, to surpass.

rhagorol *a.* excellent, splendid.

rhai 1 *rhag.* ones. **y rhai da** the good ones. **2** *a.* some. **Mae rhai pobl yn oer** Some people are cold.

rhaid *e.g. ll.* **rheidiau** necessity, need. **Mae rhaid i ti fynd** You must go.

rhain, y *rhag.* these. **Ble mae'r rhain i fod?** Where are these to go? **y rheina** those.

rhamantus: rhamantaidd *a.* romantic.

rhan *e.b. ll.* **-nau** part, share; rôle. **y rhan fwyaf** the greatest part.

rhanbarth *e.g. ll.* **-au** division, region, area, district.

rhandir *e.g. ll.* **-oedd** region, division, district; allotment.

rhandiroedd *gw.* **rhandir.**

rhaniad *e.g. ll.* **-au** division; parting.

rhannau *gw.* **rhan.**

rhannu *be.* **(rhannaf)** to divide, to share, to distribute.

rhaw *e.b. ll.* **-iau, rhofiau** shovel; spade.

rhecsyn *e.g. ll.* **rhacs** rag.

rhedeg *be.* **(rhedaf)** to run; to flow.

rhedwr *e.g. ll.* **rhedwyr** runner.

rhedyn *e.ll.* fern, bracken. *gw.* **rhedynen.**

rhedynen *e.b. ll.* **rhedyn** fern.

rheg *e.b. ll.* **-feydd** curse, swearword.

rhegfeydd *gw.* **rheg.**

rhegi *be.* **(rhegaf)** to curse, to swear.

rheidiau *gw.* **rhaid.**

rheiddiadur *e.g. ll.* **-on** radiator.

rheilffordd *e.b. ll.* **rheilffyrdd** railway.

rheiffyrdd *gw.* **rheilffordd.**

rheina, y *gw.* **rhain.**

rheini, y *rhag.* those (*not present*.)

rheol *e.b. ll.* **-au** rule, order. **Rheolau'r Ffordd Fawr** the Highway Code.

rheolaidd *a.* regular, constant, orderly, proper.

rheoli *be.* **(rheolaf)** to control, to manage.

rheolwr   **rhyfeddu**

rheolwr *e.g. ll.* **rheolwyr** manager, ruler, controller, governor; referee.
rheolwyr *gw.* **rheolwr.**
rhes *e.b. ll.* **-i** row, rank; stripe, line.
rhesi *gw.* **rhes.**
rhestr *e.b. ll.* **-au, -i** row, rank; list.
rhestr fer short list.
rhestrau *gw.* **rhestr.**
rhestri *gw.* **rhestr.**
rheswm *e.g. ll.* **rhesymau** reason, cause. **y rheswm dros** the reason for.
rhesymau *gw.* **rheswm.**
rhesymol *a.* reasonable.
rhew *e.g. ll.* **-iau, -ogydd** frost, ice.
rhewbwynt freezing-point.
rhewfwyd frozen food; **rhewlif** glacier; **Siôn Rhew** Jack Frost.
rhewgell *eb. ll.* **-oedd** deep freeze cabinet, freezer.
rhewi *be.* **(rhewaf)** to freeze.
rhewiau *gw.* **rhew.**
rhewlif *e.g. ll.* **-iau** glacier.
rhewogydd *gw.* **rhew.**
rhëydr *gw.* **rhaeadr.**
rhiant *e.g. ll.* **rhieni** parent.
rhieni *gw.* **rhiant.**
rhif *e.g. ll.* **-au** number, numeral.
rhifau *gw.* **rhif.**
rhifo *be.* **(rhifaf)** to count, to number, to reckon.
rhifyddeg *e.b.g.* arithmetic.
rhifyn *e.g. ll.* **-nau** number (*of magazine*).
rhifynnau *gw.* **rhifyn.**
rhigwm *e.g. ll.* **rhigymau** rhyme; rigmarole.
rhigymau *gw.* **rhigwm.**
rhiniog *e.b. ll.* **-au** threshold.
rhinwedd *e.b.g. ll.* **-au** virtue.
rhisgl *e.ll.* bark (*of tree*).
rhiw *e.b. ll.* **-iau** hill, ascent, slope (*S.W.*).
rhodd *e.b. ll.* **-ion** gift, donation.
rhoddi: rhoi *be.* **(rhoddaf: rhoiaf)** to give, to bestow, to put. **rhoi benthyg** to lend; **rhoi'r gorau i** to relinquish. *gw. At. Berfau.*
rhoddion *gw.* **rhodd.**
rhofion *gw.* **rhaw.**
rhoi *gw.* **rhoddi.**
rholio *be.* **(rholiaf)** to roll.

rhos *e.b. ll.* **-ydd.** moor, heath, plain. *gw.* **rhosyn.**
rhosod *gw.* **rhosyn.**
rhosydd *gw.* **rhos.**
rhosyn *e.g. ll.* **-nau, rhos, rhosod** rose.
rhosynnau *gw.* **rhosyn.**
Rhufain *e.b.* Rome.
Rhufeinig *a.* Roman.
rhugl *a.* fluent.
rhuo *be.* **(rhuaf)** to roar, to bellow.
rhuthro *be.* **(rhuthraf)** to rush.
rhwbio *be.* **(rhwbiaf)** to rub.
rhwng *ardd.* (*personal forms:* **rhyngo, rhyngot, rhyngddo/rhyngddi, rhyngom, rhyngoch, rhyngddyn**) between, among. *gw. At. Arddodiaid.*
rhwyd *e.b. ll.* **-au, -i** net, snare.
rhwydd *a.* easy; fluent; generous; fast (*S.W.*).
rhwyfo *be.* **(rhwyfaf)** to row.
rhwyfus *a.* restless.
rhwygo *be.* **(rhwygaf)** to tear, to rip.
rhwym *a.* bound, tied; constipated.
rhwymo *be.* **(rhwymaf)** to bind, to tie; to constipate.
rhwystr *e.g. ll.* **-au** hindrance, obstacle.
rhwystrau *gw.* **rhwystr.**
rhy 1 *e.g.* excess. **2** *ad.* too. **yn rhy drwm** too heavy.
rhybudd *e.g. ll.* **-ion** warning, notice, caution.
rhybuddio (rhag) *be.* **(rhybuddiaf)** to warn, to caution.
rhyd *e.b. ll.* **-au** ford.
Rhydychen *e.b.* Oxford.
rhydd *a. ll.* **-ion** free, liberal. **Y Seiri Rhyddion** Freemasons.
rhyddhau *be.* **(rhyddhaf)** to free, to release, to loose.
rhyddid *e.g.* freedom, liberty.
rhyddion *gw.* **rhydd.**
rhyfedd: rhyfeddol *a.* wonderful, strange.
rhyfeddod *e.g. ll.* **-au** wonder, surprise.
rhyfeddol *gw.* **rhyfedd.**
rhyfeddu (at) *be.* **(rhyfeddaf)** to wonder, to marvel.

rhyfel *e.g.b.* *ll.* **-oedd** war, warfare.
Rhyfel y Gwlff The Gulf War; **Yr Ail Ryfel Byd** The Second World War; **Y Rhyfel Mawr** The Great War.
rhyngo i *gw.* **rhwng.**
rhyngwladol *a.* international.
rhyw 1 *e.b.g.* *ll.* **-au** sort, kind; sex; gender. **2** *a.* some, certain. **Roedd rhyw ddyn yma ddoe** A certain man was here yesterday.

rhywbeth *e.g.* something.
rhywbryd *ad.* sometime.
rhywdro *ad.* sometime.
rhywfaint *e.g.* some amount.
rhywiol *a.* sexual.
rhywle *ad.* somewhere, anywhere.
rhywrai *gw.* **rhywun.**
rhywsut *ad.* somehow, anyhow.
rhywun *e.g.* *ll.* **rhywrai** someone, anyone. **rhywun neu'i gilydd** someone or other; **rhywrai** some.

Sabath: Saboth *e.g. ll.* **-au** Sabbath.
sach *e.b. ll.* **-au** sack. **sach gysgu** sleeping bag.
Sadwrn *e.g. ll.* **Sadyrnau.** Saturn; Saturday.
saer *e.g. ll.* **seiri** carpenter, joiner; wright; mason. **saer coed** carpenter; **saer maen** stonemason; **pensaer** architect.
Saesneg 1 *e.b.* English (*language*). **2** *a.* English (*in language*).
Saesnes *e.b. ll.* **-au** Englishwoman.
Saeson *gw.* **Sais.**
saeth *e.b. ll.* **-au** arrow.
saethu (at) *be.* **(saethaf)** to shoot, to fire.
saethwr *e.g. ll.* **saethwyr** shooter; archer; goal shooter.
safbwynt *e.g. ll.* **-iau** standpoint, viewpoint, perspective.
safle *e.g. ll.* **-oedd** position, station, situation, rank.
safon *e.b. ll.* **-au** standard, class; criterion. **Y Safon Aur** The Gold Standard; **Safon A** A level.
safonol *a.* standard.
saib *e.g. ll.* **seibiau** pause, rest.
sail *e.b. ll.* **seiliau** base, foundation; ground. **ar sail** on the basis of.
saim *e.g. ll.* **seimiau** grease, fat. **saim gŵydd** goose grease.
sain *e.b. ll.* **seiniau** sound, tone.

saint *gw.* **sant.**
Sais *e.g. ll.* **Saeson** Englishman.
saith *a. & e.g.* seven.
sâl 1 *a.* poorly, sick; mean. **2** *e.g.* sale (*N.W.*).
salm *e.b. ll.* **-au** psalm. **salmdôn** chant.
salw *a.* ugly, vile, mean (*S.W.*).
salwch *e.g.* illness.
sanctaidd *a.* holy.
sant *e.g. ll.* **saint, seintiau** saint. **Dewi Sant** Saint David; **Sant Ioan** Saint John.
santes *e.b. ll.* **-au** female saint; **Santes Dwynwen** Saint Dwynwen, patron saint of lovers.
sarff *e.b. ll.* **seirff** serpent.
sarhad *e.g. ll.* **-au** insult, disgrace.
sarnu (ar) *be.* **(sarnaf)** to trample, to litter, to spill (*S.W.*).
sathru (ar) *be.* **(sathraf)** to trample, to tread. **sathru dan draed** to trample underfoot; **sathru ar gyrn** to offend.
sawdl *e.g.b. ll.* **sodlau** heel.
sawl *rhag. & ad.* (*followed by a singular noun*) he that, (*the one*) who, that which; several, a number (of); how many? many. **Sawl car sy 'da chi?** How many cars do you have? **Sawl tŷ sy ar y bryn?** How many houses are there on the hill? **Roedd sawl llyfr yn y pentwr** There were many books in the pile; **Y sawl a gododd a gollodd ei le** The one that got up lost his seat.
saws *e.g. ll.* **-iau** sauce.
Sbaen *e.g.* Spain.
Sbaeneg *e.b.* Spanish language.
Sbaenes *e.b. ll.* **-au** Spanish woman.
Sbaenwr *e.g. ll.* **-wyr** Spanish man, Spaniard.
sbardun *e.g. ll.* **-au** accelerator; spur.
sbectol *e.b.* spectacles.
sbon *ad.* (*as used with the adjective* **newydd**) wholly. **newydd sbon** brand new.
sbot: sbotyn *e.g. ll.* **sbotiau** spot.
sebon *e.g. ll.* **-au** soap. **sebon dannedd** toothpaste.

sedd   **sgrym**

sedd *e.b. ll.* **-au** seat, pew. **sedd
fawr** deacon's pew.
sef *c.* namely, that is to say.
sefydliad *e.g. ll.* **-au** establishment,
institution, induction.
sefydlog *a.* fixed, settled, stationary.
sefydlu *be.* **(sefydlaf)** to establish,
to settle.
sefyll (am) *be.* **(safaf)** to stand; to
stop; to stay, to wait (for) (*S.W.*).
sefyll arholiad to sit an
examination.
sefyllfa *e.b. ll.* **-oedd** situation,
position.
segur *a.* idle.
segura *be.* **(seguraf)** to idle.
segurdod *e.g.* idleness.
sengl *a.* single.
seiat *e.b. ll.* **seiadau** fellowship,
meeting, society.
seibiant *e.g. ll.* **-au, seibiannau**
leisure, respite, pause.
seibiannau *gw.* **seibiant.**
seibiau *gw.* **saib.**
seicoleg *e.b.g.* psychology.
seiliau *gw.* **sail.**
seilio *be.* **(seiliaf)** to base, to found,
to ground.
seimiau *gw.* **saim.**
seimlyd: seimllyd *a.* greasy.
seiniau *gw.* **sain.**
seindorf *eb. ll.* **-eydd, seindyrf.**
band (*musical*). **seindorf bres** brass
band; **band un dyn** one-man band.
seintiau *gw.* **sant.**
seirff *gw.* **sarff.**
seiri *gw.* **saer.**
Seisnig *a.* English, pertaining to
England.
Seisnigeiddio: Seisnigo *be.*
(Seisnigeiddiaf: Seisnigaf) to
Anglicise.
seithfed *a.* seventh.
sêl *e.b.* zeal.
Seland Newydd *e.b.* New Zealand.
seld *e.b. ll.* **-au** dresser.
sen *e.b. ll.* **-nau** rebuke, snub,
censure. **bwrw sen ar** to cast a
rebuke at.
senedd *e.b. ll.* **-au** parliament,
senate.

sennau *gw.* **sen.**
sêr *gw.* **seren.**
serch 1 *e.g. ll.* **-iadau** love. 2 *c.* &
ardd. although, notwithstanding.
serch ei fod e'n briod although he
was married.
serchog *a.* affectionate, loving.
serchus *a.* affectionate, loving;
pleasant.
seremoni *e.b. ll.* **seremonïau**
ceremony.
seren *e.b. ll.* **sêr** star; asterisk.
seren wib shooting star.
serennog *a.* starry.
serth *a.* steep; unclean; obscene.
set *e.b. ll.* **-iau** set. **set deledu**
television set.
sêt *e.b. ll.* **seti** seat, pew: **sêt fawr**
deacons' seat.
seti *gw.* **sêt.**
setiau *gw.* **set.**
setio *be.* **(setiaf)** to settle.
sgarff *e.b. ll.* **-iau** scarf.
sgert *e.b. ll.* **-i, -iau** skirt. *gw.* **sgyrt.**
sgets *e.b. ll.* **-ys** sketch.
sgi *e.b.g.* ski.
sgil *e.g. ll.* **-iau** skill, device, trick.
sgil *ad.* in the wake of, behind.
Daeth tlodi yn sgil y rhyfel There
was poverty in the wake of the war.
sgïo *be.* **(sgïaf)** to ski.
sgipio *be.* **(sgipiaf)** to skip.
sgiw 1 *e.b. ll.* **-iau** settle.
2 *a.* askew.
sgïwr *e.g. ll.* **sgïwyr** skier.
sglefrio *be.* **(sglefriaf)** to skate, to
slide.
sglodion *gw.* **sglodyn.**
sglodyn *e.g. ll.* **sglodion** chips.
pysgod a sglodion fish and chips.
sgôr *e.b. ll.* **sgoriau** score.
sgorio *be.* **(sgoriaf)** to score.
sgrech *e.b. ll.* **-iadau** yell, scream.
sgrech y coed jay.
sgrechain: sgrechian *be.*
(sgrechaf: sgrechiaf) to yell, to
scream.
sgrifennu: ysgrifennu (ar, at) *be.*
(sgrifennaf: ysgrifennaf) to write.
sgript *e.b. ll.* **-iau** script.
sgrym *e.b. ll.* **-iau** scrum (*rugby*).

sgrymio

sgrymio *be.* **(sgrymiaf)** to scrum.
sgubo *be.* **(sgubaf)** to sweep, to brush.
sgwâr *e.g.b.* *ll.* **-iau** square.
sgwd *e.g.* *ll.* **sgydau** waterfall, cataract.
sgwrs *e.b.* *ll.* **sgyrsiau** talk, chat; conversation.
sgwrslo (â) *be.* **(sgwrsiaf)** to talk, to chat.
sgydau *gw.* **sgwd.**
sgyrsiau *gw.* **sgwrs.**
sgyrt *e.b.* *ll.* **-iau, -is** skirt. *gw.* **sgert.**
si *e.g.* *ll.* **sïon** buzz, rumour, murmur.
siaced *e.b.* *ll.* **-i** jacket, coat.
sialc *e.g.* *ll.* **-iau** chalk. **sialciau lliw** coloured chalks.
siampl *e.b.* *ll.* **-au** example.
sianel *e.b.* *ll.* **-i** channel. **Sianel Pedwar Cymru** S4C (Welsh TV Channel 4).
siâp *e.g.* *ll.* **-iau** shape.
siâr *e.b.* share. **Ga i siâr o'r bwyd?** May I have a share of the food?
siarad *be.* **(siaradaf)** to talk, to speak. **siarad â** to speak with; **siarad am** to speak about.
siaradwr *e.g.* *ll.* **siaradwyr** talker, speaker.
sibrwd *be.* **(sibrydaf)** to whisper.
sicr: siŵr *a.* sure, certain; secure.
sicrhau *be.* **(sicrhaf)** to assure, to confirm, to obtain, to fix, to secure.
sicrwydd *e.g.* certainty, assurance, security.
sidan *e.g.* *ll.* **-au** silk.
siswrn *e.g.* *ll.* **sisyrnau** scissors.
siwd *gw.* **sut.**
siwg: jwg *e.g.* *ll.* **-iau** jug. **siwg laeth** milk jug.
siwgr *e.g.* sugar; **siwgr brown** brown sugar.
siŵr *gw.* **sicr.**
siwrnai 1 *e.g.* *ll.* **siwrneiau, siwrneion** journey. **Siwrnai dda ichi!** Have a good trip! **2** *ad.* once. **Siwrnai roedd tawelwch, fe gododd i siarad** Once there was silence he rose to speak (*S.W.*).

stumog

sliper *e.b.* *ll.* **-i** slipper.
smotyn *e.g.* *ll.* **smotiau** spot.
sodlau *gw.* **sawdl.**
sôn (am) 1 *be.* **(soniaf)** to mention, to talk, to rumour. **2** *e.g.* mention, talk, rumour: **Does dim sôn amdani** There is no sign of her.
sosban *e.b.* *ll.* **-au, sosbenni** saucepan.
sosbenni *gw.* **sosban.**
soser *e.b.* *ll.* **-i** saucer.
sosialaeth *e.b.* socialism.
sosialaidd *a.* socialist.
sosialwyr *gw.* **sosialydd.**
sosialydd *e.g.* *ll.* **sosialwyr** socialist.
sothach *e.torf.* trash, rubbish.
stabl *e.b.* *ll.* **-au** stable.
stafell: ystafell *e.b.* *ll.* **-oedd** room. **stafell ffrynt** front room; **stafell gefn** back room; **stafell wely** bedroom; **stafell ymolchi** bathroom.
stamp *e.g.* *ll.* **-iau** stamp.
stampio *be.* **(stampiaf)** to stamp.
stôl *e.b.* *ll.* **stolau** stool.
stondin *e.b.* *ll.* **-au** stall. **stondin farchnad** market stall.
stopio *be.* **(stopiaf)** to stop.
stôr *e.g.* *ll.* **storau** store. **stôr celfi** furniture store.
stordy *e.g.* *ll.* **stordai** storehouse, warehouse.
storfa *e.b.* *ll.* **storfeydd** store; storage.
stori *eb.* *ll.* **storiáu, storïau, straeon** story. **stori arswyd** horror story; **stori fer** short story.
storiáu: storïau *gw.* **stori.**
storïwr *e.g.* *ll.* **storïwyr** storyteller.
storm *e.b.* *ll.* **-ydd** storm.
stormus *a.* stormy, tempestuous.
stormydd *gw.* **storm.**
straeon *gw.* **stori.**
strategaeth *e.b.* strategy.
streic *e.b.* *ll.* **-iau** strike.
strwythur *e.g.* *ll.* **-au** structure.
strwythuro *be.* **(strwythuraf)** to structure.
stryd *e.b.* *ll.* **-oedd** street.
stumog *e.b.* *ll.* **-au** stomach.

stumogi

stumogi *be.* **(stumogaf)** to stomach.
stŵr *e.g.* stir, noise, bustle, fuss.
su *e.g. ll.* **suon** buzz, murmur,
rumour. *gw.* **si.**
suddo *be.* **(suddaf)** to sink, to dive;
to invest.
sugno *be.* **(sugnaf)** to suck, to
absorb.
Sul *e.g. ll.* **-iau** Sunday. **Dydd Sul**
Sunday; **Sul y Blodau** Palm
Sunday; **Sul y Mamau** Mothering
Sunday.
Sulgwyn *e.g.* Whitsunday.
Suliau *gw.* **Sul.**
suo *be.* **(suaf)** to hum, to buzz; to
lull.
suon *gw.* **su.**
sur *a. ll.* **-ion** sour, bitter, acid.
suro *be.* **(suraf)** to sour.
sut: siwd *rhag.gof.* how? **Sut/Siwd**
mae? How are things?
sw *e.g.* zoo.
swil *a.* shy, bashful.
Swistir Y, *e.b.* Switzerland.
swm *e.g. ll.* **symiau** sum.
sŵn *e.g. ll.* **synau** sound, noise.
swnio *be.* **(swniaf)** to sound, to
pronounce.
swper *e.g.b. ll.* **-au** supper: **Y**
Swper Olaf The Last Supper.
sws *e.g.* kiss (*N.W.*).
swydd *e.b. ll.* **-i** post, office, job;
county (*in England*). gw. **sir. Swydd**
Gaerloyw Gloucestershire; **swydd**
Buckingham Buckinghamshire.
swyddfa *e.b. ll.* **swyddfeydd**
office. **Y Swyddfa Gymreig** The
Welsh Office.
swyddfeydd *gw.* **swyddfa.**
swyddi *gw.* **swydd.**
swyddog *e.g. ll.* **-ion** officer,
official. **swyddog prawf** probation
officer. **swyddog y llys** officer of
the court.
swyddogol *a.* official. **llythyr**
swyddogol official letter.
swyn *e.g. ll.* **-ion** charm, magic,
spell.
swyno *be.* **(swynaf)** to charm, to
enchant, to bewitch.
swynol *a.* charming, fascinating.

synhwyrol

sy: sydd *bf.* is, are. *gw.* **bod.**
sych *a.* dry. **tywydd sych** dry
weather.
syched *e.g.* thirst: **mae syched ar**
Tom Tom is thirsty.
sychedig *a.* thirsty, parched.
sychu *be.* **(sychaf)** to dry, to dry up;
to wipe.
sydyn *a.* sudden, abrupt.
sydd *gw.* **sy.**
syfrdanol *a.* stupefying, stunning.
sylfaen *e.b. ll.* **sylfeini** foundation,
base.
sylfaenol *a.* basic, fundamental.
sylfeini *gw.* **sylfaen.**
sylw *e.g. ll* **-adau** notice, remark,
observation, attention. **Gadewch e**
dan sylw. Don't take notice of him.
sylwadau *gw.* **sylw.**
sylwebaeth *e.b. ll.* **-au**
commentary.
sylwebu (ar) *be.* **(sylwebaf)** to give
a commentary (on).
sylwebydd: sylwebwr *e.g. ll.*
sylwebwyr commentator.
sylwedd *e.g. ll.* **-au** substance,
foundation.
sylweddol *a.* substantial.
sylweddoli *be.* **(sylweddolaf)** to
realise.
sylwi (ar) *be.* **(sylwaf)** to observe, to
notice. **Sylwch arnyn nhw** Notice
them.
syllu (ar) *be.* **(syllaf)** to gaze.
symiau *gw.* **swm.**
syml *a.* simple.
symud 1 *be.* **(symudaf)** to move, to
remove; **2** *e.g.* movement, action.
symudiad *e.g. ll.* **-au** movement,
removal.
symudol *a.* mobile, portable. **ffôn**
symudol mobile phone.
syn *a.* amazed, astonishing,
surprising.
synau *gw.* **sŵn.**
syndod *e.g. ll.* **-au** surprise,
amazement.
synhwyrau *gw.* **synnwyr.**
synhwyro *be.* **(synhwyraf)** to sense;
to sniff, to smell.
synhwyrol *a.* sensible.

syniad   **sythu**

syniad *e.g.* *ll.* **-au** idea, notion, thought.
synnu (at) *be.* **(synnaf)** to be surprised, to marvel, to wonder. **Rwy'n synnu atoch chi** I'm surprised at you.
synnwyr *e.g.* *ll.* **synhwyrau** sense.
syr *e.g.* sir. **Annwyl Syr** Dear Sir.
syrcas *e.b.* *ll.* **-au** circus.
syrffed *e.g.* surfeit.
syrffedu (ar) *be.* **(syrffedaf)** to surfeit, to be fed up (with).
syrthio *be.* **(syrthiaf)** to fall. **syrthio mewn cariad** to fall in love; **syrthio ar fai** to admit to blame.
syth *a.* stiff, straight, erect. **Dewch yn syth** Come at once.
sythlyd *a.* cold, chilled.
sythu *a.* to become chilled, to straighten (*S.W.*). **Rwyf bron â sythu** I'm perished.

tabl *e.g. ll.* **-au** table.
tabled *e.b. ll.* **-au, -i** tablet.
tacl *e.b.g. ll.* **-au** tackle, gear.
taclo *be.* **(taclaf)** to tackle.
taclu *be.* **(taclaf)** to put in order; to dress *(S.W.)*.
taclus *a.* neat, tidy.
tacluso *be.* **(taclusaf)** to trim, to tidy.
taclwr *e.g. ll.* **taclwyr** tackler *(rugby)*.
tacsi *e.g. ll.* **-s** taxi.
Tachwedd *e.g.* November.
tad *e.g. ll.* **-au** father: **tad maeth** foster-father; **llystad** stepfather; **tad-yng-nghyfraith** father in law.
tad-cu *e.g. ll.* **tadau-cu** grandfather *(S.W.). gw.* **taid** *(N.W.)*.
tafarn *e.g.b. ll.* **tafarnau** tavern, public house, inn.
tafarnwr *e.g. ll.* **tafarnwyr** publican, inn-keeper.
tafell *e.b. ll.* **-au, -i, tefyll** slice, slab.
taflegryn *e.g. ll.* **taflegrau** missile.
taflen *e.b. ll.* **-ni** leaflet, list, table. **taflen amser** timetable.
taflu (at) *be.* **(taflaf)** to throw (to), to fling, to cast; to dislocate.
tafod *e.g. ll.* **-au** tongue, tang, spit.
tafodiaith *e.b. ll.* **tafodieithoedd** dialect.
tafodieithoedd *gw.* **tafodiaith.**
tafol *e.b. ll.* **-au** scales.

tagfa *e.b. ll.* **tagfeydd** strangulation, choking; bottleneck.
tagu *be.* **(tagaf)** to strangle, to choke.
tangnefedd *e.g.b.* peace.
tai *gw.* **tŷ.**
taid *e.g. ll.* **teidiau** grandfather *(N.W.); gw.* **tad-cu** *(S.W.)*.
tair *a.b. & e.b.* three. **tair merch** three girls. *gw.* **tri.**
taith *e.b. ll.* **teithiau** journey, tour, voyage.
tal *a.* tall, lofty, high.
tâl 1 *e.g. ll.* **taloedd, taliadau** pay, payment, charge, rates. **Tâl Cymunedol** Community Charge. **2** *e.g. ll.* **talau** forehead, front, end.
talai *e.g. ll.* **taleion** payee.
talaith *e.b. ll.* **taleithiau** province, state. **Yr Unol Daleithiau** The United States.
talcen *e.g. ll.* **-nau, -ni** forehead; gable, pine-end. **talcen tŷ** pine-end of house.
talcennau *gw.* **talcen.**
talcenni *gw.* **talcen.**
taleb *e.b. ll.* **-au, -ion** receipt.
taleion *gw.* **talai.**
taleithiau *gw.* **talaith.**
talent *e.b. ll.* **-au** talent.
talentog *a.* gifted, talented.
talfyriad *e.g. ll.* **-au** abbreviation.
taliadau *gw.* **tâl.**
taloedd *gw.* **tâl.**
talu (am) *be.* **(talaf)** to pay.
talwr *e.g. ll.* **talwyr** payer.
talwrn *e.g. ll.* **talyrnau** spot, place; cock-fighting pit: **Talwrn y Beirdd** the Poet's Place *(for competition)*.
tamaid *e.g. ll.* **tameidiau** piece, bit bite. **tamaid i aros pryd** temporary provision while awaiting arrival of something more substantial.
tameidiau *gw.* **tamaid.**
tan *ardd. (followed by soft mutation)* until, as far; under. *gw.* **dan.**
tân *e.g. ll.* **tanau** fire, light. **tân siafins** short-lived enthusiasm and transitory zeal *(lit. a blaze of wood shavings)*.
tanau *gw.* **tân.**

tanbaid | **teimlo**

tanbaid *a.* hot, fervent, fiery, brilliant.
tanc *e.g. ll.* **-iau** tank.
tancer *e.g. ll.* **-i** tanker.
tanddaear: tanddaearol *a.* subterranean, underground.
tanfor *a.* submarine. **llong danfor** submarine.
tanio *be.* **(taniaf)** to ignite, to fire, to stoke, to light. **tanio'r dychymyg** to fire the imagination.
tanlinellu *be.* **(tanlinellaf)** to underline.
tanlwybr *e.g. ll.* **-au** subway.
tanllyd *a.* fiery, fervent.
tannau *gw.* **tant.**
tanseilio *be.* **(tanseiliaf)** to sap, to undermine.
tant *e.g. ll.* **tannau** chord, string. **tant telyn** harp string.
tanwydd *e.g.* fuel, firewood.
tap *e.g. ll.* **-iau** tap. **tap dŵr oer** cold water tap.
tâp *e.g. ll.* **tapiau** tape.
tapiau *gw.* **tap, tâp.**
taran *e.b. ll.* **-au** (peal of) thunder. **mellt a tharanau** thunder and lightning.
taranu *be.* **(taranaf)** to thunder, to threaten.
tarddiad *e.g. ll.* **-au** source, derivation.
tarddu *be.* **(tarddaf)** to spring, to sprout, to derive from, to issue.
targed *e.g. ll.* **-au** target.
tarian *e.b. ll.* **tariannau** shield.
tariannau *gw.* **tarian.**
taro 1 *be.* **(trawaf)** to strike, to hit, to tap; to suit. **Mae e'n dy daro'n iawn** It suits you well.
2 *e.g.* difficulty, crisis; **mewn taro** in an emergency.
tarw *e.g. ll.* **teirw** bull. **llwybr tarw** a short cut.
tasg *e.b. ll.* **-au**
tasgu *be.* **(tasgaf)** to splash, to start, to bolt; to spark; to lose one's temper. **Roedd e'n tasgu pan glywodd e** He was mad when he heard.
taten *e.b.* **tatws, tato** potato. **tatws**

drwy'r croen/pil jacket potatoes; **tatws rhost** roast potatoes; **tatws wedi'u berwi** boiled potatoes; **tatws wedi'u ffrio** fried potatoes; **creision tatws** potato crisps.
tato: tatws *gw.* **taten.**
tawel *a.* quiet, calm, still, peaceful.
tawelu *be.* **(tawelaf)** to calm, to grow calm.
tawelwch *e.g.* quiet, calm, stillness, tranquillity.
tawelydd *e.g. ll.* **-ion** tranquillizer.
tawelyddion *gw.* **tawelydd.**
tawelyn *e.g. ll.* **-nau** tranquillizer.
tawelynnau *gw.* **tawelyn.**
te *e.g.* tea.
tebot *e.g. ll.* **-au** teapot.
tebyg *a.* like, similar, likely. **yn debyg i** like, similar to; **yn debyg o** likely to.
tebygol *a.* likely, probable. **yn debygol o ennill** likely to win.
tebygrwydd *e.g.* likeness, similarity, resemblance.
tecell: tegell *e.g. ll.* **-au, -i** kettle.
techneg *e.b. ll.* **-au** technique.
technegol *a.* technical.
technegwr *e.g. ll.* **technegwyr** technician.
technoleg *e.b.* technology.
teg *a.* fair, fine, beautiful. **chwarae teg** fair play; **teg o bryd** beautiful in appearance.
tegan *e.g. ll.* **-au** toy, plaything.
tegell *gw.* **tecell.**
tegwch *e.g.* beauty, fairness.
tei *e.g.b. ll.* **teis** tie.
teiar *e.g. ll.* **-s** tyre.
teidiau *gw.* **taid.**
teigr *e.g. ll.* **-od** tiger.
teiliwr *e.g. ll.* **teilwriaid** tailor.
teilsen *e.b. ll.* **teils** tile.
teilwng *a.* worthy, deserved. **yn deilwng o** worthy of.
teilwres *e.b. ll.* **-au** tailoress.
teilwriaid *gw.* **teiliwr.**
teilyngdod *e.g. ll.* **-au** merit, worthiness.
teimlad *e.g. ll.* **-au** feel, emotion, feeling, sensation.
teimlo *be.* **(teimlaf)** to feel, to

teipiadur   **toll**

handle, to touch. **teimlo fel** to feel
like.
teipiadur *e.g. ll.* **-on** typewriter.
teirgwaith *ad.* three times.
teirw *gw.* **tarw.**
teis *gw.* **tei.**
teisen *e.b. ll.* **-nau** cake, tart. **teisen
ddwbl** sandwich cake; **teisen
ffrwythau** fruit cake; **teisennau cri**
Welsh cakes.
teitl *e.g. ll.* **-au** title.
teithiau *gw.* **taith.**
teithio *be.* **(teithiaf)** to travel, to
journey.
teithiwr *e.g. ll.* **teithwyr** traveller.
telediad *e.g. ll.* **-au** telecast.
teledu 1 *be.* **(teledaf)** to televise.
2 *e.g.* television. **set deledu lliw**
colour television set.
teleffon *e.g. ll.* **-au** telephone. *gw.*
ffôn.
teleffonio: ffonio *be.* **(teleffoniaf:
ffoniaf)** to telephone, to phone.
telyn *e.b. ll.* **-au** harp.
telyneg *e.b. ll.* **-ion** lyric.
telynor *e.g. ll.* **-ion** harpist.
telynores *e.b. ll.* **-au** female harpist.
telynorion *gw.* **telynor.**
teml *e.b. ll.* **-au** temple.
tenau *a.* thin, slender, lean; rare.
terfyn *e.g. ll.* **-au** end, boundary,
extremity.
terfynol *a.* ultimate, last. **y taliad
terfynol** the last instalment.
terfysg *e.g. ll.* **-oedd** tumult,
commontion, riot.
terfysgaeth *e.g.* terrorism.
terfysgwr *e.g. ll.* **terfysgwyr**
terrorist.
term *e.g. ll.* **-au** term. **termau
technegol** technical terms.
tes *e.g.* heat, sunshine, haze.
tesog *a.* hot, sunny.
testun *e.g. ll.* **-au** text, subject.
testun sgwrs subject for debate;
testun siarad subject of gossip.
teulu *e.g. ll.* **-oedd** family.
tew *a.* fat.
teyrnas *e.b. ll.* **-oedd** kingdom.
Teyrnas Nefoedd Kingdom of
Heaven; **Y Deyrnas Unedig** The

United Kingdom.
ti *rhag.* you *(singular).*
ticed *e.g. ll.* **-i** ticket.
tîm *e.g. ll.* **timau** team.
tip *e.g. ll.* **-iau** tip.
tipiau *gw.* **tip, tipyn.**
tipyn *e.g. ll.* **-nau, tipiau** little, bit.
tipyn bach a little; **bob yn dipyn**
little by little.
tir *e.g. ll.* **-oedd** land, earth, ground,
territory. **tir neb** no man's land;
colli tir to lose ground.
tirion *a.* tender, kind, gentle,
gracious.
tirlun *e.g. ll.* **-iau** landscape.
tiroedd *gw.* **tir.**
tisian *be.* **(tisiaf)** to sneeze.
tithau *rhag.* you also *(singular).*
tiwtor *e.g. ll.* **-iaid** tutor.
tlawd *a. ll.* **tlodion** poor, needy. **y
tlodion** the poor.
tlodi *e.g.* poverty.
tlodion *gw.* **tlawd.**
tlos *a.b.* pretty. **merch dlos** a
pretty girl *(N.W.). gw.* **tlws.**
tlws 1 *e.g. ll.* **tlysau** gem, jewel,
brooch. **tlws aur** a gold brooch;
tlws yr eira snowdrop; **clustlysau**
ear-rings. **2** *a.g.* pretty. *gw.* **tlos.**
tlysau. *gw.* **tlws.**
to 1 *e.g. ll.* **-eau, -eon** roof.
2 *e.g.b.* generation. **y to sy'n codi**
the rising generation.
tocyn *e.g. ll.* **-nau** ticket, token.
tocyn dwyffordd return ticket.
tocynnau *gw.* **tocyn.**
tocynnwr *e.g. ll.* **tocynwyr** ticket
collector, conductor.
tocynwyr *gw.* **tocynnwr.**
toddi *be.* **(toddaf)** to melt, to thaw,
to dissolve.
toeau *gw.* **to.**
toeon *gw.* **to.**
toes *e.g.* dough. **toesenni**
doughnuts; **tylino toes** to knead
dough.
toiled *e.g. ll.* **-au** toilet.
tolc *e.g. ll.* **-iau** dent.
tolcio *be.* **(tolciaf)** to dent.
toll *e.b. ll.* **-au** toll, custom, duty.
tollborth/tollglwyd toll-gate.

tom   **treial**

tom *e.b.* manure.
ton *e.b. ll.* **tonnau** wave, breaker.
tôn *e.b. ll.* **tonau** tune. **tôn gron** a round (tune).
tonau *gw.* **tôn.**
tonfedd *e.b. ll.* **-i** wavelength.
tonnau *gw.* **ton.**
torch *e.b. ll.* **-au** wreath, coil, torque.
toreithiog *a* abundant, teeming.
toreth *e.b.* abundance.
torf *e.b.* **-eydd** crowd, multitude.
torfeydd *gw.* **torf.**
torfol *a.* collective, mass. **enw torfol** collective noun.
torheulo *be.* **(torheulaf)** to sunbathe.
Tori *e.g. ll.* **Torïaid** Tory.
toriad *e.g. ll.* **-au** break, cut.
Torïaid *gw.* **Tori.**
Torïaidd *a.* Tory, Conservative.
torri *be.* **(torraf)** to break, to cut, to sever; to go bankrupt. **torri ar draws** to interrupt; **torri enw** to sign; **torri gwynt** to break wind.
tors *e.g.b. ll.* **tyrs** torch.
torth *e.b. ll.* **-au** loaf. **torth wen** white loaf.
tosau *gw.* **tosyn.**
tost 1 *a.* severe, sharp, sore; ill *(S.W.).* 2 *e.g.* toast (bread).
tostrwydd *e.g.* illness, severity.
tosyn *e.g. ll.* **tosau** pimple *(S.W.).*
tra 1 *ad.* extremely, over, very. **Dw i'n dra diolchgar** I'm very grateful; 2 *c.* while, whilst. **Ewch tra bod heddwch** Go whilst there is peace.
trachefn *gw.* **drachefn.**
trachwant *e.g. ll.* **-au** lust, greed, covetousness.
trachwantus *a.* covetous, lustful.
traddodiad *e.g. ll.* **-au** tradition; delivery.
traddodiadol *a.* traditional.
traed *gw.* **troed.**
traeth *e.g. ll.* **-au** beach, shore.
traethau *gw.* **traeth.**
traethawd *e.g. ll.* **traethodau** essay, treatise, tract.
traethodau *gw.* **traethawd.**
trafnidiaeth *e.b.* traffic, commerce.
trafod *be.* **(trafodaf)** to handle, to

discuss, to negotiate, to transact.
cylch trafod discussion group.
trafferth *e.b.g. ll.* **-ion** trouble, toil, bother.
trafferthu (i) *be.* **(trafferthaf)** to trouble, to bother, to take pains.
trafferthus *a.* troublesome, laborious; troubled.
traffordd *e.b. ll.* **traffyrdd** motorway.
traffyrdd *gw.* **traffordd.**
tragwyddol *a.* eternal, everlasting. **o dragwyddol bwys** of everlasting importance.
trai *e.g. ll.* **treiau** ebb, decrease. **trai a llanw** ebb and flow.
trais *e.g. ll.* **treisiau** violence, oppression; rape.
trallod *e.g. ll.* **-au, -ion** tribulation, trouble.
trallodau *gw.* **trallod.**
trallodion *gw.* **trallod.**
trallwysiad *e.g. ll.* **-au** transfusion. **Gwasanaeth Trallwyso Gwaed** Blood Transfusion Service.
tramor *a.* overseas, foreign.
trannoeth *ad.* next day. **Daeth e drannoeth** He came the next day.
trap *e.g. ll.* **-iau** trap.
traul *e.b. ll.* **treuliau** wear; cost, expense.
trawsblannu *be.* **(trawsblannaf)** to transplant.
trawst *e.g. ll.* **-iau** beam, crossbar.
tre *gw.* **tref.**
trechu *be.* **(trechaf)** to overcome, to defeat.
tref: tre *e.b. ll.* **-i, -ydd** town, home. **tua thre** homeward: **tre farchnad** market town.
trefi *gw.* **tref.**
trefn *e.b. ll.* **-au** order, arrangment, system, method. **dweud y drefn** to scold.
trefnu (i) *be.* **(trefnaf)** to order, to arrange, to organise, to sort.
trefnus *a.* orderly, methodical.
trefnydd *e.g. ll.* **-ion** organiser.
trefol *a.* urban.
trefydd *gw.* **tref.**
treial *e.g. ll.* **-on** trial, contest.

treiau   **troswr**

treialon cŵn defaid sheepdog
trials.
treiau *gw.* **trai.**
treiglad *e.g. ll.* **-au** mutation;
rolling. **treiglad llaes** spirant
mutation; **treiglad meddal** soft
mutation; **treiglad trwynol** nasal
mutation.
treiglo *be.* **(treiglaf)** to mutate; to
roll.
treisgar *a.* violent.
treisiau *gw.* **trais.**
treisio *be.* **(treisiaf)** to force, to
violate, to oppress; to rape.
trem *e.b. ll.* **-iau** sight, look.
trên *e.g. ll.* **trenau** train.
trenau *gw.* **trên.**
trennydd *ad.* two days hence.
treth *e.b. ll.* **-i** rate, tax, levy; strain.
treth ar werth value added tax;
treth incwm income tax; **treth y
pen** community charge/poll tax;
treth gyngor council tax; **Roedd
e'n dreth ar fy amynedd** He was a
strain on my patience.
trethdalwr *e.g. ll.* **trethdalwyr**
ratepayer.
trethu *be.* **(trethaf)** to tax, to rate.
treuliau *gw.* **traul.**
treulio *be.* **(treuliaf)** to wear; to
spend; to digest.
tri *a.g. & e.g.* **-oedd** *(followed by
spirant mutation)* three. **tri chap**
three caps; **tri pheint** three pints; **tri
thŷ** three houses; **tri chynnig i
Gymro** three tries for a Welshman.
gw. At. Treigladau. gw. **tair.**
triawd *e.g. ll.* **-au** trio, threesome.
tric *e.g. ll.* **-iau** trick.
tridiau *e.ll.* three days.
trigain *a. & e.g.* sixty. **trigain
mlynedd yn ôl** sixty years ago. *gw.
At. Treiglad Trwynol.*
trigfan *e.b. ll.* **-nau** dwelling-place.
trigo *be.* **(trigaf)** to dwell, to reside;
to die (of animal).
trigolion *e.ll.* inhabitants.
trin *be.* **(triniaf)** to treat; to handle; to
dress; to till; to revile. **siop trin
gwallt** hairdresser's shop; **trin y tir**
to cultivate the land.

trindod *e.b. ll.* **-au** trinity. **Coleg y
Drindod** Trinity College.
trioedd *e.ll.* triads.
triongl *e.g.b. ll.* **-au** triangle.
trist *a.* sad, sorrowful, unhappy.
tristwch *e.g.* sadness, sorrow.
tristwch o'r mwyaf the greatest
sorrow.
tro *e.g. ll.* **troeau, troeon** turn,
twist, bend; conversion. **gweld tro
ar fyd** to experience a change in
circumstances. **llygad tro** a squint;
tro gwael an unworthy act; **tro yn
ei gwt** a twist in his tail.
trochi *be.* **(trochaf)** to dip, to plunge;
to soil *(S.W.);* to bathe *(N.W.).*
troeau *gw.* **tro.**
troed *e.g.b. ll.* **traed** foot, base;
handle.
troedfedd *e.b. ll.* **-i** foot *(measure).*
troedffordd *e.g. ll.* **troedffyrdd**
footpath.
troëdig *a.* turned, converted.
tröedigaeth *e.b. ll.* **-au** conversion,
turning.
troedio *be.* **(troediaf)** to walk, to
tread, to trudge.
troednoeth *a.* barefooted.
troeon *gw.* **tro.**
trogylch *e.g. ll.* **-oedd, -au**
roundabout.
troi *be.* **(troaf)** to turn, to revolve, to
convert; to plough; to translate. *gw.
At. Berfau.*
tros *gw.* **dros.**
trosedd *e.b. ll.* **-au** crime, offence,
transgression.
troseddu *be.* **(troseddaf)** to offend,
to transgress.
troseddwr *e.g. ll.* **troseddwyr**
criminal, transgressor.
trosgais *e.g. ll.* **trosgeisiau**
converted try *(rugby).*
trosglwyddo *be.* **(trosglwyddaf)** to
convey, to transfer.
trosi *be.* **(trosaf)** to turn, to translate,
to transfer; to convert *(rugby).*
trosiad *e.b. ll.* **-au** translation;
conversion *(rugby).*
troswr *e.g. ll.* **troswyr** switch
(electricity).

trothwy *e.g. ll.* **-au, -on** threshold.
ar drothwy'r Nadolig on the
threshold of Christmas.
trowsus *e.g. ll.* **-au** trousers.
trowsus byr short trousers.
truan *e.g. ll.* **trueiniaid** wretch.
Druan ohono! Poor fellow! **Jac
druan!** Poor Jack!
trueiniad *gw.* **truan.**
trueni *e.g.* wretchedness, pity,
misery. **trueni ei fod** a pity that;
trueni iddo a pity that.
truenus *a.* wretched, miserable.
trugaredd *e.g. ll.* **-au** mercy,
compassion. **drwy drugaredd**
fortunately.
trugarhau (wrth) *be.* **(trugarhaf)** to
be merciful (to), to take pity (on).
trwbl *e.g.* trouble.
trwchus *a.* thick; dense.
trwm *a. ll.* **trymion** heavy, sad,
wretched.
trwser *e.g. ll.* **-i** trousers. *gw.*
trowsus.
trwsio *be.* **(trwsiaf)** to mend, to trim,
to dress.
trwsiwr *e.g. ll.* **trwswyr** repairer.
trwy *gw.* **drwy.**
trwydded *e.b. ll.* **-au** licence,
dispensation. **trwydded yrru**
driving licence.
trwyn *e.g. ll.* **-au** nose, snout; point,
cape.
trwynol *a.* nasal.
trychineb *e.g.b. ll.* **-au** disaster,
calamity.
trydan 1 *e.g.* electric. **Y Bwrdd
Trydan** The Electricity Board.
trydanol *a.* electrical.
trydanwr *e.g. ll.* **trydanwyr**
electrician.
trydedd *a.b. (used before feminine
nouns)* third. **y drydedd bennod**
the third chapter.
trydydd *a.g. (used before masculine
nouns)* third. **y trydydd tro** the
third time.
trydyddol *a.* tertiary. **Coleg
Trydyddol** Tertiary College.
tryloyw *a.* transparent.
trymaidd *a.* heavy, close, sultry.

trymion *gw.* **trwm.**
trysor *e.b. ll.* **-au** treasure.
trysorfa *e.b.* **trysorfeydd**
treasury, fund.
trysori *be.* **(trysoraf)** to treasure.
trysorydd *e.g. ll.* **-ion** treasurer.
trywydd *e.g. ll.* **-ion** scent, trail.
ar drywydd on the trail of.
tu *e.g.* side, region. **tu draw i: tu
hwnt** beyond; **tu fewn: tu mewn**
inside; **tu faes *(S.W.): tu allan**
(N.W.).* outside.
tua: tuag *ardd. (followed by spirant
mutation)* towards; about. **tua thre:
adre** homewards; **tuag at** towards;
tua mis about a month.
tudalen *e.g.b. ll.* **-nau** page.
tudalen flaen front page. *gw.* **dalen.**
tueddiad *e.g. ll.* **-au** tendency,
proneness.
tun 1 *e.g.* **-iau** tin, can. **2** *a.* tin.
tunnell *e.g. ll.* **tunelli** ton.
twlc *e.g. ll.* **tylciau** sty. **twlc
mochyn** pigsty.
twll *e.g. ll.* **tyllau** hole.
twmffat *e.g.* funnel.
twmpath *e.g. ll.* **-au** tump, hillock.
Twmpath Dawns Folk Dancing
event.
twndis *e.g. ll.* **-au** funnel.
twnel *e.g. ll.* **-au, -i** tunnel.
twp *a.* dull, stupid *(S.W.).*
twpsyn *e.g.* stupid person.
twr *e.g. ll.* **tyrrau** heap; group;
crowd.
twˆr *e.g. ll.* **tyrau** tower.
twrci *e.g. ll.* **twrcïod, tyrcwn**
turkey.
twristiaeth *e.b.* tourism. **Y Bwrdd
Croeso** The Tourist Board.
twrw *e.g. ll.* **tyrfau** noise, tumult,
roar, crash. **tyrfau: taranau**
thunder.
twt *a.* neat, tidy. **tŷ bach twt** a
Wendy house *(lit. a neat little
house);* **twt a lol** nonsense, rubbish.
twyll *e.g.* deceit, fraud, treachery.
twyllo *be.* **(twyllaf)** to deceive, to
cheat, to defraud.
twyllodrus *a.* deceitful, false,
fraudulent.

twym *a.* warm *(S.W.).* **twym iawn**
hot *(S.W.).*
twymo *be.* **(twymaf)** to warm.
twymyn *e.b. ll.* **-au** fever.
tŷ *e.g. ll.* **tai** house. **tŷ newydd** new
house; **tŷ bach** toilet; **tŷ tafarn**
public house; **tŷ cwrdd** religious
meeting house.
tybed *ad.* I wonder: is that so?
Tybed a ddaw hi? I wonder
whether she will come?
tybied: tybio *be.* **(tybiaf)** to
suppose, to think, to imagine.
tydi *rhag.* you yourself.
tyddyn *e.g. ll.* **-nod, -nau** small
holding, small farm, croft. **ty'n
cwm: tyddyn y cwm** the valley
smallholding; **ty'n y waun** the moor
croft.
tyddynnwr *e.g. ll.* **tyddynwyr**
smallholder, crofter.
tyddynwyr *gw.* **tyddynnwr.**
tyfiannau *gw.* **tyfiant.**
tyfiant *e.g. ll.* **tyfiannau** growth,
increase.
tyfu *be.* **(tyfaf)** to grow, to increase.
tynged *e.b. ll.* **tynghedau** destiny,
fate.
tyngedfennol *a.* fateful, fatal.
tynghedau *gw.* **tynged.**
tyngu *be.* **(tyngaf)** to swear, to vow.
tylciau *ge.* **twlc.**
tyle *e.g. ll.* **-au** hill, ascent, slope
(S.W.).
tylino *be.* **(tylinaf)** to knead *(dough).*
tylwyth *e.g. ll.* **-au** family, ancestry,
kindred. **Tylwyth Teg** fairies.
tyllau *gw.* **twll.**
tyllu *be.* **(tyllaf)** to hole, to bore, to
perforate.
tylluan *e.b. ll.* **-od** owl *(N.W.).* *gw.*
gwdihŵ.
tymer *e.b. ll.* **tymherau** temper,
temperament.
tymereddau *gw.* **tymheredd.**
tymestl *e.b. ll.* **tymhestloedd**
tempest, storm.

tymherau *gw.* **tymer.**
tymheredd *e.g. ll.* **tymereddau**
temperature, temperament.
tymhestloedd *gw.* **tymestl.**
tymhestlog *a.* tempestuous, stormy.
tymhorau *gw.* **tymor.**
tymor *e.g. ll.* **tymhorau** season,
term. **Tymor yr Haf** Summer Term;
yn el thymor in season *(of animal).*
tyn 1 *a.* tight, mean, perverse.
2 *bf.* pull! tighten! *gw.* **tynnu**
tyner *a.* gentle, tender.
tynerwch *e.g.* gentleness, tenderness.
tynnu *be.* **(tynnaf)** to pull, to draw,
to remove; take off. **Tynnwch eich
cot** Take off your coat.
tyrau *gw.* **tŵr.**
tyrfa *e.b. ll.* **-oedd** crowd, multitude.
tyrfau *gw.* **twrw.**
tyrrau *gw.* **twr.**
tyst *e.g. ll.* **-ion** witness.
tystio *be.* **(tystiaf)** to testify, to
witness. **tystio bod** to testify that.
tystiolaeth *e.b. ll.* **-au** evidence;
testimony.
tystion *gw.* **tyst.**
tystysgrif *e.b. ll.* **-au** certificate.
tystysgrif geni birth certificate;
tystysgrif marwolaeth death
certificate; **tystysgrif priodi**
marriage certificate.
tywel *e.g. ll.* **-ion** towel.
tywod *e.g.* sand.
tywydd *e.g.* weather. **tywydd mawr**
stormy weather; **tywydd teg** fair
weather.
tywyll *a.* dark, obscure; blind, sad.
tywyllu *be.* **(tywyllaf)** to darken.
tywyllwch *e.g.* darkness.
tywys *be.* **(tywysaf)** to lead, to
guide.
tywysydd *e.g. ll.* **-ion** guide.
tywysog *e.g. ll.* **-ion** prince.
Tywysog Cymru Prince of Wales.
tywysoges *e.b. ll.* **-au** princess.
Tywysoges Cymru Princess of
Wales.

thawelyn

th

thabl *gw.* tabl.
thabled *ge.* tabled.
thacl *gw.* tacl.
thaclo *gw.* taclo.
thaclu *gw.* taclu.
thaclus *gw.* taclus.
thacluso *ge.* tacluso.
thaclwr *gw.* taclwr.
thacsi *gw.* tacsi.
Thachwedd *gw.* Tachwedd.
thad *gw.* tad.
thad-cu *gw.* tad-cu.
thafarn *gw.* tafarn.
thafarnwr *gw.* tafarnwr.
thafell *gw.* tafell.
thaflegryn *gw.* taflegryn.
thaflen *gw.* taflen.
thaflu *gw.* taflu.
thafod *gw.* tafod.
thafodiaith *gw.* tafodiaith.
thafodieithoedd *gw.* tafodiaith.
thafol *gw.* tafol.
thagfa *gw.* tagfa.
thagu *gw.* tagu.
thangnefedd *gw.* tangnefedd.
thai *gw.* tŷ.
thaid *gw.* taid.
thair *gw.* tair.
thaith *gw.* taith.
thai *gw.* tai.
thâl *gw.* tâl.
thalai *gw.* talai. *gw.* talu.
thalaith *gw.* talaith.

thalcen *gw.* talcen.
thalcennau: thalcenni *gw.* talcen.
thaleb *gw.* taleb.
thalent *gw.* talent.
thalentog *gw.* talentog.
thaliadau: thaloedd *gw.* tâl.
thalu *gw.* talu.
thalwr *gw.* talwr.
thalwrn *gw.* talwrn.
thamaid *gw.* tamaid.
thameidiau *gw.* tamaid.
than *gw.* dan.
thân *gw.* tân.
thanau *gw.* tân.
thanbaid *gw.* tanbaid.
thanc *gw.* tanc.
thancer *gw.* tancer.
thanddaear *gw.* tanddaear.
thanddaearol *gw.* tanddaear.
thanfor *gw.* tanfor.
thanio *gw.* tanio.
thanlinellu *gw.* tanlinellu.
thanlwybr *gw.* tanlwybr.
thanllyd *gw.* tanllyd.
thannau *gw.* tant.
thanseilio *gw.* tanseilio.
thant *gw.* tant.
thanwydd *gw.* tanwydd.
thap *gw.* tap.
thâp *gw.* tâp.
thapiau *gw.* tap. *gw.* tâp.
tharan *gw.* taran.
tharanu *gw.* taranu.
tharddiad *gw.* tarddiad.
tharddu *gw.* tarddu.
tharged *gw.* targed.
tharian *gw.* tarian.
tharianau *gw.* tarian.
tharo *gw.* taro.
tharw *gw.* tarw.
thasg *gw.* tasg.
thasgu *gw.* tasgu.
thaten *gw.* taten.
thato *gw.* taten.
thatws *gw.* taten.
thawel *gw.* tawel.
thawelu *gw.* tawelu.
thawelwch *gw.* tawelwch.
thawelydd *gw.* tawelydd.
thawelyddion *gw.* tawelydd.
thawelyn *gw.* tawelyn.

the *gw.* te.
theatr *eb. ll.* -au theatre, playhouse.
thebot *gw.* tebot.
thebyg *gw.* tebyg.
thebygrwydd *gw.* tebygrwydd.
thecell *gw.* tecell.
thechneg *gw.* techneg.
thechnegol *gw.* technegol.
thechnegwr *gw.* technegwr.
thechnoleg *gw.* technoleg.
theg *gw.* teg.
thegan *gw.* tegan.
thegell *gw.* tecell.
thegwch *gw.* tegwch.
thei *gw.* tei.
theiar *gw.* teiar.
theidiau *gw.* taid.
theigr *gw.* teigr.
theiliwr *gw.* teiliwr.
theilsen *gw.* teilsen.
theilwng *gw.* teilwng.
theilwres *gw.* teilwres.
theilwriaid *gw.* teiliwr.
theilyngdod *gw.* teilyngdod.
theimlad *gw.* teimlad.
theimlo *gw.* teimlo.
theipiadur *gw.* teipiadur.
theirgwaith *gw.* teirgwaith.
theirw *gw.* tarw.
theis *gw.* tei.
theisen *gw.* teisen.
theitl *gw.* teitl.
theithiau *gw.* taith.
theithio *gw.* teithio.
theithiwr *gw.* teithiwr.
thelediad *gw.* telediad.
theledu *gw.* teledu.
theleffon *gw.* teleffon.
theleffonio *gw.* teleffonio.
thelyn *gw.* telyn.
thelyneg *gw.* telyneg.
thelynor *gw.* telynor.
thelynores *gw.* telynores.
thelynorion *gw.* telynor.
thema *e.b ll.* themâu theme.
theml *gw.* teml.
thenau *gw.* tenau.
therapydd *e.g. ll.* -ion therapist.
therfyn *gw.* terfyn.
therfysg *gw.* terfysg.
therfysgaeth *gw.* terfysgaeth.

therfysgwr *gw.* terfysgwr.
therm *gw.* term.
thermomedr *e.g. ll.* -au
   thermometer.
thes *gw.* tes.
thesog *gw.* tesog.
thestun *gw.* testun.
theulu *gw.* teulu.
thew *gw.* tew.
theyrnas *gw.* teyrnas.
thi *gw.* ti.
thiced *gw.* ticed.
thîm *gw.* tîm.
thipiau *gw.* tip. *gw.* tipyn.
thipyn *gw.* tipyn.
thir *gw.* tir.
thirion *gw.* tirion.
thirlun *gw.* tirlun.
thiroedd *gw.* tir.
thisian *gw.* tisian.
thithau *gw.* tithau.
thiwtor *gw.* tiwtor.
thlawd *gw.* tlawd.
thlodi *gw.* tlodi.
thlodion *gw.* tlawd.
thlos *gw.* tlos.
thlws *gw.* tlws.
thlysau *gw.* tlws.
tho *gw.* to.
thocyn *gw.* tocyn.
thocynnau *gw.* tocyn.
thocynnwr *gw.* tocynnwr.
thocynwyr *gw.* tocynnwr.
thoddi *gw.* toddi.
thoeau *gw.* to.
thoeon *gw.* to.
thoes *gw.* toes.
thoiled *gw.* toiled.
tholc *gw.* tolc.
tholcio *gw.* tolcio.
tholl *gw.* toll.
thom *gw.* tom.
thon *gw.* ton.
thôn *gw.* tôn.
thonau *gw.* tôn.
thonfedd *gw.* tonfedd.
thonnau *gw.* ton.
thorch *gw.* torch.
thoreithiog *gw.* toreithiog.
thoreth *gw.* toreth.
thorf *gw.* torf.

thorfeydd   **throsgais**

thorfeydd *gw*. torf.
thorfol *gw*. torfol.
thorheulo *gw*. torheulo.
Thori *gw*. Tori.
thoriad *gw*. toriad.
Thorïaid *gw*. Tori.
Thorïaidd *gw*. Torïaidd.
thorri *gw*. torri.
thors *gw*. tors.
thorth *gw*. torth.
thosau *gw*. tosyn.
thost *gw*. tost.
thostrwydd *gw*. tostrwydd.
thosyn *gw*. tosyn.
thrachefn *gw*. trachefn.
thrachwant *gw*. trachwant.
thrachwantus *gw*. trachwantus.
thraddodiad *gw*. traddodiad.
thraddodiadol *gw*. traddodiadol.
thraed *gw*. troed.
thraeth *gw*. traeth.
thraethau *gw*. traeth.
thraethawd *gw*. traethawd.
thraethodau *gw*. traethawd.
thrafnidiaeth *gw*. trafnidiaeth.
thrafod *gw*. trafod.
thrafferth *gw*. trafferth.
thrafferthu *gw*. trafferthu.
thrafferthus *gw*. trafferthus.
thraffordd *gw*. traffordd.
thraffyrdd *gw*. traffordd.
thragwyddol *gw*. tragwyddol.
thrai *gw*. trai.
thrais *gw*. trais.
thrallod *gw*. trallod.
thrallodau *gw*. trallod.
thrallodion *gw*. trallod.
thrallwysiad *gw*. trallwysiad.
thramor *gw*. tramor.
thrannoeth *gw*. trannoeth.
thrap *gw*. trap.
thraul *gw*. traul.
thrawsblannu *gw*. trawsblannu.
thrawst *gw*. trawst.
thre *gw*. tref.
threchu *gw*. trechu.
thref *gw*. tref.
threfi *gw*. tref.
threfn *gw*. trefn.
threfnu *gw*. trefnu.
threfnus *gw*. trefnus.

threfnydd *gw*. trefnydd.
threfol *gw*. trefol.
threfydd *gw*. tref.
threial *gw*. treial.
threiau *gw*. trai.
threiglad *gw*. treiglad.
threiglo *gw*. treiglo.
threisgar *gw*. treisgar.
threisiau *gw*. trais.
threisio *gw*. treisio.
threm *gw*. trem.
thrên *gw*. trên.
threnau *gw*. trên.
thrennydd *gw*. trennydd.
threth *gw*. treth.
threthdalwr *gw*. trethdalwr.
threthu *gw*. trethu.
threuliau *gw*. traul.
threulio *gw*. treulio.
thri *gw*. tri.
thriawd *gw*. triawd.
thric *gw*. tric.
thridiau *gw*. tridiau.
thrigain *gw*. trigain.
thrigfan *gw*. trigfan.
thrigo *gw*. trigo.
thrigolion *gw*. trigolion.
thrin *gw*. trin.
thrindod *gw*. trindod.
thrioedd *gw*. trioedd.
thriongl *gw*. triongl.
thrist *gw*. trist.
thristwch *gw*. tristwch.
thro *gw*. tro.
throchi *gw*. trochi.
throeau *gw*, tro.
throed *gw*. troed.
throedfedd *gw*. troedfedd.
throedffordd *gw*. troedffordd.
throëdig *gw*. troëdig.
thröedigaeth *gw*. tröedigaeth.
throedio *gw*. troedio.
throednoeth *gw*. troednoeth.
throeon *gw*. tro.
throgylch *gw*. trogylch.
throi *gw*. troi.
thros *gw*. tros.
throsedd *gw*. trosedd.
throseddu *gw*. troseddu.
throseddwr *gw*. troseddwr.
throsgais *gw*. trosgais.

throsglwyddo   **thyrrau**

throsglwyddo *gw.* trosglwyddo.
throsi *gw.* trosi.
throsiad *gw.* trosiad.
throswr *gw.* troswr.
throthwy *gw.* trothwy.
throwsus *gw.* trowsus.
thruan *ge.* truan.
thrueiniaid *gw.* truan.
thrueni *gw.* trueni.
thruenus *gw.* truenus.
thrugaredd *gw.* trugaredd.
thrugarhau *gw.* trugarhau.
thrwbl *gw.* trwbl.
thrwchus *gw.* trwchus.
thrwm *gw.* trwm.
thrwser *gw.* trwser.
thrwsio *gw.* trwsio.
thrwsiwr *gw.* trwsiwr.
thrwy *gw.* drwy.
thrwydded *gw.* trwydded.
thrwyn *gw.* trwyn.
thrwynol *gw.* trwynol.
thrychineb *gw.* trychineb.
thrydan *gw.* trydan.
thrydanol *gw.* trydanol.
thrydanwr *gw.* trydanwr.
thrydedd *gw.* trydedd.
thrydydd *gw.* trydydd.
thrydyddol *gw.* trydyddol.
thryloyw *gw.* tryloyw.
thrymaidd *gw.* trymaidd.
thrymion *gw.* trwm.
thrysor *gw.* trysor.
thrysorfa *gw.* trysorfa.
thrysorydd *gw.* trysorydd.
thrywydd *gw.* trywydd.
thu *gw.* tu.
thua *gw.* tua.
thuag *gw.* tua.
thudalen *gw.* tudalen.
thueddiad *gw.* tueddiad.
thun *ge.* tun.
thunnell *gw.* tunnell.
thus *e.g.* frankincense.
thwlc *gw.* twlc.
thwll *gw.* twll.
thwmpath *gw.* twmpath.
thwndis *gw.* twndis.
thwnel *gw.* twnel.
thwp *gw.* twp.
thwpsyn *gw.* twpsyn.

thwr *gw,* twr.
thŵr *gw.* tŵr.
thwrci *gw.* twrci.
thwristiaeth *gw.* twristiaeth.
thwrw *gw.* twrw.
thwt *gw.* twt.
thwyll *gw.* twyll.
thwyllo *gw.* twyllo.
thwyllodrus *gw.* twyllodrus.
thwym *gw.* twym.
thwymo *gw.* twymo.
thwymyn *gw.* twymyn.
thŷ *gw.* tŷ.
thybied *gw.* tybied.
thybio *gw.* tybied.
thydi *gw.* tydi.
thyddyn *gw.* tyddyn.
thyddynnwr *gw.* tyddynnwr.
thyddynwyr *gw.* tyddynnwr.
thyfiannau *gw.* tyfiant.
thyfiant *gw.* tyfiant.
thyfu *gw.* tyfu.
thynged *gw.* tynged.
thyngedfennol *gw.* tyngedfennol.
thynghedau *gw.* tynged.
thyngo *gw.* tyngu.
thylciau *gw.* twlc.
thyle *gw.* tyle.
thylino *gw.* tylino.
thylwyth *gw.* tylwyth.
thyllau *gw.* twll.
thyllu *gw.* tyllu.
thylluan *gw.* tylluan.
thymer *gw.* tymer.
thymereddau *gw.* tymheredd.
thymestl *gw.* tymestl.
thymherau *gw.* tymer.
thymheredd *gw.* tymheredd.
thymhestloedd *gw.* tymestl.
thymhestlog *gw.* tymhestlog.
thymhorau *gw.* tymor.
thymor *gw.* tymor.
thyn *gw.* tyn.
thyner *gw.* tyner.
thynerwch *gw.* tynerwch.
thynnu *gw.* tynnu.
thyrau *gw.* tŵr.
thyrfa *gw.* tyrfa.
thyrfaoedd *gw.* tyrfa.
thyrfau *gw.* twrw.
thyrrau *gw.* twr.

thyst *gw.* tyst.
thystio *gw.* tystio.
thystiolaeth *gw.* tystiolaeth.
thystion *gw.* tyst.
thystysgrif *gw.* tystysgrif.
thystysgrifau *gw.* tystysgrif.
thywel *gw.* tywel.
thywod *gw.* tywod.

thywydd *gw.* tywydd.
thywyll *gw.* tywyll.
thywyllu *gw.* tywyllu.
thywyllwch *gw.* tywyllwch.
thywys *gw.* tywys.
thywysog *gw.* tywysog.
thywysoges *gw.* tywysoges.

turn; once; **yr un** the one, the same;
yr un faint as much, the same; **yr
un pryd** the same time.
unawd *e.g. ll.* **-au** solo.
unawdwr: unawdydd *e.g. ll.*
unawdwyr soloist.
unben *e.g. ll.* **-iaid** dictator, despot.
undeb *e.g. ll.* **-au** union, unity.
Undeb yr Athrawon the Teachers'
Union; **Undeb y Mamau** the
Mothers' Union.
undebwr *e.g. ll.* **undebwyr** unionist.
undod *e.g. ll.* **-au** unit, unity.
Undodwr *e.g. ll.* **Undodwyr**
Unitarian.
undonog *a.* monotonous.
undydd *a.* one-day. **ysgol undydd**
a one-day school.
uned *e.b. ll.* **-au** unit.
unedig *a.* united.
unfarn *a.* unanimous.
unfryd: unfrydol *a.* unanimous.
unffordd *a.* one-way. **stryd
unffordd** one-way street.
uniaethu (â) *be.* **(uniaethaf)** to
identify (with).
unig *a. (precedes noun and causes
soft mutation)* only, sole; alone,
lonely. **yr unig fab** the only son;
mab unig lonely son.
unigol *a.* singular; individual.
unigolyn *e.g. ll.* **unigolion**
individual.
unigrwydd *e.g.* loneliness.
unigryw *a.* unique.
union *a.* direct, straight; exact. **yr
union fan** the exact place.
unioni *be.* **(unionaf)** to rectify, to
straighten.
unman *ad.* anywhere.
unnos *a.* of or for one night. **tŷ
unnos** habitable cabin built
between dusk and dawn.
uno *be.* **(unaf)** to unite, to join.
unrhyw *a.* same; any; homogeneous.
mewn unrhyw wlad in any
country; **unrhyw beth** anything.
unwaith *ad.* once. **ar unwaith** at
once; **unwaith ac am byth** once
and for all.
urdd *e.b. ll.* **-au** order, guild. **Urdd**

---

uchaf *a.* uppermost, highest; loudest.
am yr uchaf for the loudest.
uchafbwynt *e.g. ll.* **-iau** climax;
zenith.
uchder *e.g. ll.* **-au** height, altitude.
uchel *a.* high; loud.
uchelder *e.g. ll.* **-au** highness.
ucheldir *e.g. ll.* **-oedd** highland.
uchelgais *e.g.b. ll.* **uchelgeisiau**
ambition.
uchelgeisiol *a.* ambitious.
uchelion *e.ll.* heights.
uchelwr *e.g. ll.* **uchelwyr**
gentleman, nobleman.
uchod *ad.* above. **yn y rhestr
uchod** in the above list.
udo *be.* **(udaf)** to howl, to moan, to
wail.
ufudd *a.* obedient.
ufuddhau (i) *be.* **(ufuddhâf)** to
obey.
uffern *e.b. ll.* **-au** hell. **Uffern dân!**
Hell fire!
uffernol *a.* infernal, hellish. **Roedd
hi'n ddrud uffernol** It was
extremely expensive.
ugain *a. & e.g. ll.* **ugeiniau** twenty.
tri ar hugain twenty-three; **deg ar
hugain** thirty.
ugeinfed *a.* twentieth. **yr ugeinfed
ganrif** the 20th century.
ugeiniau *gw.* **ugain.**
un *a. & e.g. ll.* **-au** one. **un tro** one.

urddas

Gobaith Cymru Welsh League of Youth.
urddas *e.g. ll.* **-au** dignity, honour.
urddo *be.* **(urddaf)** to obtain, to bestow honour on.
us *e.ll.* chaff.
ustus *e.g. ll.* **-iaid** magistrate.
uwch *a.* higher, senior, superior; advanced. **uwchgapten** major (army officer); **uwchnormal** superior. *gw.* **uchel.**
uwchben *ardd. & ad.* above.
uwchfarchnad *e.b. ll.* **-oedd** supermarket.
uwchlaw *ardd.* above.
uwchradd *a.* secondary. **ysgol uwchradd** secondary school.
uwd *e.g. ll.* **-iau** porridge.

weddill

w

wadu *gw.* **gwadu.**
waed *gw.* **gwaed.**
waedu *gw.* **gwaedu.**
waedd *gw.* **gwaedd.**
wael *gw.* **gwael.**
waelod *gw.* **gwaelod.**
waeth *gw.* **drwg.**
waethaf *gw.* **drwg.**
waethed *gw.* **drwg.**
waethygu *gw.* **gwaethygu.**
wag *gw.* **gwag.**
wagedd *gw.* **gwagedd.**
wagio *gw.* **gwagio.**
wagle *gw.* **gwagle.**
wagu *gw.* **gwagio.**
wahân *gw.* **gwahân.**
wahanlaeth *gw.* **gwahaniaeth.**
wahaniaethu *gw.* **gwahaniaethu.**
wahanol *gw.* **gwahanol.**
wahanu *gw.* **gwahanu.**
wahardd *gw.* **gwahardd.**
wahodd *gw.* **gwahodd.**
wahoddedig *gw.* **gwahoddedig.**
wahoddedigion *gw.* **gwahoddedig.**
wahoddiad *gw.* **gwahoddiad.**
wahoddion *gw.* **gwahodd.**
wair *gw.* **gwair.**
waith *gw.* **gwaith.**
wal *e.b. ll.* **-au** wall. *gw.* **gwal.**
wâl *gw.* **gwâl.**
walau *gw.* **gwâl.**
waliau *gw.* **gwal, wal.**
wall *gw.* **gwall.**

wallgof *gw.* **gwallgof.**
wallt *gw.* **gwallt.**
wallus *gw.* **gwallus.**
wan *gw.* **gwan.**
wanwyn *gw.* **gwanwyn.**
war *gw.* **gwar.**
wâr *gw.* **gwâr.**
warchod *gw.* **gwarchod.**
waredu *gw.* **gwaredu.**
waredwr *gw.* **gwaredwr.**
wario *gw.* **gwario.**
warrau *gw.* **gwar.**
wartheg *gw.* **gwartheg.**
warthus *gw.* **gwarthus.**
was *gw.* **gwas.**
wasanaeth *gw.* **gwasanaeth.**
wasanaethu *gw.* **gwasanaethu.**
wasg *gw.* **gwasg.**
wasgedd *gw.* **gwasgedd.**
wasgfa *gw.* **gwasgfa.**
wasgod *gw.* **gwasgod.**
wasgu *gw.* **gwasgu.**
wastad *gw.* **gwastad.**
wastraff *gw.* **gwastraff.**
wastraffu *gw.* **gwastraffu.**
wats *e.g. ll.* **-ys** watch.
wau *gw.* **gwau.**
waun *gw.* **gwaun.**
wawd *gw.* **gwawd.**
wawdio *gw.* **gwawdio.**
wawr *gw.* **gwawr.**
wawrio *gw.* **gwawrio.**
wawroedd *gw.* **gwawr.**
wdihŵ *gw.* **gwdihŵ.**
wddf *gw.* **gwddf.**
wddwg *gw.* **gwddwg.**
we *gw.* **gwe.**
wedi *ardd.* after. **wedi deg** after
ten; **Mae wedi chwech arno** He
has lost his chance; *the preposition is
also used as follows:* (forms of **bod**)
+ (**wedi**) + *(be.);* **Rydw i wedi
blino** I am tired; **Dwyt ti ddim
wedi cysgu** You have not slept;
Roedd ef wedi troi He turned;
Maen nhw wedi marw They are
dead.
wedyn *ad.* afterwards, then.
weddi *gw.* **gweddi.**
weddïau *gw.* **gweddi.**
weddill *gw.* **gweddill.**

weddïo   **wleidyddiaeth**

weddïo *gw.* **gweddïo.**
weddol *gw.* **gweddol.**
weddw *gw.* **gweddw.**
wefus *gw.* **gwefus.**
weiddi *gw.* **gweiddi.**
weigion *gw.* **gwag.**
weiniaid *gw.* **gwan.**
weinidog *gw.* **gweinidog.**
weinion *gw.* **gwan.**
weinydd *gw.* **gweinydd.**
weinyddes *gw.* **gweinyddes.**
weiriau *gw.* **gwair.**
weisg *gw.* **gwasg.**
weision *gw.* **gwas.**
weithdy *gw.* **gweithdy.**
weithgar *gw.* **gweithgar.**
weithiau *ad.* sometimes. *gw.* **gwaith.**
weithio *gw.* **gweithio.**
weithiwr *gw.* **gweithiwr.**
weithred *gw.* **gweithred.**
weithredu *gw.* **gweithredu.**
weithwyr *gw.* **gweithiwr.**
wel *ebych.* well!
welâu *gw.* **gwely.**
weld *gw.* **gweld.**
wele *ebych.* behold!
weled *gw.* **gweld.**
welw *gw.* **gwelw.**
wely *gw.* **gwely.**
welyau *gw.* **gwely.**
welydd *gw.* **gwal.**
well *gw.* **gwell.**
wella *gw.* **gwella.**
wellt *gw.* **gwellt.**
welltyn *gw.* **gwelltyn.**
wen *gw.* **gwen.**
wên *gw.* **gwên.**
wenau *gw.* **gwên.**
wendid *gw.* **gwendid.**
Wener *gw.* **Gwener.**
wenith *gw.* **gwenith.**
wennol *gw.* **gwennol.**
Went *gw.* **Gwent.**
wenu *gw.* **gwenu.**
wenwyn *gw.* **gwenwyn.**
wenwynig *gw.* **gwenwynig.**
wenwynol *gw.* **gwenwynig.**
wenyn *gw.* **gwenynen.**
wenynen *gw.* **gwenynen.**
wêr *gw.* **gwêr.**
werdd *gw.* **gwerdd.**

werin *gw.* **gwerin.**
weriniaeth *gw.* **gweriniaeth.**
wers *gw.* **gwers.**
werslyfr *gw.* **gwerslyfr.**
wersyll *gw.* **gwersyll.**
werth *gw.* **gwerth.**
werthfawr *gw.* **gwerthfawr.**
werthfawrogi *gw.* **gwerthfawrogi.**
werthfawrogiad *gw.*
  gwerthfawrogiad.
werthiant *gw.* **gwerthiant.**
werthu *gw.* **gwerthu.**
werthwr *gw.* **gwerthwr.**
werthwyr *gw.* **gwerthwr.**
westai *gw.* **gwestai.** *gw.* **gwesty.**
westeion *gw.* **gwestai.**
westeiwr *gw.* **gwesteiwr.**
westeiwyr *gw.* **gwesteiwr.**
westy *gw.* **gwesty.**
weu *gw.* **gweu.**
weunydd *gw.* **gwaun.**
wg *gw.* **gwg.**
wgu *gw.* **gwgu.**
whilber *e.b. ll.* **-au** wheelbarrow.
  gw. **berfa.**
wiail *gw.* **gwialen.**
wialen *gw.* **gwialen.**
wialennod *gw.* **gwialen.**
wiced *e.b. ll.* **-i** wicket.
wicedwr *e.g. ll.* **wicedwyr** wicket-
  keeper.
widw *e.b. ll* **-od** widow *(S.W.).*
win *gw.* **gwin.**
winwnsyn *e.g. ll.* **winwns** onion.
wir *gw.* **gwir.**
wirionedd *gw.* **gwirionedd.**
wisg *gw.* **gwisg.**
wisgo *gw.* **gwisgo.**
wiwer *gw.* **gwiwer.**
wlad *gw.* **gwlad.**
wladfa *gw.* **gwladfa.**
wladgarwr *gw.* **gwladgarwr.**
wladol *gw.* **gwladol.**
wlân *gw.* **gwlân.**
wlanen *gw.* **gwlanen.**
wledig *gw.* **gwledig.**
wledydd *gw.* **gwlad.**
wledd *gw.* **gwledd.**
wledda *gw.* **gwledda.**
wleidydd *gw.* **gwleidydd.**
wleidyddiaeth *gw.* **gwleidyddiaeth.**

wleidyddol   **wyll**

wleidyddol *gw.* **gwleidyddol.**
wlith *gw.* **gwlith.**
wlyb *gw.* **gwlyb.**
wlybaniaeth *gw.* **gwlybaniaeth.**
wlychu *gw.* **gwlychu.**
wn *gw.* **gwn.**
ŵn *gw.* **gŵn.**
wneud *gw.* **gwneud.**
wneuthur *gw.* **gwneud.**
wniadyddes *gw.* **gwniadyddes.**
wnïo *gw.* **gwnïo.**
wniyddes *gw.* **gwniadyddes.**
wobr *gw.* **gwobr.**
wobrwyo *gw.* **gwobrwyo.**
ŵr *gw.* **gŵr.**
wrach *gw.* **gwrach.**
wragedd *gw.* **gwraig.**
wraidd *gw.* **gwreiddyn.**
wraig *gw.* **gwraig.**
wrandawaid *gw.* **gwrandawiad.**
wrandawr *gw.* **gwrandawr.**
wrando *gw.* **gwrando.**
wreichion *gw.* **gwreichionen.**
wreichionen *gw.* **gwreichionen.**
wreiddiau *gw.* **gwreiddyn.**
wreiddio *gw.* **gwreiddio.**
wreiddiol *gw.* **gwreiddiol.**
wreiddyn *gw.* **gwreiddyn.**
wres *gw.* **gwres.**
wresog *gw.* **gwresog.**
wresogi *gw.* **gwresogi.**
wresogydd *gw.* **gwresogydd.**
wrido *gw.* **gwrido.**
wridog *gw.* **gwridog.**
wrol *gw.* **gwrol.**
wrtaith *gw.* **gwrtaith.**
wrth *ardd.* by; with; to; because;
  since. **wrth gwrs** of course; **wrth**
  law at hand, in reserve; **wrth lwc**
  luckily.
wrthblaid *gw.* **gwrthblaid.**
wrthchwyswr *gw.* **gwrthchwyswr.**
wrthdaro *gw.* **gwrthdaro.**
wrthdystio *gw.* **gwrthdystio.**
wrthglocwedd *gw.* **gwrthglocwedd.**
wrthod *gw.* **gwrthod.**
wrthrych *gw.* **gwrthrych.**
wrthrychol *gw.* **gwrthrychol.**
wrthryfel *gw.* **gwrthryfel.**
wrthryfela *gw.* **gwrthryfela.**
wrthwyneb *gw.* **gwrthwyneb.**

wrthwynebu *gw.* **gwrthwynebu.**
wrthwynebwr *gw.* **gwrthwynebwr.**
wryw *gw.* **gwryw.**
wrywaidd *gw.* **gwrywaidd.**
wrywgydiaeth *gw.* **gwrywgydiaeth.**
wrywol *gw.* **gwrywaidd.**
wthiad *gw.* **gwthiad.**
wthio *gw.* **gwthio.**
wthiwr *gw.* **gwthiwr.**
wy *e.g. ll.* **-au** egg. **wy clwc** addled
  egg; **wy Pasg** Easter egg; **wy**
  wedi'i falu beaten egg; **wy wedi'i**
  ferwi boiled egg; **wy wedi'i ffrio**
  fried egg.
wybedyn *gw.* **gwybedyn.**
wybod *gw.* **gwybod.**
wybodaeth *gw.* **gwybodaeth.**
wybren *e.b. ll.* **-nau, -nydd** sky,
  firmament *(literary usage).*
wybrennau *gw.* **wybren.**
wybrennydd *gw.* **wybren.**
wych *gw.* **gwych.**
wydr *gw.* **gwydr.**
wydrau *gw.* **gwydr.** *gw.* **gwydryn.**
wydryn *gw.* **gwydryn.**
ŵydd *gw.* **gŵydd.**
wyddau *gw.* **gŵydd.**
wyddbwyll *gw.* **gwyddbwyll.**
Wyddel *gw.* **Gwyddel.**
Wyddeleg *gw.* **Gwyddeleg.**
Wyddeles *gw.* **Gwyddeles.**
Wyddelig *gw.* **Gwyddelig.**
Wyddfa, Yr *e.b.* Snowdon.
Wyddgrug, Yr *e.b.* Mold.
wyddoniaeth *gw.* **gwyddoniaeth.**
wyddonol *gw.* **gwyddonol.**
wyddonydd *gw.* **gwyddonydd.**
wyddor *gw.* **gwyddor.**
wyf (i) *bf.* I am. *gw.* **bod.**
wyfyn *gw.* **gwyfyn.**
ŵyl *gw.* **gŵyl.**
wylan *gw.* **gwylan.**
wyliadwrus *gw.* **gwyliadwrus.**
wyliau *gw.* **gŵyl.**
wylio *gw.* **gwylio.**
wyliwr *gw.* **gwyliwr.**
wylnos *gw.* **gwylnos.**
wylo *be.* **(wylaf)** to weep, to cry
  (N.W.).
wylwyr *gw.* **gwyliwr.**
wyll *gw.* **gwyll.**

wyllt *gw.* **gwyllt.**
wylltio *gw.* **gwylltio.**
wylltu *gw.* **gwylltio.**
wymon *gw.* **gwymon.**
wyn *gw.* **gwyn.**
ŵyn *gw.* **oen.**
wyneb *e.g. ll.* **-au** face; surface.
  dauwynebog deceitful; **wyneb-**
  ddalen title page; **wynebgaled**
  barefaced; **wyneb i waered** upside-
  down.
wynebu *be.* **(wynebaf)** to face, to
  confront.
Wynedd *gw.* **Gwynedd.**
wynegon *gw.* **gwynegon.**
wynegu *gw.* **gwynegu.**
wynfa *gw.* **gwynfa.**
wynfyd *gw.* **gwynfyd.**
wyngalch *gw.* **gwyngalch.**
wynion *gw.* **gwyn.**
wynnu *gw.* **gwynnu.**
wynt *gw.* **gwynt.**
wyntog *gw.* **gwyntog.**
wŷr *gw.* **gwŷr.**
ŵyr *e.g. ll.* **wyrion** grandson.
wyrion *gw.* **ŵyr.**
wyrdd *gw.* **gwyrdd.**
wyres *e.b. ll.* **-au** grand-daughter.

wyresau *gw.* **wyres.**
wyriad *gw.* **gwyriad.**
wyrio *gw.* **gwyro.**
wyro *gw.* **gwyro.**
wyrth *gw.* **gwyrth.**
wyrthiol *gw.* **gwyrthiol.**
wyryf *gw.* **gwyryf.**
wŷs *gw.* **gwŷs.**
Wysg *e.b.* Usk (river).
wystl *gw.* **gwystl.**
wyt (ti) *bf.* you are *(singular).* **Wyt ti**
  gartref? Are you at home? *gw.*
  bod.
wyth *a. & e.g.* eight. **wyth deg**
  eighty.
wythawd *e.g. ll.* **-au** octave; octet.
wythfed *a.* eighth.
wythnos *e.b. ll.* **-au** week. **yr**
  wythnos diwethaf last week; **yr**
  wythnos hon this week; **yr**
  wythnos nesaf next week.
wythnosol *a.* weekly. **cyfarfod**
  wythnosol weekly meeting; **papur**
  wythnosol weekly paper.
wythwr *e.g. ll.* **wythwyr** number
  eight *(rugby forward).*
wythwyr *gw.* **wythwr.**
wywo *gw.* **gwywo.**

y: yr: 'r, **1** *y fan.* the. **y** *before a consonant:* **y dyn** the man; **y ferch** the girl; **y tai** the houses; **yr** *before a vowel and h:* **yr afal** the apple; **yr esgid** the shoe; **yr haul** the sun; **yr heol** the road; **'r** *after a vowel:* **a'r plant** and the children; **o'r llyfr** from the book; **i'r cae** to the field; *y and* **'r** *are followed by soft mutation of feminine singular nouns:* **y dorth** the loaf; **tŷ'r fam** the mother's house; **gyda'r gath** with the cat; *nouns beginning with ll and rh do not mutate after* **y** *and* **'r**. *gw. At. Treiglad Meddal.* **2** *geir. used with forms of the verb* **bod: y mae...; yr oedd...; rwyf...**
y: yr *geir. perth.* **Dyma'r tŷ y trigaf ynddo** Here is the house in which I live.
ychwaith *gw.* **chwaith.**
ychwaneg *gw.* **chwaneg.**
ychwanegu: chwanegu *be.* **(ychwanegaf: chwanegaf)** to add, to augment.
ychydig *a.* little, few. **ychydig o lyfrau** a few books; **ychydig fara** a little bread; **ychydig lai** a little less.
ŷd *e.g. ll.* **ydau** corn. **creision ŷd** cornflakes.
ydy *bf.* is, are. *gw.* **bod.**
yddfau *gw.* **gwddf.**
yfed *be.* **(yfaf)** to drink.

yfory: fory *ad.* tomorrow.
yfflon *e.ll.* fragments, pieces, bits *(S.W.).* **yn yfflon racs** in smithereens. *gw.* **yfflyn.**
yfflyn *e.g. ll.* **yfflon** fragment, piece, bit. **heb yfflyn o wahaniaeth** without a scrap of difference.
ygau *gw.* **gwg.**
yng *gw.* **yn.**
ynghanol *ardd.* in the midst of.
ynghyd *ad.* together. **ynghyd â** together with.
ynghylch *ardd.* about, concerning.
ynglŷn (â) *ad.* in connection (with), concerning.
ym *gw.* **yn.**
yma *ad.* here, this.
ymadael (â) *be.* **(ymadawaf)** to depart.
ymadrodd *e.g. ll.* **-ion** speech, saying, expression.
ymaelodi (â) *be.* **(ymaelodaf)** to become a member, to join.
ymaith *ad.* away.
ymarfer (â) 1 *be.* **(ymarferaf)** to practise. **2** *e.b.g. ll.* **-ion** practice, exercise. **ymarfer corff** physical exercise.
ymarferiad *e.g. ll.* **-au** practice, exercise.
ymarferol *a.* practical.
ymateb 1 *be.* **(ymatebaf)** to respond. **2** *e.g. ll.* **-ion** reaction; response.
ynbelydredd *e.g.* radiation.
ymbelydrol *a.* radioactive.
ymchwil *e.b.* research, search, quest.
ymchwiliad *e.g. ll.* **-au** investigation; inquiry.
ymchwilio (i) *be.* **(ymchwiliaf)** to research; to search.
ymdaith 1 *e.b. ll.* **ymdeithiau** journey, march. **2** *be.* **(ymdeithiaf)** to travel, to march.
ymdrech *e.b. ll.* **-ion** effort, endeavour, struggle: **ymdrech deg** valiant effort.
ymdrechu (i) *be.* **(ymdrechaf)** to strive, to endeavour.
ymdrin (â) *be.* **(ymdriniaf)** to deal (with).
ymddangos (i) *be.* **(ymddangosaf)**

to appear, to seem.
ymddangosiad *e.g. ll.* **-au**
appearance.
ymddeol *be.* **(ymddeolaf)** to retire.
ymddeoliad *e.g. ll.* **-au** retirement.
ymddiheuriad *e.g. ll.* **-au** apology.
ymddiheuro *be.* **(ymddiheuraf)** to
apologise.
ymddiried (yn) *be.* **(ymddiriedaf)** to
trust, to confide *(in)*.
ymddirledaeth *e.b. ll.* **-au** trust,
confidence.
ymddiriedolaeth *e.b. ll.* **-au** trust
(charity).
ymddiriedolwr *e.b. ll.*
ymddiriedolwyr trustee.
ymddiswyddiad *e.g. ll.* **-au**
resignation.
ymddiswyddo *be.* **(ymddiswyddaf)**
to resign.
ymddwyn *be.* **(ymddygaf)** to
behave.
ymddygiad *e.g. ll.* **-au** behaviour.
ymennydd *e.g. ll.* **ymenyddion**
brain.
ymenyddion *gw.* **ymennydd.**
ymenyn: menyn *e.g.* butter. **bara
menyn** bread and butter.
ymerodraeth *e.b. ll.* **-au** empire.
ymestyn (at) *be.* **(ymestynnaf)** to
stretch, to reach, to extend.
ymfudo *be.* **(ymfudaf)** to emigrate.
ymfudwr *e.g. ll.* **ymfudwyr**
emigrant.
ymffrost *e.g.* boast.
ymffrostio (yn) *be.* **(ymffrostiaf)** to
boast.
ymffrostiwr *e.g. ll.* **ymffrostwyr**
boaster.
ymffrostwyr *gw.* **ymffrostiwr.**
ymgais *e.b.* effort, attempt.
ymgeiswyr *gw.* **ymgeisydd.**
ymgeisydd *e.g. ll.* **ymgeiswyr**
candidate, applicant. **ymgeisydd
seneddol** parliamentary candidate.
ymgeledd *e.g. ll.* **-au** care, succour.
ymgeledd parod first aid.
ymgom *e.b. ll.* **-ion** conversation,
chat. **ymgom â** a conversation with.
ymgomio (â) *be.* **(ymgomiaf)** to
chat, to converse.

ymgorffori *be* **(ymgorfforaf)** to
incorporate.
ymgrymu *be.* **(ymgrymaf)** to stoop,
to bow down.
ymgynghori (â) *be.* **(ymgynghoraf)**
to consult, to confer.
ymgymryd (â) *be.* **(ymgymeraf)** to
undertake.
ymgyrch *e.g.b. ll.* **-oedd** campaign,
expedition.
ymhel (â) *be.* **(ymhelaf)** to be
concerned; to meddle *(with)*.
ymhell *ad.* far, afar.
ymhellach *ad.* furthermore, further.
ymhlith *ardd.* among.
ymholi *be.* **(ymholaf)** to inquire.
ymholiad *e.g. ll.* **-au** inquiry.
ymlacio *be.* **(ymlaciaf)** to relax.
ymladd (â) 1 *be.* **(ymladdaf)** to fight
(with). 2 *e.g. ll.* **-au** fight, battle.
ymladdwr *e.g. ll.* **ymladdwyr**
fighter.
ymlaen *ad.* on, onward. **yn ôl ac
ymlaen** backward and forward.
ymolch: ymolchi *be.* **(ymolchaf)** to
wash oneself.
ymosod (ar) *be.* **(ymosodaf)** to
attack.
ymosodiad *e.g. ll.* **-au** attack.
ymosodiadau awyr air attacks.
ymosodwr *e.g. ll.* **ymosodwyr**
attacker.
ymosodwyr *gw.* **ymosodwr.**
ymostwng (i) *be.* **(ymostyngaf)** to
stoop; to submit, to capitulate.
ymryson (â) 1 *be.* **(ymrysonaf)** to
contend; to strive, to compete.
2 *e.g. ll.* **-au** competition, rivalry;
strife, contention. **Ymryson y
Beirdd** poets' contest.
ymuno (â) *be.* **(ymunaf)** to unite; to
join.
ymweld (â) *be.* **(ymwelaf)** to visit.
ymweliad *e.g. ll.* **-au** visit,
visitation.
ymwelwr: ymwelydd *e.g. ll.*
ymwelwyr visitor.
ymwelwyr *gw.* **ymwelwr.**
ymwelydd *gw.* **ymwelwr.**
ymwneud (â) *be.* **(ymwnaf)** to deal
(with), to be connected (with).

ymyl   **ysgol**

ymyl *e.g.b. ll.* **-on** edge, border,
margin. **ymyl y ddalen** edge of the
page; **yn ymyl** close by, near.
ymyrraeth *e.b. ll.* **ymyrraethau**
interference, intervention.
ymyrru: ymyrryd (â) *be.* **(ymyrraf)**
to interfere, to intervene, to meddle.
ymysg *ardd.* among, amid.
yn:'n yng: ym 1 *ardd. (personal
forms:* **yno, ynot, ynddo/ynddi,
ynom, ynoch, ynddyn)** in, at, into;
for; *the prepostion* **yn** *is followed by
nasal mutation:* **yn** + Corwen **yng
Nghorwen** in Corwen; **yn** + Pen-bre
ym Mhen-bre in Pen-bre; **yn** +
Treorci **yn Nhreorci** in Treorchy;
yn + Gŵyr **yng Ngŵyr** in Gower;
yn + Dinbych **yn Ninbych** in
Denbigh; **yn** + Bangor **ym Mangor**
in Bangor. *gw. At. Treiglad Trwynol.*
2 *geiryn.* (not translated). *An
adjective or noun following the
predicative particle* **yn** *takes soft
mutation:* **Mae Twm yn ddoniol**
Tom is amusing; **Ydy Alun yn ddyn
da?** Is Alun a good man? *gw. At.
Treiglad Meddal. No mutation
occurs when* **yn** *is followed by a be.*
(verb-noun): **Mae'r ci yn cyfarth**
The dog is barking; **Mae'r gath yn
cysgu** The cat is sleeping; **Mae
Mair yn canu** Mair is singing;
Rydw i'n darllen I am reading;
Maen nhw'n gwrando They are
listening.
yna *ad.* there; then; thereupon; that.
ynad *e.g. ll.* **-on** judge, justice,
magistrate. **Ynad Heddwch (Y.H.)**
Justice of the Peace (J.P.).
Llys yr Ynadon the Magistrates'
Court.
ynau *gw.* **gŵn.**
yn awr *ymadrodd ad.* now, at
present. *gw.* **rwan.**
ynn *gw.* **onnen.**
ynnau *gw.* **gwn.**
ynni *e.g.* energy, vigour.
yno *ad.* there. *gw.* **yn.**
yntau *rhag.* he, he also.
ynte: ynteu *c.* or, or else, otherwise;
then.

ynys *e.b. ll.* **-oedd** island. **Ynys
Bŷr** Caldey Island; **Ynys Enlli**
Bardsey Island; **Ynys Wyth** Isle of
Wight; **Ynysoedd Heledd** the
Hebrides.
ynysoedd *gw.* **ynys.**
yr *gw.* **y.**
yrfa *gw.* **gyrfa.**
yrfeydd *gw.* **gyrfa.**
yrru *gw.* **gyrru.**
yrrwr *gw.* **gyrrwr.**
yrwyr *gw.* **gyrrwr.**
ysbardun *e.g. ll.* **-au** spur,
accelerator *(in car).*
ysbïo *be.* **(ysbïaf)** to spy, to look.
ysbïwr *e.g. ll.* **ysbïwyr** spy.
ysbïwyr *gw.* **ysbïwr.**
ysblander *e.g.* splendour, glory.
ysbryd *e.g. ll* **-ion, -oedd** spirit,
ghost. **Yr Ysbryd Glân** The Holy
Spirit.
ysbrydion *gw.* **ysbryd.**
ysbrydoedd *gw.* **ysbryd.**
ysbrydol *a.* spiritual; high-spirited.
ysbrydoli *be.* **(ysbrydolaf)** to
inspire; to spiritualise.
ysbwriel *e.g.* refuse, rubbish.
ysbytai *gw.* **ysbyty.**
ysbyty *e.g. ll.* **ysbytai** hospital,
hospice.
ysfa *e.b. ll.* **ysfeydd** itching;
hankering; urge.
ysfeydd *gw.* **ysfa.**
ysgafn *a.* light *(weight).*
ysgafnhau: ysgafnu *be.*
(ysgafnhaf: ysgafnaf) to lighten.
ysgall *gw.* **ysgallen.**
ysgallen *e.b. ll.* **ysgall** thistle.
ysgariad *e.g. ll.* **-au** divorce.
ysgol *e.b. ll.* **-ion** school; ladder.
ysgol annibynnol independent
school; **ysgol arbennig** special
school; **ysgol breifat** private
school; **ysgol breswyl** boarding
school; **ysgol feithrin** nursery
school; **ysgol gyfun** comprehensive
school; **ysgol Gymraeg** Welsh
medium school; **ysgol gynradd**
primary school; **ysgol iau** junior
school; **ysgol nos** night-school;
ysgol Sul Sunday school; **ysgol**

171

uwchradd secondary school.
ysgolfeistr *e.g. ll.* **-i** schoolmaster.
ysgolfeistres *e.b. ll.* **-au**
schoolmistress.
ysgolhaig *e.g. ll.* **ysgolheigion**
scholar.
ysgolheigion *gw.* **ysgolhaig.**
ysgolor *e.g. ll.* **-ion** scholar.
ysgoloriaeth *e.b. ll.* **-au**
scholarship.
ysgolorion *gw.* **ysgolor.**
ysgrech *e.b. ll.* **-feydd** scream,
shriek.
ysgrechfeydd *gw.* **ysgrech.**
ysgrif *e.b. ll.* **-au** article, essay.
ysgrifennu (ar, at) *be.* **(ysgrifennaf)**
to write.
ysgrifennydd *e.g. ll.*
ysgrifenyddion secretary.
ysgrifenyddes *e.b. ll.* **-au** female
secretary.
ysgrifenyddion *gw.* **ysgrifennydd.**
ysgrythur *e.b. ll.* **-au** scripture.
ysgubo *be.* **(ysgubaf)** to sweep.
ysgubor *e.b. ll.* **-iau** barn.
ysgwyd *be.* **(ysgydwaf)** to shake, to
sway, to wag.
ysgwydd *e.b. ll.* **-au** shoulder.
ysgyfaint *e.ll.* lungs.
ysgyfarnog *e.b. ll.* **-od** hare. **codi**
ysgyfarnog to raise a red herring
(fig. – irrelevant diversion).
ysgytwad *e.g. ll* **-au** shock, shaking.
ysmala *a.* funny, amusing; droll.
ystadegau *e.ll.* statistics.
ystafell *e.b. ll.* **-oedd** room. **ystafell**

ddosbarth classroom; **ystafell**
wely bedroom; **ystafell ymolchi**
bathroom.
ystlum *e.g. ll.* **-od** bat *(animal).*
ystlys *e.b. ll.* **-au** side, flank;
touchline.
ystlyswr *e.g. ll.* **ystlyswyr**
linesman; sidesman.
ystod *e.b. ll.* **-ion, -au** course, space
of time, span, range; swath. **yn**
ystod during; **ystod oed** age
range.
ystrydeb *e.b. ll.* **-au** cliché;
stereotype.
ystwyth *a.* flexible, supple, agile,
pliant.
ystyr *e.g.b. ll.* **-on** sense, meaning.
ystyriaeth *e.b. ll.* **-au** consideration,
heed.
ystyried *be.* **(ystyriaf)** to consider,
to heed.
ystyriol *a.* heedful, mindful.
ystyrlon *a.* meaningful.
ysu *be.* **(ysaf)** to consume, to crave,
to itch. **yn ysu am wybod** itching
to know.
yswiriannau *gw.* **yswiriant.**
yswiriant *e.g. ll.* **yswiriannau**
insurance. **yswiriant cyfun**
comprehensive insurance; **yswiriant**
trydydd person third-party
insurance.
yswirio: yswiro *be.* **(yswiriaf:**
yswiraf) to insure.
yw *bf.* is, are. *gw.* **bod.** *gw.* **ywen.**
ywen *e.b. ll.* **yw** yew.

DICTIONARY
English–Welsh

ABBREVIATIONS
BYRFODDAU

a.	adjective	*ansoddair*
ad.	adverb	*adferf*
c.	conjunction	*cysylltair*
def. art.	definite article	*y fannod*
e.g. (exempli gratia)	for example	*er enghraifft*
i.	interjection	*ebychiad*
int. pn.	interrogative pronoun	*rhagenw gofynnol*
n.	noun	*enw*
coll.	collective	*torfol*
f.	feminine	*benywaidd*
m.	masculine	*gwrywaidd*
n.pl.	noun plural	*enw lluosog*
N.W.	North Wales	*Gogledd Cymru*
pn.	pronoun	*rhagenw*
prp.	preposition	*arddodiad*
px.	prefix	*rhagddodiad*
rel. pn.	relative pronoun	*rhagenw perthynol*
S.W.	South Wales	*De Cymru*
v.	verb	*berf*

If the gender of the Welsh noun is not specified, that noun has the same gender as the noun(s) immediately following it in the definition.

abbreviation *n.* byrfodd, talfyriad *m.*
abdomen *n.* bol *m.*
ability *n.* gallu *m.*
able *a.* galluog, medrus. **to be able** gallu, medru.
abode *n.* cartref, preswyl, preswylfod *m.*
abolish *v.* dileu.
abort *v.* erthylu.
abortion *n.* erthyliad *m.*
about *prp. & ad.* am, o gwmpas, oddeutu, tua, ogylch, ynghylch.
above **1** *prp.* dros, i fyny, uwchben, uwchlaw. **2** *ad.* uchod.
abrupt *a.* sydyn, cwta. **abrupt reply** ateb cwta.
absent *a.* absennol.
abstract *a.* haniaethol.
abundance *n.* toreth *f.*
abundant *a.* helaeth, aml, toreithiog.
accelerate *v.* cyflymu.
accelerator *n.* cyflymydd, sbardun *m.*
accent *n.* acen *f.*
accept *v.* derbyn, cymryd.
acceptable *a.* derbyniol.
access *n.* mynedfa *f.* mynediad *m.*
accident *n.* damwain *f.*

accommodation *n.* llety, lle *m.*
accomplish *v.* cyflawni, gorffen.
account *n.* cyfrif, cownt; adroddiad *m.*
accountant *n.* cyfrifydd *m.*
accusation *n.* cyhuddiad.
accuse *v.* cyhuddo.
accustom *v.* cyfarwyddo, arfer.
ache **1** *n.* poen *mf,* dolur *m.* **2** *v.* poeni, brifo, gwynegu.
acid **1** *n.* asid *m.***2** *a.* sur.
acknowledge *v.* cydnabod.
acorn *n.* mesen *f.*
acquaintance *n.* cydnabod *m.*
acre *n.* erw, acer *f.*
across *prp.* draw, ar draws.
act **1** *n.* act *(drama)*; deddf *(law)*; gweithred *f.* **2** *v.* actio *(drama)*; gweithredu.
active *a.* bywiog, heini.
actor *n.* actor, chwaraewr *m.*
add *v.* ychwanegu, chwanegu.
address **1** *n.* cyfeiriad. *m.* **2** *n.* annerch.
adequately *ad.* digonol.
adhere *v.* glynu wrth.
adjective *n.* ansoddair *m.*
adjudge *v.* dyfarnu.
adjudicate *v.* beirniadu.
adjudicator *n.* beirniad *m.*
admire *v.* edmygu.
admit *v.* derbyn, cyfaddef.
adolescence *n.* llencyndod *m.*
adult *n.* oedolyn *m.*
advantage *n.* mantais *f.* **to take advantage** manteisio.
advantageous *a.* llesol, manteisiol.
adventure *n.* antur *mf.*
adventurous *a.* anturus.
advertise *v.* hysbysebu.
advertisement *n.* hysbyseb *f.*
advertiser *n.* hysbysebwr *m.*
advice *n.* cyngor *m.*
advise *v.* cynghori.
adviser *n.* ymgynghorwr *m.*
aeroplane *n.* awyren *f.*
afar *ad.* ymhell.
affair *n.* carwriaeth.
affectation *n.* maldod *m.*
affection *n.* cariad, serch *m.*
affectionate *a.* serchus, serchog,

cariadus.
after 1 *ad.* wedyn, yna. **2** *prp.* ar ôl, wedi.
after-care *n.* ôl-ofal *m.*
afternoon *n.* prynhawn *m.*
afterwards *ad.* wedyn, wedi hynny.
again *ad.* eto, drachefn, eilwaith.
against *prp.* erbyn, yn erbyn.
age 1 *n.* oed, oedran *m;* oes *f.*
2 *v.* heneiddio.
aged *a.* hen, oedrannus. **the aged** yr oedrannus, yr henoed.
agency *n.* cyfrwng *m*, asiantaeth *f.*
agent *n.* asiant, cyfrwng *m.*
agile *a.* heini.
agitated *a.* cynhyrfus.
ago *ad.* yn ôl.
agony *n.* ing, poen mawr *m.*
agree *v.* cytuno (â).
agreement *n.* cytundeb *m.*
agriculturalist *n.* ffarmwr, ffermwr, amaethwr *m.*
agriculture *n.* amaethyddiaeth *f.*
aid 1 *n.* cymorth, help *m.* **2** *v.* helpu.
First Aid Cymorth Cyntaf.
ailment *n.* afiechyd, dolur *m.*
aim *n.* amcan, bwriad, diben, nod *m.*
air *n.* awyr; aer; alaw *f.* **fresh air** awyr iach.
alarm *n.* braw, ofn; larwm *m.* **alarm-clock** cloc larwm.
alien *n.* & *a.* estron *m.*
all 1 *n.* pawb; y cwbl, y cyfan *m.* **2** *a.* holl, i gyd, pob. **3** *ad.* yn hollol.
allege *v.* honni.
alleged *a.* honedig.
alliance *n.* cynghrair *m.*
allotment *n.* rhandir *m.*
allow *v.* caniatáu, goddef, gadael (i).
allowance *n.* lŵans, lwfans *m.*
allure *v.* hudo.
ally *n.* cynghreiriad *m.*
almighty *a.* hollalluog. **Almighty God** Hollalluog Dduw.
almost *ad.* bron, braidd, lled.
alone *a.* unig, ar ei ben ei hun, wrtho'i hun.
along 1 *ad.* ymlaen; ar hyd. **2** *prp.* ar hyd.
all along o'r cychwyn.
alphabet *n.* yr wyddor, abiéc *f.*

already *ad.* eisoes, yn barod.
also *ad.* & *c.* hefyd.
alter *v.* newid.
although *prp.* & *c.* serch, er.
altitude *n.* uchder *m.*
altogether *ad.* yn gyfan gwbl, i gyd.
always *ad.* bob amser, yn wastad.
am, I *v.* rydw i, dw i.
amazed *a.* syn.
amazement *n.* syndod *m.*
amazing *a.* rhyfedd, rhyfeddol.
ambassador *n.* llysgennad *m.*
ambition *n.* uchelgais *m.*
ambitious *a.* uchelgeisiol.
ambulance *n.* ambiwlans *m.*
amend *v.* gwella, diwygio, cywiro.
American 1 *n.* Americanwr *m*, Americanes *f.* **2** *a.* Americanaidd.
amid *prp.* ymhlith, rhwng, ynghanol, ymysg.
among *prp.* rhwng, ymhlith, ymysg.
amount *n.* swm, cyfanswm, cyfrif *m.*
ample *a.* helaeth, digon, digonedd.
amuse *v.* difyrru.
amusing *a.* difyr, difyrrus, digrif, ysmala.
analyse *v.* dadansoddi.
ancestor *n.* hynafiad *m.*
ancient *a.* hynafol, hen iawn.
ancient monument henebyn.
and *c.* a, ac.
anecdote *n.* hanesyn *m.*
angel *n.* angel *m.*
angle *n.* ongl *m.* **right angle** ongl sgwâr.
Anglesey *n.* Môn *f.*
Anglicise *v.* Seisnigeiddio, Seisnigo.
Anglo- *a.* Eingl-
Anglo-Welshman *n.* Eingl-Gymro *m.*
angry *a.* crac, dig.
anguish *n.* ing *m.*
angular *a.* onglog.
animal *n.* anifail *m.*
animate *a.* byw.
ankle *n.* migwrn, pigwrn *m.*
announce *v.* cyhoeddi; datgan; hysbysu.
announcement *n.* cyhoeddiad, hysbysiad *m.*
announcer *n.* cyhoeddwr *m.*

anoint *v.* iro.
another *a. & pn.* arall, llall.
answer *n. & v.* ateb *m.*
ant *n.* morgrugyn *m.*
antagonist *n.* gwrthwynebwr,
gwrthwynebydd *m.*
anthology *n.* blodeugerdd *f,*
detholiad *m.*
anti- *px.* gwrth-, yn erbyn.
anticlockwise *a.* gwrthglocwedd.
antiperspirant *n.* gwrthchwyswr.
anxiety *n.* pryder *m.*
any *a.* unrhyw, rhyw, peth, dim. **I
don't see her any longer/more** Ni
fyddaf yn ei gweld mwyach.
anyone *n. & pn.* rhywun, unrhyw un,
neb *m.*
anywhere *ad.* unman, rhywle,
unrhyw le.
apart *ad.* ar wahân, o'r neilltu.
ape *n.* epa *m.*
aperture *n.* agoriad, twll *m.*
apologise *v.* ymddiheuro.
apology *n.* ymddiheuriad *m.*
apparatus *n.* offer *m.*
apparition *n.* drychiolaeth *f,* ysbryd
m.
appear *v.* ymddangos.
appearance *n.* ymddangosiad *m.*
appendix *n.* atodiad *m.*
apple *n.* afal *m.*
applicant *n.* ymgeisydd *m.*
appoint *v.* penodi; trefnu, nodi.
appointed *a.* penodedig.
appointment *n.* penodiad *m.*
appreciate *n.* gwerthfawrogi.
appreciation *n.* gwerthfawrogiad *m.*
apprentice *n.* prentis *m.*
apprenticeship *n.* prentisiaeth *f.*
approach *v.* agosáu, nesáu.
appropriate *a.* addas, priodol.
approximate *a.* bras, agos.
April *n.* Ebrill *m.*
archer *n.* saethwr *m.*
architect *n.* pensaer, cynlluniwr,
cynllunydd *m.*
are *v.* mae, maen, maent, oes, sy,
sydd, ydy, ydynt, ydyw, yw. *see* **bod.**
argue *v.* dadlau.
argument *n.* dadl *f.*
arithmetic *n.* rhifyddeg *f.*

ark *n.* arch *f.* **Noah's Ark** Arch Noa.
arm *n.* braich *f;* arf *m.* **nuclear arms**
arfau niwclear.
armed *a.* arfog. **armed forces**
lluoedd arfog.
army *n.* byddin *f.*
around *ad. & prp.* am, o amgylch, o
gwmpas, o gylch.
arrange *v.* trefnu.
arrive at *v.* cyrraedd.
arrow *n.* saeth *f.*
art *n.* celf *f.* **art exhibition**
arddangosfa gelf.
article *n.* erthygl, ysgrif *f;* nwydd *m.*
definite article y fannod (y, yr, 'r).
as *c. & ad.,* â, ag, fel, mor, cyn. **as if**
fel pe bai, fel petai, fel petasai.
ascent *n.* rhiw *f,* tyle *m.*
ash *n.* lludw *m;* onnen *f.*
ashes *n.* llwch, lludw *m.*
aside *ad.* o'r neilltu.
ask *v.* gofyn, holi, gwahodd.
askew *a.* ar gam, gŵyr.
asleep *ad.* yn cysgu, yng nghwsg.
ass *n.* asyn *m.*
assembly *n.* cymanfa *f.* cynulliad *m.*
assert *v.* honni, haeru.
assertion *n.* honiad *m.*
assess *v.* asesu.
assist *v.* helpu.
assistance *n.* cymorth, help *m.*
assistant *n.* cynorthwywr,
cynorthwy-ydd *m.*
association *n.* cymdeithas *f.*
assurance *n.* sicrwydd *m.*
assure *v.* sicrhau.
asterisk *n.* seren *f.*
astonishing *a.* rhyfedd, rhyfeddol,
syn.
astronaut *n.* gofodwr *m,* gofodwraig
f.
at *prp.* am, ar, ger, wrth, yn, yng, ym.
atonement *n.* iawn *m.*
atrocious *a.* erchyll.
attack 1 *n.* ymosodiad *m.*
2 *v.* ymosod (ar).
attacker *n.* ymosodwr *m.*
attain *v.* ennill, cyrraedd.
attempt 1 *n.* cais, cynnig *m;* ymgais *f.*
2 *v.* ceisio, cynnig.
attend *v.* mynychu.

attendance *n.* presenoldeb *m.*
attention *n.* sylw *m.*
attitude *n.* agwedd *m.*
attract *v.* denu, tynnu.
attractive *a.* deniadol, atyniadol.
augment *v.* ychwanegu at, chwanegu
　at.
August *n.* Awst *m.*
aunt *n.* modryb *f.*
author *n.* awdur, llenor *m.*
authoress *n.* awdures, llenores, *f.*

authority *n.* awdurdod *m:* **Education**
　Authority Awdurdod Addysg.
autobiography *n.* hunangofiant *m.*
autumn *n.* hydref *m.*
autumnal *a.* hydrefol.
avenge *v.* dial (ar).
avoid *v.* osgoi.
awake 1 *v.* deffro, dihuno, **2** *a.* effro.
away *ad.* ymaith, i ffwrdd.
awful *a.* ofnadwy.
awkward *a.* lletchwith; chwithig.

baby *n.* baban, babi *m.*
baby-sit *v.* gwarchod. **babysitter** *n.*
gwarchodwr babanod *m.*
bachelor *n.* dyn dibriod, hen lanc *m.*
back 1 *n.* cefn; cefnwr *m.* 2 *ad.* yn
ôl.
background *n.* cefndir *m.*
bacon *n.* cig moch, bacwn *m.*
bad *a.* drwg, drygionus; sâl, gwael.
badge *n.* bathodyn *m.*
bag *n.* bag, cwd, cwdyn *m.*
bail *n.* mechnïaeth *f.*
bake *v.* crasu, pobi.
baked *a.* cras, pob.
bakehouse *n.* popty *m.*
baker *n.* pobydd *m.*
bald *a.* moel, penfoel.
baldness *n.* moelni *m.*
ball *n.* dawns; pêl *f.* **football** pêl
droed; **rugby ball** pêl rygbi.
ballad *n.* balad *f.* **ballad-monger**
baledwr.
ballot *n.* balot *m.*
banana *n.* banana *m.*
band *n.* band *m.;* seindorf *f.* **brass**
band band pres.
bangle *n.* breichled *f.*
bank 1 *n.* glan *f.;* clawdd; banc *m.*
2 *v.* bancio. **bank statement**
adroddiad banc.
banner *n.* baner *f.*
banquet 1 *n.* gwledd *f.* 2 *v.* gwledda.
Baptist *n.* Bedyddiwr *m.*

baptise *v.* bedyddio.
bar 1 *n.* bar *m.* 2 *v.* atal.
barbecue *n.* barbeciw *m.*
bard *n.* bardd *m.*
bare *a.* noeth, llwm, moel, prin.
barefooted *a.* troednoeth.
barely *ad.* prin.
bareness *n.* moelni *m.*
bark 1 *n.* cyfarthiad; rhisgl *m.*
2 *v.* cyfarth.
barley *n.* haidd, barlys *m.coll.*
barn *n.* ysgubor *f.*
barrel *n.* casgen *f,* baril *mf.*
barrow *n.* berfa, whilber *f.*
base 1 *n.* bôn, gwaelod; sail, sylfaen;
canolfan *m.* 2 *a.* isel. 3 *v.* seilio.
bashful *a.* swil.
basic *a.* sylfaenol.
basin *n.* basn *m.*
basket *n.* basged *f.*
Basque Country *n.* Gwlad y Basg *f.*
bass *n.* bas, baswr *m.*
baste *v.* iro.
bat 1 *n.* ystlum; bat *m.* 2 *v.* batio.
bath *n.* bath, baddon *m.*
bathe *v.* ymolch, ymolchi, golchi.
bathroom *n.* ystafell ymolchi *f.*
battle 1 *n.* ymladdfa *m,* brwydr *f.*
2 *v.* ymladd *m.*
bay *n.* bae *m.* **Swansea Bay** Bae
Abertawe.
be *v.* bod.
beach *n.* traeth *m,* glan y môr *f.*
beam *n.* pelydr: trawst *m.*
bean *n.* ffäen, ffeuen *f.*
bear 1 *n.* arth *m,* arthes *f.* 2 *v.* cario;
geni; goddef. **polar bear** arth gwyn.
beard *n.* barf *f.*
beat *v.* taro; gorchfygu.
beautiful *a.* hardd, glân, teg, prydferth.
beauty *n.* harddwch, prydferthwch,
tegwch *m.*
because *prp.* er, oherwydd, o achos,
gan, am, oblegid.
become *v.* dyfod, dod yn.
bed *n.* gwely *m.*
bedding *n.* dillad gwely *m.*
bedroom *n.* ystafell wely, llofft *f.*
bedsitter *n.* ystafell un gwely *f.*
bee *n.* gwenynen *f.*
beech *n.* ffawydden *f.*

been, I have v. bues i, fues i, bûm, *see* bod.
beer n. cwrw m.
beeswax n. cwyr m.
beetle n chwilen f.
before 1 prp. cyn, gerbron, o flaen, rhag.
2 ad. o'r blaen. **before long** cyn bo hir.
beforehand ad. ymlaen llaw.
beg v. erfyn (ar).
begin v. cychwyn, dechrau.
beginning n. dechreuad m.
behave v. ymddwyn.
behaviour n. ymddygiad m.
behind 1 prp. tu ôl (i), tu cefn (i), **2** ad. ar ôl.
behold 1 i. wele! **2** v. gweld, edrych.
being n. bod m.
Belgium n. Gwlad Belg f.
believe v. credu (yn).
bell n. cloch f.
bellow v. rhuo.
belly n. bol, bola m.
belong v. perthyn (i).
beloved 1 n. anwylyd mf. **2** a. annwyl, anwylaf, cariadus, cu, hoff. **beloved ones** anwyliaid.
below prp. islaw, dan.
bend 1 n. tro m. **2** v. plygu.
beneath prp. islaw, dan.
beneficial a. llesol.
benefit 1 n. elw, lles m. **2** v. elwa.
berry n. aeronen, mwyaren f.
berserk a. gwyllt.
beside prp. ger, gerllaw, wrth, heibio, yn ymyl.
besides prp. heb, heblaw.
best a. gorau.
bestow v. rhoddi, rhoi, cyflwyno.
betrothal n. dyweddïad m.
better 1 a. gwell. **2** ad. yn well.
between prp. rhwng.
beverage n. diod f.
bewitch v. swyno.
beyond prp. draw, dros, tu hwnt.
Bible n. Beibl m.
bicker v. cweryla, ffraeo.
bicycle n. beic m.
bid n & v. cynnig m.
bide v. aros, disgwyl.

big a. mawr. **bigger** mwy; **biggest** mwyaf.
bilingual a. dwyieithog.
bilingualism n. dwyieithrwydd m.
bill n. bil; mesur m; rhaglen f.
bin n. bin m. **rubbish bin** bin ysbwriel.
bind v. rhwymo, clymu.
biological a. biolegol.
biology n. bioleg, bywydeg f.
birch n. bedwen, bedw f.
bird n. aderyn m.
birthday n. pen-blwydd m. **birthday card** cerdyn pen-blwydd.
biscuit n. bisged, bisgïen f.
bishop n. esgob m.
bit n. tamaid, darn, tipyn, yfflyn m.
bite 1 n. tamaid m. **2** v. cnoi.
bitter a. chwerw, sur.
bizarre a. od, rhyfedd, chwithig.
black 1 n. du; dyn du m. **2** a. du, tywyll. **3** v. duo.
blackberry n. mwyaren f.
blackbird n. aderyn du m.
blackboard n. bwrdd du m.
blacken v. duo.
blacksmith n. gof m.
Blackwood n. Y Coed-duon f.
blade n. eginyn; llafn m.
blame 1 n. bai m. **2** v. beio.
blameless a. di-fai.
blanch v. gwynnu.
blank a. gwag; syn. **blank cheque** siec wag.
blanket n. blanced, planced.
blaze n. fflam f.
bleach 1 n. cannydd m. **2** v. cannu, gwynnu.
bleed v. gwaedu.
blemish n. nam; bai m.
blend v. cymysgu.
blessed a. bendigedig.
blessedness n. gwynfyd m.
blessing n. bendith f.
blind 1 a. dall, tywyll. **2** n. person dall m. **3** v. dallu.
bliss n. gwynfyd f.
blizzard n. storm o wynt ac eira f.
blood n. gwaed m. **blood pressure** pwysedd gwaed.

bloom *n.* blodyn *m.*
blossom *n.* blodyn *m.*
blouse *n.* blows, blowsen *f.*
blow 1 *n.* ergyd *mf.* **2** *v.* chwythu.
blow-dry *v.* chwythu'n sych.
blue *n.* & *a.* glas *m.*
blush *v.* gwrido, cochi.
blushing *a.* gwridog.
blustery *a.* stormus.
board *n.* bwrdd *m,* bord *f;* bwyd *m.*
boarding house *n.* llety *m.*
boast 1 *n.* ymffrost *m.* **2** *v.* ymffrostio.
boaster *n.* ymffrostiwr *m.*
boat *n.* bad, cwch *m.*
bodily *a.* corfforol.
body *n.* corff *m.*
boil *v.* berwi.
boiling *n.* & *a.* berw *m.*
bold *a.* hyf.
boldness *n.* hyfdra *m.*
bolster *n.* clustog hir *f,* gobennydd mawr *m.*
bolt 1 *n.* bollt *m.* **2** *v.* bolltio.
bomb 1 *n.* bom *m.* **2** *v.* bomio.
bone *n.* asgwrn *m.*
book *n.* llyfr *m;* cyfrol *f.*
booklet *n.* llyfryn *m.*
boot *n.* esgid *f.*
booth *n.* caban *m.* stondin *f.*
border *n.* ffin *f,* ymyl *mf.* border *m.*
bordering *a.* ffiniol.
bore 1 *n.* twll; dyn diflas *m.* **2** *v.* tyllu; blino.
boring *a.* diflas.
born *a.* wedi ei eni; ganed.
borough *n.* bwrdeistref *f.* **Borough Council** Cyngor Bwrdeistref.
borrow *v.* benthyca, cael benthyg.
boss *n.* meistr, pennaeth, bos *m.*
botanical *a.* llysieuol.
both *a.* & *ad.* &. *pn.* y ddau, y ddwy. **they both** ill dau, ill dwy.
bother 1 *n.* helynt *f,* trafferth *m.* **2** *v.* trafferthu.
bottle *n.* potel *f.*
bottleneck *m.* tagfa *f.*
bottom *n.* gwaelod: godre *m.*
boulder *n.* carreg fawr *f.*
bound 1 *n.* llam; terfyn *m,* ffin *f.* **2** *v.* llamu, neidio; ffinio.

boundary *n.* ffin *f,* terfyn *m.*
bow *v.* plygu, ymgrymu.
bowl 1 *n.* bowlen, powlen *f.* **2** *v.* bowlio.
box *n.* blwch, bocs; pren bocs *m.* **box office** swyddfa docynnau.
boy *n.* bachgen, hogyn, mab; gwas *m.*
boyish *a.* bachgennaidd.
brace *n.* bres; pâr *m.*
braces *n.* bresys *m.*
bracelet *n.* breichled *f.*
brain *n.* ymennydd *m.*
branch *n.* cangen *f.*
brandy *n.* brandi *m.*
brass *n.* pres *m.*
brave *a.* dewr, gwrol.
bread *n.* bara *m.* **daily bread** bara beunyddiol.
breadth *n.* lled *m.*
break 1 *n.* egwyl, hoe *f,* toriad *m.* **2** *v.* torri.
breaker *n.* ton *f.*
breakfast *n.* brecwast *m.*
breast *n.* bron; brest *f.*
breath *n.* anadl *mf,* gwynt *m.*
breathe *v.* anadlu, chwythu.
breed *v.* magu, bridio.
breeze *n.* awel *f.*
brewery *n.* bragdy *m.*
bride *n.* priodferch *f.*
bridge 1 *n.* pont *f.* **2** *v.* pontio.
brief *a.* byr, cryno.
bright *a.* disglair, gloyw, llachar, llewyrchus.
brightness *n.* llewyrch, disgleirdeb *m.*
brilliant 1 *n.* gem *f.* **2** *a.* disglair, llachar; gwych.
bring *v.* dwyn, dod (â).
brink *n.* ymyl *mf,* min *m.*
Britain *n.* Prydain *f.*
British *a.* Prydeinig.
Brittany *a.* Llydaw *f.*
broad *a.* llydan, eang, bras.
broadcast 1 *n.* darllediad *m.* **2** *v.* darlledu.
brochure *n.* llyfryn *m.*
bronze *n.* pres, efydd *m.*
brooch *n.* tlws *m.*
brook *n.* nant *f.*
broom *n.* brws, brwsh *m,* ysgub *f.*

broth *n.* cawl *m.*
brother *n.* brawd *m.* **brother-in-law**
brawd-yng-nghyfraith.
brow *n.* ael *f,* talcen *m;* crib *mf.*
brown *a.* brown.
brush 1 *n.* brws, brwsh *m,* ysgub *f.*
2 *v.* brwsio, brwshio, sgubo, ysgubo.
paint brush brws paent, brwsh
paent.
bucket *n.* bwced *m.*
bud 1 *n.* blaguryn *m.* **2** *v.* blaguro.
bug *n.* byg *m.*
build *v.* adeiladu, codi.
builder *n.* adeiladwr *m.*
building *n.* adeilad *m.*
bull *n.* tarw *m.* **bulldozer** tarw dur.
bungalow *n.* tŷ unllawr, byngalo *m.*
burden 1 *n.* baich, llwyth *m.*
2 *v.* llwytho.
burdened *a.* llwythog.
bureau *n.* swyddfa *f.*
burn 1 *n.* llosg *m;* nant *f.* **2** *a.* llosg.
3 *v.* llosgi.

burner *n.* llosgydd *m.*
burrow 1 *n.* twll cwningen *m.* **2** *v.*
tyllu.
bus *n.* bws *m.* **bus-stop** arhosfan *f.*
bysus.
bush *n.* llwyn *m,* perth *f.*
business *n.* busnes *m.*
busy *a.* prysur.
but *c.* ond, onid.
butcher *n.* cigydd.
butter *n.* menyn, ymenyn *m.*
butterfly *n.* glöyn byw *m,* iâr fach yr
haf, pili-pala *f.*
button 1 *n.* botwm *m.* **2** *v.* botymu.
buy *v.* prynu.
buyer *n.* prynwr *m.*
buzz 1 si, su, sŵn gwenyn *n.* **2** *v.* sio,
suo.
by *prp.* erbyn, ger, gerllaw, drwy,
trwy, gan, heibio, wrth, â.
by-election *n.* is-etholiad *m.*
bypass *n.* ffordd osgoi *f.*

cabbage *n.* bresychen; bresych *f.*
cabin *n.* caban *m* .
café *n.* caffe *m.*
cake *n.* cacen, teisen *f.* **birthday cake** teisen pen-blwydd.
calamity *n.* trychineb *mf.*
calculate *v.* cyfrif, rhifo.
calculation *n.* cyfrif *m.*
calculator *n.* cyfrifiannell *m.*
calendar *n.* calendar *m.*
calf *n.* llo (anifail) *m;* croth (coes) *f.*
call 1 *n.* galwad *mf,* galw *m.* 2 *v.* galw, ymweld (â).
calling *n.* galwad *mf;* galwedigaeth *f.*
calm 1 *n.* tawelwch; hedd *m.* 2 *a.* tawel; 3 *v.* tawelu, distewi.
camera *n.* camera *m.*
camp 1 *n.* gwersyll *m.* 2 *v.* gwersyllu.
campaign *n.* ymgyrch *mf.*
can *n.* can, tun *m.*
candidate *n.* ymgeisydd *m.*
candle *n.* cannwyll *f.*
candlestick *n.* canhwyllbren *m.*
cane *n.* gwialen *f.*
canoe 1 *n.* canŵ *m.* 2 *v.* canŵio.
cap *n.* cap *m.*
capital 1 *n.* prifddinas *f;* corff (arian), cyfalaf *m;* priflythyren *f.* 2 *a.* prif, pen.
capitulate *v.* ymostwng, ildio.
captain *n.* capten *m.*
captivate *v.* swyno, hudo, denu.

capture *v.* dal, dala.
car *n.* car *m.* **car park** maes parcio.
caravan *n.* carafán *f.* **caravan site** maes carafanau *m.*
card *n.* cerdyn *m,* carden *f.*
Cardiff *n.* Caerdydd *f.*
care 1 *n.* gofal, pryder *m.* 2 *v.* gofalu, carco, hidio, pryderu.
career 1 *n.* gyrfa *f.* 2 *v.* rhuthro.
careful *a.* carcus, gofalus, manwl.
careless *a.* diofal, esgeulus.
caretaker *n.* gofalwr *m.*
caring *a.* gofalus.
Carmarthen *n.* Caerfyrddin *f.*
carol *n.* carol *f.*
carpenter *n.* saer coed *m.*
carpet 1 *n.* carped *m.* 2 *v.* carpedu.
carrot *n.* moronen *f.*
carry *v.* cario.
carve *v.* cerfio.
case *n.* cas; achos; cyflwr *m;* dadl *f.*
cash 1 *n.* arian parod *m.* 2 *v.* newid.
casing *n.* plisgyn; casin *m.*
cast *v.* taflu.
castle *n.* castell *m.*
cat *n.* cath *f.*
catalogue *n.* catalog *m.*
cataract *n.* rhaeadr *f,* sgwd *m;* pilen *(ar lygad) f.*
catch *v.* dal, dala.
catchment *n.* dalgylch.
catechism *n.* holwyddoreg *f.*
caterpillar *n.* lindysen *m.*
cathedral *n.* eglwys gadeiriol *f.*
catholic 1 *n.* pabydd *m.* 2 *a.* pabyddol; catholig.
cattle *n.pl.* gwartheg, da.
cauliflower *n.* blodfresychen *f.*
cause 1 *n.* achos; achlysur; rheswm *m.* 2 *v.* achosi, peri.
caution 1 *n.* pwyll; rhybudd *m.* 2 *v.* rhybuddio.
cautious *a.* gofalus, gwyliadwrus.
cave *n.* ogof *f.*
cavity *n.* gwagle *m.*
cease *v.* peidio (â).
ceiling *n.* nen *f.*
celebrate *v.* dathlu.
celebrated *a.* enwog.
celebration *n.* dathliad *m.*
cell *n.* cell *f.*

Celtic *a.* Celtaidd.
cemetery *n.* mynwent *f.*
censure 1 *n.* cerydd *m*, sen *f.*
2 *v.* ceryddu.
centenary *n.* canmlwyddiant *m.*
centigrade *a.* canradd, sentigred.
20°C ugain gradd Celsius.
central *a.* canol, canolog. **central
heating** gwres canolog.
centre *n.* canol *m;* canolfan *f;*
canolwr *m.* **shopping centre**
canolfan siopa; **job centre** canolfan
gwaith.
centurion *n.* canwriad *m.*
century *n.* cant *m;* canrif *f.*
ceremony *n.* seremoni *f.*
certain *a.* sicr, siŵr; rhyw, rhai.
certainly *ad.* yn sicr, yn siŵr.
certainty *n.* sicrwydd *m.*
certificate *n.* tystysgrif *f.*
chaff *n.* us *m.coll.*
chaffinch *n.* ji-binc, asgell fraith *f.*
chain 1 *n.* cadwyn *f.* 2 *v.* cadwyno.
chair 1 *n.* cadair, stôl *f.* 2 *v.* cadeirio,
llywyddu. **Chairing of the Bard**
Cadeirio'r Bardd.
chaired *a.* cadeiriol.
Chairman *n.* cadeirydd *m.*
chalet *n.* hafoty, bwthyn (haf) *m.*
chalk 1 *n.* sialc *m.* 2 *v.* sialcio.
challenge 1 *n.* her *f.* 2 *v.* herio.
chamber *n.* ystafell, siambr *f.*
chamber orchestra cerddorfa
siambr.
champion *n.* pencampwr *m.*
chance 1 *n.* hap, siawns, lwc *f*, cyfle
m, damwain *f.* 2 *v.* digwydd.
change *n.* & *v.* newid *m.*
changing-room *n.* ystafell newid *f.*
channel *n.* sianel *f.* gwely *m.*
chapel *n.* capel *m.*
chapter *n.* pennod *f.*
character *n.* cymeriad, nod *m;*
llythyren *f.*
characteristic 1 *n.* nodwedd *f.*
2 *a.* nodweddiadol.
charge 1 *n.* gofal; gorchymyn; pris,
tâl; ergyd *m.* 2 *v.* gofalu, gorchymyn;
codi.
charm 1 *n.* hud, swyn *m.* 2 *v.* hudo,
swyno.

charming *a.* swynol.
chase 1 *n.* helfa *f.* 2 *v.* hel, hela,
erlid.
chat 1 *n.* sgwrs *f*, siarad, sôn *m*,
ymgom *mf.* 2 *v.* sgwrsio, siarad,
ymgomio.
chatter *v.* clebran.
cheap *a.* rhad.
cheat 1 *n.* twyllwr *m.* 2 *v.* twyllo.
cheek *n.* grudd *mf*, boch *f*,
haerllugrwydd *m.*
cheerful *a.* llawen, llon, siriol.
cheese *n.* caws *m.*
cheers! *i.* iechyd da!
chemist *n.* fferyllydd; cemegwr *m.*
chemistry *n.* cemeg *f.*
Chepstow *n.* Cas-Gwent *f.*
cheque *n.* siec *f.* **cheque book** llyfr
sieciau; **cheque card** cerdyn
sieciau.
cherry *n.* ceiriosen *f.*
chest *n.* cist; brest *f;*
Chester *n.* Caer *f.*
chew *v.* cnoi.
chick *n.* cyw *m.*
chicken *n.* cyw iâr *m.* ffowlyn *f.*
chickenpox brech yr ieir.
chief 1 *n.* pen, pennaeth *m.* 2 *a.* prif,
pen, pennaf. **chief bard** prifardd.
child *n.* plentyn *m.*
childish *a.* plentynnaidd.
chill 1 *a.* oer. 2 *v.* oeri.
chilled *a.* sythlyd, wedi ei oeri.
chilly *a.* oer, oerllyd.
chimney *n.* simdde, simnai *f.,* corn
(mwg) *m.*
chin *n.* gên *f.*
China *n.* Tseina, China *f.*
china *n.* llestri te *m.*
chip *n.* sglodyn *m.* **fish and chips**
pysgod a sglodion.
chocolate *n.* siocled *m.*
choice *n.* dewis *m.*
choir *n.* côr *m.*
choke *v.* tagu.
choose *v.* dewis, ethol.
chop *v.* torri.
chord *n.* tant, cord *m.*
chorus *n.* cytgan *f;* côr, corws *m.*
Christ *n.* Crist *m.*
christen *v.* bedyddio, enwi.

Christian 1 *n.* Cristion *m.* **2** *a.*
Cristnogol. **Christian Aid** Cymorth
Cristnogol; **Christian name** enw
bedydd.
Christmas *n.* y Nadolig *m.*
Christmas Day Dydd Nadolig;
Christmas Eve Noswyl Nadolig;
Christmas Holidays gwyliau'r
Nadolig; **Christmas presents**
anrhegion Nadolig; **Christmas tree**
coeden Nadolig.
chum *n.* cyfaill, ffrind *m.*
church *n.* eglwys, llan *f.*
churchyard *n.* mynwent *f.*
chute *n.* llithren *f.*
cigar *n.* sigâr *f.*
cigarette *n.* sigarét *f.*
cinema *n.* sinema *f.*
circle *n.* cylch *m.*
circular 1 *n.* cylchlythyr *m.*
2 *a.* cylchog.
circumflex *n.* hirnod *mf.*
circus *n.* syrcas *f.*
citizen *n.* dinesydd *m.*
city *n.* dinas *f.*
civic *a.* dinesig.
civil *a.* gwladol; cwrtais.
civilian *n.* dinesydd *m.*
civil war *n.* rhyfel cartref *mf.*
claim 1 *n.* hawl *m.* **2** *n.* hawlio.,
clamber *v.* dringo.
clash *v.* gwrthdaro.
class 1 *n.* dosbarth *m;* adran *f,* cylch
m, safon *f.* **2** *v.* dosbarthu.
classic *n.* clasur, campwaith *m.*
classical *a.* clasurol.
classics *n.* clasuron *m.pl.*
clause *n.* cymal *m.* adnod, adran *f.*
clay *n.* clai *m.*
clean 1 *a.* glân. **2** *v.* glanhau.
cleanliness *n.* glendid *m.*
cleanly *ad.* yn lân.
clear 1 *a.* amlwg, clir, eglur, gloyw.
2 *v.* clirio.
clef *n.* allwedd *f,* cleff *m.*
clerk *n.* clerc *m.*
clever *a.* medrus, clyfar.
cliché *n.* ystrydeb *f.*
cliff *n.* clogwyn *m,* craig *f.*
climate *n.* hinsawdd *f.*
climax *n.* uchafbwynt *m.*

climb *v.* dringo.
climber *n.* dringwr *m.*
cling *v.* glynu, cydio.
clinic *n.* meddygfa *f,* clinig *m.*
cloak *n.* clogyn *m,* mantell *f.*
clock *n.* cloc *m.* **o'clock** o'r gloch;
six o'clock chwech o'r gloch.
clockwise *a.* clocwedd.
close 1 *n.* diwedd, terfyn *m.* **2** *v.* cau.
close 1 *n.* clos, buarth *m,* iard *f.* **2** *a.*
agos, clòs, tyn.
cloth *n.* brethyn, defnydd, lliain,
clwtyn *m.*
clothes *n.pl.* dillad *m.pl.,* gwisgoedd
f.pl.
clothing *n.* dillad *m.*
cloud 1 *n.* cwmwl *m.* **2** *v.* cymylu.
cloudy *a.* cymylog.
clown *n.* clown *m.*
clumsy *a.* lletchwith.
coach 1 *n.* hyfforddwr *m;* coets *f.*
2 *v.* hyfforddi.
coal *n.* glo *m.*
coarse *a.* garw, bras.
coast *n.* arfordir *m,* glan môr *f.*
coat *n.* cot, siaced *f.*
cobweb *n.* gwe. *f.*
cockerel *n.* ceiliog *m.*
coffee *n.* coffi *m.*
coffin *n.* arch, coffin *f.*
cog *n.* dant, còg *m.*
coil 1 *n.* torch *m.* **2** *v.* torchi.
coin 1 *n.* darn arian *m.* **2** *v.* bathu;
pound coin darn punt.
cold 1 *n.* oerfel; annwyd *m.* **2** *a.* oer,
sythlyd. **to become cold** oeri; **to
catch a cold** dal annwyd.
collar *n.* coler *f.* **collar bone** pont yr
ysgwydd.
collect 1 *n.* colect *m (gweddi).*
2 *v.* casglu, crynhoi, hel.
collection *n.* casgliad *m.*
college *n.* coleg *m.*
collide *v.* gwrthdaro.
collier *n.* glöwr *m;* llong lo *f.*
colliery *n.* glofa *f,* pwll glo, gwaith
glo *m.*
colloquial *a.* llafar.
colony *n.* gwladfa *f.*
colour 1 *n.* lliw *m.* **2** *v.* lliwio, lliwio,
coluro.

coloured *a.* lliwiog.
colourful *a.* lliwgar.
colt *n* . ebol *m.*
column *n.* colofn *f,* piler *m.*
columnist *n.* newyddiadurwr *m.*
comb 1 *n.* crib *mf.* **2** *v.* cribo.
combat *n.* gornest, brwydr *f.*
come *v.* dod, dyfod. **to come
across** dod ar draws; **to come to
an end** dod i ben.
comely *a.* teg, glân, hardd.
comfort 1 *n.* cysur *m.* **2** *v.* cysuro.
comfortable *a.* cyfforddus,
cyffyrddus, cysurus.
command *n.* & *v.* gorchymyn *m.*
commandment *n.* gorchymyn *m:*
The Ten Commandments Y Deg
Gorchymyn.
commence *v.* dechrau.
commend *v.* canmol.
comment 1 *n.* sylw *m.* **2** *v.* sylwi,
esbonio.
commentary *n.* sylwebaeth *f;*
esboniad *m.* **to commentate**
sylwebu.
commentator *n.* sylwebydd,
sylwebwr *m.*
committee *n.* pwyllgor *m.*
common *a.* cyffredin. **common
sense** synnwyr cyffredin.
commons *n.* y cyffredin *m.pl.*
House of Commons Tŷ'r
Cyffredin.
commotion *n.* terfysg *m.*
communion *n.* cymun, cymundeb *m.*
community *n.* cymdeithas,
cymuned *f.*
compact *a.* cryno. **compact disc**
cryno ddisg.
companion *n.* cyfaill *m,* cyfeilles *f.*
company *n.* cwmni *m.*
compare *v.* cymharu (â).
compassion *n.* trugaredd *f.*
compel *v.* gorfodi.
compensate *v.* talu iawn.
compensation *n.* iawn, iawndal *m.*
compete *v.* cystadlu.
competition *n.* cystadleuaeth *f,*
ymryson *m.*
competitor *n.* cystadleuwr,
cystadleuydd *m.*

complain *v.* cwyno.
complaint *n.* cwyn *mf.*
complete *a.* hollol, llwyr.
completely *ad.* yn hollol, yn llwyr.
complex *a.* cymhleth.
complexity *m.* cymhlethdod *m.*
complicate *v.* cymhlethu *m.*
complicated *a.* cymhleth.
complication *n.,* cymhlethdod *m.*
compose *v.* cyfansoddi.
composer *n.* cyfansoddwr *m.*
comprehensive *a.* cyfun,
cynhwysfawr. **Comprehensive
School** Ysgol Gyfun.
compulsion *n.* gorfod *m,*
gorfodaeth *f.*
compulsory *a.* gorfodol.
computer *n.* cyfrifiadur *m.*
conceal *v.* cuddio.
concentrate *v.* canolbwyntio.
concerning *prp.* ynglŷn â, ynghylch.
concert *n.* cyngerdd *mf.*
concession *n.* lŵans, lwfans *m.*
conclude *v.* gorffen.
conclusion *n.* casgliad; diwedd,
diweddglo *m.*
concrete *n.* concrit *m.*
condition *n.* cyflwr *m;* amod *mf.*
conduct 1 *n.* ymddygiad *m.*
2 *v.* arwain.
conductor *n.* arweinydd; tocynnwr *m.*
cone *n.* côn *m.*
confer *v.* ymgynghori.
conference *n.* cynhadledd *f.*
confide *v.* ymddiried (yn).
confidence *n.* hyder *m,*
ymddiriedaeth *f.* **self-confidence**
hunanhyder.
confident *a.* hyderus: **to be
confident** hyderu.
confidential *a.* cyfrinachol.
confine *v.* cyfyngu, carcharu.
confined *a.* cyfyng.
confluence *n.* cymer *m.*
confront *v.* wynebu.
confuse *v.* drysu, cymysgu.
congratulate *v.* llongyfarch.
congratulation *n.* llongyfarchiad *m.*
Congratulations!
Llongyfarchiadau!
congregation *n.* cynulleidfa *f.*

Congregationalist *n.*
Annibynnwr *m.*
conjecture *v.* dychmygu, dyfalu.
conjunction *n.* cysylltair *m.*
connection *n.* cysylltiad *m,*
perthynas *mf.* **in connection with**
ynglŷn â.
conquer *v.* gorchfygu, trechu.
conquest *n.* buddugoliaeth,
concwest *f.*
conscientious *a.* cydwybodol.
conscription *n.* gorfodaeth filwrol *f.*
consent 1 *n.* caniatâd *m.* **2** *v.*
caniatáu.
conservative 1 *n.* ceidwadwr;
Tori *m.* **2** *a.* cadwrol, ceidwadol.
conservatory *n.* tŷ gwydr *m.*
conserve *v.* cadw, amddiffyn.
consider *v.* ystyried.
considerable *a.* cryn.
consideration *n.* ystyriaeth *f.*
considering *prp.* ag ystyried.
consolation *n.* cysur *m.*
consolation prize gwobr gysur.
console *v.* cysuro.
consonant *n.* cytsain *f.*
constituency *n.* etholaeth *f.*
construct *v.* ffurfio, llunio, adeiladu.
consult *v.* ymgynghori (â).
consume *v.* bwyta; defnyddio;
treulio.
contact *v.* cyffwrdd (â).
contain *v.* cynnwys, dal.
contaminate *v.* llygru.
contamination *n.* llygredd *m.*
content *n.* cynnwys *m.*
content 1 *a.* bodlon. **2** *v.* bodloni.
contention *n.* ymryson *m.*
contents *n.* cynnwys *m.pl.*
contest 1 *n.* gornest, ornest,
cystadleuaeth, ymryson *f.*
2 *v* ymryson; ymladd.
contestant *n.* cystadleuwr,
cystadleuydd *m.*
context *n.* cyd-destun *m.*
continual *a.* parhaus.
continually *ad.* byth a hefyd.
continuation *n.* parhad *m.*
continue *v.* para, parhau, dal (ati).
continuous *a.* parhaol.
contra- *px.* gwrth-, croes- (*followed*

by soft mutation).
contradiction *n.* gwrthddywediad m.
contract *n.* cytundeb *m.*
contrary *a.* gwrthwyneb, croes. **on**
the contrary i'r gwrthwyneb.
contribute *v.* cyfrannu.
contrite *a.* edifeiriol.
control *v.* rheoli.
controller *n.* rheolwr *m.*
convenient *a.* cyfleus, hwylus.
conversation *n.,* ymgom *mf,* sgwrs *f.*
converse 1 *n.* gwrthwyneb *m.*
2 *v.* ymgomio, sgwrsio, ymddiddan.
conversion *n.* trosiad *m;*
tröedigaeth *f.*
convert *v.* troi, newid, trosi.
converted *a.* wedi ei addasu.
converted try trosgais.
convey *v.* cyfleu; trosglwyddo.
cook 1 *n.* cogydd *m;* cogyddes *f.*
2 *v* coginio, gwneud bwyd.
cool 1 *a.* oer. **2** *v.* oeri.
copy 1 *n.* copi *m.* **2** *v.* copïo.
copyright *n.* hawlfraint *f.*
cord *n.* cordyn *m;* lein *f,* llinyn *m.*
corgi *n.* corgi *m.*
corn *n.* llafur, corn, ŷd *m.*
corner *n.* cornel *mf,* cwr *m,* congl *f.*
cornflakes *n.* creision ŷd *m.pl.*
corpse *n.* corff *m.*
correct 1 *a.* cywir, iawn, priodol.
2 *n.* cywiro.
correction *n.* cywiriad *m.*
corrupt 1 *a.* llygredig. **2** *v.* llygru.
corruption *n.* llygredd,
llygredigaeth *m.*
cost 1 *n.* pris *m,* traul, cost *f.*
2 *v.* costio.
costume *n.* gwisg *f.*
cottage *n.* bwthyn *m.*
cotton *n.* cotwm *m;* edau *f.* **cotton**
wool gwlân cotwm.
cough 1 *n.* peswch, pesychiad *m.*
2 *v.* peswch.
council *n.* cyngor *m.* **council house**
tŷ cyngor; **county council** cyngor
sir.
councillor *n.* cynghorwr *m.* **County**
Councillor Cynghorwr Sir.
counsel 1 *n.* cyngor *m.* **2** *v.* cynghori.
count 1 *n.* cyfrif; iarll *m.*

2 *v.* rhifo; cyfrif.
counter- *px.* gwrth- (*followed by soft mutation*): **counteract** gwrthweithio; **counterclockwise** gwrthgloc.
counterfeit *n. & a.* ffug *m.*
counterfoil *n.* bôn *m* (*siec/ derbynneb . . .*).
countess *n.* iarlles *f.*
country *n.* gwlad, bro *f.* **Country Music** Canu Gwlad.
county *n.* sir, swydd (*English county*) *f:* **Carmarthenshire** Sir Gaerfyrddin, Sir Gâr; **Lancashire** Swydd Gaerhirfryn; **Yorkshire** Swydd Efrog; **Buckinghamshire** Swydd Buckingham.
courageous *a.* dewr, gwrol.
course *n.* cwrs *m,* hynt; ystod; gyrfa *f.* **in the course of** yn ystod; **of course** wrth gwrs; **crash course** cwrs carlam.
court 1 *n.* llys *m.* **2** *v.* caru, canlyn.
courteous *a.* cwrtais.
cousin *n.* cefnder *m;* cyfnither *f.*
cover 1 *n.* clawr *m.* **2** *v.* gorchuddio.
covetous *a.* trachwantus.
covetousness *n.* trachwant *m.*
cow *n.* buwch *f.*
cowardly *a.* llwfr.
crack 1 *n.* crac *m.* **2** *v.* cracio.
cradle *n.* crud *m.*
craft *n.* crefft; llong; awyren *f.*
craftsman *n.* crefftwr *m.*
crafty *a.* cyfrwys.
crag *n.* craig *f,* clogwyn *m.*
cream *n.* hufen *m.*
crematorium *n.* amlosgfa *f.*
cress *n.* berw *m.*
crest *n.* brig *m,* crib *mf.*
crew *n.* criw *m.*
crib *n.* preseb *m.*
cricket *n.* criced; cricsyn *m.*
cricketer *n.* cricedwr *m.*
crime *n.* trosedd *f.*
criminal *n.* troseddwr *m.*
crisps *n.* creision (tatws) *m.pl.*
critic *n.* beirniad *m.*

criticise *v.* beirniadu.
crockery *n.* llestri *pl.m.*
croft *n.* tyddyn *m.*
crook *n.* troseddwr; ffon fugail *m.*
crooked *a.* cam.
cross 1 *n.,* croes *f.* **2** *v.* croesi.
cross-examine *v.* croesholi.
crossing *n.* croesfan *f.*
crossroad *n.* croesffordd *f.*
crossword *n* . croesair, pos croeseiriau *m.*
crow *n.* brân *f.*
crowd *n.* torf *f,* twr *m,* tyrfa *f,* llu *m.*
crown 1 *n.* coron *f.* **2** *v.* coroni; **Crown land** tir y Goron; **Triple Crown** Coron Driphlyg.
cruel *a.* creulon.
cruelty *n.* creulondeb *m.*
crumb *n.* briwsionyn *m.*
crumble *v.* chwalu; briwsioni.
crush *v.* malu, gwasgu.
crust *n.* crwst, crystyn *m.*
cry 1 *n.* cri *mf,* llef, sgrech *f.* **2** *v.* crio, llefain, wylo.
cuckoo *n.* cog, cwcw *f.*
cultured *a.* gwâr.
cunning *a.* cyfrwys.
cup *n.* cwpan *mf,* dysgl *f.*
cupboard *n.* cwpwrdd *m.*
cure *v.* gwella, iacháu.
curly *a.* cyrliog.
current 1 *n.* ffrwd *f.* llif *m.* **2** *a.* cyfoes: **current affairs** materion cyfoes.
currently *ad.* ar hyn o bryd.
curse 1 *n.* llw *m,* melltith, rheg *f.* **2** *v.* rhegi.
curtain *n.* llen *f.*
cushion *n.* clustog *f.*
custom *n.* arfer, cwstwm *m;* toll *f.*
customary *a.* arferol.
customer *n.* cwsmer *m.*
customs *n.* y tollau *f.pl.* **customs officer** swyddog tollau.
cut 1 *n.* toriad *m.* **2** *v.* torri.
cycle 1 *n.* cylch; beic *m.* **2** *v.* seiclo.
cylinder *n.* silindr *m.*
cylindrical *a.* silindrog.

dad: daddy *n.* tad *m.*
daffodil *n.* cenhinen Bedr *f*, daffodil *m.*
daisy *n.* llygad y dydd *m.*
dale *n.* cwm, dyffryn *m*, dôl, bro *f.* **hill and dale** bryn a dôl.
damage *n.* niwed, difrod *m.*
damages *n.pl.* iawndal, iawn *m.*
damp *a.* llaith.
damson *n.* eirinen ddu *f.*
dance 1 *n.* dawns *f.* 2 *v.* dawnsio. **public folk dance** twmpath dawns.
dandelion *n.* dant y llew *m.*
danger *n.* perygl *m.*
dangerous *a.* peryglus.
dank *a.* llaith, gwlyb.
dare *v.* beiddio, meiddio, mentro.
dark *a.* tywyll.
darkness *n.* tywyllwch, gwyll *m.*
darling 1 *n.* anwylyd *mf*, cariad *m.* 2 *v.* annwyl.
date *n.* dyddiad *m.*
daughter *n.* merch *f.*
dawn 1 *n.* gwawr *f.* 2 *v.* gwawrio.
day *n.* diwrnod, dydd *m.* **day before yesterday** echdoe; **yesterday** doe, ddoe; **today** heddiw; **tomorrow** yfory; **day after tomorrow** trennydd; **three days hence** tradwy; **by day** liw dydd; **next day** trannoeth; **Good day!** Dydd da!
daybreak *n.* gwawr *f*, toriad dydd *m.*
daylight *n.* golau dydd *m.*

dazzle *v.* dallu; disgleirio.
dazzling *a.* llachar, disglair.
deacon *n.* diacon; blaenor *m.* **deaconess** diacones.
dead *n.* & *a.* marw, meirw, meirwon *m.pl.*
deadly *a.* marwol.
deaf *n.* & *a.* byddar *m.*
deal *v.* ymwneud (â), delio (â), ymdrin (â).
dear 1 *n.* anwylyd *mf*, cariad *m.* 2 *a.* annwyl, bach, cu, ffel, hoff; drud.
dearest *n.* & *a.* anwylaf *mf.* **dearest ones** anwyliaid.
death *n.* angau *m*, marwolaeth *f.*
debate 1 *n.* dadl *f.* 2 *v.* dadlau, ymryson.
debt *n.* dyled *f.*
decade *n.* degawd *m.*
decay *v.* pydru.
deceased *a.* y diweddar.
deceit *n.* twyll *m.*
deceitful *a.* twyllodrus.
deceive *v.* twyllo.
decelerate *v.* arafu.
December *n.* Rhagfyr *m.*
decentralise *v.* datganoli.
decide *v.* penderfynu, dyfarnu.
decision *n.* penderfyniad, dyfarniad *m.*
deck *n.* bwrdd; dec *m.*
declaration *n.* datganiad *m.*
declare *v.* datgan, mynegi.
decompose *v.* pydru.
decree *n.* gorchymyn *m.*
dedicate *v.* cyflwyno; cysegru.
deed *n.* gweithred *f.*
deep 1 *n.* dyfnder *m.* 2 *a.* dwfn. **deep freeze cabinet** rhewgell.
Deeside *n.* Glannau Dyfrdwy *f.*
defeat *v.* gorchfygu, trechu.
defect *n.* nam, diffyg, gwall *m.*
defence *n.* amddiffyn, amddiffyniad *m;* amddiffynfa *f.*
defend *v.* amddiffyn.
defiance *n.* her *f.*
define *v.* diffinio.
definite *a.* pendant.
definitely *ad.* yn bendant.
definition *n.* diffiniad *m.*

defraud v. twyllo.
defrost v. dadrewi.
deft a. medrus.
degree n. gradd f.
de-ice v. toddi.
deity n. duwdod; duw m.
delay v. oedi.
delectable a. hyfryd.
delegate 1 n. dirprwy m. **2** v. dirprwyo.
delegation n. dirprwyaeth f.
delete v. dileu.
delicious a. blasus.
delightful a. hyfryd, braf.
deliver v. gwaredu (rhag); danfon, trosglwyddo.
deliverer n. gwaredwr.
demand f. **2** v. mynnu, gofyn.
demi- px. hanner.
demise n. marwolaeth f.
den n. ffau f.
denomination n. enw, enwad m.
dense a. trwchus; hurt.
dent 1 n. pant, tolc m. **2** v. tolcio.
dentist n. deintydd m.
dentures n. dannedd gosod, dannedd dodi m.pl.
deny v. gwadu, gwrthod.
depart v. ymadael (â); cychwyn.
department n. adran f. dosbarth m.
depend v. dibynnu (ar).
deplore v. gresynu.
depose v. diswyddo; tystio.
deposit n. ernes f. blaendal m.
depressed a. isel, digalon.
depth n. dyfnder m.
deputation n. dirprwyaeth f.
deputy n. dirprwy m. **Deputy Director** Dirprwy Gyfarwyddwr; **Deputy Headteacher** Dirprwy Brifathro, Dirprwy Brifathrawes.
derivation n. tarddiad m.
derive v. derbyn, cael; tarddu.
descend v. disgyn.
describe v. disgrifio, darlunio.
description n. disgrifiad m.
desert n. anialwch m.
desert v. cilio, ffoi (rhag).
deserter n. ffoadur m.
deserve v. haeddu.
deserved a. teilwng.

design 1 n. cynllun m. **2** v. cynllunio.
designer n. cynlluniwr, cynllunydd m.
desirable a. dymunol.
desire 1 n. dymuniad, chwant, ewyllys m. **2** v. dymuno.
desirous a. awyddus.
desk n. desg f.
desolate a. gwag.
despite prp. er, er gwaethaf.
despot n. unben m.
dessert n. pwdin, melysfwyd m.
destiny n. tynged f.
destroy v. dinistrio, difetha.
detached a. ar wahân.
detail 1 n. manylyn m. **2** v. manylu. **details** manylion; **in detail** yn fanwl.
detective n. ditectif m. **detective story** stori dditectif.
determination n. penderfyniad m.
determine v. penderfynu.
determined a. penderfynol.
detest v. casáu.
develop v. datblygu.
development n. datblygiad m.
deviate v. gwyro, gwyrio.
deviation n. gwyriad m.
devil n. diafol, diawl m.
devilish a. diawledig.
devolution n. datganoli m.
devolve v. datganoli.
devour v. llyncu, ysu.
dew 1 n. gwlith m. **2** v. gwlitho.
diagnose v. adnabod.
diagnosis n. diagnosis m.
dialect n. tafodiaith f.
dialogue n. deialog, sgwrs f.
diarrhoea n. dolur rhydd m.
diary n. dyddiadur m.
dictator n. unben m.
dictionary n. geiriadur m.
die v. marw, darfod, trigo.
differ v. gwahaniaethu.
difference n. gwahaniaeth m.
different a. gwahanol.
difficult a. anodd, caled.
difficulty n. anhawster m.
dig v. palu.

digest *v.* treulio.
dignity *n.* urddas *m.*
diligent *a.* prysur, diwyd.
dimension *n.* maint *m.*
diminish *v.* lleihau.
diminutive *a.* bychan.
dingle *n.* cwm, glyn, pant *m.*
dinner *n.* cinio *mf.*
dip *v.* trochi, golchi.
direct 1 *a.* union. **2** *v.* cyfeirio.
direction *n.* cyfeiriad;
hyfforddiant *m.*
directly *ad.* yn union.
director *n.* cyfarwyddwr *m.*
directory *n.* cyfarwyddiadur *m.*
dirt *n.* baw, llacs *m.*
dirty *a.* brwnt, budr.
disability *n.* anabledd *m.*
disabled *a.* anabl, methedig.
disappear *v.* diflannu.
disappoint *v.* siomi.
disappointed *a.* siomedig.
disappointing *a.* siomedig.
disappointment *n.* siom *mf.*
disarm *v.* diarfogi.
disaster *n.* trychineb *mf.*
disc *n.* disg *mf.*
disciple *n.* disgybl *m.*
discipline *n.* disgyblaeth *f.*
disclaim *v.* gwadu.
disclose *v.* datguddio.
discontented *a.* anfodlon.
discover *v.* darganfod.
discretion *n.* doethineb, pwyll *m.*
discuss *v.* trafod.
discussion *n.* trafodaeth, sgwrs *f.*
disease *n.* afiechyd, clefyd, dolur *m.*
haint *f.*
disembark *v.* glanio.
dish *n.* dysgl *f.*
disinfectant *n.* diheintydd *m.*
disk *n.* disg *mf.*
dislike *v.* casáu.
dismiss *v.* diswyddo; rhyddhau;
gwrthod.
disown *v.* gwadu, diarddel.
dispatch 1 *n.* neges *f.* **2** *v.* anfon,
danfon.
dispute 1 *n.* dadl *f.* **2** *v.* dadlau,
amau, ymryson.
disseminate *v.* hau.

dissimilar *a.* annhebyg, gwahanol.
dissolve *v.* toddi; datod.
distance *n.* pellter *m.*
distant *a.* pell, hirbell. **from far** o
hirbell.
distasteful *a.* diflas.
distinct *a.* arbennig; eglur; gwahanol.
distribute *v.* rhannu, dosbarthu.
district *n.* ardal *f.* dosbarth, cylch,
rhanbarth, rhandir *m.*
ditch *n.* ffos *f.*
diverse *a.* gwahanol.
divide *v.* rhannu.
diviner *n.* dewin, dyn hysbys *m.*
division *n.* adran, rhan *f,* rhaniad,
rhanbarth, rhandir *m.*
divorce *n.* ysgariad *m.*
do *v.* gwneud, gwneuthur.
dock *n.* doc *m.*
doctor *n.* meddyg, doctor *m.* **Dr
John Jones** y Dr John Jones.
document *n.* dogfen *f.*
dog *n.* ci *m.*
doll *n.* dol *f.*
domesticated *a.* dof.
donation *n.* rhodd *f,* cyfraniad *m.*
donkey *n.* asyn, mul *m.*
door *n.* drws, porth *m.*
double *a.* dwbl.
doubt 1 *n.* amheuaeth, amau.
2 *v.* amau.
dough *n.* toes *m.*
down *ad.* i lawr.
dozen *n.* dwsin, deuddeg *m.*
drag *v.* llusgo.
dragon *n.* draig *f.*
drama *n.* drama *f.* **drama festival**
gŵyl ddrama.
dramatist *n.* dramodydd *m.*
draw *v.* darlunio, llunio, tynnu, llusgo.
drawing *n.* llun *m.*
dread 1 *n.* ofn *m.* **2** *v.* ofni.
dreadful *a.* ofnadwy.
dream 1 *n.* breuddwyd *mf.*
2 *v.* breuddwydio.
dregs *n.* gwaelodion *m.pl.,*
gwaddodd *m.*
dress 1 *n.* gwisg *f,* dilledyn *m,* ffrog *f.*
2 *v.* gwisgo, taclu; trin.
dresser *n.* seld, dreser, dresel *f;*
gwisgwr *m.*

dressmaker *n.* gwniadyddes, gwniyddes *f.*
drink 1 *n.* diod *f.* **2** *v.* yfed; diota.
drive 1 *n.* dreif *m.* **2** *v.* gyrru, hala.
driver *n.* gyrrwr *m.*
driving licence *n.* trwydded yrru *f.*
droll *a.* ysmala, digrif.
drop 1 *n.* cwymp; diferyn *m.*
  2 *v.* cwympo. **drop goal** gôl adlam.
drown *v.* boddi.
drug *n.* cyffur *m.*
drum *n.* drwm.
drunk *a.* meddw. **to get drunk** meddwi.
drunkard *n.* meddwyn.
dry 1 *a.* sych, cras. **2** *v.* sychu.
Dublin *n.* Dulyn *f.*
duck *n.* hwyad, hwyaden *f.* **duckling** cyw hwyaden *m.*

due 1 *n.* dyled, hawl *f,* tâl *m.* **2** *a.* dyledus.
duel *n.* gornest *f.*
duet *n.* deuawd *mf.*
dull *a.* dwl, hurt; diflas, cymylog.
  dull man dyn dwl; **dull day** diwrnod cymylog.
dumb *a.* mud.
dummy-pass *n.* ffug-bas *f.*
during *prp.* yn ystod.
dust *n.* llwch, dwst *m.* **dustbin** bin ysbwriel *m.*
duty *n.* dyletswydd; toll *f.*
dwell *v.* cartrefu, trigo, byw.
dwelling *n.* preswylfa, trigfa, trigfan *f.*
dye *v.* lliwio, lliwo.
dyke *n.* clawdd, morglawdd *m:* **Offa's Dyke** Clawdd Offa.

each *a. & pn* pob un, pob.
eager *a.* awyddus.
eagle *n.* eryr *m.*
ear *n.* clust *f.*
earl *n.* iarll *m.*
earliest *a.* cyntaf.
early 1 *a.* cynnar, bore, boreol.
2 *a.* yn fore.
ear-mark 1 *n.* clustnod *mf.*
2 *v.* clustnodi, neilltuo.
earn *v.* ennill.
earner *n.* enillwr, enillydd *m.*
earnings *n.* enillion *pl.*
ear-ring *n.* clustlws *m.*
earshot *n.* clyw *m.*
earth *n.* daear, Y Ddaear *f,* pridd, tir,
y byd *m.*
earthquake *n.* daeargryn *mf.*
earthwork *n.* clawdd *m.*
east 1 *n.* dwyrain *m.* **2** *a.* dwyreiniol.
Easter *n.* y Pasg *m.* **Easter egg** wy
Pasg; **Easter holidays** gwyliau'r
Pasg.
easy *a.* hawdd, rhwydd.
easy chair *n.* cadair esmwyth *f.*
eat *v.* bwyta.
ebb *n.* trai *m.*
echo *n.* adlais, atsain *m.* carreg ateb *f.*
economics *n.* economeg *f.*
economise *v.* cynilo.
edge *n.* cwr, blaen, min *m,* ymyl *mf.*
Edinburgh *n.* Caeredin *f.*
edit *v.* golygu.

edition *n.* argraffiad *m.*
editor *n.* golygydd *m.*
education *n.* addysg *f.*
effect 1 *n.* effaith *f.* **2** *v.* effeithio.
effective *a.* effeithiol.
effeminate *a.* merchetaidd.
effort *n.* ymdrech, ymgais *f.*
e.g. *(exempli gratia), ad.*
er enghraifft *(e.e.).*
egg *n.* wy *m.*
egg cup *n.* cwpan wy *mf.*
eight *n. & a.* wyth *m.*
eighteen *n. & a.* deunaw, un deg
wyth *m.*
eighth *n. & a.* wythfed *m.*
eighty *n. & a.* wyth deg, pedwar
ugain *m.*
either 1 *a. & pn.* un o'r ddau, naill ai
. . . neu. **2** *ad. & c.* na, nac, chwaith,
ychwaith.
elbow *n.* penelin *mf.*
elderly *a.* oedrannus.
elect *v.* ethol, dewis.
election *n.* etholiad *m.*
electorate *n.* etholaeth *f.*
electric *n. & a.* trydan *m.* **electric
fire** tân trydan.
electrical *a.* trydanol.
electrician *n.* trydanwr *m.*
electricity *n.* trydan *m.*
element *n.* elfen *f.*
elementary *a.* elfennol.
elephant *n.* eliffant.
eleven *n. & a.* un ar ddeg *m.*
eleventh *n. & a.* unfed ar ddeg *m.*
ellipse *n.* hirgylch *m.*
else *ad.* arall.
e-mail *n.* e-bost.
embankment *n.* clawdd, cob *m.*
embassy *n.* llysgenhadaeth *f.*
embrace *v.* cofleidio.
emigrant *n.* ymfudwr *m.*
emigrate *v.* ymfudo.
eminent *a.* enwog, amlwg.
emphasis *n.* pwys, pwyslais *m.*
emphatic *a.* pendant.
empire *n.* ymerodraeth *f.*
employ *v.* cyflogi.
employee *n.* gŵr cyflog *m.*
employer *n.* cyflogwr *m.*
employment *n.* gwaith *m.*

empty 1 *a.* gwag. **2** *v.* gwagio, arllwys. **empty-handed** gwaglaw.
enchant *v.* swyno, hudo.
enchanting *a.* hudol, swynol.
enchantment *n.* lledrith, swyn *m.*
enclose *v.* amgáu.
enclosed *a.* amgaeëdig.
encore 1 *n.* encôr *m.* **2** *ad.* eto.
end 1 *n.* diwedd, diben, pen, terfyn *m.* **2** *v.* dibennu, gorffen.
endeavour 1 *n.* ymdrech *f.* **2** *v.* ymdrechu.
endless *a.* diddiwedd.
endure *v.* dioddef, goddef.
enemy *n.* gelyn *m.*
energetic *a.* egnïol.
energy *n.* egni, ynni *m.*
enforce *v.* gorfodi.
enforced *a.* gorfod.
enforcement *n.* gorfodaeth *f.*
engagement *n.* dyweddïad; ymrwymiad *m.*
engine *n.* peiriant *m,* injan, injin *f.*
England *n.* Lloegr *f.*
English 1 *n.* Saesneg *f.* **2** *a.* Saesneg, Seisnig.
Englishman *n.* Sais *m.*
Englishwoman *n.* Saesnes *f.*
enjoy *v.* mwynhau, joio.
enjoyment *n.* mwynhad *m.*
enlighten *v.* goleuo; hysbysu.
enormous *a.* enfawr, anferth.
enough 1 *n.* digon, digonedd *m.* **2** *a.* & *ad.* digon.
enquire *v.* gofyn, holi.
entangle *v.* drysu.
enter *v.* mynd i mewn.
entertain *v.* difyrru.
entertaining *a.* difyr, difyrrus.
entertainment *n.* adloniant *m.*
enthusiastic *a.* brwdfrydig.
entice *v.* denu, hudo.
enticing *a.* deniadol, dengar.
entire *a.* cyfan, hollol, llwyr.
entirely *ad.* yn gyfan gwbl, yn hollol, yn llwyr.
entrails *n.* perfedd *pl.*
entrance *n.* mynedfa *f.* mynediad, drws, porth; tâl *m.*
entrance *v.* swyno.
entreat *v.* erfyn.

entry *n.* mynediad *m,* mynedfa *f.*
envelop *v.* amgáu.
envelope *n.* amlen *f.*
environment *n.* amgylchedd *m.*
environs *n.* amgylchoedd *pl.*
envoy *n.* negesydd, cennad *m.*
epilogue *n.* diweddglo, epilog *m.*
epistle *n.* llythyr, epistol *m.*
equal *a.* cydradd, yr un faint, hafal.
equation *n.* hafaliad *m.* **simple equation** hafaliad syml.
equipment *n.* offer *m.pl.*
erase *v.* dileu.
erect 1 *a.* syth. **2** *v.* codi.
errand *n.* neges *f.*
error *n.* camsyniad; bai, gwall *m.*
escape *v.* dianc, ffoi.
escort *v.* hebrwng.
especial *a.* arbennig, enwedig, neilltuol.
especially *ad.* yn arbennig, yn enwedig.
essay *n.* traethawd *m.* ysgrif *mf.*
essential *a.* hanfodol.
establish *v.* sefydlu.
establishment *n.* sefydliad *m.*
estate *n.* eiddo *m,* ystad, stad *f.*
estuary *n.* aber *m.*
eternal *ad.* yn dragwyddol, yn oes oesoedd.
Europe *n.* Ewrop *f.*
evade *v.* osgoi.
eve *n.* min nos *m,* noswyl *f.*
even 1 *n.* yr hwyr *m.* **2** *a.* gwastad, llyfn; tawel. **3** *ad.* hyd yn oed.
evening *n.* hwyr *m,* noson, noswaith *f.* **evening class** dosbarth nos.
event *n.* digwyddiad *m.*
eventually *ad.* o'r diwedd.
ever *ad.* byth, erioed.
evergreen *n.* & *a.* bythwyrdd *m.*
everlasting *a.* tragwyddol.
evermore *ad.* byth, byth bythoedd.
every *a.* pob.
everybody *pn.* pawb, pob un.
everyday *a.* bob dydd.
everyone *pn* pawb, pob un.
everything *pn.* pob peth, popeth.
everywhere *ad.* ym mhobman.
evidence *n.* tystiolaeth *f,* prawf *m.*
evident *a.* amlwg, eglur.

evil 1 *n.* drwg, drygioni *m.* **2** *a.* drwg, drygionus.
evolve *v.* datblygu; esblygu.
ewe *n.* dafad, mamog *f.*
ex- *px.* cyn-.
exact *a.* cywir, manwl, union. **to be exact** manylu.
exactly *ad.* yn union, i'r dim.
examination *n.* arholiad, archwiliad *m.*
examine *v.* arholi, chwilio, archwilio.
examiner *n.* arholwr, holwr *m.*
example *n.* enghraifft, esiampl *f.* **for example, e.g.** er enghraifft, e.e.
excavator *n.* jac-codi-baw *m.*
excel *v.* rhagori.
excellent *a.* ardderchog, campus, godidog, gwych, penigamp, rhagorol.
except 1 *v.* eithrio. **2** *prp.* ac eithrio. **3** *pn.* eithr.
excess *n.* gormod.
exciting *a.* cyffrous, cynhyrfus.
exclaim *v.* llefain, gweiddi, bloeddio.
exclamation *n.* llef, gwaedd *f.*
exclude *v.* eithrio, cau allan.
excuse 1 *n.* esgus *m.* **2** *v.* esgusodi.
execute *v.* gweithredu; dienyddio.
exercise 1 *n.* ymarfer *f,* ymarferiad *m.* **2** *v.* ymarfer. **exercise book** llyfr ymarfer, llyfr ysgrifennu.
exile 1 *n.* alltud *m.* **2** *v.* alltudio.
exist *v.* bod.
existence *n.* bod *m,* bodolaeth *f.*
exit 1 *n.* allanfa *f,* mynediad allan *m.*

2 *v.* mynd allan.
expect *v.* disgwyl.
expediency *n.* hwylustod *m.*
expedient *a.* hwylus, cyfleus.
expense *n.* traul, cost *f.*
expenses *n.* treuliau *f.pl.*
expensive *a.* costus, drud.
experience *n.* profiad *m.*
experienced *a.* profiadol.
explain *v.* egluro, esbonio.
explanation *n.* esboniad, eglurhad *m.*
explode *v.* ffrwydro.
expose *v.* amlygu, dinoethi.
exposed *a.* agored, noeth.
exposition *n.* esboniad *m.*
express 1 *a.* cyflym. **2** *v.* mynegi. **3** *n.* trên cyflym *m.*
extend *v.* estyn, ymestyn.
extension *a.* estyniad *m.*
extensive *a.* eang, helaeth.
extent *n.* maint, hyd, mesur *m.* **to some extent** i raddau.
exterior 1 *n.* y tu allan *m.* **2** *a.* allanol.
external *a.* allanol.
extinguish *v.* diffodd; dileu.
extreme 1 *n.* eithaf *m.* **2** *a.* eithafol.
extremely *ad.* dros ben, gor-.
extremity *n.* eithaf, terfyn, pen *m.*
eye 1 *n.* llygad *mf.* **2** *v.* llygadu, sylwi ar.
eyesight *n.* golwg *mf.*
eyewitness *n.* llygad-dyst *m.*

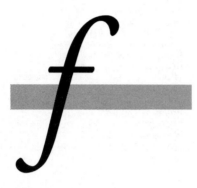

fable *n.* chwedl *f.*
fabric *n.* defnydd *m.*
face 1 *n.* wyneb *m.* **2** *v.* wynebu.
 face-cloth clwtyn ymolch.
facilitate *v.* hwyluso.
fact *n.* ffaith *f,* gwirionedd *m.* **as a**
 matter of fact mewn gwirionedd.
factor *n.* elfen, ffactor *f.*
factory *n.* ffatri *f.*
fade *v.* gwywo, colli lliw.
fail *v.* methu, ffaelu.
failure *n.* methiant *m.*
faint 1 *a.* gwan. **2** *v.* llewygu.
fair 1 *n.* ffair *f.* **2** *a.* teg, glân;
 gweddol; golau.
fairly *ad.* yn deg, yn lân, yn weddol,
 eithaf-, go-, lled-. **fairly good** eithaf
 da, go dda, lled dda. **fairly rare** go
 brin. **fairly quiet** lled dawel;
 see Appendix for mutation of
 Adjectives following certain Adverbs.
fairness *n.* harddwch; tegwch *m.*
faith *n.* ffydd *f.*
faithful *a.* ffyddlon, cywir.
faithfully *ad.* yn ffyddlon, yn gywir.
 Yours faithfully Yr eiddoch yn
 gywir.
fake 1 *a.* ffug. **2** *v.* ffugio.
falcon 1 *a.* hebog *m.*
fall 1 *n.* cwymp *m.* **2** *v.* cwympo,
 syrthio.
false *a.* ffug, gau, twyllodrus. **false**
 teeth dannedd gosod, dannedd dodi.

fame *n.* enwogrwydd, clod *m.*
familiarise *v.* cyfarwyddo.
family *n.* teulu *m.*
famine *n.* newyn *m.*
famish *v.* llwgu.
famous *a.* enwog.
fanciful *a.* ffansïol.
fancy 1 *n.* dychymyg *m,* ffansi *f,*
 serch *m.* **2** *v.* dychmygu, ffansïo,
 serchu.
fantasy *n.* ffantasi *f.*
far *a. & ad.* pell, ymhell. **as far as**
 hyd at: **from afar** o hirbell.
farewell 1 *n.* ffárwel, ffarwél *f.*
 2 *v.* ffarwelio. **to bid farewell**
 canu'n iach.
farm 1 *n.* ffarm, fferm *f.* **2** *v.* ffarmio,
 ffermio.
farmer *n.* amaethwr, ffarmwr,
 ffermwr *m.*
farmhouse *n.* ffermdy, tŷ ffarm *m.*
farming *n.* ffermio, gwaith ffarm *m,*
 amaethyddiaeth *f.*
farmyard *n.* buarth, clos *m.*
farthest *a.* pellaf, eithaf.
fascinate *v.* hudo, swyno.
fascinating *a.* hudol, swynol.
fashion 1 *n.* llun, ffasiwn *m;* arfer *mf.*
 2 *v.* llunio, ffurfio, gwneud.
fast *a.* cyflym, buan; tyn.
fat 1 *n.* braster, saim *m.* **2** *v.* bras,
 tew. **fat meat** cig bras, cig gwyn.
fatal *a.* marwol.
fatality *n.* marwolaeth *f.*
fate *n.* tynged *f.*
fateful *a.* tyngedfennol.
father *n.* tad *m.* **father-in-law** tad-
 yng-nghyfraith; **stepfather** llystad.
 Father Christmas *n.* Siôn Corn *m.*
fault *n.* bai, nam, diffyg *m.*
faultless *a.* di-fai.
faulty *a.* gwallus.
favour *n.* cymwynas, ffafr *f.*
favourite 1 *n.* ffefryn *m.* **2** *a.* hoff.
fear 1 *n.* ofn, braw *m.* **2** *v.* ofni.
feast 1 *n.* gwledd, gŵyl *f.*
 2 *v.* gwledda.
feat *n.* camp *f.*
feather 1 *n.* pluen, plufyn *m.*
 2 *v.* pluo, plufio.
feature *n.* nodwedd.

fee *n.* tâl *m,* cyflog *mf,* ffi *f.*
February *n.* Chwefror, Mis Bach *m.*
feeble *a.* gwan, egwan, bregus.
feed *v.* bwydo, bwyda; bwyta.
feel 1 *n.* teimlad *m.* **2** *v.* teimlo, clywed.
feeling *n.* teimlad *m,* naws *f.*
feign *v.* cymryd ar; ffugio.
fell *v.* cwympo, syrthio, torri.
female 1 *n.* benyw, menyw *f.*
  2 *a.* benywaidd, menywaidd.
feminine *a.* benywaidd, menywaidd.
fence 1 *n.* clawdd *m,* ffens *f.*
  2 *v.* cau, amgáu.
fern *n.* rhedynen *f,* rhedyn *pl.*
ferocious *a.* ffyrnig, gwyllt.
fertile *a.* ffrwythlon, bras, toreithiog.
fertilise *v.* ffrwythloni; gwrteithio.
fertiliser *n.* gwrtaith *m.*
fervent *a.* gwresog, tanllyd, tanbaid, selog.
festival *n.* gŵyl, dydd gŵyl *m.*
  singing festival cymanfa ganu.
fetch *v.* hôl, nôl, hercyd.
fever *n.* twymyn *f,* clefyd, gwres *m.*
few *a.* ychydig.
fiancé *n.* darpar-ŵr, dyweddi *m.*
fiancée *n.* darpar wraig, dyweddi *f.*
fiction *n.* ffluglen *f.*
fictitious *a.* ffug, ffugiol.
field *n.* cae, maes, parc *m.*
fierce *a.* ffyrnig.
fiery *a.* tanllyd, tanbaid.
fifteen *n.* & *a.* pymtheg *m.*
fifteenth *n.* & *a.* pymthegfed *m.*
fifth *n.* & *a.* pumed *m.*
fifty *n.* & *a.* hanner cant, pum deg *m.*
fight 1 *n.* brwydr *f.* ymladd *m.*
  2 *v.* brwydro, ymladd.
fighter *n.* ymladdwr *m.*
fighting *n.* ymladd *m.*
figure 1 *n.* ffigur *mf,* ffurf *f,* llun *m.*
  2 *v.* ffurfio; rhifo.
fill *v.* llanw, llenwi.
film 1 *n.* ffilm *f.* **2** *v.* ffilmio.
filth *n.* baw, budreddi, mochyndra *m.*
final 1 *n.* rownd derfynol *f. a.* terfynol, olaf.
finally *ad.* o'r diwedd, yn olaf.
find *v.* darganfod, cael, dod o hyd.
fine 1 *n.* dirwy *f.* **2** *v.* dirwyo.
  3 *a.* mân, manwl; main; braf; gwych;

hardd, hyfryd, teg.
finger *n.* bys *m.* **fingerprint** ôl bys.
finish 1 *n.* diwedd, terfyn *m.*
  2 *v.* gorffen, dibennu, cwpla.
fir *n.* ffynidwydden *f.*
fire 1 *n.* tân *m.* **2** *v.* tanio; saethu.
  fire-brigade brigâd dân *f.* **fire exit** allanfa dân *f.*
fireplace *n.* lle tân *m.*
firewood *n.* coed tân *f.pl.*
fireworks *n.* tân gwyllt *m.pl.*
firm 1 *n.* cwmni, ffyrm *m.*
  2 *a.* cadarn, cryf. **3** *v.* nerthu, cryfhau.
firmament *n.* ffurfafen *f.*
first 1 *n.* & *a.* cyntaf *m.*
  2 *ad.* yn gyntaf.
fish 1 *n.* pysgodyn *m.* **2** *v.* pysgota.
fisherman *n.* pysgotwr *m.*
fishing *n.* pysgota *m.*
fist *n.* dwrn *m.*
fitting *a.* addas, priodol.
five *n.* & *a.* pump *m.*
fix *v.* gosod, sicrhau, sefydlu.
fixed *a.* sefydlog.
flabby *a.* llac, llipa, llaes.
flag *n.* baner *f.* **Union Jack** Jac-yr-Undeb.
flakes *n.* creision *m.pl.* **cornflakes** creision ŷd; **snowflakes** plu eira.
flame 1 *n.* fflam *f.* **2** *v.* fflamio.
flank *n.* ystlys, ochr *f.*
flannel *n.* gwlanen *f.*
flap 1 *n.* llabed *f.* fflap *m.* **2** *v.* fflapio.
flash 1 *n.* fflach *f.* **2** *v.* fflachio.
flat 1 *n.* fflat *f.* **2** *a.* fflat, gwastad.
flavour 1 *n.* blas *m.* **2** *v.* blasu.
flaw *n.* bai, diffyg, nam *m.*
flea *n.* chwannen *f.*
flee *v.* cilio, dianc, ffoi.
fleet *n.* llynges *f.*
flesh *n.* cig, cnawd *m.* **flesh and blood** cig a gwaed.
flexible *a.* hyblyg, ystwyth.
fling *v.* taflu.
flock *n.* haid *f;* praidd *m.*
flood 1 *n.* llif *m.* **2** *v.* llifo, gorlifo.
floor *n.* llawr *m.*
flour *n.* blawd, can *m.*
flow 1. *n.* llif *m.* **2** *v.* llifo, rhedeg.
flower *n.* blodyn *m.* **flower pot** pot blodau.

flowing *a.* llithrig; llaes, llac, rhydd.
fluent *a.* rhwydd, llithrig, rhugl.
fluid *n. & a.* hylif *m.*
fly 1 *n.* cleren *f*, pryf, gwybedyn *m.*
  2 *v.* hedfan.
foam *n.* ewyn *m.*
focus 1 *n.* canolbwynt, ffocws *m.*
  2 *a.* canolbwyntio.
foe *n.* gelyn *m.*
fog *n.* niwl, ffog *m.* **thick fog** niwl
  trwchus.
foggy *a.* niwlog.
fold *v.* plygu.
folk *n.* gwerin *coll.f.,* pobl *f.*
folklore *n.* llên gwerin.
folksong *n.* cân werin *f.*
follow *v.* dilyn.
follower *n.* dilynwr *m.*
folly *n.* ffolineb *m.*
fond *a.* hoff, cu, annwyl.
fondle *v.* anwesu, anwylo.
fondness *n.* hoffter; anwes *m.*
food *n.* bwyd *m.*
fool 1 *n.* ffŵl *m.* **2** *v.* twyllo.
foolish *a.* ffôl, dwl.
foolishness *n.* ffolineb, dwli *m.*
foot *n.* troed *mf;* troedfedd *f.*
football *n.* pêl-droed *f.* **footballer**
  pêldroediwr *m.*
footpath *n.* troedffordd *f*, llwybr *m.*
  public footpath llwybr cyhoeddus.
footprint *n.* ôl troed *m.*
for 1 *prp.* am, dros, tros, er, ers,
  erbyn, hyd, i, yn, lle. **2** *c.* achos, gan,
  oblegid, oherwydd.
force *n.* grym; llu *m.* **armed forces**
  lluoedd arfog.
ford *n.* rhyd *f.* **Ammanford**
  Rhydaman: **Oxford** Rhydychen.
forehead *n.* talcen, tâl *m.*
foreign *a.* estron, tramor. **foreign**
  affairs materion tramor.
foreigner *n.* estron *m.*
forest *n.* coedwig, fforest *f.*
foretaste *n.* rhagflas, rhagbrawf *m.*
forge 1 *n.* gefail *f.* **2** *v.* ffugio, twyllo.
forget *v.* anghofio. **forget-me-not**
  glas y gors.
forgive *v.* maddau.
fork *n.* fforc, fforch *f.*
form 1 *n.* ffurf *f;* modd, dull *m;*

ffurflen *f;* dosbarth *m.* **2** *v.* ffurfio,
llunio. **application form** ffurflen
gais *f.*
former *px.* cyn.
formerly *ad.* gynt.
fort *n.* caer *f.*
forthcoming *a.* ar ddod, gerllaw.
fortnight *n.* pythefnos *mf.*
fortnightly *ad.* bob pythefnos.
fortunate *a.* ffodus, lwcus.
fortunately *ad.* yn ffodus, yn lwcus.
fortune *n.* ffortiwn *f.*
forty *n. & a.* deugain, pedwar deg *m.*
forward 1 *n.* blaenwr *m.* **2** *a.* blaen;
  eofn. **3** *ad.* ymlaen. **4** *v.* anfon
  ymlaen. **wing forward**
  blaenasgellwr: **number eight**
  wythwr.
foster *v.* meithrin, rhoi ar faeth.
foster-mother *n.* mam-faeth *f.*
foul *a.* brwnt, budr, ffiaidd.
found *v.* dechrau, sefydlu.
foundation *n.* sail *f*, sylfaen *mf.*
fountain *n.* ffynnon, ffynhonnell *f.*
four *n. & a.* pedair, pedwar *m.*
fourteen *n. & a.* pedwar ar ddeg,
  pedair ar ddeg, un deg pedwar *m.*
fourth *n. & a.* pedwaredd,
  pedwerydd *m.*
fowl *n.* ffowlyn *m.*
fox *n.* cadno, llwynog. **vixen**
  cadnawes, cadnöes, llwynoges.
fraction *n.* ffracsiwn *m.*
fragment *n.* darn, tamaid *m,* yfflyn
  m.
France *n.* Ffrainc *f.*
frankincense *n.* thus *m.*
fraud *n.* twyll *m.*
fraudulent *a.* twyllodrus.
free 1 *a.* rhad, rhydd, di-dâl.
  2 *v.* rhyddhau. **free kick** cic rydd.
  free phone rhadffôn; **freepost**
  rhadbost.
freedom *n.* rhyddid *m.*
freely *ad.* yn rhydd.
freeze *v.* rhewi.
freezer *n.* rhewgell *f.*
freight *n.* llwyth *m.*
French 1 *n.* Ffrangeg *f.*
  2 *a.* Ffrengig.
Frenchman *n.* Ffrancwr *m.*

Frenchwoman *n.* Ffrances *f.*
frequent *a.* aml.
fresh *a.* ffres, newydd.
Friday *n.* dydd Gwener.
friend *n.* cyfaill *m,* cyfeilles *f,*
ffrind *m.*
friendly *a.* cyfeillgar.
friendship *n.* cyfeillgarwch *m.*
fright *n.* braw, ofn *m.*
frighten *v.* codi ofn ar, brawychu.
frightful *a.* dychrynllyd.
frigid *a.* oer, rhewllyd.
frivolity *n.* lol *f.*
frock *n.* ffrog *f.*
frog *n.* broga, ffroga *m.*
from *prp.* o, oddi, gan, oddi wrth,
rhag.
front 1 *n.* ffrynt, talcen, tu blaen *m.*
2 *a.* ffrynt, blaen. **front door** drws
ffrynt: **front page** tudalen flaen;
front room ystafell flaen: **front row**
rhes flaen: **cold front** ffrynt oer:
warm front ffrynt cynnes.
frontier *n.* ffin *f.*
frost *n.* rhew *m.* **hoarfrost** barrug;
to cast hoar frost llwydrewi.
frosty *a.* rhewllyd.
froth *n.* ewyn *m.*
frown 1 *n.* gwg *m.* **2** *v.* gwgu.
frozen *a.* wedi rhewi.

fruit *n.* ffrwyth *m,* ffrwythau *pl.* **fruit
juice** sudd ffrwythau *m.*
fruitful *a.* ffrwythlon.
fry *v.* ffrio.
frying pan *n.* padell ffrio *f.*
fuel *n.* tanwydd *m.*
fugitive *n.* ffoadur *m.*
full *a.* llawn.
full-back *n.* cefnwr *m.*
fullness *n.* llawnder, cyflawnder *m.*
fully *ad.* yn gyfan gwbl, yn hollol.
fun *n.* hwyl *f,* miri *m.*
fund *n.* cronfa *f.*
fundamental *a.* sylfaenol.
funeral *n.* angladd *mf.*
funnel *n.* twndis, corn, twmffat *m.*
funny *a.* digrif, ysmala, doniol.
fur *n.* ffwr, blew *m.*
furious *a.* ffyrnig, yn gacwn wyllt,
crac.
furnace *n.* ffwrn, ffwrnais *f.*
furnishings *n.* dodrefn *pl.*
furniture *n.* celfi, dodrefn *pl.* **piece
of furniture** celficyn, dodrefnyn.
furry *a.* blewog.
further *ad.* bellach, ymhellach.
further education addysg bellach.
fuss *n.* helynt *f,* trafferth, ffws,
stŵr *m.*
future *n. & a.* dyfodol *m.*

gain 1 *n.* elw, ennill *m,* enillion *pl.*
 2 *v.* elwa, ennill.
gale *n.* gwynt cryf *m.* tymestl *f.*
gallery *n.* oriel *f,* galeri *m,* llofft *f.*
gallon *n.* galwyn *m.*
gallop *v.* carlamu.
gamble *v.* hapchwarae, gamblo.
game *n.* gêm *f,* chwarae *m,* camp *f.*
gang *n.* mintai *f,* torf, haid, gang *f.*
gaol 1 *n.* carchar *m.* **2** *v.* carcharu.
gap *n.* bwlch, adwy *m.*
garage *n.* garej *f.*
garbage *n.* ysbwriel, sothach *m.*
garden 1 *n.* gardd *f.* **2** *v.* garddio.
gardener *n.* garddwr *m.*
garlic *n.* garlleg *m.*
garment *n.* pilyn *m,* gwisg *f,* dilledyn *m.*
gas *n* nwy *m.* **Gas Board** Bwrdd Nwy **gas mask** mwgwd nwy.
gate *n.* clwyd, gât, iet, llidiart *f.*
gateway *n.* mynedfa *f.*
gather *v.* casglu, crynhoi, cynnull, hel.
gathering *n.* casgliad, cynulliad *m.*
gaunt *a.* llwm, tenau.
gauntlet *n.* maneg *f.*
gay *a.* llon, bywiog, hoyw.
gaze *v.* edrych, syllu, rhythu.
gear *n.* gêr *mf,* offer *pl.*
gem *n.* gem *f,* tlws *m.*
gender *n.* rhyw *mf,* cenedl *f.*
gene *n.* genyn *m.*

general 1 *n.* cadfridog *m.*
 2 *a.* cyffredin, cyffredinol. **general election** etholiad cyffredinol.
generally *ad.* yn gyffredinol.
generation *n.* cenhedlaeth to *m.*
generosity *n.* haelioni *m.*
generous *a.* hael, haelionus.
genetic *a.* genetig.
genial *a.* tyner, tirion, hynaws.
genteel *a.* bonheddig.
gentle *a.* tyner, mwyn.
gentleman *n.* bonheddwr, gŵr bonheddig, uchelwr *m.*
gentleness *n.* tynerwch, addfwynder *m.*
gently *ad.* yn dyner, yn addfwyn; gan bwyll.
gents *n.* toiledau dynion *m.pl.*
genuine *a.* diffuant, cywir, pur.
geography *n.* daearyddiaeth *f.*
geology *n.* daeareg *f.*
geometry *n.* geometreg *mf.*
German 1 *n.* Almaeneg *(iaith) f.* Almaenwr *(person) m.*
 2 *a.* Almaenaidd.
Germany *n.* yr Almaen *f.*
get *v.* cael, ennill.
ghost *n.* ysbryd *m,* drychiolaeth *f.*
giant *n.* cawr *m.*
gift *n.* anrheg, rhodd *f.*
gifted *a.* talentog, dawnus.
gigantic *a.* anferth.
gipsy *n.* sipsi *m.*
giraffe *n.* jiráff *m.*
girder *n.* trawst *m.*
girl *n.* merch, geneth, croten, hogen, llances *f.*
give *v.* rhoddi, rhoi. **to give generously** rhoi'n hael. **to give up** rhoi'r gorau i.
glad *a.* llawen, llon, balch.
gladly *ad.* yn llawen, â phleser.
Glamorgan *n.* Morgannwg *f.* **Mid Glamorgan** Morgannwg Ganol; **South Glamorgan** De Morgannwg; **West Glamorgan** Gorllewin Morgannwg.
glance *n.* cipolwg *m,* trem *f,* cip *m.*
glass *n.* gwydr, gwydryn *m.*
gleam 1 *n.* llewyrch *m.*
 2 *v.* llewyrchu.

glen *n.* glyn, cwm, dyffryn *m.*
glide 1 *n.* llithriad *m.* **2** *v.* llithro
dros.
glitter *v.* disgleirio, serennu.
glorious *a.* gogoneddus.
glory *n.* gogoniant, ysblander *m.*
Gloucester *n.* Caerloyw *f.*
glove *n.* maneg *f.*
glower *v.* gwgu, cuchio.
glue 1 *n.* glud *m.* **2** *v.* gludo, gludio,
glynu.
gnat *n.* gwybedyn *m.*
go *v.* cer! dos! *(unigol)*; cerwch!
ewch! *(lluosog); see* mynd.
goal *n.* gôl *f.* **goalkeeper**
golgeidwad, golwr *m.*
goat *n.* gafr *f.*
god *n.* duw *m.* **God** Duw.
goddess *n.* duwies *f.*
godly *a.* duwiol.
gold *n.* aur *m.*
golden *a.* euraid, euraidd.
goldfish *n.* **pysgod aur** *m.pl.*
golf *n.* golff *m.* **golf course** maes
golffio.
golfer *n.* golffwr *m.*
good *n. & a.* da. **good afternoon**
prynhawn da; **good day** dydd da;
good evening noswaith dda; **good
morning** bore da; **good night** nos
da; **good luck** lwc dda; **Good
gracious!** Bobol annwyl! **Good
health!** Iechyd da!
goodbye 1 *n.* ffarwél *m.*
2 *i.* da bo chi! hwyl! yn iach!
goodness *n.* daioni *m.*
goods *n.* eiddo *m*, nwyddau, da *m.pl.*
goodwill *n.* ewyllys dâ *m.*
goose *n.* gŵydd *f.*
gosling *n.* cyw gŵydd *m.*
gospel *n.* efengyl *f.* **the Gospel
according to John** yr Efengyl yn
ôl Ioan.
govern *v.* llywodraethu, rheoli.
government *n.* llywodraeth *f.*
governor *n.* llywodraethwr, rheolwr.
Gower *n.* Gŵyr *f.*
gown *n.* gŵn *f.*
grace *n.* gras *m.*
graceful *a.* lluniaidd, urddasol.
grade 1 *n.* gradd, safon *f.*

2 *v.* graddio.
gradual *a.* graddol.
graduate 1 *n.* gŵr gradd *m.* **2** *v.*
graddio.
gram *n.* gram *m.*
grammar *n.* gramadeg *m.* **Grammar
School** Ysgol Ramadeg.
grammatical *a.* gramadegol.
grand *a.* mawreddog, ardderchog,
crand; prif, uchel. **grand concert**
cyngerdd mawreddog.
grandchild *n.* ŵyr *m*, wyres *f.*
granddaughter *n.* wyres *f.*
grandeur *n.* mawredd *m.*
grandfather *n.* tad-cu, taid *m.*
grandmother *n.* mam-gu, nain *f.*
grandson *n.* ŵyr *m.*
grant 1 *n.* rhodd *f*, grant, cymhorthdal
m. **2** *v.* caniatáu.
grapefruit *n.* grawnffrwyth *m.*
grapes *n.pl.* grawnwin.
grass *n.* glaswellt *m*, porfa *f:*
grasshopper ceiliog y rhedyn,
sioncyn y gwair.
grateful *a.* diolchgar.
gratefulness *n.* diolchgarwch *m.*
gratitude *n.* diolchgarwch *m.*
grave 1 *n.* bedd *m.* **2** *a.* difrifol,
dwys, prudd.
gravestone *n.* carreg fedd *f.*
graveyard *n.* mynwent *f.*
graze *v.* pori.
grease 1 *n.* saim *m.* **2** *v.* iro.
greasy *a.* seimlyd, seimllyd.
great *a.* mawr. **a great many** llawer
iawn.
great-grandfather *n.* hen dad-cu,
hendaid *m.*
great-grandmother *n.* hen fam-gu,
hennain *f.*
greatly *ad.* yn fawr.
greatness *n.* mawredd *m.*
Grecian 1 *n.* Groegwr *m.* **2** *v.*
Groegaidd.
Greece *n.* Groeg, Gwlad Groeg *f.*
greed *n.* trachwant *m.*
greedy *a.* trachwantus.
Greek 1 *n.* Groeg *f (iaith)*; Groegwr
m. (person). **2** *a.* Groeg, Groegaidd.
green 1 *a.* gwyrdd, gwerdd, glas.
2 *v.* glasu.

greenhouse *n.* tŷ gwydr *m.*
greet *v.* cyfarch, annerch.
greeting *n.* cyfarchiad *m.*
grey *a.* llwyd, glas: **to turn grey** llwydo, britho, brithio.
greyhound *n.* milgi *m.*
grief *n.* galar, gofid, hiraeth *m.*
grievance *n.* cwyn *mf.*
grieve *v.* gofidio, hiraethu.
grievous *a.* gofidus, poenus, blin, difrifol.
grind *v.* malu.
grip 1 *n.* gafael *f.* 2 *v.* gafael (yn), gwasgu.
gripping *a.* gafaelgar.
groan *v.* ochneidio, griddfan.
gross 1 *n.* gros *m.* 2 *a.* bras. **gross weight** pwysau gros.
ground 1 *n.* daear *f,* tir *m;* sail *f;* cae chwarae *m.* 2 *v.* gwreiddio, seilio.
groundless *a.* di-sail.
group *n.* grŵp, twr *m.*
grove *n.* llwyn *m,* celli *f.*
grow *v.* tyfu, prifio, codi.
growing *a.* yn tyfu.

growth *n.* tyfiant *m.*
grubby *a.* brwnt, budr.
guard 1 *n.* gwyliwr, gard *m.* 2 *v.* gwarchod, gwylio.
guerilla *n.* herwfilwr *m.*
guess 1 *n.* amcan, dyfaliad *m.* 2 *v.* dyfalu.
guest *n.* gwestai, gŵr gwadd *m,* gwraig wadd *f.*
guests *n.* gwesteion, gwahoddedigion *m.pl.*
guide 1 *n.,* arweinydd, hyfforddwr, tywysydd *m.* 2 *v.* arwain, tywys.
guild *n.* cymdeithas, urdd *f.*
guilt *n.* euogrwydd, bai *m.*
guilty *a.* euog.
guitar *n.* gitâr *m.*
gulf *n.* gwlff *m.*
gull *n.* gwylan *f.*
gulp *v.* llyncu, traflyncu.
gum *n* gwm, glud; cig (y dannedd) *m.*
gun *n.* dryll, gwn *m.*
guts *n.* perfedd *m.*
gymnasium *n.* campfa *f.*

habit *n.* arfer *mf;* gwisg *f.*
had, he/she/it *v.* cafodd. **I had** ces i, cefais: *see* cael.
hag *n.* gwrach *f.*
hail 1 *n.* cesair, cenllysg *coll.& pl.* 2 *v.* bwrw cesair; cyfarch, galw. 3 *i.* henffych well!
hailstones *n.* cesair *coll. & pl.*
hair *n.* gwallt; blewyn *m.*
hairbrush *n.* brwsh gwallt *m.*
hairy *a.* blewog.
half *n.* hanner *m.*
half-back *n.* hanerwr *m.*
hall *n.* neuadd *f,* llys, plas; cyntedd *m.*
Hallowe'en *n.* Nos Galan Gaeaf *f.*
hammer 1 *n.* morthwyl *m.* 2 *v.* morthwylio.
hand *n.* llaw *f; (of clock)* bys *m.* **hands** dwylo. **in hand** mewn llaw, ar waith.
handbag *n.* bag llaw *m.*
handbook *n.* llawlyfr *m.*
handful *n.* dyrnaid *m,* llond llaw *f.*
handkerchief *n.* cadach *m,* hances, neisied *f,* macyn *m.*
handle *n.* dolen *f.* 2 *v.* trafod, trin.
handsome *a.* hardd, glân, prydferth, golygus.
handwork *n.* gwaith llaw *m.*
handwriting *b.* llawysgrifen *f.*
hang *v.* hongian; crogi.
hankering *n.* ysfa *f.*
happen *v.* digwydd.

happening *n.* digwyddiad *m.*
happily *ad.* yn hapus.
happiness *n.* hapusrwydd, llawenydd *m.*
happy *a.* dedwydd, hapus, llawen, wrth ei fodd, wrth ei bodd.
harbour 1 *n.* harbwr *m,* hafan *f,* porth, porthladd *m.* 2 *v.* llochesu.
hard *a.* caled, anodd.
harden *v.* caledu.
hardly *ad.* o'r braidd.
hardness *n.* caledwch *m.*
hardship *n.* caledi *m.*
hard shoulder *n.* llain galed *f.*
hard-up *a.* prin o arian.
hardwood *n.* pren caled *m.*
hardworking *a.* gweithgar.
hardy *a.* caled.
hare *n.* ysgyfarnog *f.*
harm *n.* cam, drwg, niwed *m.*
harmless *a.* diniwed.
harp 1 *n.* telyn *f.* 2 *v.* canu'r delyn.
harpist *n.* telynor *m.,* telynores *f.*
harsh *a.* llym, garw, cras.
harvest *n.* cynhaeaf.
haste 1 *n.* brys, prysurdeb *m.* 2 *v.* brysio, prysuro, cyflymu.
hasten *v.* brysio.
hastily *ad.* yn frysiog.
hasty *a.* brysiog.
hat *n.* het *f.*
hate 1 *n.* cas, casineb *m.* 2 *v.* casáu.
hatred *n.* cas, casineb *m.*
haul *v.* tynnu, llusgo.
have, I *v.* caf. **he/she/it will have** caiff; *see* cael.
haven *n.* hafan *f.*
hawk *n.* hebog *m.*
hawthorn *n.* draenen wen *f.*
hay *n.* gwair *m,* porfa *f.*
hazard *n.* perygl *m,* antur *mf.*
haze *n.* niwl, tawch *m.*
hazel *n.* collen *f.*
hazy *a.* niwlog.
he *pn.* ef, fe, efe, efô, fo, yntau.
head 1 *n.* pen, pennaeth *m.* 2 *a.* prif.
headache *n.* pen tost, cur yn y pen *m.*
heading *n.* pennawd, teitl *m.*
headland *n.* penrhyn *m.*
headline *n.* pennawd, teitl *m.* **news headlines** penawdau'r newyddion.

headmaster *n.* prifathro *m.*
headmistress *n.* prifathrawes *f.*
headquarters *n.* pencadlys *m.*
heal *v.* iacháu, gwella.
health *n.* iechyd. **Health Service** Gwasanaeth Iechyd.
healthy *a.* iach, iachus.
heap *n.* pentwr, twr *m.*
hear *v.* clyw! *(unigol)*, clywch! *(lluosog); see* clywed.
hearer *n.* gwrandawr *m.*
hearing *n.* clyw; gwrandawiad *m.* **hearing aid** cymorth clywed.
heart *n.* calon *f.* **heart attack** trawiad ar y galon.
hearth *n.* aelwyd *f.*
heat 1 *n.* gwres *m.* 2 *v.* poethi, twymo, gwresogi.
heater *n.* gwresogydd *m.*
heath *n.* rhos *f*, rhostir *m.*
heather *n.* grug *m.*
heave 1 *n.* gwthiad, hwb *m.* 2 *v.* gwthio, codi.
heaven *n.* nef, nefoedd, nen *f.*
heavenly *a.* nefol, nefolaidd.
heavens *n.* ffurfafen, wybren *f.*
heavy *a.* trwm, trymaidd.
Hebrew 1 *n.* Hebraeg *f. (iaith);* Hebrëwr, *m.* Hebrëes *f.* 2 *a.* Hebraeg, Hebreig.
hedge *n.* perth *f*, clawdd, gwrych *m.*
hedgehog *n.* draenog *m.*
heed 1 *n.* sylw *m.* ystyriaeth *f.* 2 *v.* sylwi, ystyried, hidio.
heedful *a.* ystyriol, gofalus.
heel 1 *n.* sawdl *mf.* 2 *v.* sodli.
height *n.* uchder, uchelder *m.*
heir *n.* aer, etifedd *m.*
heiress *n.* aeres, etifeddes *f.*
helicopter *n .* hofrennydd *f.*
hell *n.* uffern *f.*
hellish *a.* uffernol.
hello *i.* helô! hylô! clyw! gwrando!
helm *n.* llyw *m.*
help 1 *n.* cymorth, help *m.* 2 *v.* cynorthwyo, helpu.
helper *n.* cynorthwywr, cynorthwy-ydd, helpwr *m.*
hem *n .* hem *f*, godre *m*, ymyl *mf.*
hen *n.* iâr *f.*
henceforth *ad.* mwyach, o hyn ymlaen.

her *pn.* ei, hi, hithau.
herb *n.* llysieuyn *m.*
herbal *a.* llysieuol.
herbs *n.* llysiau pêr, perlysiau *m.pl.*
herd *n.* gyr *m*, cenfaint *f.*
here *ad* yma, yn y man hwn.
hermit *n.* meudwy *m.*
hero *n.* arwr *m.*
heroine *n* arwres *f.*
hers *pn.* ei, ei heiddo.
hew *v.* torri, naddu.
hexagon *n.* hecsagon *m.*
hiccup *n.* yr ig *m.*
hide 1 *n.* crown *m.* 2 *v.* cuddio. **hide and seek** chwarae mig.
high *a.* uchel; mawr; cryf; llawn. **most high** goruchaf.
higher *a.* uwch.
highest *a.* uchaf.
highland *n.* ucheldir *m.*
highly *ad.* yn fawr, yn uchel.
highness *n.* uchder, uchelder; mawrhydi *m.* **His Highness** Ei Fawrhydi.
highway *n.* priffordd *f.*
highwayman *n.* lleidr penffordd *m.*
hijack 1 *n.* herwgipiad *m.* 2 *v.* herwgipio.
hill *n.* allt *f*, bryn *m*, rhiw *f*, tyle *m.*
hillock *n.* bryncyn, twmpath *m.*
him *pn.* ef, fe, efe, efô, fo, yntau.
hindrance *n.* rhwystr *m.*
hint 1 *n.* awgrym *m.* 2 *v.* awgrymu.
hip *n.* clun *f.*
hire 1 *n.* cyflog *mf.* 2 *v.* cyflogi, llogi.
his *pn.* ei, ei eiddo.
historian *n.* hanesydd, haneswr *m.*
history *n.* hanes *m.* **History of Wales** Hanes Cymru.
hit 1 *n.* ergyd *mf*, trawiad *m.* 2 *v.* taro.
hoarfrost *n.* llwydrew, barrug *m.*
hoary *a.* llwyd.
hoax 1 *n.* tric, twyll *m.* 2 *v.* twyllo.
hold 1 *n.* gafael *f.* 2 *v.* dal, dala, gafael.
hole 1 *n.* twll *m;* ffau *f.* 2 *v.* tyllu.
holiday *n.* gŵyl *f.*
holidays *n.* gwyliau *pl.* **Christmas holidays** gwyliau Nadolig: **summer holidays** gwyliau haf.

hollow 1 *n.* pant *m.* **2** *a.* gwag, cau.
holly *n.* celyn *pl,* celynnen *f.* **holly bush** llwyn celyn.
holy *a.* sanctaidd, glân, gwyn: **Holy Spirit** Ysbryd Glân.
Holyhead *n.* Caergybi *f.*
home 1 *n.* cartref *m,* aelwyd *f.*
2 *ad.* adref, tua thref. **at home** gartref: **going home** mynd adref, mynd tua thref.
homeless *a.* digartref.
homesick *a.* hiraethus.
homesickness *n.* hiraeth *m.*
homestead *n.* tyddyn *m.*
homeward *ad.* adref, tua thref.
homework *n.* gwaith cartref *m.*
homework book llyfr gwaith cartref.
homosexuality *n.* gwrywgydiaeth *f.*
honest *a.* cywir, gonest, onest.
honesty *n.* gonestrwydd, onestrwydd *m.*
honey *n.* mêl *m.*
honeymoon *n.* mis mêl *m.*
honour 1 *n.* anrhydedd *mf.*
2 *v.* anrhydeddu; urddo; cydnabod.
hook 1 *n.* bach, bachyn; cryman *m.*
2 *v.* bachu.
hoop *n.* cylch *m.*
hooray *i.* & *n.* hwrê.
hope 1 *n.* gobaith *m.* **2** *v.* gobeithio.
horizon *n.* gorwel *m.*
horn *n.* corn *m. (automobile).*
horrendous *a.* dychrynllyd, ofnadwy.
horrible *a.* ofnadwy.
horse *n.* ceffyl, march *m.*
horseman *n.* marchog *m.*
horseshoe *n.* pedol *f.*
hospice *n.* ysbyty, lletty *m.*
hospitable *a.* croesawus, lletygar.
hospital *n.* ysbyty *m.*
host *n.* llu *m,* byddin *f;* gwesteiwr, lletywr *m.*
hostage *n.* gwystl *m.*
hostel *n.* neuadd breswyl *f.*
hostess *n.* gwesteiwraig *f.*

hot *a.* twym, poeth, gwresog.
hot-water bottle potel ddŵr twym/poeth.
hotel *n.* gwesty *m.*
hotelier *n.* gwestywr *m.*
hound 1 *n.* ci hela, helgi *m.*
2 *v.* hela, erlid.
hour *n.* awr *f.*
hourly *ad.* bob awr.
house *n.* tŷ *m.*
housework *n.* gwaith tŷ *m.*
housewife *n.* gwraig tŷ *f.*
housing *n.* tai *pl.*
how *ad.* sut, pa fodd, pa.
however *ad.* sut bynnag, er hynny, pa fodd bynnag.
howl *v.* udo.
hue *n.* lliw *m.* gwawr *f.*
hug *v.* cofleidio, gwasgu.
huge *a.* anferth, enfawr.
hum 1 *n.* si, sibrwd *m.* **2** *v.* mwmian.
humble *a.* gostyngedig, isel.
humorous *a.* doniol.
humour *n.* hiwmor *m,* hwyl *f.*
hundred 1 *n.* cant *m.* **2** *a.* can.
hundred years old canmlwydd.
hundredth *n.* & *a.* canfed.
hunger 1 *n.* newyn, chwant bwyd *m.*
2 *v.* newynu.
hunt *n.* helfa *f.* **2** *v.* hel, hela, erlid.
hunter *n.* heliwr; ceffyl hela *m.*
hunting *n.* hela *m.* **hunting horn** corn hela.
hurricane *n.* corwynt *m.*
hurry 1 *n.* brys, prysurdeb *m.*
2 *v.* brysio, prysuro.
hurt 1 *n.* niwed, dolur *m.* **2** *v.* anafu, brifo.
husband *n.* gŵr, priod, gŵr priod *m.*
hut *n.* caban, cwt *m.*
hutch *n.* cwt, cwb *m.*
hydrogen *n.* hydrogen *m.*
hymn *n.* emyn, hymn *m.*
hymnal *n.* llyfr emynau *m.*
hymn-tune *n.* emyn-dôn *f.*
hypermarket *n.* archfarchnad *f.*
hyphen *n.* cyplysnod, cysylltnod *m.*

I *pn.* mi, myfi; fi, i; minnau, innau.
ice *n.* iâ, rhew *m.* **Ice Age** Oes yr Iâ.
iceberg *n.* mynydd iâ *m.*
ice-cream *n.* hufen iâ *m.*
Iceland *n.* Gwlad yr Iâ *f.*
icy *a.* rhewllyd.
idea *n.* syniad *m.*
identical *a.* yr un *(fath).*
identify *v.* abnabod *(fel yr un un),* enwi, nodi; uniaethu (â).
idiom *n.* priod-ddull, idiom *f.*
idle 1 *a.* segur, diog, dioglyd. 2 *v.* segur, diogi.
idler *n.* diogyn, pwdryn *m.*
idol *n.* delw *f.*
if *c.* os, pe.
ignite *v.* tanio.
ill *a.* claf, gwael, sâl, tost; drwg.
ill-mannered *a.* anfoesgar.
illness *n.* afiechyd, clefyd, dolur, salwch, tostrwydd *m.*
illustrate *v.* darlunio; egluro, esbonio.
illustration *n.* darlun *m.*
image *n.* delw, llun *m.*
imagination *n.* dychymyg *m.*
imagine *v.* dychmygu, tybied, tybio.
immediately *ad.* ar unwaith, yn union, yn y man.
immense *a.* anferth, eang.
imminent *a.* agos, gerllaw, wrth y drws.
immunisation *n.* imwneiddiad *m.*
immunise *v.* imwneiddio.

immunity *n.* imwnedd *m.*
impart *v.* cyfrannu, rhoi.
imperative 1 *n.* gorchymyn *m.* 2 *a.* gorchmynnol, gorfodol.
imperfect *a.* amherffaith.
impinge *v.* taro yn erbyn, cyffwrdd â.
implement 1 *n.* offeryn. arf *m.* 2 *v.* gweithredu.
implore *v.* erfyn (ar).
imply *v.* cyfleu, awgrymu.
importance *n.* pwys, pwysigrwydd *m.*
important *a.* pwysig.
impossible *a.* amhosibl.
impress 1 *n.* argraff *f.* 2 *v.* argraffu, pwyso (ar).
impression *n.* argraff.
imprison *v.* carcharu.
improve *v.* gwella.
impudence *n.* haerllugrwydd *m.*
impudent *a.* haerllug, eofn.
in 1 *prp.* yn, yng, ym, mewn. 2 *ad.* i mewn. **in the midst of** ynghanol: **in time** mewn pryd.
inaccurate *a.* anghywir, gwallus.
inasmuch *ad.* yn gymaint (â).
inch *n.* modfedd *f.*
incident *n.* digwyddiad *m.*
incinerator *n.* llosgydd *m,* ffwrnais *f.*
include *v.* cynnwys.
included *a.* cynwysedig.
including *prp.* gan gynnwys.
inclusive *a.* gan gynnwys, cynwysedig.
income *n.* enillion *pl,* incwm *m.* **Income Tax** Treth Incwm.
incorporate *v.* ymgorffori.
incorrect *a.* anghywir.
indebted *a.* dyledus.
indeed *ad.* yn wir, iawn.
indemnity *n.* iawndal *m.*
independence *n.* annibyniaeth *f.*
independent *n.* annibynnwr *m.*
independent *a.* annibynnol.
independently *ad.* yn annibynnol, ar wahân.
index *n.* mynegai *m.*
India *n.* Yr India *f.*
Indian 1 *n.* Indiad *m.* 2 *a.* Indiaidd.
indicate *v.* dangos, mynegi.
indigestion *n.* diffyg traul *m.*

individual 1 *n.* un, unigolyn *n.*
2 *a.* unigol.
indolent *a.* diog, dioglyd, segur,
  pwdr.
indoor *a.* i mewn, dan do.
induct *v.* sefydlu.
induction *n.* sefydliad *m.*
indulgence *n.* maldod *m.*
industrious *a.* gweithgar.
industry *n.* diwydiant; diwydrwydd *m.*
ineffectual *a.* aneffeithiol.
inevitable *a.* anochel.
inexpensive *a.* rhad.
inexperience *n.* diffyg profiad *m.*
inexperienced *a.* dibrofiad.
infant *n.* baban, maban *m.* **Infants'**
  school ysgol fabanod: **Infants'**
  teacher athrawes fabanod.
infection *n.* haint *f.*
inferior *a.* is, israddol.
infinitive *n.* berfenw *m.*
infirm *a.* gwan.
infirmity *n.* gwendid, llesgedd *m.*
inflammation *n.* llid *m.*
inflate *v.* chwyddo, rhoi awyr yn.
inflation *n.* chwyddiant *m.*
influence 1 *n.* dylanwad *m.*
  2 *v.* dylanwadu.
influenza *n.* ffliw *m.*
inform *v.* hysbysu.
information *n.* gwybodaeth *f.*
infrequent *a.* anaml.
ingredients *n.* defnyddiau,
  cynhwysion *m.pl.*
inhabitants *n.* trigolion,
  preswylwyr *pl.*
inhale *v.* anadlu.
inherit *v.* etifeddu.
iniquity *n.* drwg, drygioni,
  anwiredd *m.*
injection *n.* chwistrelliad, pigiad *m.*
injure *v.* anafu, niweidio.
injury *n.* niwed, cam, clwyf, anaf *m.*
inn *n.* tafarn *mf,* gwesty *m.*
inner *a.* mewnol.
inn-keeper *n.* tafarnwr, gwestywr *m.*
innocent *a.* diniwed.
inoculation *n.* brechiad *m.*
inquire *v.* gofyn, holi, ymholi.
inquiry *n.* ymchwiliad, ymholiad *m.*
inquisition *n.* ymchwiliad *m.*

insane *a.* gwallgof.
insect *n.* pryf, pryfedyn, pryfyn *m.*
in-service *a.* mewn swydd. **in-**
  service training hyfforddiant mewn
  swydd.
inside 1 *n.* tu mewn *m.* **2** *a.* mewnol.
  3 *ad,* i mewn, o fewn. **4** *prp.* y tu
  mewn.
inside-out *ad.* o chwith.
insist *v.* mynnu.
insolence *n.* haerllugrwydd *m.*
insolent *a.* haerllug.
inspire *v.* ysbrydoli.
instantaneous *a.* yn y man.
instead *ad.* yn lle.
institution *n.* sefydliad *m.*
instruct *v* . cyfarwyddo, dysgu,
  hyfforddi.
instruction *n.* hyfforddiant *m.*
instructor *n.* hyfforddwr *m.*
instrument *n.* offeryn, arf *m.*
  musical instrument offeryn, arf *m.*
instrumental *a.* offerynol; yn
  gyfrwng.
insult *n.* sarhad *m.*
insurance *n.* yswiriant *m.*
insure *v.* yswiro, yswirio.
insurrection *n.* terfysg, gwrthryfel *m.*
intellect *n.* deall *m.*
intelligent *a.* deallus.
intelligentsia *n.* y deallus *m,*
  deallusion *m.pl.*
intend *v.* bwriadu, golygu.
intense *a.* dwys.
intent *n.* bwriad, amcan; diben *m;*
  ystyr *f.*
intention *n.* bwriad *m.*
interest *n.* diddordeb; llog; budd *m.*
  interest rates cyfraddau llog.
interests *n.pl.* diddordebau *m.*
interfere *v.* ymhel, ymyrru, ymyrryd.
interference *n.* ymyrraeth *f.*
interior 1 *n.* tu mewn, canol *m.*
  2 *a.* mewnol.
include *n.* egwyl *f.*
intermediate *a.* canol, canolradd.
internal *a.* mewnol.
international *a.* rhyngwladol.
interpreter *n.* cyfieithydd *m.*
interrogate *v.* holi.
interrogator *n.* holwr *m.*

interrupt *v.* torri ar, torri ar draws, ymyrru, ymyrryd.
interval *n.* egwyl *f,* saib *m.*
intervene *v.* ymyrru, ymyrryd.
interview 1 *n.* cyfweliad *m.*
 2 *v.* cyfweld.
into *prp.* i, i mewn.
intoxicate *v.* meddwi.
invalid *n.* un afiach, un methedig *mf.*
invalid *a.* di-rym.
invest *v.* buddsoddi.
investigate *v.* ymchwilio, chwilio.
investigation *n.* ymchwiliad *m.*
investigator *n.* ymchwiliwr, ymchwilydd *m.*
invisible *a.* anweledig.
invitation *n.* gwahoddiad, gwahodd *m.*
invite *v.* gwahodd.
invited *a.* gwahoddedig.
involved *a.* cymhleth, astrus, cywrain.
inward *a.* mewnol.
Ireland *n.* Iwerddon, Yr Ynys Werdd *f.*
Irish 1 *n.* Gwyddeleg *f. (iaith).*
 2 *a.* Gwyddelig.

Irishman *n.* Gwyddel *m.*
Irishwoman *n.* Gwyddeles *f.*
iron 1 *n.* & *a.* haearn *m.*
 2 *v.* smwddio.
ironing board *n.* bwrdd smwddio *m.*
irritable *a.* pigog, piwis.
irritation *n.* poen *mf,* llid, *m,* enynfa *f.*
is *v.* ydy, yw, mae, oes, sy, sydd.
island *n.* ynys *f.* **Caldy Island** Ynys Bŷr: **Bardsey Island** Ynys Enlli.
Israel *n.* Israel *f.*
Israelite *n.* Israeliad *m.*
issue 1 *n.* llif, tarddiad; plant; cyhoeddiad *m.* **2** *v.* tarddu; cyhoeddi.
it *pn.* ef, efe, fe, efo, fo; hi.
Italian *n.* Eidaleg *f. (iaith);* Eidalwr *m,* Eidales *f.*
Italy *n.* Yr Eidal *f.*
itch 1 *n.* crafu *m,* ysfa *f.* **2** *v.* cosi, ysu.
item *n.* eitem *f.*
its *pn.* ei.
itself *pn.* ei hun, ei hunan.
ivy *n.* iorwg, eiddew *m.*

jackdaw *n.* jac-y-do *m.*
jacket *n.* siaced *f.*
jail *n.* carchar *m.*
jam 1 *n.* jam *m.;* tagfa *f.* **2** *v.* gwasgu, tagu.
January *n.* Ionawr *m.*
Japan *n.* Siapan *f.*
Japanese 1 *n.* Siapaneg *f. (iaith);* Siapanead *m.* **2** *a.* Siapaneaidd.
jar 1 *n* jar, jâr *f.* **2** *v.* ysgwyd.
jaundice *n.* y clefyd melyn *m.*
jaw *n.* gên, cern *f.*
jay *n.* sgrech y coed *m.*
jealous *a.* cenfigennus.
jeer 1 *n.* gwawd *m.* **2** *v.* gwawdio.
jelly *n.* jeli *m.*
jerk 1 *n.* plwc *m.* **2** *v.* plycio.
jersey *n.* jersi, jyrsi, siersi *f.*
Jerusalem *n.* Caersalem, Jerwsalem *f.*
Jesus *n.* Iesu *m.* **Jesus Christ** Iesu Grist: **Jesus Son of God** Iesu Mab Duw.
Jew *n.* Iddew *m.*
Jewess *n.* Iddewes *f.*
jewel *n.* gem *f,* tlws *m.*
Jewish *a.* Iddewig.
jingle *n.* rhigwm; tinc *m.*

job *n.* job, jobyn, gwaith *m,* swydd *f.*
Job Centre Canolfan Gwaith *mf.*
jobless *a.* diwaith.
jog *v.* loncian.
jogger *n.* lonciwr *m.*
join *v.* cydio; ymuno; uno; ymaelodi.
joiner *n.* saer coed *m.*
joint 1 *n.* cyswllt, cymal *m.* **2** *a.* cyd.
joint of meat darn o gig *m.*
joke 1 *n.* jôc *f.* **2** *v.* jocan, cellwair.
jolly *a.* braf, llawen, llon.
journalist *n.* newyddiadurwr *m.*
journey 1 *n.* hynt, siwrnai, taith *f.* **2** *v.* teithio.
joy *n.* llawenydd *m.*
joyful 1 *a.* llawen, llon. **2** *v.* llawenhad.
jubilation *n .* llawenydd, gorfoledd *m.*
jubilee *n.* jiwbilî *f.*
Judaism *n.* Iddewaeth *f.*
judge 1 *n.* barnwr; beirniad; dyfarnwr *m.* **2** *v.* beirniadu; dyfarnu.
judgement *n.* barn *f.* dyfarniad *m.*
jug *n.* jwg, siwg *f.*
juice *n.* sudd *m.*
juicy *a.* llawn sudd.
July *n.* Gorffennaf *m.*
jumble 1 *n.* cymysgwch *m,* cymysgfa *f.* **2** *v.* cymysgu: **jumble sale** ffair sborion *f.*
jump 1 *n.* naid *f.* llam *m.* **2** *v.* neidio, llamu.
jumper *n.* neidiwr *m;* jersi, jyrsi, siwmper *f.*
junction *n.* cydiad *m;* cyffordd *f.*
June *n.* Mehefin *m.*
junior *a.* iau; ieuaf. **junior school** ysgol iau.
just 1 *a.* cyfiawn, cywir, iawn, teg. **2** *ad.* braidd, yn union, newydd. **just now** gynnau (fach).
justice *n.* cyfiawnder; ynad *m.* **Justice of the Peace** Ynad Heddwch.
juvenile *a.* ieuanc, ifanc.

kangaroo *n.* cangarŵ *m.*
keep 1 *n.* cadw *m;* amddiffynfa *f.*
  2 *v.* cadw; cynnal.
keeper *n.* ceidwad *m.*
kennel *n.* cwb, cenel *m.*
kerchief *n.* cadach *m,* hances *f,*
  macyn *m,* neisied *f.*
kettle *n.* tegell *m.*
key *n.* agoriad *m,* allwedd *f;* cywair
  m. **keyhole** twll clo.
kick 1 *n.* cic *f.* **2** *v.* cicio. **drop kick**
  cic adlam.
kidnap 1 *n.* herwgydiad *m.*
  2 *v.* herwgydio.
kidnapper *n.* herwgydiwr *m.*
kidney-beans *n.pl.* ffa dringo,
  cidnabêns *pl.*
kill *v.* lladd.
killer *n.* lladdwr *m.*
kilogram *n.* kilogram (kg.) *m.*
kilometre *n.* kilometr (km.) *m.*
kilowatt *n.* kilowat (kW.) *m.*
kin *n.* perthynas *mf.*

kind *n.* math, rhyw *m.*
kind *a.* caredig.
kindergarten *n.* ysgol feithrin *f.*
kindliness *n.* caredigrwydd *m.*
kindly *a.* caredig, tirion.
kindness *n.* caredigrwydd *m;*
  cymwynas *f.*
kindred *n.* perthynas *mf;*
  perthnasau *pl.*
king *n.* brenin *m.*
kingdom *n.* teyrnas *f.* **Kingdom of**
  Heaven Teyrnas Nefoedd: **United**
  Kingdom Teyrnas Unedig.
kingfisher *n.* glas y dorlan *m.*
kingly *a.* brenhinol.
kipper *n.* ciper *m.*
kiss 1 *n.* cusan *mf,* sws *m*
  2 *v.* cusanu.
kitchen *n.* cegin *f.*
kitchenette *n.* cegin fach *f.*
kitchen garden *n.* gardd lysiau *f.*
kitten *n.* cath fach *f.*
knead *v.* tylino.
knee *n.* glin *mf,* pen-glin, pen-lin *m.*
kneel *v.* penlinio.
knife *n.* cyllell *f.* **bread knife** cyllell
  fara: **pocket knife** cyllell boced.
knight *n.* marchog *m.*
knit *v.* gwau.
knock 1 *n.* cnoc, ergyd *mf.*
  2 *v.* cnocio, curo, taro.
knot 1 *n.* clwm, cwlwm *m.*
  2 *v.* clymu.
know *v.* adnabod; gwybod: **I know**
  gwn, mi wn, rydw i'n gwybod; **to**
  know well gwybod yn iawn.
knowing *a.* gwybodus; ffel.
knowingly *ad.* yn fwriadol.
knowledge *n.* gwybodaeth *f.*
knuckle *n.* migwrn, cymal *m.*

label 1 *n.* llabed, label, *f.* **2** *v.* labelu.
laboratory *n* labordy *m.* **language laboratory** labordy iaith.
laborious *a.* llafurus.
labour 1 *n.* llafur, gwaith *m.*
2 *v.* llafurio, gweithio. **the Labour Party** y Blaid Lafur.
labourer *n.* labrwr, gweithiwr *m.*
lace 1 *n.* les *m.* **2** *v.* cau *(esgidiau).*
lack 1 *n.* eisiau, diffyg *m.* **2** *v.* bod mewn eisiau.
lad *n.* llanc, hogyn, gwas, bachgen *m.*
ladder *n.* ysgol *f.*
laden *a.* llwythog.
ladies *n.* arglwyddesau; boneddigesau; toiledau merched *pl.*
lady *n.* arglwyddes; boneddiges *f.*
lair *n.* ffau, gwâl, lloches *f.*
lake *n.* llyn *m.*
lamb *n.* oen *m.* **Paschal Lamb** Oen y Pasg.
lame 1 *a.* cloff. **2** *v.* cloffi.
lameness *n.* cloffi, cloffni *m.*
lamp *n.* lamp *f.* **lampshade** lamplen *f.*
lamp post *n.* postyn lamp, polyn lamp *m.*
land 1 *n.* tir *m,* daear, gwlad, glan *f.*
2 *v.* glanio.
landlady *n.* gwraig llety *f.*
landlord *n.* meistr tir, lletywr, tafarnwr *m.*
landscape *n.* tirlun *m.*

lane *n.* lôn *f.* **escape lane** lôn ddianc.
language *n.* iaith *f.* **first language** iaith gyntaf, mamiaith; **second language** ail iaith; **foreign language** iaith dramor, iaith estron.
lantern *n.* llusern *f.*
lap 1 *n.* arffed *f,* glin *mf.* **2** *v.* lapio.
lapel *n.* llabed *f.*
large *a.* mawr; eang; helaeth.
largely *ad.* gan mwyaf.
lark *n.* ehedydd, hedydd, uchedydd *m.*
laryngitis *n.* llwnc tost *m.*
lass *n.* geneth, hogen, llances, merch *f.*
last 1 *a.* diwethaf; olaf. **2** *ad.* yn ddiwethaf, yn olaf. **3** *v.* para, parhau, dal, dala. **last night** neithiwr; **last week** yr wythnos diwethaf; **last month** mis diwethaf; **last year** y llynedd; **at last** o'r diwedd; **the last word** y gair olaf.
late *a.* hwyr; diweddar.
lately *ad.* yn ddiweddar.
later *ad.* wedyn, eto, yn ddiweddarach.
latest *a.* diweddaraf.
Latin *n.* Lladin *f.*
latter *a.* diwethaf, olaf.
laugh *n.* & *v.* chwerthin *m.*
laughable *a.* chwerthinllyd.
laughter *n.* chwerthin *m.*
launderette *n .* golchdy *m.*
lavatory *n.* tŷ-bach *m,* ystafell ymolchi *f,* toiled *m.*
lavender *n.* lafant *m.*
law *n.* cyfraith, deddf *f.*
lawn *n.* lawnt *f.*
lawyer *n.* cyfreithiwr *m.*
lax *a.* llac; esgeulus.
lay *v.* gosod, dodi; dodwy.
layer *n.* haenen *f.*
laze *v.* diogi, segura.
laziness *n.* diogi *m.*
lazy *a.* diog, dioglyd, pwdr.
lead *n.* plwm *m.*
lead *v.* arwain, tywys.
leaden *a.* plwm.
leader *n.* arweinydd; blaenwr *m.*
leaf *n.* deilen; dalen *f.*
leaflet *n.* taflen *f.*

league *n.* cynghrair *m.*
leak *v.* gollwng, colli, diferu.
lean 1 *n.* cig coch *m.* **2** *a.* main,
tenau. **3** *v.* pwyso (ar).
leap 1 *n.* llam *m,* naid *f.* **2** *v.* llamu,
neidio. **leap year** blwyddyn naid.
learn *u.* dysgu.
learned *a.* dysgedig, hyddysg.
learner *n.* dysgwr *m.*
learning 1 *n.* dysg *f.* **2** *v.* dysgu.
lease *n.* les, prydles *f.*
least *a.* lleiaf; *see* bach. **at least** o
leiaf.
leather *n.* lledr *m.*
leave 1 *n.* caniatâd *m.* **2** *v.* gadael,
ymadael.
leaven *n.* lefain *m.*
lecture 1 *n.* darlith *f.* **2** *v.* darlithio.
lecturer *n.* darlithiwr, darlithydd *m.*
ledge *n.* silff *f;* crib *mf.*
leek *n.* cenhinen *f.*
left *a.* chwith. **left-handed**
llawchwith.
leg *n.* coes *f.*
legend *n.* chwedl *f.*
legislate *v.* deddfu.
leisure *n.* hamdden *f.*
leisurely *a.* hamddenol.
lemon *n.* lemwn *m.* **lemonade** diod
lemwn; **lemon juice** sudd lemwn.
lend *v.* benthyca, rhoi benthyg.
length *n.* hyd *m.* **at length** o'r
diwedd.
lengthen *v.* estyn, ymestyn.
lengthy *a.* hir.
less 1 *a.* & *n.* llai *m.* **2** *ad.* yn llai.
lesson *n.* gwers *f.* **history lesson**
gwers hanes; **Welsh lesson** gwers
Gymraeg.
lest *c.* rhag, rhag ofn, fel na.
let *v.* caniatáu; gadael; gosod; rhentu.
lethal *a.* marwol.
letter *n.* llythyr *m;* llythyren *f.*
lettuce *n.* letysen *f.*
level *n.* & *a.* gwastad *m.* lefel *f.* **spirit
level** lefelydd.
level crossing *n.* croesfan *f.*
liable *a.* agored, atebol.
liar *n.* celwyddgi *m.*
liberal *a.* hael, haelionus.
liberty *n.* rhyddid *m.*

librarian *n.* llyfrgellydd *m.*
library *n.* llyfrgell *f.*
licence *n.* trwydded *f.* **driving
licence** trwydded yrru.
lick *v.* llyfu, llio.
lid *n.* clawr *m.*
lie 1 *n.* celwydd, anwiredd *n.* **2** *v.*
dweud celwydd, dweud anwiredd;
gorwedd.
life *n.* bywyd, byw *m.*
lifeboat *n.* bad achub *m.*
life insurance *n.* yswiriant bywyd *m.*
lifeless *a.* marwaidd.
lifetime *n.* oes *f.*
lift 1 *n.* lifft *m.* **2** *v.* codi.
ligament *n.* gewyn.
light 1 *n.* golau, goleuni, llewyrch *m.*
2 *a.* golau; ysgafn. **3** *v.* goleuo;
tanio.
lighten *v.* ysgafnhau, ysgafnu.
lighthouse *n.* goleudy *m.*
lightning *n.* mellt, lluched *pl.*
like 1 *a.* tebyg. **2** *prp.* fel. **3** *v.* hoffi,
caru.
likeable *a.* dymunol.
likely *a.* & *ad.* tebygol, tebyg.
likeness *n.* tebygrwydd *m.*
likewise 1 *n.* yn yr un modd. **2** *c.*
hefyd.
liking *n.* hoffter *m.*
lily *n.* lili *f.* **lilly of the valley** lili'r
dyffrynnoedd.
limb *n.* aelod *m;* cangen *f;* cymal *m.*
limit *n.* ffin *f,* terfyn *m.*
limp 1 *a.* llipa. **2** *v.* cloffi.
line *n.* llinell *f,* llinyn *m,* lein *f.*
linen *n.* lliain *m.*
linesman *n.* llinellwr, ystlyswr *m.*
link 1 *n.* dolen *f.* **2** *v.* cydio.
lion *n.* llew *m.*
lioness *n.* llewes *f.*
lip *n.* gwefus *f,* min *m.*
lipstick *n.* minlliw *m.*
liquid 1 *n.* hylif *m.* **2** *a.* hylif; gwlyb.
list *n.* rhestr *f.*
listen *v.* gwrando.
listener *n.* gwrandawr *m.*
literary *a.* llenyddol.
literate *a.* llythrennog.
literature *n.* llên, llenyddiaeth *f.*
litre *n.* litr *m.*

litter 1 *n.* sbwriel, ysbwriel *m.* **2** *v.*
sarnu.
littérateur *n.* llenor *m.*
little *a.* bach, bychan, bechan; mân,
tamaid, ychydig.
live *a.* & *v.* byw.
lively *a.* bywiog, heini.
liver *n.* iau *m*, afu *mf.*
Liverpool *n.* Lerpwl *f.*
living *a.* byw, yn fyw.
load 1 *n.* baich, llwyth *m.* **2** *v.*
llwytho.
loaf *n.* torth *f.*
loathsome *a.* ffiaidd.
lobby *n.* cyntedd, porth *m.*
local *a.* lleol. **Local Government**
Llywodraeth Leol.
locality *n.* lle *m*, ardal, cymdogaeth *f.*
localise *v.* lleoli.
locate *v.* lleoli, gosod.
location *n.* lleoliad *m.*
loch *n.* llyn, llwch *m.*
lock 1 *n.* clo *m.* **2** *v.* cloi.
locked *a.* ar glo, dan glo, ynghlo.
lodge 1 *n.* llety *m.* **2** *v.* lletya.
lodger *n.* lletywr *m.*
lodging(s) *n.* *(pl).* llety *m.*
loft *n.* llofft *f.*
loin *n.* llwyn *f.*
London *n.* Llundain *f.*
loneliness *n.* unigrwydd *m.*
lonely *a.* unig.
long 1 *n.* hir, maith. **2** *v.* hiraethu.
　long since ers amser.
longing *n.* hiraeth *m.*
look 1 *n.* golwg *mf,* trem **2** *v.* edrych,
ysbîo.
loose 1 *a.* llac, llaes, rhydd.
　2 *v.* datod, llacio, rhyddhau.

loosen *v.* llacio, rhyddhau, datod.
lord *n.* arglwydd *m.* **The Lord** Yr
Arglwydd; **the Lord's Prayer**
Gweddi'r Arglwydd; **House of
Lords** Tŷ'r Arglwyddi.
lord mayor *n.* arglwydd faer *m.*
lorry *n.* lorri *f.*
lorry driver *n.* gyrrwr lorri *m.*
lose *v.* colli.
loss *n.* colled *mf.*
loud *a.* uchel.
loudest *a.* uchaf.
Loughor *n.* Casllwchwr *f.*
lounge 1 *n.* lolfa *f.* **2** *v.* lolian.
louse *n.* lleuen *f.*
love 1 *n.* cariad, serch *m.* **2** *v.* caru:
　love-letter llythyr caru.
lovely *a.* hyfryd, teg, prydferth; braf.
lover *n.* cariad *mf,* carwr *m.*
loving *a.* cariadus, serchus, serchog.
low *a.* isel.
lower 1 *a.* is. **2** *v.* gostwng, gollwng.
lowest *a.* isaf; lleiaf.
loyal *a.* ffyddlon, teyrngar.
lozenge *n.* losinen, losen *f.*
luck *n.* lwc, ffortiwn *f.* **best of luck**
lwc dda, pob hwyl.
luckily *ad.* yn ffodus, yn lwcus.
lucky *a.* ffodus, lwcus.
lull 1 *n.* gosteg *m.* **2** *v.* suo.
lullaby *n.* hwiangerdd *f.*
luminous *a.* golau, disglair, llachar.
lungs *n.* ysgyfaint *pl.*
lupins *n.* bysedd y blaidd *pl.*
lust *n.* chwant, trachwant *m.*
lustful *a.* trachwantus.
lustre *n.* llewyrch *m.*
luxurious *a.* moethus.
lyric *n.* telyneg *f.*

m

machine *n.* peiriant *m.* **machinery**
peiriannau.
mackintosh *n.* cot law *f.*
mad *a.* gwyllt, gwallgof.
magazine *n.* cylchgrawn *m.*
magic *n.* hud, lledrith, swyn *m.*
magician *n.* dewin *m.*
magistrate *n.* ustus, ynad *m.*
magnificent *a.* gwych.
magnifying glass *n.* chwyddwydr *m.*
magnitude *n.* maint, ehangder *m.*
magpie *n.* pioden *m.*
maid *n.* morwyn, merch *f.* **old maid**
hen ferch.
mail 1 *n.* y post *m.* **2** *v.* postio.
main *a.* pennaf, prif, mwyaf. **main
road** ffordd fawr, priffordd;
mainland y tir mawr.
mainly *ad.* yn bennaf.
majesty *n.* mawredd; mawrhydi *m.*
Her Majesty Ei Mawrhydi.
major 1 *n.* uwchgapten *m.* **2** *a.* prif,
mwyaf.
majority *n.* mwyafrif; oedran llawn
m.
make *v.* gwneud, gwneuthur.
make-up *n.* & *v.* coluro *m.*
male *n.* gwryw *m.*
man *n.* dyn, gŵr, mab *m.* **man of
letters** llenor.
manage *v.* rheoli, trin; llwyddo.
manager *n.* rheolwr *m.*
manger *n.* preseb *m.*

manifest *v.* dangos, egluro.
manipulate *v.* trin, trafod.
manner *n.* modd, dull *m.*
manners *n.* moesau *pl.* **good
manners** moesau da.
manse *n.* tŷ gweinidog, mans *m.*
mansion *n.* plas, plasty *m.*
mantle *n.* mantell *f.*
manual 1 *n.* llawlyfr *m.*
2 *a.* perthynol i'r llaw.
manure *n.* gwrtaith, tail *m.* tom *f.*
manuscript *n.* llawysgrif *f.*
many 1 *n.* llawer *m.* **2** *a.* llawer, aml,
sawl. **how many** sawl. **too many**
gormod.
map *n.* map *n.*
March *n.* Mawrth *m.*
march 1 *n.* ymdaith *f.*
2 *v.* ymdeithio.
margin *n.* ffin *f,* ymyl *mf.*
mariner *n.* llongwr, morwr *m.*
mark 1 *n.* nod, nam, ôl, marc *m.*
2 *v.* nodi, marcio.
market 1 *n.* marchnad *f.*
2 *v.* marchnata.
marriage *n.* priodas *f.*
married *a.* priod.
marrow *n.* mêr *m.* **vegetable
marrow** pwmpen *f.*
marry *v.* priodi.
Mars *n.* Mawrth *m.*
mart *n.* mart *m.*
martyr *n.* merthyr *m.*
marvel 1 *n.* rhyfeddod *m.*
2 *v.* rhyfeddu, synnu.
marvellous *a.* rhyfeddol, gwych.
masculine *a.* gwryw, gwrywaidd,
gwrywol.
mask 1 *n.* mwgwd *m.* **2** *v.* cuddio.
mass *n.* pentwr *m;* pwysau *pl;*
offeren *f.*
massive *a.* anferth.
master 1 *n.* meistr, capten *(llong) m.*
2 *v.* meistroli.
masterpiece *n.* campwaith *m.*
mat *n.* mat *m.*
match *n.* matsien; gêm; gornest;
priodas *f.*
material *n.* defnydd, nwydd *m.*
mathematical *a.* mathemategol.
mathematician *n.* mathemategwr *m.*

mathematics *n.* mathemateg *f.*
matrimony *n.* priodas *f.*
matter *n.* mater *m.* **What's the matter?** Beth sy'n bod?
mature 1 *a.* aeddfed. **2** *v.* aeddfedu.
maximum *n.* uchafswm, uchafrif, uchafbwynt *m.*
May *n.* Mai *m.* **May Day** Calan Mai.
maybe *ad.* efallai, hwyrach.
mayor *n.* maer *f.*
mayoress *n.* maeres *f.*
me *pn.* myfi, mi, fi, i; minnau.
mead *n.* medd *m.*
meadow *n.* dôl, gwaun *f,* maes *m.*
meagre *a.* cul, llwm, tenau, prin.
meal *n.* pryd o fwyd; blawd *m.*
mean 1 *n.* cyfrwng, modd; canol *m.* **2** *a.* sâl; gwael; tynn. **3** *v.* bwriadu, golygu, meddwl.
meaning *n.* ystyr *mf,* meddwl *m.*
meaningful *a.* ystyrlon.
means *n.* modd, moddion, cyfrwng; cyfoeth *m.* **by all means** ar bob cyfrif, wrth gwrs.
measles *n.* y frech goch *f.*
measure *n.* mesur *m.*
meat *n.* cig *m.*
medal *n.* bathodyn *m,* medal *f.*
meddle *v.* ymhél, ymyrru, ymyrryd.
media *n.* cyfryngau *pl.*
medicine *n.* moddion, ffisig *m;* meddyginiaeth *f.*
mediate *v.* myfyrio.
meditation *n.* myfyrdod *m.*
medium 1 *n.* cyfrwng; canol *m.* **2** *a.* canol.
medley *n.* cadwyn o alawon *f;* cymysgwch *m.*
meet *v.* cyfarfod, cwrdd (â); cyffwrdd.
meeting *n.* cyfarfod, cwrdd *m;* oedfa *f.*
melody *n.* alaw, tôn *f.*
melt *v.* toddi.
member *n.* aelod *m.* **to become a member** ymaelodi: **Member of Parliament (M.P.)** Aelod Seneddol (A.S.).
membership *n.* aelodaeth *f.*
memory *n.* cof *m.*
mend *v.* gwella, trwsio, cyweirio.

meningitis *n.* llid yr ymennydd *m.*
menstruation *n.* y misglwyf *m.*
mention *n.* & *v.* sôn (am) *mf.*
menu *n.* bwydlen *f.*
merchant *n.* masnachwr *m.*
merciful *a.* trugarog.
mercifully *ad.* drwy drugaredd.
Mercury *n.* Mercher *m.*
mercury *n.* arian byw, mercwri *m.*
mercy *n.* trugaredd *f.* **to be merciful** trugarhau.
merit 1 *n.* teilyngdod *m.* **2** *v.* haeddu.
mermaid *n.* môr-forwyn *f.*
merriment *n.* miri *m.*
merry *a.* llawen, llon.
mess *n.* llanast(r) *m.*
message *n.* neges *f.*
messenger *n.* negesydd *m.*
metal *n.* metel *m.*
meteor *n.* seren wib *f.*
meter *n.* mesurydd *m.*
method *n.* dull, modd *m,* trefn *f.* **new methods** dulliau newydd.
methodical *a.* trefnus.
metre *n.* mesur; metr *m.* **kilometre** kilometr (km.).
metric *a.* metrig. **metric scale** graddfa fetrig.
mew *v.* mewian.
micro-chip *n.* meicro-sglodyn *m.*
microphone *n.* meic, meicroffon *m.*
microscope *n.* meicrosgop *m.*
microwave *n.* meicrodon *f.*
mid *a.* canol.
midday *n.* canol dydd, hanner dydd *m.*
middle *n.* canol *m.*
middle-aged *a.* canol oed.
midland *n.* canolbarth *m.* **the Midlands** Canolbarth Lloegr: **Mid Wales** Canolbarth Cymru.
midnight *n.* canol nos, hanner nos *f.*
midst 1 *n.* canol, plith *m.* **2** *prp.* rhwng.
might *n.* nerth, gallu *m.*
mighty *a.* grymus.
mild *a.* mwyn, tyner, meddal, gwan. **become mild** mwynhau, tyneru.
mile *n.* milltir *f:* **milestone** carreg filltir *f.*

milk 1 *n.* llaeth, llefrith *m.* **2** *v.* godro.
milkman dyn llaeth.
mill *n.* melin *f.*
million *n.* miliwn *m.* **millionaire** miliynydd.
mime 1 *n.* meim *m.* **2** *v.* meimio.
mind 1 *n.* meddwl, bryd, bwriad *m.* **2** *v.* gwylio, gofalu, hidio.
mindful *a.* gofalus, ystyriol.
mine 1 *n.* pwll, mwynglawdd *m.* **2** *pn.* fy, yr eiddof i.
miner *n.* glöwr, mwynwr *m.*
mineral *n.* mwyn *m.*
minimum *n.* lleiafswm, isafrif, isafbwynt *m.*
minister 1 *n.* gweinidog *m.* **2** *v.* gwasanaethu.
minority *n.* lleiafrif *m.*
mint *n.* bathdy; mint, mintys *m.* **Royal Mint** Bathdy Brenhinol.
minute *n.* munud *mf;* cofnod *m.* **minute book** llyfr cofnodion.
minute *a.* bach, mân, manwl.
miracle *n.* gwyrth *f.*
miraculous *a.* gwyrthiol.
mirror *n.* drych *m.*
miscarriage *n.* erthyliad *m.*
miscarry *v.* erthylu; colli.
mischief *n.* drwg, drygioni *m.*
mischievous *a.* drygionus.
miserable *a.* gwael, truenus, diflas.
misery *n.* trallod, trueni, diflastod *m.*
mislead *v.* camarwain, twyllo.
miss *v.* colli, methu, gweld eisiau.
missile *n.* taflegryn *m.*
mission *n.* cenhadaeth *f.*
missionary 1 *n.* cenhadwr *m;* cenhades *f.* **2** *a.* cenhadol.
mist *n.* niwl *m.*
mistake *n.* camsyniad, gwall, camgymeriad *m.*
mistress *n.* meistres, athrawes *f:* **headmistress** prifathrawes.
misty *a.* niwlog.
misunderstand *v.* camddeall.
mix *v.* cymysgu.
mixed *a.* cymysg.
mob *n.* torf, tyrfa, haid *f.*
mobile *a.* symudol. **mobile phone** ffôn symudol.
mock *v.* gwawdio.

mode *n.* modd, dull *m.*
modern *a.* diweddar, modern.
moist *a.* llaith, gwlyb.
moisten *v.* gwlychu.
moisture *n.* gwlybaniaeth *f.*
Mold *n.* Yr Wyddgrug *f.*
moment *n.* eiliad *f,* ennyd *mf,* moment *f.*
monarch *n.* brenin *m.*
monastery *n.* mynachlog *f.*
Monday *n.* dydd Llun *m.*
money *n.* arian, pres *m.*
monk *n.* mynach *m.*
monkey *n.* mwnci *m.*
monoglot 1 *n.* person uniaith *m.* **2** *a.* uniaith.
monotonous *a.* undonog.
monstrous *a.* anferth.
month *n.* mis *m.*
monthly 1 *n.* misolyn *m.* **2** *a.* misol.
mood *n.* tymer, hwyl *f.*
moon *n.* lleuad, lloer *f.* **moonlight** golau leuad.
moor *n.* rhos *f,* rhostir *m,* gwaun *f.*
moral *a.* moesol.
morals *n.* moesau *pl.*
more 1 *n.* rhagor, ychwaneg, chwaneg *m.* **2** *a* & *ad.* mwy, mwyach. **more than** mwy na.
morning 1 *n.* bore *m.* **2** *a.* bore, boreol. **Monday morning** bore dydd Llun: **every morning** bob bore; **Morning Service** Gwasanaeth Boreol; **next morning** bore trannoeth.
morrow *ad.* trannoeth.
mortal 1 *n.* dyn; un marwol *m.* **2** *a.* marwol.
mortgage *n.* morgais *m.*
most *a.* mwyaf, amlaf.
mostly *ad.* gan mwyaf.
moth *n.* gwyfyn *m.*
mother *n.* mam *f.* **mother-in-law** mam-yng-nghyfraith.
mother tongue *n.* mamiaith *f.*
motor *n.* modur, car *m.* **motor bike** beic modur.
motorist *n.* modurwr *m.*
motorway *n.* traffordd *f.*
mountain *n.* mynydd *m.*
mountaineer *n.* mynyddwr *m.*

mountainous *a.* mynyddig.
mourn *v.* galaru.
mourning *n.* galar *m.*
mouse *n.* llygoden *f.*
moustache *n.* mwstash *m.*
mouth *n.* ceg *f*, genau *pl.m.*
move *v.* symud.
movement *n.* mudiad; symudiad, symud *m.*
moving *a.* yn symud, cyffrous.
mow *v.* lladd gwair.
much 1 *n.* llawer. 2 *a.* llawer, mawr. 3 *ad.* yn fawr, llawer *(with comparative a.):* **much better** llawer gwell: **too much** gormod.
mud *n.* llacs *m.*
muddy *a.* llacsog.
multiply *v.* lluosi.
multitude *n.* llu *m*, torf, tyrfa *f.*
munch *v.* cnoi.
murder 1 *n.* llofruddiaeth *f.* 2 *v.* llofruddio.

murderer *n.* llofrudd *m.*
muscular *a.* cyhyrog.
museum *n.* amgueddfa *f.*
mushroom *n.* madarchen *f.*
music *n.* cerddoriaeth, cerdd, caniadaeth, alaw, miwsig *f.*
musical *a.* cerddorol.
musician *n.* cerddor *m.*
must *n. & v.* rhaid *m.*
mutate *v.* treiglo.
mutation *n.* treiglad, cyfnewidiad *m.*
mute *a.* mud, distaw.
mutilate *v.* anafu, llurgunio.
mutiny *n.* gwrthryfel, terfysg *m.*
mutton *n.* cig dafad, cig gwedder *m.*
my *pn.* fy; 'm.
myrrh *n.* myrr *m.*
myself *pn.* fy hunan, mi fy hunan, myfi fy hun.
mysterious *a.* rhyfedd, dirgel.
mystery *n.* dirgelwch.
myth *n.* chwedl, dameg, myth *f.*

n

nail 1 *n.* ewin *mf;* hoel, hoelen *f.*
  2 *a.* hoelio.
naked *a.* noeth; llwm: **stark naked**
  noethlymun, porcyn.
name 1 *n.* enw *m.* **2** *v.* enwi, galw.
namely *ad.* sef.
nape *n.* gwar *m.*
napkin *n.* cewyn, clwt *m.*
narrate *v.* adrodd (hanes).
narration *n.* adroddiad *m.*
narrative *n.* chwedl *f,* hanes *m,* stori *f.*
narrow 1 *a.* cul, cyfyng.
  2 *v.* cyfyngu.
narrow-minded *a.* cul.
nasal *a.* trwynol.
nasty *a.* cas, brwnt, budr, ffiaidd.
nation *n.* cenedl *f.*
national *a.* cenedlaethol; gwladol.
  National Assistance Cymorth
  Gwladol: **National Museum**
  Amgueddfa Genedlaethol.
nationalism *n.* cenedlaetholdeb *m.*
nationalist *n.* cenedlaetholwr *m.*
nationality *n.* cenedligrwydd *m.*
native 1 *n.* brodor *m.* **2** *a.* brodorol.
nativity *n.* genedigaeth *f.*
natural *a.* naturiol.
nature *n.* natur, naws *f.*
naught *n.* dim; sero *m.*
naughtiness *n.* drygioni *m.*
naughty *a.* drwg, drygionus.
navy *n.* llynges *f.* **navy blue**
  glasddu.

near 1 *a.* agos. **2** *ad.* yn agos, braidd.
  3 *v.* agosáu, nesáu. **4** *prp.* ger, yn
  agos at.
nearby *a. & ad.* yn ymyl, gerllaw.
nearly *ad.* bron.
neat *a.* twt, del, taclus, trefnus.
Neath *n.* Castell-nedd *f.*
necessary *a.* angenrheidiol.
necessitate gwneud yn
  angenrheidiol, gorfodi.
necessity *n.* anghenraid, rhaid *m.*
neck *n.* gwddf, gwddwg.
necklace *n.* neclis *f.* mwclis *pl.*
née *a.* gynt, cyn priodi. **Mair Puw,**
  née Rhys Mair Puw, gynt Rhys.
need *n.* eisiau, rhaid. *m.*
needle *n.* nodwydd; gwaell *f.*
needy *a.* tlawd.
negative *a.* negyddol.
neglect *v.* esgeuluso.
negligence *n.* esgeulustod *m.*
negligent *a.* esgeulus.
negotiate *v.* trafod, trefnu.
negro *n.* dyn du, negro *m.*
neighbour *n.* cymydog *m.*
neighbouring *a.* cyfagos.
neither 1 *ad. & c.* na, nac, chwaith,
  ychwaith. **2** *pn.* nid y naill na'r llall,
  nid un o'r ddau.
nephew *n.* nai *m.*
nerve *n.* gewyn, nerf *m.*
nervous *a.* nerfus, ofnus.
nest *n.* nyth *mf.*
nestle *v.* nythu.
nestling *n.* aderyn bach, cyw *m.*
net *n.* rhwyd *f.*
netball *n.* pêl rwyd *f.*
Netherlands, The *n.* Yr Iseldiroedd *f.*
never *ad.* byth, erioed.
nevertheless *ad.* er hynny, eto.
new *a.* newydd. **New Year**
  Blwyddyn Newydd; **New York**
  Efrog Newydd; **New Zealand**
  Seland Newydd; **brand new**
  newydd sbon.
newcomer *n.* newydd-ddyfodiad *m.*
Newport (Pembs.) *n.* Trefdraeth *f.*
Newport (Mon.) *n.* Casnewydd *f.*
Newquay *n.* Ceinewydd *f.*
news *n.pl.* newyddion *pl,* newydd,
  hanes *m.* **good news** newyddion da;

six o'clock news newyddion chwech.

newspaper *n.* papur newydd. *m.*

next 1 *a.* nesaf. **2** *prp.* nesaf at. **next door** y drws nesaf; **Next, please** Y nesaf, os gwelwch yn dda; **next week** wythnos nesaf; **next year** y flwyddyn nesaf.

nice *a.* braf, hyfryd, neis, dymunol.

nickname 1 *n.* llysenwi *m.* **2** *v.* llysenw.

niece *n.* nith *f.*

nigh *a, ad* & *prp.* agos, gerllaw, yn agos.

night *n.* nos; noson, noswaith *f.* **night and day** nos a dydd; **night before last** echnos; **last night** neithiwr; **the last night** y noson olaf; **Good night!** Nos Da!

night-dress *n.* gŵn nos, coban *f.*

night-gown *n.* gŵn nos, coban *f.*

nightingale *n.* eos *f.*

nightmare *n.* hunllef *f.*

nil *n.* dim *m.*

nimble *a.* heini, sionc, ystwyth.

nine *n.* & *a.* naw *m.*

nineteen *n.* & *a.* pedwar ar bymtheg, un deg naw *m.*

ninety *n.* & *a.* naw deg *m.*

ninth *n.* & *a.* nawfed *m.*

no 1 *a.* ni, nid, neb, dim. **2** *ad.* na, nad, ni, nid, nac oes, naddo, nage, nac ydy . . . *(Welsh uses the verb forms to answer yes/no)* e.g. **Nia? No.** Nia? Nage. **Was she there? No** Oedd hi yno? Nac oedd. **Is Non at home? No** Ydy Non gartre? Nac ydy. **Is there food here? No** Oes bwyd yma? Nac oes. **Will they be out? No** Fyddan nhw allan? Na fyddan.

noble *a.* bonheddig, ardderchog.

nobleman *n.* bonheddwr, uchelwr *m.*

nobody *n.* neb *m.*

noise *n.* sŵn, mwstwr, stŵr, sain, twrw *m.*

noisy *a.* swnllyd, stwrllyd.

nom de plume *n.* ffugenw *m.*

none *pn.* neb, dim, dim un.

nonsense *n.* lol *f.*

nook *n.* cornel, congl *f.*

noon *n.* hanner dydd, canol dydd *m.*

no one *pn.* neb.

nor *ad.* & *c.* na, nac.

Norman 1 *n.* Norman *m.* **2** *a.* Normanaidd: **Norman church** eglwys Normanaidd.

north 1 *n.* gogledd *m.* **2** *a.* gogleddol. **North Pole** Pegwn y Gogledd: **North Wales** Gogledd Cymru.

northerly *a.* gogleddol.

northern *a.* gogleddol. **Northern Ireland** Gogledd Iwerddon.

Northerner *n.* Gogleddwr *m.*

nose 1 *n.* trwyn *m.* **2** *v.* trwyno.

nostalgia *n.* hiraeth *m.*

nostril *n.* ffroen *f.*

not *ad.* na, nac, nad, ni, nid.

notable *a.* hynod, enwog, nodedig.

note 1 *n.* nodyn, nod *m.* **2** *v.* nodi, sylwi. **ten pound note** papur decpunt.

noted *a.* nodedig, enwog, hynod.

nothing *n.* dim *m.* **nothing at all** dim byd, dim o gwbl, dim yn y byd.

notice 1 *n.* rhybudd, hysbysebiad, sylw *m.* **2** *v.* sylwi.

notion *n.* syniad, amcan *m.*

notwithstanding 1 *ad.* er hynny. **2** *prp.* er, er gwaethaf, serch.

noun *n.* enw *m.* **collective noun** enw torfol; **common noun** enw cyffredin; **plural noun** enw lluosog.

novel 1 *n.* nofel *f.* **2** *a.* newydd.

novelist *n.* nofelwr, nofelydd *m.*

November *n.* Tachwedd *m.*

now *ad.* yn awr, nawr, rŵan, bellach, y pryd hwn. **now and again** nawr ac yn y man. **nowadays** *ad.* yn y dyddiau hyn. **nowhere** *ad.* dim yn unlle.

nuance *n.* naws *f.*

nuclear *a.* niwclear. **nuclear energy** egni niwclear: **nuclear power station** atomfa.

numb *a.* cwsg.

number 1 *n.* nifer *mf,* rhif; rhifyn *m.* **2** *v.* rhifo, cyfrif.

numeral *n.* rhifol, rhifnod *m.*

numerous *a.* lluosog, niferus; aml.

nun *n.* lleian *f.*

nurse 1 *n.* gweinyddes, nyrs *f.*

2 *v.* magu, nyrsio, meithrin.
nursery *n.* meithrinfa *f.* **nursery**
  class dosbarth meithrin; **nursery**
  nurse gweinyddes feithrin; **nursery**
  school ysgol feithrin.
nurseryman *n.* garddwr *m.*
nursery-rhyme *n.* hwiangerdd *f.*

nurture *v.* meithrin.
nut *n.* cneuen; nyten *f.* **coconut**
  cneuen goco; **hazelnuts** cnau cyll;
  monkey nuts cnau mwnci; **walnut**
  cneuen ffrengig; **hexagonal nut**
  nyten hecsagonal; **square nut** nyten
  sgwâr; **nut and bolt** nyten a bollt.

oak 1 *n.* derwen *f.* **2** *a.* derw. **oak-trees** derw, deri.
oath *n.* llw *m.*
obedient *a.* ufudd.
obey *v.* ufuddhau.
object 1 *n.* gwrthrych, nod, amcan *m.* **2** *v.* gwrthwynebu.
objective 1 *n.* amcan, nod *m.* **2** *a.* gwrthrychol.
objector *n.* gwrthwynebwr *m.*
obligation *n.* dyletswydd, gorfodaeth *f.*
oblige *v.* gorfodi.
obscene *a.* serth, brwnt.
obscure 1 *a.* aneglur, tywyll **2.** *v.* tywyllu.
observation *n.* sylw *m.*
observe *v.* sylwi, edrych; cadw.
obstacle *n.* rhwystr, maen tramgwydd *m.*
obstruct *v.* cau, tagu; rhwystro.
obtain *v.* cael, ennill.
obvious *a.* eglur, amlwg.
occasion 1 *n.* achlysur, achos *m,* adeg *f.* **2** *v.* achosi, peri.
occasional *a.* ambell.
occasionally *ad.* ambell waith.
occupation *n.* gwaith *m,* galwedigaeth *f.*
occur *v.* digwydd, taro.
occurrence *n.* digwyddiad, achlysur *m.*
ocean *n.* môr, cefnfor, eigion *m.*

o'clock *ad.* o'r gloch.
octagon *n.* wythongl *f,* octagon *m.*
octave *n.* wythawd *m.*
octet *n.* wythawd *m.*
October *n.* Hydref *m.*
octogenarian *n.* person pedwar ugain mlwydd oed *m.*
odd *a.* od, hynod, rhyfedd.
ode *n.* cerdd, awdl *f.*
odious *a.* cas, ffiaidd.
of *prp.* o, gan, am, ynghylch. **of course** wrth gwrs.
off 1 *a.* tu allan, tu faes. **2** *ad.* ymaith, i ffwrdd. **3** *prp.* oddi ar, oddi am, oddi wrth.
offence *n.* trosedd *f.*
offend *v.* troseddu.
offender *n.* troseddwr *m.*
offer *n.* & *v.* cynnig *m.*
office *n.* swydd; swyddfa *f.*
officer *n.* swyddog *m.*
official 1 *n.* swyddog *m.* **2** *a.* swyddogol.
offspring *n.* hil *f,* plant *pl.*
often *ad.* yn aml.
oil 1 *n.* olew, oel *m.* **2** *v.* iro, oelio. **oil field** maes olew; **oil rig** llwyfan olew.
old *a.* hen, oedrannus. **old age** henoed, henaint; **old fashioned** henffasiwn; **old man** hen ŵr, henwr; **of old** gynt.
omelette *n.* omled *m.*
on 1 *ad.* ymlaen. **2** *prp.* ar.
once *ad.* unwaith, un tro, gynt. **at once** ar unwaith.
one 1 *n.* rhywun *m.* **2** *a.* un, naill, unig. **3** *pn.* naill: **one by one** bob yn un.
one-way *a.* un-ffordd, unffordd. **one-way street** heol unffordd.
onion *n.* winwnsyn, nionyn *m.*
only 1 *a.* unig. **2** *ad.* yn, dim ond. **the only one** yr unig un; **one only** un yn unig.
open 1 *a.* agored, ar agor. **2** *v.* agor; **open air** awyr agored; **wide open** lled y pen.
opening *n.* agoriad *m.*
opera *n.* opera *f.*
operate *v.* gweithredu, gweithio.

operation *n.* gweithred *f.*, gweithrediad *m;* triniaeth lawfeddygol *f.*
opinion *n.* barn *f,* meddwl *m.*
opponent *n.* gwrthwynebwr, gwrthwynebydd *m.*
opportunity *n.* achlysur, cyfle *m,* siawns *f.*
oppose *v.* gwrthwynebu.
opposite *a.* & *prp.* cyferbyn, cyferbyniol.
opposition *n.* gwrthwyneb, gwrthwynebiad *m;* gwrthblaid *f.*
optician *n.* optegwr, optegydd *m.*
option *n.* dewis, dewisiad *m.*
or *c.* neu, ynte, ynteu, ai, naill ai.
oral *a.* llafar. **oral examination** arholiad llafar.
orally *ad.* ar lafar.
orange *n.* & *a.* oren *mf.*
orchard *n.* perllan *f.*
orchestra *n.* cerddorfa *f.*
ordain *v.* ordeinio, urddo; penderfynu.
ordeal *n.* prawf llym *m.*
order 1 *n.* trefn; urdd; rheol *f,* gorchymyn *m;* archeb *f.* **2** *v.* trefnu; gorchymyn; archebu.
orderly *a.* rheolaidd, trefnus.
ordinarily *ad.* fel rheol.
ordinary *a.* cyffredin, arferol.
ore *n.* mwyn *m.*
organ *n.* organ *f,* offeryn *m.*
organic *a.* organig.
organist *n.* organydd *m.*
organisation *n.* trefn; cyfundrefn *f.*
organise *v.* trefnu.
organiser *n.* trefnydd *m.*
origin *n.* ffynnon, ffynhonnell *f,* dechreuad *m.*
original *a.* gwreiddiol.
originate *v.* dechrau, tarddu, hannu.
other 1 *a.* arall, eraill. **2** *pn.* arall, y llall. **each other** ei gilydd.
our *pn.* ein, ein – ni; 'n. **Our Father** Ein Tad. **our house** ein tŷ, ein tŷ ni.
ours *pn.* eiddom ni, yr eiddom.

out *ad.* allan.
outcrop *n.* brig *m.*
outdoor *a.* yn yr awyr agored.
outline *n.* braslun *m.*
outside 1 *n.* tu allan, tu faes. *mf.* **2** *a.* & *ad.* allan, oddi allan. **3** *prp.* tu allan i, tu faes i.
outside-half *n.* maswr *m.*
outskirts *n.* cyrrau, cyrion *pl.*
outward *a.* allanol.
oven *n.* ffwrn *f,* popty *m.* **electric oven** ffwrn drydan; **gas oven** ffwrn nwy; **microwave oven** meicrodon.
over 1 *n.* pelawd *m.* *(criced).* **2** *ad.* dros ben, drosodd. **3** *prp.* dros, uwch, uwchben.
over- *px.* gor-, rhag-, rhy-, tra-.
overcast *a.* cymylog.
overcoat *n.* cot fawr, cot uchaf *f.*
overcome *v.* gorchfygu, trechu, cael y gorau ar.
overcrowded *a.* gorlawn.
overdo *v.* gor-wneud.
overdraw *v.* gordynnu.
overflow 1 *n.* gorlif *m.* **2** *v.* gorlifo.
overflowing *a.* gorlawn.
overhead *a.* & *ad.* uwchben.
overjoyed *a.* llawen iawn.
overlook *v.* esgeuluso; edrych dros.
overnight *ad.* dros nos.
overpower *v.* trechu.
overseas *ad.* dros y môr, tramor.
overshadow *v.* cysgodi.
overweight *a.* gor-drwm.
overwork *v.* gorweithio.
owe *v.* bod mewn dyled.
owing *a.* dyledus.
owl *n.* gwdihŵ *m,* tylluan *f.* **barn owl, white owl** tylluan wen; **little owl** tylluan fechan; **long-eared owl** tylluan glustiog.
own 1 *a.* eiddo dyn ei hun, priod. **2** *v.* meddu (ar).
owner *n.* perchen, perchennog *m.*
Oxford *n.* Rhydychen *f.*
oxygen *n.* ocsigen *m.*

pace 1 *n.* cam *m.* **2** *v.* camu, cerdded.
Pacific Ocean *n.* Môr Tawel *m.*
pack 1 *n.* pac *m.* **2** *v.* pacio.
package *n.* paced, pecyn *m.*
packet *n.* paced, pecyn *m.*
pact *n.* cytundeb, cynghrair *m.*
padlock *n.* clo *m.*
pagan *n.* pagan *m.*
page *n.* tudalen *mf.*
pageant *n.* pasiant *m.*
pail *n.* bwced *m.*
pain 1 *n.* poen *mf,* dolur *m.* **2** *v.* poeni.
painful *a.* poenus.
painstaking *a.* gofalus.
paint 1 *n.* paent, lliw *m.* **2** *v.* peintio, lliwo.
painter *n.* peintiwr, arlunydd *m.*
painting *n.* llun, darlun *m.*
pair *n.* pâr, dau, cwpl *m.*
palace *n.* llys, plas, palas, plasty *m.*
pale *a.* llwyd, glas, gwelw.
Palestine *n.* Palestina *f.*
palm *n.* palmwydden *f.* **Palm Sunday**
Sul y Blodau, Sul y Palmwydd.
pamper *n.* maldodi, anwesu.
pampering *n.* maldod, anwes *m.*
pamphlet *n.* pamffled, llyfryn *m.*
pan *n.* padell *f.*
pancake *n.* crempog, ffroesen *f.*
pane *n.* cwarel, chwarel *mf.*
panel *n.* panel *m.*

paper 1 *n.* papur *m.* **2** *v.* papuro.
newspaper papur newydd; **toilet paper** papur toiled, papur tŷ bach; **wallpaper** papur wal; **writing paper** papur ysgrifennu.
paperbacks *n.* llyfrau clawr meddal *m.pl.*
papist *n.* pabydd *m.*
parable *n.* dameg *f.*
paradise *n.* gwynfa, gwynfyd *m,* paradwys *f.*
paragraph *n.* paragraff *m.*
paramount *a.* pen, pennaf, prif.
parcel *n.* parsel *m.*
parch *v.* crasu, sychu.
parched *a.* cras, crasboeth; sychedig.
pardon 1 *n.* pardwn, maddeuant *m.* **2** *v.* maddau.
parent *n.* tad neu fam, rhiant *mf.*
parish *n.* plwyf *m.*
park 1 *n.* parc *m.* **2** *v.* parcio. **car park** maes parcio; **caravan park** maes carafanau.
parliament *n.* senedd *f.* **Member of Parliament** Aelod Seneddol (A.S.).
parsley *n.* persli *m.*
parsnip *n.* panasen *f.*
parson *n.* offeiriad, person *m.*
part 1 *n.* darn *m,* rhan *f;* peth *m.* **2** *v.* rhannu; gwahanu; ymadael.
particular *a.* neilltuol.
particularise *v.* manylu.
parting *n.* ymadael *m.*
partner *n.* cymar *m.*
party *n.* parti *m;* plaid *f.* **birthday party** parti pen-blwydd; **Christmas party** parti Nadolig; **Conservative party** Plaid Geidwadol; **Green Party** Plaid Werdd; **Labour Party** Plaid Lafur.
pass 1 *n.* bwlch; caniatâd, pás *m.* **2** *v.* mynd heibio (i); llwyddo.
passion *n.* dioddefaint; nwyd *m.*
past 1 *n. & a.* gorffennol *m.* **2** *ad.* heibio.
pastor *n.* bugail *(eglwys),* gweinidog *m.*
pasture *n.* porfa *f.*
path *n.* llwybr *m;* **public footpath** llwybr cyhoeddus.
patience *n.* amynedd *m.* **the patience of Job** amynedd Job.

patient 1 *n.* claf *m.* 2 *a.* amyneddgar.
patriot *n.* gwladgarwr *m.*
patron *n.* noddwr *m.*
patronage *n.* nawdd *m.*
pattern *n.* patrwm, patrwn *m.*
pause 1 *n.* hoe *f,* saib, seibiant *m.*
  2 *v.* pwyllo, aros, gorffwys.
pavement *n.* pafin *m.*
pavilion *n.* pabell *f,* pafiliwn *m.*
paw *n.* pawen *f.*
pay 1 *n.* cyflog *mf,* tâl *m.* 2 *v.* talu.
payee *n.* talai *m.*
payer *n.* talwr *m.*
payment *n.* tâl, taliad *m.*
pea *n.* pysen *f.*
peace *n.* hedd, heddwch, llonyddwch
  m; tangnefedd *mf.*
peaceful *a.* tawel, llonydd,
  tangnefeddus.
peak *n.* brig, copa *m.*
pear *n.* peren *f.*
pearl *n.* perl *m.*
peasant *n.* gwerinwr *m.*
peasantry *n.* y werin *f.*
peat *n.* mawn *m.*
peck 1 *n.* pigiad *m.* 2 *v.* pigo.
peculiar *a.* od, hynod, arbennig.
pedestrian 1 *n.* cerddwr *m.* 2 *a.* ar
  draed. **pedestrian crossing**
  croesfan *f.*
peel 1 *n.* croen, pil *m.* 2 *v.* pilio.
peep 1 *n.* cipolwg, cip.
  2 *v.* cipedrych, sbîo.
peg *n.* peg *m.*
pen *n.* pin ysgrifennu *m.*
penalise *v.* cosbi.
penalty *n.* cosb *f.*
pence *n.* ceiniogau *pl.*
pencil *n.* pensil *m.*
pendulum *n.* pendil *m.*
penitent *a.* edifar, edifeiriol.
penknife *n.* cyllell boced *f.*
penniless *a.* heb geiniog.
penny *n.* ceiniog *f.*
pension *n.* pensiwn *m.*
pensioner *n.* pensiynwr *m.*
pensive *a.* meddylgar.
people *n.* pobl, gwerin *f.*
pepper *n.* pupur *m.*
per *prp.* trwy, wrth, yn ôl.
perceive *v.* deall, gweld, gweled.

percentage *n.* hyn a hyn y cant,
  canran *m.*
perfect 1 *a.* perffaith. 2 *v.*
  perffeithio.
perfection *n.* perffeithrwydd *m.*
perfectly *ad.* yn berffaith.
perforate *v.* tyllu.
perforated *a.* tyllog.
perforation *n.* twll *m.*
perfume *n.* arogl; persawr *m.*
perhaps *ad.* efallai, hwyrach.
period *n.* adeg *f,* amser; misglwyf,
  cyfnod *m.*
permanent *a.* sefydlog, parhaol.
permission *n.* caniatâd *m,* hawl *f.*
permit *v.* caniatáu.
perpetuate *v.* parhau.
persecute *v.* erlid.
person *n.* person *m.*
personal *a.* personol.
personality *n.* personoliaeth *f.*
perspective *n.* safbwynt, persbectif *m.*
perspiration *n.* chwys *m.*
perspire *v.* chwysu.
pester *v.* blino, poeni.
pet *n.* anifail anwes *m.*
petite *a.* bychan, bechan.
petition *n.* deiseb *f.*
petrol *n.* petrol *m.* **petrol pump**
  pwmp petrol; **petrol station** gorsaf
  betrol; **unleaded petrol** petrol
  di-blwm.
petticoat *n.* pais *f.*
petty *a.* bach, bychan, mân, gwael.
pew *n.* sedd, sêt *f,* côr *m.*
pharmacist *n.* fferyllydd *m.*
pharmacy *n.* fferyllfa *f.*
phone 1 *n.* ffôn. teleffon *m.* 2 *v.*
  ffonio. **phone call** galwad ffôn.
photocopier *n.* llungopïydd,
  ffotogopïydd *m.*
photocopy *n.* llungopi, ffotogopi *m.*
photograph *n.* llun, ffotograff *m.*
photographer *n.* ffotograffydd *m.*
phrase 1 *n.* cymal, ymadrodd *m.*
  2 *v.* geirio, mynegi.
physical *a.* corfforol, materol.
  physical education addysg
  gorfforol.
physics *n.* ffiseg *f.*
pianist *n.* pianydd *m.*

piano

piano

piano *n.* piano *mf.*
pick *v.* dewis, pigo, casglu (blodau/
ffrwythau).
pick up *v.* codi.
picture *n.* darlun, llun, pictiwr *m.*
piece *n.* darn, pisyn *m,* rhan *f,*
tamaid *m.*
pig *n.* mochyn *m.* **piglet** mochyn
bach.
pile *n* . pentwr *m.*
pilgrim *n.* pererin *m.*
pill *n.* pilsen *f.*
pillar *n.* colofn *f.* piler *m.*
pillow *n.* clustog *f,* gobennydd *m.*
pilot *n.* peilot *m.*
pimple *n.* tosyn, ploryn *m.*
pin 1 *n.* pin *m.* **drawing pin** pin
bawd. 2 *v.* pinio, hoelio.
pinch 1 *n.* pinsiad *m.* gwasgfa *f.*
2 *v.* pinsio, gwasgu.
pine *n.* ffynidwydden *f,* ffynidwydd
pl; pinwydden *f,* pinwydd *pl;* **red
pine** ffynidwydd coch.
pineapple *n.* afal pîn, pîn-afal *m.*
pine-end *n.* talcen tŷ *m.*
pink *n.* & *a.* pinc *m.*
pint *n.* peint *m.* **pint of milk** peint o
laeth.
pious *a.* duwiol, crefyddol.
pipe *n.* pib, piben, pibell *f.*
pirate *n.* môr-leidr *m.*
pit *n.* pwll *m.* **coal-pit** pwll glo.
pity *n.* trueni, gresyn, piti *m.* **to take
pity** trugarhau.
place 1 *n.* lle, llecyn, man *m.*
2 *v.* dodi, gosod, lleoli.
plague *n.* haint *f,* pla *m.*
plain 1 *a.* amlwg; eglur.
2 *n.* gwastad *m.*
plan 1 *n.* cynllun, plan *m.*
2 *v.* cynllunio.
planet *n.* planed *f.*
planner *n.* cynlluniwr, cynllunydd *m.*
planning *n.* cynllunio *m.*
plant 1 *n.* planhigyn *m;* offer *pl.*
2 *v.* plannu; gosod.
plate *n.* plât *m.*
platform *n.* llwyfan, platfform *m.*
play 1 *n.* chwarae *m,* drama *f.* **play
group** grŵp chwarae. **fair play**
chwarae teg. **playtime** amser

politics

chwarae. 2 *v.* chwarae, canu
(offeryn).
player *n.* chwaraewr *m.*
plaything *n.* tegan *m.*
pleasant *a.* pleserus, dymunol,
hyfryd, serchus, siriol; braf.
please *v.* bodloni, plesio. **if you
please** os gwelwch yn dda.
pleased *a.* bodlon, hapus.
pleasurable *a.* pleserus, dymunol.
pleasure *n.* pleser, boddhad *m.*
pledge 1 *n.* addewid *mf;* ernes *f.*
2 *v.* addo.
plentiful *a.* helaeth.
plenty *n.* digonedd, digon *m.*
pliable *a.* hyblyg.
pliant *a.* ystwyth.
plot 1 *n.* cynllun; cynllwyn; darn o
dir *m.* 2 *v.* cynllunio; cynllwynio.
plough *v.* aredig, troi.
plum *n.* eirinen *f.*
plumage *n.* plu *pl.*
plume 1 *n.* pluen *f,* plufyn *m.*
2 *v.* pluo, plufio.
plural *n.* lluosog *m.*
pocket 1 *n.* poced *mf.* **pocket
money** arian poced. 2 *v.* pocedu.
pod *n.* plisgyn *m,* coden *f.*
poem *n.* cerdd, cân *f.*
poet *n.* bardd *m.*
poetry *n.* barddoniaeth *f.*
point 1 *n.* pwynt, blaen *m.*
2 *v.* dangos.
pointless *a.* dibwynt.
poison 1 *n.* gwenwyn *m.*
2 *v.* gwenwyno.
poisonous *a.* gwenwynig,
gwenwynol.
Poland *n.* Gwlad Pwyl *f.*
pole *n.* polyn; pegwn *m.* **Pole Star**
Seren y Gogledd.
police *n.* heddlu *m.*
policeman *n.* heddwas, plisman,
plismon.
policewoman *n.* heddferch,
pliswraig, plismones *f.*
Polish 1 *n.* Pwyleg *f.* 2 *a.* Pwylaidd.
polish 1 *n.* cwyr *m.* 2 *v.* cwyro.
political *a.* gwleidyddol, politicaidd.
politician *n.* gwleidydd *m.*
politics *n.* gwleidyddiaeth *f.*

227

pollute v. llygru.
polluted a. llygredig.
pollution n. llygredd m.
pond n. pwll, pwllyn, pownd m.
Pontypool n. Pont-y-pŵl f.
pony n. merlyn m, merlen f. **pony-trekking** merlota; **pony-trekker** merlotwr.
pool n. pwll, pwllyn m. **swimming pool** pwll nofio.
poor a. gwael, llwm, tlawd.
poorly a. gwael, sâl, tost.
Pope n. Pab m.
poppy n. pabi f.
popular a. poblogaidd.
population n. poblogaeth f.
porch n. cyntedd, porth m.
porridge n. uwd m.
port n. porth, porthladd m.
portable a. symudol.
portrait n. llun, darlun, portread m.
portrayal n. portread m.
pose v. sefyll, ymddangos, cymryd ar.
position n. safle m, sefyllfa, swydd f.
positive a. pendant, cadarnhaol.
possess v. meddu.
possession n. eiddo, meddiant m.
possessor n. perchen, perchennog m.
possibility n. posibilrwydd m.
possible a. posibl.
possibly ad. efallai.
post 1 n. post; postyn m; swydd f. **postcode** côd post. **2** v. postio.
postal a. post. **postal order** archeb bost.
posthumous a. ar ôl marw.
postman n. postman, postmon m.
postmaster n. postfeistr m.
post office n. swyddfa'r post f, llythyrdy m.
postpone v. oedi.
postscript n. ôl-nodiad m.
potato n. taten f.
pound n. punt f. (£); pwys m. (lb.); ffald m.
pour v. arllwys; bwrw.
pout v. pwdu.
poverty n. tlodi, eisiau m.
poverty-stricken a. tlawd, llwm.
powder n. llwch, powdr, powdwr m.

power n. gallu, nerth, pŵer, grym m.
powerful a. cryf, galluog, grymus, nerthol.
powerless a. dirym.
power station n. pwerdy.
pox n. brech f. **chicken pox** brech yr ieir.
practical a. ymarferol.
practice n. ymarfer f, ymarferiad, practis m, arfer mf.
practise v. arfer, ymarfer.
practising a. ymarferol.
praise 1 n. canmoliaeth f, clod, mawl m. **2** v. canmol, clodfori, moli.
pram n. pram m.
pray v. gweddïo.
prayer n. gweddi f.
preach v. pregethu.
preacher n. pregethwr.
precarious a. ansicr, peryglus.
precious a. gwerthfawr, drud, prid; annwyl.
precis n. crynodeb mf.
precise a. manwl.
preface n. rhagair, rhagymadrodd m.
preference n. dewis m, ffafriaeth f.
preferential a. ffafriol.
prefix n. rhagddodiad m.
pregnant a. beichiog.
prejudice 1 n. rhagfarn f; niwed m. **2** v. rhagfarnu; niweidio.
prejudiced a. rhagfarnllyd.
premier 1 n. prif weinidog m. **2** a. prif, pennaf, blaenaf.
premium n. gwobr f, tâl, taliad m.
preparation n. paratoad m.
prepare v. paratoi m.
prepared a. parod.
preposition n. arddodiad m.
prescription n. presgripsiwn, rysáit m.
presence n. presenoldeb, gŵydd m.
present 1 n. anrheg, rhodd f; presennol m. **2** v. anrhegu, cyflwyno, dangos. **at present** ar hyn o bryd, yn awr, nawr, rŵan.
presently ad. yn y man, yn union.
preserve 1 n. jam m. **2** v. cadw.
preside v. llywyddu.
president n. llywydd, arlywydd m.
press 1 n. gwasg f. **2** v. gwasgu.

pressure *n.* gwasgiad, pwysedd *m.*
presumably *ad.* yn ôl pob tebyg.
presume *v.* tybio; beiddio.
pretence *n.* esgus *m.*
pretend *v.* ffugio, cymryd ar; honni.
pretext *n.* esgus *m.*
prevent *v.* atal, rhwystro (rhag).
preview *n.* rhagolwg *m.*
previous *a.* cynt; diwethaf.
price 1 *n.* pris *m.* **price list** rhestr prisoedd. 2 *v.* prisio.
prick 1 *n.* pigiad *m.* 2 *v.* pigo.
prickly *a.* pigog.
pride *n.* balchder *m.*
priest *n.* offeiriad *m.*
primary *a.* cynradd; prif. **primary education** addysg gynradd; **primary school** ysgol gynradd.
prime *a.* prif, cyntaf; gorau.
prince *n.* tywysog *m.*
princess *n.* tywysoges *f.*
principal 1 *n.* pen, prifathro *m,* prifathrawes *f.* 2 *a.* prif.
principle *n.* egwyddor *f.*
print 1 *n.* argraff *f,* print, ôl *m.* 2 *a.* argraffu, printio.
printing-press *n.* gwasg argraffu.
prison *n.* carchar *m.*
prisoner *n.* carcharor *m.*
private *a.* cyfrinachol, preifat.
privilege *n.* braint *f.*
prize *n.* gwobr *f.*
probable *a.* tebyg, tebygol.
probation *n.* prawf *m.* **probation officer** swyddog prawf; **probation service** gwasanaeth prawf.
problem *n.* problem *f.*
procedure *n.* trefn *f,* arfer *mf,* dull *m.*
proceed *v.* mynd ymlaen.
proceeds *n.* enillion *pl,* elw *m.*
procession *n.* gorymdaith *f.*
proclaim *v.* cyhoeddi, datgan *m.*
proclamation *n.* cyhoeddiad *m.*
prodigious *a.* anferth.
produce *n.* cynnyrch *m.*
professor *n.* athro *m.*
profit 1 *n.* elw, ennill, enillion, proffid *m.* 2 *v.* elwa, ennill, manteisio.
profitable *a.* proffidiol.
profound *a.* dwfn, dwys.

programme *n.* rhaglen *f.*
prohibit *v.* gwahardd.
project 1 *n.* bwriad, cynllun; cywaith; prosiect, project *m.* 2 *v.* bwriadu; ymestyn.
proletariat *n.* y werin *f.*
prologue *n.* rhagair, prolog *m.*
prominent *a.* amlwg.
promise 1 *n.* addewid *mf.* 2 *v.* addo.
promontory *n.* penrhyn, pentir *m.*
proneness *n.* tueddiad *m.*
pronoun *n.* rhagenw *m.*
pronounce *v.* cyhoeddi, datgan.
pronouncement *n.* cyhoeddiad, datganiad *m.*
proof *n.* prawf *m.*
proper *a.* addas, priod, priodol, rheolaidd.
property *n.* eiddo *m.*
prophesy *v.* proffwydo.
prophet *n.* proffwyd *m.*
proportional *a.* cyfrannol. **Proportional Representation** Cynrychiolaeth Gyfrannol.
proposal *n.* cynnig *m.*
propose *v.* cynnig, bwriadu.
proposition *n.* cynigiad; gosodiad *m.*
proprietor *n.* perchennog *m.*
prose *n.* rhyddiaith *f.*
prosecute *v.* erlyn.
prosecution *n.* erlyniad *m.*
prosecutor *n.* erlynydd *m.*
prospect *n.* golwg *mf,* golyfga *f,* rhagolwg *m.*
prosper *v.* llwyddo.
prosperity *n.* llwyddiant *m.*
prosperous *a.* llwyddiannus, llewyrchus.
protect *v.* amddiffyn.
protest *v.* gwrthdystio.
Protestant 1 *n.* Protestant *m.* 2 *a.* Protestannaidd.
proud *a.* balch.
prove *v.* profi.
proverb *n.* dihareb *f.*
province *n.* talaith *f;* cylch, maes *m.*
proviso *n.* amod *mf.*
provoke *v.* profocio, pryfocio, procio.
proxy *n.* dirprwy *m.*
prudent *a.* call, doeth, synhwyrol.

pry *v.* chwilota, busnesa.
psalm *n.* salm *f.*
psalter *n.* llyfr salmau *m,* sallwyr *f.*
pseudonym *n.* ffugenw *m.*
psychologist *n.* seicolegwr *m.*
psychology *n.* seicoleg *f.*
public 1 *n.* y cyhoedd *m.*
  2 *a.* cyhoeddus. **public hall** neuadd
  gyhoeddus; **public house** tŷ tafarn;
  public place man cyhoeddus.
publican *n* tafarnwr *m.*
publication *n.* cyhoeddiad *m.*
publicity *n.* cyhoeddusrwydd *m.*
publicly *ad.* yn gyhoeddus.
publish *v.* cyhoeddi.
publisher *n.* cyhoeddwr *m.*
pudding *n.* pwdin *m.* **Christmas**
  pudding pwdin Nadolig.
puddle *n.* pwllyn *m.*
pull 1 *n.* plwc; tynfa *f.* **2** *v.* tynnu.
pulpit *n.* pulpud *m.*
pulse *n.* curiad *m.*
pump 1 *n.* pwmp *m.* **2** *v.* pwmpio.
punctual *a.* prydlon.
punctuality *n.* prydlondeb *m.*
puncture 1 *n.* twll *m.* **2** *v.* tyllu.
punish *v.* cosbi; poeni.

punishment *n.* cosb, cosbedigaeth *f.*
pup *n.* ci bach; cenau *m.*
pupil *n.* disgybl *m;* cannwyll llygad *f.*
puppet *n.* pyped *m.*
purchase 1 *n.* pryniant *m.* **2** *v.* prynu.
pure *a.* pur, glân, gwir.
purge *v.* puro, glanhau.
purify *v.* puro.
purple *n.* & *a.* porffor, piws *m.*
purpose *n.* bwriad, pwrpas, amcan,
  diben *m.*
purr *v.* canu grwndi, canu crwth;
  grwnan.
purse *n.* cwd, cwdyn, pwrs *m.*
pursue *v.* dilyn, erlid, erlyn, hel,
  hela.
pursuer *n.* erlidiwr *m.*
puffin *n.* pâl *m.*
push 1 *n.* gwthiad, hwp *m.*
  2 *v.* gwthio, hwpio.
pusher *n.* gwthiwr.
put *v.* dodi, gosod, rhoddi, rhoi;
  mynegi.
puzzle *n.* pos *m.* **crossword puzzle**
  pos croeseiriau.
pyjamas *n.pl.* pyjamas *pl,* gwisg
  nos *f.*

quagmire *n.* siglen, cors *f.*
quaint *a.* od, henffasiwn.
quake *v.* crynu, ysgwyd.
Quaker *n.* Crynwr *m.* **Quakers Yard** Mynwent y Crynwyr.
qualification *n.* cymhwyster *m.*
qualified *a.* cymwys.
quality *n.* rhinwedd *mf,* ansawdd *m.*
quantity *n.* swm *m,* nifer *mf,* maint, mesur *m.*
quarrel 1 *n.* cweryl, ffrae *f.*
2 *v.* cweryla, ffraeo.
quarry *n.* chwarel *f,* cwar *m.*
quarryman chwarelwr.
quart *n.* chwart, cwart *m.*

quarter *n.* chwarter, cwarter; cwr, man *m.* **quarter of an hour** chwarter awr.
quay *n.* cei *m.* **New Quay (Ceredigion)** Ceinewydd.
queen *n.* brenhines *f.*
queer *a.* od, hynod, ysmala.
quench *v.* diffodd; torri (syched).
query 1 *n.* cwestiwn, ymholiad *m.*
2 *v.* holi, ymholi, amau.
quest *n.* ymchwil *f,* cwest *m.*
question 1 *n.* cwestiwn *m.* **question mark** gofynnod **2** *v.* cwestiyna, holi.
questioner *n.* holwr *m.*
questionnaire *n.* holiadur *m.*
queue 1 *n.* ciw *m;* cwt *mf.*
2 *v.* ciwio.
quick *a.* cyflym, buan, byw. **to the quick** i'r byw.
quickly *ad.* yn fuan.
quiet 1 *n.* tawelwch, llonyddwch *m.*
2 *a.* tawel, distaw, llonydd.
3 *v.* tawelu.
quietness *n.* tawelwch *m.*
quilt 1 *n.* cwilt, cwrlid *m.*
2 *v.* cwiltio.
quintet *n.* pumawd *m.*
quit *v.* gadael, symud, ymadael.
quite *ad.* hollol, llwyr, eithaf.
quiver *ad.* crynu.
quiz 1 *n.* pos, cwis *m.* **2** *v.* holi, profocio.
quotation *n.* dyfyniad *m.* **quotation marks** dyfynodau.

rabbit *n.* cwningen *f.*
race *n.* gyrfa, ras; hil *f.*
racial *a.* hiliol.
racket *n.* raced *mf.*
radiator *n.* rheiddiadur *m.*
radio *n.* radio *m.* **radio programme** rhaglen radio; **radio station** gorsaf radio.
rag *n.* clwtyn, rhecsyn *m.* **rag doll** doli glwt *f.*
rail *n.* cledr, cledren, rheilen; canllaw *f.* **rails (of railway)** cledrau.
railway *n.* rheilffordd *f.* **railway station** gorsaf reilffordd.
raiment *n.* dillad *m.* gwisg *f.*
rain 1 *n.* glaw *m.* **2** *v.* glawio, bwrw glaw.
rainbow *n.* enfys *f.*
raincoat *n.* cot law *f.*
rainy *a.* glawog, glawiog.
rake 1 *n.* rhaca *mf.* **2** *v.* crafu, rhacanu.
ram *n.* hwrdd, maharen *m.*
range *n.* amrediad; cwmpas; ystod *f.* **range of temperature** amrediad tymheredd: **age range** ystod oed.
rank *n.* rhes, rhestr, rheng, gradd *f.*
ransom *n.* pridwerth *m.*
rape 1 *n.* trais *m.* **2** *v.* treisio.
rapid *a.* cyflym, buan, gwyllt.
rare *a.* prin; anaml.
raspberry *n.* afanen, afansen, mafonen *f.*

rat *n.* llygoden fawr, llygoden Ffrengig *f.*
rate 1 *n.* treth *f,* tâl; cyflymder; cyfradd *m.* **2** *v.* trethu.
ratepayer *n.* trethdalwr *m.*
rather *ad.* braidd, go, lled, yn hytrach.
raw *a.* noeth, garw; amrwd.
ray *n.* pelydr, pelydryn *m.*
re *prp.* ynglŷn â, mewn perthynas â.
re- *px.* ail-; eto.
reach 1 *n.* cyrraedd *m.* **2** *v.* cyrraedd, estyn, hercyd.
reaction *n.* ymateb, adwaith *m.*
read *v.* darllen.
re-address *v.* ailgyfeirio.
reader *n.* darllenwr, darllenydd; llyfr darllen *m.*
readily *ad.* yn barod, yn union, yn rhwydd.
reading *n.* darllen *m.*
reading-room *n.* ystafell ddarllen *f.*
ready *a.* parod, rhwydd.
real *a.* gwir, real, go-iawn.
realise *v.* sylweddoli; gwerthu.
reality *n.* gwirionedd, realiti *m.*
really *ad.* yn wir, mewn gwirionedd.
realm *n.* teyrnas, gwlad, bro *f.*
reap *v.* medi, cywain.
rear 1 *n.* cefn, pen ôl, y tu ôl *m.* **2** *v.* codi, magu, meithrin.
reason 1 *n.* rheswm, achos *m.* **2** *v.* rhesymu.
reasonably *a.* rhesymol.
rebel 1 *n.* gwrthryfelwr *m.* **2** *v.* gwrth ryfela.
rebellion *n.* gwrthryfel *m.*
rebuke 1 *n.* cerydd *m,* sen *f.* **2** *v.* ceryddu.
recall *v.* galw yn ôl, galw i gof, cofio.
receipt *n.* derbynneb, taleb *f.*
receive *n.* derbyn.
receiver *n.* derbynnydd *m.*
recent *a.* diweddar.
receptionist *n.* derbynnydd *m.*
receptive *a.* derbyniol.
recipe *n.* rysait *f.*
recitation *n.* adroddiad *m.*
recite *v.* adrodd, datgan.
reckon *v.* cyfrif, rhifo; barnu.
recline *v.* gorwedd, gorffwys.

recluse *n.* meudwy *m.*
recognise *v.* adnabod.
recollect *v.* galw i gof, cofio.
record 1 *n.* record *f.* **2** *v.* cofnodi, recordio.
recording *n.* recordiad *m.*
re-count *v.* ailgyfrif.
reaction *n.* adloniant *m.*
rectify *n.* unioni, cywiro.
recurrence *n.* ailddigwyddiad, ailymddangosiad *m.*
recycle *v.* ailgylchu.
red *n.* & *a.* coch *m.*
redeem *v.* gwaredu, achub, prynu (yn ôl).
redeemer *n.* prynwr, gwaredwr *m.*
reduce *v.* gostwng.
reduction *n.* gostyngiad *m.*
redundant *a.* di-swydd.
refer *v.* cyfeirio, cyfarwyddo.
referee 1 *n.* canolwr, rheolwr *m.* **2** *v.* dyfarnu.
reference *n.* cyfeiriad; geirda *m.*
refine *v.* puro.
refinery *n.* purfa *f.*
reflect *v.* meddwl, myfyrio, ystyried.
reform 1 *n.* diwygiad *m.* **2** *v.* diwygio, gwella.
reformation *n.* diwygiad *m;*
Protestant Reformation Diwygiad Protestannaidd.
refresh *v.* adfywio.
refrigerator *n.* oergell *f.*
refuge *n.* lloches, noddfa *f.*
refugee *n.* ffoadur *m.*
refuse *n.* ysbwriel, sothach *m.* **refuse bin** bin ysbwriel.
refuse *v.* gwrthod, pallu.
region *n.* ardal, cylch; rhanbarth *f;* rhandir *m.*
register 1 *n.* cofrestr *f.* **2** *v.* cofrestru.
registrar *n.* cofrestrydd *m.*
regular *a.* rheolaidd, cyson.
rehearsal *n.* rihyrsal, practis *m.*
reimburse *v.* talu yn ôl, ad-dalu.
rejoice *v.* llawenhau.
rejoicing *n.* llawenydd *m.*
relate *v.* adrodd, mynegi; perthyn.
related *a.* yn perthyn; wedi ei ddweud.
relating to *prp.* yn ymwneud â.

relation *n.* perthynas *mf.*
relationship *n.* perthynas *mf.*
relative 1 *n.* perthynas *mf.*
2 *a.* perthynol; cymharol: **relative pronoun** rhagenw perthynol.
relax *v.* llacio, llaesu, ymlacio.
release *v.* gollwng, rhyddhau.
relevant *a.* perthnasol.
religion *n.* crefydd *f.*
religious *a.* crefyddol.
relish 1 *n.* blas *m.* **2** *v.* blasu, hoffi, mwynhau.
rely *v.* dibynnu (ar).
remain *v.* aros, bod ar ôl.
remainder *n.* gweddill *m.*
remains *n.* olion, gweddillion *pl.*
remark 1 *n.* sylw *m.* **2** *v.* sylwi, dweud.
remarkable *a.* hynod, nodedig; rhyfedd, od.
remedy 1 *n.* meddyginiaeth *f.*
2 *v.* gwella.
remember *v.* cofio.
remembrance *n.* cof, coffa *m.*
remind *v.* atgoffa, atgofio, cofio.
remiss *a.* esgeulus, diofal.
remnant *n.* gweddill *m.*
remote *a.* pell, diarffordd, anghysbell.
remotely *ad.* o bell.
removal *n.* symudiad *m.*
remove *v.* symud.
remunerate *v.* talu, gwobrwyo; cydnabod.
rendering *n.* datganiad; trosiad *m.*
rendezvous *n.* man cyfarfod *m.*
renowned *a.* enwog, adnabyddus.
repairer *n.* trwsiwr, cyweiriwr *m.*
repeat *v.* ailadrodd.
reply 1 *n.* ateb, atebiad *m.* **2** *v.* ateb.
report 1 *n.* adroddiad; sŵn ergyd *m.*
2 *v.* adrodd.
reporter *n.* gohebydd *m.*
representation *n.* cynrychiolaeth *f.*
Proportional Representation Cynrychiolaeth Gyfrannol.
republic *n.* gweriniaeth *f.*
reputed *a.* honedig.
request 1 *n.* cais, dymuniad *m,* arch *f.*
2 *v.* ceisio, dymuno.
require *v.* ceisio, gofyn.

requirements *n.* gofynion *pl.*
rescue *v.* achub.
research *n.* ymchwil *f.* **research work** gwaith ymchwil.
 2 *v.* ymchwilio.
researcher *n.* chwilotwr *m.*
resemblance *n.* tebygrwydd *m.*
reserve *v.* neilltuo, cadw wrth gefn.
reserved *a.* swil; wedi ei gadw.
 reserved seats seddau cadw.
reservoir *n.* cronfa *f.*
reside *v.* trigo, byw, preswylio.
resident *n.* preswylydd *m.*
residential *a.* preswyl. **residential school** ysgol breswyl.
residue *n.* gweddill *m.*
resign *v.* ymddiswyddo.
resignation *n.* ymddiswyddiad *m.*
resist *v.* gwrthwynebu, gwrthsefyll.
resolute *a.* penderfynol.
resolution *n.* penderfyniad *m.*
resolve 1 *n.* penderfyniad *m.*
 2 *v.* penderfynu.
resources *n.* adnoddau *pl.*
respect 1 *n.* parch *m.* **2** *v.* parchu.
respectable *a.* parchus.
respectful *a.* boneddigaidd.
respectfully *ad.* yn barchus.
respiration *n.* anadliad *m.*
respire *v.* anadlu.
respite *n.* egwyl *f,* seibiant *m,* hoe *f.*
respond *v.* ateb, ymateb.
response *n.* ateb, atebiad *m.*
responsibility *n.* cyfrifoldeb *m.*
responsible *a.* cyfrifol.
rest 1 *n.* gorffwys, saib *m,* hoe *f;* gweddill *m.* **2** *v.* gorffwyso, pwyso.
restaurant *n.* tŷ bwyta; bwyty *m.*
restless *a.* rhwyfus, aflonydd.
restore *v.* adfer.
restrict *v.* cyfyngu.
result *n.* canlyniad, ateb *m.*
retain *v.* cadw, dal; llogi.
retard *v.* arafu.
retire *v.* ymddeol.
retired *a.* wedi ymddeol.
retirement *n.* ymddeoliad *m.*
retiring *a.* swil.
return *v.* dychwelyd.
returns *n.* enillion *pl.*
reveal *v.* datguddio, dangos, egluro,

datgelu.
revenge *n.* & *v.* dial *m.*
reverend *a.* parchedig: **Revd Ifan Puw** Parchg. Ifan Puw.
revise *v.* diwygio, cywiro.
revival *n.* diwygiad *m.*
revive *v.* adfer.
revolution *n.* chwyldro, chwyldroad *m.*
revolve *v.* troi.
reward 1 *n.* gwobr *f,* tâl *m.*
 2 *v.* gwobrwyo.
rheumatism *n.* gwynegon, cryd cymalau *m.*
rhyme 1 *n.* odl *f;* rhigwm *m.*
 2 *v.* odli; rhigymu.
ribbon *n.* ruban *m.*
rice *n.* reis *m.*
rich *a.* cyfoethog, bras, ffrwythlon.
riches *n.* cyfoeth, golud *pl.*
rickety *a.* simsan, sigledig.
rid *v.* gwaredu, cael gwared o.
riddle *n.* pos *m.*
ridge *n.* crib *mf,* cefn *m.*
rifle *n.* dryll, reiffl *m.*
right 1 *n.* hawl, iawn *m.* braint *f.*
 2 *a.* iawn, cywir; de. **3** *ad.* yn gywir, yn iawn. **right angle** ongl sgwâr; **right hand** llaw dde.
righteous *a.* cyfiawn.
righteousness *n.* cyfiawnder *m.*
rim *n.* ymyl *mf.*
ring 1 *n.* cylch *m;* modrwy *f;* caniad *(ffôn) m.* **wedding ring** modrwy briodas. **2** *v.* canu cloch.
rinse *v.* golchi.
riot *n.* terfysg *m.*
rip *v.* rhwygo.
ripe *a.* aeddfed.
rise 1 *n.* codiad *m.* **2** *v.* codi.
river *n.* afon *f.* **River Severn** Afon Hafren; **River Tawe** Afon Tawe; **River Wye** Afon Gwy.
road *n.* ffordd, heol, hewl *f.* **main road** ffordd fawr, heol fawr; **narrow road** ffordd gul, heol gul; **straight road** heol syth; **winding road** heol droellog; **bypass** ffordd osgoi.
roar *v.* rhuo.
roast 1 *n.* rhost. **roast potatoes** tatws rhost. **2** *v.* rhostio.
rob *v.* lladrata, dwyn, dwgyd.

robber *n.* lleidr *m.*
robbery *n.* lladrad *m.*
robe *n.* gwisg, gŵn *f.*
robin *n.* robin goch *m.*
rock 1 *n.* craig *f;* roc *m.* **2** *v.* siglo.
rocky *a.* creigiog.
rôle *n.* rhan, rôl *f.*
roll 1 *n.* rhôl, rhestr *f.* **2** *v.* rholio, treiglo.
Roman 1 *n.* Rhufeiniwr *m.*
  2 *v.* Rhufeinig. **Roman Catholic** Pabydd *n.*
romance *n.* carwriaeth *f.*
romantic *a.* rhamantus, rhamantaidd.
Rome *n.* Rhufain *f.*
roof *n.* to *m,* nen *f.*
room *n.* lle *m,* ystafell, stafell *f.*
rooster *n.* ceiliog *m.*
root *n.* gwreiddyn *m.*
rope 1 *n.* rhaff *f.* **2** *v.* rhaffu, rhwymo.
rose *n.* rhosyn *m.*
rosy-cheeked *a.* gwridog.
rot *v.* pydru.
rotten *a.* pwdr, drwg, sâl.
rough *a.* garw, bras.
round *a.* cron *f,* crwn *m.*
roundabout 1 *n.* cylchfan *f,* trogylch *m.* **2** *a.* o amgylch.
route *n.* llwybr *m,* taith, ffordd *f.*
row 1 *n.* rhes, rhestr *f.* **2** *v.* rhwyfo.
  rowing boat cwch rhwyfo.
row *n.* ffrae *f,* terfysg *m.*
royal *a.* brenhinol.
rub *v.* rhwbio.

rubber *n.* rwber *m.*
rubbish *n.* ysbwriel, sothach *coll,* lol *f;* **rubbish bin** bin ysbwriel.
rudder *n.* llyw *m.*
ruddy *a.* coch, gwridog.
rude *a.* anfoesgar, haerllug.
rudiment *n.* egwyddor, gwyddor, elfen *f.*
rudimentary *a.* elfennol.
rugby *n.* rygbi *m.* **rugby ball** pêl rygbi; **rugby match** gêm rygbi.
rugged *a.* garw.
ruin 1 *n.* dinistr *m;* adfail *mf.*
  2 *v.* dinistrio, difetha.
rule 1 *n.* llywodraeth; rheol *f;* arfer *mf;* riwl, riwler *m.* **2** *v.* llywodraethu, rheoli.
ruler *n.* llywodrodaethwr, llyw, rheolwr; riwl, riwler, pren mesur *m.*
ruling *n.* dyfarniad *m.*
rummage *v.* chwilota.
rummager *n.* chwilotwr *m.*
rumour *n.* & *v.* si, su, *m,* sôn *mf,* chwedl *f.*
run 1 *n.* rhediad *m.* **2** *v.* rhedeg, rheoli.
runaway *n.* ffoadur *m.*
runner *n.* rhedwr *m.*
running *n.* rhediad *m.*
rural *a.* gwledig.
rush 1 *n.* rhuthr *m.* **2** *v.* rhuthro.
Russia *n.* Rwsia *f.*
Russian 1 *n.* Rwsiad *m (person)*; Rwsieg *f (iaith).* **2** *a.* Rwsiaidd.

Sabbath *n.* Sabath, Saboth *m.*
sack *n.* cwd, cwdyn *m,* sach *f.*
sacred *a.* sanctaidd, glân.
sacrifice 1 *n.* aberth *mf.* 2 *v.* aberthu.
sad *a.* trist, blin, truenus, trwm,
prudd.
sadly *ad.* yn drist, yn flin, yn brudd.
sadness *n.* tristwch, trymder *m.*
safe 1 *n.* cist, cell *f.* 2 *a.* diogel, saff.
said 1 *n.* hwyl *f.* 2 *v.* hwylio, morio.
sailing *n.* hwylio *m.* **sailing boat**
llong hwylio.
sailor *n.* llongwr, morwr *m.*
saint *n.* sant *m;* santes *f.* **Saint David**
Dewi Sant; **Saint John** Sant Ioan;
Saint Mary y Santes Fair; **Saint
David's** Tyddewi.
sake *n.* mwyn *m.* **for the sake of** er
mwyn.
salary *n.* cyflog *mf.*
sale *n.* gwerthiant *m;* sâl, sêl *f,*
arwerthiant *m.* **For Sale** Ar Werth.
salesman *n.* gwerthwr *m.*
saliva *n.* poer, poeri *m.*
salt 1 *n.* halen *m.* **salt cellar** llestr
halen. 2 *a.* hallt. **salt water** dŵr
hallt; dŵr y môr. 3 *v.* halltu.
salvation *n.* iachawdwriaeth *f.*
Salvation Army Byddin yr
Iachawdwriaeth.
same *a.* yr un, yr unrhyw, yr un fath.
sand *n.* tywod *m.* **sand castles**
cestyll tywod.

sandwich 1 *n.* brechdan *f.* 2 *v.*
gwthio rhwng.
Santa Claus *n.* Siôn Corn *m.*
sap 1 *n.* sudd. 2 *v.* sugno; tanseilio.
satellite *n.* lloeren *f.*
satisfaction *n.* boddhad *m.*
satisfy *v.* bodloni.
Saturday *n.* dydd Sadwrn *m.*
Saturn *n.* Sadwrn *m.*
sauce *n.* saws *m.*
saucepan *n.* sosban *f.* **small
saucepan** sosban fach; **big
saucepan** sosban fawr.
saucer *n.* soser *f.*
savage 1 *n.* dyn gwyllt *m.* 2 *a.*
ffyrnig, gwyllt.
save 1 *v.* achub, arbed, gwaredu;
cynilo. 2 *prp.* & *c.* ond.
savings *n.* cynilion *pl.*
saviour *n.* gwaredwr, iachawdwr *m.*
savoury *a.* blasus.
saw 1 *n.* llif *f.* **sawdust** blawd llif;
hand-saw llawlif. 2 *v.* llifio.
say *v.* dweud (wrth). **to tell
someone** dweud wrth rywun.
saying *n.* dywediad, ymadrodd *m.*
scale *n.* graddfa; clorian, tafol *f.*
Celsius scale graddfa Celsius.
scales *n.* clorian, tafol *f.*
scarce *a.* prin, anaml.
scarcely *ad.* braidd, prin, o'r braidd.
scarcity *n.* prinder *m.*
scare 1 *n.* braw, ofn *m.* 2 *v.* ofni,
dychryn.
scarf *n.* sgarff *f.*
scatter *v.* chwalu.
scene *n.* lle, man *m.* golygfa *f.*
scenery *n.* golygfa *f.*
scent 1 *n.* arogl, aroglau; gwynt;
trywydd *m.* 2 *v.* arogli; gwynto;
sawru.
scheme 1 *n.* cynllun *m.* 2 *v.*
cynllunio.
scholar *n.* ysgolhaig, ysgolor *m.*
scholarship *n.* ysgoloriaeth *f.*
school *n.* ysgol *f.* **bilingual school**
ysgol ddwyieithog; **local school**
ysgol leol; **night-school** ysgol nos;
summer school ysgol haf; **Welsh
school** ysgol Gymraeg; **primary
school** ysgol gynradd;

comprehensive school ysgol gyfun.
schoolboy *n* . bachgen ysgol *m*.
schooldays *n*. dyddiau ysgol *pl*.
schoolgirl *n*. merch ysgol *f*.
schoolhouse *n*. tŷ ysgol *m*.
schoolmaster *n*. athro ysgol, ysgolfeistr *m*.
schoolmistress *n*. athrawes, ysgolfeistres *f*.
science *n*. gwyddoniaeth, gwyddor *f*.
science fiction ffuglen wyddonol.
scientific *a*. gwyddonol.
scientist *n*. gwyddonydd *m*.
scissors *n*. siswrn *m*.
scorch *v*. crasu; rhuddo.
scorched *a*. cras.
score 1 *n*. sgôr; ugain *m*. **2** *v*. sgorio.
scorn 1 *n*. gwawd *m*. **2** *v*. gwawdio.
Scotland *n*. Yr Alban *f*.
scowl 1 *n*. gwg *m*. **2** *v*. gwgu.
scratch 1 *n*. crafiad *m*. **2** *v*. crafu.
scream 1 *n*. sgrech, ysgrech *f*. **2** *v*. sgrechian, sgrechain.
screw 1 *n*. sgriw *f*. **2** *v*. sgriwio.
script *n*. sgript *f*.
scripture *n*. ysgrythur *f*, y Beibl *m*.
scrum 1 *n*. sgrym *f*. **2** *v*. sgrymio.
scrum-half *n*. mewnwr *m*.
sea *n*. môr *m*. **sea-level** lefel y môr; **sea water** dŵr y môr.
seagull *n*. gwylan *f*.
seal *n*. morlo *m;* sêl *f*.
seaman *n*. morwr, llongwr *m*.
sea-marsh *n*. morfa *m*.
seamstress *n*. gwniadyddes, gwniyddes *f*.
search 1 *n*. ymchwil *f*. **2** *v*. chwilio, edrych, ymchwilio.
searcher *n*. chwiliwr *m*.
sea-shore *n*. glan y môr *f*.
seasickness *n*. salwch (y) môr. *m*.
season *n*. adeg *f*, amser, pryd, tymor *m*. **season ticket** tocyn tymor.
seat 1 *n*. sedd, sêt *f*. **2** *v*. eistedd.
seaweed *n*. gwymon *m*.
second 1 *n*. ail *m*; eiliad *f*. **2** *a*. ail. **second class** ail ddosbarth; isradd; **second-hand** ail-law.
secret 1 *n*. cyfrinach *f*. **2** *a*. cyfrinachol.

secretary *n*. ysgrifennydd *m*, ysgrifenyddes *f*. **Secretary of State** Ysgrifennydd Gwladol.
section *n*. adran, rhan *f*.
secure 1 *a*. diogel, sicr, siŵr. **2** *v*. sicrhau.
security *n*. sicrwydd, diogelwch; ernes. **Social Security** Nawdd Cymdeithasol.
sediment *n*. gwaelodion, gwaddod *m*.
see 1 *n*. esgobaeth *f*. **2** *v*. gweld, gweled.
seed 1 *n*. had *coll*, hadyn, hedyn *m*. **2** *v*. hadu.
seek *v*. ceisio, chwilio.
seem *v*. ymddangos.
seemly *a*. addas.
seething *n*. & *a*. berw *m*.
seize *v*. gafael, dal. **to seize the opportunity** achub y cyfle.
seldom *ad*. anaml.
select *a*. & *v*. dewis, dethol.
selection *n*. detholiad *m*.
self *pn*. & *n*. hun, hunan *m*.
self-catering *a*. hunan arlwyol.
self-cleaning *a*. hunan lanhaol.
self-confident *a*. hunan hyderus.
selfish *a*. hunanol.
self-respect *n*. hunan-barch *m*.
sell *v*. gwerthu.
seller *n*. gwerthwr.
semi- *px*. hanner-, go-, lled-.
semicircle *n*. hanner cylch *m*.
semi-final *a*. cynderfynol.
senate *n*. senedd *f*.
send *v*. anfon, danfon, gyrru, hala.
sender *n*. gyrrwr *m*.
senile *a*. oedrannus, hen.
senility *n*. henaint.
senior *a*. hŷn, uwch, uchaf.
sense 1 *n*. synnwyr, pwyll *m*, ystyr *mf*. **2** *v*. synhwyro.
sensible *a*. synhwyrol, call.
sentence 1 *n*. brawddeg; barn *f*. **2** *v*. dedfrydu.
sentry *n*. gwyliwr *m*.
separate 1 *a*. ar wahân. **2** *v*. gwahanu.
separately *ad*. ar wahân.
separation *n*. gwahaniad *m*.

September *n.* Medi *m.*

serenity *n.* tawelwch, hedd, heddwch *m.*

serial 1 *n.* cyfres *f.* **2** *a.* cyfresol.

series *n.* cyfres, rhes *f.*

serious *a.* difrifol, prudd, prysur.

seriously *ad.* yn ddifrifol.

sermon *n.* pregeth *f.*

serpent *n.* sarff *f.*

servant *n.* gwas *m,* morwyn *f.* **civil servant** gwas sifil.

serve *v.* gwasanaethu.

service *n.* gwasanaeth *m;* oedfa *f.*

set 1 *n.* set; *f.* **2** *v.* trefnu, gosod, dodi.

setting *n.* machlud; lleoliad *m.*

settle 1 *n.* sgiw, setl *f.* **2** *v.* sefydlu; penderfynu; talu, cytuno, setlo.

settled *a.* sefydlog.

settlement *n.* gwladfa *f.*

seven *n. & a.* saith *m.*

seventeen *n. & a.* dau ar bymtheg, un deg saith *m.*

seventh *n. & a.* seithfed *m.*

seventy *n. & a.* deg a thrigain, saith deg *m.*

sever *v.* torri.

several *a.* amryw.

severe *a.* caled, llym, hallt, tost.

severity *n.* caledi *m.*

Severn *n.* Afon Hafren *f.*

sew *v.* gwnïo, pwytho.

sewing machine *n.* periant gwnïo.

sex *n.* rhyw *m.*

sexual *a.* rhywiol.

shade 1 *n.* cysgod *m.* **2** *v.* cysgodi.

shadow *n.* cysgod *m.*

shady *a.* cysgodol.

shake *v.* ysgwyd, siglo, crynu.

shaking *n.* ysgytwad *m.*

shaky *a.* sigledig.

shallow *a.* bas.

sham *a.* ffug, gau.

shame *n.* cywilydd.

shameful *a.* gwarthus, cywilyddus.

shape 1 *n.* ffurf *f,* llun *m,* siâp *f.* **2** *v.* ffurfio, llunio.

shapely *a.* lluniaidd.

share 1 *n.* rhan, siâr *f.* **2** *v.* rhannu.

sharp *a.* llym, miniog, siarp.

shawl *n.* siôl *f.*

she *pn.* hi, hithau, hyhi.

shed *n.* sied, cwts *m.*

sheep 1 *n.* dafad *f.* **2** *n.* defaid *pl.*

sheer *a.* pur; glân; noeth.

sheet *n.* llen *f,* lliain *m.* dalen *f,* taflen *f.*

shelf *n.* silff *f.*

shell *n.* cragen *f;* plisgyn *m.*

shelter 1 *n.* cysgod *m,* lloches *f.* **2** *v.* cysgodi, llochesu.

shepherd 1 *n.* bugail *m.* **2** *v.* bugeilio.

shield 1 *n.* tarian *f.* **2** *v.* cysgodi; amddiffyn.

shift 1 *n.* newid, symudiad; tro *m;* shifft *f.* **2** *v.* newid, symud.

shine *v.* disgleirio, llewyrchu.

shiny *a.* gloyw, disglair.

ship *n.* llong *f.*

shipshape *a.* taclus, trefnus, twt.

shire *n.* sir (Wales), swydd (England) *f.* **Pembrokeshire** Sir Benfro (Cymru); **Gloucestershire** Swydd Gaerloyw (Lloegr).

shirk *v.* osgoi.

shirt *n.* crys *m.*

shiver *v.* crynu.

shivering *n.* cryd *m.*

shoal *n.* haig *f.*

shock *n.* ysgytwad, sioc *m.*

shoe *n.* esgid *f.* **pair of shoes** pâr o esgidiau.

shoot 1 *n.* eginyn *m.* **2** *v.* saethu.

shooter *n.* saethwr *m.*

shooting *n.* saethu.

shop 1 *n.* siop *f.* **2** *v.* siopa.

shopkeeper *n.* siopwr *m.*

shopper *n.* prynwr *m.*

shopping *n.* siopa *m.*

shore *n.* glan *f,* traeth *f.*

short *a.* byr, cwta, prin.

shot *n.* ergyd *mf.*

shoulder *n.* ysgwydd *f.*

shout 1 *n.* bloedd *m.* gwaedd *f.* **2** *v.* bloeddio, crio, gweiddi.

shove 1 *n.* hwp *m.* **2** *v.* gwthio.

shovel *n.* rhaw *f.*

show 1 *n.* sioe *f.* **2** *v.* dangos, arddangos.

shower *n.* cawod *f.*

shriek 1 *n.* sgrech, ysgrech *f.* **2** *v.* sgrechian, sgrechain.

shrill *a.* main, llym.
shut *v.* cau.
shy *a.* swil.
sick 1 *n.pl.* cleifion *m.* **2** *a.* claf, gwael, sâl, tost.
sickness *n.* afiechyd, clefyd, dolur, anhwyldeb, anhwylder, tostrwydd *m.*
side 1 *n.* ochr *f,* ymyl, ystlys; tu *mf,* plaid *f.* **2** *v.* ochri.
sidesman *n.* ystlyswr *m.*
sideways *ad.* tua'r ochr.
sigh 1 *n.* ochenaid *f.* **2** *v.* ochneidio.
sight 1 *n.* golwg *mf,* golygfa *f.* **2** *v.* gweld, gweled.
sign 1 *n.* arwydd *m.* **2** *v.* arwyddo, llofnodi.
signal *n.* arwydd *m.*
signature *n.* llofnod *m.*
silage *n.* silwair *m.*
silence 1 *n.* distawrwydd, tawelwch *m.* **2** *v.* distewi.
silencer *n.* distewydd *m.*
silent *a.* distaw, tawel.
silk *n.* sidan *m.*
silly *a.* ffôl, dwl, twp.
silver *n.* arian *m.* **silversmith** gof arian; **silver wedding** priodas arian.
similar *a.* tebyg.
similarity *n.* tebygrwydd *m.*
simple *a.* syml; diniwed.
sin 1 *n.* pechod *m.* **2** *v.* pechu.
since 1 *c.* am, gan, oherwydd. **2** *prp.* er, ers, er pan.
sincere *a.* diffuant, cywir, pur.
sinew *n.* gewyn *m.*
sing *v.* canu.
singer *n.* canwr, cantwr, cantor *m;* cantores *f.*
singing *n.* caniad, caniadaeth *f,* canu *m.*
single *a.* sengl, un; dibriod.
singular *a.* unigol; hynod.
sink 1 *n.* sinc *m.* **2** *v.* suddo.
sinner *n.* pechadur *m.*
sir *n.* syr *m.*
sister *n.* chwaer *f.*
sister-in-law *n.* chwaer-yng-nghyfraith *f.*
sit *v.* eistedd.
situation *n.* lle, safle *m;* sefyllfa *f.*
six *n.* & *a.* chwe, chwech *m.*

sixteen *n.* & *a.* un ar bymtheg, un deg chwech *m.*
sixth *n.* & *a* chweched *m.*
sixty *n.* & *a.* trigain, chwe deg *m.*
size *n.* maint *m.*
skate 1 *n.* sgêt *f.* **2** *v.* sglefrio.
skateboard bwrdd sglefrio.
sketch 1 *n.* llun, braslun *m;* sgets *f.* **2** *v.* braslunio.
ski 1 *n.* sgi *f.* **2** *v.* sgïo.
skier *n.* sgïwr *m.*
skilful *a.* medrus.
skill *n.* sgil *m,* crefft *f.*
skim *v.* tynnu, codi (hufen).
skimmed milk *n.* llaeth glas *m.*
skin 1 *n.* croen *m.* **2** *v.* blingo.
skip *v.* sgipio.
skirt *n.* sgert, sgyrt *f.*
sky *n.* wybren, awyr, ffurfafen, nen *f.*
skylark *n.* ehedydd, uchedydd, hedydd *m.*
slack 1 *n.* glo mân *m.* **2** *a.* llac, diofal, esgeulus.
slacken *v.* llacio, llaesu.
slate *n.* llechen *n.*
slaughter *v.* lladd.
slaughterhouse *n.* lladd-dy *m.*
slave *n.* caethwas *m.*
slay *v.* lladd.
sleek *a.* llyfn.
sleep 1 *n.* cwsg *m.* **2** *v.* cysgu, huno.
sleeping bag sach gysgu.
sleepy *a.* cysglyd.
sleet *n.* eirlaw *m.*
sleeve *n.* llawes *f.*
slender *a.* main, tenau.
slice *n.* tafell, sleisen. **slice of bread and butter** tafell o fara menyn; **slice of bacon** sleisen o gig moch.
slide 1 *n.* llithren *f.* **2** *v.* llithro, sglefrio.
slim *a.* main.
slip 1 *n.* llithriad *m.* **2** *v.* llithro dros.
slipper *n.* sliper *f.*
slippery *a.* llithrig, slic.
slipshod *a.* anniben.
slovenly *a.* anniben.
slope *n.* rhiw *f,* tyle, llethr *m.*
slow 1 *a.* araf. **2** *v.* arafu.
slug *n.* malwoden *f.* slyg *m.*
sluggard *n.* diogyn, pwdryn *m.*

sluggish *a.* diog, dioglyd.
slumber 1 *n.* cwsg *m.* **2** *v.* cysgu.
slur 1 *n.* llithriad *m.* **2** *v.* llithro dros.
sly *a.* cyfrwys.
small *a.* bach, mân, bychan *m.*
bechan *f.*
smallest *a.* lleiaf; *see* **bach.**
smallholder *n.* tyddynnwr *m.*
smallholding *n.* tyddyn *m.*
smash *v.* malu.
smell 1 *n.* arogl *m,* aroglau *pl,* gwynt
m. **2** *v.* arogli, clywed arogl, gwynto.
smile 1 *n.* gwên *f.* **2** *v.* gwenu.
smith *n.* gof *m.* **smithy** gefail.
smoke 1 *n.* mwg *m.* **2** *v.* mygu,
ysmygu.
smoky *a.* myglyd.
smooth *a.* llyfn; esmwyth.
smother *v.* mogi, mygu.
snack *n.* byrbryd *m.*
snag *n.* rhwystr.
snail *n.* malwoden *f.*
snake *n.* neidr *f.*
snarl *v.* chwyrnu.
sneeze *v.* tisian.
snobs *n.pl.* crachach *m.*
snore *v.* chwyrnu.
snout *n.* trwyn *m.*
snow *n.* eira *m.* **snowball** pelen eira;
snowdrift lluwch, lluwchfa, lluchfa;
snowflake pluen eira.
Snowdon *n.* Yr Wyddfa *f.*
Snowdonia *n.* Eryri *f.*
snowdrop *n.* eirlys, tlws yr eira, lili
wen fach *m.*
snub *n.* sen *f.*
so *ad.* & *c.* fel, felly, mor.
soap *n.* sebon *m.* **soap powder**
powdr golchi.
soccer *n.* pêl-droed *f.*
socialism *n.* sosialaeth *f.*
socialist 1 *n.* sosialydd *m.*
2 *a.* sosialaidd.
society *n.* cymdeithas *f.*
sociology *n.* cymdeithaseg *f.*
sock *n.* hosan *f.*
soft *a.* meddal. **soft drinks** diodydd
ysgafn.
soften *v.* meddalu.
software *n.* meddalwedd *f.*
soil 1 *n.* pridd *m;* daear *f.*

2 *v.* trochi, sarnu.
soldier *n.* milwr *m.*
sole 1 *n.* gwadn *m.* **2** *a.* unig, unigol,
un.
solemn *a.* difrifol, dwys.
solicitor *n.* cyfreithiwr *m.*
solo 1 *n.* unawd *m.* **2** *a.* unigol.
soloist *n.* unawdwr, unawdydd *m.*
solve *v.* datrys, datod.
some 1 *a.* rhyw, rhai, peth, ychydig.
2 *pn.* rhai, rhywrai, rhywfaint. **3** *ad.*
rhyw, tua, ynghylch.
somebody *n.* & *pn.* rhywun *m.*
someone *n.* & *pn.* rhywun *m.*
Somerset *n.* Gwlad yr Haf *f.*
something *n.* rhywbeth *m.*
sometime *ad.* rhywbryd, rhywdro,
gynt.
sometimes *ad.* weithiau, ambell
waith, ar brydiau.
somewhat *ad.* go, lled, braidd.
somewhere *ad.* rhywle.
son *n.* mab *m.*
son-in-law *n.* mab-yng-nghyfraith *m.*
soon *ad.* yn fuan, ar fyr o dro.
sooner *ad.* yn gynt.
soot *n.* huddygl *m.*
sore *a.* blin, tost.
sorrow 1 *n.* gofid, tristwch, galar *m.*
2 *v.* gofidio, hiraethu.
sorrowful *a.* trist.
sorry *a.* blin, drwg gan, edifar, trist.
sort 1 *n.* math, modd, dosbarth *m.*
2 *v.* dosbarthu, trefnu.
soul *n.* enaid *m.*
sound 1 *n.* sain *f,* sŵn *m.* **2** *a.* iach;
cyfan. **3** *v.* swnio, seinio.
soup *n.* cawl *m.*
sour 1 *a.* sur. **2** *v.* suro.
source *n.* ffynhonnell *f,* tarddiad *m.*
south 1 *n.* & *a.* de *mf,* deau *m;*
South Wales De Cymru. **2** *ad.*
tua'r de.
southern *a.* deheuol.
sow *n.* hwch *f.*
sow *v.* hau.
sower *n.* heuwr *m.*
space *n.* gofod, gwagle, bwlch *m.*
spaceman *n.* gofodwr *m.*
spaceship *n.* llong ofod *f.*
spade *n.* pâl, rhaw *f.*

Spain *n.* Sbaen *f.*
Spanish 1 *n.* Sbaeneg *f. (iaith).*
2 *a.* Sbaenaidd.
spare 1 *a.* sbâr. **2** *v.* arbed.
spark *n.* gwreichionen *f.*
speak *v.* llefaru, siarad.
speaker *n.* llefarwr, llefarydd,
siaradwr *m.*
special *a.* arbennig, neilltuol.
species *n.* math *m.*
specified *a.* nodedig.
specify *v.* enwi.
spectacle *n.* golygfa *f.*
spectacles *n.* sbectol *pl.*
speech *n.* araith *f;* llafar *m,*
ymadrodd *m.*
speechless *a.* mud.
speed *n.* cyflymder *m.*
speedy *a.* buan, cyflym.
spell 1 *n.* egwyl, hoe, sbel *f;* hud,
swyn *m.* **2** *v.* cael hoe; sillafu. **to
cast a spell** swyno.
spend *v.* gwario, hala *(arian);* treulio
(amser).
spiced *a.* llysieuol.
spider *n.* corryn, pryf copyn *m.*
spill *v.* colli.
spine *n.* asgwrn cefn *m.*
spirit *n.* ysbryd *m.*
spirited *a.* ysbrydol, nwyfus.
spiritual *a.* ysbrydol.
spiritualise *v.* ysbrydoli.
spit *n.* & *v.* poeri *m.*
spittle *n.* poer, poeri *m.*
splash *v.* tasgu.
splendid *a.* rhagorol, ardderchog,
penigamp, campus, gwych.
splendour *n.* ysblander *m.*
split 1 *n.* cwmni, ffyrm *m.*
2 *a.* cadarn, cryf. **3** *v.* nerthu, cryfhau.
spokesman *n.* llefarwr, llefarydd *m.*
spoon 1 *n.* llwy *f.* **2** *v.* llwyo.
spoonful *n.* llwyaid *f.*
sport *n.* sbort *f.* chwarae *m,* hwyl *f.*
sports *n.* mabolgampau *pl,*
chwaraeon.
spot 1 *n.* man *mf,* lle, llecyn, sbot,
sbotyn, smotyn *m.* **2** *v.* adnabod;
smotio.
spread *v.* lledu.
spring 1 *n.* ffynnon, ffynhonnell;

sbring; gwanwyn; neidio *f.*
2 *v.* tarddu; neidio.
sprout *n.* eginyn *m,* egin *pl.*
Brussels sprouts ysgewyll Brwsel.
spur *n.* ysbardun; clogwyn *m.*
sputnik *n.* lloeren *f.*
spy 1 *n.* ysbïwr *m.* **2** *v.* ysbïo.
square *n.* sgwâr *f.*
squash 1 *n.* sboncen *f.* **2** *v.* gwasgu.
squirrel *n.* gwiwer *f.*
stable 1 *n.* stabl *f.* **2** *a.* sefydlog,
diogel.
staff *n.* ffon; staff *f.*
stag *n.* hydd *f.*
stage 1 *n.* llwyfan *m;* lefel *f.*
2 *v.* llwyfannu.
stair *n.* gris *m,* staer *f.*
stall *n.* stondin *f;* côr *m.*
stamp 1 *n.* stamp *m.* **2** *v.* stampio.
stand 1 *n.* stondin *f.* **2** *v.* sefyll.
standard 1 *n.* safon; baner *f.*
2 *a.* safonol.
standpoint *n.* safbwynt *m.*
stanza *n.* pennill *m.*
star 1 *n.* seren *f.* **2** *v.* serennu.
starlight *n.* golau'r sêr.
starling *n.* drudwy *m.*
starry *a.* serennog.
start *n.* & *v.* cychwyn, dechrau *m.*
starve *v.* llwgu.
state 1 *n.* cyflwr *m,* ffurf; talaith *f.*
2 *v.* mynegi, dweud.
statesman *n.* gwleidydd *m.*
station *n.* gorsaf *f.* safle *m,* sefyllfa *f.*
railway station gorsaf reilffordd.
stationary *a.* sefydlog.
stationer *n.* gwerthwr papurau *m.*
stationery *n.* papur ysgrifennu *m.*
statistics *n.pl.* ystadegau.
statue *n.* cerflun *m,* delw *f.*
statute *n.* deddf, cyfraith, act *f.*
stay 1 *n.* arhosiad *m.* **2** *v.* aros, oedi,
sefyll.
steal *v.* lladrata, dwyn.
steel *n.* dur *m.*
steep *a.* serth.
steer *v.* llywio; cyfeirio.
stench *n.* drewdod, drewi *m.*
step 1 *n.* cam, gris **2** *v.* camu.
step- *px.* llys-.
stepdaughter *n.* llysferch *f.*

stepfather *n.* llystad *m.*
stepmother *n.* llysfam *f.*
stepsister *n.* llyschwaer *f.*
stepson *n.* llysfab *f.*
steward 1 *n.* stiward *m.* 2 *v.* stiwardio.
stick 1 *n.* ffon, gwialen *f,* pren *m.*
  2 *v.* glynu.
stiff *a.* syth.
stiffen *v.* sythu.
still 1 *a.* llonydd, tawel. 2 *ad.* eto, er
  hynny; byth.
stillness *n.* tawelwch, heddwch,
  llonyddwch *m.*
sting 1 *n.* pigiad *m.* 2 *v.* pigo.
stink 1 *n.* drewdod, drewi *m.*
  2 *v.* drewi.
stitch 1 *n.* pwyth *m;* 2 *v.* pwytho,
  gwnïo.
stocking *n.* hosan *f.*
stoke *v.* tanio, gofalu am dân.
stomach 1 *n.* stumog *f,* bol *m.*
  2 *v.* stumogi.
stone *n.* carreg *f.*
stool *n.* stôl *f.*
stoop *v.* plygu, ymostwng.
stop 1 atalfa *f,* stop *m.* **full stop**
  atalnod. 2 *v.* atal; stopio; cau; aros,
  sefyll; peidio (â).
storage *n.* stôr *m,* storfa *f.*
store 1 *n.* stôr *m,* storfa *f.* 2 *v.* storio.
storehouse *n.* stordy *m.*
storm *a.* storm, tymestl *f.*
stormy *a.* stormus, tymhestlog.
story *n.* stori *f,* hanes, hanesyn *m,*
  chwedl *f.*
stove *n.* ffwrn, stof *f.*
straight *a.* syth, union.
straighten *v.* sythu, unioni.
straightway *ad.* yn y man, yn syth.
strange *a.* dieithr, rhyfedd,
  rhyfeddol, od, estron.
stranger *n.* dieithryn, estron *m.*
strangle *v.* tagu.
straw *n.* gwelltyn; gwellt *m.*
strawberry *n.* mefusen *f.*
stream 1 *n.* ffrwd *f,* llif *m,* nant *f.*
  2 *v.* llifo.
streamer *n.* ruban *m,* baner *f.*
street *n.* stryd, heol, hewl, ffordd *f.*
strength *n.* nerth, grym *m.*
stretch *v.* estyn, ymestyn.

strict *a.* cyfyng, llym, manwl.
stride 1 *n.* cam *m.* 2 *v.* camu.
strife *n.* ymryson *m.*
strike 1 *n.* streic *f.* 2 *v.* streicio; taro.
striker *n.* streiciwr *m.*
strip *n.* llain *f.* **landing strip,**
  airstrip llain lanio.
string *n.* cordyn, llinyn; tant *m.*
strive *v.* ymdrechu.
strong *a.* cryf, grymus.
structure 1 *n.* adeilad; strwythur *m.*
  2 *v.* strwythuro.
struggle 1 *n.* ymdrech *f.*
  2 *v.* ymdrechu.
student *n.* myfyriwr *m.*
study *v.* myfyrio, astudio.
stump *n.* bôn *m.*
stunning *a.* syfrdanol.
stupefying *a.* syfrdanol.
stupid *a.* twp, dwl, hurt. **stupid**
  person twpsyn, hurtyn.
sty *n.* twlc *m.* **pigsty** twlc mochyn.
stye *n.* llefelyn, llyfelyn *m,*
  llefrithen *f.*
subconscious 1 *n.* isymwybod *m.*
  2 *a.* isymwybodol.
submarine 1 *n.* llong danfor *f.*
  2 *a.* tanfor, tanforol.
submit *v.* ymostwng; anfon; cyflwyno.
subordinate *a.* israddol.
substance *n.* sylwedd *m.*
substantial *a.* sylweddol.
substantiate *v.* profi.
substitute *n.* dirprwy, un yn lle
  arall *m.*
subterranean *a.* tanddaear,
  tanddaearol.
suburb *n.* maestref *f.*
subway *n.* isffordd *f,* tanlwybr *m.*
succeed *v.* llwyddo; dilyn, canlyn.
success *n.* llwydd, llwyddiant *m.*
successful *a.* llwyddiannus.
succour *n.* ymgeledd, swcwr *m.*
such *a.* y fath, cyfryw.
suck *v.* sugno.
sudden *a.* sydyn.
sue *v.* erlyn.
suffer *v.* dioddef, caniatáu, goddef.
suffering *n.* dioddef *m,* poen *mf.*
sufficient 1 *n.* digon *m.* 2 *a.* digon,
  digonol.

sufficiently *ad.* digon.
suffocate *v.* mogi, mygu, tagu.
sugar 1 *n.* siwgr *m.* 2 *v.* siwgro.
suggest *v.* awgrymu.
suggestion *n.* awgrym, awgrymiad *m.*
suicide *n.* hunanladdiad *m.*
suitable *a.* addas, priodol.
suite *n.* cyfres *f.*
sulk *v.* pwdu.
sultry *a.* clòs, trymaidd.
sum 1 *n.* swm *m.* 2 *v.* crynhoi.
summarise *v.* crynhoi.
summary *n.* crynodeb *mf.*
summer *n.* haf *m.* **midsummer** canol haf; **a summer's day** hafddydd; **summer dwelling** hafdy, hafod; tŷ haf.
summery *a.* hafaidd.
summit *n.* brig, pen *m,* ban *mf,* copa *m.*
summon *v.* galw, gwysio.
summons *n.* gwŷs *f.*
sumptuous *a.* moethus.
sun *n.* haul *m.*
sunbathe *v.* torheulo.
sunburn *n.* llosg haul *m.*
Sunday *n.* dydd Sul *m.*
sunflower *n.* blodyn yr haul *m.*
sunglasses *n.* sbectol haul *f.*
sunny *a.* heulog.
sunrise *n.* codiad haul *m.*
sunset *n.* machlud haul *m.*
sunshine *n.* heulwen *f.*
superb *a.* ardderchog, rhagorol.
superior *a.* uwch, gwell.
supermarket *n.* archfarchnad *f.*
supernatural *a.* goruwchnaturiol.
superstition *n.* ofergoel, ofergoeledd, ofergoeliaeth *f.*
superstitious *a.* ofergoelus.
supper *n.* swper *m.* **the Last Supper** y Swper Olaf.
supple *a.* ystwyth, hyblyg.
supplement 1 *n.* atodiad *m.* 2 *v.* ychwanegu.
supplementary *a.* atodol, ychwanegol.
support *v.* cynnal, cefnogi.
suppose *v.* tybied, tybio.
supreme *a.* goruchaf, prif, pennaf.

sure *a.* sicr, siŵr.
suretyship *n.* mechnïaeth *f.*
surface *n.* wyneb, arwyneb, arwynebedd.
surfeit 1 *n.* syrffed *m.* 2 *v.* syrffedu.
surgeon *n.* llawfeddyg *m.*
surgery *n.* llawfeddygaeth, llawdriniaeth; meddygfa *f.*
surgical *a.* llawfeddygol.
surname 1 *n.* cyfenw *m.* 2 *v.* cyfenwi.
surpass *v.* rhagori ar, trechu.
surprise 1 *n.* rhyfeddod, syndod *m.* 2 *v.* synnu.
surprising *a.* rhyfedd, rhyfeddol, syn.
surround *v.* amgylchynu.
suspect *v.* amau.
suspend *v.* crogi; atal.
suspension bridge *n.* pont grog *f.*
swallow 1 *n.* llwnc *m;* gwennol *f.* 2 *v.* llyncu.
swamp 1 *n.* siglen, cors *f.* 2 *v.* gorlifo.
swan *n.* alarch *m.*
swarm 1 *n.* haid, torf *f.* 2 *v.* heidio, tyrru.
swathe 1 *n.* ystod *f.* 2 *v.* rhwymo.
sway *v.* siglo.
swear *v.* tyngu, rhegi.
sweat 1 *n.* chwys *m.* 2 *v.* chwysu.
swede *n.* erfinen, sweden, meipen *f.*
Swede *n.* Swediad *m.*
Sweden *n.* Sweden *f.*
Swedish *a.* Swedaidd.
sweep 1 *n.* ysgubwr, sgubwr *f.* 2 *v.* ysgubo, sgubo, brwsio, brwshio.
sweet 1 *n.* losinen, losen *f.* 2 *a.* melys.
sweetheart *n.* cariad *mf.*
sweets *n.* losin *pl.*
swell *v.* chwyddo.
swerve *v.* osgoi, gwyro, troi.
swift 1 *n.* gwennol ddu *f.* 2 *a.* buan, cyflym.
swiftness *n.* cyflymder *m.*
swim 1 *n.* nofiad *m.* 2 *v.* nofio.
swimmer *n.* nofiwr *m.*
swimming *n.* nofio *m.*
swimming pool *n.* pwll nofio *m.*
swimsuit *n.* gwisg nofio *f.*

swing 1 *n.* siglen *f.* **2** *v.* siglo.
switch *n.* troswr *f.* *(trydan)*, swits *mf.*
Switzerland *n.* Y Swistir *f.*
swoon *v.* llewygu.
syllable *n.* sillaf *f.*
syllabus *n.* maes llafur *m.*

sympathy *n.* cydymdeimlad *m.*
symptom *n.* arwydd *m.*
synonym *n.* cyfystyr *m.*
synonymous *a.* cyfystyr (â).
system *a.* cyfundrefn; trefn, system *f.*

tape-recorder *n.* recordydd tâp *m.*
tapering *a.* pigfain.
target *n.* targed, nod *m.*
tart *n.* tarten, pastai *f.* **apple tart** pastai afalau; **jam tart** pastai jam.
task *n.* tasg *m.*
taste **1** *n.* blas *m.* **2** *v.* blasu, clywed, profi.
tasty *a.* blasus.
tavern *n.* tafarn *mf,* tŷ tafarn *m.*
tax **1** *n.* treth *f.* **Income tax** Treth Incwm; **Value Added Tax** Treth Ar Werth. **2** *v.* trethu.
taxi *n.* tacsi *m.*
tea *n.* te *m.* **tea-bags** cydau te; **teacup** cwpan te, dysgl de; **tea-leaves** dail te.
teach *v.* dysgu.
teacher *n.* athro *m;* athrawes *f.*
team *n.* tîm *m.*
tea-party *n.* téparti *m.*
teapot *n.* tebot *m.*
tear *n.* deigryn *m.*
tear **1** *n.* rhwyg *m.* **2** *v.* rhwygo.
tease *v.* poeni.
teaspoon *n.* llwy de *f.*
teaspoonful *n.* llond llwy de *m.*
technical *a.* technegol.
technician *n.* technegwr *m.*
technique *n.* techneg *m.*
technology *n.* technoleg *f.*
teddy-bear *n.* tedi *m.*
teenager *n.* un yn yr arddegau *mf.*
teens *n.pl.* arddegau.
teetotaller *n.* llwyrymwrthodwr *m.*
telecast *n.* telediad *m.*
telephone **1** *n.* teleffon, ffôn *m.* **telephone call** galwad ffôn. **2** *v.* teleffonio, ffonio.
television *n.* teledu *m.*
tell *v.* dweud (wrth), mynegi. **to tell the truth** dweud y gwir.
temper *n.* tymer, natur *m.*
temperature *n.* tymheredd *m.*
tempest *n.* tymestl *f.*
tempestuous *a.* tymhestlog.
temple *n.* teml; arlais *f.*
ten *n.* & *a.* deg, deng *m.*
tendency *n.* tueddiad *m.*
tender *a.* tyner, mwyn, meddal, tirion.

tabernacle *n.* tabernacl *m,* pabell *f.*
table *n.* bord *f,* bwrdd; tabl *m;* taflen *f.* **tableful** bordaid, byrddaid.
tablecloth *n.* lliain bord, lliain bwrdd *m.*
tablespoon *n.* llwy fawr, llwy fwrdd *f.*
tablet *n.* tabled *m.*
tackle **1** *n.* offer *pl,* gêr, tacl *m.* **2** *v.* taclo.
tackler *n.* taclwr *m.*
tail *n.* cynffon *f.*
tailback *n.* tagfa *f.*
tailor *n.* teiliwr *m.*
tailoress *n.* teilwres *f.*
take *v.* cymryd, cael, dwyn, dal.
take hold *v.* cydio.
tale *n.* chwedl *f,* hanes, hanesyn *m,* stori *f.*
talent **1** *n.* talent, dawn *f.* **2** *a.* talentog, dawnus.
talk **1** *n.* sgwrs *f,* siarad *m.* sôn *mf.* **2** *v.* sgwrsio, siarad, sôn.
talker *n.* siaradwr *m.*
tall *a.* tal, uchel.
tallow *a.* gwêr *m.*
talon *n.* ewin *mf,* crafanc *f.*
tame **1** *n.* dof. **2** *v.* dofi.
tang *n.* tafod *m.*
tank *n.* tanc *m.*
tanker *n.* tancer *m;* llong olew *f.*
tap **1** *n.* tap *m.* **2** *v.* taro, tapio.
tape *n.* tâp, incil *m.*
tape measure *n.* tâp mesur *m.*

tenderness *n.* tynerwch *m.*
tendon *n.* gewyn, tendon *m.*
tennis *n.* tenis *m.* **tennis ball** pêl denis; **tennis court** cwrt tenis; **tennis racket** raced denis.
tense 1 *n.* amser *m.* *(gramadeg).* **2** *v.* tyn, tynn.
tent *n.* pabell *f.*
tenth *n.* & *a.* degfed *m.*
term 1 *n.* tymor; term; amod *m.* **2** *v.* enwi, galw.
terminus *n.* terfyn *m.*
terrace *n.* rhes dai *f,* teras *m.*
terrible *a.* dychrynllyd, ofnadwy, erchyll.
terrifying *a.* dychrynllyd.
territory *n.* tir *m.*
terror *n.* braw, ofn *m.*
terrorism *n.* terfysgaeth *f.*
terrorist *n.* terfysgwr *m.*
tertiary *a.* trydyddol. **tertiary college** coleg trydyddol.
test rhagbrawf; **reading test** prawf darllen; **spelling test** prawf sillafu.
testament *n.* testament *m.* **New Testament** Testament Newydd.
testify *v.* tystio.
testimony *n.* tystiolaeth *f.*
text *n.* testun *m.* **text-book** gwerslyfr.
than *c.* na, nag.
thank *v.* diolch. **Thanks** Diolch! **Thanks very much** Diolch yn fawr.
thankful *a.* diolchgar.
thankfulness *n.* diolchgarwch *m.*
thankless *a.* diddiolch.
thanksgiving *n.* diolchgarwch *m.* **Thanksgiving Service** Gwasanaeth Diolchgarwch.
that 1 *a.* hwnnw, honno, hynny, yna, acw. **2** *pn.* hwn, hon, yna, hwn acw, hon acw, hyna, dacw; a, y, yr. **3** *c.* mai, taw, fel y, fel yr.
thaw *v.* toddi, meddalu, meirioli, dadmer, dadlaith.
the *def. art.* y, yr, 'r.
theatre *n.* theatre *f.*
thee *pn.* ti, tydi, tithau.
theft *n.* lladrad *m.*
their *pn.* eu.
theirs *pn.* eiddynt, yr eiddynt.

them *pn.* hwy, hwynt, hwythau, nhw.
themselves *pn.* eu hunain.
then 1 *ad.* wedyn, yna, y pryd hwnnw. **2** *c.* yna, ynte, ynteu.
thereafter *ad.* wedyn.
thereat *ad.* ar hynny, yna.
thereby *ad.* trwy hynny.
therefore *c.* am hynny, gan hynny, felly.
therefrom *ad.* oddi yno.
therein *ad.* yno, ynddo, yn hynny.
thereupon *ad.* ar hynny.
therewith *ad.* gyda hynny.
thermometer *n.* thermomedr *f.*
these *pn.* & *a.* y rhai hyn, y rhain.
they *pn.* hwy, hwynt, hwythau, nhw.
thick *a.* tew, trwchus.
thief *n.* lleidr *m.*
thieve *v.* lladrata, dwyn, dwgyd.
thigh *n.* clun, morddwyd *f.*
thin *a.* main, tenau, cul.
thing *n.* peth, gwrthrych *m.*
think *v.* meddwl, tybied, tybio.
third *n.* & *a.* trydydd *m;* trydedd *f.*
thirst 1 *n.* syched *m.* **2** *v.* sychedu.
thirsty *a.* sychedig.
thirteen *n.* & *a.* tri ar ddeg, un deg tri *m.*
thirty *n.* & *a.* deg ar hugain, tri deg *m.*
this *a.* & *pn.* hwn, hon, hyn; yma. **this minute** y funud hon, y funud yma; **this hour, (now, at present)** yr awr hon, **this day** y dydd hwn; **this week** yr wythnos hon; **this month** y mis hwn; **this year** eleni.
thistle *n.* ysgallen *f.*
thorn *n.* draen, draenen *f;* **thorns** drain.
those 1 *pn.* hynny, y rhai hynny, y rheini, y rheiny. **2** *a.* hynny, yna.
though 1 *ad.* er, serch hynny. **2** *prp.* er, pe, cyd.
thought *n.* meddwl, syniad *m.*
thoughtful *a.* meddyglar.
thousand *n.* & *a.* mil *f.*
thread *n.* edau *f,* llinyn *m.*
three *n.* & *a.* tri *m,* tair *f.* **three times** teirgwaith.
threesome *n.* triawd *m.*

threshold *n.* trothwy *m.* rhiniog *f.*
thrill *n.* ias *f.*
thrilling *a.* iasol.
throat *n.* gwddf, gwddwg, llwnc *m.*
throne *n.* gorsedd *f.*
through 1 *ad.* trwodd. **2** *prp* drwy, trwy.
throw 1 *n.* tafliad *m.* **2** *v.* taflu.
thrush *n.* bronfraith *f.*
thrust 1 *n.* gwthiad, hwp *m.*
  2 *v.* gwthio.
thumb 1 *n.* bawd *m.* **2** *v.* bodio.
thunder 1 *n.* taran *f,* tyrfau *pl.*
  2 *v.* taranu.
thunderbolt *n.* bollt *m,* mellten, llucheden *f.*
thunderclap *n.* taran *f.*
thunderstorm *n.* storm fellt a tharanau *f.*
Thursday *n.* dydd Iau.
thus *ad.* fel hyn, felly.
thy *pn.* dy, 'th.
ticket *n.* tocyn, ticed *m.* **ticket collector** tocynnwr; **ticket office** swyddfa docynnau.
tide *n.* llanw *m:* **high-tide** penllanw; **ebb-tide** trai.
tidy 1 *a.* cryno, taclus, twt.
  2 *v.* tacluso.
tie 1 *n.* tei; clwm, cwlwm *m.*
  2 *v.* clymu, rhwymo.
tiger *n.* teigr *m.*
tight *a.* tyn, tynn; cyfyng.
tile *n.* teilsen *f.*
timber *n.* coed, pren *m.*
time *n.* adeg *f,* oed; amser, pryd *m.* **at times** ar adegau, ar brydiau; **in time** mewn pryd.
timetable *n.* amserlen *f.*
timid *a.* llwfr, ofnus.
tin *n.* tun; alcam *m.* **tin of paint** tun o baent; **tin of peas** tun o bys.
tinge *n.* naws, gwawr *f.*
tinted *a.* lliwiog.
tiny *a.* bach, bychan, bitw, mân.
tip *n.* tip *m,* tomen *f;* cyngor *m;* gwobr *f;* cil-dwrn *m.* **rubbish tip** tomen ysbwriel, tip ysbwriel.
tire *v.* blino.
tired *a.* blinedig, blin.
title *n.* teitl, enw *m;* hawl *f.* **title-**

page wyneb ddalen.
to *prp.* at, hyd at, i, er mwyn, tua, wrth, yn.
toad *n.* llyffant *m.*
toadstools *n.* madarch, caws llyffant, bwyd y boda *pl.*
toast 1 *n.* tost; llwncdestun *m.*
  2 *v.* tostio; cynnig llwncdestun.
today *ad.* heddiw.
together *ad.* gyda'i gilydd, ynghyd.
toil 1 *n.* llafur *m.* **2** *v.* llafurio.
toilet *n.* toiled, tŷ-bach, lle chwech, jeriw *m.*
token *n.* arwydd; tocyn *m.*
tolerate *v.* goddef, caniatáu.
toll 1 *n.* toll, treth *f.* **2** *v.* canu cloch.
toll-gate *n.* tollborth *m,* tollglwyd *f.*
tomato *n.* tomato *m.*
tomb *n.* bedd, beddrod *m.*
tomcat *n.* cwrcath, gwrcath, cwrcyn, gwrcyn *m.*
tomorrow *ad.* fory, yfory.
ton *n.* tunnell *f.* **tonne** tunnell fetrig.
tone *n.* tôn; naws *f.*
tongue *n.* tafod *m;* tafodiaith, iaith *f.*
tonight *ad.* heno.
too *ad.* hefyd; rhy. **too much** gormod; **too little** rhy fach; **too late** rhy hwyr.
tool *n.* arf, erfyn, offeryn *m.*
tooth *n.* dant *m.*
toothache *n.* dannoedd *f.*
toothbrush *n.* brwsh dannedd *m.*
toothpaste *n.* sebon dannedd, past dannedd *m.*
top *n.* pen, brig, copa, top *m.*
topic *n.* pwnc, testun *m.*
torch *n.* tors *m.*
torch-light *n.* golau tors *m.*
torment *v.* poeni, poenydio.
tormentor *n.* poenydiwr *m.*
torque *n.* torch *m.*
torrid *a.* cras, poeth, crasboeth.
tortoise *n.* crwban *m.*
torture *v.* poenydio.
Tory 1 *n.* Tori, Ceidwadwr *m.*
  2 *a.* Torïaidd.
total 1 *n.* cyfanswm, y cyfan *m.*
  2 *a.* cyfan, hollol, llwyr.
tottering *a.* sigledig, simsan.
touch 1 *n.* teimlad *m.* **2** *v.* cyffwrdd (â), teimlo.

touch judge *n.* ystlyswr *m.*
touchline *n.* llinell ystlys *f.*
tour **1** *n.* taith *f*, tro *m.* **2** *v.* teithio.
tourism *n.* twristiaeth *f.*
tourist **1** *n.* teithiwr, ymwelwr, ymwelydd *m.* **2** *a.* twristaidd.
Tourist Board Bwrdd Croeso.
towards *prp.* tua, at, tuag at.
towel *n.* lliain, tywel *m.*
tower *n.* tŵr *m.*
town *n.* tref, tre *f.* **Carmarthen Town** Tre Caerfyrddin; **town centre** canol y dre; **town council** cyngor y dre; **town hall** neuadd y dre.
toy **1** *n.* tegan *m.* **2** *v.* chwarae.
trace *v.* olrhain.
track **1** *n.* llwybr, ôl, trac *m.* **2** *v.* olrhain.
tracksuit *n.* tracwisg *f.*
trade *n.* masnach; crefft *f.*
tradesman *n.* masnachwr, siopwr; crefftwr.
tradition *n.* traddodiad *m.*
traditional *a.* traddodiadol.
traffic *n.* trafnidiaeth, traffig *f.* **traffic jam** tagfa.
trail **1** *n.* trywydd *m.* **2** *v.* llusgo.
train **1** *n.* trên *m.* **2** *v.* hyfforddi; ymarfer.
trainer *n.* hyfforddwr.
training *n.* hyfforddiant *m*, ymarfer *f.* **in-service training** hyfforddiant mewn swydd.
tramp **1** *n.* crwydryn *m.* **2** *v.* crwydro.
trample *v.* sathru, sarnu.
tranquillity *n.* hedd, heddwch, tawelwch, llonyddwch *m.*
tranquilliser *n.* tawelyn *m.*
transact *v.* trafod, trin, gwneud.
transfer *v.* trosglwyddo.
transfusion *n.* trallwysiad *m.* **blood transfusion** trallwysiad gwaed.
transgress *v.* troseddu.
transgression *n.* trosedd *f.*
transgressor *n.* troseddwr *m.*
translate *v.* cyfieithu, trosi.
translation *n.* cyfieithiad, trosiad *m.*
translator *n.* cyfieithydd *m.*
transparent *a.* tryloyw.

transplant *v.* trawsblannu.
trap **1** *n.* trap *m.* **2** *v.* dal, trapio.
trash *n.* sothach, ysbwriel *m.*
travel *v.* teithio.
traveller *n.* teithiwr *m.*
travelling *a.* teithiol.
treachery *n.* brad, twyll *m.*
treasure **1** *n.* trysor *m.* **2** *v.* trysori.
treasurer *n.* trysorydd *m.*
treasury *n.* trysorfa *f.* **the Treasury** y Trysorlys.
treat **1** *n.* gwledd *m.* **2** *v.* trin.
treatise *n.* traethawd *m.*
tree *n.* coeden *f*, pren *m.*
tremendous *a.* dychrynllyd, ofnadwy, anferth.
trench *n.* ffos *f.*
triad *n.* tri *m.*
triads *n.* trioedd *pl.*
trial *n.* prawf; treial *m.* **sheepdog trials** treialon cŵn defaid.
triangle *n.* triongl *mf.*
triangular *a.* trionglog.
tribe *n.* llwyth, tylwyth *m.*
tribulation *n.* trallod *m.*
trick *n.* tric *m.*
trickery *n.* twyll *m.*
tricky *a.* anodd.
trim *v.* tacluso, trwsio.
trinity *n.* trindod *f.*
trio *n.* triawd *m.*
triplet *n.* tripled *m*; triban *f.*
trouble **1** *n.* gofid *m*, helynt *f*, picil, picl, trafferth, trallod, trwbl *m.* **2** *v.* blino, gofidio, trafferthu.
troublesome *a.* trafferthus.
trousers *n.* trowsus, trwser *pl.*
trowel *n.* trywel *m.*
trudge *v.* troedio, cerdded.
true *a.* gwir, cywir, iawn.
truly *ad.* yn wir, yn gywir. **Yours truly** Yr eiddoch yn gywir.
trunk *n.* bôn *m*; cist *f*; trwnc *m.*
trust **1** *n.* ymddiriedaeth, ymddiriedolaeth *f.* **2** *v.* ymddiried (yn).
trustee *n.* ymddiriedolwr *m.*
trusteeship *n.* ymddiriedolaeth *f.*
trusty *a.* ffyddlon, cywir.
truth *n.* gwirionedd, gwir, iawn *m.*
try **1** *n.* cais *(mewn rygbi)*, cynnig *m.*

converted try trosgais. **2** *v.* ceisio, cynnig, profi.
T-shirt *n.* crys-T *m.*
Tuesday *n.* dydd Mawrth *m.*
tug 1 *n.* plwc; tynfa *m.* **2** *v.* llusgo, tynnu.
tuition *n.* addysg *f,* hyfforddiant *m.*
tumble 1 *n.* cwymp *m.* **2** *v.* cwympo.
tumbler *n.* gwydryn *m.*
tummy *n.* bola *m.*
tumult *n.* twrw, mwstwr, terfysg, cythrwfl *m.*
tune *n.* alaw, tôn *f.*
tunnel *n.* twnnel *m.*
turkey *n.* twrci *m.*
Turkey *n.* Twrci *f.*
Turkish *a.* Twrcaidd.
turmoil *n.* berw, trafferth *m.*
turn 1 *n.* tro *m.* **2** *v.* troi.
turning *n.* tro *m.* tröedigaeth *m.*
turning-point *n.* trobwynt *m.*
turnip *n.* erfinen, meipen *f.*

tutor 1 *n.* athro, tiwtor, hyfforddwr *m.*
2 *v.* dysgu, hyfforddi.
twelfth *n. & a.* deuddegfed *m.*
twelve *n. & a.* deuddeg, un deg dau *m.*
twentieth *n. & a.* ugeinfed *m.*
twenty *n. & a.* ugain, dau ddeg *m.*
twice *ad.* dwywaith.
twig *n.* brigyn, brig *m.*
twilight *n.* cyfnos, cyfddydd *m.*
twin 1 *n.* gefell *m.* gefeilles *f.*
2 *v.* gefeillio.
twine *n.* llinyn *m.*
twist 1 *n.* tro *m.* **2** *v.* troi.
two *n. & a.* dau *m:* dwy *f;* pâr *m.* **in twos, two by two** yn ddeuoedd, yn ddau a dau.
typescript *n.* teipysgrif *f.*
typewriter *n.* teipiadur *m.*
typhoon *n.* corwynt *m.*
typist *n.* teipydd *m.*
tyre *n.* teiar *m.*

ubiquitous *a.* ym mhob man.
ugliness *n.* hagrwch *m.*
ugly *a.* hagr, hyll, salw.
ultra 1 *a.* eithafol. **2** *px.* gor-, dros ben, tu hwnt i.
ultra-modern *a.* tra modern, modern iawn.
umbrella *n.* ambarél, ymbarél, ymbrelo *m.*
umpire 1 *n.* dyfarnwr, canolwr *m.* **2** *v.* dyfarnu.
unaccompanied *a.* heb gwmni; heb gyfeiliant.
unaccustomed *a.* anghyfarwydd.
unacquainted *a.* anghyfarwydd.
unanimous *a.* unfryd, unfrydol, unfarn.
unanimously *ad.* yn ynfryd.
unceasing *a.* di-baid, diddiwedd.
uncertain *a.* ansicr.
uncivil *a.* anfoesgar.
unclad *a.* noeth.
uncle *n.* ewyrth, ewythr *m.*
unclean *a.* aflan, brwnt, budr.
uncommon *a.* anghyffredin.
uncover *v.* datguddio.
uncultivated *a.* heb ei drin.
under 1 *prp.* dan, tan, o dan, is, islaw. **2** *ad.* danodd, oddi tanodd. **3** *px.* is-, tan-.
underclothing *n.* dillad isaf *m.*
undercurrent *n.* islif *m.*
undergo *v.* dioddef.

underground *a.* tanddaear, tanddaearol.
underline *v.* tanlinellu, pwysleisio.
undermine *v.* tanseilio.
underneath 1 *prp.* dan, tan, oddi tan. **2** *ad.* oddi tanodd.
underpass *n.* tanffordd *f.*
underskirt *n.* sgert isaf, sgyrt isaf, pais *f.*
understand *v.* deall.
understanding *n.* deall, dealltwriaeth.
undertake *v.* ymgymryd (â).
undertake *n.* trefnydd angladdau *m.*
undo *v.* datod; difetha.
undress *v.* dadwisgo.
unearned *a.* heb ei ennill.
uneasy *a.* anesmwyth, pryderus.
unemployed 1 *n.* y diwaith *m.* **2** *a.* di-waith, segur.
unemployment *n.* diweithdra *m;*
unemployment benefit budd-dâl diwaith.
unending *a.* diddiwedd, diderfyn.
unfair *a.* annheg.
unfaithful *a,* anffyddlon.
unfamiliar *a.* anghyfarwydd, dieithr.
unfasten *v.* datod.
unfit *a.* anaddas, anghymwys.
unfortunate *a.* anffodus.
unfortunately *ad.* yn anffodus.
unhappy *a.* anhapus, trist.
unhealthy *a.* afiach.
uniform 1 *n.* gwisg swyddogol *f.* **2** *a.* unffurf.
unimportant *a.* dibwys.
uninteresting *a.* anniddorol.
union *n.* undeb *m.*
unionist *n.* undebwr *m.*
unique *a.* unigryw.
unit *n.* uned *f;* un, rhif un; undod *m.*
Unitarian *n.* Undodwr *m.*
unite *v.* uno, cysylltu, cyfuno.
united *a.* unedig, unol. **the United Kingdom** y Deyrnas Unedig; **United States of America** Unol Daleithiau America.
unity *n.* undod *m.*
universe *n.* bydysawd, cyfanfyd, yr hollfyd *m.*
university *n.* prifysgol *f.* **University**

of **Wales** Prifysgol Cymru.
unjust *a.* anghyfiawn.
unjustly *ad.* ar gam.
unkind *a.* angharedig.
unleaded *a.* di-blwm. **unleaded petrol** petrol di-blwm.
unless *c.* oni, onid.
unlike *a.* annhebyg.
unlimited *a.* diderfyn.
unlucky *a.* anffodus, anlwcus.
unmannerly *a.* anfoesgar.
unmarried *a.* dibriod.
unnatural *a.* annaturiol.
unoccupied *a.* gwag, segur.
unopened *a.* heb ei agor.
unprepared *a.* amharod.
unravel *v.* datod, datrys.
unready *a.* amharod.
unreasonable *a.* afresymol.
unsatisfied *a.* anfodlon.
unseen *a.* anweledig.
unsightly *a.* diolwg, hyll, salw.
unsteady *a.* simsan.
unsuitable *a.* anaddas, anghymwys.
untidy *a.* anniben.
untie *v.* datod.
until *prp.* & *c.* hyd, hyd oni, nes, tan.
untrue *a.* celwyddog.
untruth *n.* celwydd, anwiredd *m.*
untruthful *a.* celwyddog.
unusual *a.* anarferol.
unwell *a.* anhwylus, afiach, claf.

unwholesome *a.* afiach.
unwilling *a.* anfodlon.
unwise *a.* annoeth, ffôl.
unworthy *a.* annheilwng.
up *ad.* & *prp.* i fyny.
uphill *ad.* i fyny.
uphold *v.* cynnal.
upon *prp.* ar, ar warthaf, ar uchaf.
upper *a.* uwch, uchaf.
uppermost *a.* & *ad.* uchaf.
upright *a.* syth, union, unionsyth; onest, cywir.
upside-down *ad.* wyneb i waered.
upstairs **1** *n.* llofft *f.* **2** *ad.* ar y llofft.
up-to-date *a.* cyfoes, hyd yn hyn.
upwards *ad.* i fyny.
urban *a.* trefol.
urge *v.* argymell.
urgency *n.* brys *m.*
us *pn.* ni, ninnau, nyni, 'n.
usage *n.* arfer *mf,* defnydd *m.*
use **1** *n.* arfer *mf,* defnydd, gwasanaeth, iws. **2** *v.* arfer, defnyddio.
useful *a.* defnyddiol.
useless *a.* diwerth.
user *n.* defnyddiwr *m.*
Usk *n.* Wysg *(river)*; Brynbuga *(town) f.*
usual *a.* arferol. **as usual** fel arfer.
utilise *v.* defnyddio.
utmost *a.* eithaf, pellaf.

V

vacancy *n.* lle gwag *m,* swydd wag *f.*
vacant *a.* gwag.
vacation *n.* gwyliau *pl.*
vaccination *n.* brechiad *m,* brech *f.*
vacuum *n.* gwagle *m.*
vain *a.* balch; ofer.
vale *n.* bro *f,* cwm, dyffryn, glyn *m.*
Vale of Glamorgan Bro
  Morgannwg.
valiant *a.* dewr.
valley *n.* cwm, dyffryn, glyn *m.*
valuable *a.* drud, gwerthfawr.
value *n* gwerth *m.* **Value Added Tax
  (VAT)** Treth Ar Werth.
van *n.* fan, men; y rheng flaenaf *f.*
vandal *n.* fandal *m.*
vandalise *v.* fandaleiddio.
vandalism *n.* fandaliaeth *f.*
vanish *v.* diflannu.
vanity *n.* gwagedd, oferedd *m.*
various *a.* amryw, gwahanol.
vary *v.* newid.
vast *a.* eang, enfawr, anferth.
veal *n.* cig llo *m.*
vegetable *n.* llysieuyn *m.*
vegetarian *n.* llysfwytäwr *m.*
  llysfwytawraig *f.*
vehicle *n.* cerbyd; cyfrwng *m.*
veil *n.* llen *f.*
velocity *n.* cyflymder *m.*
vengeance *n.* dial, dialedd *m.*
venom *n.* gwenwyn *m.*
venture 1 *n.* antur *m,* menter *f.*

2 *v.* mentro, beiddio, meiddio.
venturesome *a.* mentrus, anturus.
Venus *n.* Gwener *m.*
verb *n.* berf *f.*
verbally *ad.* mewn geiriau.
verb-noun *n.* berfenw *m.*
verdict *n.* dyfarniad, dedfryd *m.*
vermin *n.* pryfed, llygod . . . *pl.*
verse *n.* adnod *f,* pennill *m;*
  barddoniaeth *f.*
version *n.* fersiwn *m.*
versus *ad.* yn erbyn.
vertical *a.* syth, unionsyth, plwm.
very *a.* & *ad.* gwir, iawn, i'r dim.
vessel *n.* llestr; llong *m.*
vestry *n.* festri *f.*
veterinary surgeon *n.* milfeddyg *m.*
vex *v.* blino, gofidio, poeni, becso.
vexation *n.* blinder, gofid *m.*
via *prp.* trwy, ar hyd.
vicar *n.* ficer *m.*
vicarage *n.* ficerdy *m.*
vice *n.* drygioni *m;* gwasg, feis *f.*
vice- *px,* is-, rhag-.
vice-chairman *n.* is-gadeirydd *m.*
vice-president *n.* is-lywydd *m.*
victor *n.* buddugwr, y buddugol,
  enillwr, enillydd *m.*
victory *n.* buddugoliaeth *f.*
view 1 *n.* golygfa *f,* golwg *mf;* barn *f.*
  2 *v.* edrych, gweld.
viewer *n.* gwyliwr *m, (teledu).*
viewpoint *n.* safbwynt *m.*
vigil *n.* gwylnos, noswyl *f.*
vigour *n.* grym, nerth, egni, ynni.
vigorous *a.* egnïol.
vile *a.* ffiaidd, gwael, salw.
village *n.* pentref *m.*
villager *n.* pentrefwr.
vinegar *n.* finegr *m.*
viola *n.* fiola *f.*
violate *v.* treisio, troseddu.
violence *n.* trais *m.*
violent *a.* treisiol, gwyllt. **non-
  violent** di-drais.
violet 1 *n.* fioled *f.* **2** *a.* dulas.
violin *n.* ffidil *f.*
virgin *n.* morwyn, gwyryf *f.* **the
  Virgin Mary** y Forwyn Fair.
virtually *ad.* i bob pwrpas.
virtue *n.* rhinwedd *f.*

virus *n.* firws *m.*
vision *n.* gweledigaeth *f;* golwg *mf;* gweled *m.*
visit 1 *n.* ymweliad *m.* **2** *v.* ymweld (â), galw.
visitor *n.* ymwelwr, ymwelydd *m.*
vitamin *n.* fitamin *m.*
vivacious *a.* bywiog, heini.
vivid *a.* byw, clir, llachar.
vixen *n.* cadnawes, cadnöes, llwynoges *f.*
vocabulary *n.* geirfa *f.*
vocal *a.* llafar; lleisiol.
vocalist *n.* cantor *m,* cantores *f,* canwr *m.*
vocally *ad.* â'r llais.
vocation *n.* galwedigaeth *f.*
vogue *n.* ffasiwn *m,* arfer *mf.*
voice 1 *n.* llais *m,* llef *f.* **2** *v.* lleisio, mynegi.

void 1 *n.* gwagle *m.* **2** *a.* di-rym. **3** *v.* gwacáu.
volcano *n.* llosgfynydd, folcano *m.*
vole *n.* llygoden y maes *f.*
volume *n.* cyfrol *f;* cyfaint; llais, sŵn; foliwm *m.*
voluntary *a.* gwirfoddol.
volunteer 1 *n.* gwirfoddolwr *m.* **2** *v.* gwirfoddoli.
vomit *v.* chwydu.
vote 1 *n.* pleidlais *f.* **2** *v.* pleidleisio.
voter *n.* pleidleisiwr *m.*
vowel *n.* llafariad *f.*
voyage 1 *n.* mordaith *f.* **2** *v.* mordeithio, mordwyo, morio.
Bon voyage Hwyl dda! Sirwrnai dda!
vulgar *a.* cyffredin; isel, brwnt; aflednais; gwerinol.
vulgarity *n.* diffyg moes *m.*

wag *v.* ysgwyd, siglo.
wage *n.* cyflog *mf.*
waist *n.* gwasg *mf,* canol *m.*
waistcoat *n.* gwasgod *f.*
wait *v.* aros, disgwyl; gweini.
waiter *n.* gweinydd *m.*
waitress *n.* gweinyddes *f.*
wake *v.* dihuno, deffro.
Wales *n.* Cymru *f.*
walk 1 *n.* tro *m.* **2** *v.* cerdded, mynd
am dro.
walker *n.* cerddwr *m.*
walking-stick *n.* ffon *f.*
wall *n.* gwal, wal *f,* mur *m.*
wallflowers *n.* blodau mam-gu *pl.*
wallpaper *n.* papur wal *m.*
want 1 *n.* eisiau, diffyg *m.* **2** *v.* bod
mewn eisiau.
wanting *a.* yn eisiau.
war 1 *n.* rhyfel *mf.* **2** *v.* rhyfela.
warehouse *n.* storfa, stôr *f,* ystordy *m.*
warfare *n.* rhyfel *mf.*
warm 1 *n.* cynnes, gwresog, twym.
2 *v.* cynhesu, twymo.
warmth *n.* gwres, cynhesrwydd *m.*
warn *v.* rhybuddio.
warning *n.* rhybudd *m.*
warship *n.* llong ryfel *f.*
wart *n.* dafaden, dafad *f.*
was, I *v.* bues i, bûm, fues i, fûm,
roeddwn; *see* bod.
wash 1 *n.* golch, golchiad *m.*
2 *v.* golchi, ymolch, ymolchi.

washer *n.* golchydd *m. see* **washing
machine.**
washing machine *n* peiriant
golchi *m.*
washing powder *n.* powdr golchi *m.*
wash-house *n.* golchdy *m.*
wasp *n.* cacynen, picwnen *f.* **wasps'
nest** nyth cacwn.
waste 1 *n.* gwastraff *m.* **nuclear
waste** gwastraff niwclear. **2** *v.*
gwastraffu.
wasteful *a.* gwastraffus.
watch 1 *n.* wats *f.* **2** *v.* gwarchod,
gwylio.
watchful *a.* gwyliadwrus.
watchman *n.* gwyliwr *m.*
watchnight *n .* gwylnos *f.*
water *n.* dŵr *m.*
waterfall *n.* rhaeadr, sgwd *f,* pistyll *m.*
wave 1 *n.* ton *f.* **2** *v.* chwifio, codi.
wavelength *n.* tonfedd *f.*
wax 1 *n.* cwyr *m.* **2** *v.* cwyro;
cynyddu, tyfu.
way *n.* ffordd, heol, hewl *f,* llwybr *m;*
hynt *f;* arfer *fm,* modd *m.*
wayside *n.* ymyl y ffordd *mf.*
we *pn.* ni, ninnau, nyni.
weak *a.* gwan.
weaken *v.* gwanhau.
weakness *n.* gwendid *m.*
wealth *n.* cyfoeth, golud, da, modd
m.
wealthy *a.* cyfoethog, cefnog.
weapon *n.* arf, erfyn *m.* **nuclear
weapons** arfau niwclear.
wear 1 *n.* gwisg; traul *f.* **2** *v.* gwisgo;
treulio.
weariness *n.* blinder *m.*
wearisome *a.* blinedig, blin, poenus.
weary 1 *a.* blinedig, blin. **2** *v.* blino,
diflasu.
weather *n.* tywydd *m,* hin *f.* **fine
weather** tywydd teg, hindda;
tempestuous weather tywydd
mawr.
weave *v.* gwau, gweu.
web *n.* gwe *f.*
wed *v.* priodi.
wedding *n.* priodas *f.*
Wednesday *n.* dydd Mercher *m.*
weed 1 *n.* chwynnyn *m* **2** *v.* chwynnu.

weeds *n.* chwyn *pl.*
week *n.* wythnos *f.* **the first week** yr wythnos gyntaf; **the second week** yr ail wythnos; **the third week** y drydedd wythnos; **the last week** yr wythnos diwethaf; **the final week** yr wythnos olaf.
weekend *n.* penwythnos *m.*
weekly *a.* wythnosol.
weep *v.* crio, wylo, llefain.
weigh *v.* pwyso.
weight *n.* pwys, pwysau *m.*
weighty *a.* pwysig; trwm.
welcome 1 *n.* croeso *m.* **2** *v.* croesawu.
welfare *n.* lles, budd *m.*
welfare state *n.* gwladwriaeth les *f.*
well 1 *n.* ffynnon *f.* **2** *v.* iach, da, iawn. **3** *v.* llifo, cronni. **4** *ad.,* yn dda. **5** *i.* wel! **fairly well** yn lled dda; **very well** o'r gorau.
Welsh *a.* Cymraeg; Cymreig: **Welsh affairs** materion Cymreig, **Welsh books** llyfrau Cymraeg; **Welsh cakes** picau ar y maen; **Welsh office** Swyddfa Gymreig; **Welsh schools** ysgolion Cymraeg; **Welsh water** dŵr Cymru.
Welsh (language) *n.* Cymraeg *f.*
Welsh (people) *n.* Cymry *pl.*
Welshman *n.* Cymro *m.*
Welshness *n.* Cymreictod *m.*
Welshwoman *n.* Cymraes *f.*
west 1 *n.* gorllewin, gorllewinol. **West Wales** Gorllewin Cymru; **west or westerly wind** gwynt y gorllewin.
western *a.* gorllewinol.
wet 1 *n.* gwlybaniaeth *f.* **2** *a.* gwlyb. **3** *v.* gwlychu.
whale *n.* morfil *m.*
what 1 *a.* pa. **2** *pn.* pa beth. **3** *i.* beth!
whatever *pn.* beth bynnag.
wheat *n.* gwenith *m.*
wheel *n.* olwyn *f.* **front wheel** olwyn flaen; **rear wheel** olwyn gefn; **spare wheel** olwyn sbâr.
wheelbarrow *n.* berfa, whilber *f.*
wheelchair *n.* cadair olwynion *f.*
when *ad., pn & c.* pan, pa bryd.

whenever *ad.* pa bryd bynnag.
where *ad.* ym mha le; yn y lle, lle.
whereabouts *ad.* ymhle.
whereas *c.* gan, yn gymaint â.
whereby *ad.* trwy yr hyn.
wherefore *ad.* paham, am hynny.
wherein *ad.* yn yr hyn.
wherever *ad.* ble bynnag.
which 1 *rel.pn.* a; y, yr. **2** *int.pn.* pa un? p'un? **3** *a.* pa.
whichever *a. & pn.* pa un bynnag.
whilst *ad.* cyhyd, tra.
whip 1 *n.* chwip *f.* **2** *v.* chwipio.
whirlpool *n.* pwll tro, trobwll *m.*
whisper 1 *n.* sisial *m.* **2** *v.* sisial, sibrwd.
whistle 1 *n.* chwiban *m.* **2** *v.* chwiban, chwibanu.
white *a.* gwyn, gwen, can.
white-lime *n.* gwyngalch *m.*
whiten *v.* gwynnu.
whitewash 1 *n.* gwyngalch *m.* **2** *v.* gwyngalchu.
Whitsunday *n.* Sulgwyn *m.*
whittle *v.* naddu.
whiz 1 *n.* si, su *m.* **2** *v.* sio, suo.
who *pn.* a, pwy; y, yr.
whole 1 *n.* cwbl, cyfan, holl *m.* **2** *a.* cyfan, holl; iach, holliach.
wholesome *a.* iach, iachus.
wholly *ad.* yn hollol, yn gyfan gwbl, yn llwyr.
whom *rel.pn.* a; y, yr.
whose *pn.* eiddo pwy? pwy biau?
whosoever *pn.* pwy bynnag.
why *ad.* paham, pam.
wicked *a.* drwg, drygionus.
wickedness *n.* drwg, drygioni *m.*
wicket *n.* wiced; clwyd *f.* **wicket-keeper** wicedwr.
wide *a.* llydan, eang.
wide-awake *a.* effro, ar ddihun.
widely *ad.* yn eang.
widen *v.* lledu, llydanu.
widow *n.* gweddw, gwidw *f.*
widower *n.* gwidman *m.*
width *n.* lled *m.*
wife *n.* gwraig, gwraig briod, priod *f.*
wild *a.* gwyllt, ffyrnig.
wilderness *n.* anialwch, diffeithwch *m.*

wildfire *n.* tân gwyllt *m.*
will 1 *n.* ewyllys *m.* **2** *v.* mynnu.
will be, he/she/it *v.* bydd; *see* bod.
willing *a.* bodlon, parod.
willow *n.* helygen *f.*
win *v.* ennill. **to win the day** cario'r dydd.
wind *n.* gwynt *m;* anadl *mf.* **cold wind** gwynt oer; **the north wind** gwynt y gogledd.
wind *v.* troi, dirwyn.
windmill *n.* melin wynt *f.*
window *n.* ffenestr *f.* **window pane** cwarel.
windy *a.* gwyntog.
wine *n.* gwin *m.* **dry red wine** gwin coch sych; **sweet white wine** gwin gwyn melys.
wineglass *n.* gwydr gwin *m.*
wing *n.* adain, aden, asgell *f;* asgellwr *m.*
winner *n.* enillwr, enillydd, y buddugol *m.*
winning *a.* buddugol.
winnings *n.* enillion *pl.*
winter *n.* gaeaf *m.* **winter dwelling** hendref, hendre.
wintry *a.* gaeafol.
wipe *v.* sychu.
wire *n.* gwifren *f.*
wisdom *n.* doethineb *m.*
wise *a.* call, doeth. **the Wise Men** y Doethion.
wish 1 *n.* dymuniad, ewyllys *m.*
  2 *v.* dymuno.
witch *n.* gwrach *f.*
with *prp.* â, ag, gyda, gydag, efo, gan.
withdraw *v.* tynnu yn ôl; cilio; codi arian.
wither *v.* gwywo.
withhold *v.* atal, dal yn ôl.
within 1 *prp.* i mewn, o fewn, yn.
  2 *ad.* tu mewn.
without 1 *prp.* heb **2** *a.* tu allan.
witness 1 *n.* tyst *m.* **2** *v.* tystio.
wits *n.* synhwyrau *pl.*
witticism *n.* jôc, ffraethineb *f.*
witty *a.* doniol, ffraeth.
wizard *n.* dewin *m.*
wolf *n.* blaidd *m.*
woman *n.* merch, menyw, gwraig, llances, dynes *f.*

wonder 1 *n.* rhyfeddod *m.*
  2 *v.* rhyfeddu, synnu. **I wonder** tybed.
wonderful *a.* rhyfedd, rhyfeddol.
wood *n.* coed *pl,* coedwig *f.* pren *m.*
wooden *a.* o goed, o bren.
woodwork *n .* gwaith coed, gwaith saer *m.*
wool *n.* gwlân *m.*
woollen *a.* gwlân, gwlanog. **woollen industry** diwydiant gwlân.
word *n.* gair *m.* **a good word** gair da; **the last word** y gair olaf; **word for word** gair am air.
work 1 *n.* gwaith, llafur *m.*
  2 *v.* gweithio, llafurio.
worker *n.* gweithiwr *m.*
working *a.* gwaith, yn gweithio. **working class** dosbarth gweithiol; **working clothes** dillad gwaith; **working party** gweithgor.
workshop *n.* gweithdy *m,* siop waith *f.*
world *n.* byd *m.*
worldly *a.* bydol.
worldwide *a.* byd-eang.
worm *n.* mwydyn, pryfyn *m.*
worried *a.* gofidus, pryderus.
worry 1 *n.* gofid *m,* helynt *f,* pryder *m.*
  2 *v.* gofidio, poeni, pryderu blino.
worse *a.* gwaeth.
worsen *v.* gwaethygu.
worship *n.* addoliad *m.*
worth *n.* gwerth *m.*
worthiness *n.* teilyngdod, gwerth.
worthless *a.* diwerth.
worthy *a.* teilwng.
wound 1 *n.* clwyf, anaf *m.*
  2 *v.* clwyfo, anafu.
wrap *v.* lapio, rhwymo. **wrapping paper** papur lapio.
wrath *n.* llid *m.*
wreath *n.* torch *f.*
wren *n.* dryw *m.*
wretch *n.* truan *m.*
wretched *a.* truan, truenus.
wretchedness *n.* trueni, trallod *m.*
wright *n.* crefftwr, saer *m.*
  cartwright saer certiau;
  wheelwright saer olwynion *(pren).*

wrist *n.* arddwrn *m.*
write *v.* sgrifennu, ysgrifennu. **to write a name** torri enw.
writer *n.* ysgrifennwr, awdur *m,* awdures *f.*

writing *n.* ysgrifen, ysgrifennu *f.*
wrong 1 *n.* cam, bai *m.* **2** *a.* anghywir, rong. **3** *v.* gwneud cam â.
wrongdoer *n.* troseddwr *m.*
wrongdoing *n.* trosedd *f.*

X-ray *n.* pelydr X, pelydryn X *m.*
X-rays pelydrau X.
xylophone *n.* seiloffon *f.*

yard *n.* buarth *m*, iard *f,* clos, cwrt *m;*
llathen *f.*
yarn *n.* chwedl, stori; edau *f.*
year *n.* blwyddyn; blwydd (oed) *f;*
blynedd *pl (after numerals).* **the first
year** y flwyddyn gyntaf; **the
second year** yr ail flwyddyn; **three
years old** tair blwydd oed; **four
years old** pedair blwydd oed; **for
five years** am bum mlynedd; **for
six years** am chwe blynedd; **last
year** y llynedd; **leap year**
blwyddyn naid; **this year** eleni;
next year y flwyddyn nesaf.
yearly *a.* blynyddol.
yearn *v.* hiraethu, dyheu.
yearning *n.* hiraeth *m.*
yell 1 *n.* sgrech, gwaedd *f.*
2 *v.* sgrechian, sgrechain, gweiddi.

yellow *a.* melyn *m.,* melen *f.* **the
yellow apple** yr afal melyn; **the
yellow dress** y wisg felen.
yes *ad.* ie, byddaf, byddan, do, oes,
oedd, oeddwn, ydw, ydy, ydyn . . .
*(Welsh uses the verb forms to answer
yes/no)* **Tom? Yes** Tom? Ie. **Was
he there? Yes** Oedd e yno? Oedd.
Is Huw late? Yes Ydy Huw'n
hwyr? Ydy. **Are there dogs here?
Yes** Oes cŵn yma? Oes. **Will they
be cold? Yes** Fyddan nhw'n oer?
Byddan.
yesterday *n. & ad.* doe, ddoe. **the
day before yesterday** echdoe.
yet *ad.* eto, er hynny.
yew *n.* ywen *f.*
yield *v.* ildio, rhoddi.
yoke *n.* iau *f.*
yolk *n.* melyn wy, melynwy m.
yonder *ad.* acw, draw.
York *n.* Efrog *f.*
you *pn.* ti; chi, chwi. **you also** tithau,
chithau, chwithau; **you yourself** tydi.
young *a.* ieuanc, ifanc.
younger *a.* iau.
youngest *a.* ifancaf.
youngster *n.* crwt, hogyn, plentyn *m.*
your *pn.* dy, 'th; eich, 'ch.
yours *pn.* eiddoch, yr eiddoch. **yours
faithfully** yr eiddoch yn ffyddlon;
yours truly yr eiddoch yn gywir.
yourself *pn.* eich hun, eich hunan.
yourselves *pn.* eich hunain.
youth *n.* llanc; ieuenctid *m.*
youthful *a.* ieuanc, ifanc.
Yuletide *n.* adeg y Nadolig *f.*

zeal *n.* sêl *f.*
zero *n.* dim, sero *m.*
zigzag *a.* igam-ogam.
zinc *n.* sinc *m.*
zip 1 *n.* sip *m.* **2** *v.* sipio.
zone *n.* cylch, rhanbarth *m.*
zoo *n.* sw *m.*
zoology *n.* sŵoleg *mf.*

SUPPLEMENT ATODIAD

VERBS
BERFAU

In this short introduction to the study of Welsh verbs, the irregular verb **bod** (*to be*) is conjugated in the Present, Imperfect, Future and Past tenses only. A fuller discussion of the subject may be found in contemporary books on Welsh grammar.

Present tense (bod *to be*)

Affirmative Form

Singular		Plural	
1 *Rydw i	*I am*	Rydyn ni	*We are*
2 Rwyt ti	*You are*	Rydych chi	*You are*
3 Mae e/o	*He/It is*	Maen nhw	*They are*
Mae hi	*She is*		

Note: 3rd Person	**mae, oes, sy,**	*is, there is*
Singular	**yw, ydyw**	*are, there are*
	Oes . . .?	*Is there . . .?*
		Are there . . .?

*Literary Form: **Yr wyf i, 'Rwyf i.** In spoken Welsh one hears **Rw i/Dw i** and also **Ryn ni/Dyn ni; Rych chi/Dych chi** (see overleaf).

Interrogative Form

Singular		Plural	
1 Ydw i?	*Am I?*	Ydyn ni?	*Are we?*
2 Wyt ti?	*Are you?*	Ydych chi?	*Are you?*
3 Ydy e/o?	*Is he/it?*	Ydyn nhw?	*Are they?*
Ydy hi?	*Is she?*		

Negative Form

Singular		Plural	
1 Dydw i ddim	*I am not*	Dydyn ni ddim	*We are not*
2 Dwyt ti ddim	*You are not*	Dydych chi ddim	*You are not*
3 Dydy e/o ddim	*He/It is not*	Dydyn nhw ddim	*They are not*
Dydy hi ddim	*She is not*		

Learners (**Dysgwyr**) of the spoken language are introduced to the following **Affirmative, Interrogative** and **Negative Forms** of the above when they first encounter the verb **bod:**

Affirmative Form

	Singular			Plural	
1	Dw i	*I am*	Dyn ni	*We are*
2	Rwyt ti	*You are*	Dych chi	*You are*
3	Mae e/hi	*He/She/It is*	Maen nhw	*They are*

Interrogative Form

	Singular			Plural	
1	Ydw i?	*Am I?*	Dyn ni?	*Are we?*
2	Wyt ti?	*Are you?*	Dych chi?	*Are you?*
3	Ydy e/hi?	*Is he/she/it?*	Dyn nhw?	*Are they?*

Negative Form

	Singular			Plural	
1	Dw i ddim	*I'm not*	Dyn ni ddim	*We're not*
2	Dwyt ti ddim	*You're not*	Dych chi ddim	*You're not*
3	Dydy e/hi ddim	*He's/She's/It's not*	Dyn nhw ddim	*They're not*

Imperfect tense   (**bod** *to be*)

Affirmative Form

	Singular			Plural	
1	*Roeddwn i	*I was/used to*	Roedden ni	*We were/used to*
2	Roeddet ti	*You were/used to*	Roeddech chi	*You were/used to*
3	Roedd e/o	*He/It was/used to*	Roedden nhw	*They are/used to*
	Roedd hi	*She was/used to*		

Note: 3rd Person Singular **roedd** *was, there was*
were, there were

*Also heard in spoken Welsh: **Rown i, Roen i; Rot ti; Roedd e/hi; Ron ni: Roch chi, Ron nhw.**

Interrogative Form

	Singular	
1	Oeddwn i?	*Was I?*
2	Oeddet ti?	*Were you?*
3	Oedd e/o?	*Was he/it?*
	Oedd hi?	*Was she?*

	Plural	
1	Oedden ni?	*Were we?*
2	Oeddech chi?	*Were you?*
3	Oedden nhw?	*Were they?*

Note: 3rd Person Singular **Oedd . . .?** *Was there . . .?*
Were there . . .?

Negative Form

Singular

1	Doeddwn i ddim	*I wasn't/I used not to*
2	Doeddet ti ddim	*You weren't/You used not to*
3	Doedd e/o ddim	*He/It wasn't/It used not to*
	Doedd hi ddim	*She wasn't/She used not to*

Plural

1	Doedden ni ddim	*We weren't/We used not to*
2	Doeddech chi ddim	*You weren't/You used not to*
3	Doedden nhw ddim	*They weren't/They used not to*

Future tense (bod *to be*)

Affirmative Form

	Singular		*Plural*	
1	Bydda i	*I shall be*	Byddwn ni	*We shall be*
2	Byddi di	*You will be*	Byddwch chi	*You will be*
3	Bydd e/o	*He/It will be*	Byddan nhw	*They will be*
	Bydd hi	*She will be*		

Note: 3rd Person Singular **bydd** *will be*

Interrogative Form

	Singular		*Plural*	
1	Fydda i?	*Shall I be?*	Fyddwn ni?	*Shall we be?*
2	Fyddi di?	*Will you be?*	Fyddwch chi?	*Will you be?*
3	Fydd e/o?	*Will he/she be?*	Fyddan nhw?	*Will they be?*
	Fydd hi?	*Will she be?*		

Negative Form

	Singular		*Plural*	
1	Fydda i ddim	*I shall not be*	Fyddwn ni ddim	*We shall not be*
2	Fyddi di ddim	*You will not be*	Fyddwch chi ddim	*You will not be*
3	Fydd e/o ddim	*He/It will not be*	Fyddan nhw ddim	*They will not be*
	Fydd hi ddim	*She will not be*		

Imperative tense (bod *to be*)

Bydd! Bydda! (singular); **Byddwch!** (plural) *Be!*

Past tense (bod *to be*)

Affirmative Form

	Singular		*Plural*	
1	*Bues i	*I was*	Buon ni	*We were*
2	Buest ti	*You were*	Buoch chi	*You were*
3	Buodd e/o	*He/It was*	Buon nhw	*They were*
	Buodd hi	*She was*		

*Literary form of 1st Person Singular Past Tense: **Bûm i**

Interrogative Form

	Singular		Plural	
1	Fues i?	*Was I?*	Fuon ni?	*Were we?*
2	Fuest ti?	*Were you?*	Fuoch chi?	*Were you?*
3	Fuodd e/o?	*Was he/it?*	Fuon nhw?	*Were they?*
	Fuodd hi?	*Was she?*		

Negative Form

	Singular		Plural	
1	Fues i ddim	*I wasn't*	Fuon ni ddim	*We weren't*
2	Fuest ti ddim	*You weren't*	Fuoch chi ddim	*You weren't*
3	Fuodd e/o ddim	*He/It wasn't*	Fuon nhw ddim	*They weren't*
	Fuodd hi ddim	*She wasn't*		

Affirmative and Negative Answers Yes and No

The entries shown in the English–Welsh section of the dictionary under **yes** and **no** may be further supplemented:

Present Tense

	Singular		Plural	
1	Ydw/Nag ydw	*Yes/No*	Ydyn/Nag ydyn	*Yes/No*
2	Wyt/Nag wyt	*Yes/No*	Ydych/Nag ydych	*Yes/No*
3	Ydy/Nag ydy	*Yes/No*	Ydyn/Nag ydyn	*Yes/No*
	Oes/Nag oes	*Yes/No*		

Imperfect Tense

	Singular		Plural	
1	Oeddwn/Nag oeddwn	*Yes/No*	Oedden/Nag oedden	*Yes/No*
2	Oeddet/Nag oeddet	*Yes/No*	Oeddech/Nag oeddech	*Yes/No*
3	Oedd/Nag oedd	*Yes/No*	Oedden/Nag oedden	*Yes/No*

Future Tense

	Singular		Plural	
1	Bydda/Na fydda	*Yes/No*	Byddwn/Na fyddwn	*Yes/No*
2	Byddi/Na fyddi	*Yes/No*	Byddwch/Na fyddwch	*Yes/No*
3	Bydd/Na fydd	*Yes/No*	Byddan/Na fyddan	*Yes/No*

With the past tense **Do** *Yes* and **Naddo** *No* are the forms relating to both singular and plural usages.

For forms such as the Pluperfect **Buaswn i, Fe/Mi faswn i** *I would (be)*, see further works on contemporary Welsh grammar.

Regular Verbs

Welsh verbs have inflected tenses, that is, the tenses have their own endings. These endings are added to the stem of the verbs. Most verbs follow a regular pattern but there are some irregular verbs.

In the Welsh–English section of this dictionary an entry for a verb is shown as follows:

canu *be.* **(canaf)** to sing, to play.

The stem derived from the verb-noun **canu** is **can-**. The Present Tense ending for the 1st Person Singular is **-af**, and when the ending is added to the stem, **can + af** becomes **canaf**, which is the form shown in the brackets, frequently written and pronounced **cana**.

The verb **bod** (*to be*) is used as an auxiliary in forming tenses of regular verbs such as **can, bwyta, cysgu** . . . The Present Tense of **canu** is formed by using the Present Tense of the verb **bod**, that is, **Rydw i, Rwyt ti, Mae e** . . . followed by **yn + canu**. It also exists in compact form as shown below.

Note: **Rydw i yn canu** becomes **Rydw i'n canu/Dw i'n canu**
Rwyt ti yn canu becomes **Rwyt ti'n canu**
Mae e yn canu becomes **Mae e'n canu** . . .

Present Tense (canu *to sing, to play*)

Singular

1	Rydw/Dw i'n canu	*I sing, I am singing*
2	Rwyt ti'n canu	*You sing, You are singing*
3	Mae e/o'n canu	*He/It sings, He/It is singing*
	Mae hi'n canu	*She sings, She is singing*

Plural

1	Rydyn/Dyn ni'n canu	*We sing, We are singing*
2	Rydych/Dych chi'n canu	*You sing, You are singing*
3	Maen nhw'n canu	*They sing, They are singing*

The Imperfect Tense is formed by using the Imperfect Tense of **bod**, that is, **Roeddwn i, Roeddet ti, Roedd e** . . . followed by **yn canu**.

Imperfect Tense (canu *to sing, to play*)

Singular

1	Roeddwn i'n canu	*I was singing*
2	Roeddet ti'n canu	*You were singing*
3	Roedd e/o'n canu	*He/It was singing*
	Roedd hi'n canu	*She was singing*

Plural

1	Roedden ni'n canu	*We were singing*
2	Roeddech chi'n canu	*You were singing*
3	Roedden nhw'n canu	*They were singing*

The Imperfect Tense also conveys the meaning of continuous action. **Roedd hi'n canu** means not only *She was singing,* but also *She was **going on** singing.* **Roedd hi'n arfer canu** *She used to sing.*

The Future Tense is formed by using the Future Tense of **bod**, that is, **Bydda i, Byddi di, Bydd e** . . . followed by **yn + canu**.

Future Tense (canu *to sing, to play*)

Singular
1	Bydda i'n canu	*I shall be singing*
2	Byddi di'n canu	*You will be singing*
3	Bydd e/o'n canu	*He/It will be singing*
	Bydd hi'n canu	*She will be singing*

Plural
1	Byddwn ni'n canu	*We shall be singing*
2	Byddwch chi'n canu	*You will be singing*
3	Byddan nhw'n canu	*They will be singing*

Imperative (canu *to sing, to play*)

Cana! (singular); **Canwch!** (plural) *Sing!*

The Past Tense of **canu** is formed by adding **-ais, -aist, -odd, -on, -och, -on** to the stem **can-**, and is used to convey completed action in the past.

Past Tense (canu *to sing, to play*)

	Singular			Plural	
1	*Cenais i	*I sang*	Canon ni	*We sang*
2	*Cenaist ti	*You sang*	Canoch chi	*You sang*
3	Canodd e/o	*He/It sang*	Canon nhw	*They sang*
	Canodd hi	*She sang*		

*In those verbs which have 'a' in the stem it is usual in literary Welsh for a > e in the 1st and 2nd Person Singular Past Tense and in the 2nd Person Singular Present and Future Tenses.

The particle Fe (S.W.)/Mi (N.W.)

The verb is placed as the first word in the normal construction of the Welsh sentence:

Cerddodd Siôn i'r siop.	*Siôn walked to the shop.*
Rydw i'n darllen llyfr.	*I'm reading a book.*
Mae ci yn y cae.	*There's a dog in the field.*
Dydyn nhw ddim yma.	*They're not here.*

Usually the particle **Fe/Mi** is placed in front of the verb merely to indicate that the verb is affirmative.

Note: The particle **Fe/Mi** is not translated, and is not placed before **mae** or **maen** but may occur before other persons of the verb in speech or informal texts. Both particles are followed by Soft Mutation.

Golchodd Mair y dillad.	
Fe olchodd Mair y dillad.	*Mair washed the clothes.*
Byddan nhw'n canu heno.	
Fe fyddan nhw'n canu heno.	*They will be singing tonight.*
Canon ni yn yr eisteddfod.	
Fe ganon ni yn yr eisteddfod.	*We sang in the eisteddfod.*

Compact Form of Verbs

The Future and Imperfect Tenses of the verb **canu** referred to above also exist in their compact forms. These inflected verb forms are more likely to be found in formal texts than in current conversational Welsh, though they may well appear in both.

The endings for the Future Tense of **canu** are **-af/-a, -i, -iff/ith, -wn, -wch, -an** and are added to the stem *can-*.

Present and Future Tenses (Compact Form) (**canu** *to sing, to play*)

Singular

1	Fe/Mi ganaf/gana i	*I shall sing*
2	Fe/Mi geni di/geni	*You will sing*
3	Fe/Mi gân/ganiff/ganith e/o	*He/It will sing*
	Fe/Mi ganiff/ganith hi	

Plural

1	Fe/Mi ganwn ni	*We shall sing*
2	Fe/Mi ganwch chi	*You will sing*
3	Fe/Mi ganan nhw	*They will sing*

The endings for the Imperfect Tense of **canu** are **-wn, -it, -ai, -en, -ech, -en** and are added to the stem **can-**.

Imperfect Tense (Compact Form) (**canu** *to sing, to play*)

Singular

1	Canwn i	*I was singing*
2	Canit ti	*You were singing*
3	Canai e/o	*He/It was singing*

Plural

1	Canen ni	*We were singing*
2	Canech chi	*You were singing*
3	Canen nhw	*They were singing*

Regular verbs follow the same pattern as **canu**. The Present, Imperfect, Future and Past Tenses of **bwyta** are shown below.

Present Tense (**bwyta** *to eat*)

Singular

1	Rydw i'n bwyta	*I am eating, I eat*
2	Rwy ti'n bwyta	*You are eating . . .*
3	Mae e'n bwyta . . .	*He/It is eating . . . etc.*

Imperfect Tense (**bwyta** *to eat*)

Singular

1	Roeddwn i'n bwyta	*I was eating*
2	Roeddet ti'n bwyta	*You are eating*
3	Roedd e'n bwyta . . .	*He/It was eating . . . etc.*

Future Tense (bwyta *to eat*)

Singular

1 Fe/Mi fydda(f) i'n bwyta   *I shall be eating*
2 Fe/Mi fyddi di'n bwyta   *You will be eating*
3 Fe/Mi fydd e'n bwyta . . .   *He/It will be eating . . . etc.*

Past Tense (Compact Form) (bwyta *to eat*)

	Singular		*Plural*
1 Fe/Mi fwytais i	*I ate*	Fe/Mi fwyton ni	*We ate*
2 Fe/Mi fwytaist ti	*You ate*	Fe/Mi fwytoch chi	*You ate*
3 Fe/Mi fwytodd e/o	*He/It ate*	Fe/Mi fwyton nhw	*They ate*
Fe/Mi fwytodd hi	*She ate*		

Future Tense (Compact Form) (bwyta *to eat*)

	Singular		*Plural*
1 Fe/Mi fwyta(f) i	*I shall eat*	Fe/Mi fwytwn ni	*We shall eat*
2 Fe/Mi fwyti di	*You will eat*	Fe/Mi fwytwch chi	*You will eat*
3 Fe/Mi fwytiff e/o	*He/It will eat*	Fe/Mi fwytan nhw	*They will eat*
Fe/Mi fwytiff hi	*She will eat*		

Imperative (bwyta *to eat*)

Bwyta! (singular); **Bwyt(e)wch!** (plural) *Eat!*

Irregular Verbs

Irregular verbs do not follow the same pattern as **canu** and have to be treated separately. Included below are: **cael, dod, gwneud, gwybod, mynd, rhoddi** and **troi.**

Present Tense (cael *to have*)

Singular

1 Rydw i'n cael   *I am having, I have*
2 Rwyt ti'n cael   *You are having, You have*
3 Mae e'n cael . . .   *He/It is having . . . etc.*

Imperfect Tense (cael *to have*)

Singular

1 Roeddwn i'n cael   *I was having*
2 Roeddet ti'n cael   *You were having*
3 Roedd e'n cael . . .   *He/It was having . . . etc.*

Future Tense (cael *to have*)

	Singular		*Plural*
1 Fe/Mi ga(f) i	*I shall have*	Fe/Mi gawn ni	*We shall have*
2 Fe/Mi gei di	*You will have*	Fe/Mi gewch chi	*You will have*
3 Fe/Mi gaiff e/o	*He/It will have*	Fe/Mi gân nhw	*They will have*
Fe/Mi gaiff hi	*She will have*		

Past Tense (cael *to have*)

Singular		Plural	
1 Fe/Mi ges i	*I had*	Fe/Mi gawson ni	*We had*
2 Fe/Mi gest ti	*You had*	Fe/Mi gawsoch chi	*You had*
3 Fe/Mi gafodd/gas e/o	*He/It had*	Fe/Mi gawson nhw	*They had*
Fe/Mi gafodd/gas hi	*She had*		

Imperative (cael *to have*)

Cymera! (singular); **Cymerwch!** (plural) *Have!*

Present Tense (dod *to come*)

Singular

1 Rydw i'n dod	*I am coming*
2 Rwyt ti'n dod	*You are coming*
3 Mae e'n dod . . .	*He/It is coming . . .* etc.

Imperfect Tense (dod *to come*)

Singular

1 Roeddwn i'n dod	*I was coming*
2 Roeddet ti'n dod	*You were coming*
3 Roedd e'n dod . . .	*He/It was coming . . .* etc.

Future Tense (dod *to come*)

Singular

1 Fe/Mi ddeuaf/ddo(f) i	*I shall come*
2 Fe/Mi ddoi di	*You will come*
3 Fe/Mi ddaw e/o	*He/It will come*
Fe/Mi ddaw hi	*She will come*

Plural

1 Fe/Mi ddown ni	*We shall come*
2 Fe/Mi ddewch/ddowch chi	*You will come*
3 Fe/Mi ddôn nhw	*They will come*

Past Tense (dod *to come*)

Singular

1 Fe/Mi ddes i	*I came*
2 Fe/Mi ddest ti	*You came*
3 Fe/Mi ddaeth e/o, hi	*He/I came, She came*

Plural

1 Fe/Mi ddaethon ni	*We came*
2 Fe/Mi ddaethoch chi	*You came*
3 Fe/Mi ddaethon nhw	*They came*

Imperative (dod *to come*)

Tyrd! *(N.W.)/***Dere!** *(S.W.)* (singular); **Dewch!** *(S.W.)/***Dowch!** *(N.W.)* (plural) *Come!*

Present Tense (gwneud *to make, to do*)

Singular
1 Rydw i'n gwneud   *I am making, I make*
2 Rwyt ti'n gwneud   *You are making, You make*
3 Mae e'n gwneud . . .   *He/It is making . . . etc.*

Imperfect Tense (gwneud *to make, to do*)

Singular
1 Roeddwn i'n gwneud   *I was making*
2 Roeddet ti'n gwneud   *You were making*
3 Roedd e'n gwneud . . .   *He/It was making . . . etc.*

Future Tense (gwneud *to make, to do*)

Singular
1 Fe/lMi wna(f) i   *I shall make*
2 Fe/Mi wnei di   *You will make*
3 Fe/Mi wnaiff e/o   *He/It will make*
   Fe/Mi wnaiff hi   *She will make*

Plural
1 Fe/Mi wnawn ni   *We shall make*
2 Fe/Mi wnewch chi   *You will make*
3 Fe/Mi wnân nhw   *They will make*

Past Tense (gwneud *to make, to do*)

	Singular			Plural	
1	Fe/Mi wnes i	*I made*	Fe/Mi wnaethon ni	*We made*
2	Fe/Mi wnest ti	*You made*	Fe/Mi wnaethoch chi	*You made*
3	Fe/Mi wnaeth e/o	*He/It made*	Fe/Mi wnaethon nhw	*They made*
	Fe/Mi wnaeth hi	*She made*		

Imperative (cael *to have*)

Gwna! (singular); **Gwnewch!** (plural) *Do! Make!*

Present Tense (gwybod *to know*)

Singular
1 Rydw i'n gwybod   *I know*
2 Rwyt ti'n gwybod   *You know*
3 Mae e/o'n gwybod . . .   *He/It knows . . . etc.*

Present Tense (Compact Form) (gwybod *to know*)

	Singular			Plural	
1	Fe/Mi wn i	*I know*	Fe/Mi wyddon ni	*We know*
2	Fe/Mi wyddost ti	*You know*	Fe/Mi wyddoch chi	*You know*
3	Fe/Mi ŵyr e/o	*He/It knows*	Fe/Mi wyddan nhw	*They know*
	Fe/Mi ŵyr hi	*She knows*		

Imperfect Tense (gwybod *to know*)

Singular

1 Roeddwn i'n gwybod   *I knew*
2 Roeddet ti'n gwybod   *You knew*
3 Roedd e'n gwybod . . .   *He/It knows . . . etc.*

Future Tense (gwybod *to know*)

Singular

1 Bydda i'n gwybod   *I shall know*
2 Byddi di'n gwybod   *You will know*
3 Bydd e'n gwybod . . .   *He/It will know . . . etc.*

The Compact Form of the Future and Past Tenses are seldom used in conversation.

Present Tense (mynd *to go*)

Singular

1 Rydw i'n mynd   *I go, I am going*
2 Rwyt ti'n mynd   *You go, You are going*
3 Mae e'n mynd . . .   *He/It goes, He/It is going . . . etc.*

Present Tense (Compact Form) (mynd *to go*)

Singular

1 Af/Â i   *I go, I am going*
2 Ei di   *You go, You are going*
3 *Aiff e/o   *He/It goes, He/It is going*
   *Aiff hi   *She goes, She is going . . . etc.*

The Present Tense follows the same pattern as the Compact Form of the Future Tense below.

Imperfect Tense (mynd *to go*)

Singular

1 Roeddwn i'n mynd   *I was going*
2 Roeddet ti'n mynd   *You were going*
3 **Roedd e'n mynd . . .   *He/It was going . . . etc.*

Future Tense (mynd *to go*)

	Singular		*Plural*	
1	Fe/Mi af/â i	*I shall go*	Fe/Mi awn ni	*We shall go*
2	Fe/Mi ei di	*You will go*	Fe/Mi ewch chi	*You will go*
3	*Fe/Mi aiff e/o	*He/It will go*	Fe/Mi ân nhw	*They will go*
	*Fe/Mi aiff hi	*She will go*		

*Literary form: **Â ef/hi** **Literary form: **Âi ef/hi**

Past Tense (mynd *to go*)

	Singular		*Plural*	
1	Fe/Mi es i	*I went*	Fe/Mi aethon ni	*We went*
2	Fe/lMi est ti	*You went*	Fe/Me aethoch chi	*You went*
3	Fe/Mi aeth e/o	*He/It went*	Fe/Mi aethon nhw	*They went*
	Fe/Mi aeth hi	*She went*		

Imperative (mynd *to go*)

Dos! *(N.W.)*/**Cer!** *(S.W.)* (singular); **Ewch!/Cerwch!** *(S.W.)* (plural) *Go!*

Present Tense (rhoi/rhoddi *to give*)

Singular
1 Rydw i'n rhoi/rhoddi   *I am giving, I give*
2 Rwyt ti'n rhoi   *You are giving, You give*
3 Mae e'n rhoi . . .   *He/It is giving, He/It gives . . . etc.*

Imperfect Tense (rhoi/rhoddi *to give*)

Singular
1 Roeddwn i'n rhoi/rhoddi   *I was giving*
2 Roeddet ti'n rhoi   *You were giving*
3 Roedd e'n rhoi . . .   *He/It was giving . . . etc.*

Future Tense (rhoi/rhoddi *to give*)

Singular
1 Fe/Mi roia/rodda(f) i   *I shall give*
2 Fe/Mi roddi di   *You will give*
3 Fe/Mi roddiff/rydd e/o   *He/It will give*
  Fe/Mi roddiff/rydd hi   *She will give*

Plural
1 Fe/Mi roddwn ni   *We shall give*
2 Fe/Mi roddech chi   *You will give*
3 Fe/Mi roddan nhw   *They will give*

Past Tense (rhoi/rhoddi *to give*)

Singular		*Plural*	
1 Fe/Mi roiais i/roddais i	*I gave*	Fe/Mi roddon ni	*We gave*
2 Fe/Mi roddaist ti	*You gave*	Fe/Mi roddoch chi	*You gave*
3 Fe/Mi roddodd e/o	*He/It gave*	Fe/Mi roddon nhw	*They gave*
Fe/Mi roddodd hi	*She gave*		

Imperative (rhoi/rhoddi *to give*)

Rhodda! Rho! (singular); **Rhoddwch!** (plural) *Give!*

Present Tense (troi *to turn*)

Singular
1 Rydw i'n troi   *I am turning, I turn*
2 Rwyt ti'n troi   *You are turning, You turn*
3 Mae e'n troi . . .   *He/It is turning, He/It turns . . . etc.*

Imperfect Tense (troi *to turn*)

Singular
1 Roeddwn i'n troi   *I was turning*
2 Roeddet ti'n troi   *You were turning*
3 Roedd e'n troi   *He/It was turning . . . etc.*

Future Tense (troi *to turn*)

	Singular		Plural	
1	Fe/Mi droaf/droia i	*I shall turn*	Fe/Mi droiwn ni	*We shall turn*
2	Fe/Mi droi-i di	*You will turn*	Fe/Mi droiwch chi	*You will turn*
3	Fe/Mi dröiff e/o	*He/It will turn*	Fe/Mi droian nhw	*They will turn*
	Fe/Mi dröiff hi	*She will turn*		

Past Tense (troi *to turn*)

	Singular		Plural	
1	Fe/Mi droais i	*I turned*	Fe/Mi droeson ni	*We turned*
2	Fe/Mi droaist ti	*You turned*	Fe/Mi droesoch chi	*You turned*
3	Fe/Mi droiodd e/o	*He/It turned*	Fe/Mi droeson nhw	*They turned*
	Fe/Mi droiodd hi	*She turned*		

Imperative (troi *to turn*)

Tro!/Troia! (singular); **Trowch!/Troiwch!** (plural) *Turn!*

cloi, paratoi and **rhoi** follow a similar pattern.

Imperative Mood

Commands – 2nd Person Singular and 2nd Person Plural

The 2nd Person Singular is formed by adding **-a** to the stem of the verb-noun, while the 2nd Person Plural is formed by adding **-wch** to the stem:

Cysga! (2nd Person Singular);
Cysgwch! (2nd Person Plural) *Sleep!*
Brysia! (2nd Person Singular);
Brysiwch! (2nd Person Plural) *Hurry!*

Commands – Other Persons

The forms **Gadewch i-** *Allow-/Let* is usually used to express commands in the other persons of the verb:

Gadewch i fi weithio!	(1st Person Singular)	*Let me work!*
Gadewch iddo fe weithio!	(3rd Person Singular)	*Let him work!*
Gadewch iddi hi weithio!	(3rd Person Singular)	*Let her work!*
Gadewch i ni weithio!	(1st Person Plural)	*Let us work!*
Gadewch iddyn nhw weithio!	(3rd Person Plural)	*Let them work!*

Verbs and Mutations

The direct object of a verb in compact form takes a Soft Mutation:

Fe welodd e **g**effyl.	*He saw a horse.*
Fe brynon nhw **f**wyd.	*They bought food.*
Mi gana i **g**arolau 'fory.	*I'll sing carols tomorrow.*
Rhoddaf **b**unt iddi.	*I'll give her a pound.*

Note: When the periphrastic form of the verb (**bod** + **yn** + verb-noun) is used *no* mutation of the object occurs, as is shown in the following sentences:

Mae e'n darllen **ll**yfr.	*He is reading a book.*
Mae nhw'n chwarae **p**êl-droed.	*They are playing football.*
Roedd Siân yn golchi **ll**estri.	*Siân was washing dishes.*
Rydw i'n rhoddi **p**unt iddo.	*I am giving him a pound.*

For examples involving the mutation of verbs following the particles **Fe** and **Mi**, the relative pronoun **a**, and the personal pronouns **mi, ti, ef . . .** see the section entitled **A Summary of the Main Rules of Mutation.**

PREPOSITIONS
ARDDODIAID

Prepositions are followed by nouns or pronouns, for example:

gyda *with*   **gyda Mam** *with Mother;* **gyda ni** *with us*
i fyny *up*   **i fyny'r bryn** *up the hill;* **i fyny'r ysgol** *up the ladder*
i lawr *down*   **i lawr y cwm** *down the valley;* **i lawr y pwll** *down the pit*
mewn *in a*   **mewn cwpan** *in a cup;* **mewn munud** *in a minute*

Some prepositions are conjugated and have personal forms:

at *to, towards* (stem **at-**)

	Singular			Plural	
1	ata i	*to me*	aton ni	*to us*	
2	atat ti	*to you*	atoch chi	*to you*	
3	ato fe/fo	*to him/it*	atyn nhw	*to them*	
	ati hi	*to her/it*			

dan *under* (stem **dan-**)

	Singular			Plural	
1	dana i	*under me*	danon ni	*under us*	
2	danat ti	*under you*	danoch chi	*under you*	
3	dano fe/fo	*under him/it*	danyn nhw	*under them*	
	dani hi	*under her/it*			

am *around* (stem **amdan-**)

	Singular			Plural	
1	amdana i	*around me*	amdanon ni	*around us*	
2	amdanat ti	*around you*	amdanoch chi	*around you*	
3	amdano fe/fo	*around him/it*	amdanyn nhw	*around them*	
	amdani hi	*around her/it*			

ar *on* (stem **arn-**)

	Singular			Plural	
1	arna i	*on me*	arnon ni	*on us*	
2	arnat ti	*on you*	arnoch chi	*on you*	
3	arno fe/fo	*on him/it*	arnyn nhw	*on them*	
	arni hi	*on her/it*			

wrth *by* (stem **wrth-**)

	Singular			Plural	
1	wrtho i	*by me*	wrthon ni	*by us*	
2	wrthot ti	*by you*	wrthoch chi	*by you*	
3	wrtho fe/fo	*by him/it*	wrthyn nhw	*by them*	
	wrthi hi	*by her/it*			

drwy *and* **heb** share a similar pattern:

drwy *through* (stem **drwydd-**)

	Singular		*Plural*	
1	drwyddo i	*through me*	drwyddon ni	*through us*
2	drwyddot ti	*through you*	drwyddoch chi	*through you*
3	drwyddo fe/fo	*through him/it*	drwyddyn nhw	*through them*
	drwyddi hi	*through her/it*		

heb *without* (stem **hebdd-**)

	Singular		*Plural*	
1	hebddo i	*without me*	hebddon ni	*without us*
2	hebddot ti	*without you*	hebddoch chi	*without you*
3	hebddo fe/fo	*without him/it*	hebddyn nhw	*without them*
	hebddi hi	*without her/it*		

yn *in* (stem **yn-**)

	Singular		*Plural*	
1	yno i	*in me*	ynon ni	*in us*
2	ynot ti	*in you*	ynoch chi	*in you*
3	ynddo fe/fo	*in him/it*	ynddyn nhw	*in them*
	ynddi hi	*in her/it*		

i *to, for*

	Singular		*Plural*	
1	i fi/mi	*to me, for me*	i ni	*to us, for us*
2	i ti	*to you . . .*	i chi	*to you . . .*
3	iddo fe/fo	*to him/it . . .*	iddyn nhw	*to them . . .*
	iddi hi	*to her . . .*		

o *from* (stem **ohon-**)

	Singular		*Plural*	
1	ohono i	*from me*	ohonon ni	*from us*
2	ohonot ti	*from you*	ohonoch chi	*from you*
3	ohono fe/fo	*from him/it*	ohonyn nhw	*from them*
	ohoni hi	*from her/it*		

rhwng *between* (stem **rhyng-**)

	Singular		*Plural*	
1	rhyngo i	*between us*	rhyngon ni	*between us*
2	rhyngot ti	*between you*	rhyngoch chi	*between you*
3	rhyngddo fe/fo	*between him/it*	rhyngddyn nhw	*between them*
	rhyngddi hi	*between her/it*		

dros *over, for*

	Singular	
1	drosto/droso i	*over me, for me*
2	drostot/drosot ti	*over you, for you*
3	drosto fe/fo	*over him/it, for him*
	drosti hi	*over her/it, for her/it*
	Plural	
1	droston/droson ni	*over us, for us*
2	drostoch/drosoch chi	*over you, for you*
3	drostyn nhw	*over them, for them*

gan *with*

	Singular		Plural	
1	gen i	*with me*	gennyn/gynnon ni	*with us*
2	gen ti	*with you*	gennych/gynnoch chi	*with you*
3	ganddo fe/fo	*with him/it*	ganddyn nhw	*with them*
	ganddi hi	*with her/it*		

Sometimes the preposition **gyda** is used instead of the conjugated preposition **gan** in South Wales.

The conjugated prepositions **am, ar, at, dan, dros, drwy/trwy, gan, heb, i, o, wrth** are used in their simple form when the object governed by the preposition is a noun or verb-noun. Soft Mutation follows these prepositions:

am dro; ar bapur; at drwyn; dan wely; dros frawd; drwy fôr; heb ddiolch; i regi; o freuddwydio; wrth lusgo.

See section **Treiglad Meddal – Soft Mutation.**

The conjugated preposition **rhwng** is **not** followed by mutation:

rhwng cyfeillion da	*between good friends*
rhwng dau frawd	*between two brothers*
rhwng gŵr a gwraig	*between husband and wife*

The conjugated preposition **yn** in its simple form is followed by Nasal Mutation. It becomes **yng** before **c** and **g**, and **ym** before **p** and **b**:

yng nghornel yr ystafell	*in the corner of the room*
yng nghwrs y flwyddyn	*in the course of the year*
yng Nghorwen	*in Corwen*
yng ngardd yr ysgol	*in the school's garden*
yng nglaw mis Ebrill	*in the April rain*
yng Nglanaman	*in Glanaman*
ym mhoced y bachgen	*in the boy's pocket*
ym mhrofiad y dyn	*in the man's experience*
ym Mhorthaethwy	*in Porthaethwy (Menai Bridge)*
ym mwyd y plant	*in the chidren's food*
ym masged y fenyw	*in the woman's basket*
ym Mangor	*in Bangor*

yn also becomes *ym* before *m*:

ym Môn; ym Mynwy; ym Môr y Gogledd; ym mynwent y plwyf

For examples of **yn** followed by Soft Mutation or by non-mutation, see section entitled **A Summary of the Main Rules of Mutation.**

ADJECTIVES
ANSODDEIRIAU

In the Welsh language the adjective usually comes after the noun:

afal **sur**	*a bitter apple*
blodyn **hyfryd**	*a beautiful flower*
cadair **uchel**	*a high chair*
siwrnai **hir**	*a long journey*

When the adjective follows a singular masculine noun no mutation occurs but when the adjective follows the singular feminine noun it takes soft mutation:

bachgen bach	*a small boy*
merch **f**ach	*a small girl*
brawd cariadus	*a loving brother*
chwaer **g**ariadus	*a loving sister*
dyn mawr	*a big man*
menyw **f**awr	*a big woman*
gŵr tenau	*a thin man/husband*
gwraig **d**enau	*a thin woman/wife*
tarw du	*a black bull*
buwch **dd**u	*a black cow*

Note: Adjectives do not mutate when they follow *plural* nouns.

When an adjective precedes a noun the noun is mutated whether it be masculine or feminine:

hen **ŵr**	*an old man*
hen **wraig**	*an old woman*
annwyl **dad**	*a dear father*
annwyl **fam**	*a dear mother*

The noun takes a soft mutation on each occasion.

The feminine form of a few adjectives is still used in everyday speech. Some are listed below:

Masculine	Feminine	
gwyn	gwen	*white*
melyn	melen	*yellow*
tlws	tlos	*pretty*
bychan	bechan	*little*
byr	ber	*short*

e.g. cot **wen;** ffrog **felen;** merch **dlos;** ynys **fechan;** stori **fer.**

The Comparison of Adjectives
Cymharu Ansoddeiriau

There are three degrees of comparison of adjectives in Welsh. These are: equative, comparative and superlative. Adjectives may be compared by two methods:

(i) Using **mor, mwy, mwya(f)** before the adjective. Adjectives of more than two syllables are also compared in this manner. Irregular adjectives, some of which are listed below, are an exception.

ffôl *(foolish)*	**mor ffôl**	**mwy ffôl**	**mwyaf ffôl**
cryno *(tidy)*	**mor *gryno**	**mwy cryno**	**mwyaf cryno**
rhesymol *(reasonable)*	**mor rhesymol**	**mwy rhesymol**	**mwyaf rhesymol**

Positive	Equative	Comparative	Superlative
amlwg	mor amlwg	mwy amlwg	mwya(f) amlwg
evident	*as evident*	*more evident*	*most evident*
amyneddgar	mor amyneddgar	mwy amyneddgar	mwya(f) amyneddgar
patient	*as patient*	*more patient*	*most patient*
blasus	mor *flasus	mwy blasus	mwya(f) blasus
tasty	*as tasty*	*more tasty*	*most tasty*
cyfeillgar	mor *gyfeillgar	mwy cyfeillgar	mwya(f) cyfeillgar
friendly	*as friendly*	*more friendly*	*most friendly*
diolchgar	mor *ddiolchgar	mwy diolchgar	mwya(f) diolchgar
thankful	*as thankful*	*more thankful*	*most thankful*
doniol	mor *ddoniol	mwy doniol	mwya(f) doniol
witty	*as witty*	*more witty*	*most witty*
dyledus	mor *ddyledus	mwy dyledus	mwya(f) dyledus
indebted	*as indebted*	*more indebted*	*most indebted*
dymunol	mor *ddymuol	mwy dymunol	mwya(f) dymunol
desirable	*as desirable*	*more desirable*	*most desirable*
gwerthfawr	mor *werthfawr	mwy gwerthfawr	mwya(f) gwerthfawr
valuable	*as valuable*	*more valuable*	*most valuable*
peryglus	mor *beryglus	mwy peryglus	mwya(f) peryglus
dangerous	*as dangerous*	*more dangerous*	*most dangerous*
llawen	mor **llawen	mwy llawen	mwya(f) llawen
cheerful	*as cheerful*	*more cheerful*	*most cheerful*

*Note: **mor** *(as, so, how)* is followed by Soft Mutation. An alternative translation in the above context would read:

> **mor amlwg** *so evident;* **mor amyneddgar** *so patient;* **mor flasus** *so tasty;* **mor gyfeillgar** *so friendly . . .*

ll and **rh** do not mutate after **mor.**

(ii) With regular adjectives the endings **-ed, -ach, -af** are added respectively to the adjective in its positive form in order to form the other degrees:

Positive	*Equative*	*Comparative*	*Superlative*
*agos	agosed	agosach	agosa(f)
near	as near	nearer	nearest
caled	caleted	caletach	caleta(f)
hard	as hard	harder	hardest
call	called	callach	calla(f)
wise	as wise	wiser	wisest
coch	coched	cochach	cocha(f)
red	as red	redder	reddest
cryf	cryfed	cryfach	cryfa(f)
strong	as strong	stronger	strongest
cyflym	cyflymed	cyflymach	cyflyma(f)
quick	as quick	quicker	quickest
eglur	eglured	eglurach	eglura(f)
clear	as clear	clearer	clearest
glân	glaned	glanach	glana(f)
clean	as clean	cleaner	cleanest
glas	glased	glasach	glasa(f)
blue	as blue	bluer	bluest
hapus	hapused	hapusach	hapusa(f)
happy	as happy	happier	happiest
oer	oered	oerach	oera(f)
cold	as cold	colder	coldest
pell	pelled	pellach	pella(f)
far	as far	further	furthest
tawel	taweled	tawelach	tawela(f)
quiet	as quiet	quieter	quietest
trwm	trymed	trymach	tryma(f)
heavy	as heavy	heavier	heaviest
tywyll	tywylled	tywyllach	tywylla(f)
dark	as dark	darker	darkest

Note: The final **f** of the Superlative is often omitted in spelling and pronunciation.

*See end of section on Adjectives for alternative forms.

In Welsh, adjectives are compared by two methods:
  (i) using **cyn**, and
  (ii) using **mor**.
cyn is used to compare adjectives which in their positive forms do not contain more than two syllables and do not end in **-en, -gar, -og, -ol** or **-us.**
cyn and **mor** are both followed by Soft Mutation, except when the adjective begins with **ll** or **rh.**

cyn agosed â/ag	yn agosach na(g)	yr agosaf
as near as	*nearer than*	*the nearest*

cyn goched â/ag	yn gochach na(g)	y cochaf
as red as	*redder than*	*the reddest*
cyn hapused â/ag	yn hapusach na(g)	yr hapusaf
as happy as	*happier than*	*the happiest*
cyn llawned â/ag	yn llawnach na(g)	y llawnaf
as full as	*fuller than*	*the fullest*

When the adjective in its positive form ends in **-g**, **-b** or **-d** these letters harden to **-c-**, **-p-** and **-t-** when the adjective is compared, as is shown below with **caled, teg, gwlyb, rhad:**

cyn galeted â/ag	yn galetach na(g)	y caletaf
as hard as	*harder than*	*the hardest*
cyn deced â/ag	yn decach na(g)	y tecaf
as fair as	*fairer than*	*the fairest*
cyn wlyped â/ag	yn wlypach na(g)	y gwlypaf
as wet as	*wetter than*	*the wettest*
cyn rhated â/ag	yn rhatach na(g)	y rhataf
as cheap/free as	*cheaper/freer than*	*the cheapest/freest*

â in the equative degree and **na** in the comparative degree are used when the following word begins with a consonant, and both cause Spirant Mutation.

ag and **nag** are used when the following word begins with a vowel:

cyn goched **â** thân	*as red as fire*
yn drymach **na** phlwm	*heavier than lead*
cyn wynned **ag** eira	*whiter than snow*
yn dywyllach **nag** uffern	*darker than hell*

Irregular adjectives

There are only a few irregular adjectives in Welsh and the most important of them are listed below:

Positive	Equative	Comparative	Superlative
bach/bychan *small*	mor fach/fychan cyn lleied	llai	lleia(f)
buan/cynnar *swift/early*	mor fuan cynt	cynted	cynta(f)
da *good*	mor dda cystal	gwell	gorau
drwg *bad*	mor ddrwg cynddrwg	gwaeth	gwaetha(f)
hawdd *easy*	mor hawdd cyn hawsed	haws	hawsa(f)
hen *old*	mor hen cyn hyned	hŷn	hyna(f)
hir *long*	mor hir cyn hired	hirach	hira(f)
ifanc/ieuanc *young*	mor ifanc cyn ieuanged	ifancach ieuangach	ifanca(f) ieuanga(f)

Positive	Equative	Comparative	Superlative
isel *low*	mor isel cyn ised	is	isa(f)
llawer/mawr *many/big*	mor fawr cymaint	mwy	mwya(f)
uchel *high*	mor uchel cyn uched	uwch	ucha(f)

Note: **cyn** *(as)* is also used in the Equative Degree of comparison with the appropriate **-ed** ending. (It is already contained in such forms as **cynt, cystal, cynddrwg** and **cymaint**.) **cyn** is followed by Soft Mutation.

Exception: **ll** and **rh** do not mutate after **mor** and **cyn**.

The adjective **agos** also has irregular equative, comparative and superlative forms:

agos	cyn nesed â	yn nes na	y nesaf
near	*as near as*	*nearer than*	*the nearest*

PERSONAL PRONOUNS
RHAGENWAU PERSONOL

There are two classes of personal pronouns in Welsh: independent and dependent.

Independent Personal Pronouns

These pronouns are not dependent on any other word in a sentence and may stand entirely alone.

Simple

	Singular			Plural	
1	fi, mi	*I, me*	ni	*we, us*
2	ti, di	*you*	chi	*you*
3	fe/e, fo/o	*he, him*	nhw	*they, them*
	hi	*she, her*		

Reduplicated

Singular

1	myfi, y fi	*I, I myself*
2	tydi, y chdi (G.C.)	*you, you yourself*
3	efe, efô, y fe, y fo	*he*
	hyhi, y hi	*she, it, she herself,*
		it itself

Plural

1	nyni, y ni	*we, we ourselves*
2	chychi, y chi	*you, you yourselves*
3	y nhw	*they, them, they themselves*

The reduplicated forms are often placed at the beginning of a sentence for emphasis:

Myfi sy'n magu'r baban.	*It is I who nurses the baby.*
Tydi, O Dduw, sy'n maddau.	*It is You, O Lord, who forgives.*
Nyni sy'n troi y meysydd.	*It is we who plough the fields.*

Conjunctive

	Singular			Plural	
1	finnau, minnau	*I, me*	ninnau	*we, us*
2	tithau	*you*	chithau	*you*
3	yntau	*he, him*	nhwthau	*they, them*
	hithau	*she, her*		

The conjunctive forms frequently possess an extra meaning beyond that of the mere pronoun, the additional meaning being expressed in English by a conjunction:

minnau may mean *I (me) also; even I (me); I (me) on the other hand; I (me) for my part; then I; but I . . .*

ninnau may mean *we (us) too, we (us) also; even we (us); we (us) on the other hand; we (us) on the contrary; we (us) for our part . . .*

Dependent Personal Pronouns

These pronouns are dependent on either a noun, another pronoun or personal ending of a verb or preposition, or a verb-noun.

Prefixed

Singular		*Plural*	
1 fy, f'	*my*	ein	*our*
2 dy, d'	*your*	eich	*your*
3 ei	*his/her*	eu	*their*

The prefixed forms, which are always in the genitive case, are used before nouns and verb-nouns:

Darllenodd y bachgen ei lyfr.	*The boy read his book.*
Clywais fy nhad yn galw.	*I heard my father calling.*
Cafodd y gân ei chanu ar y radio.	*The song was sung on the radio.*

Affixed

Singular		*Plural*	
1 i, fi	*I, me*	ni	*we, us*
2 di, ti	*you*	chi	*you*
3 e, fe, o, fo	*he, him*	nhw	*they, them*
hi	*she, her*		

For examples of Affixed forms and a fuller discussion of the subject of Welsh pronouns the reader is referred to specific works on Welsh grammar.

Words beginning with the vowels **a, e, i, o, u w** and **y** are aspirated and acquire an initial **h** when preceded by the following pronouns (or their abbreviated forms):

1 ei, 'i, 'w	*her (feminine singular)*
2 eu, 'u, 'w	*their*
3 ein, 'n	*our*

ysgol >   **ei h**ysgol (hi) *her school;*
Dyma **'i h**ysgol *Here is her school;*
dewch i**'w h**ysgol *Come to her school.*

ardal >   **eu h**ardal (nhw) *their district;*
Dyna **'u h**ardal *That is their district;*
Mi af i**'w h**ardal *I shall go to their district.*

ewyllys >   **ein h**ewyllys *our will;* a**'n h**ewyllys da *and our goodwill.*

annwyl >   **ein h**annwyl blentyn *our dear child;* **eu h**annwyl wlad *their dear country;*
ei hannwyl fam *her dear mother.*

For the mutations after the dependent personal pronouns:
fy, dy, ei (masculine) and **ei** (feminine)
see the section entitled **A Summary of the Main Rules of Mutation.**

A SUMMARY OF THE MAIN RULES OF MUTATION RHEOLAU TREIGLO

Nine initial consonants mutate. They are:
c, p, t, g, b, d, ll, m, rh.
They mutate in the manner shown in the box below:

Initial consonant	Soft	Nasal	Spirant
cath *cat*	dy **g**ath di *your cat*	fy **ngh**ath i *my cat*	ei **ch**ath hi *her cat*
pen *head*	dy **b**en di *your head*	fy **mh**en i *my head*	ei **ph**en hi *her head*
tad *father*	dy **d**ad di *your father*	fy **nh**ad i *my father*	ei **th**ad hi *her father*
*****g**ardd *garden*	dy ardd di *your garden*	fy **ng**ardd i *my garden*	
bys *finger*	dy **f**ys di *your finger*	fy **m**ys i *my finger*	
dant *tooth*	dy **dd**ant di *your tooth*	fy **n**ant i *my tooth*	
llyfr *book*	dy **l**yfr di *your book*		
mam *mother*	dy **f**am di *your mother*		
rhaff *rope*	dy **r**aff di *your rope*		

*The consonant **g** disappears when Soft Mutation occurs, leaving the next letter (vowel or consonant) as the initial letter of the mutated word, as in:

gair > air; **g**lo > lo; **g**wair > wair; **g**wddf > wddf; **g**wyrdd > wyrdd . . .

Soft Mutation Treiglad Meddal

Nine consonants are affected by Soft Mutation:

c > g; p > b; t > d; g > (disappears); b > f; d > dd; ll > l; m > f; rh > r.

Nouns

1 Feminine singular nouns after the definite article **y, yr, 'r**:
   y **g**ot, y **b**êl, y **d**aith, yr **a**rdd, y **f**raich, o'r **dd**afad, i'r **f**am.
   ll and **rh** do not mutate after the definite article:
   y llaw, y llwy, y rhaglen, y rhaff, i'r rhos.

2 Nouns when preceded by adjectives:
   hen **ŵ**r *(an old man)*; annwyl **f**rawd *(a dear brother)*; hoff **l**e *(a favourite place)*; unig **f**erch *(an only daughter)*.

3 Nouns and verb-nouns after the prepositions **am, ar, at, dan, dros, drwy, gan, heb, hyd, i, o, wrth**:
   am **f**lwyddyn *(for a year)*; ar **f**wrdd *(on a table)*; at **dd**rws *(towards a door)*; dan **g**oeden *(under a tree)*; dros **G**ymru *(for/over Wales)*; drwy **dd**ŵr *(through water)*; gan **dd**weud *(by saying)*; heb **g**ysgu *(without sleeping)*; wrth **g**anu *(by singing)*. The verb-nouns **dweud, cysgu** and **canu** mutate as nouns in this context.

4 Nouns after **dyma, dyna, dacw, wele**:
   Dyma **l**e da *(Here's a good place)*. Dyna **d**ŷ hyfryd *(There's a beautiful house)*. Dacw **g**i defaid *(There's a sheepdog yonder)*. Wele **f**aban! *(Behold a babe!)*

5 Feminine singular nouns after the numeral **un** except those nouns beginning in **ll** and **rh**; nouns after the numerals **dau** and **dwy**; and nouns after the numerals **saith** and **wyth** beginning in **c, p, t, ll** and **rh**:
   un **f**erch *(one girl)*; un **w**raig *(one woman)*; un **g**adair *(one chair)*; dau **f**achgen *(two boys)*; dau **g**ae *(two fields)*; dwy **g**ath *(two cats)*; dwy **d**ref *(two towns)*; saith **g**ant *(seven hundred)*; wyth **d**udalen *(eight pages)*. Exceptions remain: **un llaw** *(one hand)*; **un llong** *(one ship)*; **un rhwyd** *(one net)*; **un rhaw** *(one shovel)*.

6 A noun when it is the direct object of an inflected verb (Compact Form):

Prynais **l**yfr.	*I bought a book.*
Gwelaf **g**astell.	*I see a castle.*
Agorodd **dd**rysau'r car.	*He opened the car's doors.*
Fe ganon nhw **g**ân hapus.	*They sang a happy song.*

   When the verb is in a periphrastic form the object does *not* mutate:

Mae Siôn yn canu cân.	*Siôn is singing a song.*
Rydw i'n ysgrifennu llythyr.	*I'm writing a letter.*

7 Nouns after the predicative **yn**:

Mae Siân **yn f**erch hyfryd.	*Siân is a lovely girl.*
Mae'r gwaith **yn f**raint.	*The work is a privilege.*
Bydd hwn **yn d**rysor am byth.	*This will be a treasure for ever.*

   Exceptions: Nouns beginning in **ll** and **rh**.

Roedd Alun yn llawen.	*Alun was happy.*

8 Nouns after the personal pronouns **dy** and **ei** (masculine) together with **'i** (masculine) and **'w** (masculine):
   dy **g**ot *(your coat)*; dy **b**oced *(your pocket)*; dy **d**afod *(your tongue)*; ei **o**lwg *(his sight)*; ei **f**raich *(his arm)*; Dyma Ifan a'i **g**ŵn. *(Here is Ifan and his dogs)*; Collodd ei frawd a'i

dad. *(He lost his brother and his father)*; Aeth e i'w d**ŷ**. *(He went to his house)*; Chwythodd y llwch i'w **l**ygaid. *(The dust blew into his eyes)*.

9 Nouns and verb-nouns after the conjunction **neu** *(or)*:
te neu **g**offi *(tea or coffee)*; mab neu **f**erch *(a son or daughter)*; ci neu **g**ath *(a dog or cat)*; ennill neu **g**olli *(win or lose)*. Inflected verbs (Compact Forms) are not mutated after **neu**.

10 Feminine singular nouns after ordinal numerals:
y drydedd **f**erch *(the third girl)*; y chweched **b**ennod *(the sixth chapter)*; y nawfed **g**yfrol *(the ninth volume)*; y ddegfed **w**ers *(the tenth lesson)*.

11 The numerals **dau** and **dwy** after the definite article **y**:
y **dd**au fachgen *(the two boys)*; y **dd**wy ferch *(the two girls)*.

12 Nouns used as adjectives after feminine singular nouns:
llwy **d**e *(teaspoon)*; gwisg **b**riodas *(wedding-dress)*; gardd **l**ysiau *(a vegetable garden)*; cadair **f**reichiau *(an armchair)*.

13 Nouns in the vocative case:
Fam annwyl! *(Mother dear!)*; **F**rodyr a chwiorydd! *(Brothers and sisters!)*; **L**öwyr, gwrandewch! *(Miners, listen!)*; **W**eithwyr y byd! *(Workers of the world!)*.

14 After a break in the normal order of words:
Roedd croeso yno.   Roedd yno **g**roeso.
Mae merch newydd yn yr ysgol.   Mae yna **f**erch newydd yn yr ysgol.

15 Nouns after **amryw, cyfryw, pa, pa fath, pa ryw, rhyw, unrhyw**:
amryw **l**iwiau *(several colours)*; cyfryw **b**ethau *(such things)*; Pa **l**e? *(What place?)*; Pa fath **f**achgen ydy e? *(What kind of a boy is he?)*.

16 Nouns after **ambell, aml, holl, naill, ychydig, y fath**:
ambell **w**aith *(sometimes)*; aml **d**ro *(frequently)*; yr holl **b**entref *(the whole village)*; y naill **g**ynllun *(the one plan)*; ychydig **f**wyd *(a little food)*; y fath **dd**yn *(such a man)*.

17 Nouns after the prefix **cyn(-)** *(former, past, ex-, pre-)*:
cyn-**b**rifathro *(former headteacher)*; cyn-**l**ywydd *(past president)*; cyn-**w**einidog *(former minister)*; cyn-**l**öwr *(ex-miner)*.

Adjectives

1 Adjectives after feminine singular nouns:
cadair **f**ach *(a small chair)*; ffordd **g**ul *(a narrow way)*; heol **f**awr *(a big road)*; merch **d**enau *(a thin girl)*; stori **dd**a *(a good story)*.

2 Adjectives after the predicative **yn**:

Mae Nia yn **g**aredig.	*Nia is kind.*
Roedd y saer yn **dd**a.	*The carpenter was good.*
Mae'r bwyd yn **dd**iflas.	*The food is distasteful.*

ll and **rh** do *not* mutate after **yn**.

3 Adjectives in comparison after **cyn** and **mor**:
cyn **g**yflymed â *(as fast as)*; mor **g**yfeillgar â *(as friendly as)*; cyn **w**ynned â *(as white as)*; mor **d**yner â *(as tender as)*. **ll** and **rh** do not mutate after **cyn** and **mor**:
cyn llawned â *(as full as)*; mor rhad â *(as cheap as)*; mor llawen â'r gog *(as happy as the cuckoo)*.

4 Adjectives after the conjunction **neu**:
da neu **dd**rwg *(good or bad)*; gwyn neu **dd**u *(white or black)*.

5 Adjectives after the adverbs **go, gweddol, lled, mor, rhy**:

go **dd**rwg	*quite/fairly bad*
gweddol **d**awel	*fairly quiet*
lled **dd**a	*quite good/fairly well*
mor **b**wysig	*so important*
rhy **l**awen	*too merry*

ll and **rh** do *not* mutate after **mor**:

mor llwyddiannus	*so successful*
mor rhwydd	*so easy*

Verbs

1 Interrogative forms of inflected verbs (Compact Forms):

Weloch chi'r papur?	*Did you see the paper?*
Fuest ti allan heddiw?	*Were you out today?*
Ddaeth e i'r ysgol mewn pryd?	*Did he come to school in time?*

2 Verbs after the particles **Fe**(S.W.) and **Mi**(N.W.):

Fe **g**anodd gân.	*He sang a song.*
Mi **g**lywais ei llais hi.	*I heard her voice.*
Fe **l**anwon nhw'r car.	*They filled the car.*
Mi **g**lywson ni'r newyddion.	*We heard the news.*

3 Verbs after the relative pronoun **a** and the negative relative pronoun **na**:

Dyma'r ferch **a dd**aeth i'r parti.	*Here's the girl who came to the party.*

The relative pronoun **a** *is frequently omitted in conversational Welsh but the mutation caused by it is retained:*

Dyna'r dyn (**a**) **w**elais i.	*There's the man whom I saw.*

The negative relative pronoun **na** causes Soft Mutation with verbs beginning in **g, b, d, ll, m, rh** and Spirant Mutation with verbs beginning in **c, p, t**:

Dyna'r ferch **na dd**aeth i'r parti.	*There's the girl who did not come to the party.*
Dyna'r dyn **na ch**anodd.	*Here's the man who did not sing.*

4 After the conjunction **pan**:

Pan **dd**aeth Guto i'r tŷ . . .	*When Guto came to the house . . .*
Bydda i'n hapus pan **dd**aw'r haf.	*I'll be happy when summer comes.*

5 Negative forms of inflected verbs (Compact Forms):

Ddarllenodd e ddim o'r Beibl.	*He didn't read the Bible.*
Welais i ddim yno.	*I didn't see anything there.*

In written Welsh, the negative particle **ni** precedes these forms, as in '**Ni dd**arllenodd e ddim o'r Beibl' and '**Ni w**elais i ddim yno', and causes Soft Mutation with verbs beginning in **g, b, d, ll, m, rh.** Inflected verbs beginning in **c, p, t** undergo Spirant Mutation.

6 Verbs after the interrogative pronouns **Beth** and **Pwy**:

Beth **w**eloch chi?	*What did you see?*
Pwy **b**rynodd y tocyn?	*Who bought the ticket?*

Nasal Mutation Treiglad Trwynol

Six consonants are affected by Nasal Mutation:
c > ngh; p > mh; t > nh; g > ng; b > m; d > n.

1 After the personal pronoun **fy**:
fy **ngh**artref *(my home)*; fy **mh**oced *(my pocket)*; fy **nh**afod *(my tongue)*; fy **ng**obaith *(my hope)*; fy **m**rawd *(my brother)*; fy **n**rws *(my door)*.

2 After the preposition **yn**:
(In certain instances **yn** itself changes to **yng** or **ym**

    yn + c > yng ngh-
    yn + g > yng ng-
    yn + p > ym mh-
    yn + b > ym m-

When **yn** precedes **m** it changes to **ym** even though there is no mutation.)

yng nghorff y dyn *(in the man's body)*; **ym mh**lwyf Llangyfelach *(in the parish of Llangyfelach)*; yn **nh**re Caerfyrddin *(in Carmarthen town)*; **yng ng**olau'r gannwyll *(in the candlelight)*; **ym m**reichiau Myfanwy *(in Myfanwy's arms)*; yn **nh**ywyllwch y nos *(in the darkness of the night)*; yng **Ngh**aerdydd; **ym Mh**ontyberem; yn **Nh**reorci; **yng Ng**orseinon; **ym M**iwmares; yn Ninbych; **ym** Mynwy; **ym** Maesteg; **ym** mis Mai.

3 **blwydd** *(a year old)*, **blynedd** *(a year)*, and **diwrnod** *(a day)* all mutate after the cardinal numbers **pum, saith, wyth, naw, deng, deuddeng, ugain** (and numbers incorporating **ugain**, such as **trigain**), and **can.**

    pum **m**lwydd oed *(five years old)*; saith **m**lynedd *(seven years)*; wyth **n**iwrnod *(eight days)*; deng **m**lwydd oed; deuddeng **m**lynedd; ugain **n**iwrnod; can **m**lynedd.

Note: Mae Siôn yn **ddwy f**lwydd oed.   *Siôn is two years old.*
    Roedd Nia yma am **ddwy f**lynedd.   *Nia was here for two years.*
    Mae **dau dd**iwrnod cyn y parti.   *There are two days before the party.*
See Soft Mutation – *Treiglad Meddal.*

Spirant Mutation Treiglad Llaes

Three consonants are affected by Spirant Mutation:
c > ch; p > ph; t > th.

1 After the personal pronouns **ei** (feminine), **'i** (feminine) and **'w** (feminine):
ei **ch**aws *(her cheese)*; ei **ph**en-blwydd *(her birthday)*; ei **th**ad-cu *(her grandfather)*; o'i **ch**artref *(from her home)*; o'i **ph**en i'w **th**raed *(from her head to her feet)*.

2 After the cardinal numbers **tri, chwe**:
tri **ch**wpan *(three cups)*; tri **ph**erson *(three persons)*; chwe **ph**lentyn *(six children)*; chwe **th**estun *(six subjects)*.

3 After the prepositions **â, gyda, tua**:
torri bara â **ch**yllell	*cutting bread with a knife*
cerdded gyda **th**ad y ferch	*walking with the girl's father*
gweithio gyda **ch**yfaill	*working with a friend*
mynd tua **Ph**entre-Bach	*going towards Pentre-Bach*
aros tua **th**ymor	*waiting about a term*

4 After the conjunctions **a** *(and)*, **na** *(nor, than)*, **oni** *(until, unless)*:

dŵr a **th**an *(water and fire)*; ci a **ch**ath *(a dog and a cat)*; na **ph**en na **ch**wt *(nor head nor tail)*; yn fwy na **ph**unt *(more than a pound)*; yn gochach na **th**ân *(redder than fire)*; oni **ch**lywaf *(unless I shall hear)*.

5 After the adverbs **â** *(as)*, **tra** *(very/exceedingly)*:

cyn drymed â **ph**lwm	*as heavy as lead*
cyn oered â **ch**lai	*as cold as clay*
tra **ch**aredig	*very kind*
tra **th**ywyll	*exceedingly dark*

6 After the negative form of the relative pronoun **na**:

Dyma'r ferch na **th**alodd am ei llyfr.   *This is the girl who did not pay for her book.*

Only verbs beginning in **c**, **p**, **t** and following **na** in this context are affected by Spirant Mutation. For verbs beginning in **g**, **b**, **d**, **ll**, **m**, **rh** after the negative pronoun **na** see Soft Mutation – *Treiglad Meddal.*

7 Negative forms of inflected verbs (Compact Forms):

Chlywais i ddim sŵn.	*I didn't hear a sound.*
Thalodd e ddim.	*He didn't pay.*
Phrynais i ddim o'r esgidiau	*I didn't buy the shoes.*

In written Welsh, the negative particle **ni** precedes these forms, as in 'Ni **ch**lywais i ddim sŵn' and 'Ni **th**alodd e ddim', and causes Spirant Mutation with verbs beginning in **c**, **p**, **t**. Inflected verbs beginning in **g**, **b**, **d**, **ll**, **m** and **rh** undergo Soft Mutation.

PRONUNCIATION
YNGANU

As Welsh is a vibrant phonetic language, learners who master the basic sounds early find that they are able to pronounce Welsh words right from the start. Of the 29 letters in the Welsh alphabet, 9 share the same sound value as their counterparts in English, these are: **b, d, j, l, m, n, p, s, t**.

Vowels

a as the **a** sound in **a**pple, **a**nt, **A**rthur
e as the **e** sound in **e**lf, **e**nd, **e**mpty
i as the **ee** sound in d**ee**p, k**ee**p
o as the **o** sound in **o**il, **o**range, n**o**t
u as for the sound in **i** above
w as the **w** sound in **w**illow, **w**ood
y (i) as for the sound in **i** above. It occurs in monosyllables and in the final syllable of polysyllables, as in bys, crys, dyn, diferyn
    (ii) as the **e** sound in **e**rr, the land. It occurs in polysyllables (except for final syllables) and in such words as **y, yng, ym, yn, dy, fy**. Additional examples: dyma, dynion, ysgolion, drygioni

Consonants

a see Vowels
b as in English
c as in **c**ap, **c**oconut
ch as in German A**ch**tung!, J.S. Ba**ch**, lo**ch**
d as in English
dd as the **th** sound in brea**th**e, **th**is
e see Vowels
f as in the **v** sound in **v**iola, **v**ideo, **v**iew
ff as in the **f** sound in **f**ury, **f**right, of**f**
g as in the **g** sound in **g**ift, **g**ood, **g**reat
ng as the **ng** sound in cli**ng**, wi**ng**
h as in the **h** sound in **h**elp, **h**ooray
i see Vowels
j as in English
l as in English
ll Place tongue as though to sound **l** emitting only breath. Try these words: **ll**o, **ll**i, **ll**w, **Llanelli**

m	as in English
n	as in English
o	see Vowels
p	as in English
ph	as the **ph** sound in trium**ph**, So**ph**ia, **Ph**iladel**ph**ia
r	as in **r**ed, **r**ich, **r**obin
rh	with greater expulsion of breath and rolled, as by the Scots
s	as in English
t	as in English
th	as the **th** sound in brea**th**, dea**th**, hea**th**
u	see Vowels
w	see Vowels
y	see Vowels

Ideally, the learner should practise pronunciation regularly with a native Welsh speaker. Welsh communities in town and country districts abound with such possibilities. Weekly programmes for learners are broadcast by Radio Cymru, Radio Wales and by local radio stations. The Welsh television channel S4C adds daily to the Welsh environment. Groups of Welsh-speaking walkers invite learners to join them on their walks. Welsh language courses at all levels of ability are comprehensively organised throughout each local education authority. The University is interested and involved in every aspect of the work. Competitions are arranged, new course-books are published, **Twmpath** dancing is celebrated and **Cymanfaoedd Canu** are joyfully attended. Facilities at the annual National and Urdd **Eisteddfodau** attract learners worldwide. **Nosweithiau llawen**, **Dawnsio gwerin**, CDs, tapes, records, videos, the Web. . . The list is endless as is the energy and enthusiasm of specialist teachers who devise these enjoyable events in order that learners may experience at first hand the joy of speaking their new language in as natural an environment as possible. For our children, Welsh-medium education from nursery group to degree level is flourishing.

Croeso i'n plith!   (Welcome to our midst!)

TEACH YOURSELF

WELSH (new edition)

Julie Brake and Christine Jones

This is a complete course in understanding, speaking and writing Welsh. If you have never learnt Welsh before, or if your Welsh needs brushing up, *Teach Yourself Welsh* will give you a thorough grounding in the basics and will take you onto a level where you can communicate with confidence. This new edition has been completely revised and updated to make the course even more enjoyable and interactive.

The course contains

- Graded units of dialogues, culture notes, grammar and exercises
- Pronunciation sections
- A Welsh–English and English–Welsh vocabulary.

By the end of the course you'll be able to communicate effectively and appreciate the culture of Welsh speakers.

Official coursebook for the Welsh Distance Learning Course of the University of Wales, Lampeter, http://welsh.lamp.ac.uk/camu.